STAR WARS®
OMNIBUS

A LONG TIME AGO. . . .
VOLUME 5

STAR WARS OMNIBUS

A LONG TIME AGO....

VOLUME 5

DARK HORSE BOOKS®

cover illustration Cynthia Martin with Art Nichols and Petra Scotese
president and publisher Mike Richardson
series editors Louise Jones and Ann Nocenti
collection editor Randy Stradley
assistant editor Freddye Lins
collection designer Heather Doornink

special thanks to Jann Moorhead, David Anderman, Troy Alders, Leland Chee, Jonathan Rinzler, and Carol Roeder at Lucas Licensing

Star Wars® Omnibus: A Long Time Ago. . . . Volume Five

This volume collects Marvel Star Wars issues #86–#107.

Published by Dark Horse Books
A division of Dark Horse Comics, Inc.
10956 SE Main Street
Milwaukie, OR 97222

DarkHorse.com | StarWars.com

To find a comics shop in your area, call the Comic Shop Locator Service toll-free at 1-888-266-4226

executive vice president Neil Hankerson • chief financial officer Tom Weddle • vice president of publishing Randy Stradley • vice president of book trade sales Michael Martens • vice president of business affairs Anita Nelson • vice president of marketing Micha Hershman • vice president of product development David Scroggy • vice president of information technology Dale LaFountain • senior director of print, design, and production Darlene Vogel • general counsel Ken Lizzi • editorial director Davey Estrada • senior managing editor Scott Allie • senior books editor Chris Warner • executive editor Diana Schutz • director of print and development Cary Grazzini • art director Lia Ribacchi • director of scheduling Cara Niece

Library of Congress Cataloging-in-Publication Data

Star Wars omnibus. A long time ago / writers, Archie Goodwin ... [et al.] ; artists, Howard Chaykin ... [et al.] ; colorists, Janice Cohen ... [et al.]. -- 1st ed.
    v. cm.
ISBN 978-1-59582-486-8 (v. 1)
1. Comic books, strips, etc. I. Goodwin, Archie. II. Dark Horse Comics. III. Title: Long time ago.
PN6728.S73S7336 2010
741.5'973--dc22
                         2010000142

Printed by 1010 Printing International, Ltd., Guangdong Province, China.

First edition: February 2012
ISBN 978-1-59582-801-9

10 9 8 7 6 5 4 3 2 1

CONTENTS

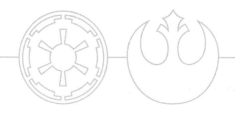

STAR WARS
TM
60¢
86
AUG
02817
APPROVED BY THE COMICS CODE AUTHORITY
STILL FEELING HIGH AND MIGHTY, *PRINCESS?*
BOB MCLEOD

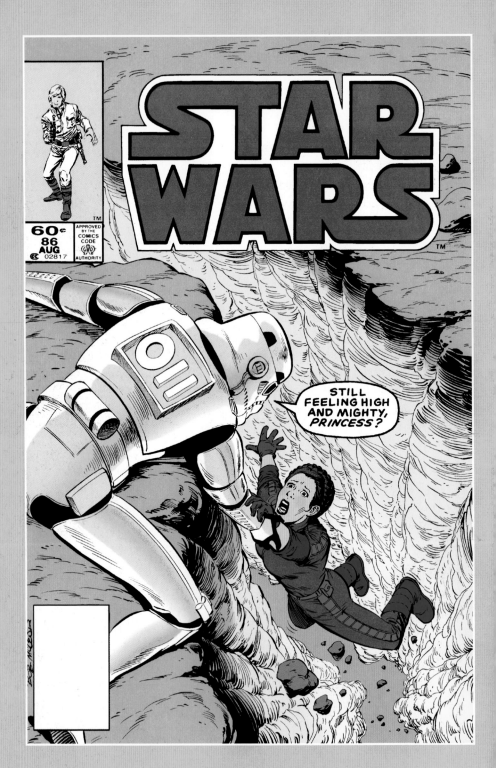

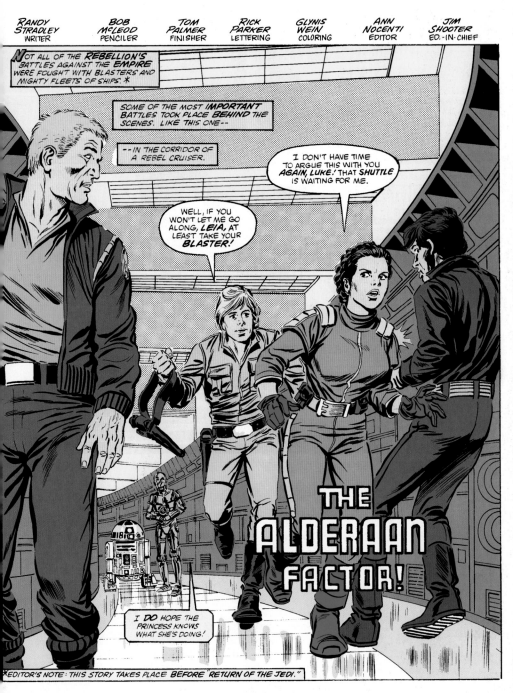

RANDY STRADLEY — WRITER
BOB McLEOD — PENCILER
TOM PALMER — FINISHER
RICK PARKER — LETTERING
GLYNIS WEIN — COLORING
ANN NOCENTI — EDITOR
JIM SHOOTER — ED.-IN-CHIEF

NOT ALL OF THE *REBELLION'S* BATTLES AGAINST THE *EMPIRE* WERE FOUGHT WITH BLASTERS AND MIGHTY FLEETS OF SHIPS. *

SOME OF THE MOST *IMPORTANT* BATTLES TOOK PLACE *BEHIND* THE SCENES. LIKE THIS ONE--

--IN THE CORRIDOR OF A REBEL CRUISER.

I DON'T HAVE TIME TO ARGUE THIS WITH YOU *AGAIN, LUKE!* THAT *SHUTTLE* IS WAITING FOR ME.

WELL, IF YOU WON'T LET ME GO ALONG, *LEIA,* AT LEAST TAKE YOUR *BLASTER!*

THE ALDERAAN FACTOR!

I *DO* HOPE THE PRINCESS KNOWS WHAT SHE'S DOING!

*EDITOR'S NOTE: THIS STORY TAKES PLACE *BEFORE* "RETURN OF THE JEDI."

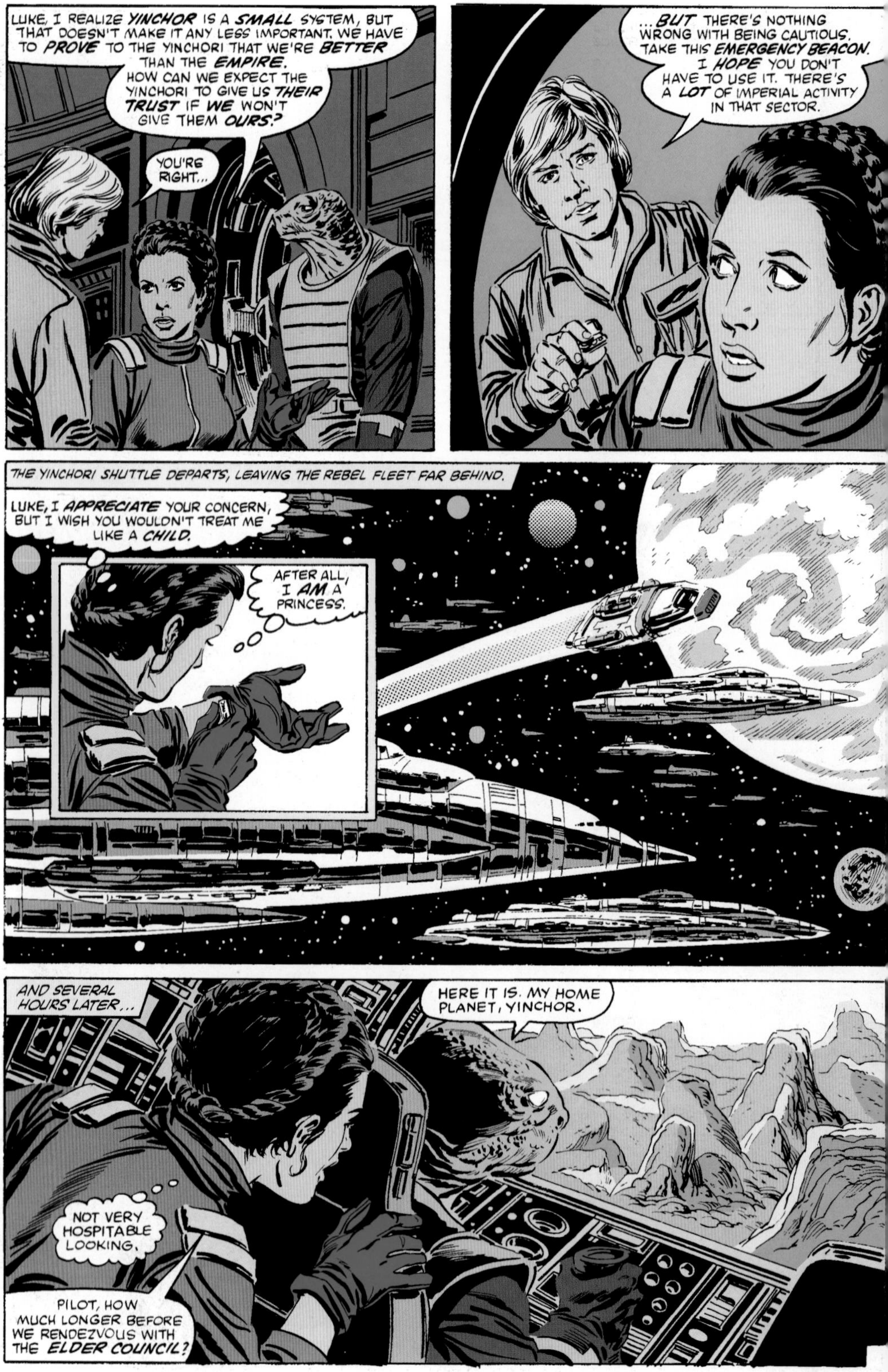

LUKE, I REALIZE YINCHOR IS A SMALL SYSTEM, BUT THAT DOESN'T MAKE IT ANY LESS IMPORTANT. WE HAVE TO PROVE TO THE YINCHORI THAT WE'RE BETTER THAN THE EMPIRE.
HOW CAN WE EXPECT THE YINCHORI TO GIVE US THEIR TRUST IF WE WON'T GIVE THEM OURS?
YOU'RE RIGHT...
...BUT THERE'S NOTHING WRONG WITH BEING CAUTIOUS. TAKE THIS EMERGENCY BEACON.
I HOPE YOU DON'T HAVE TO USE IT. THERE'S A LOT OF IMPERIAL ACTIVITY IN THAT SECTOR.
THE YINCHORI SHUTTLE DEPARTS, LEAVING THE REBEL FLEET FAR BEHIND.
LUKE, I APPRECIATE YOUR CONCERN, BUT I WISH YOU WOULDN'T TREAT ME LIKE A CHILD.
AFTER ALL, I AM A PRINCESS.
AND SEVERAL HOURS LATER...
HERE IT IS. MY HOME PLANET, YINCHOR.
NOT VERY HOSPITABLE LOOKING.
PILOT, HOW MUCH LONGER BEFORE WE RENDEZVOUS WITH THE ELDER COUNCIL?

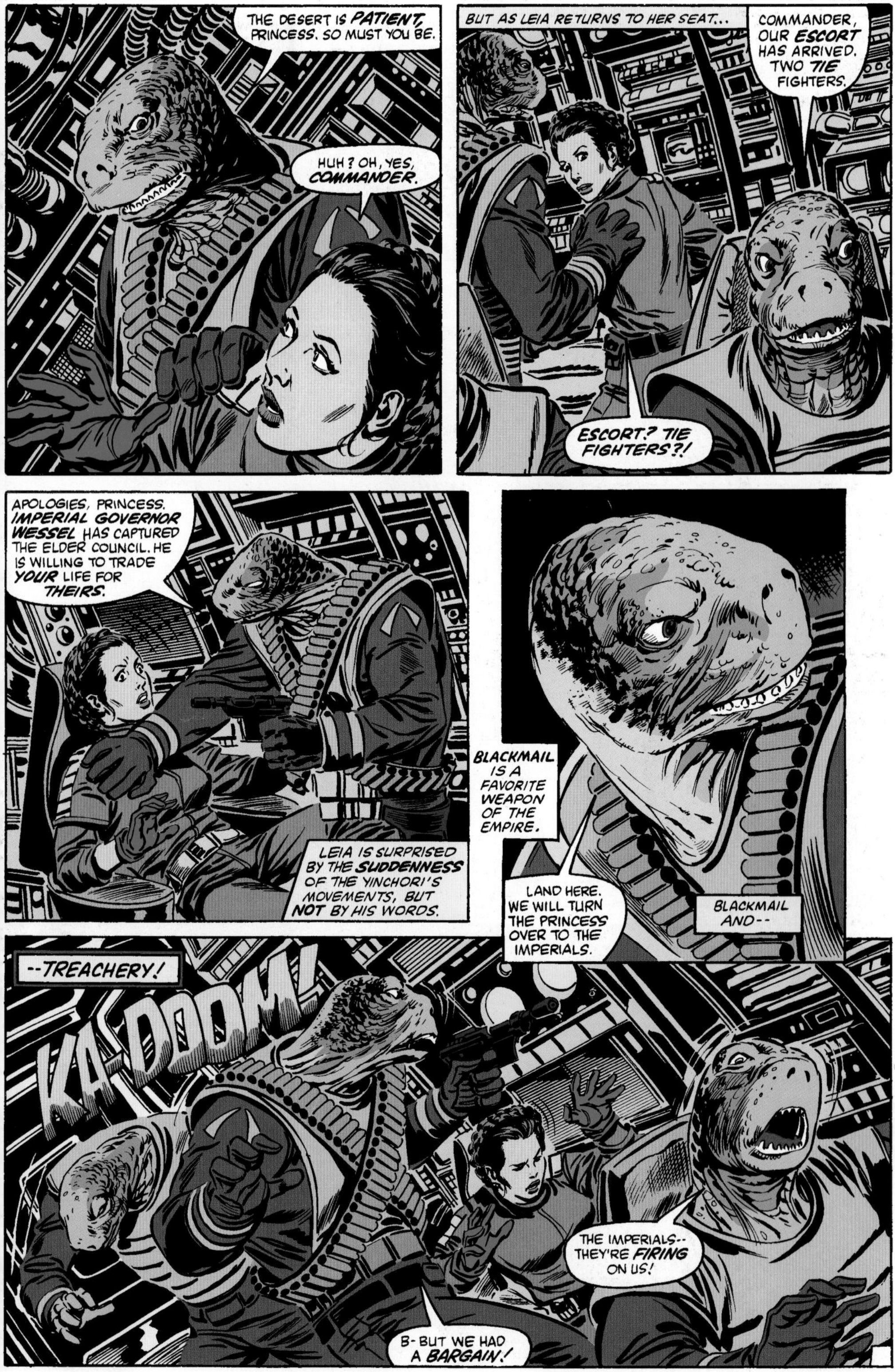
THE DESERT IS PATIENT, PRINCESS. SO MUST YOU BE.
HUH? OH, YES, COMMANDER.
BUT AS LEIA RETURNS TO HER SEAT...
COMMANDER, OUR ESCORT HAS ARRIVED. TWO TIE FIGHTERS.
ESCORT? TIE FIGHTERS?!
APOLOGIES, PRINCESS. IMPERIAL GOVERNOR WESSEL HAS CAPTURED THE ELDER COUNCIL. HE IS WILLING TO TRADE YOUR LIFE FOR THEIRS.
LEIA IS SURPRISED BY THE SUDDENNESS OF THE YINCHORI'S MOVEMENTS, BUT NOT BY HIS WORDS.
BLACKMAIL IS A FAVORITE WEAPON OF THE EMPIRE.
LAND HERE. WE WILL TURN THE PRINCESS OVER TO THE IMPERIALS.
BLACKMAIL AND--
--TREACHERY!
KA-DOOM!
THE IMPERIALS-- THEY'RE FIRING ON US!
B-BUT WE HAD A BARGAIN!

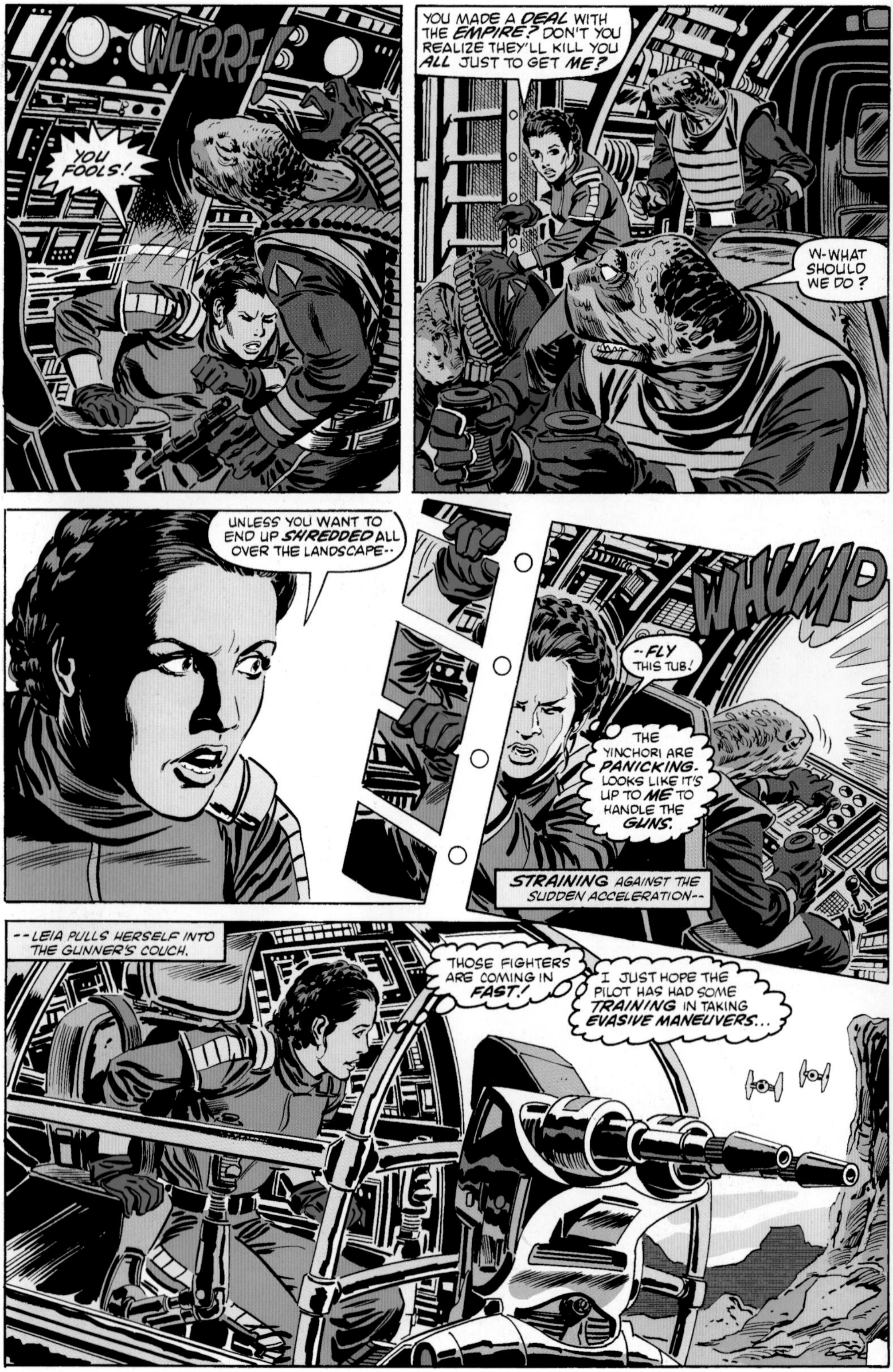
WURRF!
YOU FOOLS!
YOU MADE A DEAL WITH THE EMPIRE? DON'T YOU REALIZE THEY'LL KILL YOU ALL JUST TO GET ME?
W-WHAT SHOULD WE DO?
UNLESS YOU WANT TO END UP SHREDDED ALL OVER THE LANDSCAPE--
WHUMP
--FLY THIS TUB!
THE YINCHORI ARE PANICKING. LOOKS LIKE IT'S UP TO ME TO HANDLE THE GUNS.
STRAINING AGAINST THE SUDDEN ACCELERATION--
--LEIA PULLS HERSELF INTO THE GUNNER'S COUCH.
THOSE FIGHTERS ARE COMING IN FAST!
I JUST HOPE THE PILOT HAS HAD SOME TRAINING IN TAKING EVASIVE MANEUVERS...

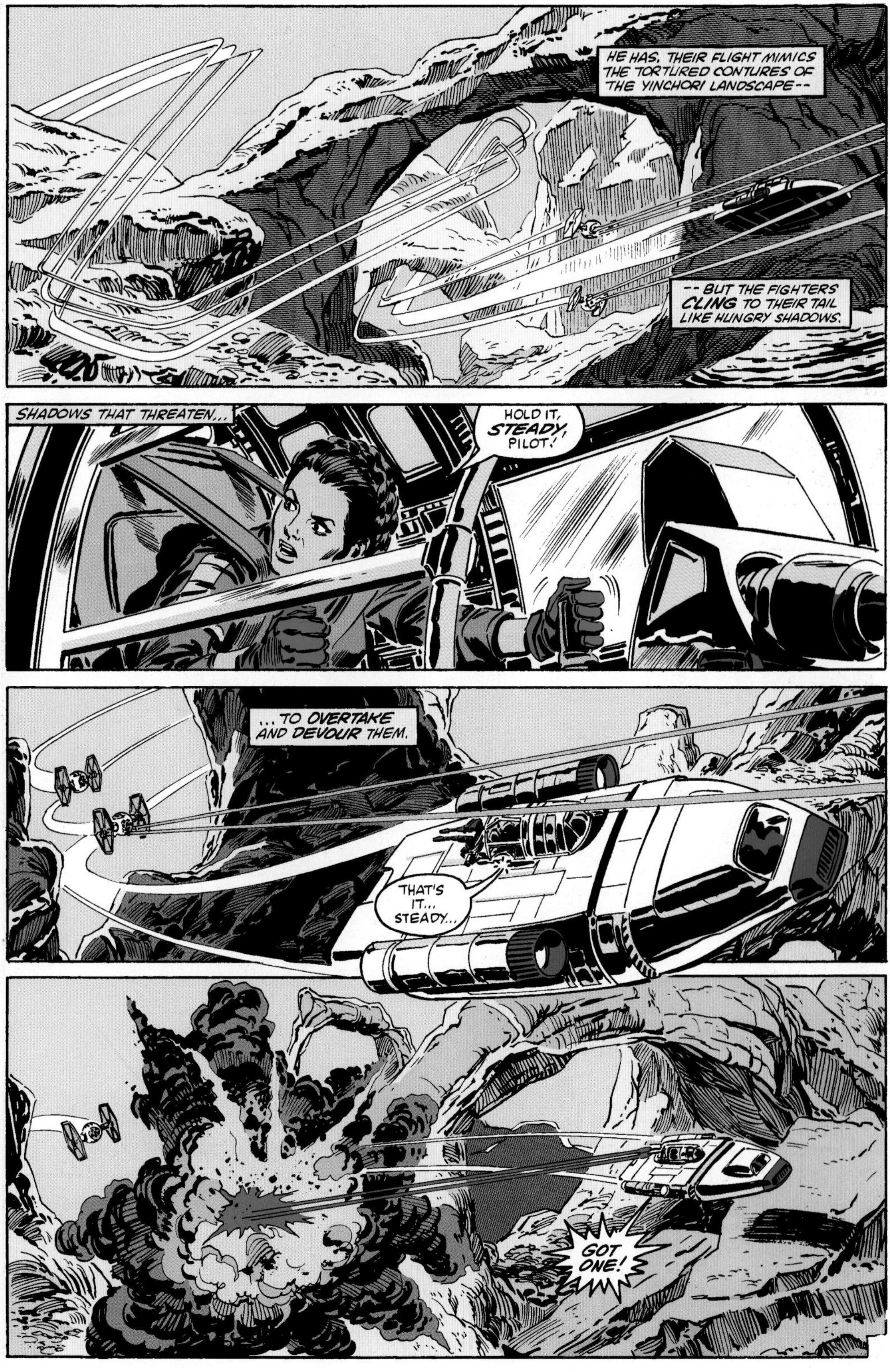
HE HAS. THEIR FLIGHT MIMICS THE TORTURED CONTURES OF THE YINCHORI LANDSCAPE--
--BUT THE FIGHTERS CLING TO THEIR TAIL LIKE HUNGRY SHADOWS.
SHADOWS THAT THREATEN...
HOLD IT, STEADY, PILOT!
...TO OVERTAKE AND DEVOUR THEM.
THAT'S IT... STEADY...
GOT ONE!

FASTER! ONE FIGHTER YET PURSUES US!

DESPERATION SHARPENS THE REFLEXES OF THE YINCHORI HELMSMEN, BUT HE IS STILL NO MATCH FOR—

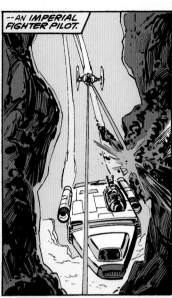

—AN IMPERIAL FIGHTER PILOT.

SKID-DOW!

THAT ONE WAS TOO CLOSE!

LUKE WAS RIGHT. I WAS FOOLISH TO COME ALONE. I CAN'T HANDLE THIS BY MYSELF!

NO. I'M A PRINCESS. I CAN HANDLE THIS!

I WILL HANDLE THIS.

THE GUNSIGHTS STEADY...

...AND LEIA FIRES—

—AN INSTANT TOO LATE.

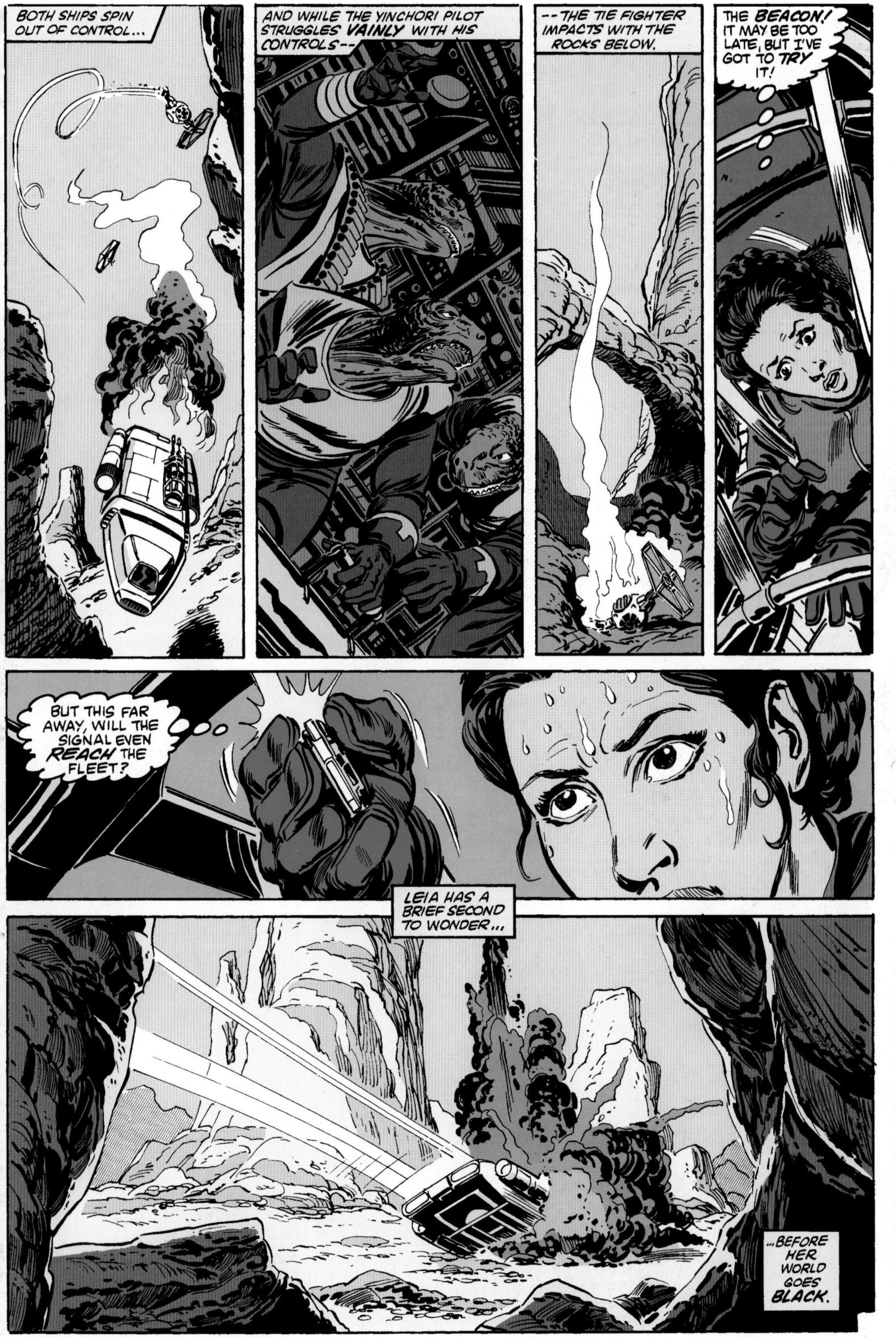
BOTH SHIPS SPIN OUT OF CONTROL...
AND WHILE THE YINCHORI PILOT STRUGGLES VAINLY WITH HIS CONTROLS--
--THE TIE FIGHTER IMPACTS WITH THE ROCKS BELOW.
THE BEACON! IT MAY BE TOO LATE, BUT I'VE GOT TO TRY IT!
BUT THIS FAR AWAY, WILL THE SIGNAL EVEN REACH THE FLEET?
LEIA HAS A BRIEF SECOND TO WONDER...
...BEFORE HER WORLD GOES BLACK.

AND FAR, FAR AWAY, WHERE THE REBEL ARMADA HAS GATHERED...

COMMANDER SKYWALKER, WE'RE PICKING UP A *SIGNAL* ON THAT CHANNEL YOU ASKED US TO MONITOR.

AND ON THE *MILLENNIUM FALCON*...

LUKE, IT *COULD* BE NOTHING. MAYBE...

NO, LANDO. THERE'S *TROUBLE*--

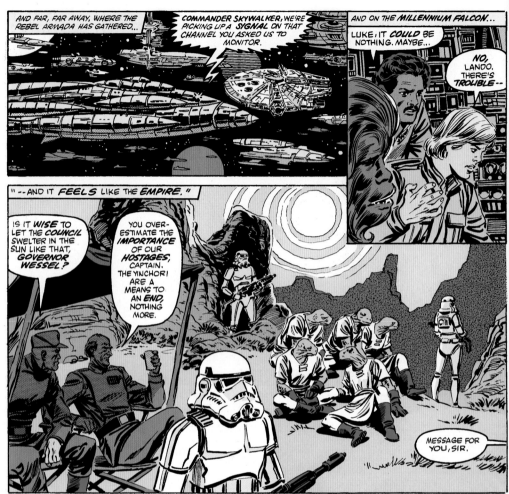

"--AND IT *FEELS* LIKE THE *EMPIRE*."

IS IT *WISE* TO LET THE *COUNCIL* SWELTER IN THE SUN LIKE THAT, *GOVERNOR WESSEL*?

YOU OVER-ESTIMATE THE *IMPORTANCE* OF OUR *HOSTAGES*, CAPTAIN. THE YINCHORI ARE A MEANS TO AN *END*, NOTHING MORE.

MESSAGE FOR YOU, SIR.

SCANNERS' REPORT THE *SHUTTLE* HAS BEEN *DOWNED* A SHORT DISTANCE FROM HERE.

GOOD. IT LOOKS AS THOUGH OUR MISSION IS A *SUCCESS.*

UH, SIR, BOTH OF *OUR* FIGHTERS WERE *ALSO* SHOT DOWN.

WHAT?!

CAPTAIN, I WANT TO *SEE* THAT CRASH SITE. I WANT TO SEE FOR MYSELF THAT THERE ARE *NO* SURVIVORS--

--AND THAT *PRINCESS LEIA* IS *DEAD.*

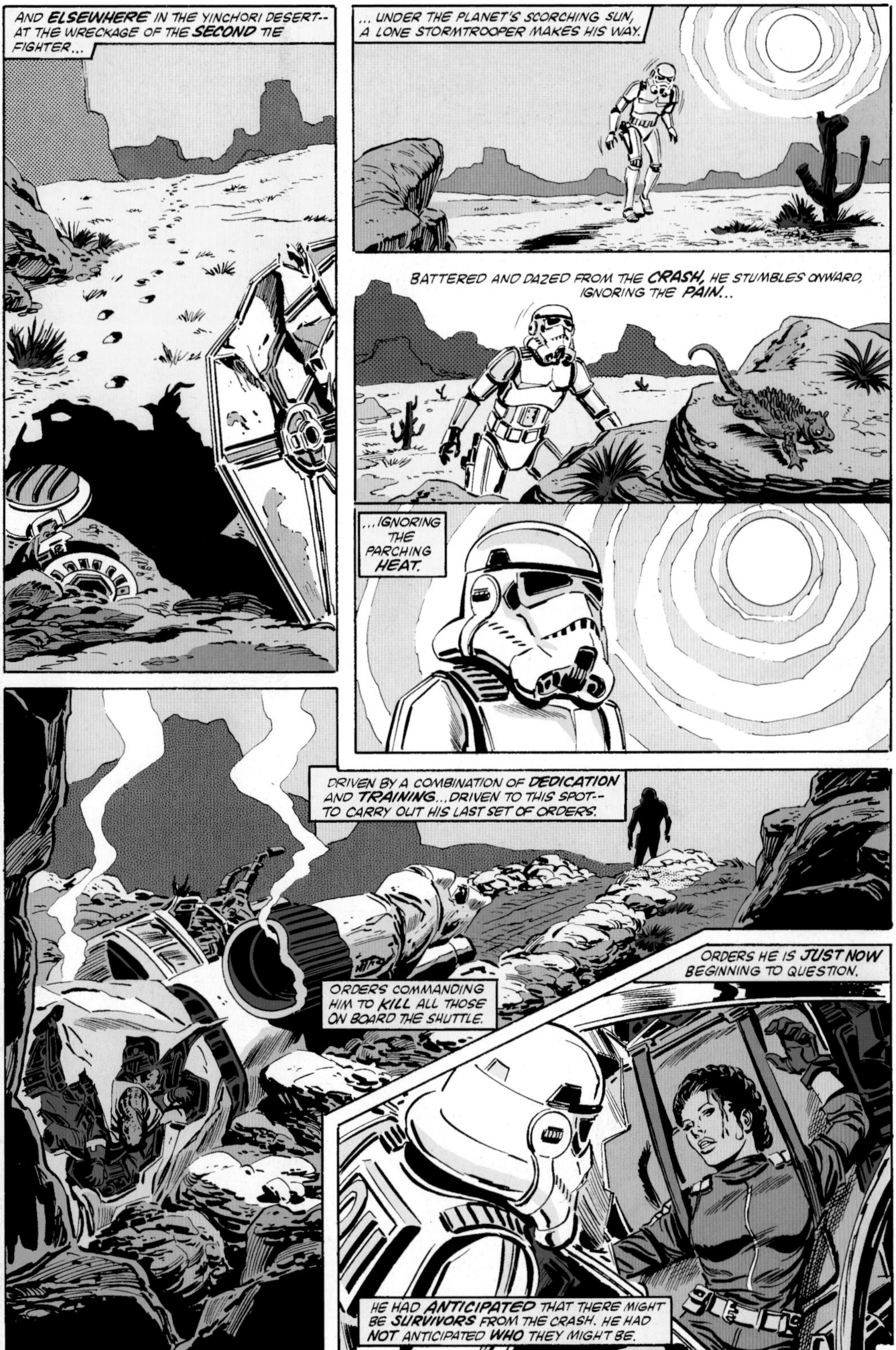
AND ELSEWHERE IN THE YINCHORI DESERT-- AT THE WRECKAGE OF THE SECOND TIE FIGHTER...
... UNDER THE PLANET'S SCORCHING SUN, A LONE STORMTROOPER MAKES HIS WAY.
BATTERED AND DAZED FROM THE CRASH, HE STUMBLES ONWARD, IGNORING THE PAIN...
...IGNORING THE PARCHING HEAT.
DRIVEN BY A COMBINATION OF DEDICATION AND TRAINING... DRIVEN TO THIS SPOT-- TO CARRY OUT HIS LAST SET OF ORDERS.
ORDERS COMMANDING HIM TO KILL ALL THOSE ON BOARD THE SHUTTLE.
ORDERS HE IS JUST NOW BEGINNING TO QUESTION.
HE HAD ANTICIPATED THAT THERE MIGHT BE SURVIVORS FROM THE CRASH. HE HAD NOT ANTICIPATED WHO THEY MIGHT BE.

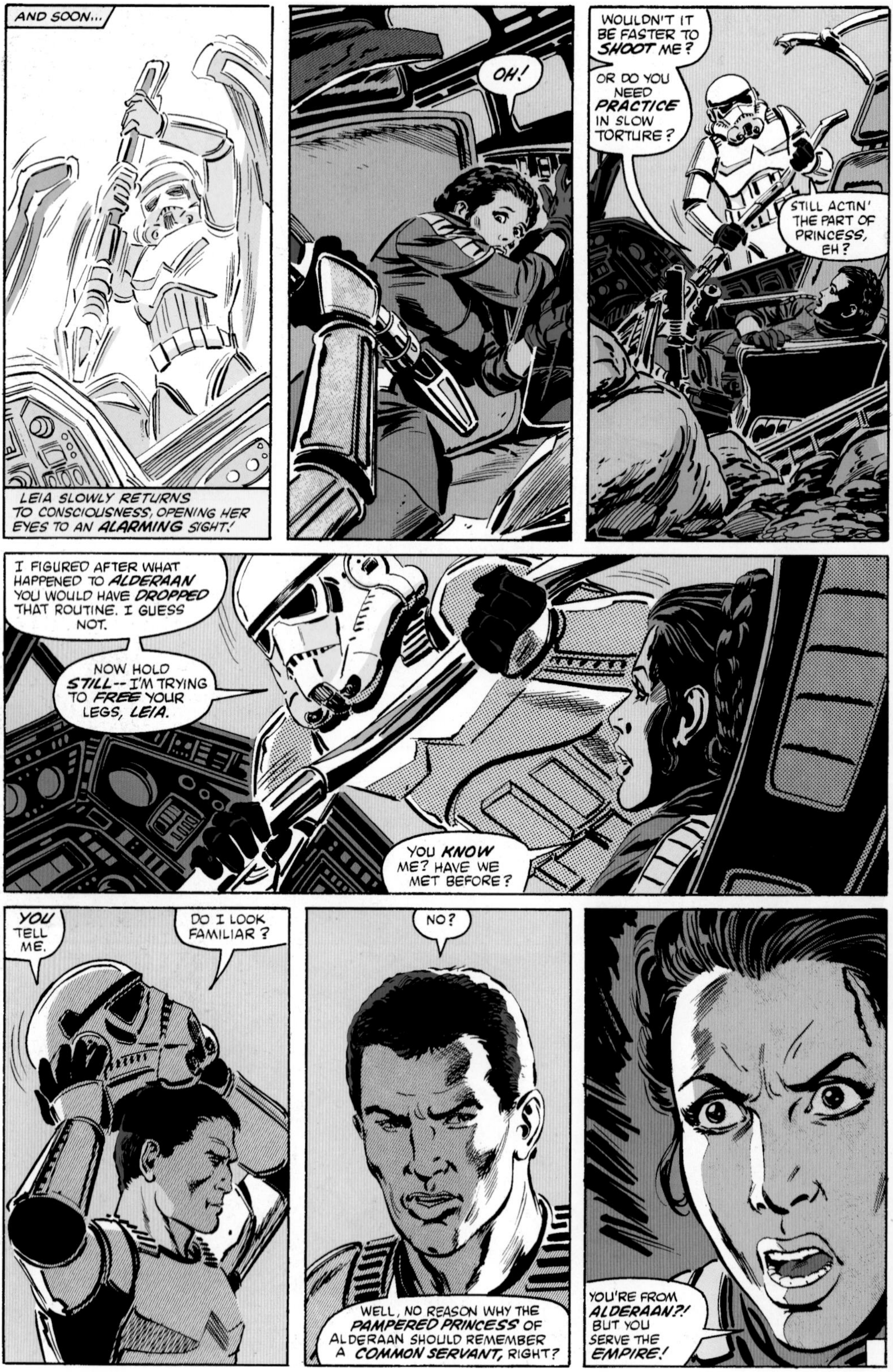

AND SOON...
LEIA SLOWLY RETURNS TO CONSCIOUSNESS, OPENING HER EYES TO AN ALARMING SIGHT!
OH!
WOULDN'T IT BE FASTER TO SHOOT ME?
OR DO YOU NEED PRACTICE IN SLOW TORTURE?
STILL ACTIN' THE PART OF PRINCESS, EH?
I FIGURED AFTER WHAT HAPPENED TO ALDERAAN YOU WOULD HAVE DROPPED THAT ROUTINE. I GUESS NOT.
NOW HOLD STILL-- I'M TRYING TO FREE YOUR LEGS, LEIA.
YOU KNOW ME? HAVE WE MET BEFORE?
YOU TELL ME.
DO I LOOK FAMILIAR?
NO?
WELL, NO REASON WHY THE PAMPERED PRINCESS OF ALDERAAN SHOULD REMEMBER A COMMON SERVANT, RIGHT?
YOU'RE FROM ALDERAAN?! BUT YOU SERVE THE EMPIRE!

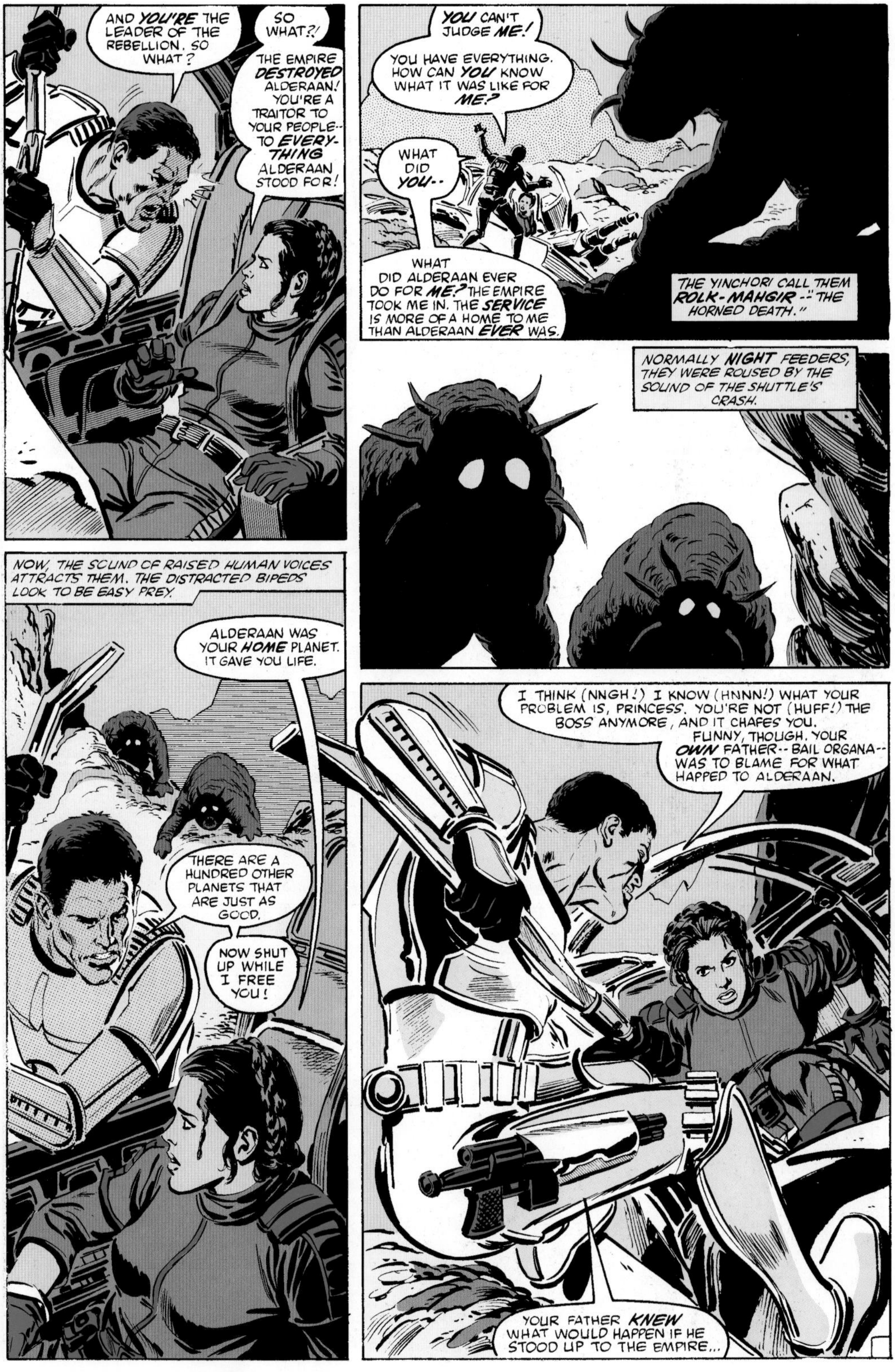
AND YOU'RE THE LEADER OF THE REBELLION. SO WHAT?
SO WHAT?!
THE EMPIRE DESTROYED ALDERAAN! YOU'RE A TRAITOR TO YOUR PEOPLE-- TO EVERY-THING ALDERAAN STOOD FOR!
YOU CAN'T JUDGE ME!
YOU HAVE EVERYTHING. HOW CAN YOU KNOW WHAT IT WAS LIKE FOR ME?
WHAT DID YOU--
WHAT DID ALDERAAN EVER DO FOR ME? THE EMPIRE TOOK ME IN. THE SERVICE IS MORE OF A HOME TO ME THAN ALDERAAN EVER WAS.
THE YINCHORI CALL THEM ROLK-MAHGIR -- "THE HORNED DEATH."
NORMALLY NIGHT FEEDERS, THEY WERE ROUSED BY THE SOUND OF THE SHUTTLE'S CRASH.
NOW, THE SOUND OF RAISED HUMAN VOICES ATTRACTS THEM. THE DISTRACTED BIPEDS LOOK TO BE EASY PREY.
ALDERAAN WAS YOUR HOME PLANET. IT GAVE YOU LIFE.
THERE ARE A HUNDRED OTHER PLANETS THAT ARE JUST AS GOOD.
NOW SHUT UP WHILE I FREE YOU!
I THINK (NNGH!) I KNOW (HNNN!) WHAT YOUR PROBLEM IS, PRINCESS. YOU'RE NOT (HUFF!) THE BOSS ANYMORE, AND IT CHAFES YOU.
FUNNY, THOUGH. YOUR OWN FATHER-- BAIL ORGANA-- WAS TO BLAME FOR WHAT HAPPED TO ALDERAAN.
YOUR FATHER KNEW WHAT WOULD HAPPEN IF HE STOOD UP TO THE EMPIRE...

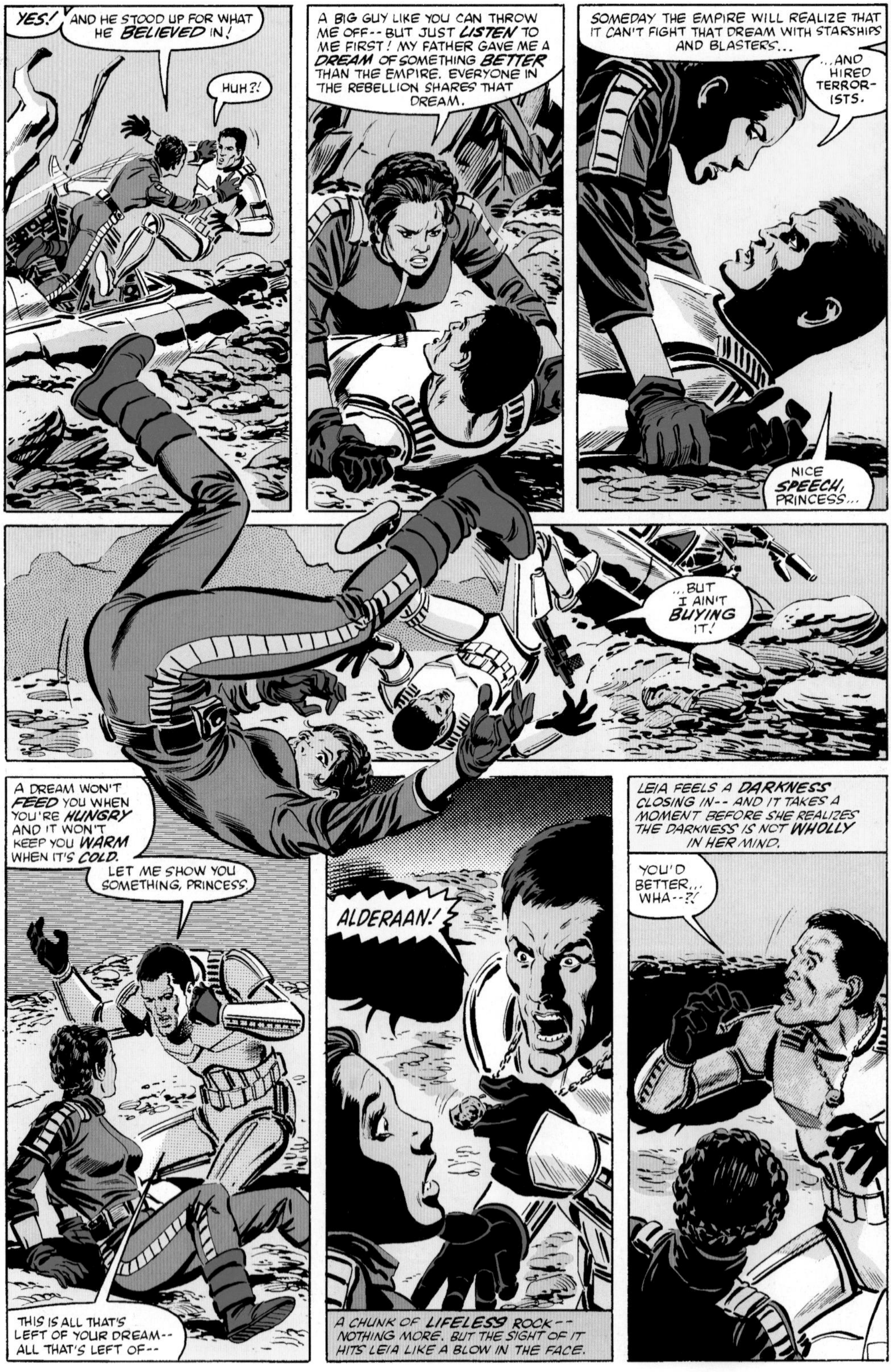
YES!
AND HE STOOD UP FOR WHAT HE BELIEVED IN!
HUH?!
A BIG GUY LIKE YOU CAN THROW ME OFF-- BUT JUST LISTEN TO ME FIRST! MY FATHER GAVE ME A DREAM OF SOMETHING BETTER THAN THE EMPIRE. EVERYONE IN THE REBELLION SHARES THAT DREAM.
SOMEDAY THE EMPIRE WILL REALIZE THAT IT CAN'T FIGHT THAT DREAM WITH STARSHIPS AND BLASTERS...
...AND HIRED TERROR-ISTS.
NICE SPEECH, PRINCESS...
...BUT I AIN'T BUYING IT!
A DREAM WON'T FEED YOU WHEN YOU'RE HUNGRY AND IT WON'T KEEP YOU WARM WHEN IT'S COLD.
LET ME SHOW YOU SOMETHING, PRINCESS.
THIS IS ALL THAT'S LEFT OF YOUR DREAM-- ALL THAT'S LEFT OF--
ALDERAAN!
A CHUNK OF LIFELESS ROCK-- NOTHING MORE. BUT THE SIGHT OF IT HITS LEIA LIKE A BLOW IN THE FACE.
LEIA FEELS A DARKNESS CLOSING IN-- AND IT TAKES A MOMENT BEFORE SHE REALIZES THE DARKNESS IS NOT WHOLLY IN HER MIND.
YOU'D BETTER... WHA--?!

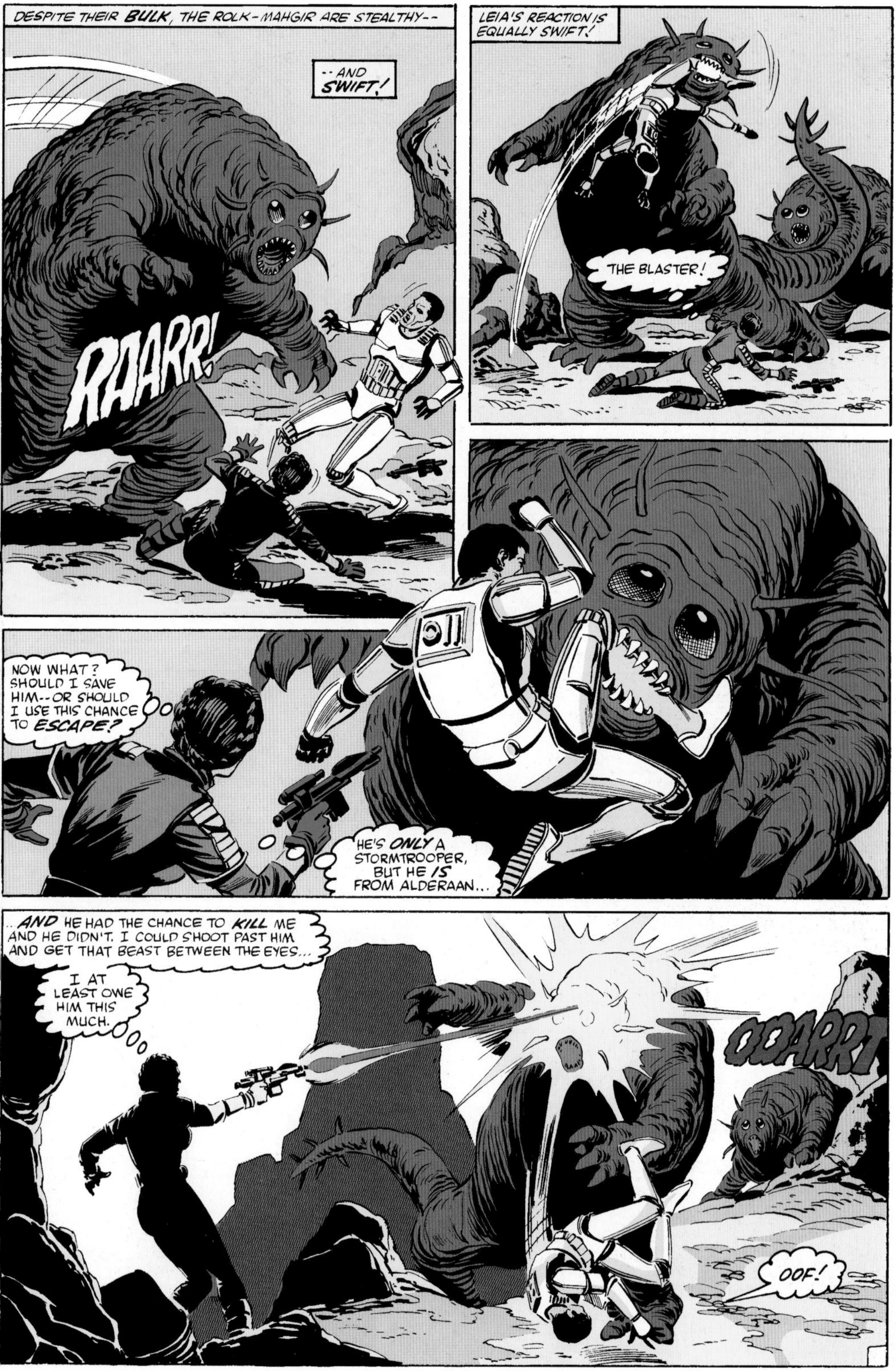
DESPITE THEIR BULK, THE ROLK-MAHGIR ARE STEALTHY--
--AND SWIFT!
RAARR!
LEIA'S REACTION IS EQUALLY SWIFT!
THE BLASTER!
NOW WHAT? SHOULD I SAVE HIM--OR SHOULD I USE THIS CHANCE TO ESCAPE?
HE'S ONLY A STORMTROOPER, BUT HE IS FROM ALDERAAN...
..AND HE HAD THE CHANCE TO KILL ME AND HE DIDN'T. I COULD SHOOT PAST HIM AND GET THAT BEAST BETWEEN THE EYES...
I AT LEAST OWE HIM THIS MUCH.
OOARRT
OOF!

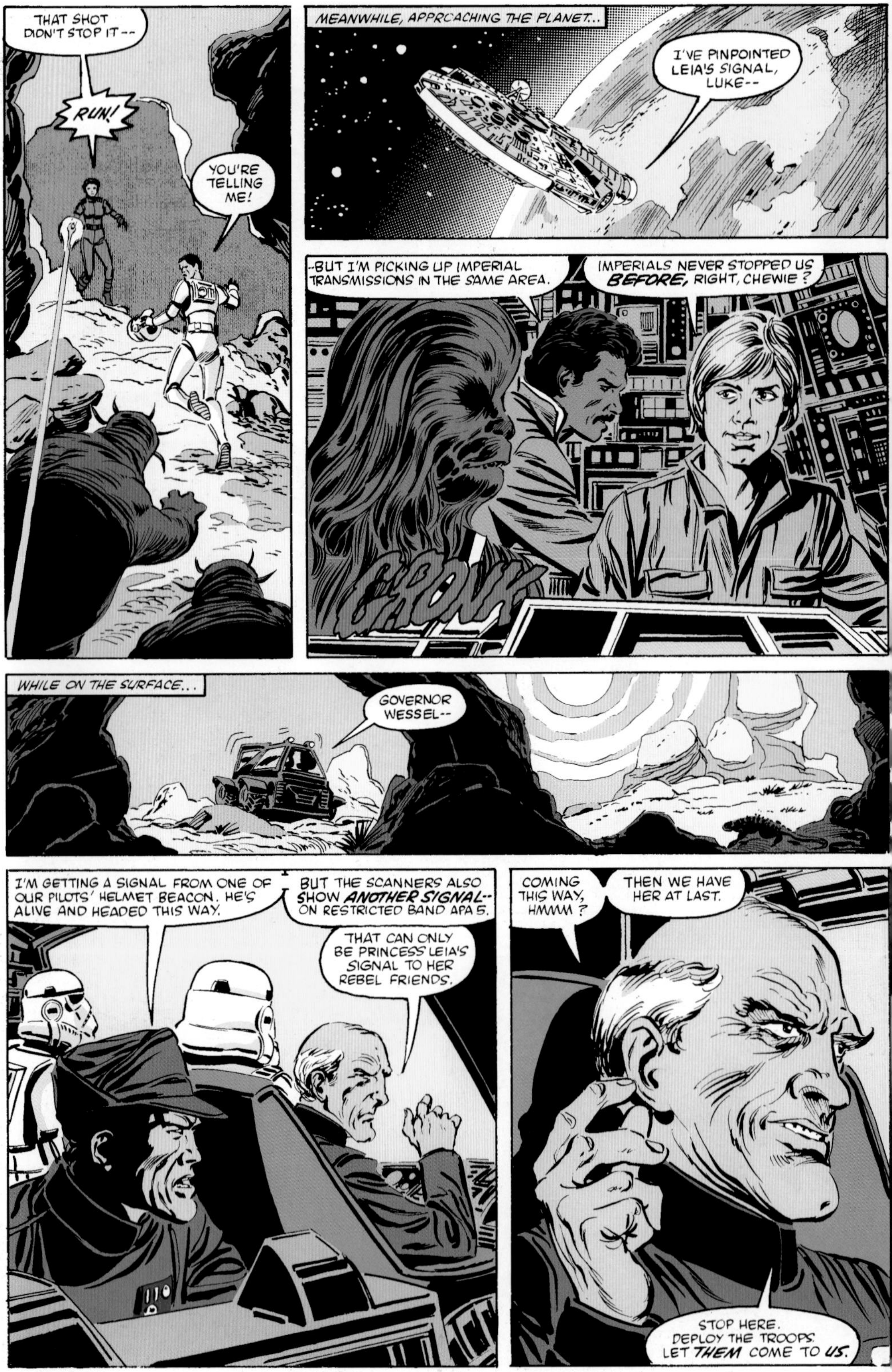
THAT SHOT DIDN'T STOP IT --
RUN!
YOU'RE TELLING ME!
MEANWHILE, APPROACHING THE PLANET...
I'VE PINPOINTED LEIA'S SIGNAL, LUKE--
--BUT I'M PICKING UP IMPERIAL TRANSMISSIONS IN THE SAME AREA.
IMPERIALS NEVER STOPPED US BEFORE, RIGHT, CHEWIE?
GRONK
WHILE ON THE SURFACE...
GOVERNOR WESSEL--
I'M GETTING A SIGNAL FROM ONE OF OUR PILOTS' HELMET BEACON. HE'S ALIVE AND HEADED THIS WAY.
BUT THE SCANNERS ALSO SHOW ANOTHER SIGNAL-- ON RESTRICTED BAND APA 5.
THAT CAN ONLY BE PRINCESS LEIA'S SIGNAL TO HER REBEL FRIENDS.
COMING THIS WAY, HMMM?
THEN WE HAVE HER AT LAST.
STOP HERE. DEPLOY THE TROOPS. LET THEM COME TO US.

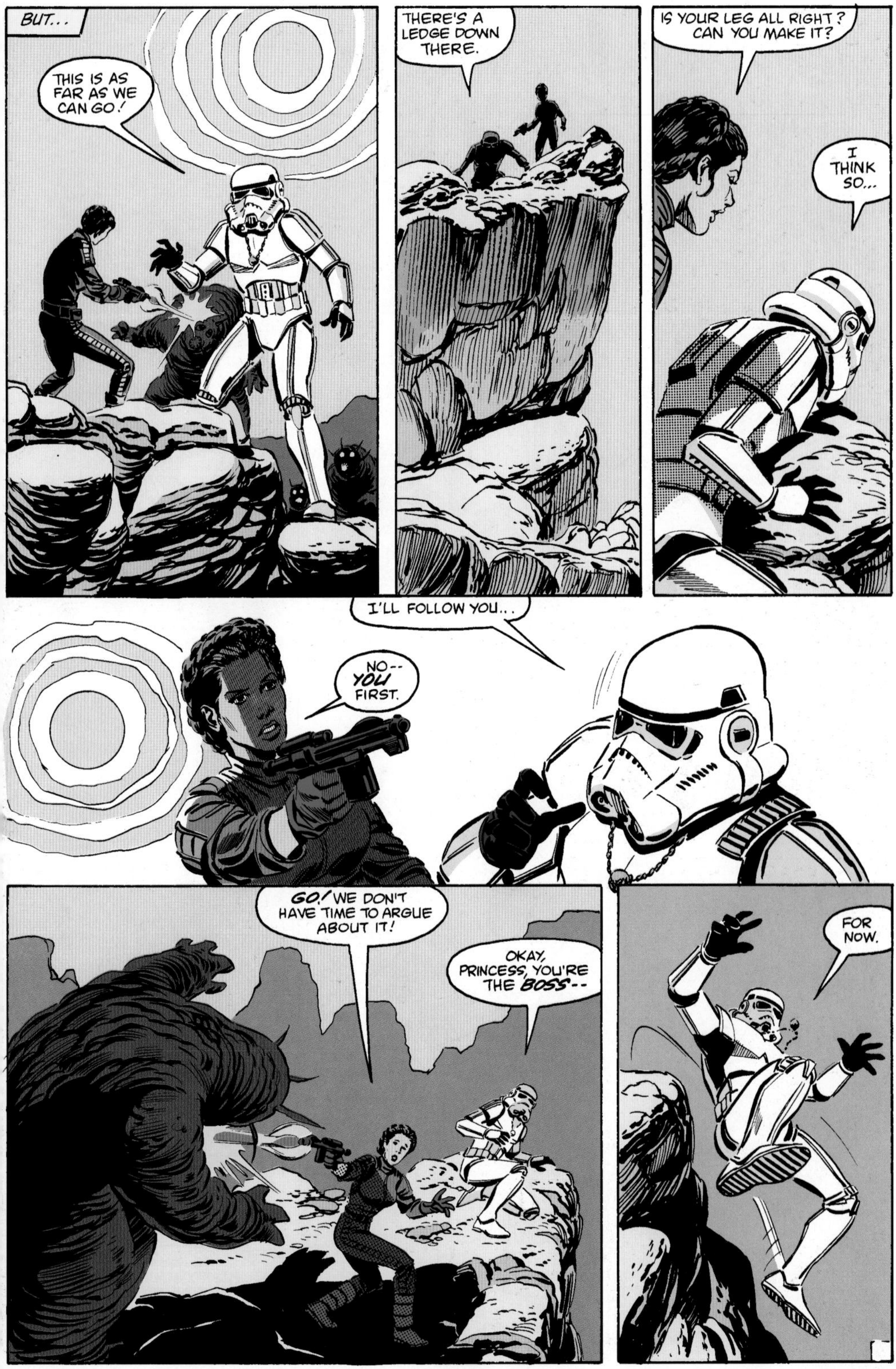
BUT...
THIS IS AS FAR AS WE CAN GO!
THERE'S A LEDGE DOWN THERE.
IS YOUR LEG ALL RIGHT? CAN YOU MAKE IT?
I THINK SO...
I'LL FOLLOW YOU...
NO-- YOU FIRST.
GO! WE DON'T HAVE TIME TO ARGUE ABOUT IT!
OKAY, PRINCESS, YOU'RE THE BOSS--
FOR NOW.

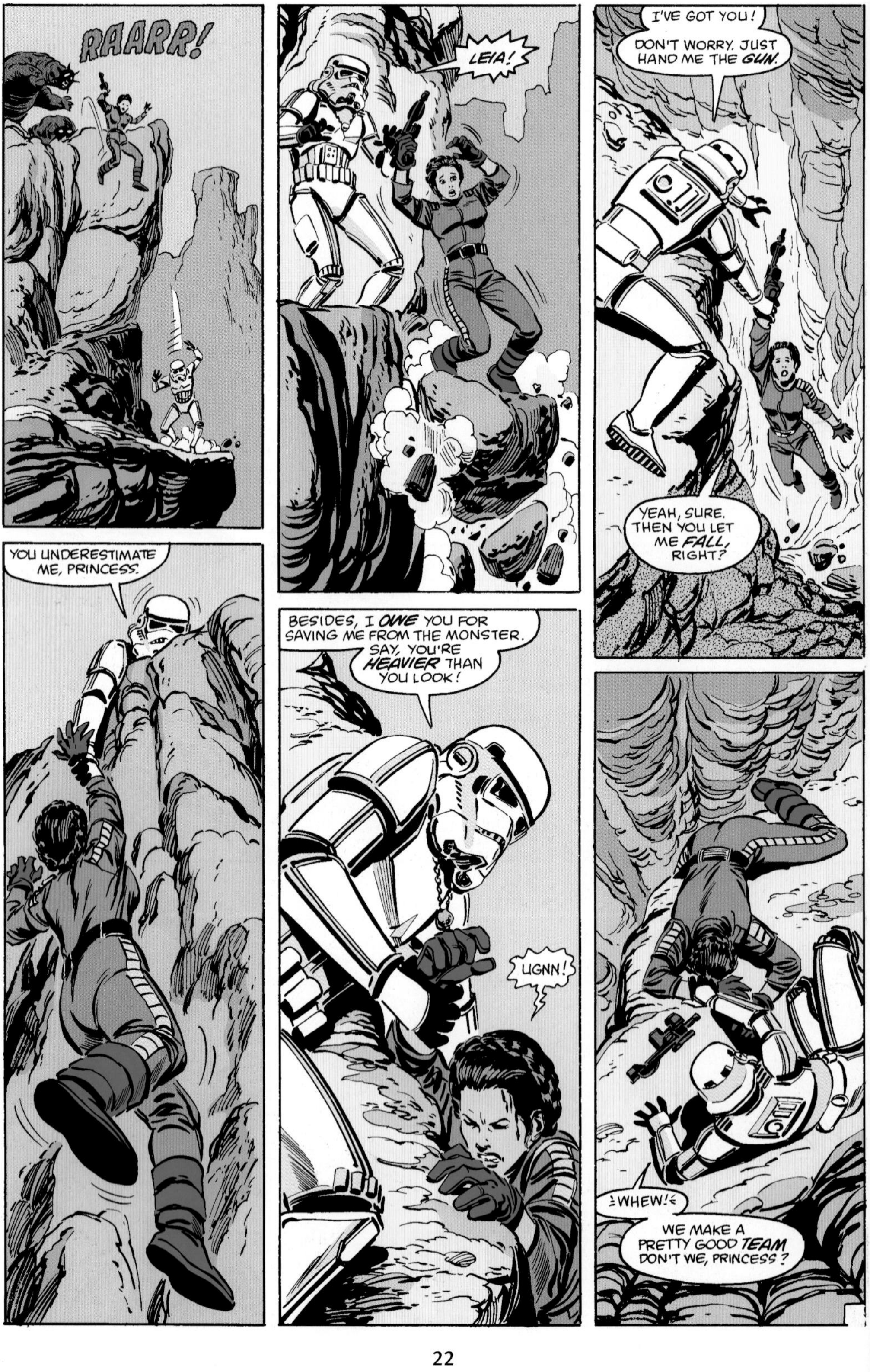
RAARR!
LEIA!
I'VE GOT YOU!
DON'T WORRY. JUST HAND ME THE GUN.
YEAH, SURE. THEN YOU LET ME FALL, RIGHT?
YOU UNDERESTIMATE ME, PRINCESS.
BESIDES, I OWE YOU FOR SAVING ME FROM THE MONSTER.
SAY, YOU'RE HEAVIER THAN YOU LOOK!
UGNN!
WHEW!
WE MAKE A PRETTY GOOD TEAM DON'T WE, PRINCESS?

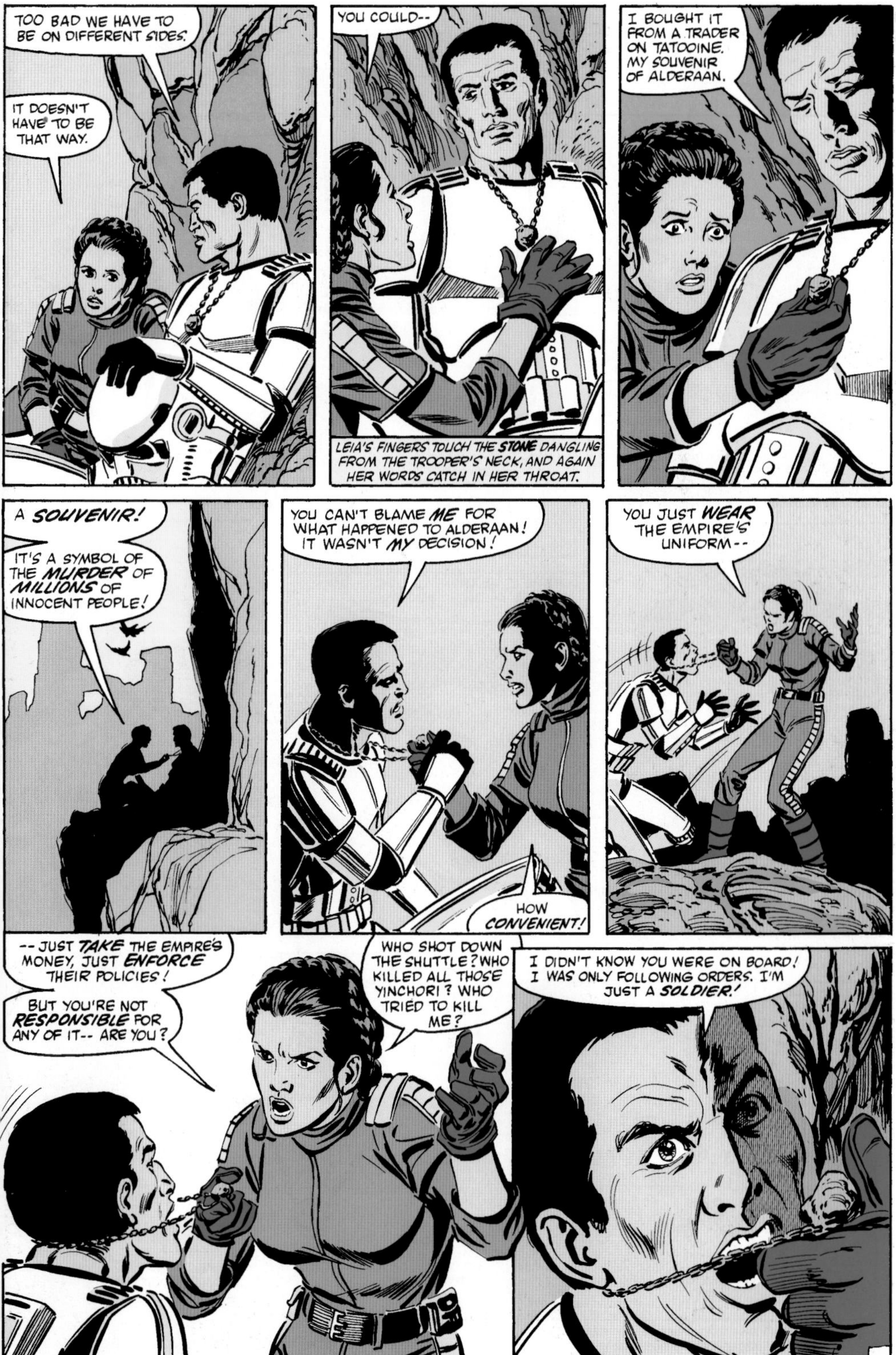
TOO BAD WE HAVE TO BE ON DIFFERENT SIDES.
IT DOESN'T HAVE TO BE THAT WAY.
YOU COULD--
LEIA'S FINGERS TOUCH THE STONE DANGLING FROM THE TROOPER'S NECK, AND AGAIN HER WORDS CATCH IN HER THROAT.
I BOUGHT IT FROM A TRADER ON TATOOINE. MY SOUVENIR OF ALDERAAN.
A SOUVENIR!
IT'S A SYMBOL OF THE MURDER OF MILLIONS OF INNOCENT PEOPLE!
YOU CAN'T BLAME ME FOR WHAT HAPPENED TO ALDERAAN! IT WASN'T MY DECISION!
HOW CONVENIENT!
YOU JUST WEAR THE EMPIRE'S UNIFORM--
--JUST TAKE THE EMPIRE'S MONEY, JUST ENFORCE THEIR POLICIES!
BUT YOU'RE NOT RESPONSIBLE FOR ANY OF IT-- ARE YOU?
WHO SHOT DOWN THE SHUTTLE? WHO KILLED ALL THOSE YINCHORI? WHO TRIED TO KILL ME?
I DIDN'T KNOW YOU WERE ON BOARD! I WAS ONLY FOLLOWING ORDERS. I'M JUST A SOLDIER!

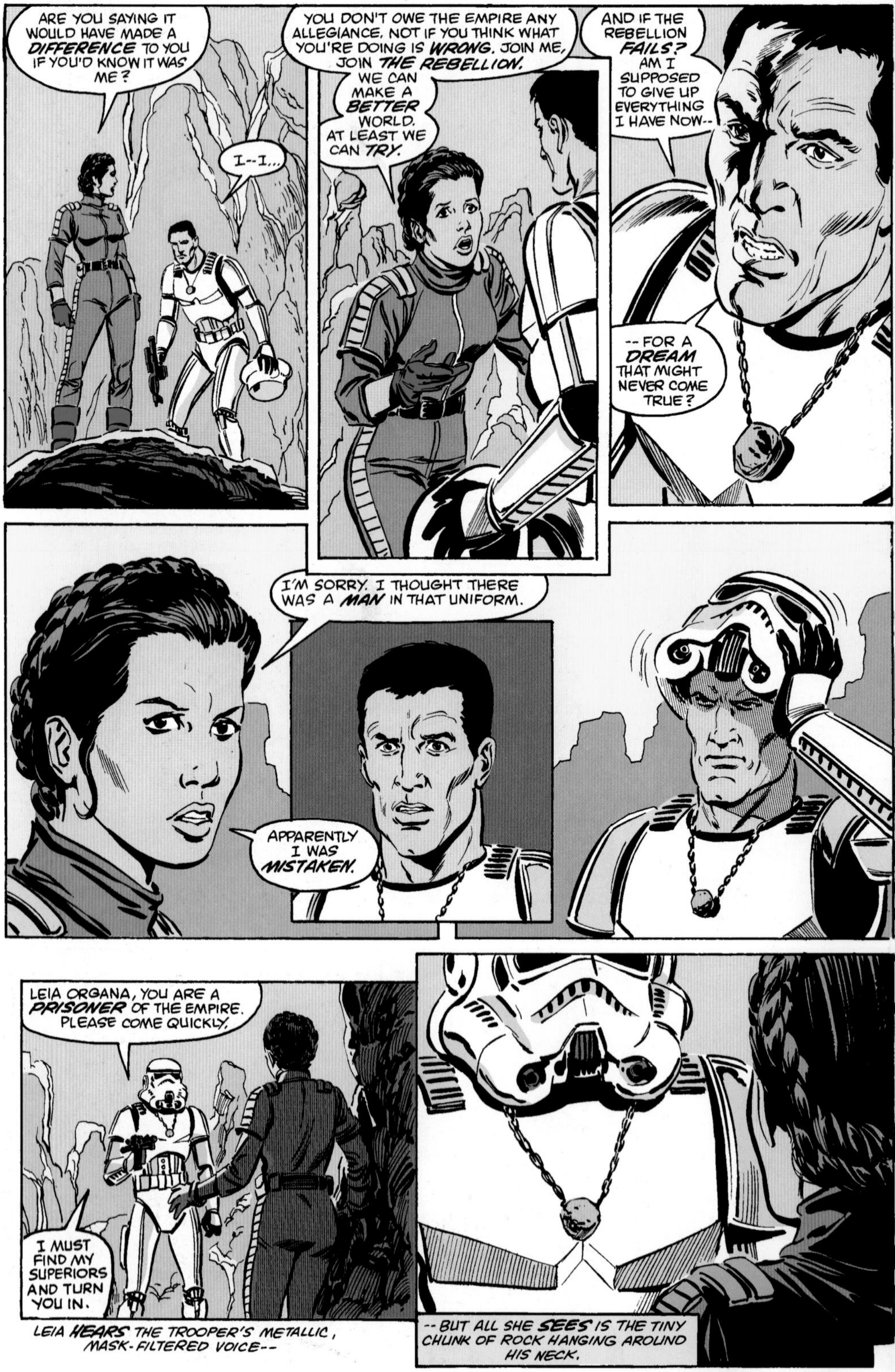
ARE YOU SAYING IT WOULD HAVE MADE A DIFFERENCE TO YOU IF YOU'D KNOW IT WAS ME?
I--I...
YOU DON'T OWE THE EMPIRE ANY ALLEGIANCE. NOT IF YOU THINK WHAT YOU'RE DOING IS WRONG. JOIN ME, JOIN THE REBELLION.
WE CAN MAKE A BETTER WORLD. AT LEAST WE CAN TRY.
AND IF THE REBELLION FAILS? AM I SUPPOSED TO GIVE UP EVERYTHING I HAVE NOW--
-- FOR A DREAM THAT MIGHT NEVER COME TRUE?
I'M SORRY. I THOUGHT THERE WAS A MAN IN THAT UNIFORM.
APPARENTLY I WAS MISTAKEN.
LEIA ORGANA, YOU ARE A PRISONER OF THE EMPIRE. PLEASE COME QUICKLY.
I MUST FIND MY SUPERIORS AND TURN YOU IN.
LEIA HEARS THE TROOPER'S METALLIC, MASK-FILTERED VOICE--
-- BUT ALL SHE SEES IS THE TINY CHUNK OF ROCK HANGING AROUND HIS NECK.

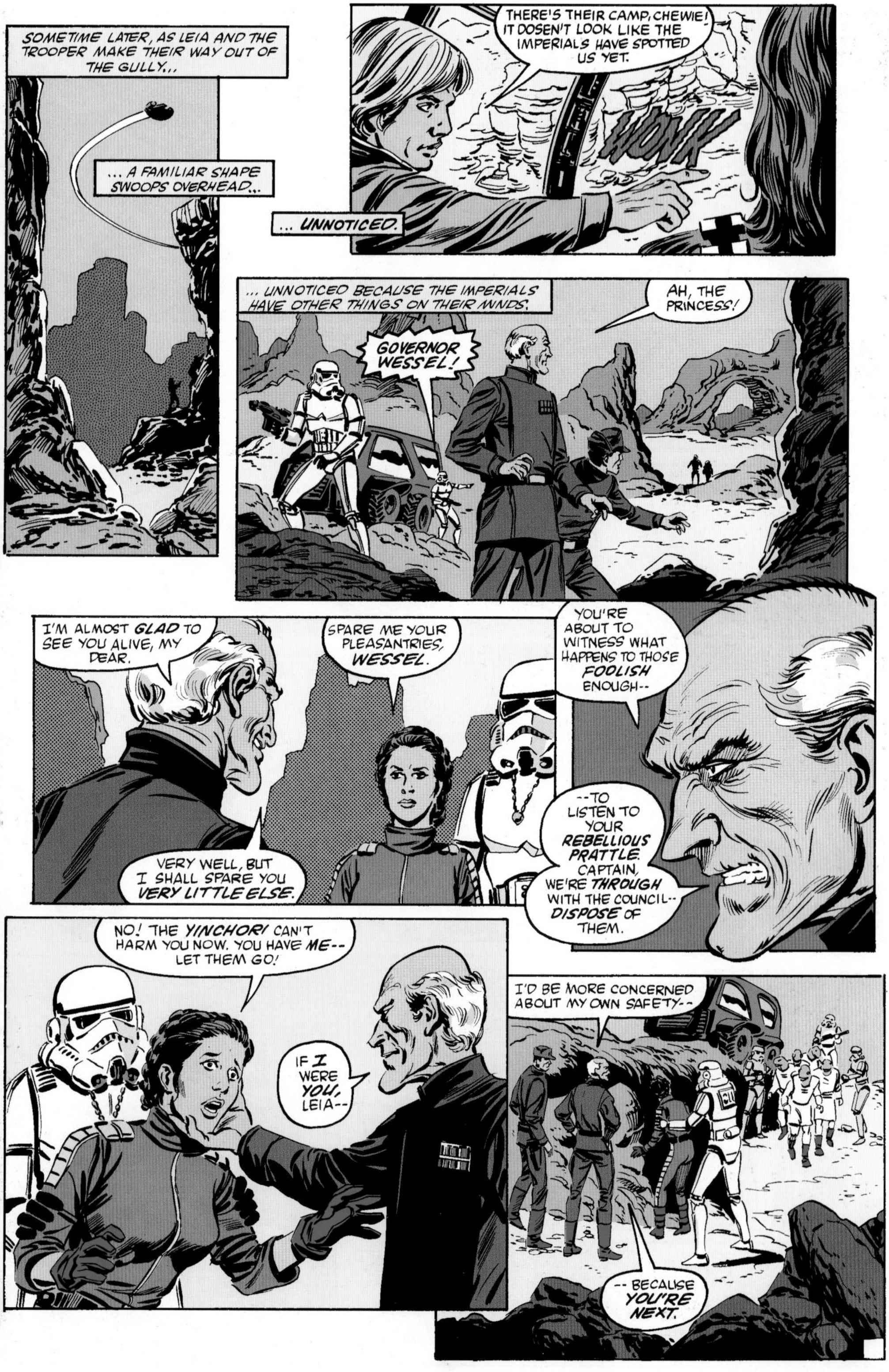
SOMETIME LATER, AS LEIA AND THE TROOPER MAKE THEIR WAY OUT OF THE GULLY...
... A FAMILIAR SHAPE SWOOPS OVERHEAD...
... UNNOTICED.
THERE'S THEIR CAMP, CHEWIE! IT DOSEN'T LOOK LIKE THE IMPERIALS HAVE SPOTTED US YET.
WONK
... UNNOTICED BECAUSE THE IMPERIALS HAVE OTHER THINGS ON THEIR MINDS.
AH, THE PRINCESS!
GOVERNOR WESSEL!
I'M ALMOST GLAD TO SEE YOU ALIVE, MY DEAR.
SPARE ME YOUR PLEASANTRIES, WESSEL.
VERY WELL, BUT I SHALL SPARE YOU VERY LITTLE ELSE.
YOU'RE ABOUT TO WITNESS WHAT HAPPENS TO THOSE FOOLISH ENOUGH--
--TO LISTEN TO YOUR REBELLIOUS PRATTLE. CAPTAIN, WE'RE THROUGH WITH THE COUNCIL-- DISPOSE OF THEM.
NO! THE YINCHORI CAN'T HARM YOU NOW. YOU HAVE ME-- LET THEM GO!
IF I WERE YOU, LEIA--
I'D BE MORE CONCERNED ABOUT MY OWN SAFETY--
-- BECAUSE YOU'RE NEXT.

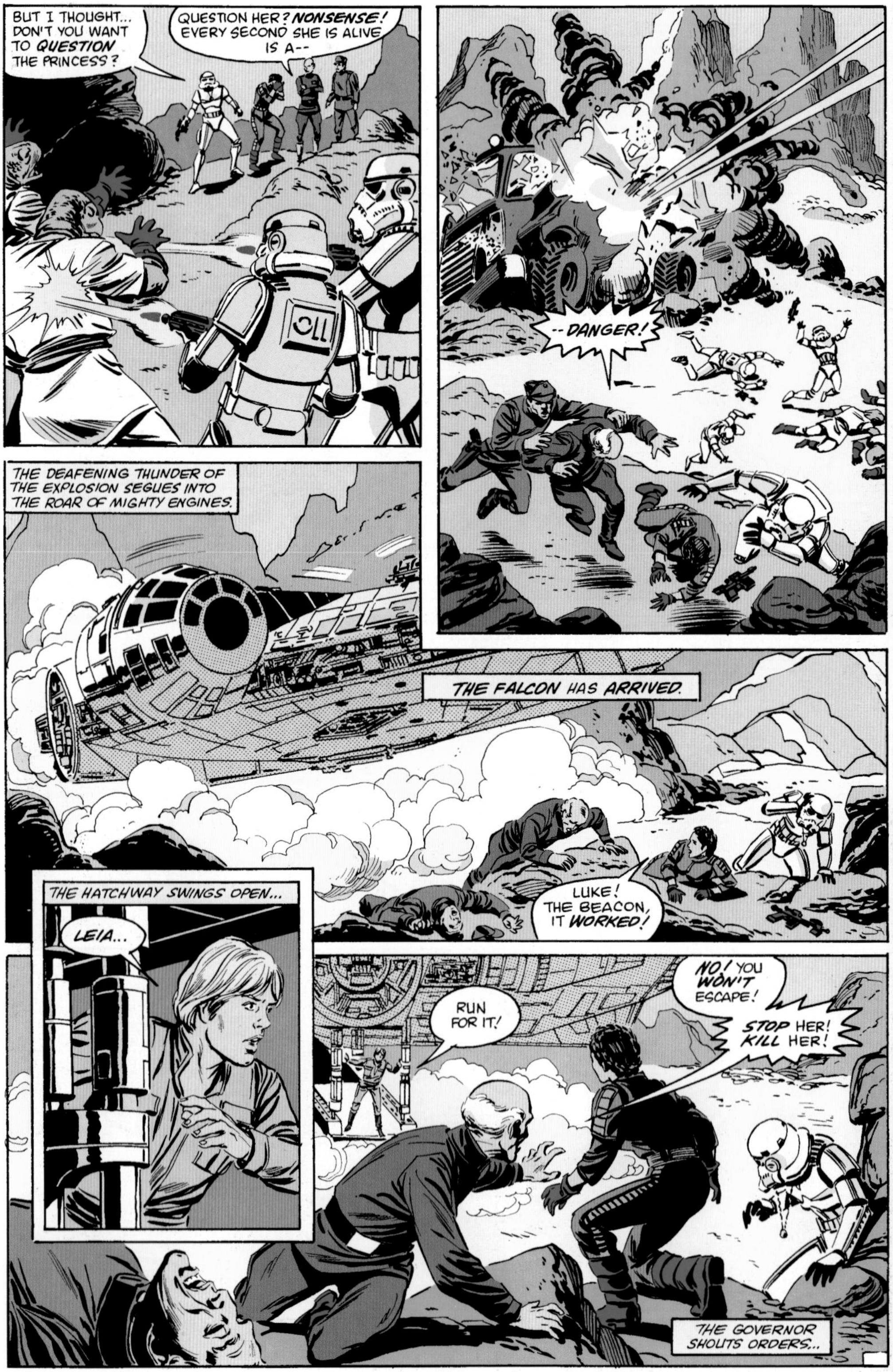

BUT I THOUGHT... DON'T YOU WANT TO QUESTION THE PRINCESS?
QUESTION HER? NONSENSE! EVERY SECOND SHE IS ALIVE IS A--
--DANGER!
THE DEAFENING THUNDER OF THE EXPLOSION SEGUES INTO THE ROAR OF MIGHTY ENGINES.
THE FALCON HAS ARRIVED.
LUKE! THE BEACON, IT WORKED!
THE HATCHWAY SWINGS OPEN...
LEIA...
RUN FOR IT!
NO! YOU WON'T ESCAPE!
STOP HER! KILL HER!
THE GOVERNOR SHOUTS ORDERS...

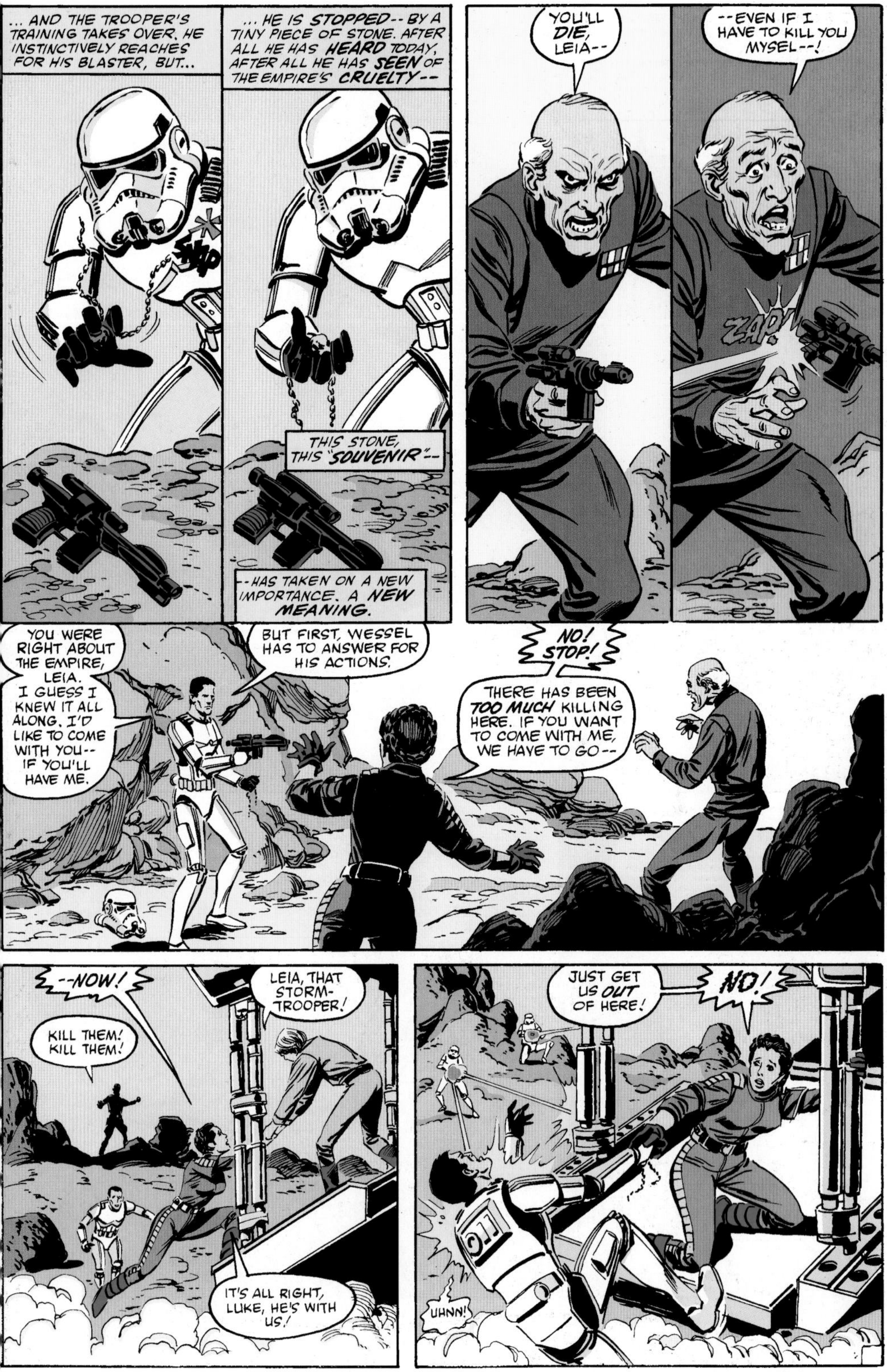

... AND THE TROOPER'S TRAINING TAKES OVER. HE INSTINCTIVELY REACHES FOR HIS BLASTER, BUT...
SNAP
... HE IS STOPPED-- BY A TINY PIECE OF STONE. AFTER ALL HE HAS HEARD TODAY, AFTER ALL HE HAS SEEN OF THE EMPIRE'S CRUELTY--
THIS STONE, THIS "SOUVENIR"--
--HAS TAKEN ON A NEW IMPORTANCE. A NEW MEANING.
YOU'LL DIE, LEIA--
--EVEN IF I HAVE TO KILL YOU MYSEL--!
ZAP!
YOU WERE RIGHT ABOUT THE EMPIRE, LEIA. I GUESS I KNEW IT ALL ALONG. I'D LIKE TO COME WITH YOU-- IF YOU'LL HAVE ME.
BUT FIRST, WESSEL HAS TO ANSWER FOR HIS ACTIONS.
NO! STOP!
THERE HAS BEEN TOO MUCH KILLING HERE. IF YOU WANT TO COME WITH ME, WE HAVE TO GO--
--NOW!
LEIA, THAT STORM-TROOPER!
KILL THEM! KILL THEM!
IT'S ALL RIGHT, LUKE, HE'S WITH US!
JUST GET US OUT OF HERE!
NO!
UHNN!

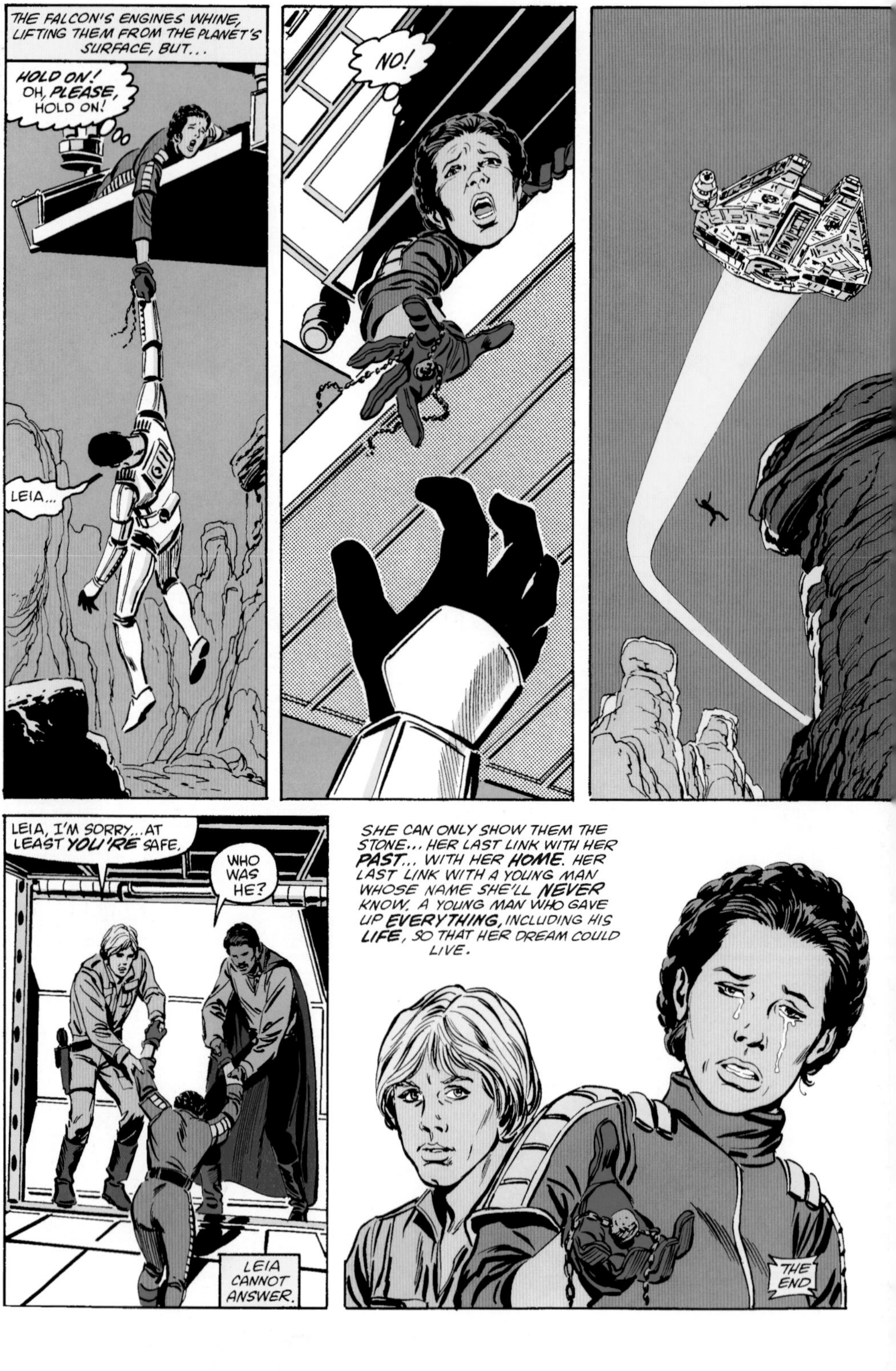
THE FALCON'S ENGINES WHINE, LIFTING THEM FROM THE PLANET'S SURFACE, BUT...
HOLD ON! OH, PLEASE, HOLD ON!
LEIA...
NO!
LEIA, I'M SORRY...AT LEAST YOU'RE SAFE.
WHO WAS HE?
LEIA CANNOT ANSWER.
SHE CAN ONLY SHOW THEM THE STONE... HER LAST LINK WITH HER PAST... WITH HER HOME. HER LAST LINK WITH A YOUNG MAN WHOSE NAME SHE'LL NEVER KNOW. A YOUNG MAN WHO GAVE UP EVERYTHING, INCLUDING HIS LIFE, SO THAT HER DREAM COULD LIVE.
THE END

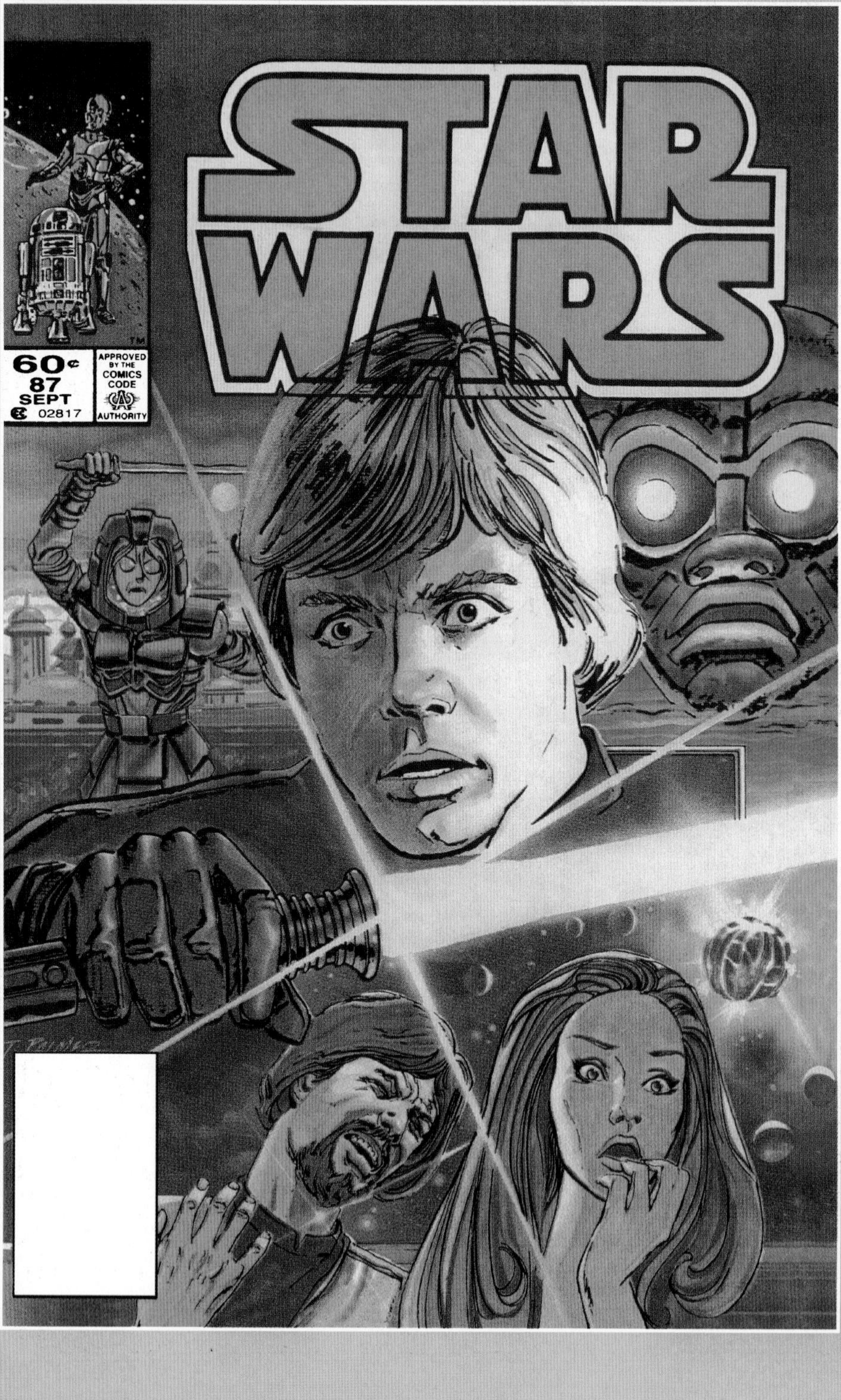
STAR WARS
60¢
87
SEPT
02817
APPROVED BY THE COMICS CODE AUTHORITY
TM

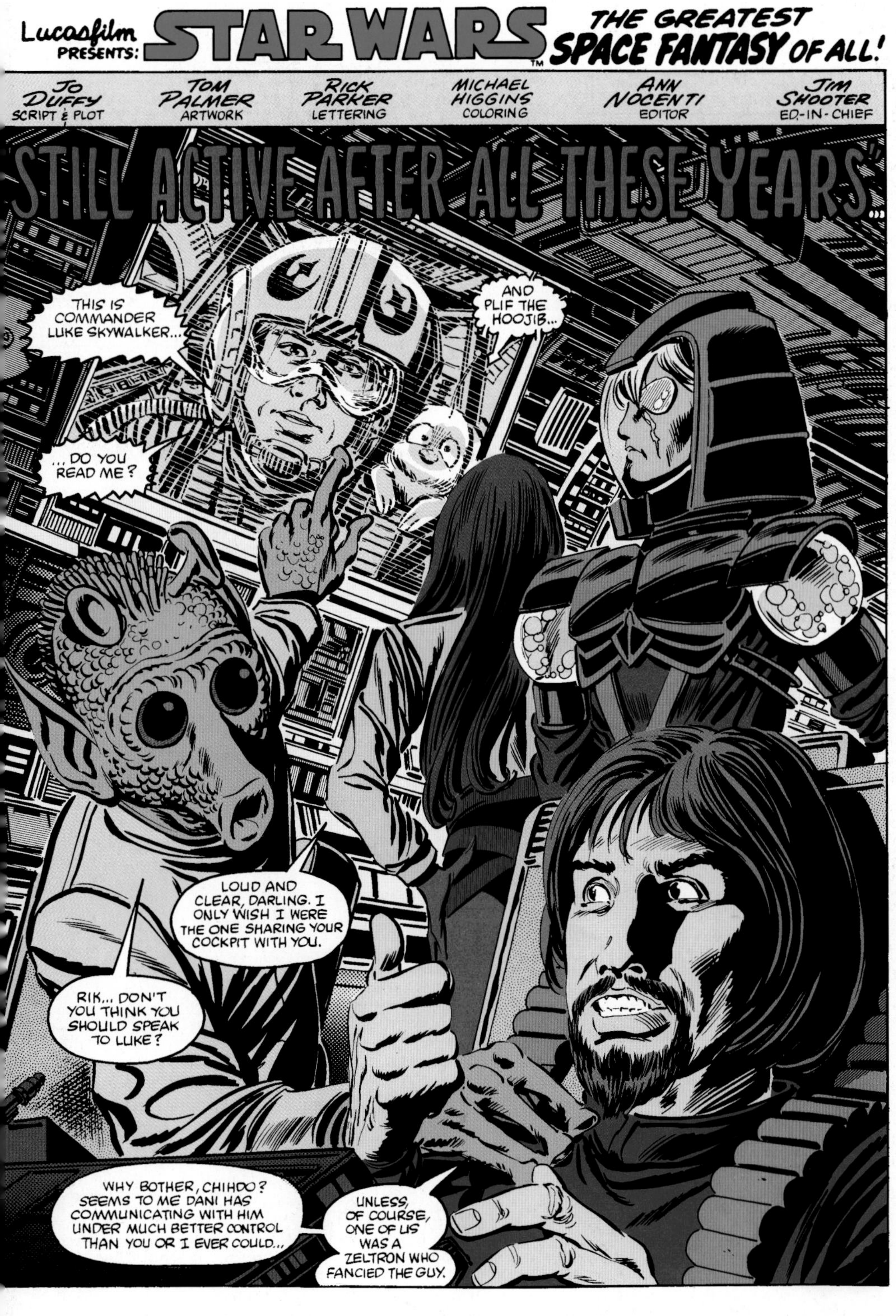
Lucasfilm PRESENTS: STAR WARS™ THE GREATEST SPACE FANTASY OF ALL!
JO DUFFY SCRIPT & PLOT
TOM PALMER ARTWORK
RICK PARKER LETTERING
MICHAEL HIGGINS COLORING
ANN NOCENTI EDITOR
JIM SHOOTER ED.-IN-CHIEF
"STILL ACTIVE AFTER ALL THESE YEARS"...
THIS IS COMMANDER LUKE SKYWALKER...
AND PLIF THE HOOJIB...
...DO YOU READ ME?
LOUD AND CLEAR, DARLING. I ONLY WISH I WERE THE ONE SHARING YOUR COCKPIT WITH YOU.
RIK... DON'T YOU THINK YOU SHOULD SPEAK TO LUKE?
WHY BOTHER, CHIHDO? SEEMS TO ME DANI HAS COMMUNICATING WITH HIM UNDER MUCH BETTER CONTROL THAN YOU OR I EVER COULD...
UNLESS, OF COURSE, ONE OF US WAS A ZELTRON WHO FANCIED THE GUY.

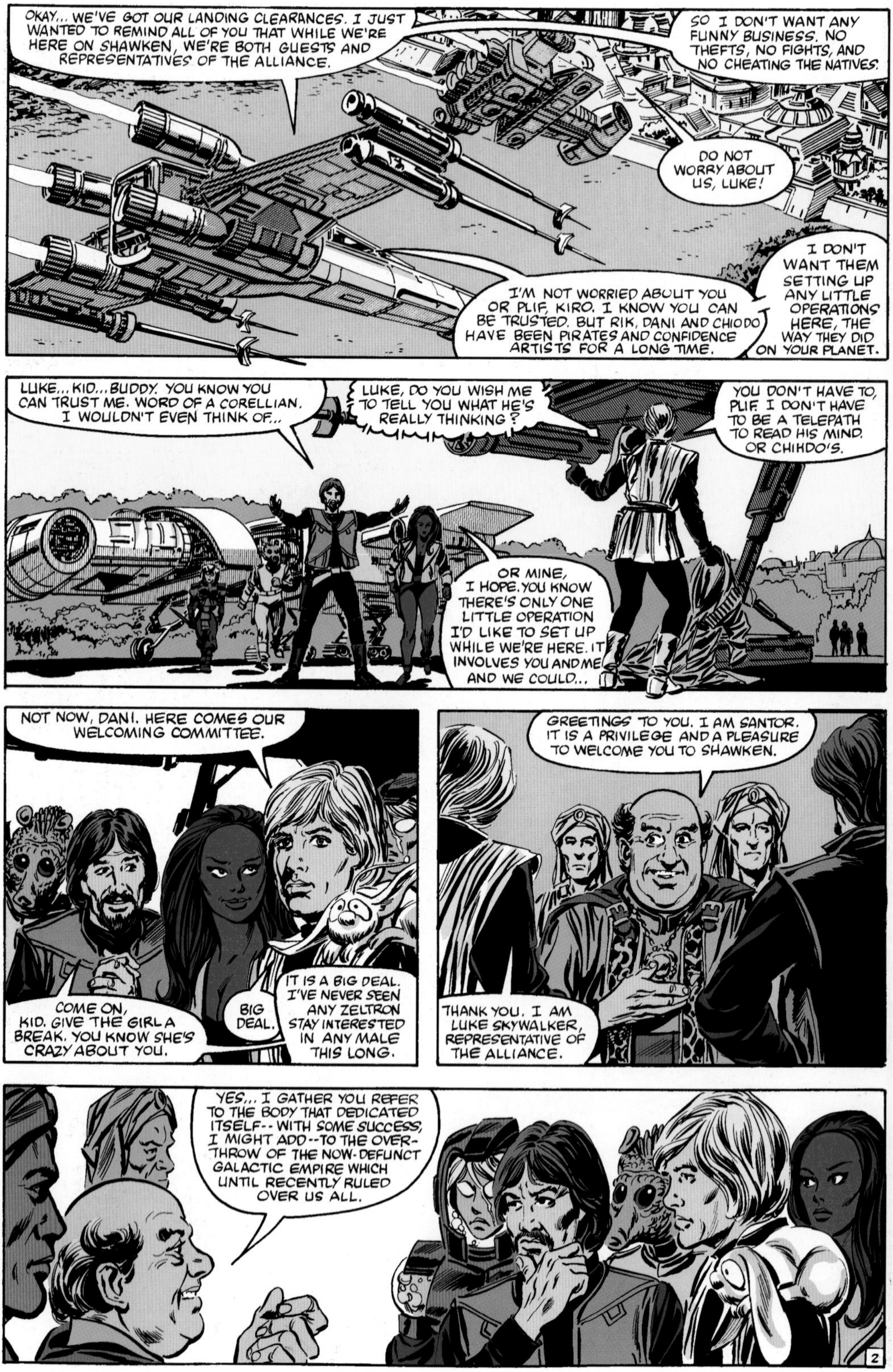
OKAY... WE'VE GOT OUR LANDING CLEARANCES. I JUST WANTED TO REMIND ALL OF YOU THAT WHILE WE'RE HERE ON SHAWKEN, WE'RE BOTH GUESTS AND REPRESENTATIVES OF THE ALLIANCE.
SO I DON'T WANT ANY FUNNY BUSINESS. NO THEFTS, NO FIGHTS, AND NO CHEATING THE NATIVES.
DO NOT WORRY ABOUT US, LUKE!
I'M NOT WORRIED ABOUT YOU OR PLIF, KIRO. I KNOW YOU CAN BE TRUSTED. BUT RIK, DANI AND CHIODO HAVE BEEN PIRATES AND CONFIDENCE ARTISTS FOR A LONG TIME.
I DON'T WANT THEM SETTING UP ANY LITTLE OPERATIONS HERE, THE WAY THEY DID ON YOUR PLANET.
LUKE... KID... BUDDY. YOU KNOW YOU CAN TRUST ME. WORD OF A CORELLIAN. I WOULDN'T EVEN THINK OF...
LUKE, DO YOU WISH ME TO TELL YOU WHAT HE'S REALLY THINKING?
YOU DON'T HAVE TO, PLIF. I DON'T HAVE TO BE A TELEPATH TO READ HIS MIND. OR CHIHDO'S.
OR MINE, I HOPE. YOU KNOW THERE'S ONLY ONE LITTLE OPERATION I'D LIKE TO SET UP WHILE WE'RE HERE. IT INVOLVES YOU AND ME AND WE COULD...
NOT NOW, DANI. HERE COMES OUR WELCOMING COMMITTEE.
COME ON, KID. GIVE THE GIRL A BREAK. YOU KNOW SHE'S CRAZY ABOUT YOU.
BIG DEAL.
IT IS A BIG DEAL. I'VE NEVER SEEN ANY ZELTRON STAY INTERESTED IN ANY MALE THIS LONG.
GREETINGS TO YOU. I AM SANTOR. IT IS A PRIVILEGE AND A PLEASURE TO WELCOME YOU TO SHAWKEN.
THANK YOU. I AM LUKE SKYWALKER, REPRESENTATIVE OF THE ALLIANCE.
YES... I GATHER YOU REFER TO THE BODY THAT DEDICATED ITSELF-- WITH SOME SUCCESS, I MIGHT ADD--TO THE OVER-THROW OF THE NOW-DEFUNCT GALACTIC EMPIRE WHICH UNTIL RECENTLY RULED OVER US ALL.
2

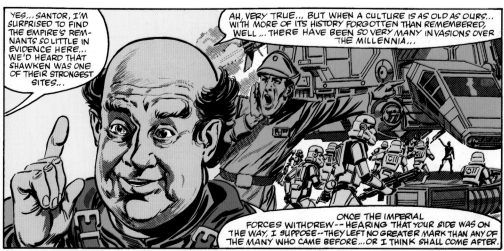

YES... SANTOR, I'M SURPRISED TO FIND THE EMPIRE'S REMNANTS SO LITTLE IN EVIDENCE HERE... WE'D HEARD THAT SHAWKEN WAS ONE OF THEIR STRONGEST SITES...

AH, VERY TRUE..., BUT WHEN A CULTURE IS AS OLD AS OURS... WITH MORE OF ITS HISTORY FORGOTTEN THAN REMEMBERED, WELL ... THERE HAVE BEEN SO VERY MANY INVASIONS OVER THE MILLENNIA...

ONCE THE IMPERIAL FORCES WITHDREW -- HEARING THAT YOUR SIDE WAS ON THE WAY, I SUPPOSE -- THEY LEFT NO GREATER MARK THAN ANY OF THE MANY WHO CAME BEFORE... OR I THINK SHALL COME AFTER.

PUH-LEEEZE! IS ALL THE TALK GONNA BE THIS LONG-WINDED AND POLITE FROM HERE ON IN... NO PRELIMINAR-IES? JUST "ON WITH THE DIPLOMACY"?

'CAUSE IF IT IS, PLEASE INCLUDE ME AND MY CREW OUT RIGHT NOW!

UH, SANTOR... HE MAY HAVE A POINT. RIK, DANI AND CHIHDO AREN'T EXACTLY PART OF THIS DELEGATION. IS THERE ANYWHERE THEY COULD--?

AH... THEY WISH AMUSEMENTS WHILE YOU AND I AND THE OTHERS TALK? THAT IS VERY SIMPLY ARRANGED.

IN TRYING TO LOOT OUR WORLD OF ITS LEGENDARY RICHES, THE IMPERIALS DID MUCH EXCAVATION.

THERE, FOR EXAMPLE, THEY UNEARTHED OLD CATACOMBS... WE NO LONGER KNOW WHAT THEY WERE ONCE FOR, THEY ARE SO OLD. I AM TOLD THEY ARE VERY INTER-ESTING AND BEAUTIFUL.

NOW... WHO WILL COME WITH US TO MY HOME?

IT WILL BE A PLEASURE.

AND I SHALL COME, TOO.

AND AN HONOR.

LET'S GO, YOU TWO... OLD, UNEXPLORED RUINS SOUND LIKE THEY GOT SOME POSSIBILITIES.

BUT... I WANT TO STAY WITH LUKE...

FORGET IT SWEETHEART, THE KID'S ON BUSINESS. HE DOESN'T WANT TO PLAY.

3

33

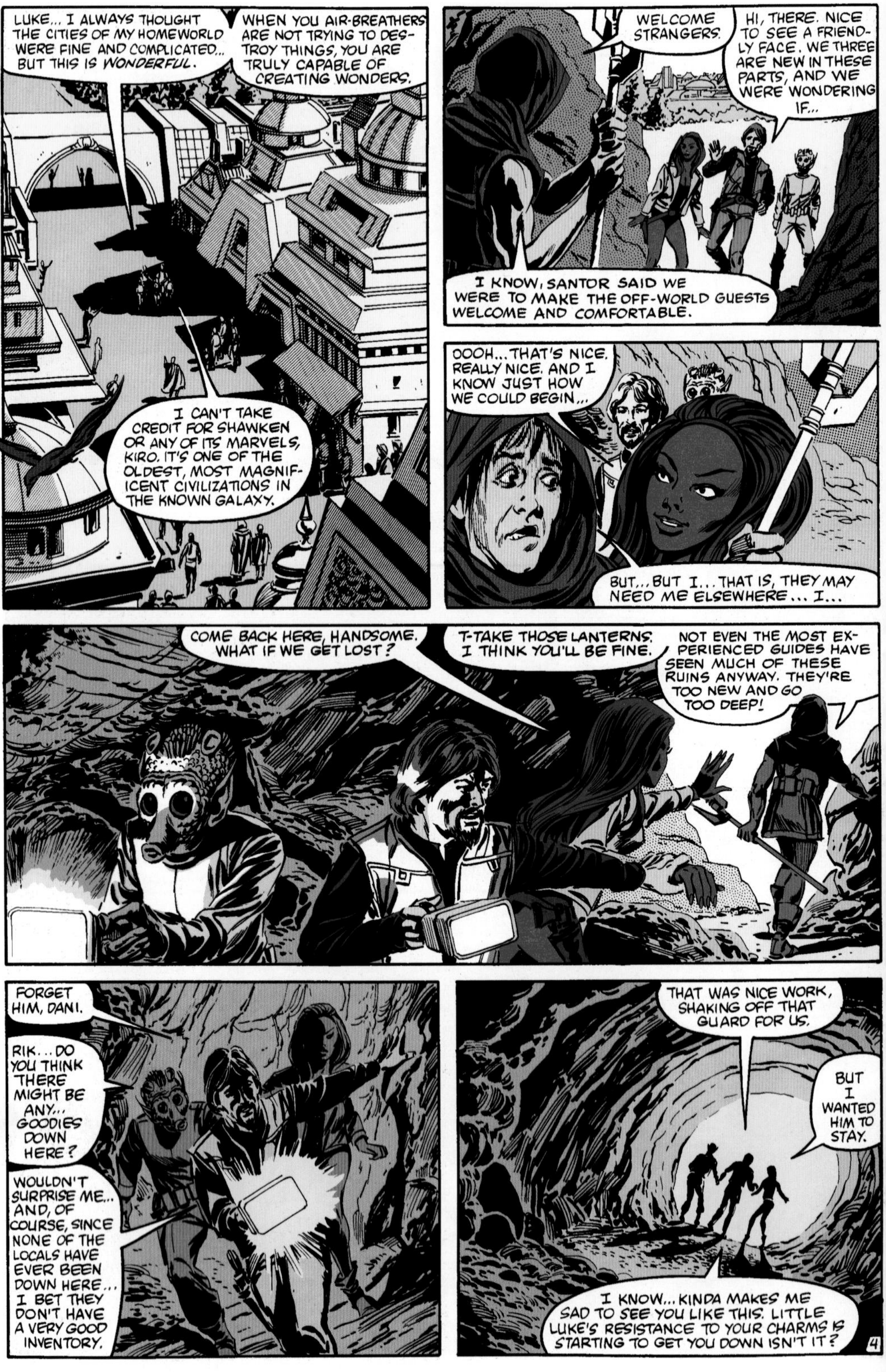

LUKE... I ALWAYS THOUGHT THE CITIES OF MY HOMEWORLD WERE FINE AND COMPLICATED... BUT THIS IS *WONDERFUL*.
WHEN YOU AIR-BREATHERS ARE NOT TRYING TO DESTROY THINGS, YOU ARE TRULY CAPABLE OF CREATING WONDERS.
I CAN'T TAKE CREDIT FOR SHAWKEN OR ANY OF ITS MARVELS, KIRO. IT'S ONE OF THE OLDEST, MOST MAGNIFICENT CIVILIZATIONS IN THE KNOWN GALAXY.
WELCOME STRANGERS.
HI, THERE. NICE TO SEE A FRIENDLY FACE. WE THREE ARE NEW IN THESE PARTS, AND WE WERE WONDERING IF...
I KNOW, SANTOR SAID WE WERE TO MAKE THE OFF-WORLD GUESTS WELCOME AND COMFORTABLE.
OOOH... THAT'S NICE. REALLY NICE. AND I KNOW JUST HOW WE COULD BEGIN...
BUT... BUT I... THAT IS, THEY MAY NEED ME ELSEWHERE... I...
COME BACK HERE, HANDSOME. WHAT IF WE GET LOST?
T-TAKE THOSE LANTERNS. I THINK YOU'LL BE FINE.
NOT EVEN THE MOST EXPERIENCED GUIDES HAVE SEEN MUCH OF THESE RUINS ANYWAY. THEY'RE TOO NEW AND GO TOO DEEP!
FORGET HIM, DANI.
RIK... DO YOU THINK THERE MIGHT BE ANY... GOODIES DOWN HERE?
WOULDN'T SURPRISE ME... AND, OF COURSE, SINCE NONE OF THE LOCALS HAVE EVER BEEN DOWN HERE... I BET THEY DON'T HAVE A VERY GOOD INVENTORY.
THAT WAS NICE WORK, SHAKING OFF THAT GUARD FOR US.
BUT I WANTED HIM TO STAY.
I KNOW... KINDA MAKES ME SAD TO SEE YOU LIKE THIS. LITTLE LUKE'S RESISTANCE TO YOUR CHARMS IS STARTING TO GET YOU DOWN ISN'T IT?
4

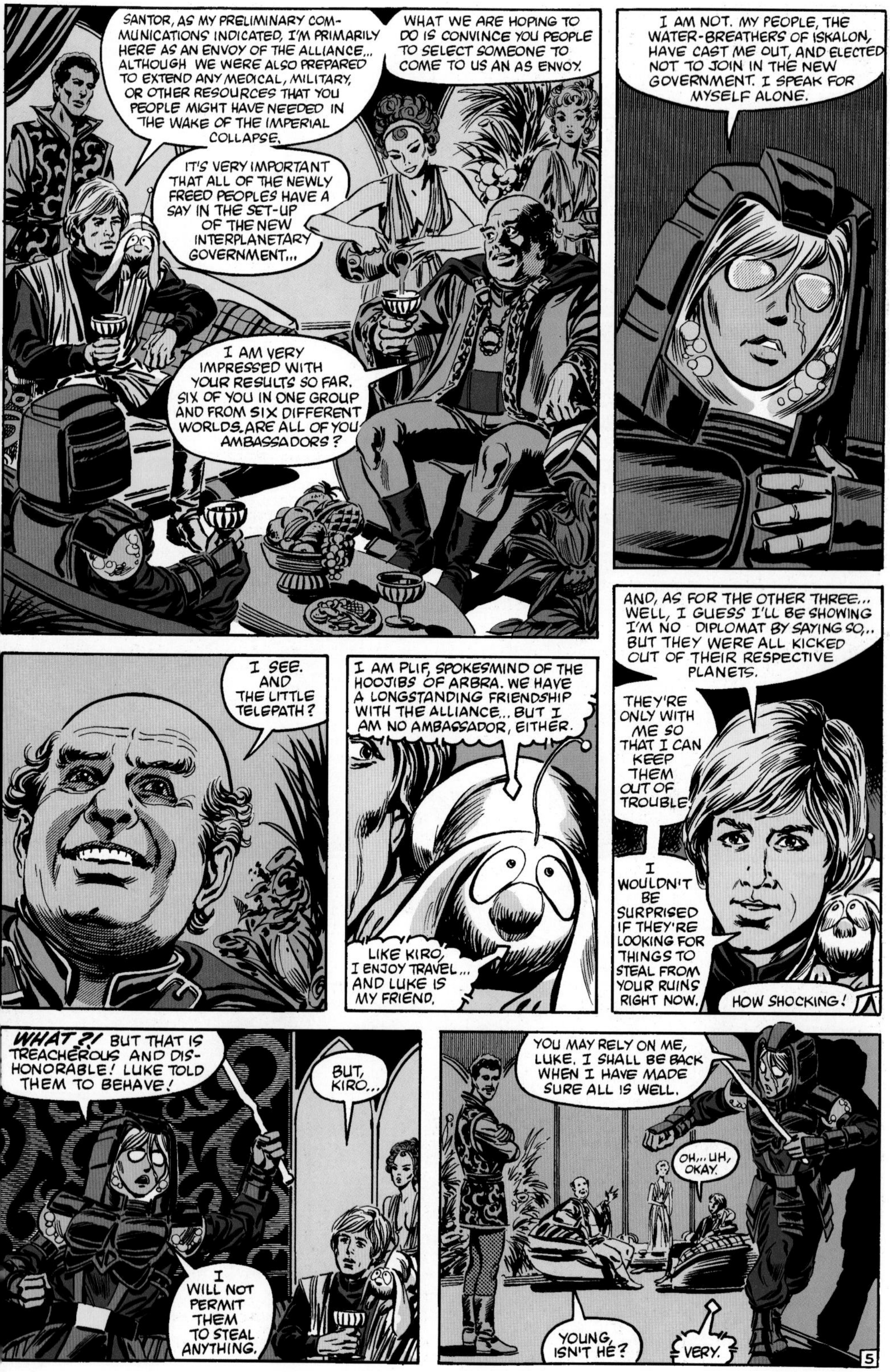
SANTOR, AS MY PRELIMINARY COMMUNICATIONS INDICATED, I'M PRIMARILY HERE AS AN ENVOY OF THE ALLIANCE... ALTHOUGH WE WERE ALSO PREPARED TO EXTEND ANY MEDICAL, MILITARY, OR OTHER RESOURCES THAT YOU PEOPLE MIGHT HAVE NEEDED IN THE WAKE OF THE IMPERIAL COLLAPSE.
IT'S VERY IMPORTANT THAT ALL OF THE NEWLY FREED PEOPLES HAVE A SAY IN THE SET-UP OF THE NEW INTERPLANETARY GOVERNMENT...
WHAT WE ARE HOPING TO DO IS CONVINCE YOU PEOPLE TO SELECT SOMEONE TO COME TO US AN AS ENVOY.
I AM VERY IMPRESSED WITH YOUR RESULTS SO FAR. SIX OF YOU IN ONE GROUP AND FROM SIX DIFFERENT WORLDS. ARE ALL OF YOU AMBASSADORS?
I AM NOT. MY PEOPLE, THE WATER-BREATHERS OF ISKALON, HAVE CAST ME OUT, AND ELECTED NOT TO JOIN IN THE NEW GOVERNMENT. I SPEAK FOR MYSELF ALONE.
I SEE. AND THE LITTLE TELEPATH?
I AM PLIF, SPOKESMIND OF THE HOOJIBS OF ARBRA. WE HAVE A LONGSTANDING FRIENDSHIP WITH THE ALLIANCE... BUT I AM NO AMBASSADOR, EITHER.
LIKE KIRO, I ENJOY TRAVEL... AND LUKE IS MY FRIEND.
AND, AS FOR THE OTHER THREE... WELL, I GUESS I'LL BE SHOWING I'M NO DIPLOMAT BY SAYING SO... BUT THEY WERE ALL KICKED OUT OF THEIR RESPECTIVE PLANETS.
THEY'RE ONLY WITH ME SO THAT I CAN KEEP THEM OUT OF TROUBLE.
I WOULDN'T BE SURPRISED IF THEY'RE LOOKING FOR THINGS TO STEAL FROM YOUR RUINS RIGHT NOW.
HOW SHOCKING!
WHAT?! BUT THAT IS TREACHEROUS AND DISHONORABLE! LUKE TOLD THEM TO BEHAVE!
BUT, KIRO...
I WILL NOT PERMIT THEM TO STEAL ANYTHING.
YOU MAY RELY ON ME, LUKE. I SHALL BE BACK WHEN I HAVE MADE SURE ALL IS WELL.
OH... UH, OKAY.
YOUNG, ISN'T HE?
VERY.
5

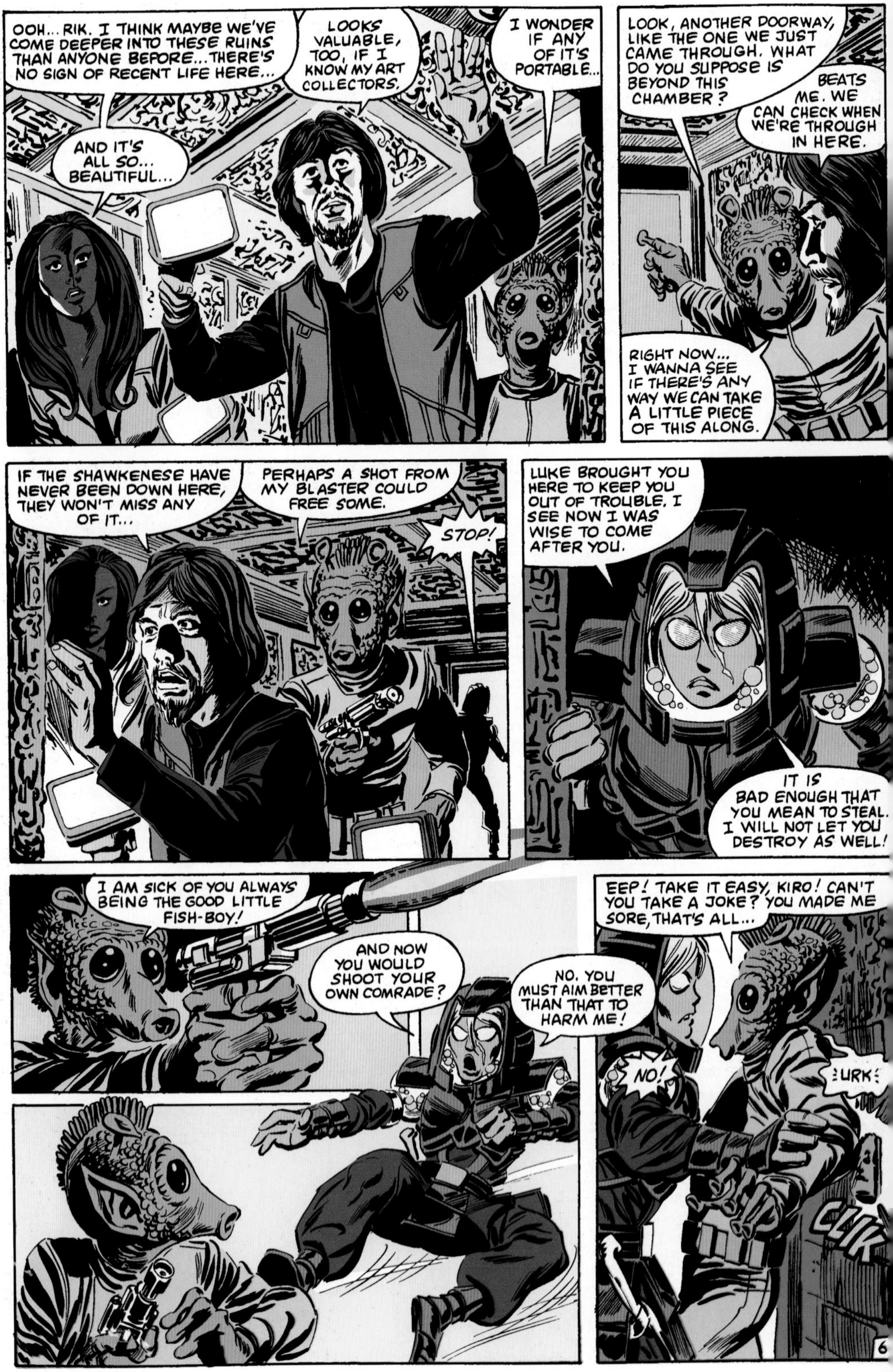
OOH... RIK. I THINK MAYBE WE'VE COME DEEPER INTO THESE RUINS THAN ANYONE BEFORE... THERE'S NO SIGN OF RECENT LIFE HERE...
LOOKS VALUABLE, TOO, IF I KNOW MY ART COLLECTORS.
I WONDER IF ANY OF IT'S PORTABLE...
AND IT'S ALL SO... BEAUTIFUL...
LOOK, ANOTHER DOORWAY, LIKE THE ONE WE JUST CAME THROUGH. WHAT DO YOU SUPPOSE IS BEYOND THIS CHAMBER?
BEATS ME. WE CAN CHECK WHEN WE'RE THROUGH IN HERE.
RIGHT NOW... I WANNA SEE IF THERE'S ANY WAY WE CAN TAKE A LITTLE PIECE OF THIS ALONG.
IF THE SHAWKENESE HAVE NEVER BEEN DOWN HERE, THEY WON'T MISS ANY OF IT...
PERHAPS A SHOT FROM MY BLASTER COULD FREE SOME.
STOP!
LUKE BROUGHT YOU HERE TO KEEP YOU OUT OF TROUBLE. I SEE NOW I WAS WISE TO COME AFTER YOU.
IT IS BAD ENOUGH THAT YOU MEAN TO STEAL. I WILL NOT LET YOU DESTROY AS WELL!
I AM SICK OF YOU ALWAYS BEING THE GOOD LITTLE FISH-BOY!
AND NOW YOU WOULD SHOOT YOUR OWN COMRADE?
NO. YOU MUST AIM BETTER THAN THAT TO HARM ME!
EEP! TAKE IT EASY, KIRO! CAN'T YOU TAKE A JOKE? YOU MADE ME SORE, THAT'S ALL...
NO!
URK
CLIK
6

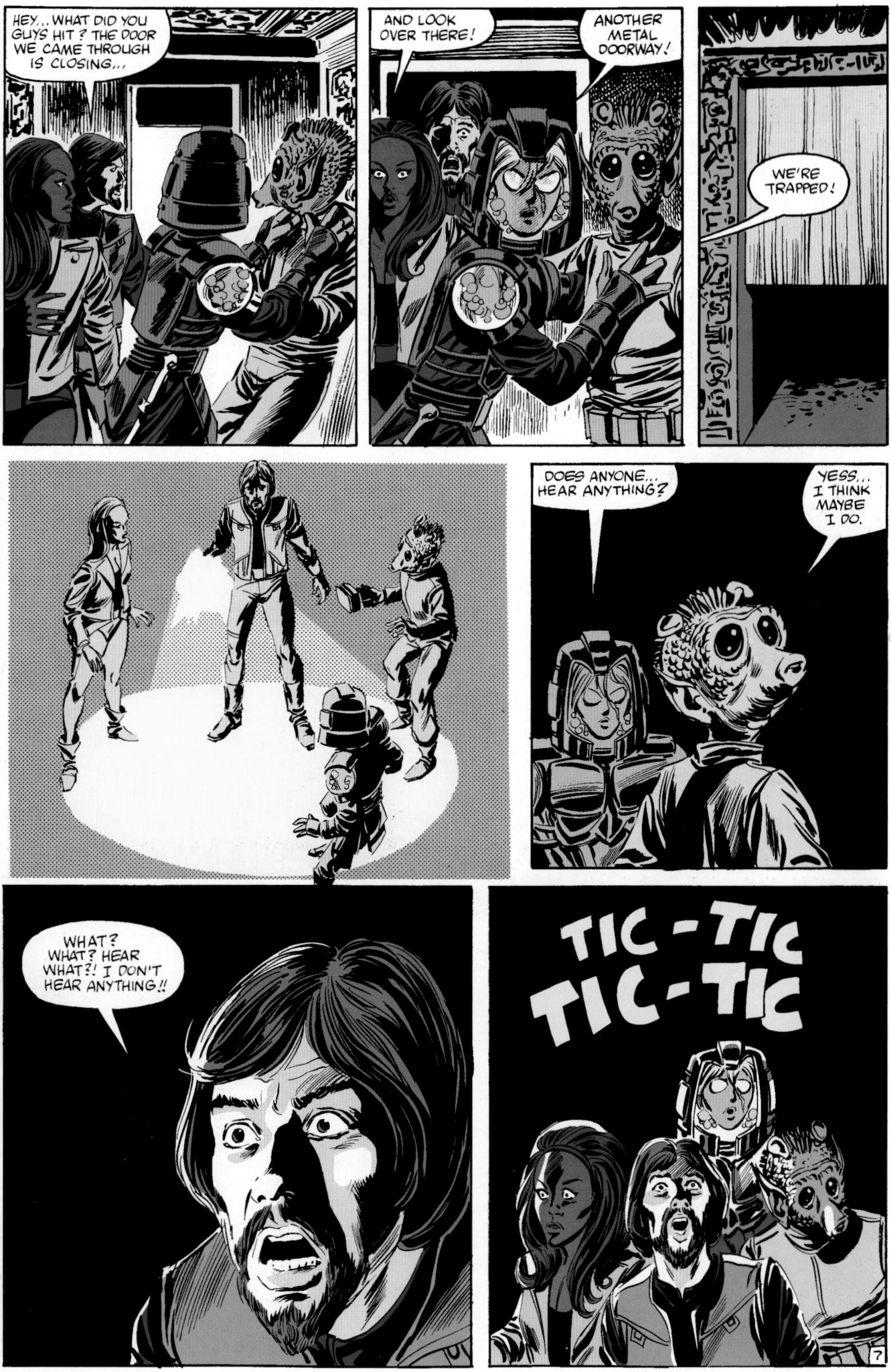
HEY... WHAT DID YOU GUYS HIT? THE DOOR WE CAME THROUGH IS CLOSING...
AND LOOK OVER THERE!
ANOTHER METAL DOORWAY!
WE'RE TRAPPED!
DOES ANYONE... HEAR ANYTHING?
YESS... I THINK MAYBE I DO.
WHAT? WHAT? HEAR WHAT?! I DON'T HEAR ANYTHING!!
TIC-TIC
TIC-TIC
7

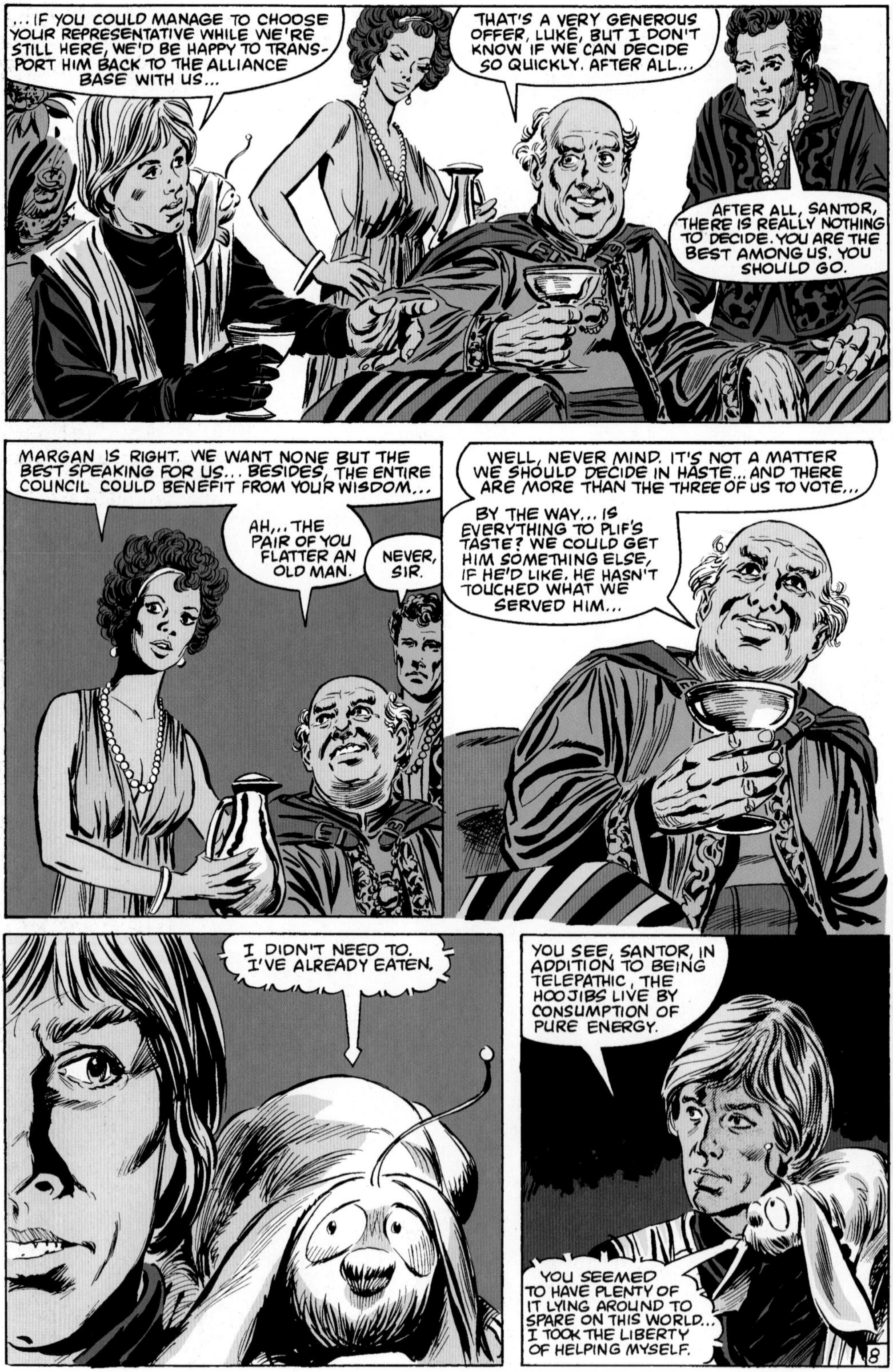
...IF YOU COULD MANAGE TO CHOOSE YOUR REPRESENTATIVE WHILE WE'RE STILL HERE, WE'D BE HAPPY TO TRANSPORT HIM BACK TO THE ALLIANCE BASE WITH US...
THAT'S A VERY GENEROUS OFFER, LUKE, BUT I DON'T KNOW IF WE CAN DECIDE SO QUICKLY. AFTER ALL...
AFTER ALL, SANTOR, THERE IS REALLY NOTHING TO DECIDE. YOU ARE THE BEST AMONG US. YOU SHOULD GO.
MARGAN IS RIGHT. WE WANT NONE BUT THE BEST SPEAKING FOR US... BESIDES, THE ENTIRE COUNCIL COULD BENEFIT FROM YOUR WISDOM...
AH,.. THE PAIR OF YOU FLATTER AN OLD MAN.
NEVER, SIR.
WELL, NEVER MIND. IT'S NOT A MATTER WE SHOULD DECIDE IN HASTE... AND THERE ARE MORE THAN THE THREE OF US TO VOTE...
BY THE WAY... IS EVERYTHING TO PLIF'S TASTE? WE COULD GET HIM SOMETHING ELSE, IF HE'D LIKE. HE HASN'T TOUCHED WHAT WE SERVED HIM...
I DIDN'T NEED TO. I'VE ALREADY EATEN.
YOU SEE, SANTOR, IN ADDITION TO BEING TELEPATHIC, THE HOOJIBS LIVE BY CONSUMPTION OF PURE ENERGY.
YOU SEEMED TO HAVE PLENTY OF IT LYING AROUND TO SPARE ON THIS WORLD... I TOOK THE LIBERTY OF HELPING MYSELF.
8

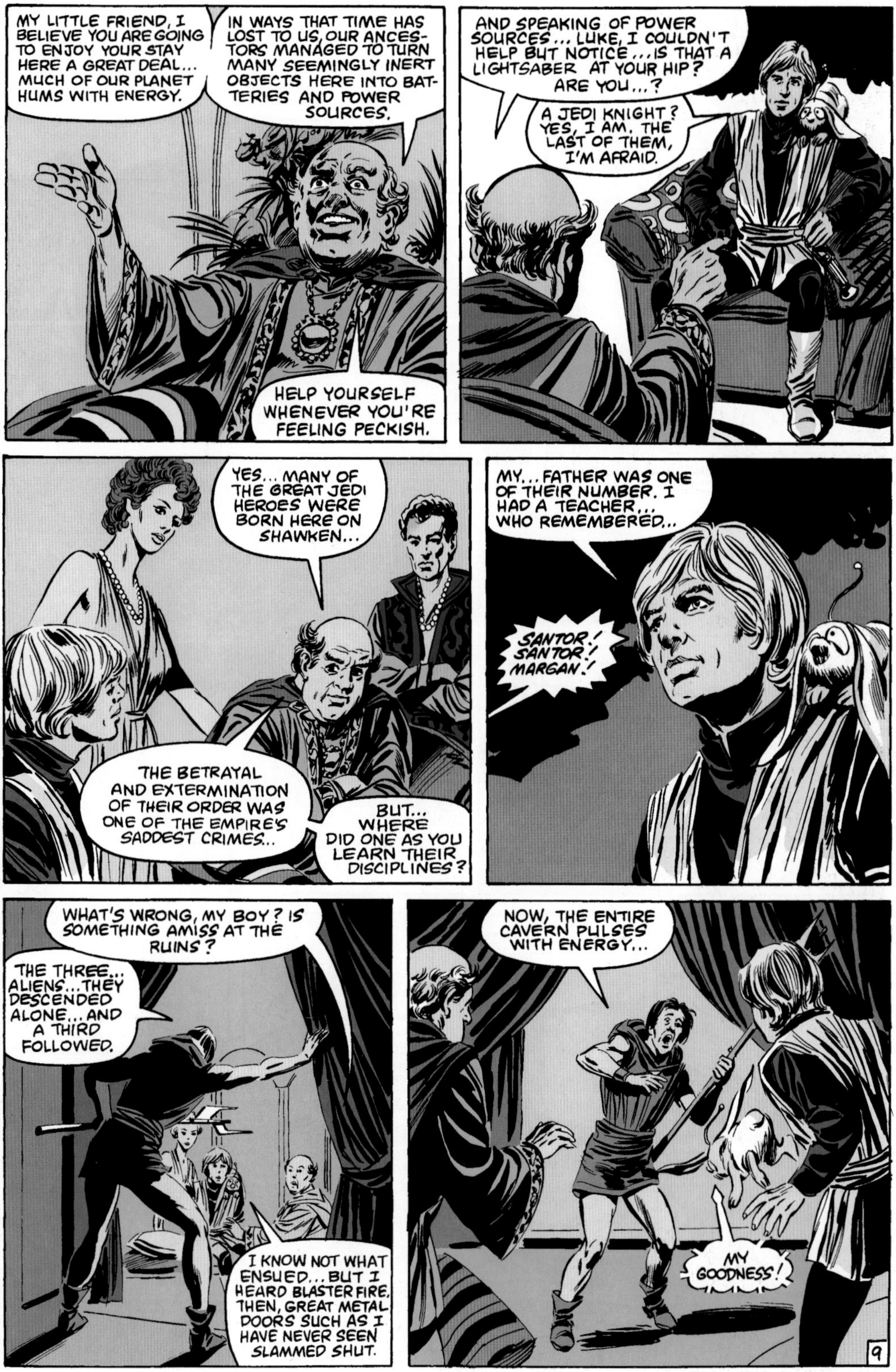
MY LITTLE FRIEND, I BELIEVE YOU ARE GOING TO ENJOY YOUR STAY HERE A GREAT DEAL... MUCH OF OUR PLANET HUMS WITH ENERGY.
IN WAYS THAT TIME HAS LOST TO US, OUR ANCESTORS MANAGED TO TURN MANY SEEMINGLY INERT OBJECTS HERE INTO BATTERIES AND POWER SOURCES.
HELP YOURSELF WHENEVER YOU'RE FEELING PECKISH.
AND SPEAKING OF POWER SOURCES... LUKE, I COULDN'T HELP BUT NOTICE... IS THAT A LIGHTSABER AT YOUR HIP? ARE YOU...?
A JEDI KNIGHT? YES, I AM. THE LAST OF THEM, I'M AFRAID.
YES... MANY OF THE GREAT JEDI HEROES WERE BORN HERE ON SHAWKEN...
THE BETRAYAL AND EXTERMINATION OF THEIR ORDER WAS ONE OF THE EMPIRE'S SADDEST CRIMES...
BUT... WHERE DID ONE AS YOU LEARN THEIR DISCIPLINES?
MY... FATHER WAS ONE OF THEIR NUMBER. I HAD A TEACHER... WHO REMEMBERED...
SANTOR! SANTOR! MARGAN!
WHAT'S WRONG, MY BOY? IS SOMETHING AMISS AT THE RUINS?
THE THREE... ALIENS... THEY DESCENDED ALONE... AND A THIRD FOLLOWED.
I KNOW NOT WHAT ENSUED... BUT I HEARD BLASTER FIRE. THEN, GREAT METAL DOORS SUCH AS I HAVE NEVER SEEN SLAMMED SHUT.
NOW, THE ENTIRE CAVERN PULSES WITH ENERGY...
MY GOODNESS!
9

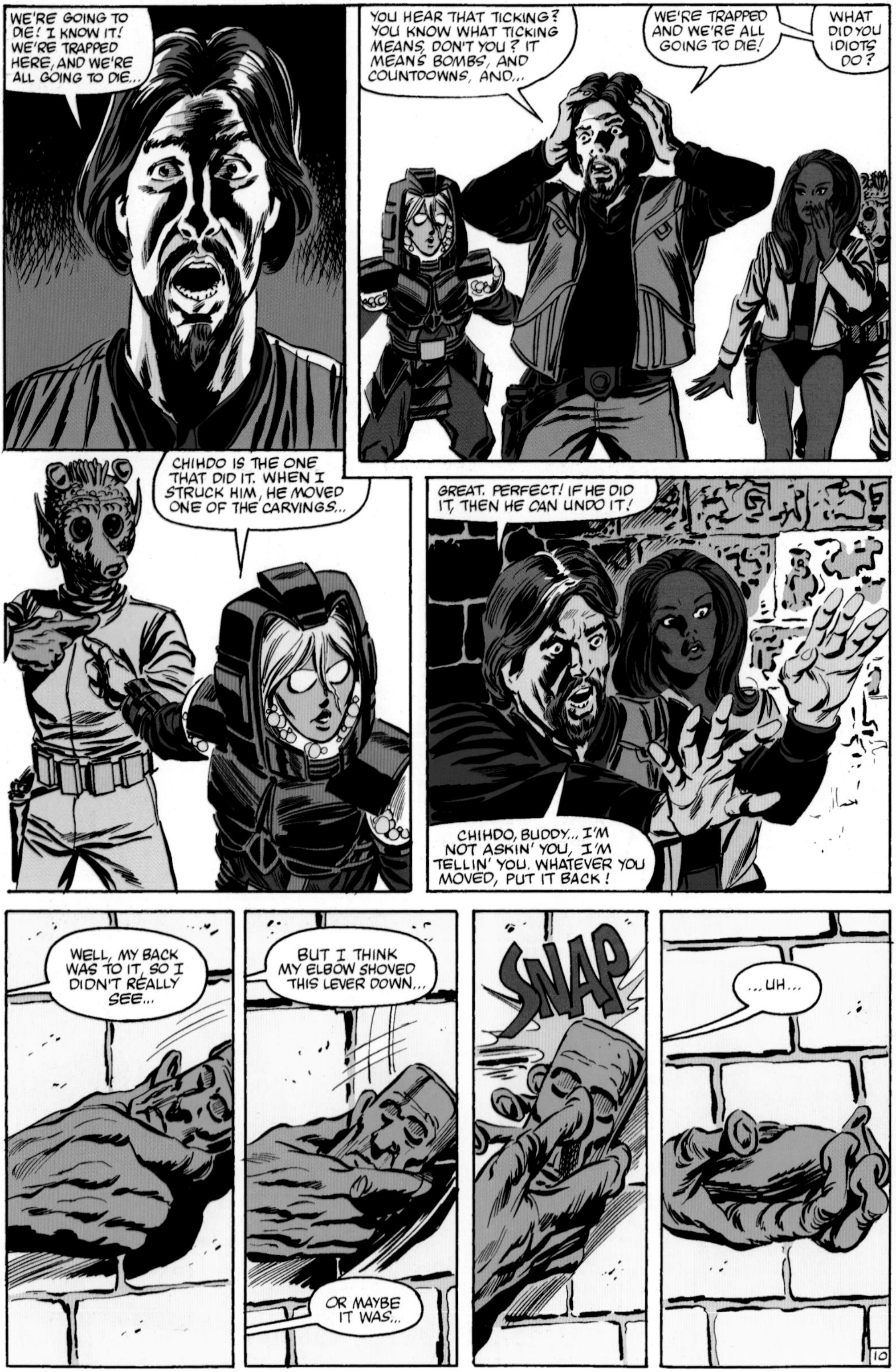
WE'RE GOING TO DIE! I KNOW IT! WE'RE TRAPPED HERE, AND WE'RE ALL GOING TO DIE...
YOU HEAR THAT TICKING? YOU KNOW WHAT TICKING MEANS, DON'T YOU? IT MEANS BOMBS, AND COUNTOWNS, AND...
WE'RE TRAPPED AND WE'RE ALL GOING TO DIE!
WHAT DID YOU IDIOTS DO?
CHIHDO IS THE ONE THAT DID IT. WHEN I STRUCK HIM, HE MOVED ONE OF THE CARVINGS...
GREAT. PERFECT! IF HE DID IT, THEN HE CAN UNDO IT!
CHIHDO, BUDDY... I'M NOT ASKIN' YOU, I'M TELLIN' YOU. WHATEVER YOU MOVED, PUT IT BACK!
WELL, MY BACK WAS TO IT, SO I DIDN'T REALLY SEE...
BUT I THINK MY ELBOW SHOVED THIS LEVER DOWN...
OR MAYBE IT WAS...
SNAP
...UH...
10

WELL...
I AM NOT READY TO DIE YET!! THERE ARE TOO MANY WORLDS I STILL HAVEN'T FLEECED!
OH, NOOOO!
WAIT A SEC... MAYBE IF I SLIDE KIRO'S KNIFE BLADE UNDER THE DOOR, I CAN...
NOPE. IT'S ABSOLUTELY FLUSH... NOTHING'LL FIT THROUGH.
I WAS RIGHT. WE'RE TRAPPED, AND WE'RE GONNA DIE.
HEY... WHAT'S WITH DANI? I THOUGHT SHE WAS ALL GUTS AND SEX APPEAL. I'VE NEVER SEEN HER CRY BEFORE.
YOU KNOW HOW GREGARIOUS ZELTRONS ARE... THEY'RE ALL TERRIFIED OF BEING ENTOMBED... ESPECIALLY ALONE...
I DON'T WANT TO DIE... NOT LIKE THIS... NOT ALONE...
YOU ARE NOT ALONE, DANI. WE ARE HERE, WITH YOU...
I'M ALONE. I'M ALL ALONE. LUKE'S NOT HERE, SO I'M ALONE.
LUKE...? *LUKE?* THIS IS ALL LUKE'S FAULT. I BLAME HIM FOR THIS.
HE'S THE ONE WHO BROUGHT US HERE, AND SENT US ALONE INTO THIS HOLE!
TRY TO BE BRAVE, RIK. HAVE CONFIDENCE. LUKE IS VERY *SMART*, AND VERY RESOURCEFUL...
BY NOW, HE MUST KNOW THAT WE ARE IN TROUBLE. IF WE CAN BE SAVED, LUKE WILL KNOW HOW TO DO IT.
OH, KIRO...
11

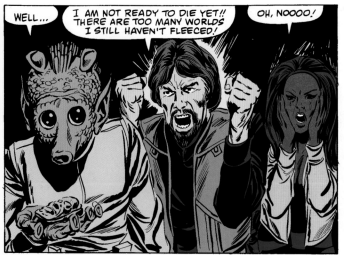

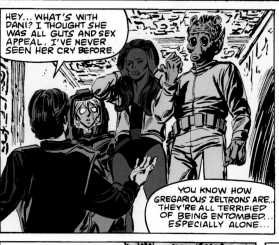

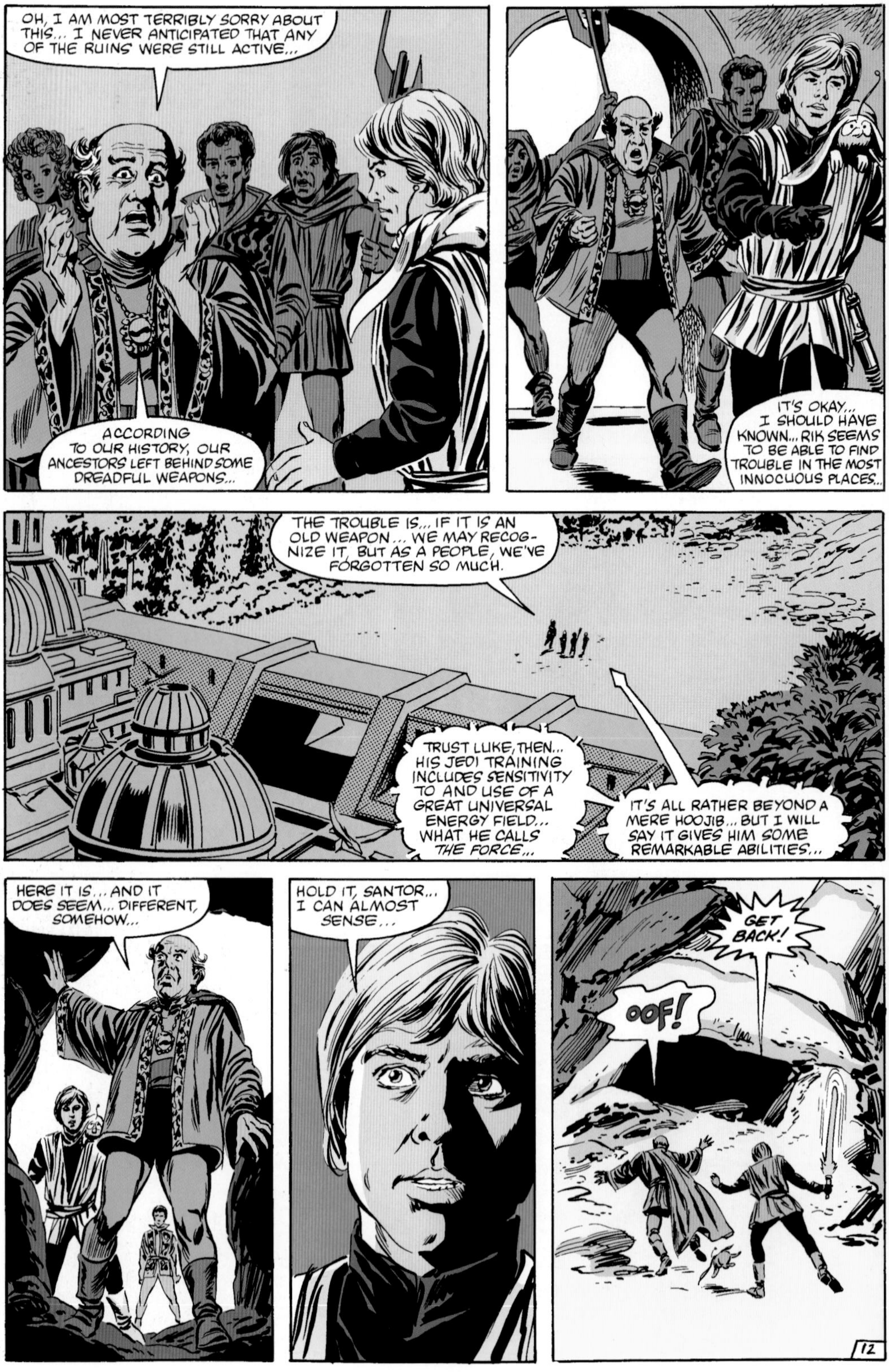
OH, I AM MOST TERRIBLY SORRY ABOUT THIS... I NEVER ANTICIPATED THAT ANY OF THE RUINS WERE STILL ACTIVE...
ACCORDING TO OUR HISTORY, OUR ANCESTORS LEFT BEHIND SOME DREADFUL WEAPONS...
IT'S OKAY... I SHOULD HAVE KNOWN... RIK SEEMS TO BE ABLE TO FIND TROUBLE IN THE MOST INNOCUOUS PLACES...
THE TROUBLE IS... IF IT IS AN OLD WEAPON... WE MAY RECOGNIZE IT, BUT AS A PEOPLE, WE'VE FORGOTTEN SO MUCH.
TRUST LUKE, THEN... HIS JEDI TRAINING INCLUDES SENSITIVITY TO AND USE OF A GREAT UNIVERSAL ENERGY FIELD... WHAT HE CALLS THE FORCE...
IT'S ALL RATHER BEYOND A MERE HOOJIB... BUT I WILL SAY IT GIVES HIM SOME REMARKABLE ABILITIES...
HERE IT IS... AND IT DOES SEEM... DIFFERENT, SOMEHOW...
HOLD IT, SANTOR... I CAN ALMOST SENSE...
GET BACK!
OOF!
12

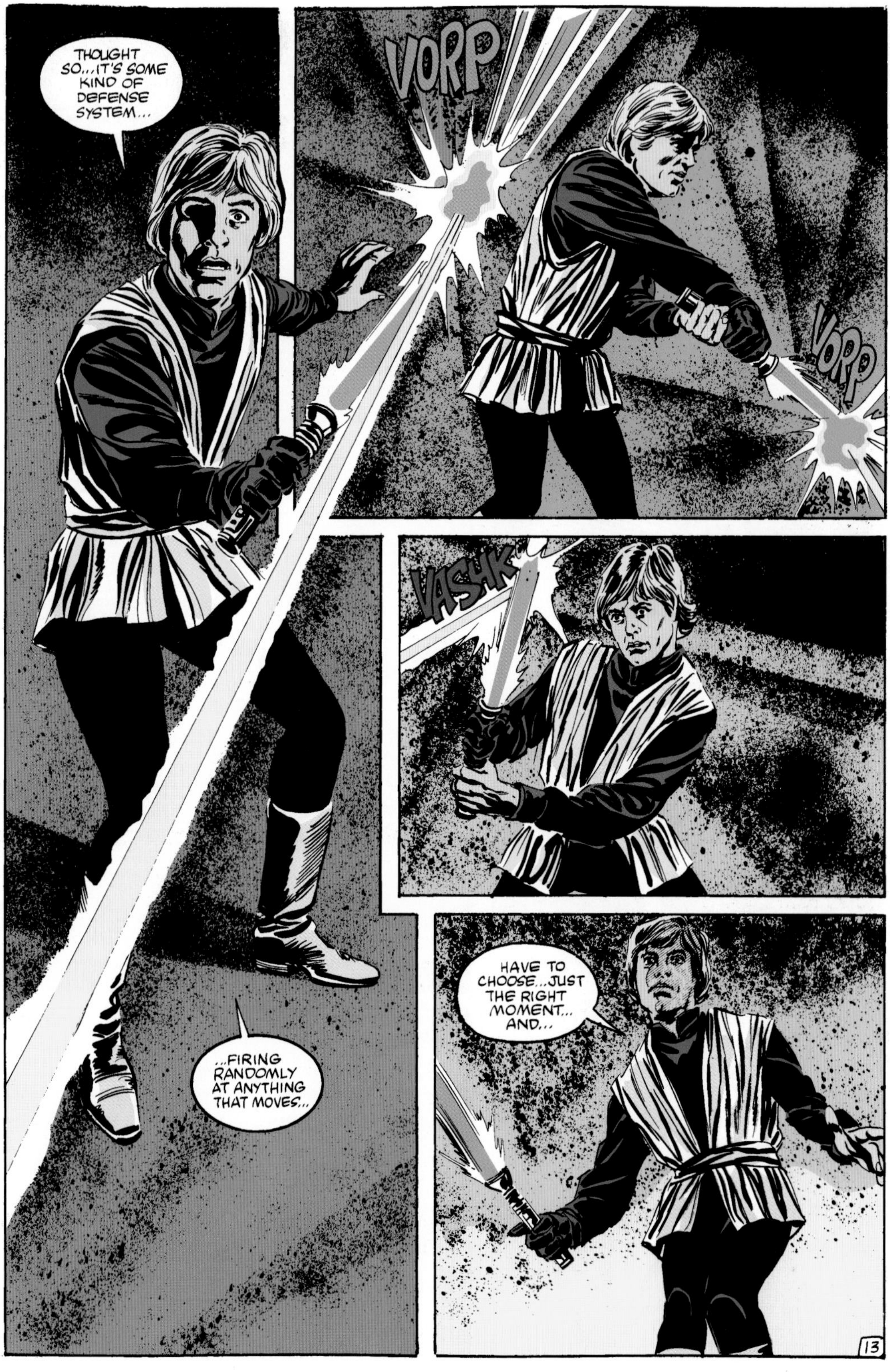
THOUGHT SO...IT'S SOME KIND OF DEFENSE SYSTEM...
VORP
VORP
...FIRING RANDOMLY AT ANYTHING THAT MOVES...
VASHK
HAVE TO CHOOSE...JUST THE RIGHT MOMENT... AND...
13

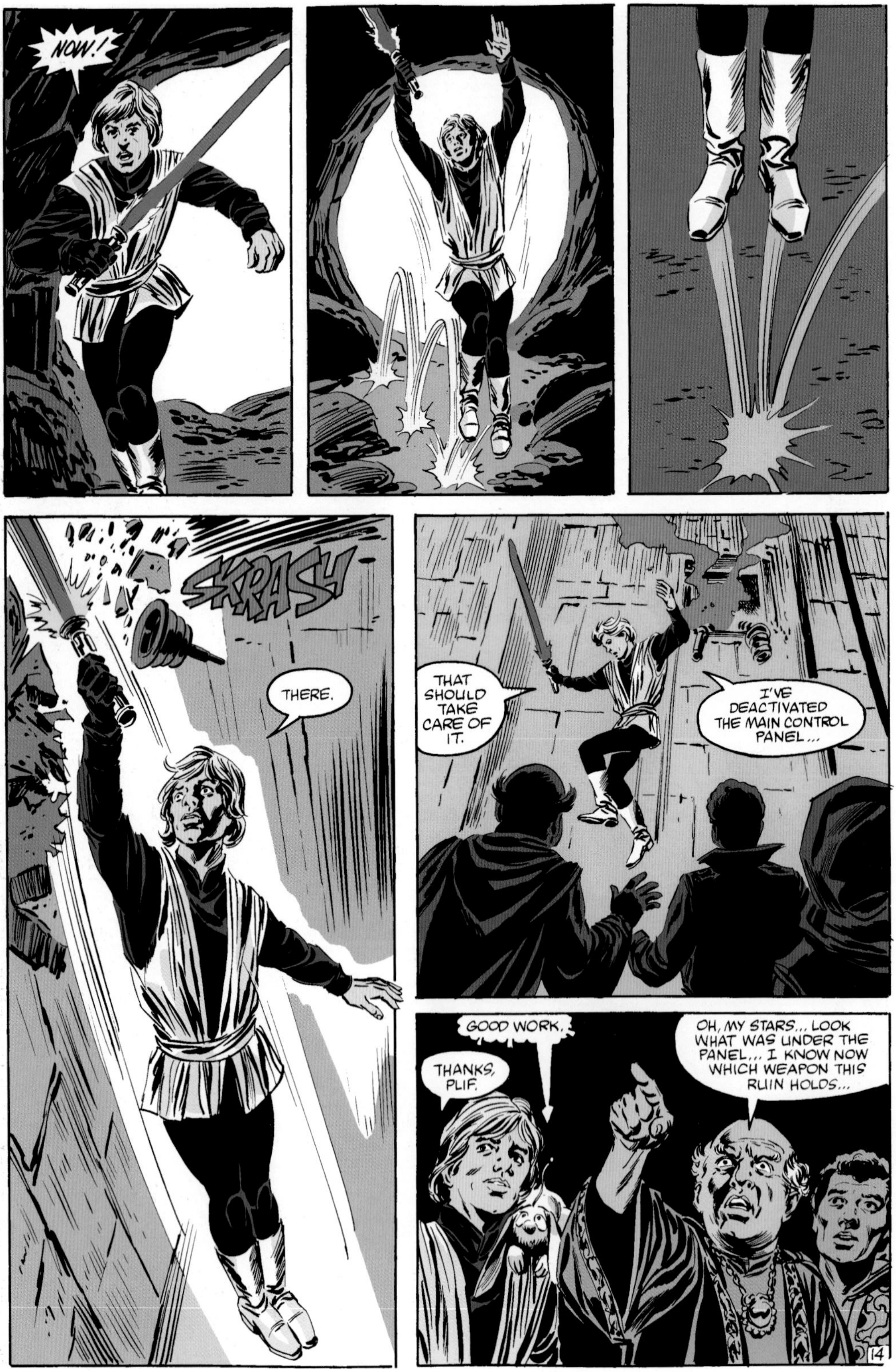
NOW!
SKRASH
THERE.
THAT SHOULD TAKE CARE OF IT.
I'VE DEACTIVATED THE MAIN CONTROL PANEL...
GOOD WORK.
THANKS, PLIF.
OH, MY STARS... LOOK WHAT WAS UNDER THE PANEL... I KNOW NOW WHICH WEAPON THIS RUIN HOLDS...
14

I DON'T UNDERSTAND...

THE CARVING BENEATH THE PANEL SHOWS WHAT THE DEVICE'S FUNCTION IS...

WHAT DOES THAT PICTURE SUGGEST TO YOU?

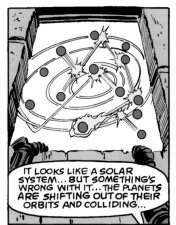

IT LOOKS LIKE A SOLAR SYSTEM... BUT SOMETHING'S WRONG WITH IT... THE PLANETS ARE SHIFTING OUT OF THEIR ORBITS AND COLLIDING...

AND THAT IS PRECISELY THE EFFECT THAT THIS MACHINE WAS DESIGNED TO ENGINEER...

BUT WHY WOULD ANYONE WANT TO BUILD SUCH A THING?

AH... IN ADDITION TO OUR TECHNOLOGY AND ARTWORK WE SHAWKENSE HAVE ALWAYS BEEN REVERED FOR STUDIES OF PHILOSOPHY...

ACCORDING TO LEGEND, ONE OF OUR GREATEST SCIENTISTS WAS ALSO A VERY SINCERE ADVOCATE OF THE DEPRESSING BELIEF OF NIHILISM...

AS YOU KNOW, NIHILISTS INSIST THAT ONCE SOMETHING HAS GONE WRONG THERE CAN BE NO CORRECTING IT...

IT IS BEST TO DESTROY EVERYTHING AND HOPE THAT SOMETHING BETTER COMES OUT OF A FRESH START.

OUR ANCESTOR BELIEVED THAT OUT OF THE UNIVERSAL ARMAGEDDON OF A NEW, ARTIFICIALLY-GENERATED *BIG BANG* MIGHT COME A BETTER TOMORROW...

LUCKILY FOR ALL HE NEVER BECAME QUITE DEPRESSED ENOUGH TO USE HIS DEVICE, AND ITS SECRETS WERE LOST WITH HIS DEATH...

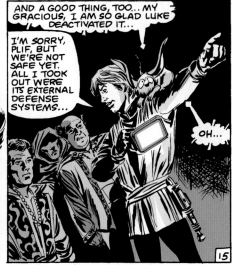

AND A GOOD THING, TOO... MY GRACIOUS, I AM SO GLAD LUKE DEACTIVATED IT...

I'M SORRY, PLIF, BUT WE'RE NOT SAFE YET. ALL I TOOK OUT WERE ITS EXTERNAL DEFENSE SYSTEMS...

OH...

15

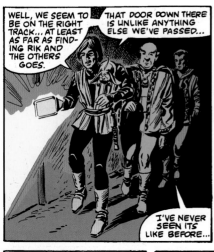

WELL, WE SEEM TO BE ON THE RIGHT TRACK... AT LEAST AS FAR AS FINDING RIK AND THE OTHERS GOES.

THAT DOOR DOWN THERE IS UNLIKE ANYTHING ELSE WE'VE PASSED...

I'VE NEVER SEEN ITS LIKE BEFORE...

PLIF, THIS POWER CEL IS PROBABLY PROVIDING ENERGY TO THE MECHANISM THAT'S KEEPING IT CLOSED. THINK YOU CAN...?

MY PLEASURE. WON'T BE A MOMENT...

WELL, PERHAPS A MOMENT OR TWO...

SO... MUCH ENERGY HERE...

FEEL A PERFECT GLUTTON...

÷WHUFF÷ ÷WHUFF÷ ÷WHUFF÷

÷URP÷

GOOD WORK, PLIF. YOU DID IT!

LUKE!

OH, DARLING... I KNEW YOU'D GET US OUT!

HAH!

GOOD OLD PLIF. I ALWAYS LIKED YOU.

ACTUALLY, IT WAS PLIF WHO DID IT.

HEY, I DON'T CARE WHO DID IT, SO LONG AS IT'S OVER...

AH, BUT IT'S NOT OVER YET...

HUNH?

WHAT ARE YOU TALKING ABOUT?!

AND UNLESS WE CAN UNRAVEL THIS DISASTER, IT WILL SOON BE OVER FOR EVERYONE, EVERYWHERE...

16

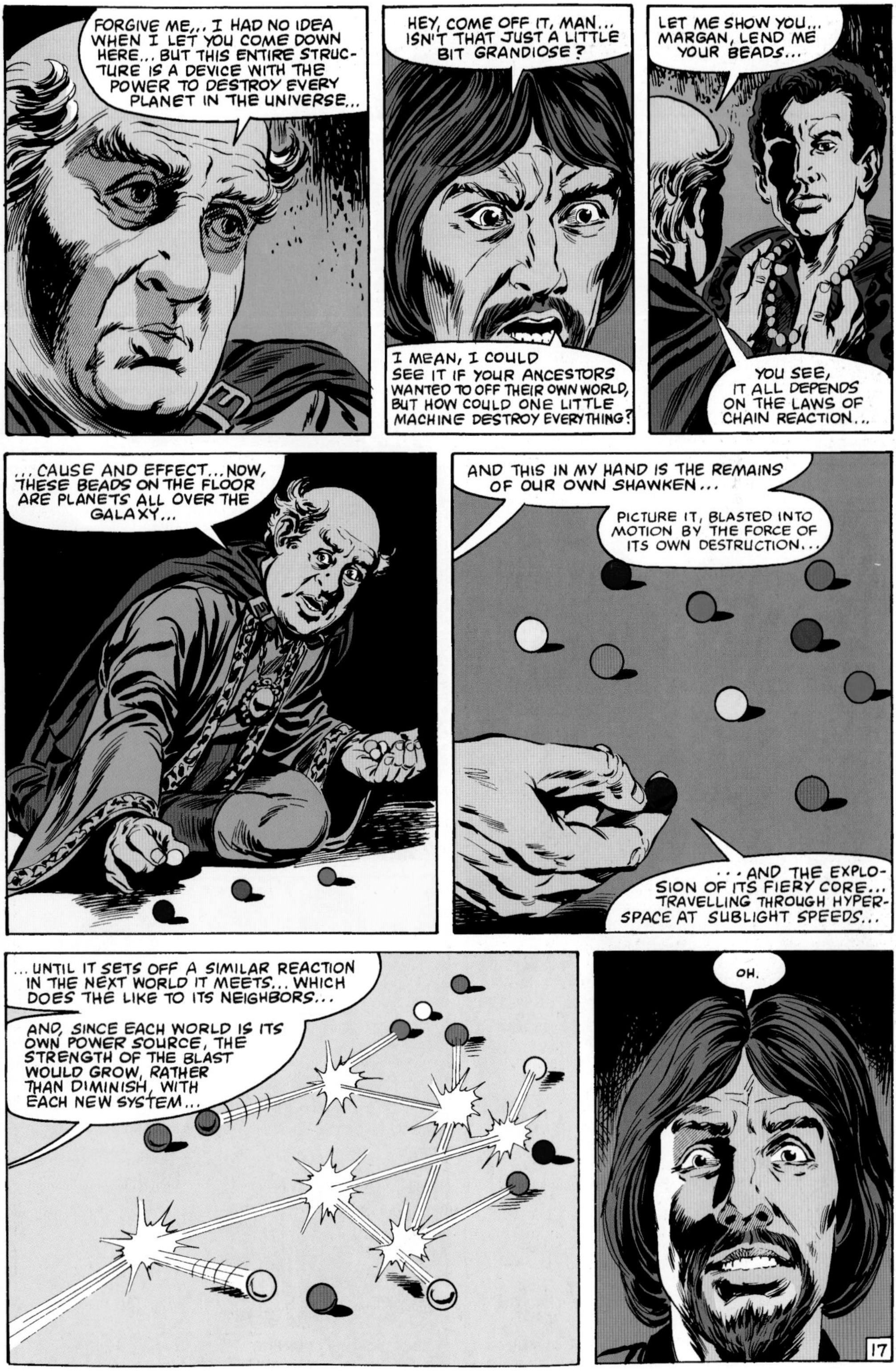
FORGIVE ME,.. I HAD NO IDEA WHEN I LET YOU COME DOWN HERE... BUT THIS ENTIRE STRUCTURE IS A DEVICE WITH THE POWER TO DESTROY EVERY PLANET IN THE UNIVERSE...
HEY, COME OFF IT, MAN... ISN'T THAT JUST A LITTLE BIT GRANDIOSE?
I MEAN, I COULD SEE IT IF YOUR ANCESTORS WANTED TO OFF THEIR OWN WORLD, BUT HOW COULD ONE LITTLE MACHINE DESTROY EVERYTHING?
LET ME SHOW YOU... MARGAN, LEND ME YOUR BEADS...
YOU SEE, IT ALL DEPENDS ON THE LAWS OF CHAIN REACTION...
...CAUSE AND EFFECT...NOW, THESE BEADS ON THE FLOOR ARE PLANETS ALL OVER THE GALAXY...
AND THIS IN MY HAND IS THE REMAINS OF OUR OWN SHAWKEN...
PICTURE IT, BLASTED INTO MOTION BY THE FORCE OF ITS OWN DESTRUCTION...
...AND THE EXPLOSION OF ITS FIERY CORE... TRAVELLING THROUGH HYPERSPACE AT SUBLIGHT SPEEDS...
...UNTIL IT SETS OFF A SIMILAR REACTION IN THE NEXT WORLD IT MEETS... WHICH DOES THE LIKE TO ITS NEIGHBORS...
AND, SINCE EACH WORLD IS ITS OWN POWER SOURCE, THE STRENGTH OF THE BLAST WOULD GROW, RATHER THAN DIMINISH, WITH EACH NEW SYSTEM...
OH.
17

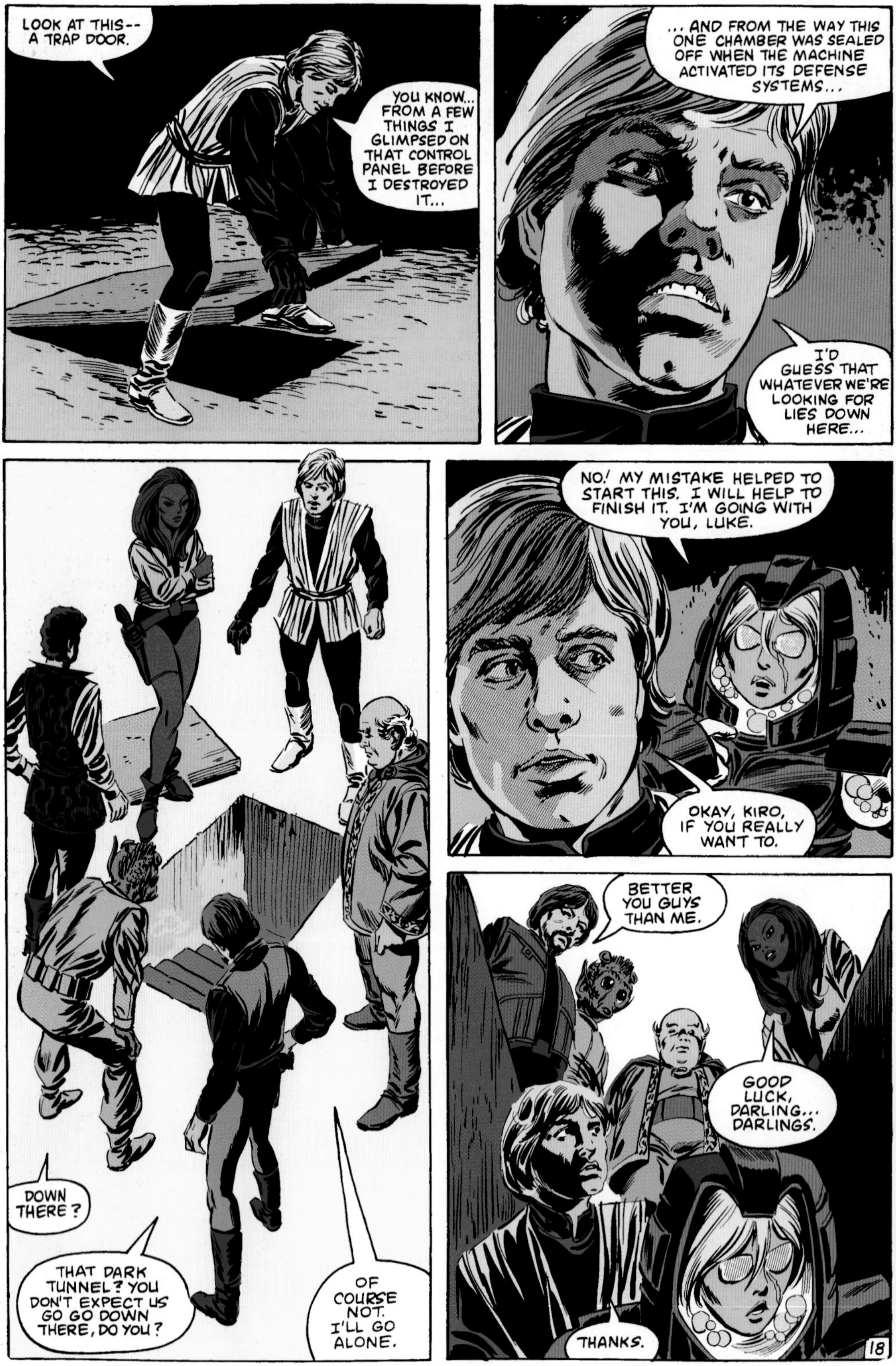
LOOK AT THIS-- A TRAP DOOR.
YOU KNOW... FROM A FEW THINGS I GLIMPSED ON THAT CONTROL PANEL BEFORE I DESTROYED IT...
... AND FROM THE WAY THIS ONE CHAMBER WAS SEALED OFF WHEN THE MACHINE ACTIVATED ITS DEFENSE SYSTEMS...
I'D GUESS THAT WHATEVER WE'RE LOOKING FOR LIES DOWN HERE...
DOWN THERE?
THAT DARK TUNNEL? YOU DON'T EXPECT US GO GO DOWN THERE, DO YOU?
OF COURSE NOT. I'LL GO ALONE.
NO! MY MISTAKE HELPED TO START THIS. I WILL HELP TO FINISH IT. I'M GOING WITH YOU, LUKE.
OKAY, KIRO, IF YOU REALLY WANT TO.
BETTER YOU GUYS THAN ME.
GOOD LUCK, DARLING... DARLINGS.
THANKS.
18

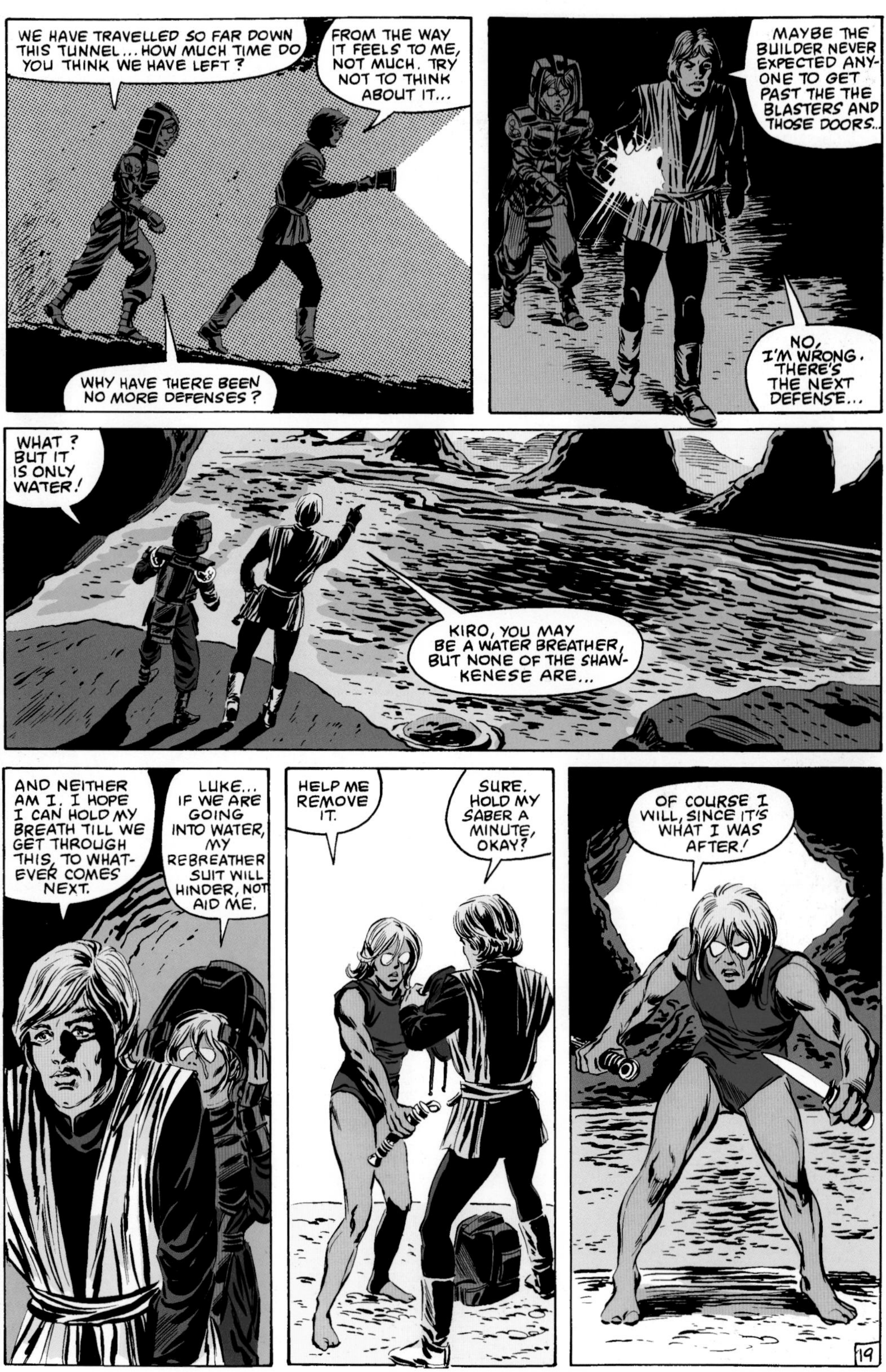

WE HAVE TRAVELLED SO FAR DOWN THIS TUNNEL... HOW MUCH TIME DO YOU THINK WE HAVE LEFT?
FROM THE WAY IT FEELS TO ME, NOT MUCH. TRY NOT TO THINK ABOUT IT...
WHY HAVE THERE BEEN NO MORE DEFENSES?
MAYBE THE BUILDER NEVER EXPECTED ANY-ONE TO GET PAST THE THE BLASTERS AND THOSE DOORS...
NO, I'M WRONG. THERE'S THE NEXT DEFENSE...
WHAT? BUT IT IS ONLY WATER!
KIRO, YOU MAY BE A WATER BREATHER, BUT NONE OF THE SHAW-KENESE ARE...
AND NEITHER AM I. I HOPE I CAN HOLD MY BREATH TILL WE GET THROUGH THIS, TO WHAT-EVER COMES NEXT.
LUKE... IF WE ARE GOING INTO WATER, MY REBREATHER SUIT WILL HINDER, NOT AID ME.
HELP ME REMOVE IT.
SURE. HOLD MY SABER A MINUTE, OKAY?
OF COURSE I WILL, SINCE IT'S WHAT I WAS AFTER!
19

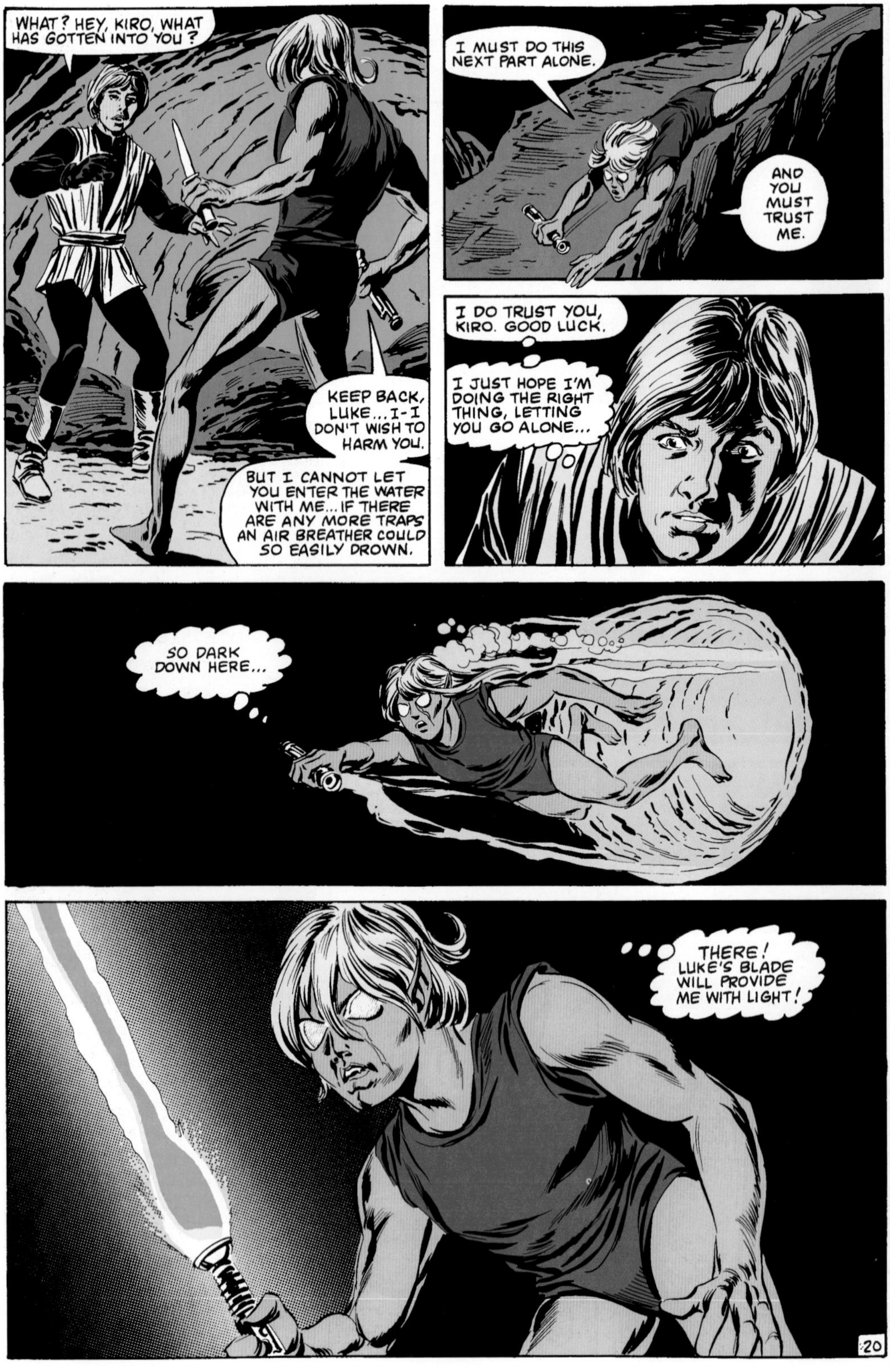
WHAT? HEY, KIRO, WHAT HAS GOTTEN INTO YOU?
KEEP BACK, LUKE... I-I DON'T WISH TO HARM YOU.
BUT I CANNOT LET YOU ENTER THE WATER WITH ME... IF THERE ARE ANY MORE TRAPS AN AIR BREATHER COULD SO EASILY DROWN.
I MUST DO THIS NEXT PART ALONE.
AND YOU MUST TRUST ME.
I DO TRUST YOU, KIRO. GOOD LUCK.
I JUST HOPE I'M DOING THE RIGHT THING, LETTING YOU GO ALONE...
SO DARK DOWN HERE...
THERE! LUKE'S BLADE WILL PROVIDE ME WITH LIGHT!
20

I... CAN GO NO FURTHER... BUT WHAT AM I LOOKING FOR?

SUDDENLY... I FEEL SO... STRANGE...

AS IF SOMETHING WERE...

...BEHIND ME!!

ZZORP

SSHRRRP

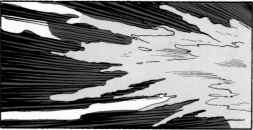

A TIDAL WAVE!

THE TICKING'S STOPPED...

SO IT HAS...

BUT WHAT ARE THOSE NEW SOUNDS, BENEATH US?

21

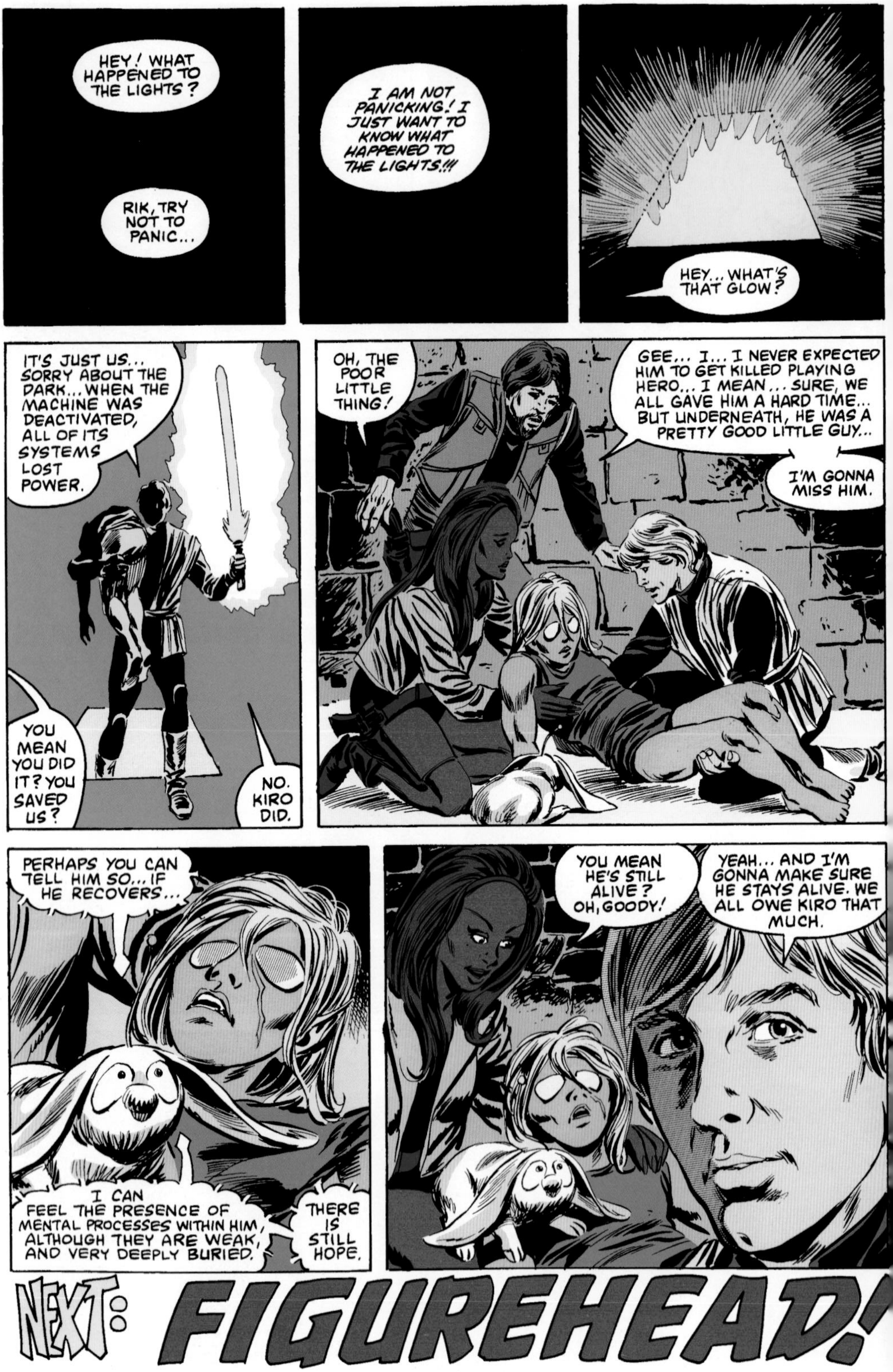
HEY! WHAT HAPPENED TO THE LIGHTS?
RIK, TRY NOT TO PANIC...
I AM NOT PANICKING! I JUST WANT TO KNOW WHAT HAPPENED TO THE LIGHTS!!!
HEY... WHAT'S THAT GLOW?
IT'S JUST US... SORRY ABOUT THE DARK... WHEN THE MACHINE WAS DEACTIVATED, ALL OF ITS SYSTEMS LOST POWER.
YOU MEAN YOU DID IT? YOU SAVED US?
NO. KIRO DID.
OH, THE POOR LITTLE THING!
GEE... I... I NEVER EXPECTED HIM TO GET KILLED PLAYING HERO... I MEAN... SURE, WE ALL GAVE HIM A HARD TIME... BUT UNDERNEATH, HE WAS A PRETTY GOOD LITTLE GUY...
I'M GONNA MISS HIM.
PERHAPS YOU CAN TELL HIM SO... IF HE RECOVERS...
I CAN FEEL THE PRESENCE OF MENTAL PROCESSES WITHIN HIM, ALTHOUGH THEY ARE WEAK, AND VERY DEEPLY BURIED.
THERE IS STILL HOPE.
YOU MEAN HE'S STILL ALIVE? OH, GOODY!
YEAH... AND I'M GONNA MAKE SURE HE STAYS ALIVE. WE ALL OWE KIRO THAT MUCH.
NEXT: FIGUREHEAD!

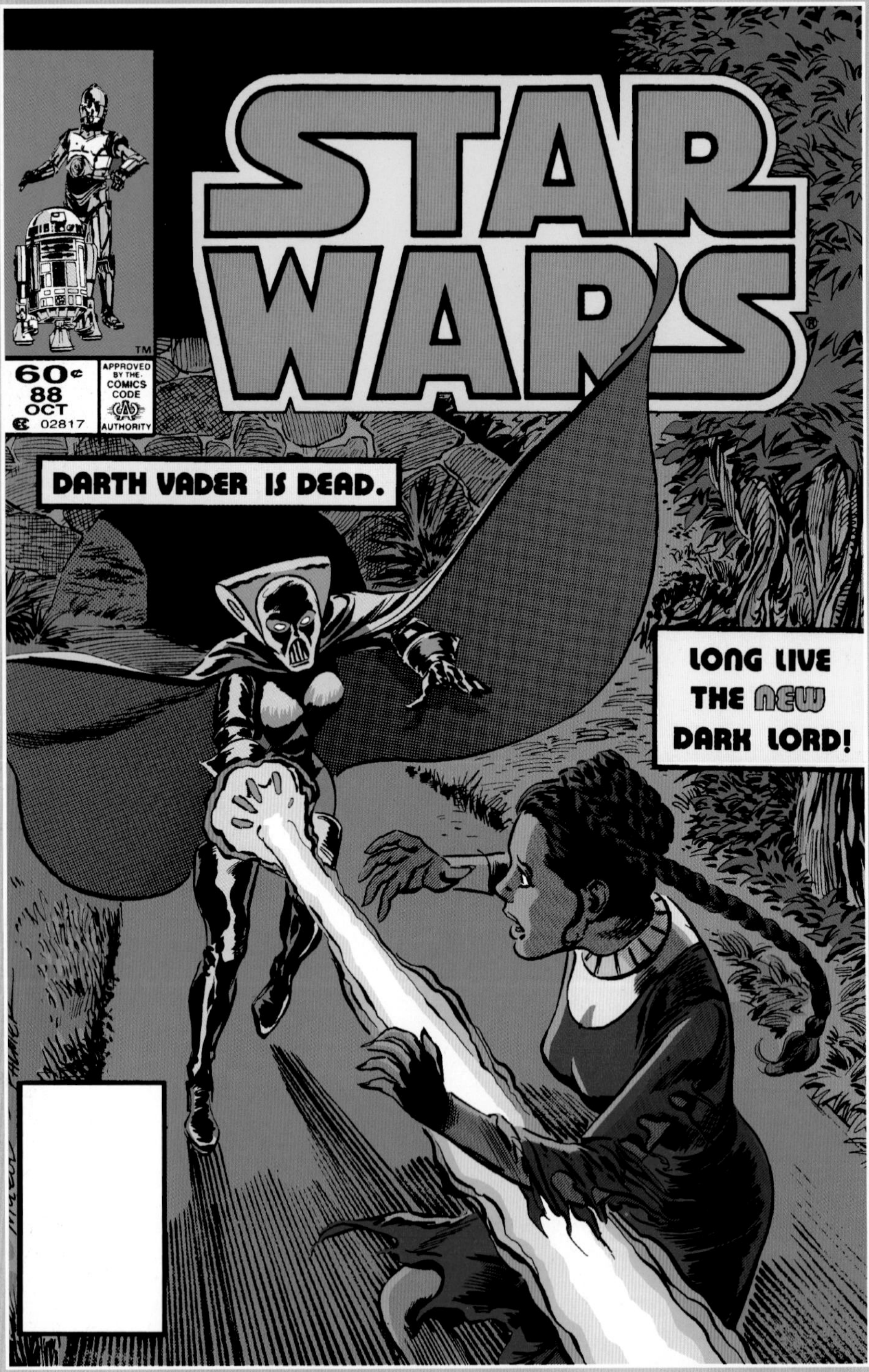
STAR WARS
TM
60¢
88
OCT
02817
APPROVED BY THE COMICS CODE AUTHORITY
DARTH VADER IS DEAD.
LONG LIVE THE NEW DARK LORD!

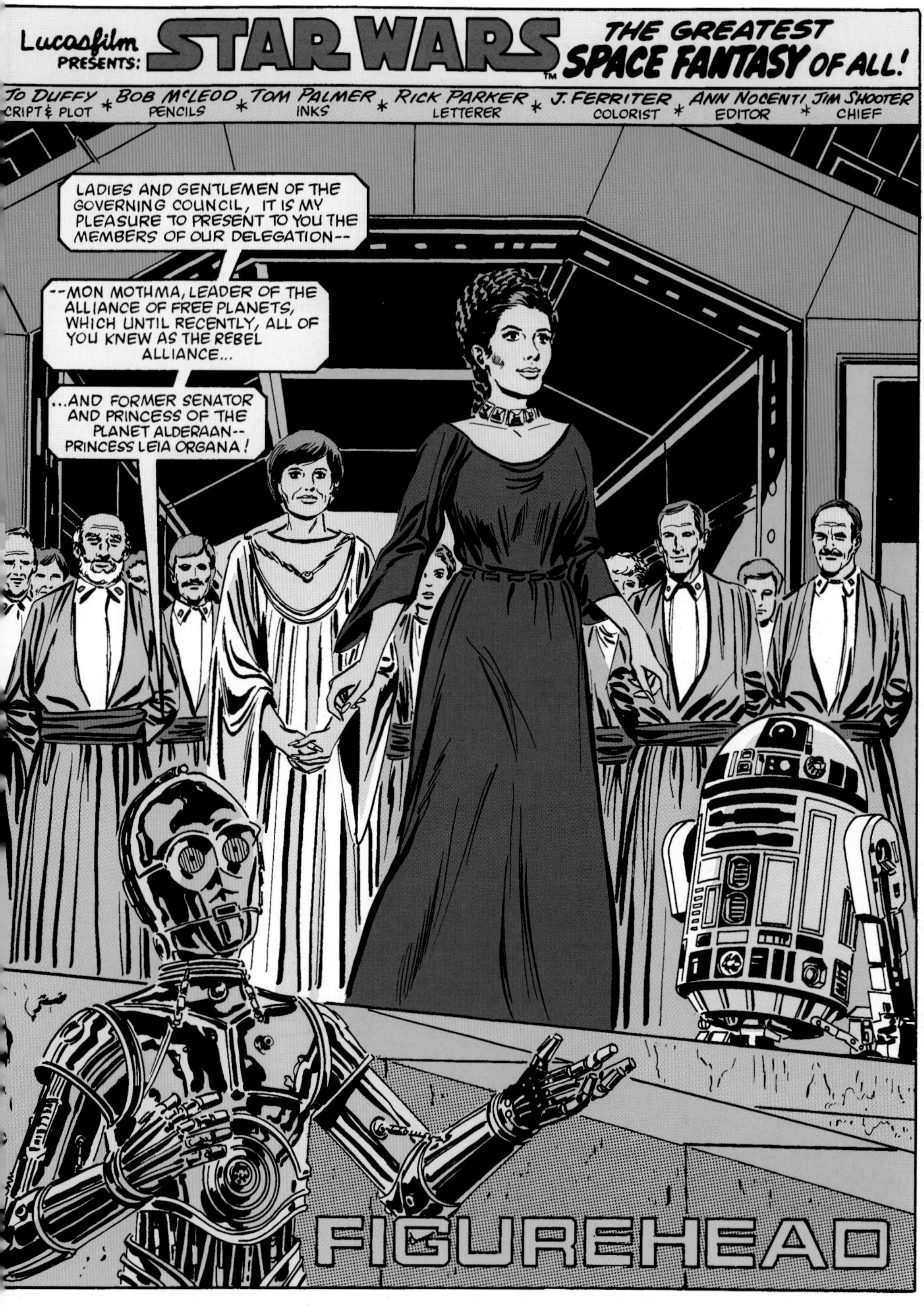

Lucasfilm PRESENTS: STAR WARS THE GREATEST SPACE FANTASY OF ALL!
JO DUFFY SCRIPT & PLOT * BOB McLEOD PENCILS * TOM PALMER INKS * RICK PARKER LETTERER * J. FERRITER COLORIST * ANN NOCENTI EDITOR * JIM SHOOTER CHIEF
LADIES AND GENTLEMEN OF THE GOVERNING COUNCIL, IT IS MY PLEASURE TO PRESENT TO YOU THE MEMBERS OF OUR DELEGATION--
--MON MOTHMA, LEADER OF THE ALLIANCE OF FREE PLANETS, WHICH UNTIL RECENTLY, ALL OF YOU KNEW AS THE REBEL ALLIANCE...
...AND FORMER SENATOR AND PRINCESS OF THE PLANET ALDERAAN-- PRINCESS LEIA ORGANA!
FIGUREHEAD

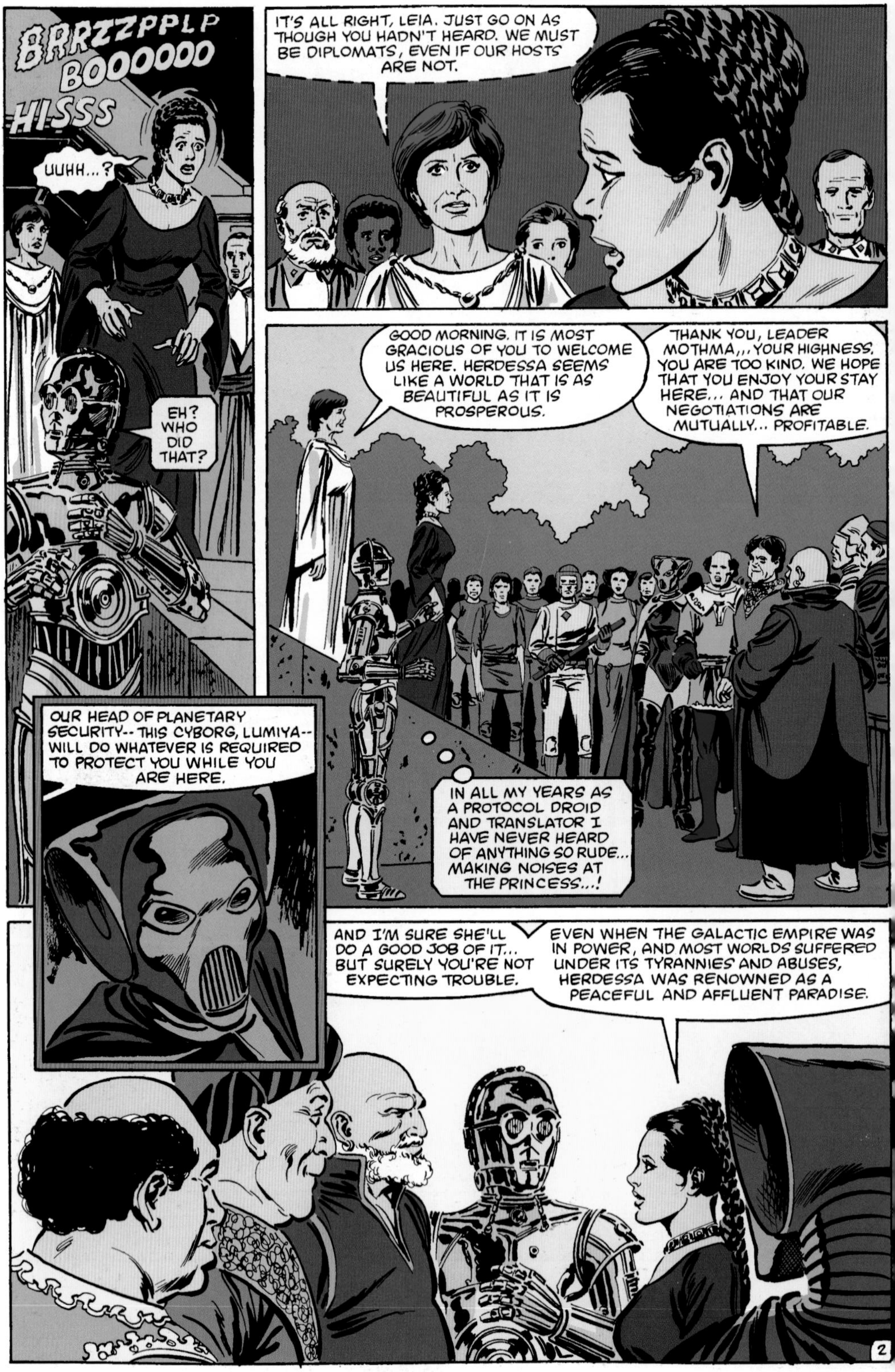
BRRZZPPLP
BOOOOOO
HISSS
UUHH...?
EH? WHO DID THAT?
IT'S ALL RIGHT, LEIA. JUST GO ON AS THOUGH YOU HADN'T HEARD. WE MUST BE DIPLOMATS, EVEN IF OUR HOSTS ARE NOT.
GOOD MORNING. IT IS MOST GRACIOUS OF YOU TO WELCOME US HERE. HERDESSA SEEMS LIKE A WORLD THAT IS AS BEAUTIFUL AS IT IS PROSPEROUS.
THANK YOU, LEADER MOTHMA,,, YOUR HIGHNESS. YOU ARE TOO KIND. WE HOPE THAT YOU ENJOY YOUR STAY HERE... AND THAT OUR NEGOTIATIONS ARE MUTUALLY... PROFITABLE.
IN ALL MY YEARS AS A PROTOCOL DROID AND TRANSLATOR I HAVE NEVER HEARD OF ANYTHING SO RUDE... MAKING NOISES AT THE PRINCESS...!
OUR HEAD OF PLANETARY SECURITY-- THIS CYBORG, LUMIYA-- WILL DO WHATEVER IS REQUIRED TO PROTECT YOU WHILE YOU ARE HERE.
AND I'M SURE SHE'LL DO A GOOD JOB OF IT... BUT SURELY YOU'RE NOT EXPECTING TROUBLE.
EVEN WHEN THE GALACTIC EMPIRE WAS IN POWER, AND MOST WORLDS SUFFERED UNDER ITS TYRANNIES AND ABUSES, HERDESSA WAS RENOWNED AS A PEACEFUL AND AFFLUENT PARADISE.
2

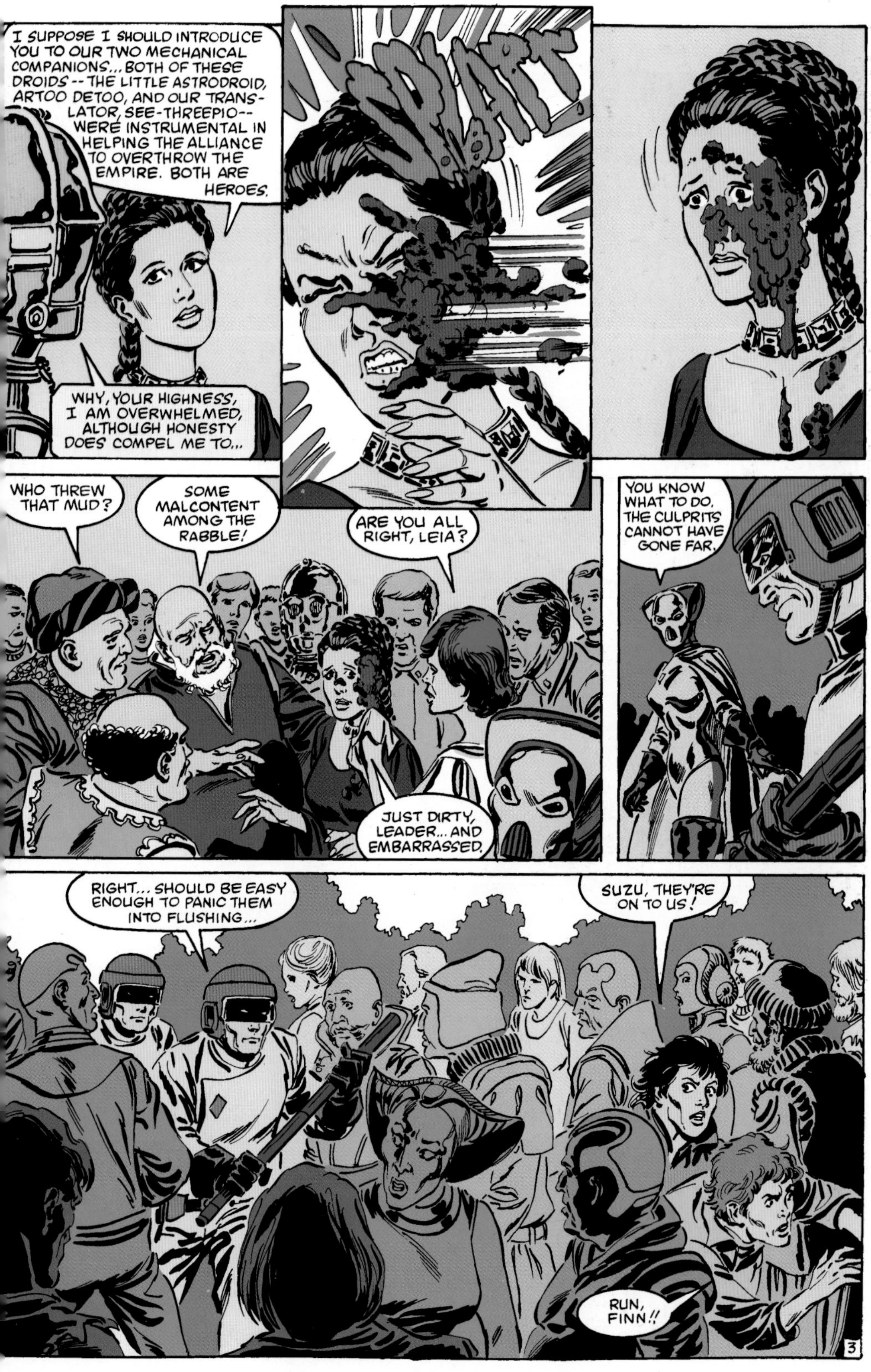
I SUPPOSE I SHOULD INTRODUCE YOU TO OUR TWO MECHANICAL COMPANIONS... BOTH OF THESE DROIDS -- THE LITTLE ASTRODROID, ARTOO DETOO, AND OUR TRANSLATOR, SEE-THREEPIO-- WERE INSTRUMENTAL IN HELPING THE ALLIANCE TO OVERTHROW THE EMPIRE. BOTH ARE HEROES.
WHY, YOUR HIGHNESS, I AM OVERWHELMED, ALTHOUGH HONESTY DOES COMPEL ME TO...
SPLAT
WHO THREW THAT MUD?
SOME MALCONTENT AMONG THE RABBLE!
ARE YOU ALL RIGHT, LEIA?
JUST DIRTY, LEADER... AND EMBARRASSED.
YOU KNOW WHAT TO DO. THE CULPRITS CANNOT HAVE GONE FAR.
RIGHT... SHOULD BE EASY ENOUGH TO PANIC THEM INTO FLUSHING...
SUZU, THEY'RE ON TO US!
RUN, FINN!!
3

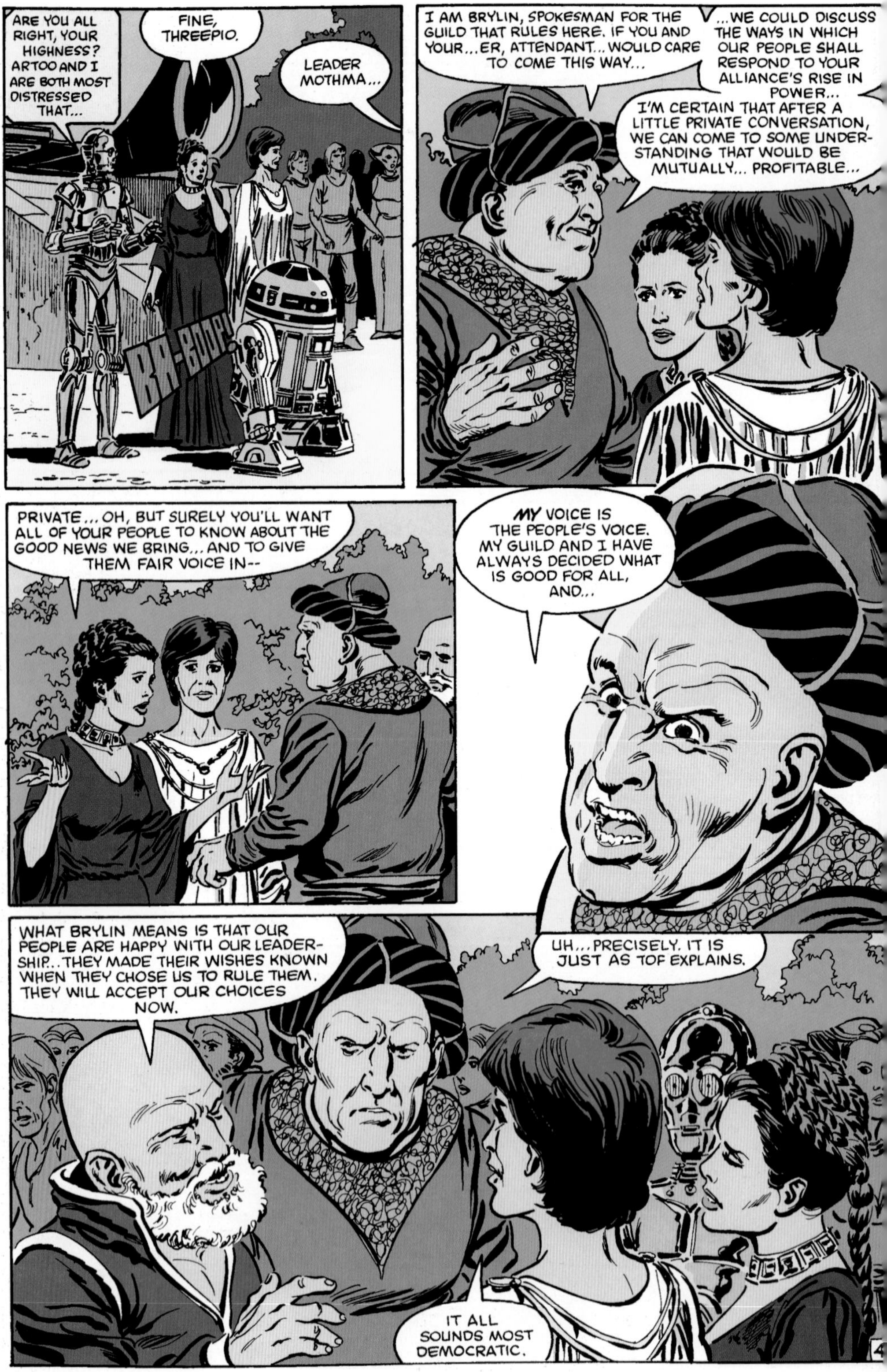

ARE YOU ALL RIGHT, YOUR HIGHNESS? ARTOO AND I ARE BOTH MOST DISTRESSED THAT...
FINE, THREEPIO.
LEADER MOTHMA...
BA-BOOP!
I AM BRYLIN, SPOKESMAN FOR THE GUILD THAT RULES HERE. IF YOU AND YOUR... ER, ATTENDANT... WOULD CARE TO COME THIS WAY...
...WE COULD DISCUSS THE WAYS IN WHICH OUR PEOPLE SHALL RESPOND TO YOUR ALLIANCE'S RISE IN POWER...
I'M CERTAIN THAT AFTER A LITTLE PRIVATE CONVERSATION, WE CAN COME TO SOME UNDERSTANDING THAT WOULD BE MUTUALLY... PROFITABLE...
PRIVATE... OH, BUT SURELY YOU'LL WANT ALL OF YOUR PEOPLE TO KNOW ABOUT THE GOOD NEWS WE BRING... AND TO GIVE THEM FAIR VOICE IN--
MY VOICE IS THE PEOPLE'S VOICE. MY GUILD AND I HAVE ALWAYS DECIDED WHAT IS GOOD FOR ALL, AND...
WHAT BRYLIN MEANS IS THAT OUR PEOPLE ARE HAPPY WITH OUR LEADERSHIP.. THEY MADE THEIR WISHES KNOWN WHEN THEY CHOSE US TO RULE THEM. THEY WILL ACCEPT OUR CHOICES NOW.
UH... PRECISELY. IT IS JUST AS TOF EXPLAINS.
IT ALL SOUNDS MOST DEMOCRATIC.

AND LATER...

...MORE TO EAT OR DRINK? THE PAIR OF YOU HAVE HARDLY TOUCHED A MORSEL...

COME NOW, LADIES, WE ARE PROUD OF THE PROSPERITY THAT TRADE HAS BROUGHT TO OUR WORLD. PERMIT US TO SHOW OFF...

BUT...WE'VE HAD SO MANY COURSES ALREADY,...AND WE CAME HERE TO ARRANGE MATTERS OF SOME POLITICAL DELICACY,...NOT TO--!

IT WAS SUMPTUOUS, GENTLEMEN. WE ARE BOTH REPLETE.

HERDESSAN HOSPITALITY IS GREATER EVEN THAN IT IS REPUTED TO BE.

COME NOW, PRETTY PRINCESS...YOU CAN'T REFUSE A GLASS OF DELTRON SPICE WINE...

IT'S EVER BEEN THE BEVERAGE OF ROYALTY.

WELL, I...THANK YOU, GAZA.

THAT'S IT. RELAX. ENJOY YOURSELVES. YOU'VE JUST ARRIVED. WE CAN TALK TOMORROW,...AFTER YOU'VE BOTH PASSED A RESTFUL NIGHT...

IN FACT...IF THERE'S ANYTHING YOU CAN DO TO MAKE IT MORE RESTFUL...

SURELY YOU'D LIKE TO SAMPLE THE LOCAL CUSTOMS...FULLY? THINK HOW WELL YOU'D SLEEP...

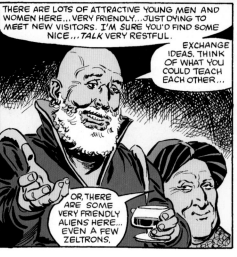

THERE ARE LOTS OF ATTRACTIVE YOUNG MEN AND WOMEN HERE...VERY FRIENDLY...JUST DYING TO MEET NEW VISITORS. I'M SURE YOU'D FIND SOME NICE...*TALK* VERY RESTFUL.

EXCHANGE IDEAS. THINK OF WHAT YOU COULD TEACH EACH OTHER...

OR, THERE ARE SOME VERY FRIENDLY ALIENS HERE... EVEN A FEW ZELTRONS,

NO ZELTRONS!!!

?

5

59

DOESN'T LIKE ZELTRONS... NOT EVEN ZELTRON BOYS?

I NEVER HEARD OF ANYONE WHO DOESN'T LIKE ZELTRONS...

I...I'M SORRY, IT'S JUST THAT A LOT OF VERY RECENT, STRESSFUL MISSIONS I'VE BEEN ON HAVE INVOLVED ZELTRONS-- ONE ZELTRON IN PARTICULAR-- IT GETS TO BE SUCH A STRAIN...

I'D NEVER HAVE THOUGHT IT OF HER...

ACTUALLY, IF WE AREN'T GOING TO SETTLE OUR AFFAIRS TONIGHT, PERHAPS I SHOULD SIMPLY TAKE A STROLL, GET SOME AIR...

YOUR HIGHNESS! WHERE ARE YOU GOING?

THREEPIO, ARTOO... I'M GOING FOR A WALK. I WANTED TO THINK A LITTLE, BY MYSELF.

I NEED SOME PEACE AND QUIET.

A MOST WISE SUGGESTION, IF I DO SAY SO MYSELF... IT HAS BEEN MY OBSERVATION THAT THE BEST WAY TO SOLVE ANY PROBLEM IS BY THINKING ABOUT IT, IN SILENCE AND SOLITUDE. YES, THERE IS NOTHING LIKE PEACE FOR--!

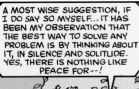

BOO-BLINK!

WHAT DO YOU MEAN, HOW WOULD I KNOW?

BUT WHAT IS TROUBLING YOU, YOUR HIGHNESS? I THOUGHT THINGS WERE GOING SPLENDIDLY.

I'VE NEVER SEEN ANY GROUP OF PLANETARY LEADERS SO EAGER TO PLEASE GUESTS AS BRYLIN AND HIS GUILD APPEAR TO BE.

THAT'S JUST THE PROBLEM. THEY'RE SO EAGER TO PLEASE AND PAMPER US, WE'RE NOT GETTING ANYTHING DONE. I HAVEN'T HAD A MOMENT TO THINK SINCE I'VE BEEN HERE. NOTHING IS BEING ACCOMPLISHED.

BUT, PRINCESS LEIA...ISN'T THAT GENERALLY HOW THINGS FUNCTION IN DIPLOMATIC CIRCLES? NOTHING EVER HAPPENS QUICKLY...

SURELY YOU LEARNED, WHEN YOU SERVED IN THE IMPERIAL SENATE...

THAT'S JUST THE TROUBLE, THREEPIO. THE SENATE'S A LONG WAY BEHIND ME NOW... I LIKED THE REBELLION... ...MAYBE I'M JUST NOT CUT OUT TO BE A DIPLOMAT ANYMORE.

6

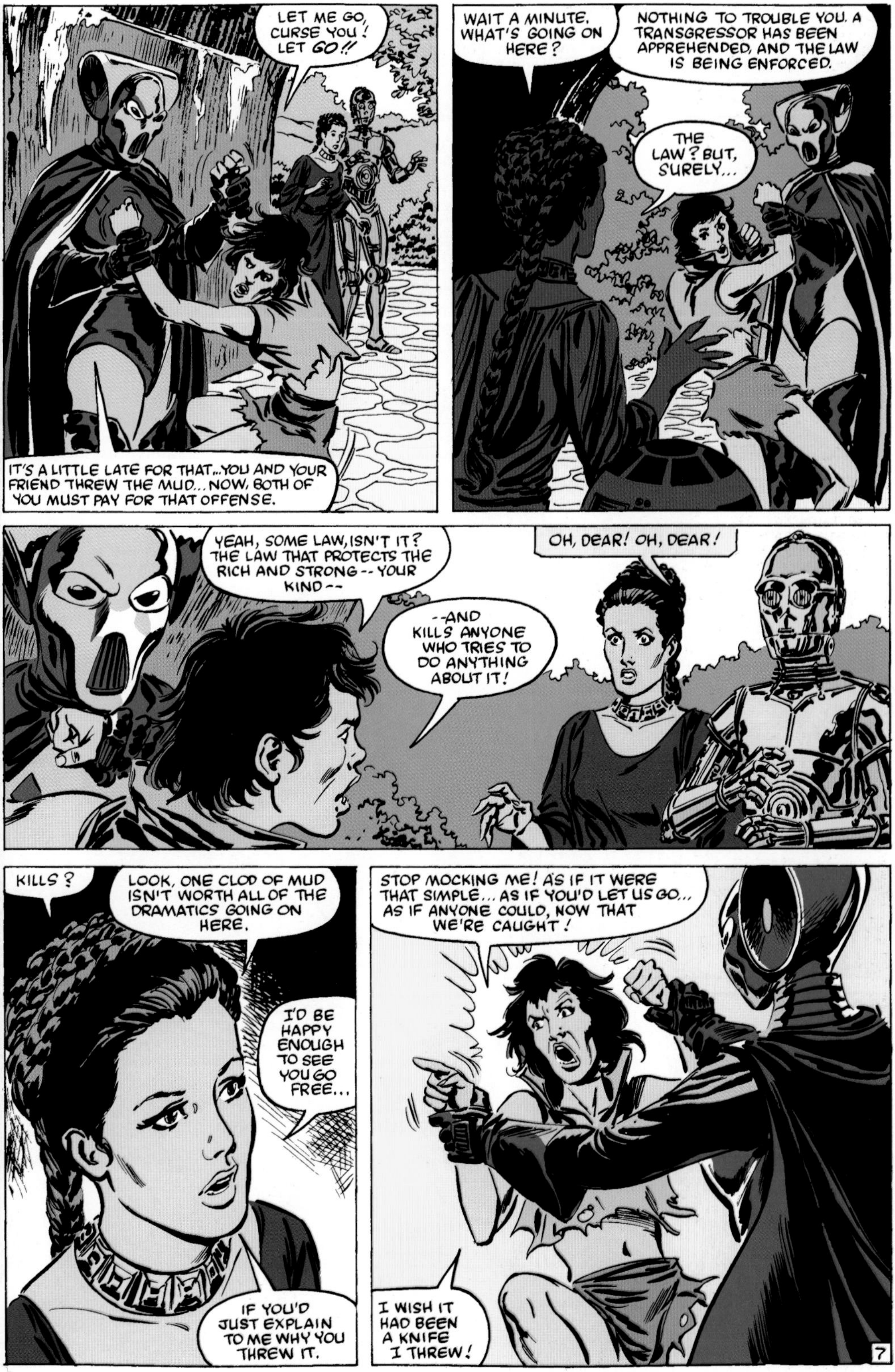
LET ME GO, CURSE YOU! LET GO!!
IT'S A LITTLE LATE FOR THAT...YOU AND YOUR FRIEND THREW THE MUD... NOW, BOTH OF YOU MUST PAY FOR THAT OFFENSE.
WAIT A MINUTE. WHAT'S GOING ON HERE?
NOTHING TO TROUBLE YOU. A TRANSGRESSOR HAS BEEN APPREHENDED, AND THE LAW IS BEING ENFORCED.
THE LAW? BUT, SURELY...
YEAH, SOME LAW, ISN'T IT? THE LAW THAT PROTECTS THE RICH AND STRONG -- YOUR KIND --
--AND KILLS ANYONE WHO TRIES TO DO ANYTHING ABOUT IT!
OH, DEAR! OH, DEAR!
KILLS?
LOOK, ONE CLOD OF MUD ISN'T WORTH ALL OF THE DRAMATICS GOING ON HERE.
I'D BE HAPPY ENOUGH TO SEE YOU GO FREE...
IF YOU'D JUST EXPLAIN TO ME WHY YOU THREW IT.
STOP MOCKING ME! AS IF IT WERE THAT SIMPLE... AS IF YOU'D LET US GO... AS IF ANYONE COULD, NOW THAT WE'RE CAUGHT!
I WISH IT HAD BEEN A KNIFE I THREW!
7

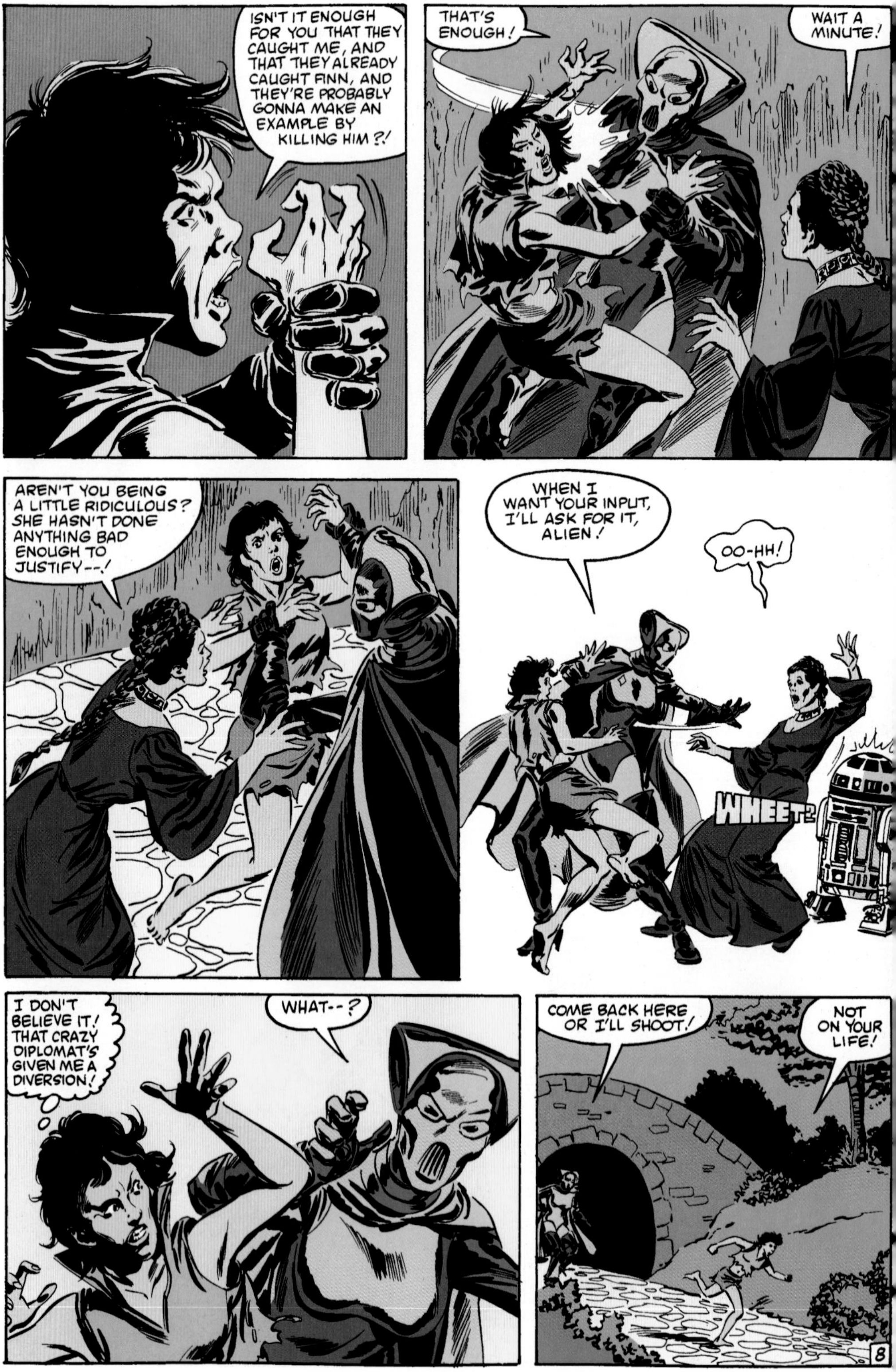
ISN'T IT ENOUGH FOR YOU THAT THEY CAUGHT ME, AND THAT THEY ALREADY CAUGHT FINN, AND THEY'RE PROBABLY GONNA MAKE AN EXAMPLE BY KILLING HIM ?!
THAT'S ENOUGH!
WAIT A MINUTE!
AREN'T YOU BEING A LITTLE RIDICULOUS? SHE HASN'T DONE ANYTHING BAD ENOUGH TO JUSTIFY--!
WHEN I WANT YOUR INPUT, I'LL ASK FOR IT, ALIEN!
OO-HH!
WHEET?
I DON'T BELIEVE IT! THAT CRAZY DIPLOMAT'S GIVEN ME A DIVERSION!
WHAT--?
COME BACK HERE OR I'LL SHOOT!
NOT ON YOUR LIFE!
8

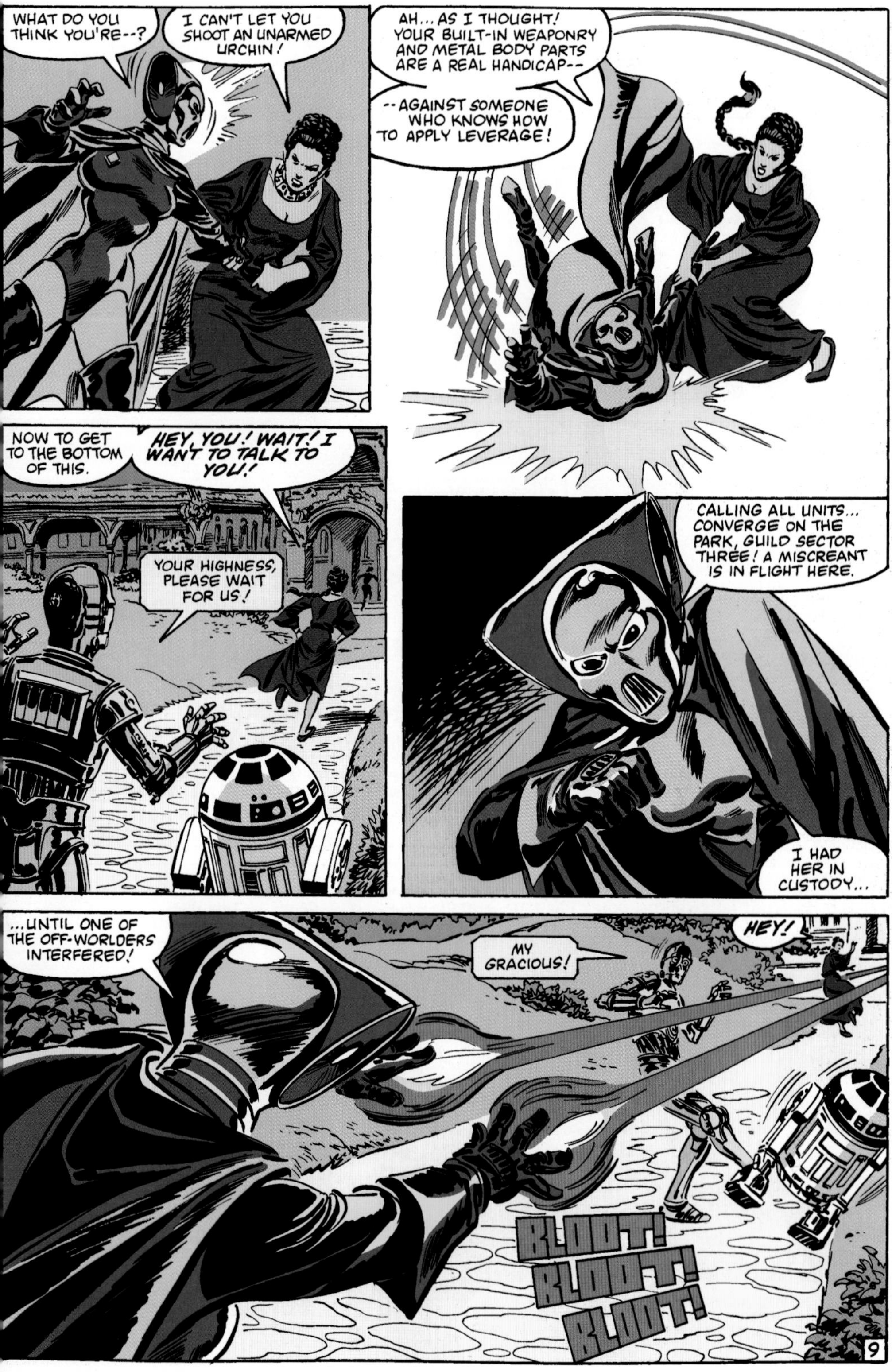
WHAT DO YOU THINK YOU'RE--?
I CAN'T LET YOU SHOOT AN UNARMED URCHIN!
AH... AS I THOUGHT! YOUR BUILT-IN WEAPONRY AND METAL BODY PARTS ARE A REAL HANDICAP--
--AGAINST SOMEONE WHO KNOWS HOW TO APPLY LEVERAGE!
NOW TO GET TO THE BOTTOM OF THIS.
HEY, YOU! WAIT! I WANT TO TALK TO YOU!
YOUR HIGHNESS, PLEASE WAIT FOR US!
CALLING ALL UNITS... CONVERGE ON THE PARK, GUILD SECTOR THREE! A MISCREANT IS IN FLIGHT HERE.
I HAD HER IN CUSTODY...
...UNTIL ONE OF THE OFF-WORLDERS INTERFERED!
MY GRACIOUS!
HEY!
BLOOT! BLOOT! BLOOT!
9

AND SOON... NOW LOOK, ALL I WANT TO DO IS TALK TO YOU! YOU LED ME QUITE A CHASE HERE, AND I FEEL I'M ENTITLED TO SOME ANSWERS.

AND YOU'LL GET THEM, I SUPPOSE, WHEN WHOEVER YOU'VE LED HERE DRAGS THEM OUT OF US, UNDER TORTURE? FORGET IT!

WHATEVER HAPPENS, WE CAN TAKE OUR REVENGE IN ADVANCE... ON YOU.

I AM GETTING A LITTLE TIRED OF LISTENING TO YOU SHOW OFF, PRACTICING YOUR TOUGH ACT.

DOESN'T MY HELPING YOU ESCAPE FROM LUMIYA PROVE A THING... UH, WHAT'S YOUR NAME, ANYWAY?

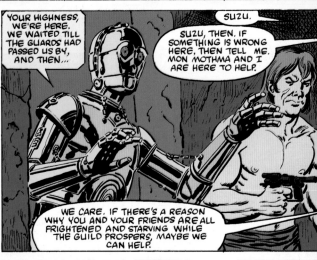

YOUR HIGHNESS, WE'RE HERE. WE WAITED TILL THE GUARDS HAD PASSED US BY, AND THEN...

SUZU.

SUZU, THEN. IF SOMETHING IS WRONG HERE, THEN TELL ME. MON MOTHMA AND I ARE HERE TO HELP.

WE CARE. IF THERE'S A REASON WHY YOU AND YOUR FRIENDS ARE ALL FRIGHTENED AND STARVING WHILE THE GUILD PROSPERS, MAYBE WE CAN HELP.

OH, SURE, YOU HELP, LIKE LADY BOUNTIFUL. THAT'S A LAUGH. ON HERDESSA, YOU LEARN YOUNG, UNLESS YOU'RE PART OF THE GUILD, TO TRUST NO ONE YOU DON'T HAVE TO, AND TO HELP YOURSELF.

WHAT DO YOU KNOW ABOUT FIGHTING OR HARDSHIP ANYWAY, *PRINCESS*? YOU'RE NOTHING BUT A FIGUREHEAD!

THAT'S IT! I HAVE TAKEN ENOUGH FROM YOU!

I HAVE BEEN MUD-BOMBED, AND HIT, AND SHOT AT, AND CHASED SINCE I CAME TO THIS WORLD. LIKE IT OR NOT, WE'RE ON THE SAME SIDE NOW.

SO, TELL ME WHAT THE FIGHT'S ALL ABOUT!

10

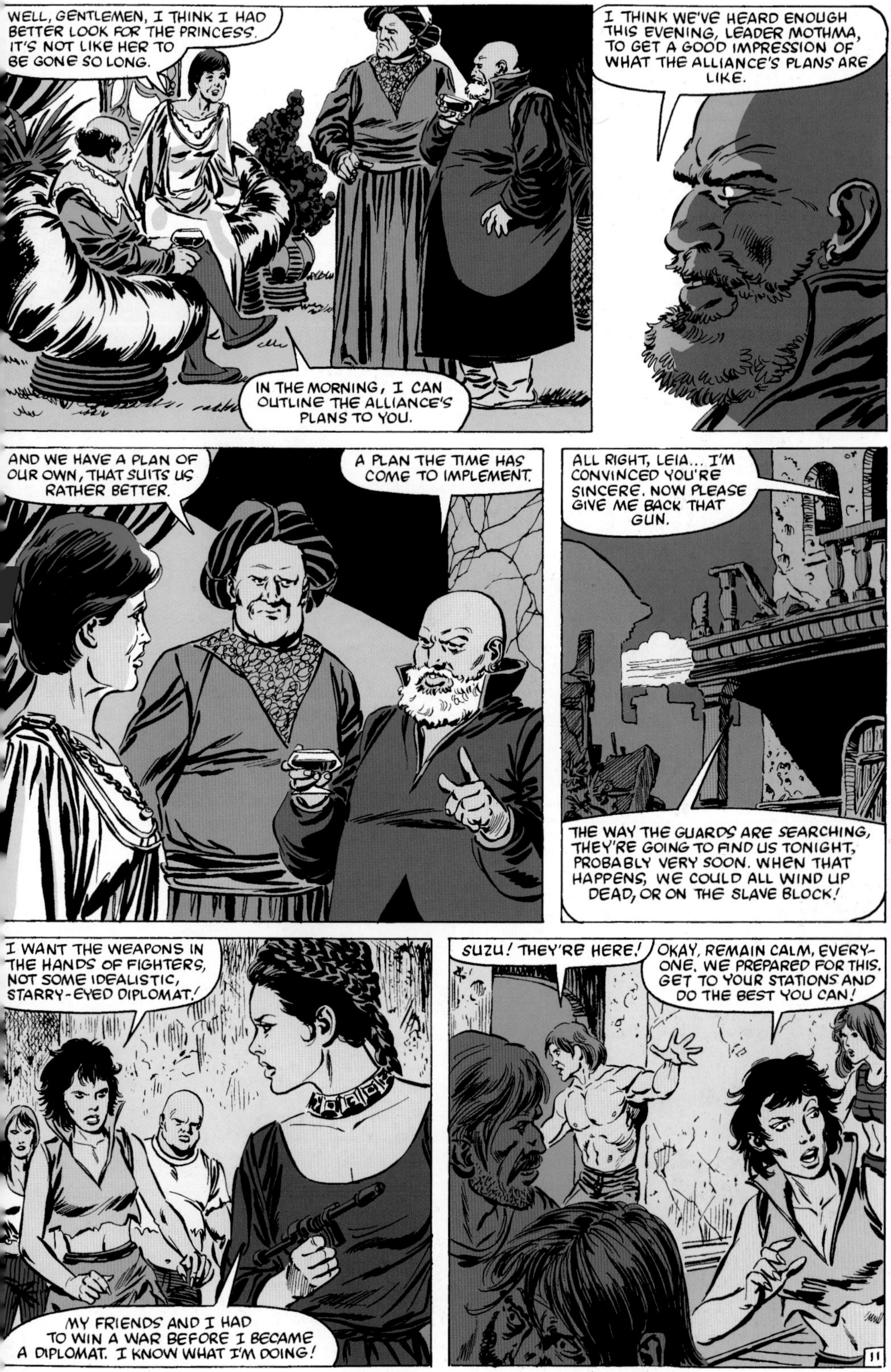
WELL, GENTLEMEN, I THINK I HAD BETTER LOOK FOR THE PRINCESS. IT'S NOT LIKE HER TO BE GONE SO LONG.
IN THE MORNING, I CAN OUTLINE THE ALLIANCE'S PLANS TO YOU.
I THINK WE'VE HEARD ENOUGH THIS EVENING, LEADER MOTHMA, TO GET A GOOD IMPRESSION OF WHAT THE ALLIANCE'S PLANS ARE LIKE.
AND WE HAVE A PLAN OF OUR OWN, THAT SUITS US RATHER BETTER.
A PLAN THE TIME HAS COME TO IMPLEMENT.
ALL RIGHT, LEIA... I'M CONVINCED YOU'RE SINCERE. NOW PLEASE GIVE ME BACK THAT GUN.
THE WAY THE GUARDS ARE SEARCHING, THEY'RE GOING TO FIND US TONIGHT, PROBABLY VERY SOON. WHEN THAT HAPPENS, WE COULD ALL WIND UP DEAD, OR ON THE SLAVE BLOCK!
I WANT THE WEAPONS IN THE HANDS OF FIGHTERS, NOT SOME IDEALISTIC, STARRY-EYED DIPLOMAT!
MY FRIENDS AND I HAD TO WIN A WAR BEFORE I BECAME A DIPLOMAT. I KNOW WHAT I'M DOING!
SUZU! THEY'RE HERE!
OKAY, REMAIN CALM, EVERY-ONE. WE PREPARED FOR THIS. GET TO YOUR STATIONS AND DO THE BEST YOU CAN!
11

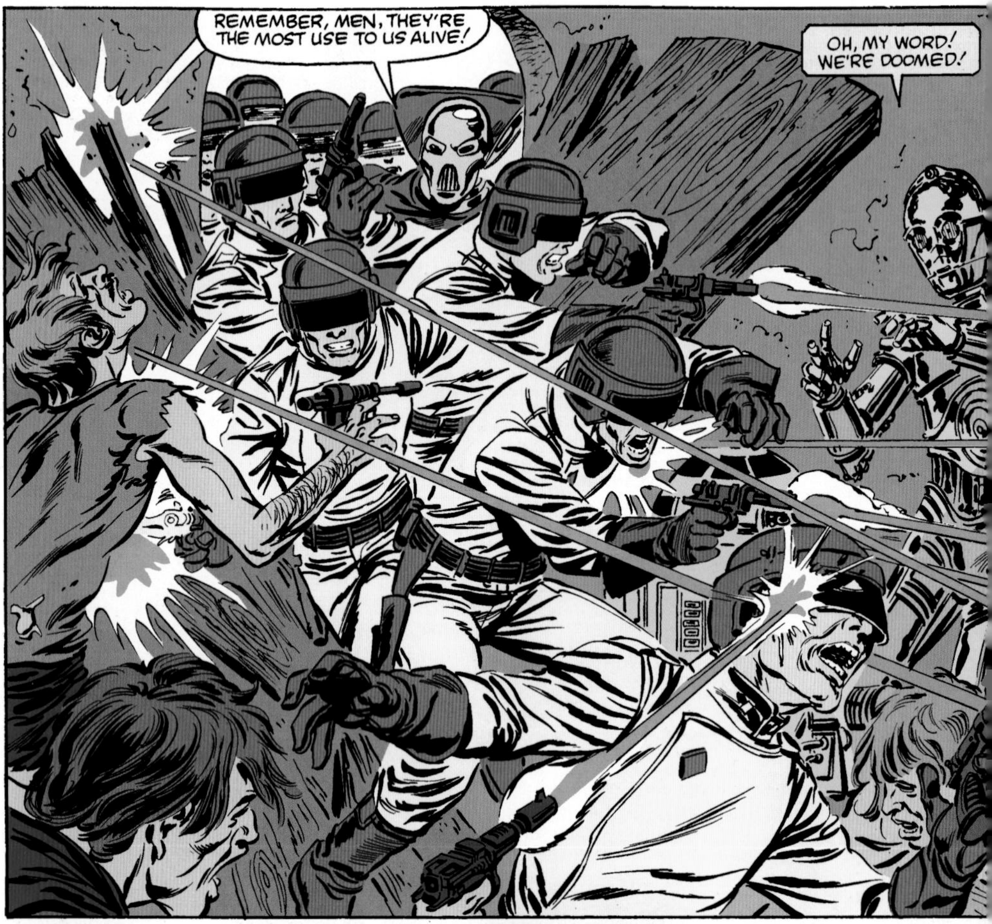
REMEMBER, MEN, THEY'RE THE MOST USE TO US ALIVE!
OH, MY WORD! WE'RE DOOMED!

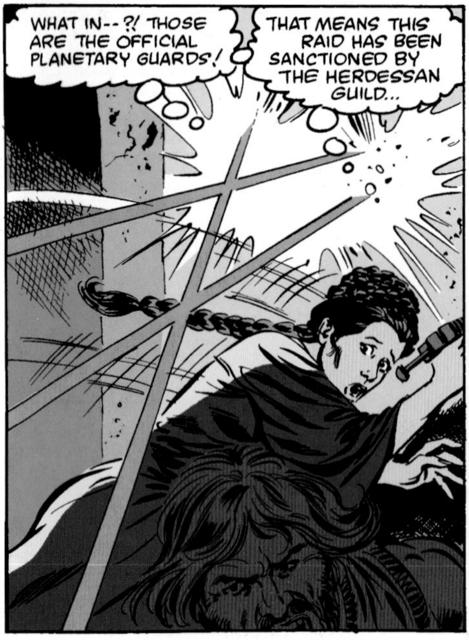
WHAT IN--?! THOSE ARE THE OFFICIAL PLANETARY GUARDS!
THAT MEANS THIS RAID HAS BEEN SANCTIONED BY THE HERDESSAN GUILD...

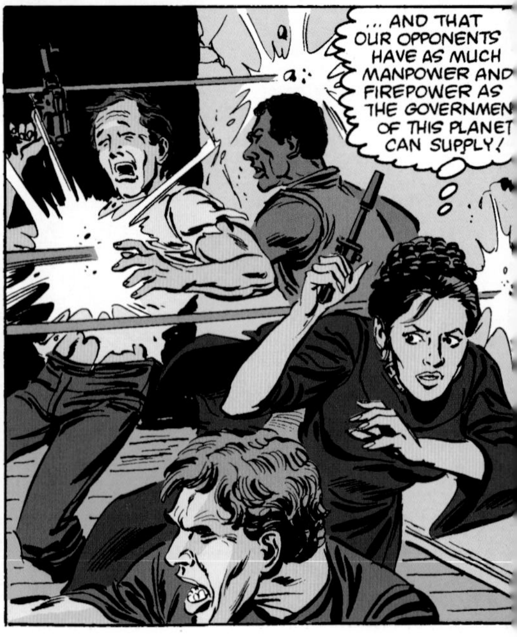
... AND THAT OUR OPPONENTS HAVE AS MUCH MANPOWER AND FIREPOWER AS THE GOVERNMEN OF THIS PLANET CAN SUPPLY!

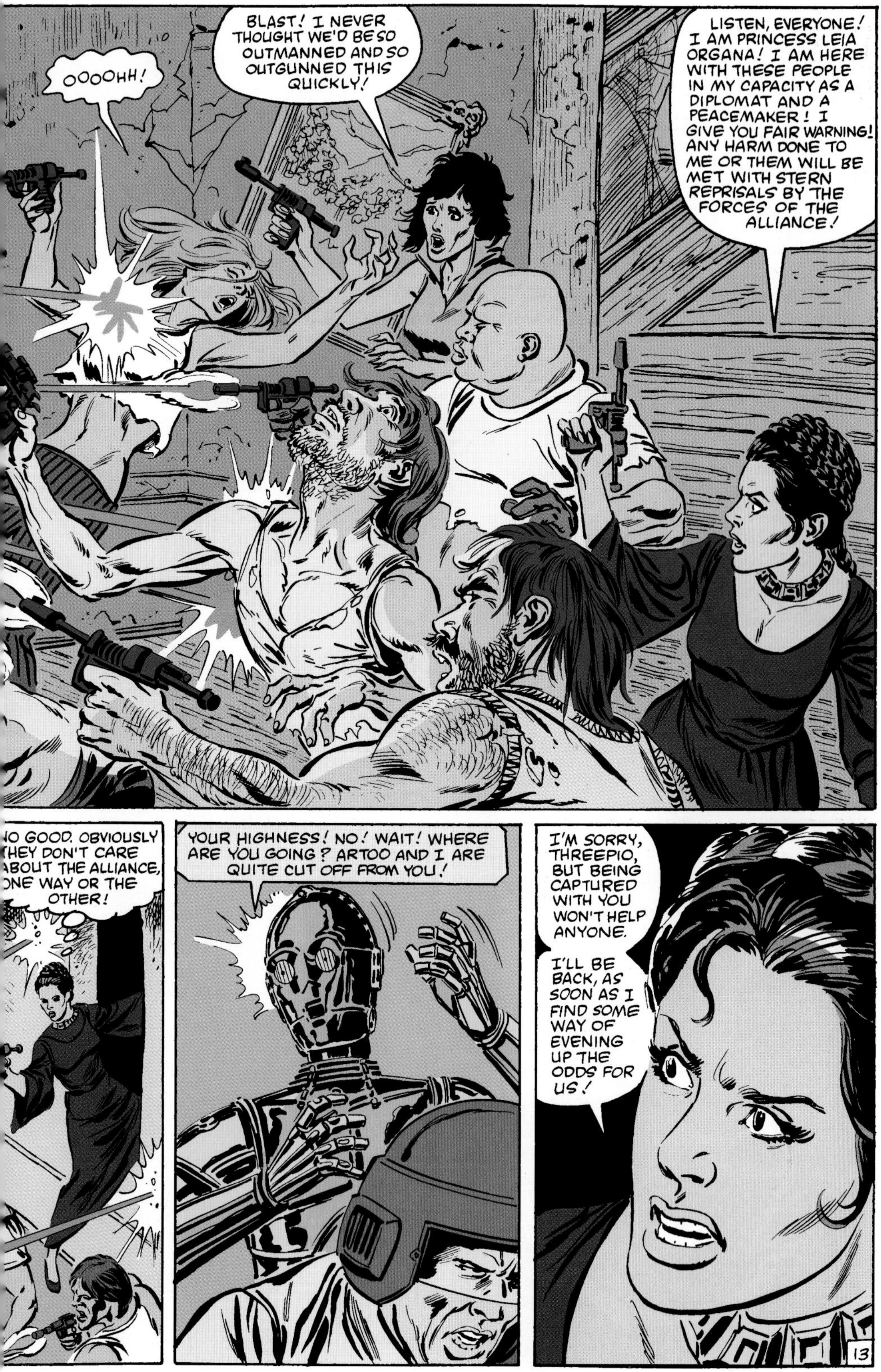
OOOOHH!
BLAST! I NEVER THOUGHT WE'D BE SO OUTMANNED AND SO OUTGUNNED THIS QUICKLY!
LISTEN, EVERYONE! I AM PRINCESS LEIA ORGANA! I AM HERE WITH THESE PEOPLE IN MY CAPACITY AS A DIPLOMAT AND A PEACEMAKER! I GIVE YOU FAIR WARNING! ANY HARM DONE TO ME OR THEM WILL BE MET WITH STERN REPRISALS BY THE FORCES OF THE ALLIANCE!
NO GOOD. OBVIOUSLY THEY DON'T CARE ABOUT THE ALLIANCE, ONE WAY OR THE OTHER!
YOUR HIGHNESS! NO! WAIT! WHERE ARE YOU GOING? ARTOO AND I ARE QUITE CUT OFF FROM YOU!
I'M SORRY, THREEPIO, BUT BEING CAPTURED WITH YOU WON'T HELP ANYONE.
I'LL BE BACK, AS SOON AS I FIND SOME WAY OF EVENING UP THE ODDS FOR US!
13

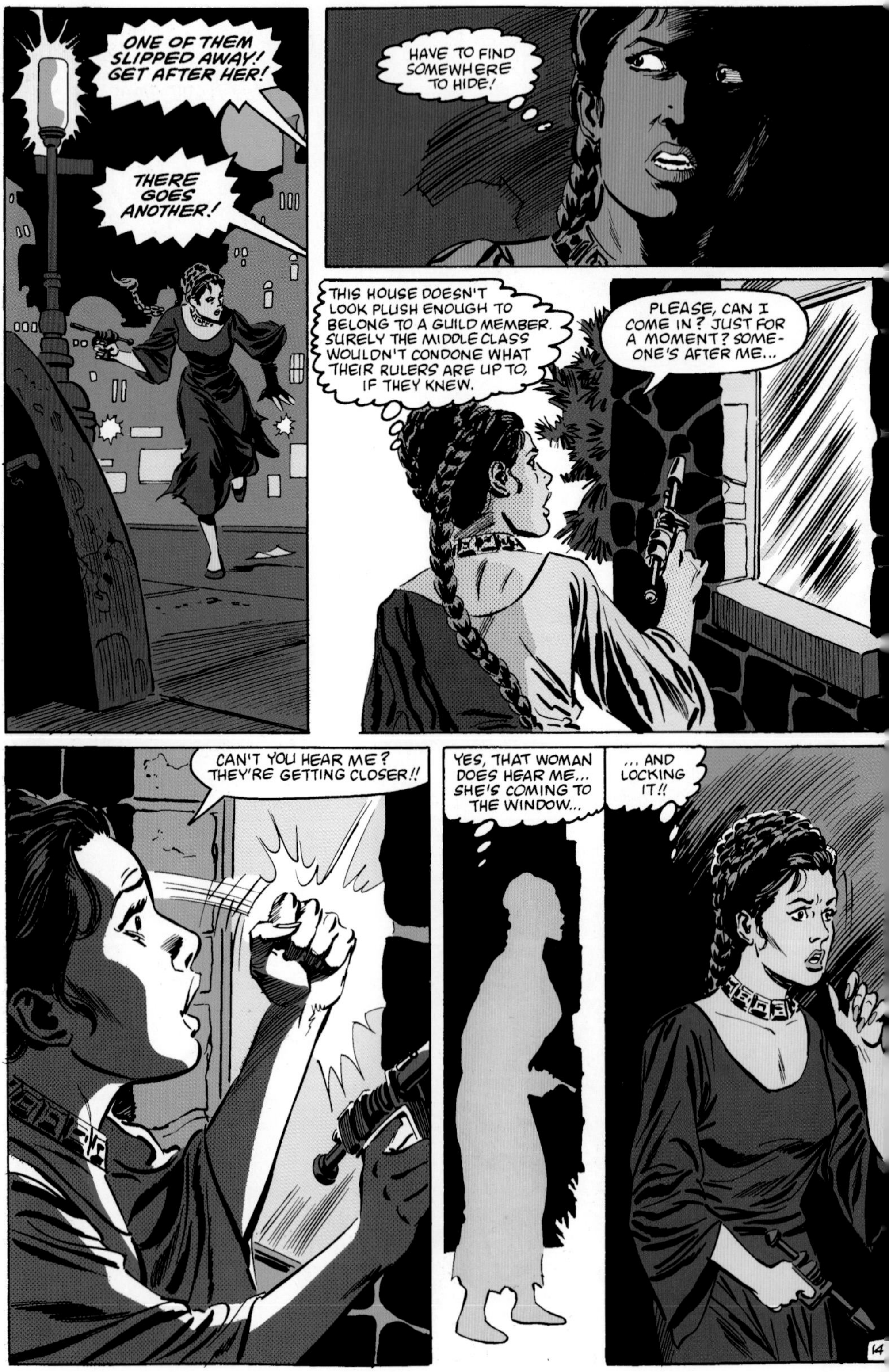
ONE OF THEM SLIPPED AWAY! GET AFTER HER!
THERE GOES ANOTHER!
HAVE TO FIND SOMEWHERE TO HIDE!
THIS HOUSE DOESN'T LOOK PLUSH ENOUGH TO BELONG TO A GUILD MEMBER. SURELY THE MIDDLE CLASS WOULDN'T CONDONE WHAT THEIR RULERS ARE UP TO, IF THEY KNEW.
PLEASE, CAN I COME IN? JUST FOR A MOMENT? SOME-ONE'S AFTER ME...
CAN'T YOU HEAR ME? THEY'RE GETTING CLOSER!!
YES, THAT WOMAN DOES HEAR ME... SHE'S COMING TO THE WINDOW...
... AND LOCKING IT!!
14

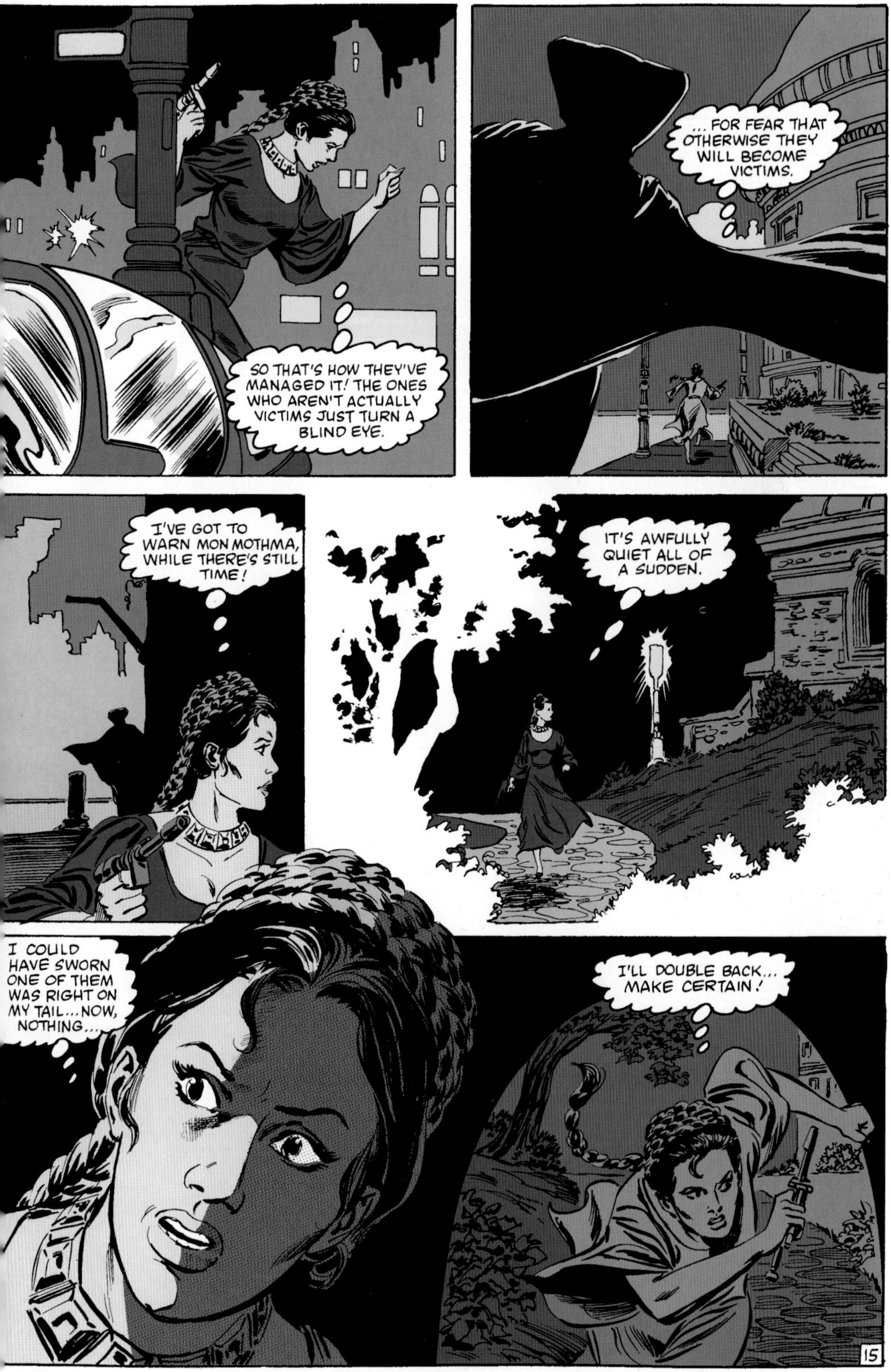
SO THAT'S HOW THEY'VE MANAGED IT! THE ONES WHO AREN'T ACTUALLY VICTIMS JUST TURN A BLIND EYE.
...FOR FEAR THAT OTHERWISE THEY WILL BECOME VICTIMS.
I'VE GOT TO WARN MON MOTHMA, WHILE THERE'S STILL TIME!
IT'S AWFULLY QUIET ALL OF A SUDDEN.
I COULD HAVE SWORN ONE OF THEM WAS RIGHT ON MY TAIL...NOW, NOTHING...
I'LL DOUBLE BACK... MAKE CERTAIN!
15

SO, THIS IS THE SOURCE OF YOUR PROSPERITY. YOU ARE *SLAVERS!* GENTLEMEN, I ASSURE YOU THAT WHATEVER YOU DO TO US, YOUR DAYS IN THIS TRADE ARE NUMBERED.

ANY MEMBER OF THE ALLIANCE IS PREPARED TO DIE AT ANY TIME. AND IF I DO NOT COME BACK, OTHERS WILL FOLLOW, AND THERE SHALL BE A RECKONING FOR ALL THE EVIL YOU HAVE DONE.

HEY... AIN'T THIS ONE OF THE KIDS WHO THREW THAT MUDBALL? YOU THINK HE LIKES PLAYING WITH MUD?

MAYBE SO. BET WE COULD ARRANGE FOR HIM TO BE SOLD TO THE LAVA MINES ON VANAN...

I'M TOO LATE. SHE'S ALREADY A PRISONER OF THOSE...

STORM TROOPERS.

WE KNEW, WHEN WE OVERTHREW THE EMPIRE, THAT SOME OF THEIR FORCES WERE BOUND TO HAVE SURVIVED...

BUT IT LOOKS LIKE THEY'RE ACTUALLY IN POWER HERE, AND IN PARTNERSHIP WITH THE GUILD SLAVERS. WE'VE GOT TO WARN THE REST OF THE ALLIANCE ABOUT IT!

ODDS DON'T LOOK TOO GOOD, DO THEY, PRINCESS?

SUZU!

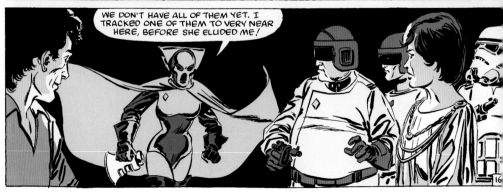

WE DON'T HAVE ALL OF THEM YET. I TRACKED ONE OF THEM TO VERY NEAR HERE, BEFORE SHE ELUDED ME!

16

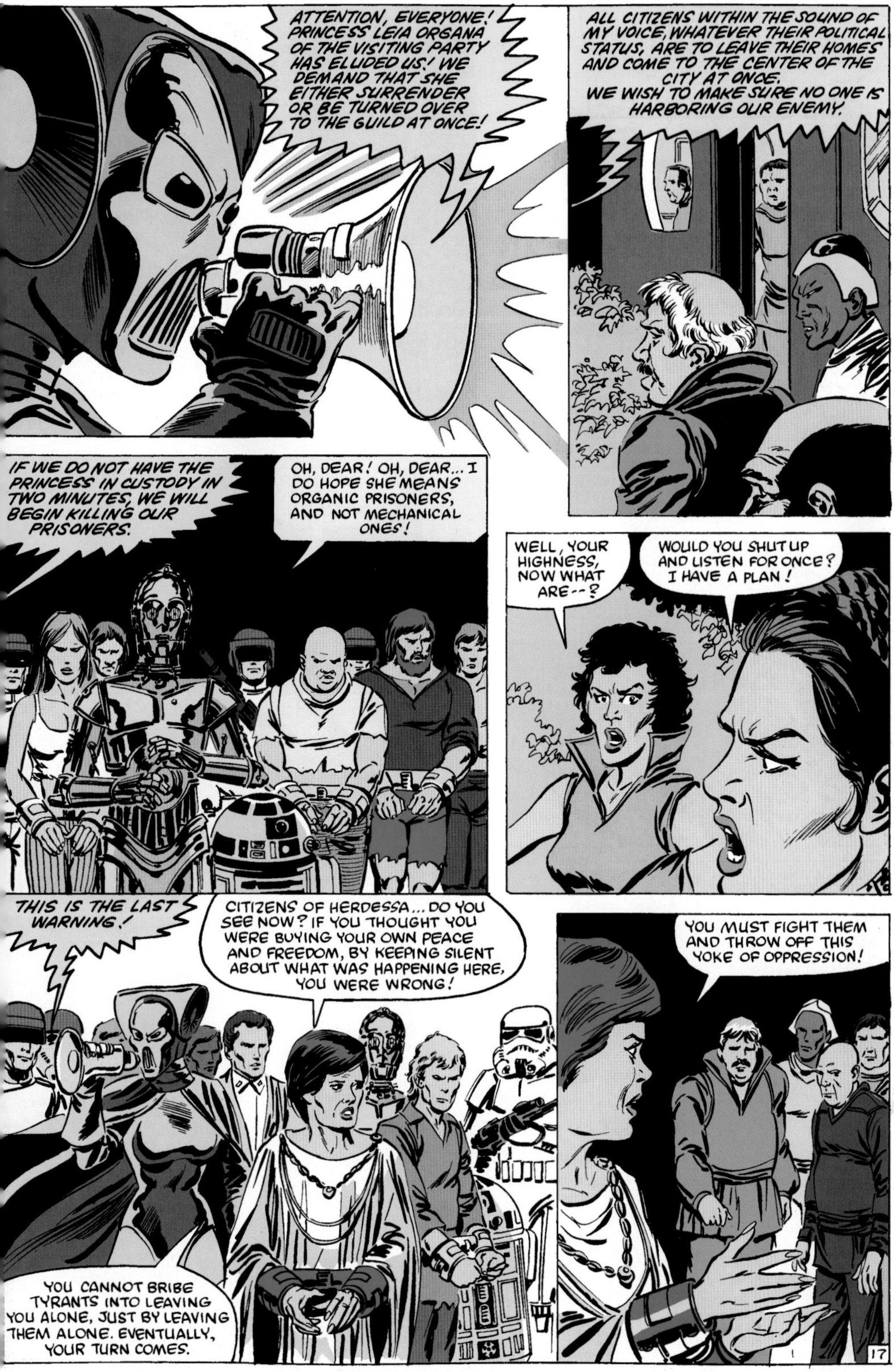
ATTENTION, EVERYONE! PRINCESS LEIA ORGANA OF THE VISITING PARTY HAS ELUDED US! WE DEMAND THAT SHE EITHER SURRENDER OR BE TURNED OVER TO THE GUILD AT ONCE!
ALL CITIZENS WITHIN THE SOUND OF MY VOICE, WHATEVER THEIR POLITICAL STATUS, ARE TO LEAVE THEIR HOMES AND COME TO THE CENTER OF THE CITY AT ONCE. WE WISH TO MAKE SURE NO ONE IS HARBORING OUR ENEMY.
IF WE DO NOT HAVE THE PRINCESS IN CUSTODY IN TWO MINUTES, WE WILL BEGIN KILLING OUR PRISONERS.
OH, DEAR! OH, DEAR... I DO HOPE SHE MEANS ORGANIC PRISONERS, AND NOT MECHANICAL ONES!
WELL, YOUR HIGHNESS, NOW WHAT ARE--?
WOULD YOU SHUT UP AND LISTEN FOR ONCE? I HAVE A PLAN!
THIS IS THE LAST WARNING!
CITIZENS OF HERDESSA... DO YOU SEE NOW? IF YOU THOUGHT YOU WERE BUYING YOUR OWN PEACE AND FREEDOM, BY KEEPING SILENT ABOUT WHAT WAS HAPPENING HERE, YOU WERE WRONG!
YOU CANNOT BRIBE TYRANTS INTO LEAVING YOU ALONE, JUST BY LEAVING THEM ALONE. EVENTUALLY, YOUR TURN COMES.
YOU MUST FIGHT THEM AND THROW OFF THIS YOKE OF OPPRESSION!
17

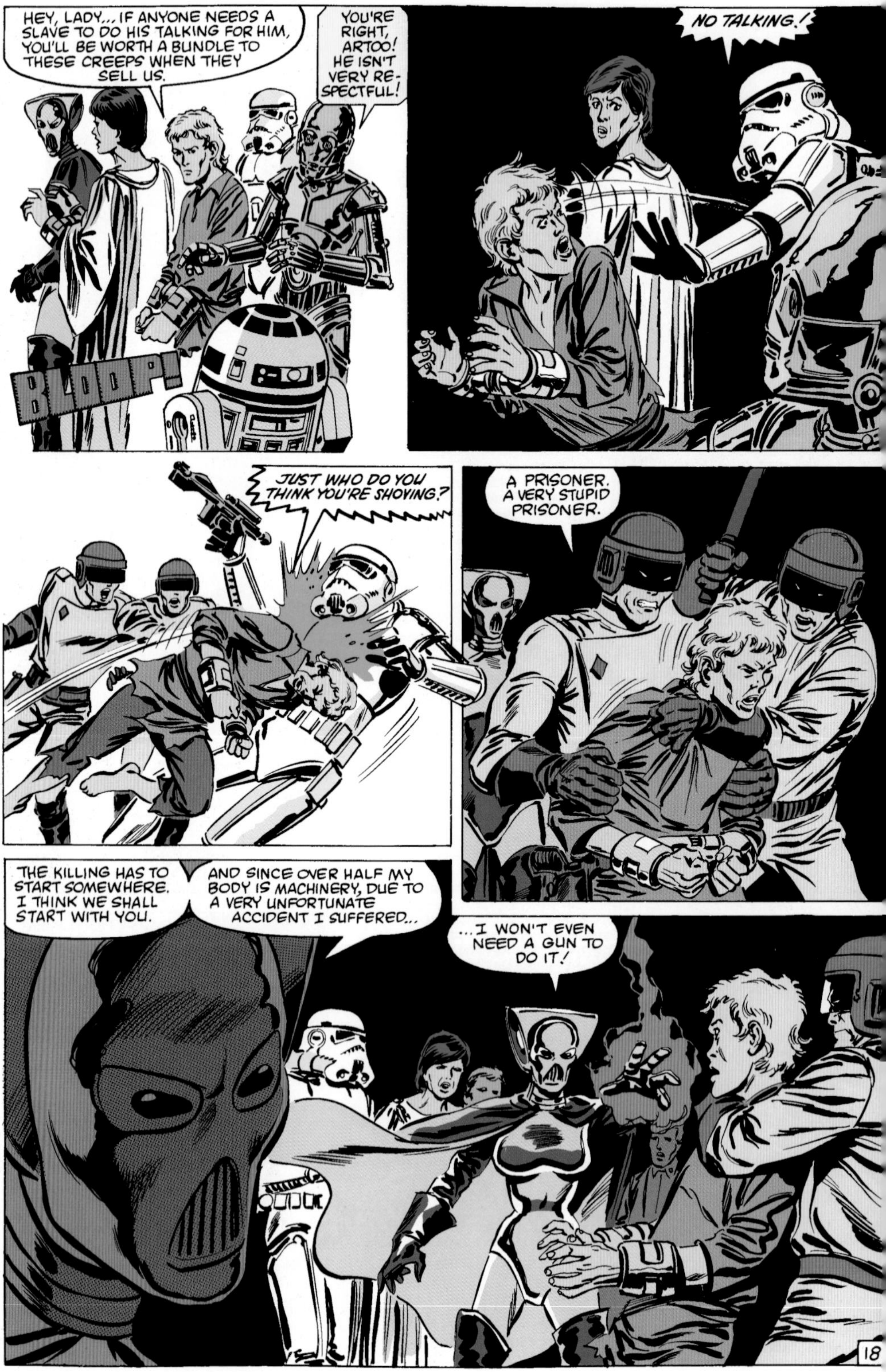
HEY, LADY... IF ANYONE NEEDS A SLAVE TO DO HIS TALKING FOR HIM, YOU'LL BE WORTH A BUNDLE TO THESE CREEPS WHEN THEY SELL US.
YOU'RE RIGHT, ARTOO! HE ISN'T VERY RE-SPECTFUL!
BLOOP!
NO TALKING!
JUST WHO DO YOU THINK YOU'RE SHOVING?
A PRISONER. A VERY STUPID PRISONER.
THE KILLING HAS TO START SOMEWHERE. I THINK WE SHALL START WITH YOU.
AND SINCE OVER HALF MY BODY IS MACHINERY, DUE TO A VERY UNFORTUNATE ACCIDENT I SUFFERED...
...I WON'T EVEN NEED A GUN TO DO IT!
18

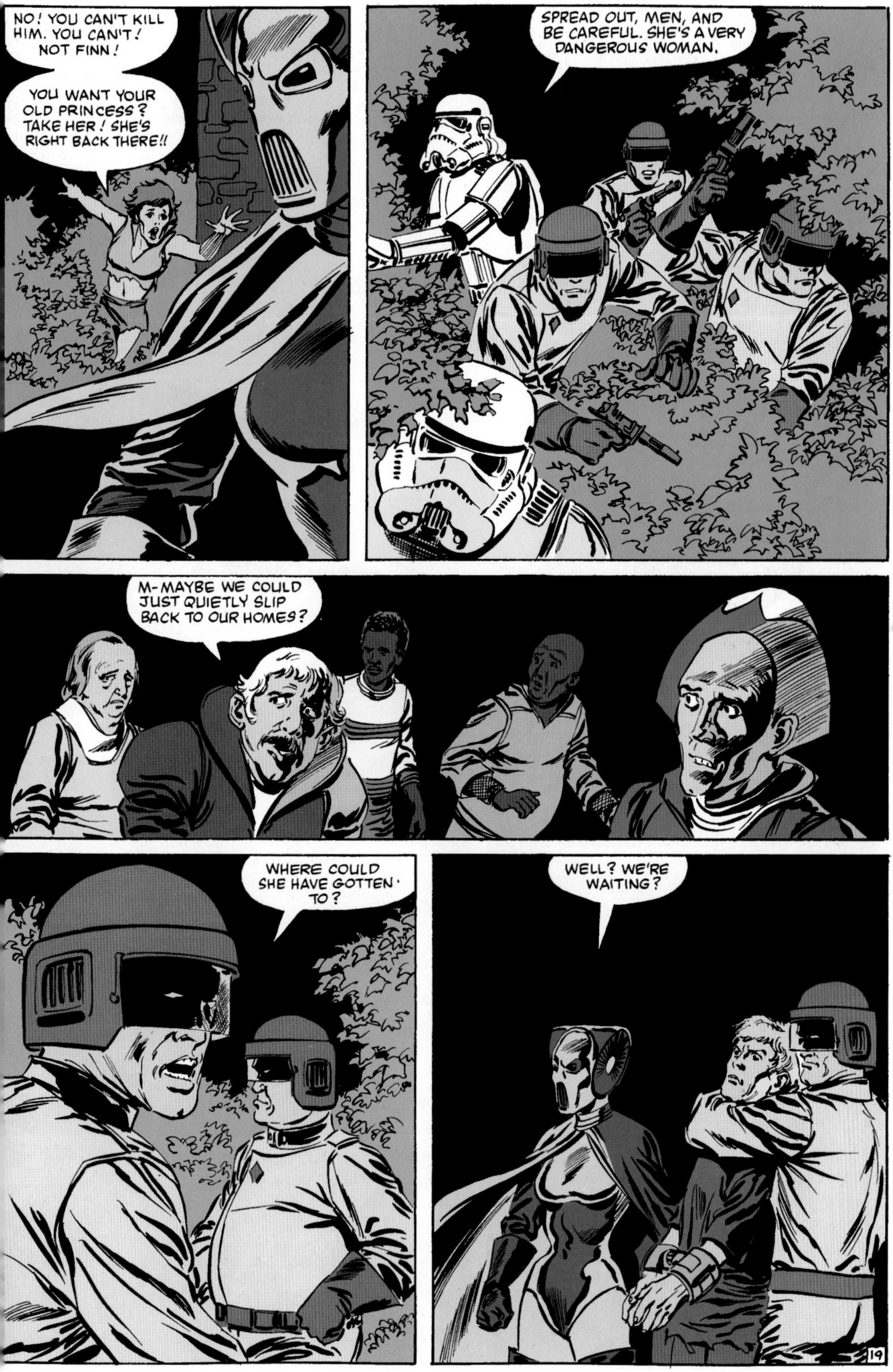
NO! YOU CAN'T KILL HIM. YOU CAN'T! NOT FINN!
YOU WANT YOUR OLD PRINCESS? TAKE HER! SHE'S RIGHT BACK THERE!!
SPREAD OUT, MEN, AND BE CAREFUL. SHE'S A VERY DANGEROUS WOMAN.
M-MAYBE WE COULD JUST QUIETLY SLIP BACK TO OUR HOMES?
WHERE COULD SHE HAVE GOTTEN TO?
WELL? WE'RE WAITING?
19

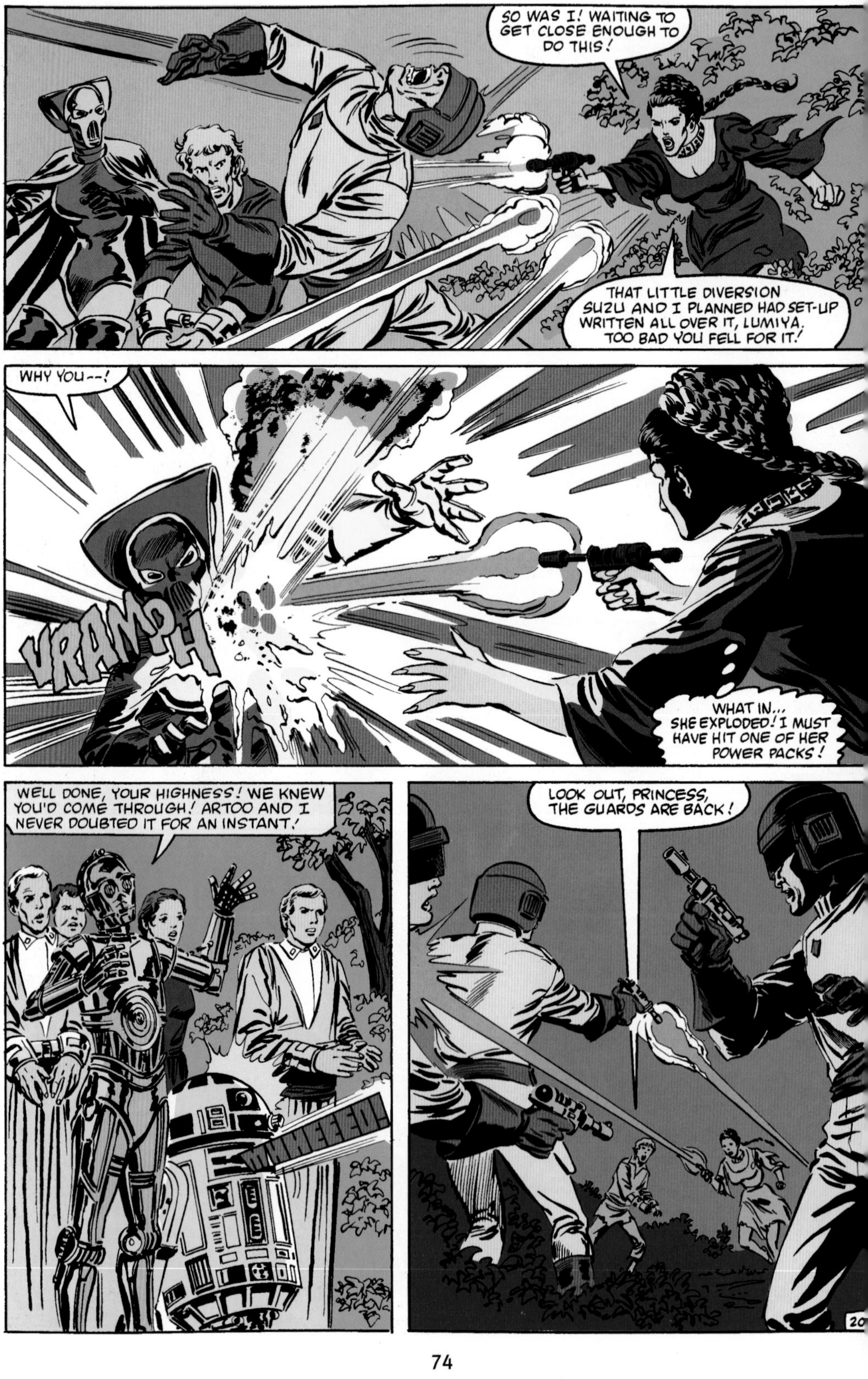
SO WAS I! WAITING TO GET CLOSE ENOUGH TO DO THIS!
THAT LITTLE DIVERSION SUZU AND I PLANNED HAD SET-UP WRITTEN ALL OVER IT, LUMIYA. TOO BAD YOU FELL FOR IT!
WHY YOU--!
VRAMPH
WHAT IN... SHE EXPLODED! I MUST HAVE HIT ONE OF HER POWER PACKS!
WELL DONE, YOUR HIGHNESS! WE KNEW YOU'D COME THROUGH! ARTOO AND I NEVER DOUBTED IT FOR AN INSTANT!
LOOK OUT, PRINCESS, THE GUARDS ARE BACK!
20

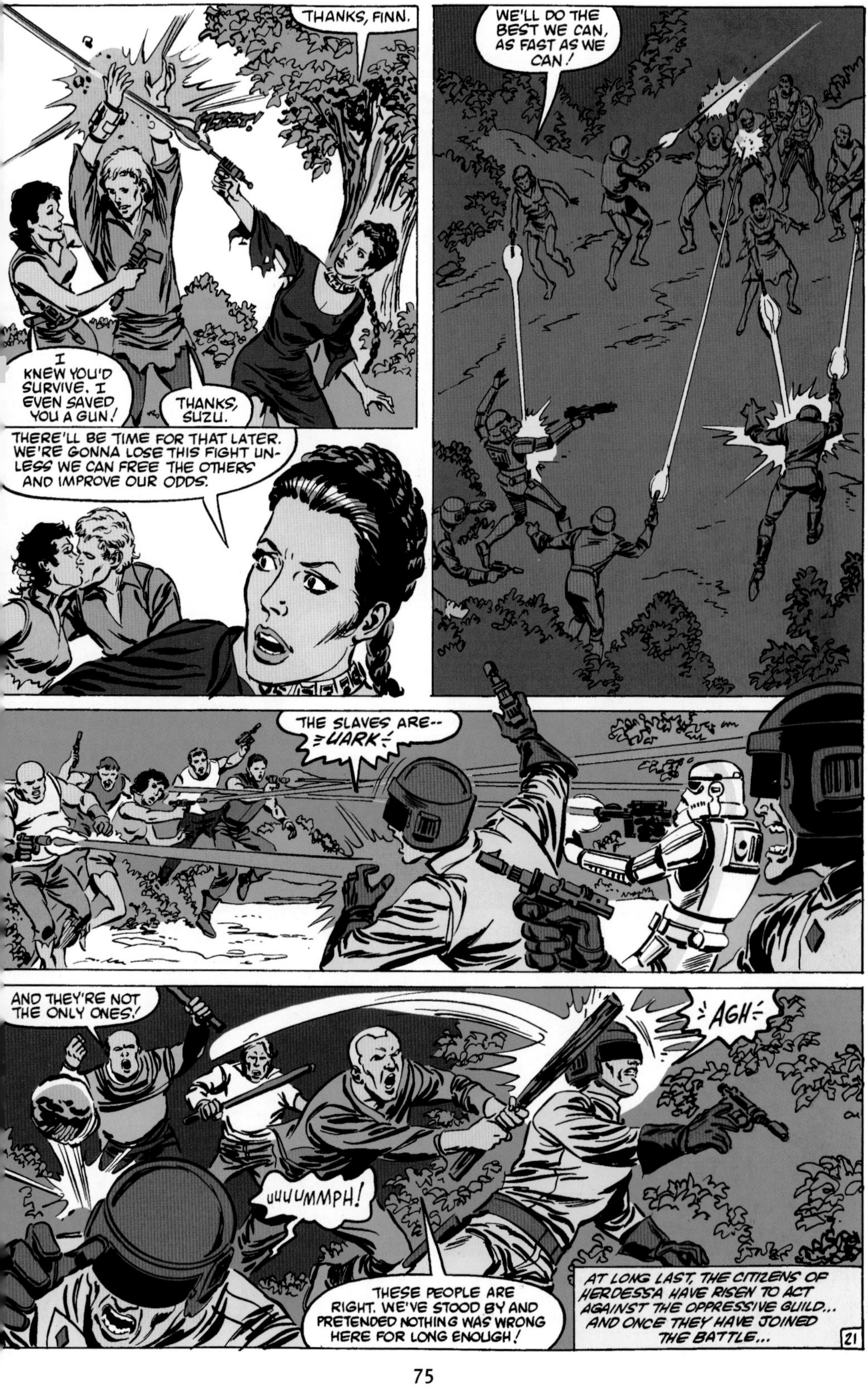
THANKS, FINN.
I KNEW YOU'D SURVIVE. I EVEN SAVED YOU A GUN!
THANKS, SUZU.
WE'LL DO THE BEST WE CAN, AS FAST AS WE CAN!
THERE'LL BE TIME FOR THAT LATER. WE'RE GONNA LOSE THIS FIGHT UNLESS WE CAN FREE THE OTHERS AND IMPROVE OUR ODDS.
THE SLAVES ARE-- UARK
AND THEY'RE NOT THE ONLY ONES!
AGH
UUUUMMPH!
THESE PEOPLE ARE RIGHT. WE'VE STOOD BY AND PRETENDED NOTHING WAS WRONG HERE FOR LONG ENOUGH!
AT LONG LAST, THE CITIZENS OF HERDESSA HAVE RISEN TO ACT AGAINST THE OPPRESSIVE GUILD... AND ONCE THEY HAVE JOINED THE BATTLE...
21

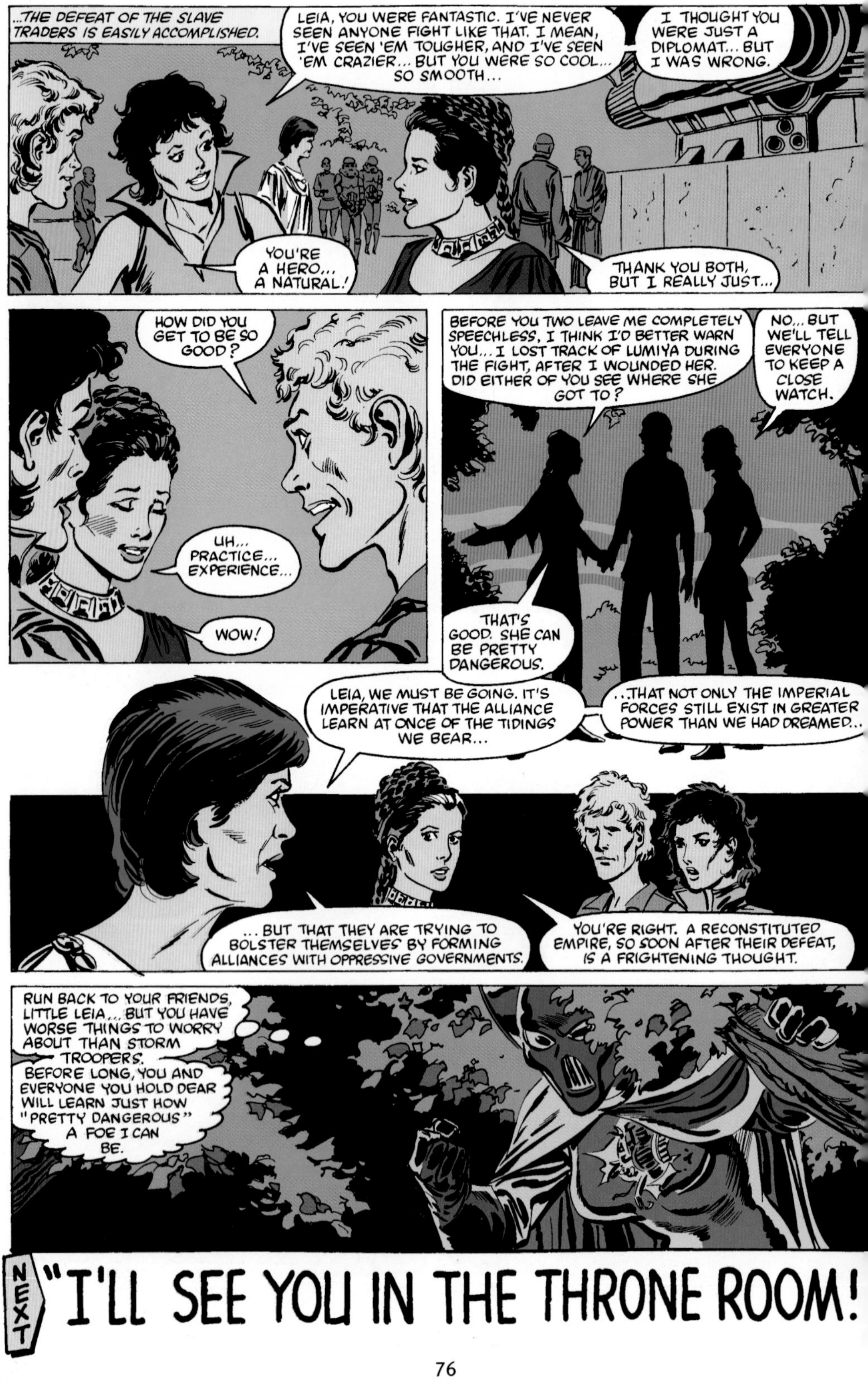
...THE DEFEAT OF THE SLAVE TRADERS IS EASILY ACCOMPLISHED.
LEIA, YOU WERE FANTASTIC. I'VE NEVER SEEN ANYONE FIGHT LIKE THAT. I MEAN, I'VE SEEN 'EM TOUGHER, AND I'VE SEEN 'EM CRAZIER... BUT YOU WERE SO COOL... SO SMOOTH...
I THOUGHT YOU WERE JUST A DIPLOMAT... BUT I WAS WRONG.
YOU'RE A HERO... A NATURAL!
THANK YOU BOTH, BUT I REALLY JUST...
HOW DID YOU GET TO BE SO GOOD?
UH... PRACTICE... EXPERIENCE...
WOW!
BEFORE YOU TWO LEAVE ME COMPLETELY SPEECHLESS, I THINK I'D BETTER WARN YOU... I LOST TRACK OF LUMIYA DURING THE FIGHT, AFTER I WOUNDED HER. DID EITHER OF YOU SEE WHERE SHE GOT TO?
NO... BUT WE'LL TELL EVERYONE TO KEEP A CLOSE WATCH.
THAT'S GOOD. SHE CAN BE PRETTY DANGEROUS.
LEIA, WE MUST BE GOING. IT'S IMPERATIVE THAT THE ALLIANCE LEARN AT ONCE OF THE TIDINGS WE BEAR...
...THAT NOT ONLY THE IMPERIAL FORCES STILL EXIST IN GREATER POWER THAN WE HAD DREAMED...
... BUT THAT THEY ARE TRYING TO BOLSTER THEMSELVES BY FORMING ALLIANCES WITH OPPRESSIVE GOVERNMENTS.
YOU'RE RIGHT. A RECONSTITUTED EMPIRE, SO SOON AFTER THEIR DEFEAT, IS A FRIGHTENING THOUGHT.
RUN BACK TO YOUR FRIENDS, LITTLE LEIA... BUT YOU HAVE WORSE THINGS TO WORRY ABOUT THAN STORM TROOPERS.
BEFORE LONG, YOU AND EVERYONE YOU HOLD DEAR WILL LEARN JUST HOW "PRETTY DANGEROUS" A FOE I CAN BE.
NEXT
"I'LL SEE YOU IN THE THRONE ROOM!

60¢
89
NOV
02817

APPROVED
BY THE
COMICS
CODE
AUTHORITY

STAR
WARS

BLEVINS

I'LL SEE YOU IN THE THRONE ROOM!

| ANN NOCENTI | BRET BLEVINS | JOE ROSEN | GLYNIS WEIN | LOUISE JONES | JIM SHOOTER |
| STORY | ART | LETTERS | COLORS | EDITOR | EDITOR-IN-CHIEF |

WHAT RIDICULOUS FIGHTERS YOU ARE! YOU'RE ALL SO OVER-ARMORED. THIS IS LIKE KNOCKING OVER SERVO-DROIDS!

SOMEONE HELP ME!

NO! RAGGOLD! *NO!* YOU WERE SO CLOSE! *WHY?!*

HE JOINED THE REBELLION AS SOON AS HE COULD WALK. NOW MUST HE *DIE* IN THE MOMENT WE WIN?!

WHY, LUKE, TELL ME WHY!?

I...DON'T KNOW...

HE WAS OUR SOURCE... OUR INSPIRATION...

I DIE HAPPY, MARY, MY WHOLE LIFE WAS REBELLION. I *AM* REBELLION. NOW I WILL SERVE AS A SYMBOL, ESPECIALLY CUT OFF NOW, IN THIS MOMENT.

NOW I WILL *TRULY* LIVE, AS A SYMBOL FOR *FREEDOM!*

WHO...WHO KILLED YOU, RAGGOLD?

A TRAITOR. A *TRAITOR* OF THE VILEST KIND IMAGINABLE -- ONE FROM OUR OWN RANKS.

YES, THERE IS A TRAITOR TO THE REBELLION. THE TRAITOR IS WITHIN...

WE'LL FIND THIS TURN-COAT SLIME AND...

HE'S... GONE.

REVENGE, LUKE?

NO, TO DESIRE REVENGE IS TO USE THE DARK SIDE OF THE FORCE. WE'LL FIND THE TRAITOR, BUT IT WILL BE FOR PEACE, FOR FREEDOM...

YES! FOR THE SPIRIT OF FREEDOM... FOR RAGGOLD!

HE WOULD HAVE WANTED US TO CELEBRATE, NOW!

TO THE THRONE ROOM!

THERE, YOU MADE IT TO THE THRONE, MY FRIEND.

LUKE! IT'S *BLACKART*, THE DETHRONED KING! HE'S CAPTURED! AND OUR COMRADES ARE MOCKING HIM!

YOU'LL NEVER WEAR A CROWN AGAIN, YOU DESPOT!

TORTURE ME ALL YOU WANT! 'CAUSE YOU SEE-- YOU MAY HAVE TOPPLED ME, BUT I SEE THAT WE DRAGGED *YOUR* KING DOWN WITH US!

AND PERHAPS *YOU* DID IT!

LUKE, WAIT!

ENOUGH VIOLENCE. IT DOESN'T MATTER WHO KILLED WHO, WE WORK FOR PEACE NOW, RIGHT? BESIDES, RAGGOLD SAID THE TRAITOR WAS *WITHIN*... FROM OUR OWN RANKS.

RAGGOLD WANTED RULE BY THE MANY, NOT THE FEW.

SO NOW EVERYBODY IS KING.

GOSH, SHE'S BEAUTIFUL.

AND SO THEY WIND THROUGH HALLS WHICH RING WITH CRIES OF FREEDOM AND JOY THE LIKES OF WHICH THESE INNER COURTS HAVE **NEVER** HEARD BEFORE!

LONG LIVE THE RULE BY THE MANY!

YEEEHA!

WE'RE FREE!

THIS IS JUST A BEGINNING! IMAGINE, TO BE *FREE* TO DO AND THINK WHATEVER WE WISH! WE'LL REVIVE THE ARTS!

BUT THE PEOPLE WILL NEED HELP. THEY DON'T KNOW WHAT FREEDOM IS!

TRUE. TO ONES ENSLAVED SO LONG, WILL THEY KNOW WHAT TO DO WITH FREEDOM?!

I GUESS IT ISN'T SO EASY TO BE FREE...

WE TOPPLED ANOTHER FIGUREHEAD. SO WHAT? IT'S NOT ENOUGH TO BE *AGAINST* SOMETHING, ONE MUST BE *FOR* SOMETHING!

YES, BUT THEY'VE EARNED THIS CELEBRATION!

THERE CAN BE NO REST TILL THE EMPIRE'S PRESENCE ON THIS PLANET IS CRUSHED, AND WE MUST FIND THAT TRAITOR-- BEFORE HE BETRAYS US AGAIN!

WHY? THAT KILLING WAS JUST A FINAL DESPERATE ACT. WE'VE WON!

LUKE, REVENGE IS THE WRONG MOTIVE, BUT YOU KNOW THAT.

SHE IS SO BRAVE AND NOBLE...AND BEAUTIFUL.

4

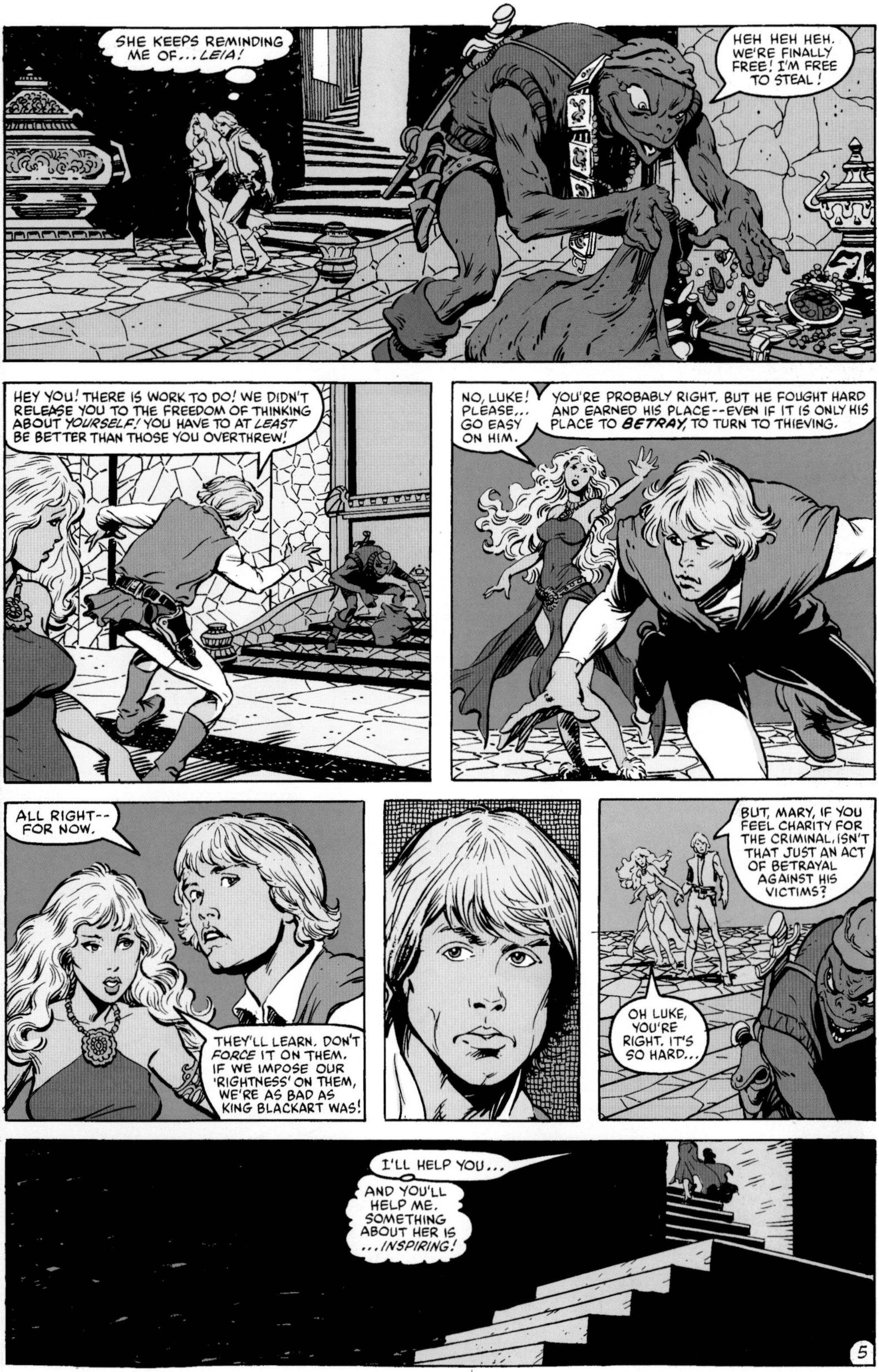
SHE KEEPS REMINDING ME OF... LEIA!
HEH HEH HEH. WE'RE FINALLY FREE! I'M FREE TO STEAL!
HEY YOU! THERE IS WORK TO DO! WE DIDN'T RELEASE YOU TO THE FREEDOM OF THINKING ABOUT YOURSELF! YOU HAVE TO AT LEAST BE BETTER THAN THOSE YOU OVERTHREW!
NO, LUKE! PLEASE... GO EASY ON HIM.
YOU'RE PROBABLY RIGHT, BUT HE FOUGHT HARD AND EARNED HIS PLACE--EVEN IF IT IS ONLY HIS PLACE TO BETRAY, TO TURN TO THIEVING.
ALL RIGHT-- FOR NOW.
THEY'LL LEARN. DON'T FORCE IT ON THEM. IF WE IMPOSE OUR 'RIGHTNESS' ON THEM, WE'RE AS BAD AS KING BLACKART WAS!
BUT, MARY, IF YOU FEEL CHARITY FOR THE CRIMINAL, ISN'T THAT JUST AN ACT OF BETRAYAL AGAINST HIS VICTIMS?
OH LUKE, YOU'RE RIGHT. IT'S SO HARD...
I'LL HELP YOU...
AND YOU'LL HELP ME. SOMETHING ABOUT HER IS ...INSPIRING!
5

AS DAYS PASS, THERE SEEMS TO BE NO END TO THE REVELRY, AND LUKE AND MARY ARE **NEVER** SEEN APART.

SOON WE MUST ORGANIZE TO WIPE OUT EVERY LAST TRACE OF THE KING AND HIS PRO-EMPIRE GOVERNMENT.

BUT THE KING IS AS GOOD AS DEAD!

NO, THE KING IS STILL HERE. THE THRONE ROOM AND INNER COURTS ARE FULL OF HIS SHADOWS AND ECHOES. I CAN FEEL IT.

COME HERE... THERE'S SO MUCH TO TEACH YOU...

I MUST TELL YOU ABOUT...

TELL YOU ABOUT...

I WANT TO... SHOW YOU...

I WANT...

MARY, CAN WE GET... AWAY FROM THE COURTS... FOR A FEW HOURS?

LET ME GO DOWN AND ARRANGE FOR A LITTLE SHIP...

SHE LEAVES, BUT NOT BEFORE OFFERING HIM HER EYES, EYES THAT PROMISE SO MUCH...

6

IT FEELS SO....*SELF-INDULGENT* TO WANT A FEW HOURS TO ENJOY MYSELF... WAIT... WHAT'S THAT RUMBLE?

NO! I *KNOW* THAT SOUND!

THE SKY IS GETTING DARK!

WHAT IS IT?

LOOK!

YES, SOMETHING DARKENS THE HORIZON, THEN BLOTS OUT THE SKY!

AN INVADING FLEET! IT'S THE *EMPIRE!*

BUT OUR FREEDOM...

...IS GONE.

WHAT...IT'S... *NO!*

THE FREEDOM... THE DREAM ...THE PEOPLE...

...*LUKE!* MUST GET BACK TO HIM!

LUKE... LUKE, I LOVE YOU...

LUKE...

ZZZP!

ZZRRP!

ZZ!

MARY!

OUT OF MY WAY!

HE WADES THROUGH A SEA OF PEOPLE. PEOPLE THAT ARE SCARED. PEOPLE THAT STRAIN FOR THEIR LAST GASPS OF FREEDOM...BEFORE THEY BEGIN TO *RUN.*

7

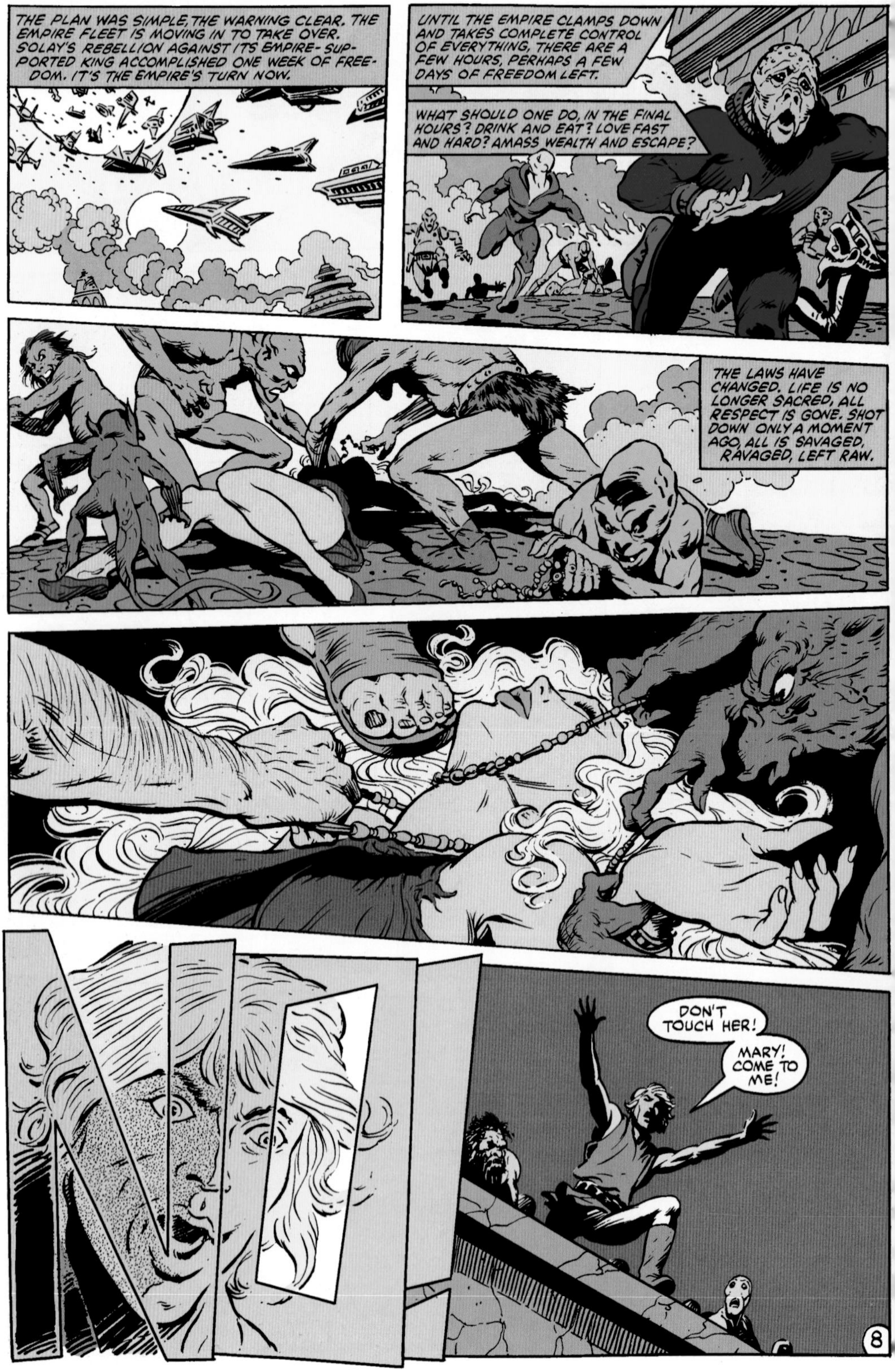
THE PLAN WAS SIMPLE, THE WARNING CLEAR. THE EMPIRE FLEET IS MOVING IN TO TAKE OVER. SOLAY'S REBELLION AGAINST ITS EMPIRE-SUPPORTED KING ACCOMPLISHED ONE WEEK OF FREEDOM. IT'S THE EMPIRE'S TURN NOW.
UNTIL THE EMPIRE CLAMPS DOWN AND TAKES COMPLETE CONTROL OF EVERYTHING, THERE ARE A FEW HOURS, PERHAPS A FEW DAYS OF FREEDOM LEFT.
WHAT SHOULD ONE DO, IN THE FINAL HOURS? DRINK AND EAT? LOVE FAST AND HARD? AMASS WEALTH AND ESCAPE?
THE LAWS HAVE CHANGED. LIFE IS NO LONGER SACRED, ALL RESPECT IS GONE. SHOT DOWN ONLY A MOMENT AGO, ALL IS SAVAGED, RAVAGED, LEFT RAW.
N
DON'T TOUCH HER!
MARY! COME TO ME!
8

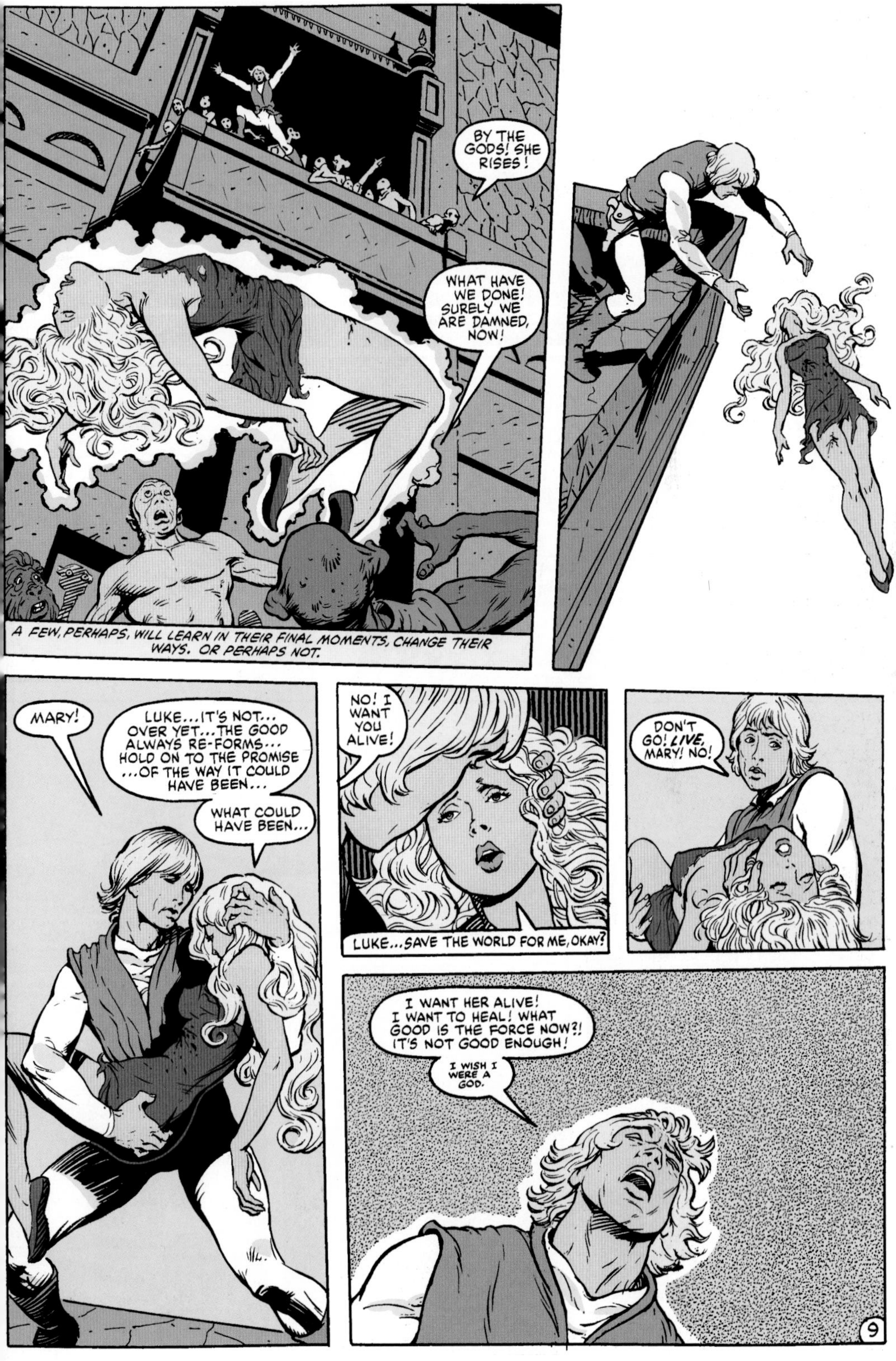
BY THE GODS! SHE RISES!
WHAT HAVE WE DONE! SURELY WE ARE DAMNED, NOW!
A FEW, PERHAPS, WILL LEARN IN THEIR FINAL MOMENTS, CHANGE THEIR WAYS. OR PERHAPS NOT.
MARY!
LUKE...IT'S NOT... OVER YET...THE GOOD ALWAYS RE-FORMS... HOLD ON TO THE PROMISE ...OF THE WAY IT COULD HAVE BEEN...
WHAT COULD HAVE BEEN...
NO! I WANT YOU ALIVE!
LUKE...SAVE THE WORLD FOR ME, OKAY?
DON'T GO! LIVE, MARY! NO!
I WANT HER ALIVE! I WANT TO HEAL! WHAT GOOD IS THE FORCE NOW?! IT'S NOT GOOD ENOUGH!
I WISH I WERE A GOD.
9

A FEW HOURS INTO THE NEW WORLD, LITTLE HAS CHANGED. FROM THE FIRST TASTE OF FREEDOM-- TO THE LAST GASPS OF IT--THE MOOD IS ONLY SLIGHTLY ALTERED.

REBELS GO INTO HIDING AND EVERY- ONE ELSE LIVES EACH MOMENT AS IF IT WERE THEIR LAST.

EXCEPT ONE MAN, ONE DANGEROUSLY GRIM AND DETERMINED SOUL.

A TRAITOR, A TRAITOR.

YOU KILLED TWO NOW. AND IN ESSENCE-- A WHOLE WORLD.

MAY THE FORCE PROTECT YOU FROM ME.

OH BOY! AN EASY MARK!

HEY!

OOOOH! UH... YOU DROPPED YOUR SABER, SIR!

I DID NOT! YOU TRIED TO *STEAL* IT!

OH, WELL, IT WAS WORTH A TRY.

HEY! I COULD USE A MAN WHO CAN HANDLE A SABER.

LOTS OF GOOD LOOT- ING THESE DAYS! AN' I *LOVE* MONEY!

LOOTING! I'VE GOT A TRAITOR TO FIND.

WHAT A WASTE OF ENERGY. UN- LESS THERE'S MONEY IN IT... WAITAMINUTE... *YEAH!*

I GOT A PLAN. I'M SCAMP, AN' YOU CAN FOLLOW ME...

HE'S TOO *LITTLE* TO BE SO SMART. I BETTER STICK WITH HIM AND KEEP HIM OUT OF TROUBLE...

10

"WHAT DO YOU WANT THE TRAITOR FOR? SO SOMEONE *SOLD OUT* THE REBELLION TO THE EMPIRE. WHO DO YOU THINK *FINANCED* THE *PHONEY REBELLION* IN THE FIRST PLACE?!"

"SOME IMPERIAL GOVERNOR USED THE REBELS TO DO HIS DIRTY WORK. HE FOUND ONE REBEL WHO HAD A PRICE... AND SET EVERYONE UP FOR A FALL. NOW SOLAY IS *HIS*."

HERE WE ARE. THE BIGGEST JERKS ARE ALWAYS FOUND AT *THESE* PLACES... YUK! LOOK AT ALL THESE *GIRLS*...

THERE-- THAT GUY-- HE'S A REBEL, BUT ALWAYS JUST FOR MONEY. NOW YOU *TORTURE* HIM AND I GET TO *ROB* HIM!

HAVING FUN?

FLAUNTING LOTS OF MONEY THERE. AREN'T YOU WORRIED THE EMPIRE WILL NOTICE?

÷GULP÷

YOU WERE A REBEL, TOO, SHOULDN'T YOU BE IN HIDING? UNLESS, OF COURSE, YOU DON'T HAVE TO HIDE?

HEY! PUT ME DOWN!

MONEY MONEY MONEY

TALK!

÷GULP÷

OBOY OBOY OBOY

WHAM

OKAY OKAY! THERE WAS A TRAITOR. ÷GULP÷ ONE OF OUR SPIES IN THE COURT, I THINK. I HEARD WE WE WERE SOLD OUT ÷GULP÷ BY THE SAME GUY WHO ASSASSINATED OLD RAGGOLD, THE REBEL LEADER! ÷GULP÷

NOW, PLEASE ÷GULP÷ GET YOUR FIST OUTTA MY THROAT-- YER *KILLIN'* ME!

HE ONLY KNOWS RUMORS ... WHAT SHOULD I DO...

11

"..THEY'VE EARNED THEIR PLACE-- EVEN IF IT'S ONLY THEIR PLACE TO BETRAY...

OKAY, MARY, THIS GUY OWES HIS LIFE TO YOUR SWEET MEMORY. I'LL LEAVE HIM IN PEACE.

YOU KNOW, SCUM-- DON'T YOU HAVE ANYTHING BETTER TO DO WITH YOUR TIME?

WHAT TIME? I'M A DEAD MAN, LET ME LIVE MY LAST HOURS MY WAY.

AND WHO ARE YOU TO TALK ANYWAY? LOOK HOW YOU'RE SPENDING YOUR TIME!

LET'S GET OUT OF HERE.

YOU KNOW, YOU HAVE NO MORAL RIGHT TO TAKE THAT MAN'S MONEY.

HEY! I ONLY STOLE FROM A THIEF! AN' BESIDES, YA WANNA HANG OUT WITH ME, DON'T GIVE ME THAT *MORALS SMORALS* GUNK, OKAY?

I GOT MY OWN 'POINT-A-VIEW' ON THINGS, AN' YOU GOT YOURS.

12

"NOW LET'S GET GOING. NEXT STOP IS THE SPACEPORT. IF I KNOW OUR EX-KING *BLACKART*, HE'S TRYING TO GET OFF-WORLD. *HE* MUST KNOW WHO THE TRAITOR IS."

GETTIN' OUTTA THEIR PRISON WAS MESSY... BUT FUN!

GOTTA GET A SHIP...

UNGH!

...AND GET OUTTA HERE! FIND A THRONE ON SOME OTHER PLANET TO SIT ON.

CRUNCH!

UGH... AW, NO!

GOT BLOOD ON MY NEW BOOTS. *BLAST!*

HEY, BLACKART!

HUH? YOU!

13

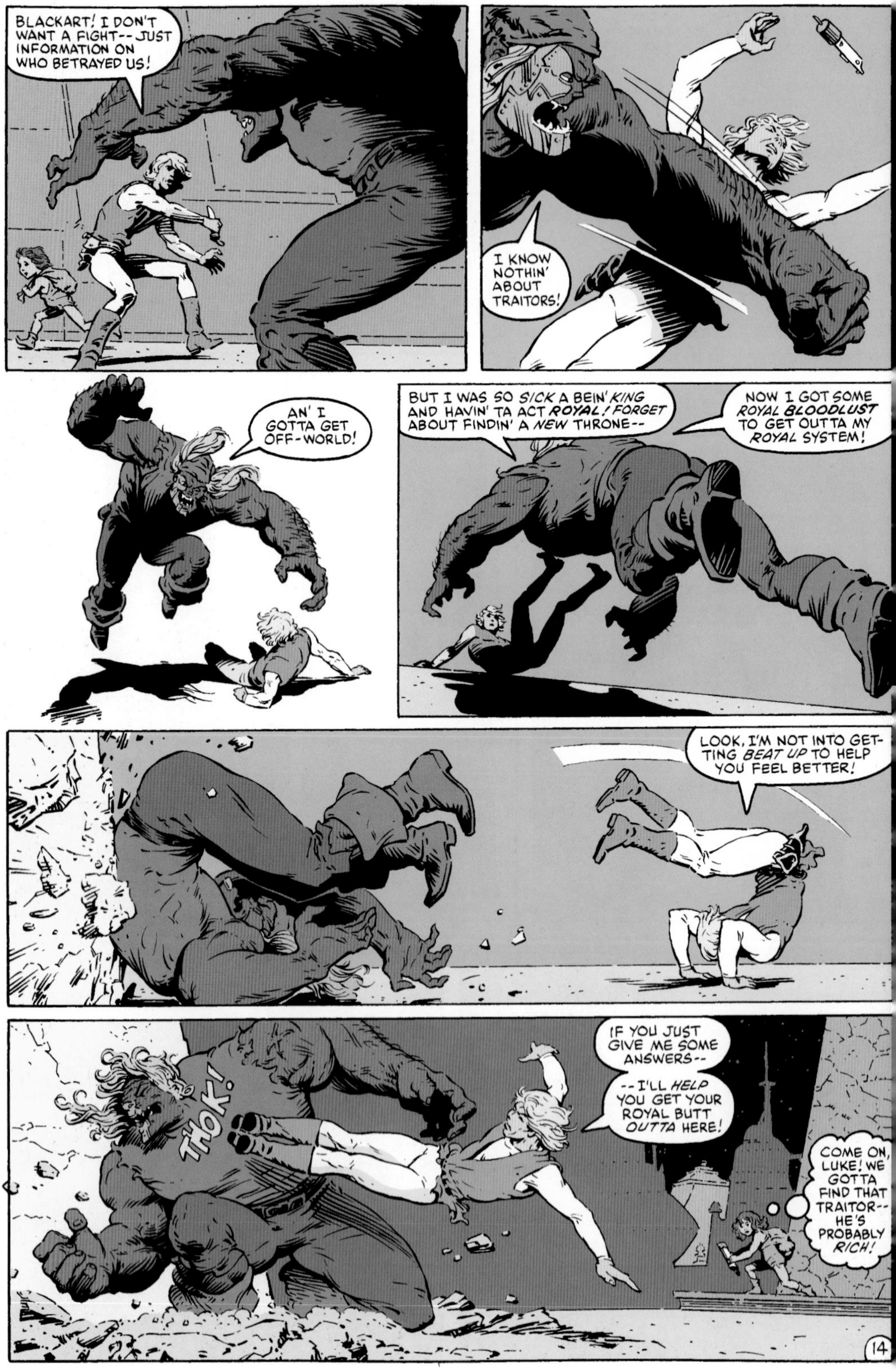
BLACKART! I DON'T WANT A FIGHT-- JUST INFORMATION ON WHO BETRAYED US!
I KNOW NOTHIN' ABOUT TRAITORS!
AN' I GOTTA GET OFF-WORLD!
BUT I WAS SO SICK A BEIN' KING AND HAVIN' TA ACT ROYAL! FORGET ABOUT FINDIN' A NEW THRONE--
NOW I GOT SOME ROYAL BLOODLUST TO GET OUTTA MY ROYAL SYSTEM!
LOOK, I'M NOT INTO GET-TING BEAT UP TO HELP YOU FEEL BETTER!
IF YOU JUST GIVE ME SOME ANSWERS--
THOK!
--I'LL HELP YOU GET YOUR ROYAL BUTT OUTTA HERE!
COME ON, LUKE! WE GOTTA FIND THAT TRAITOR--HE'S PROBABLY RICH!
14

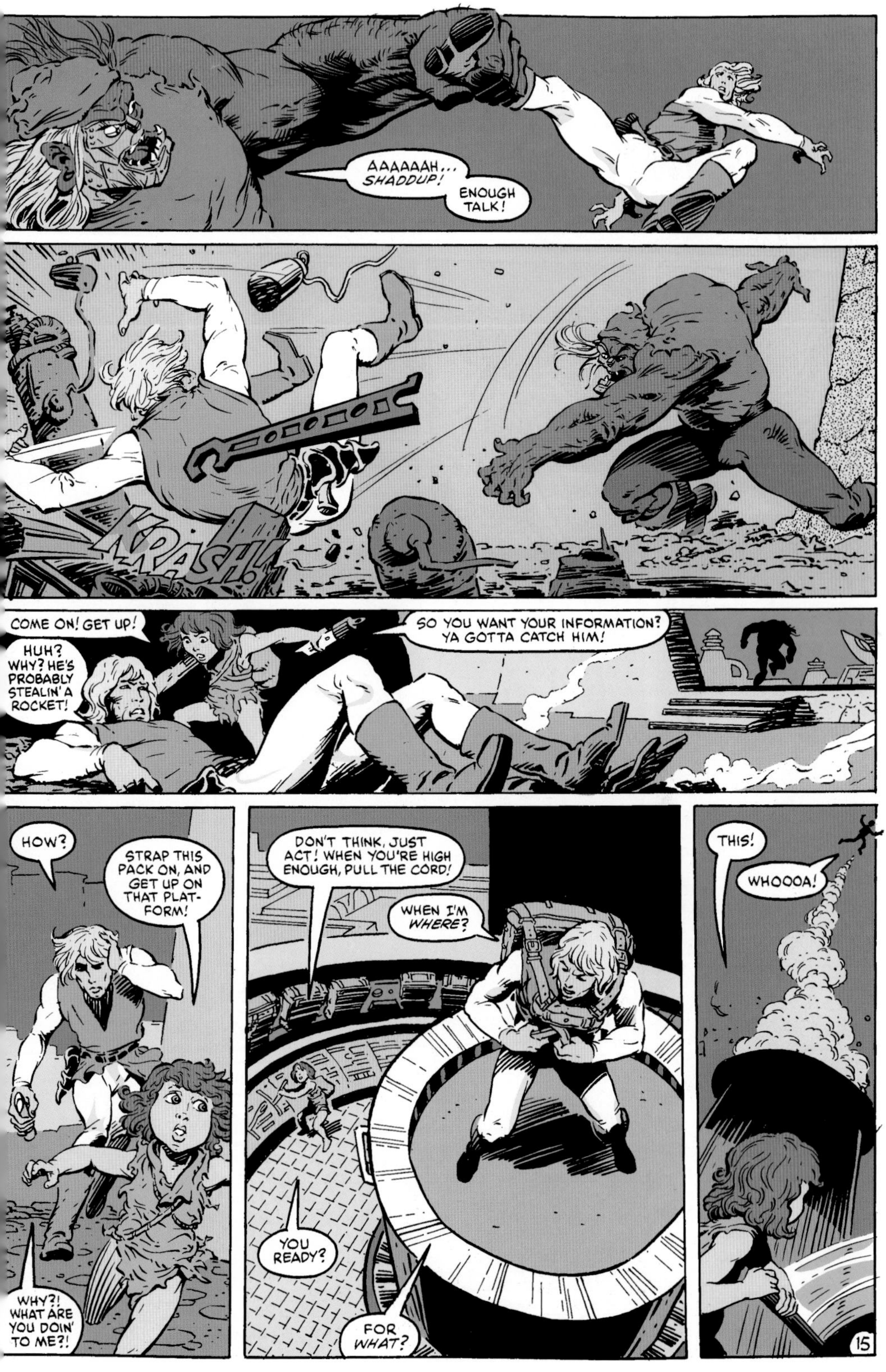
AAAAAAH... SHADDUP!
ENOUGH TALK!
KRASH!!
COME ON! GET UP!
HUH? WHY? HE'S PROBABLY STEALIN' A ROCKET!
SO YOU WANT YOUR INFORMATION? YA GOTTA CATCH HIM!
HOW?
STRAP THIS PACK ON, AND GET UP ON THAT PLAT-FORM!
WHY?! WHAT ARE YOU DOIN' TO ME?!
DON'T THINK, JUST ACT! WHEN YOU'RE HIGH ENOUGH, PULL THE CORD!
WHEN I'M WHERE?
YOU READY?
FOR WHAT?
THIS!
WHOOOA!
15

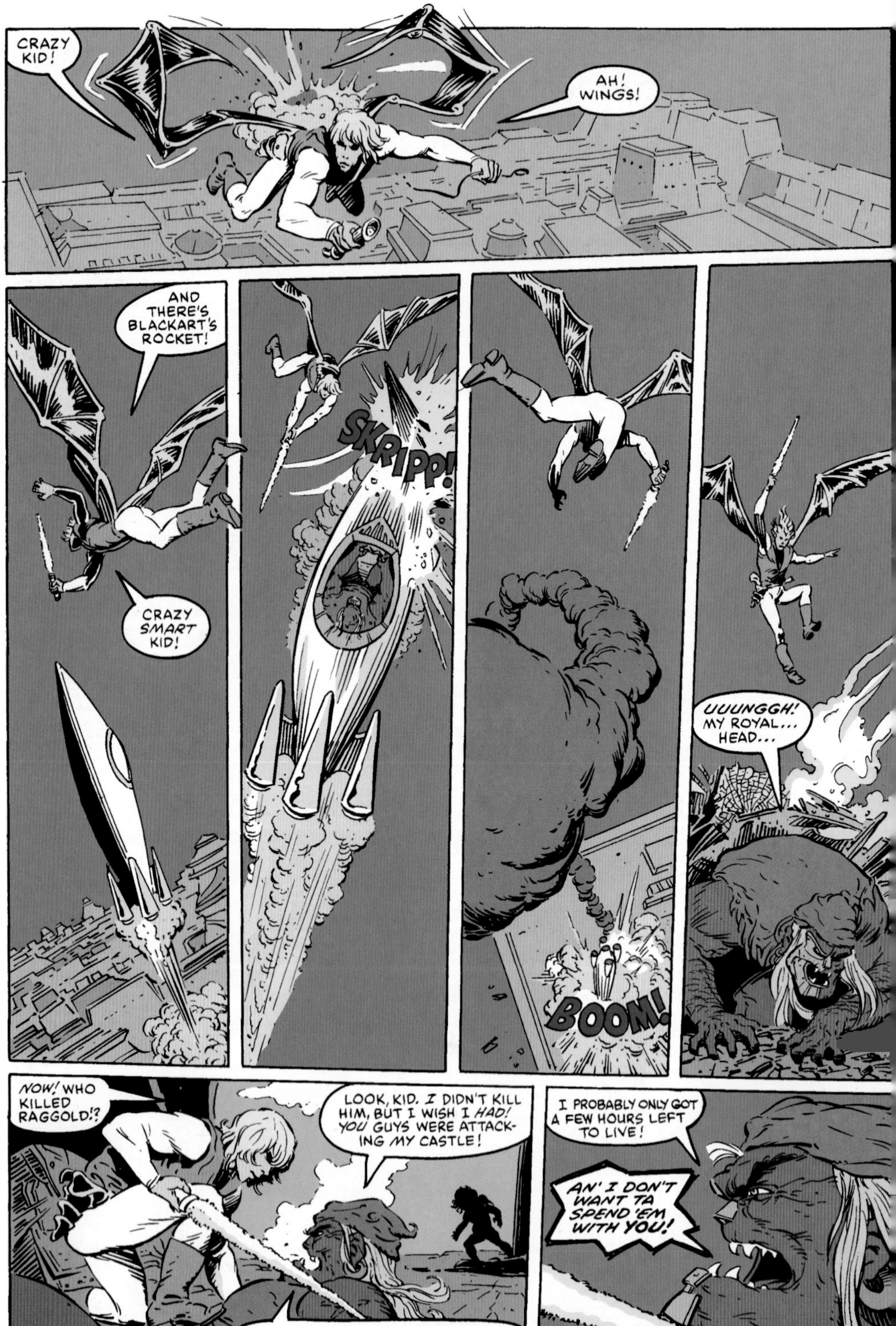
CRAZY KID!
AH! WINGS!
AND THERE'S BLACKART'S ROCKET!
CRAZY SMART KID!
SKRIPP!
BOOM!
UUUNGGH! MY ROYAL... HEAD...
NOW! WHO KILLED RAGGOLD!?
LOOK, KID. I DIDN'T KILL HIM, BUT I WISH I HAD! YOU GUYS WERE ATTACKING MY CASTLE!
AS FOR THE EMPIRE, THEY BETRAYED ME! THEY GOT ME DETHRONED! THEY BACKED THE REBELS! ANY WAY YOU LOOK AT IT, I LOSE!
I PROBABLY ONLY GOT A FEW HOURS LEFT TO LIVE!
AN' I DON'T WANT TA SPEND 'EM WITH YOU!
16

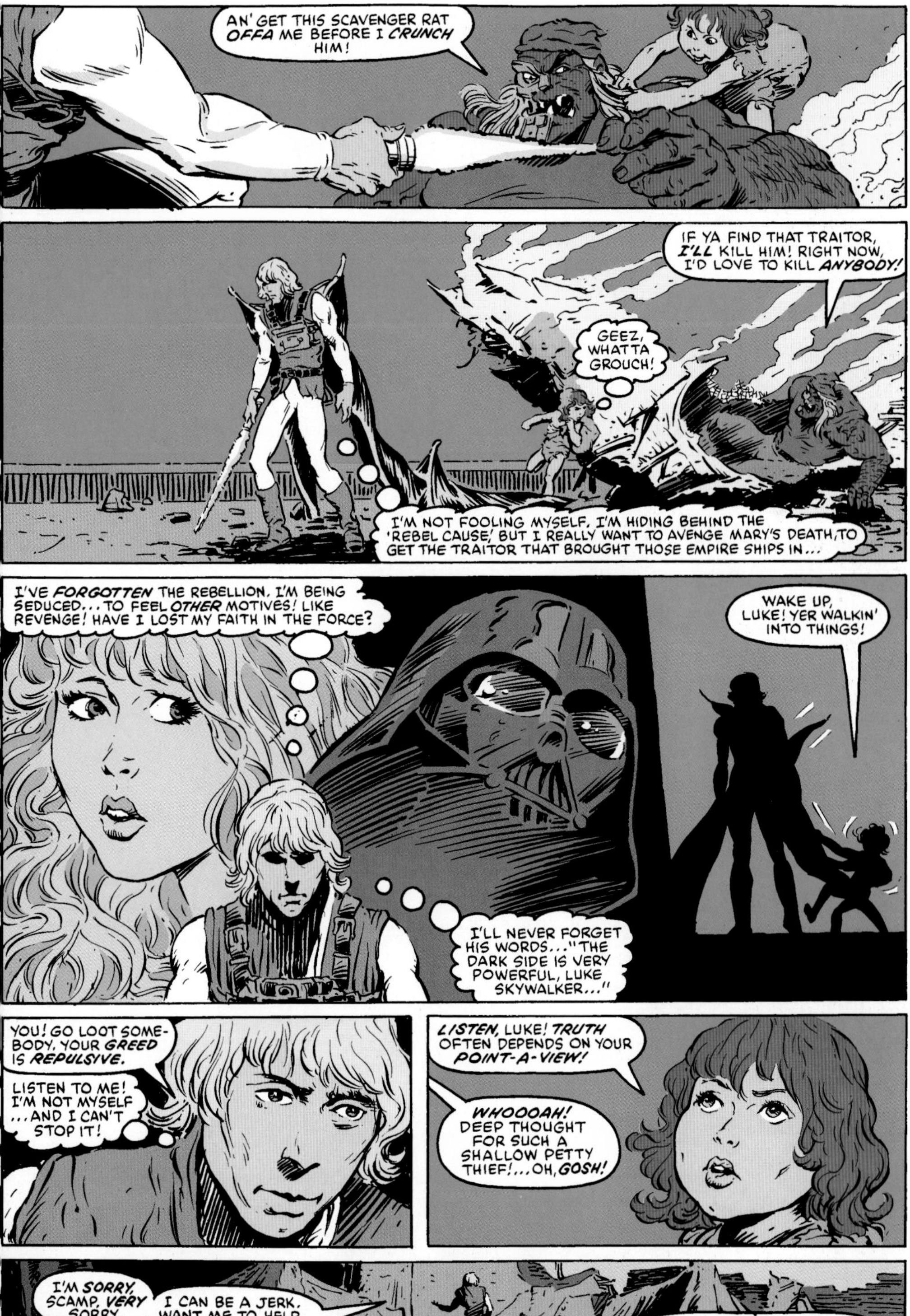

AN' GET THIS SCAVENGER RAT OFFA ME BEFORE I CRUNCH HIM!
IF YA FIND THAT TRAITOR, I'LL KILL HIM! RIGHT NOW, I'D LOVE TO KILL ANYBODY!
GEEZ, WHATTA GROUCH!
I'M NOT FOOLING MYSELF. I'M HIDING BEHIND THE 'REBEL CAUSE,' BUT I REALLY WANT TO AVENGE MARY'S DEATH, TO GET THE TRAITOR THAT BROUGHT THOSE EMPIRE SHIPS IN...
I'VE FORGOTTEN THE REBELLION. I'M BEING SEDUCED... TO FEEL OTHER MOTIVES! LIKE REVENGE! HAVE I LOST MY FAITH IN THE FORCE?
WAKE UP, LUKE! YER WALKIN' INTO THINGS!
I'LL NEVER FORGET HIS WORDS... "THE DARK SIDE IS VERY POWERFUL, LUKE SKYWALKER..."
YOU! GO LOOT SOMEBODY. YOUR GREED IS REPULSIVE.
LISTEN TO ME! I'M NOT MYSELF ...AND I CAN'T STOP IT!
LISTEN, LUKE! TRUTH OFTEN DEPENDS ON YOUR POINT-A-VIEW!
WHOOOAH! DEEP THOUGHT FOR SUCH A SHALLOW PETTY THIEF!... OH, GOSH!
I'M SORRY, SCAMP, VERY SORRY.
I CAN BE A JERK. WANT ME TO HELP YOU UNLOAD SOME OF YOUR LOOT AT YOUR STASH?
NAH... MY STASH? HEY, SURE. IN FACT, THAT'S A GREAT IDEA. YOU MIGHT BE INTERESTED TO SEE MY 'STASH.'
17

AND SOON...

A *BAR*! SCAMP, YOU'RE TOO YOUNG! YOU CAN'T GET IN! LET *ME* HANDLE THIS.

PRIVATE CLUB, BUDDY, GET LOST.

IT'S OKAY, HE'S WITH *ME*.

SORRY, SCAMP, I DIDN'T SEE YA. GO RIGHT IN.

OKAY, LUKE -- YOU'RE GONNA MEET *BRAXAS* NOW. HIS BODY'S NO GOOD BUT HIS MIND IS *FULL* OF STUFF!

WHY DIDN'T YOU TAKE ME HERE SOONER?

I HAD TO SEE IF YOU HAD ANYTHING TO OFFER BRAXAS IN RETURN.

DO I?

YEAH. GOT ONE FOR YA, BRAXAS.

THAT'S MY BOY, SCAMP!

HE'S ALL YOURS!

SCAMP ALREADY TOLD ME YOUR STORY. YOU WONDER WHAT HELP A TWISTED COOT LIKE ME CAN OFFER?

I MAKE IT MY BUSINESS TO KNOW *EVERYTHING*. THAT WAY I GOT GOODS ON *ALL* MEN, AND NO ONE *DARES* TOUCH ME.

19

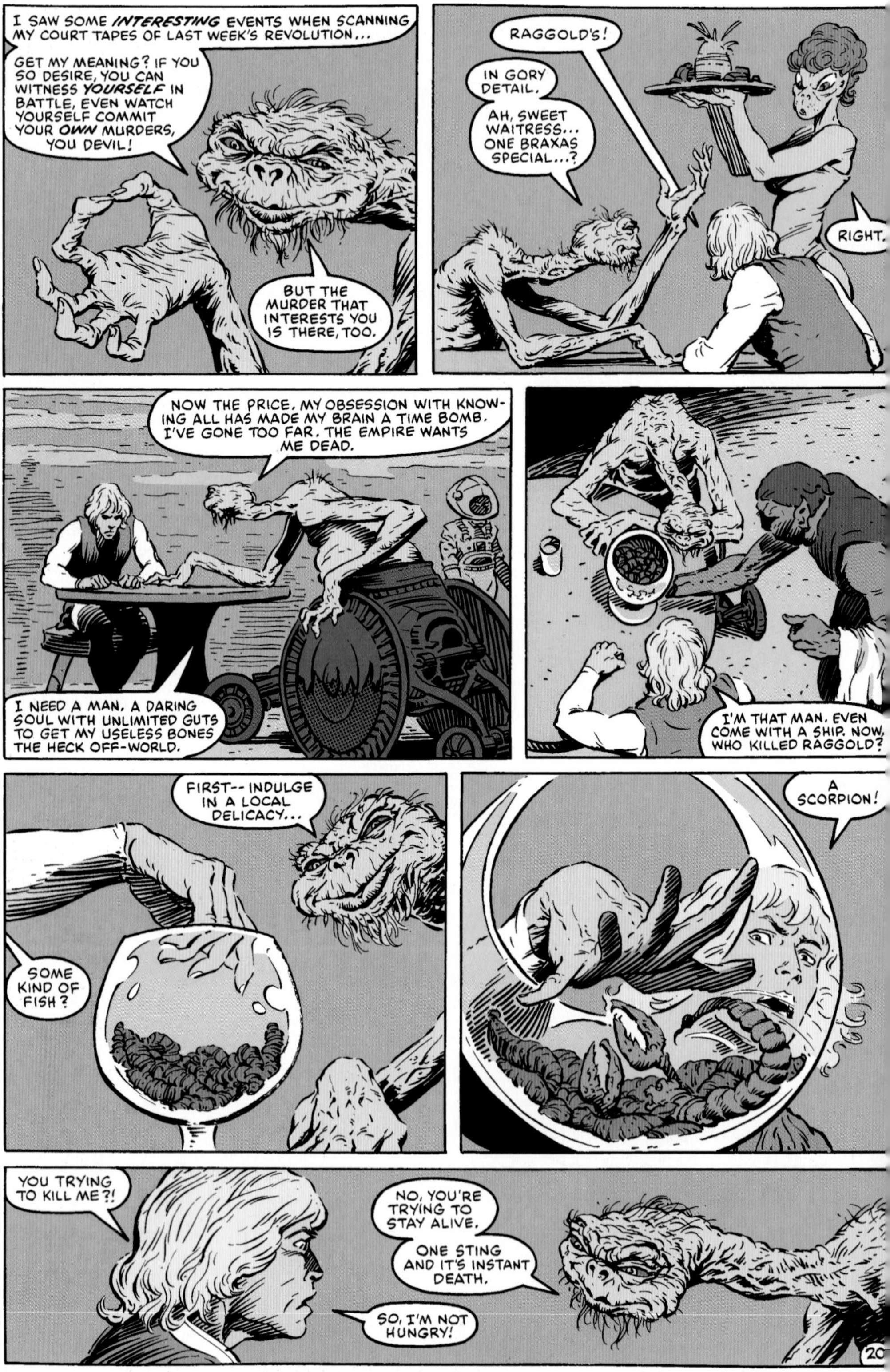

I SAW SOME *INTERESTING* EVENTS WHEN SCANNING MY COURT TAPES OF LAST WEEK'S REVOLUTION...
GET MY MEANING? IF YOU SO DESIRE, YOU CAN WITNESS *YOURSELF* IN BATTLE, EVEN WATCH YOURSELF COMMIT YOUR *OWN* MURDERS, YOU DEVIL!
BUT THE MURDER THAT INTERESTS YOU IS THERE, TOO.
RAGGOLD'S!
IN GORY DETAIL.
AH, SWEET WAITRESS... ONE BRAXAS SPECIAL...?
RIGHT.
NOW THE PRICE. MY OBSESSION WITH KNOWING ALL HAS MADE MY BRAIN A TIME BOMB. I'VE GONE TOO FAR. THE EMPIRE WANTS ME DEAD.
I NEED A MAN. A DARING SOUL WITH UNLIMITED GUTS TO GET MY USELESS BONES THE HECK OFF-WORLD.
I'M THAT MAN. EVEN COME WITH A SHIP. NOW, WHO KILLED RAGGOLD?
FIRST-- INDULGE IN A LOCAL DELICACY...
SOME KIND OF FISH?
A SCORPION!
YOU TRYING TO KILL ME?!
NO, YOU'RE TRYING TO STAY ALIVE.
ONE STING AND IT'S INSTANT DEATH.
SO, I'M NOT HUNGRY!
20

WANT YOUR TAPE?

IT'S AN OLD MAN'S TEST OF GUTS... AND *LUCK*.

FINISH YOUR MEAL, SKY-WALKER.

HUH?! *LEFT* HAND, LUKE. THAT MECHANICAL RIGHT OF YOURS WOULD JUST BREAK HIS LITTLE STINGER.

HOW DID YOU *KNOW!?*

AND A LITTLE *ETI-QUETTE,* PLEASE ...USE *THESE.*

AH, CHOP-STICKS...

SUCH AN ELEGANT UTENSIL.

MAKES THE RITUAL OF EATING SO EXQUISITELY... *EXCITING.*

TRUST IT, TRUST MYSELF.

DON'T TOUCH ME, YOU VERMIN.

FOR YOU, MARY...

FOR MARY ...AND FOR THE FORCE!

MY LOSS OF FAITH IN THE FORCE...I MUST BELIEVE AGAIN!

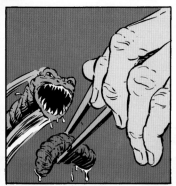

MIND IF I DON'T EAT THIS ONE?

NO... *ANYTHING* FOR MY NEW PILOT!

21

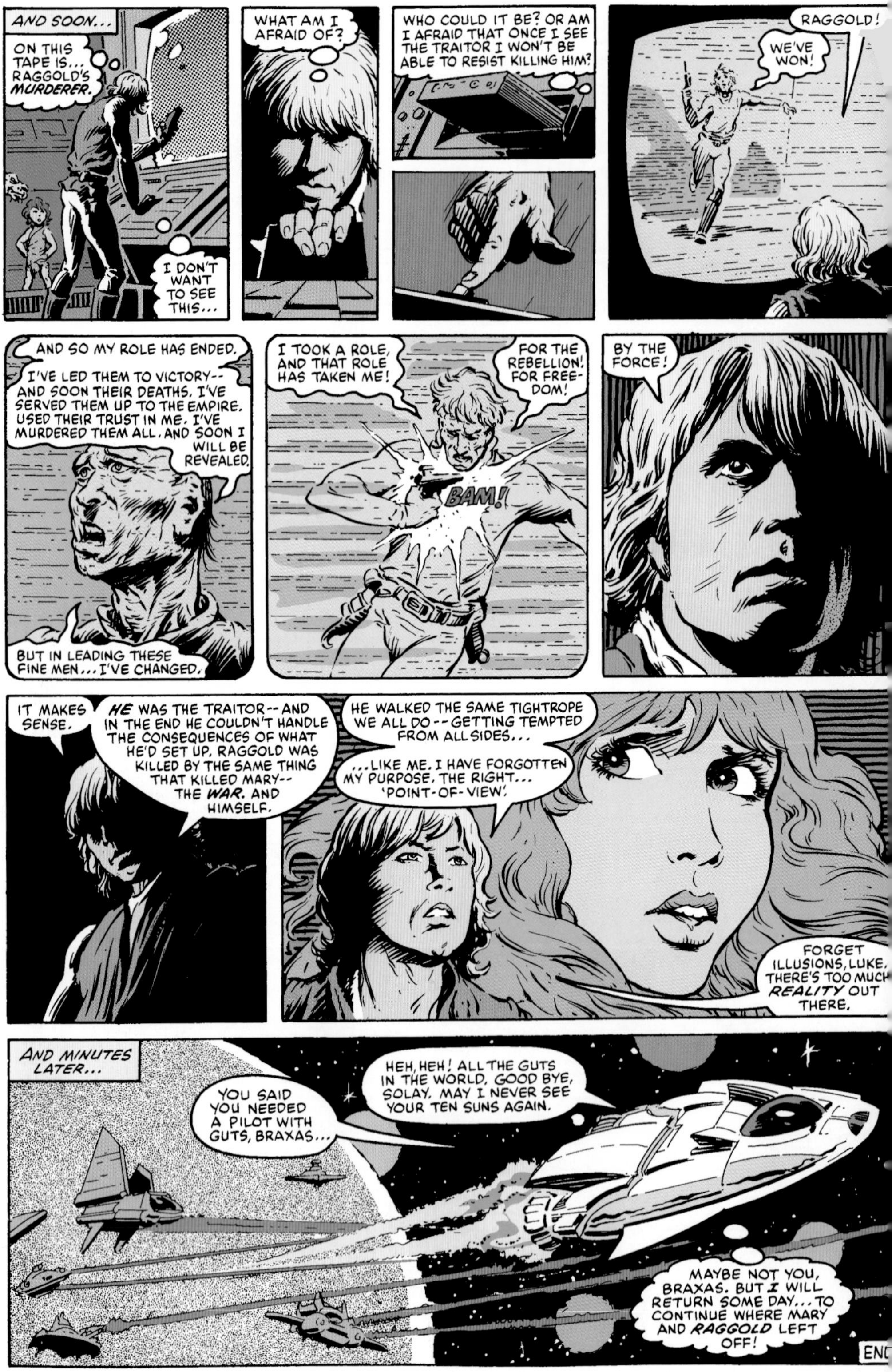
AND SOON...
ON THIS TAPE IS... RAGGOLD'S MURDERER.
I DON'T WANT TO SEE THIS...
WHAT AM I AFRAID OF?
WHO COULD IT BE? OR AM I AFRAID THAT ONCE I SEE THE TRAITOR I WON'T BE ABLE TO RESIST KILLING HIM?
RAGGOLD!
WE'VE WON!
AND SO MY ROLE HAS ENDED.
I'VE LED THEM TO VICTORY-- AND SOON THEIR DEATHS. I'VE SERVED THEM UP TO THE EMPIRE. USED THEIR TRUST IN ME. I'VE MURDERED THEM ALL. AND SOON I WILL BE REVEALED.
BUT IN LEADING THESE FINE MEN... I'VE CHANGED.
I TOOK A ROLE, AND THAT ROLE HAS TAKEN ME!
FOR THE REBELLION! FOR FREE-DOM!
BAM!
BY THE FORCE!
IT MAKES SENSE.
HE WAS THE TRAITOR--AND IN THE END HE COULDN'T HANDLE THE CONSEQUENCES OF WHAT HE'D SET UP. RAGGOLD WAS KILLED BY THE SAME THING THAT KILLED MARY-- THE WAR. AND HIMSELF.
HE WALKED THE SAME TIGHTROPE WE ALL DO--GETTING TEMPTED FROM ALL SIDES...
...LIKE ME. I HAVE FORGOTTEN MY PURPOSE. THE RIGHT... 'POINT-OF-VIEW'.
FORGET ILLUSIONS, LUKE. THERE'S TOO MUCH REALITY OUT THERE.
AND MINUTES LATER...
YOU SAID YOU NEEDED A PILOT WITH GUTS, BRAXAS...
HEH, HEH! ALL THE GUTS IN THE WORLD. GOOD BYE, SOLAY. MAY I NEVER SEE YOUR TEN SUNS AGAIN.
MAYBE NOT YOU, BRAXAS. BUT I WILL RETURN SOME DAY... TO CONTINUE WHERE MARY AND RAGGOLD LEFT OFF!
END

STAR WARS

™

60¢
90
DEC
02817

APPROVED BY THE COMICS CODE AUTHORITY

®

THE CHOICE!

Long ago in a galaxy far, far away. . .there exists a state of cosmic *civil war*. A brave alliance of *underground freedom fighters* has challenged the tyranny and oppression of the awesome *Galactic Empire*. This is their story!

Lucasfilm PRESENTS: STAR WARS THE GREATEST SPACE FANTASY OF ALL!

JO DUFFY SCRIPT/PLOT * BOB McLEOD BREAKDOWNS * TOM PALMER FINISHES * RICK PARKER LETTERING * BOB SHAREN COLORING * ANN NOCENTI EDITING * J. SHOOTER CHIEF

ARTOO? ARTOO-DETOO? WILL YOU PAY ATTENTION? DON'T YOU HEAR THAT?

BR-WHEET!

WHAT DO YOU MEAN, HEAR WHAT? A SHIP'S LANDING! IT'S HER HIGHNESS! PRINCESS LEIA HAS COME BACK TO ENDOR!

THE CHOICE!

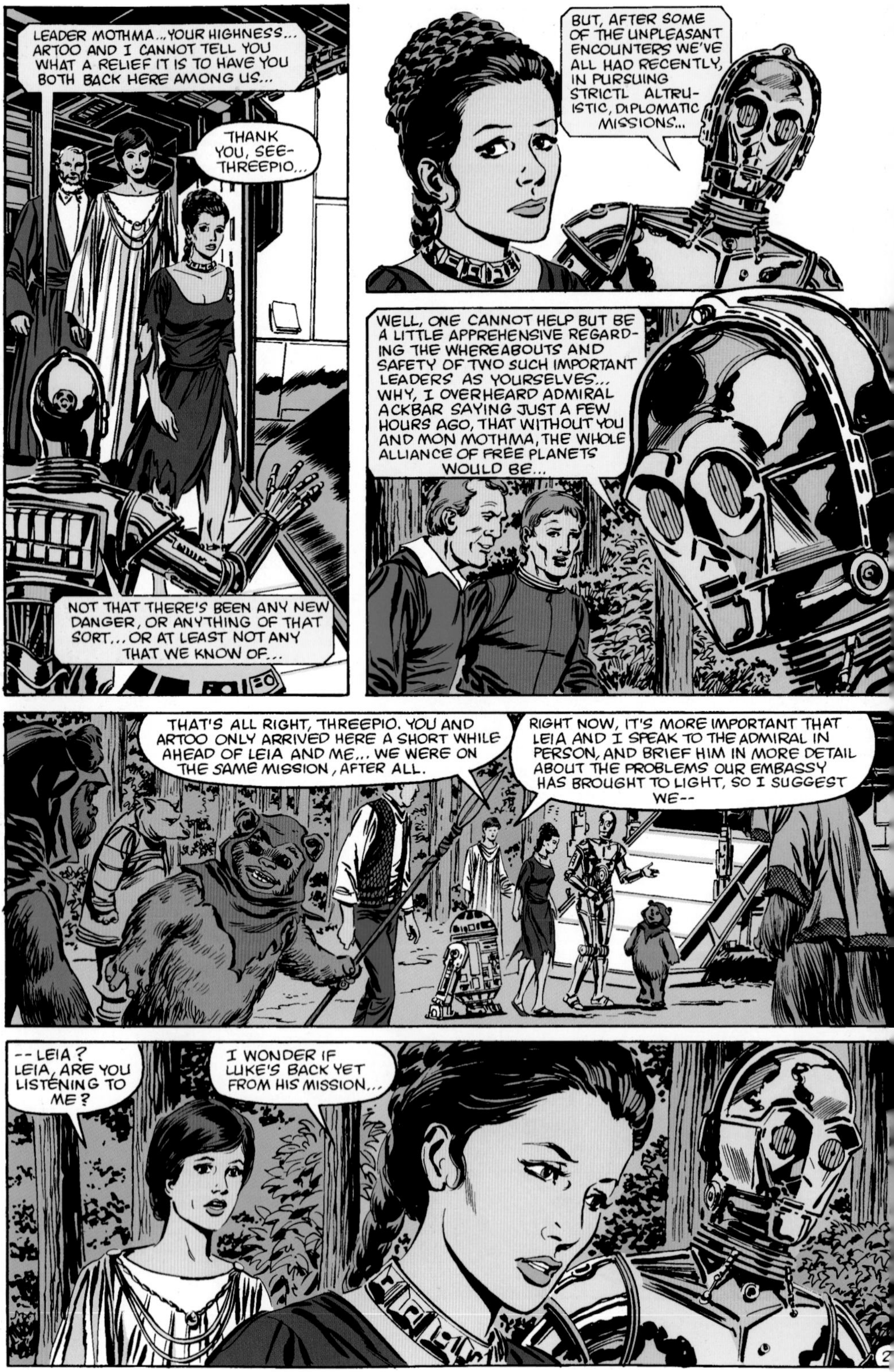

LEADER MOTHMA... YOUR HIGHNESS... ARTOO AND I CANNOT TELL YOU WHAT A RELIEF IT IS TO HAVE YOU BOTH BACK HERE AMONG US...
THANK YOU, SEE-THREEPIO...
NOT THAT THERE'S BEEN ANY NEW DANGER, OR ANYTHING OF THAT SORT... OR AT LEAST NOT ANY THAT WE KNOW OF...
BUT, AFTER SOME OF THE UNPLEASANT ENCOUNTERS WE'VE ALL HAD RECENTLY, IN PURSUING STRICTL ALTRU-ISTIC, DIPLOMATIC MISSIONS...
WELL, ONE CANNOT HELP BUT BE A LITTLE APPREHENSIVE REGARD-ING THE WHEREABOUTS AND SAFETY OF TWO SUCH IMPORTANT LEADERS AS YOURSELVES... WHY, I OVERHEARD ADMIRAL ACKBAR SAYING JUST A FEW HOURS AGO, THAT WITHOUT YOU AND MON MOTHMA, THE WHOLE ALLIANCE OF FREE PLANETS WOULD BE...
THAT'S ALL RIGHT, THREEPIO. YOU AND ARTOO ONLY ARRIVED HERE A SHORT WHILE AHEAD OF LEIA AND ME... WE WERE ON THE SAME MISSION, AFTER ALL.
RIGHT NOW, IT'S MORE IMPORTANT THAT LEIA AND I SPEAK TO THE ADMIRAL IN PERSON, AND BRIEF HIM IN MORE DETAIL ABOUT THE PROBLEMS OUR EMBASSY HAS BROUGHT TO LIGHT, SO I SUGGEST WE--
-- LEIA? LEIA, ARE YOU LISTENING TO ME?
I WONDER IF LUKE'S BACK YET FROM HIS MISSION...

MASTER LUKE? WELL, FROM WHAT I'VE BEEN ABLE TO LISTENING IN TO THE CONVERSATIONS OF THE OTHER PILOTS, HE AND THE PARTY HE WAS TRAVELLING WITH ARE DUE IN AT ANY TIME.

IS ANYTHING THE MATTER?

NOT REALLY.. NOTHING ANYONE BUT LUKE COULD HELP ME WITH, ANY WAY...

BALOOT?

NO,... THANKS FOR THE OFFER, ARTOO, BUT, I DON'T THINK A DROID COULD ADVISE ME ABOUT THIS.

YOUR HIGHNESS, LEADER MOTHMA! WELCOME BACK!

HELLO, ADMIRAL.

YOU SEE!? I TOLD YOU HE WAS CONCERNED!

THOSE SHIPS--THAT'S LUKE'S X-WING!

HE'S BACK!

LEIA, WAIT! THE ADMIRAL AND I HAVE GOT TO...

OH, DEAR, OH, DEAR!

TELL ME, MON... IS THE MESSAGE THAT WAS RELAYED TO ME CORRECT? IS IT TRUE THAT REMNANTS OF THE GALACTIC EMPIRE STILL EXIST IN STRENGTH IN SOME QUADRANTS, DESPITE THEIR RECENT OVERTHROW...

I'M AFRAID THAT IS CORRECT... NOT ALL OF OUR OLD ENEMIES HAVE ABIDED BY THEIR LEADERS' CAPITULATION...

AND, AS YOU CAN SEE... WE MAY HAVE ANOTHER SERIOUS PROBLEM, AS WELL...

3

LUKE! LUKE!

LEIA!

LUKE, I'M SO GLAD YOU'RE BACK! I HAVE TO SPEAK TO YOU...

EXCUSE ME, YOUR HIGHNESS... I KNOW HOW HAPPY YOU ARE TO SEE COMMANDER SKYWALKER, BUT CAN'T YOU SPARE A FEW FRIENDLY THOUGHTS FOR A LONELY TELEPATHIC HOOJIB?

OF COURSE, I CAN, PLIF... I'M SORRY... IT'S JUST THAT...

LUKE, SOME THINGS CAME UP WHILE I WAS ON MY LAST MISSION, AND I THOUGHT YOU...

I KNOW, LEIA. I NEED TO TALK TO YOU, TOO. IT'S JUST THAT RIGHT NOW, I HAVE SOMETHING TO DO, AND IT'S SOMETHING THAT WON'T WAIT...

PLIF... MASTER LUKE... ARTOO AND I WOULD LIKE TO SAY THAT WE'RE--!

WE ACQUIRED SOME COMPANY, WHILE PURSUING OUR DUTIES AS AMBASSADORS...

WELL... THE KID DIDN'T TELL US YOU WERE GONNA BE HERE! HOW YOU DOIN,' GORGEOUS? I LIKE THE DRESS!

LEIA...

RIK DUEL... AND CHIHDO. LUKE, YOU KNOW THEY'RE PIRATES AND SWINDLERS... WHY DID YOU BRING THEM HERE?

I WENT OUT AS A DIPLOMAT, REMEMBER? THEIR CON GAMES WERE ON THE VERGE OF STARTING AN INTERPLANETARY INCIDENT, SO I WANTED TO KEEP MY EYES ON THEM...

NOR ARE THOSE TWO THE ONLY COMPANY WE ACQUIRED!

LEIA!

D-D-DANI...?

IT'S GONNA BE JUST LIKE OLD TIMES' AGAIN, LEIA! YOU AND ME AND A PLANET FULL OF LONELY, GULLIBLE MEN!

TO THINK I WAS LOOKING FORWARD TO SEEING HIM... AND HE BROUGHT THIS ZELTRON MAN-TRAP ALONG WITH HIM...

YOU MEN, BE CAREFUL WITH THAT. RIK WAS PACKING A VERY SPECIAL CARGO IN HIS SHIP...

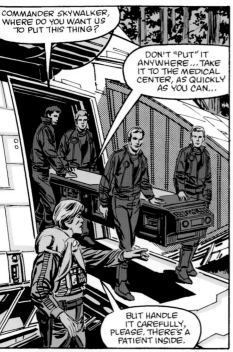

COMMANDER SKYWALKER, WHERE DO YOU WANT US TO PUT THIS THING?

DON'T "PUT" IT ANYWHERE... TAKE IT TO THE MEDICAL CENTER, AS QUICKLY AS YOU CAN...

BUT HANDLE IT CAREFULLY, PLEASE, THERE'S A PATIENT INSIDE.

A PATIENT...? IT'S KIRO!

LUKE, WHAT'S WRONG WITH HIM? IS HE GOING TO BE ALL RIGHT?

I HOPE SO, LEIA. THAT'S WHY COMMANDER SKYWALKER INSISTED ON BRINGING HIM BACK TO ENDOR, YOUR HIGHNESS... SO THAT HE'D GET THE BEST POSSIBLE MEDICAL CARE...

SHOO... GET AWAY, YOU GUYS...

OOHH?

RRUF

HEY, NOW... YOU CAN'T JUST SHOO THE EWOKS AWAY. THIS IS THEIR HOME PLANET WE'RE ON, AFTER ALL!

AAARROOK?

NO, IT IS NOT SOMETHING GOOD TO EAT. IF YOU'D LOOKED MORE CLOSELY, YOU'D HAVE REALIZED THAT CANISTER CONTAINS A *MAN!* WELL, A MAN OF SORTS, ANYWAY.

5

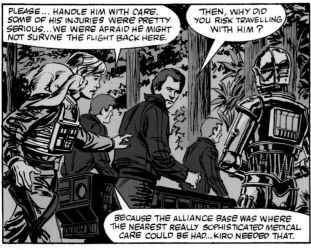

PLEASE... HANDLE HIM WITH CARE. SOME OF HIS INJURIES WERE PRETTY SERIOUS... WE WERE AFRAID HE MIGHT NOT SURVIVE THE FLIGHT BACK HERE.

THEN, WHY DID YOU RISK TRAVELLING WITH HIM?

BECAUSE THE ALLIANCE BASE WAS WHERE THE NEAREST REALLY SOPHISTICATED MEDICAL CARE COULD BE HAD... KIRO NEEDED THAT.

AND DESERVES IT AS WELL! I'LL HAVE YOU KNOW THAT KIRO'S WOUNDS WERE INCURRED MOST SELFLESSLY...

WHY, HE DID NOTHING LESS THAN SAVE US ALL FROM UNIVERSAL ANNIHILATION!

UNIVERS--? WHY, PLIF, I'M SURPRISED AT YOU. I DIDN'T KNOW THAT HOOJIBS INDULGED IN POETIC HYPERBOLE.

WE DON'T, MY DEAR.

HE'S RIGHT, LEIA. IT'S NO EXAGGERATION. I STILL HAVE SOME QUESTIONS ABOUT HOW HE DID IT... BUT KIRO MANAGED TO DEACTIVATE A GALAXY-WIDE BOOBY-TRAP THAT COULD HAVE BEEN THE END OF EVERYTHING.

AND WONDERING ABOUT KIRO HAS GOTTEN ME THINKING ABOUT A LOT OF OTHER THINGS... THERE ARE QUESTIONS AND PROBLEMS I'VE BEEN AVOIDING...

IS THERE SOMEWHERE WE CAN GO AND TALK LATER?

AND SOON...

ENDOR'S A BEAUTIFUL WORLD.

AS BEAUTIFUL AS ANY I'VE EVER VISITED.

NICE TO HAVE SOME PEACE AND QUIET FOR A CHANGE, ISN'T IT?

FOR A CHANGE, YES... BUT I'M BEGINNING TO WONDER IF IT'S REALLY WHAT I WANT PERMANENTLY.

LUKE... DON'T YOU EVER HAVE REGRETS... ABOUT THE COURSE WE'VE CHOSEN FOR OURSELVES?

REGRET JOINING THE REBELLION AND HELPING TO OVERTHROW THE EMPIRE?

SOMETIMES I FEEL SO PURPOSELESS! A JOKE. I'M A PRINCESS OF A PEOPLE WHO WERE ANNIHILATED, AND A SENATOR FROM A RULING BODY THAT WAS DISBANDED BY THE EMPIRE A LONG TIME AGO...

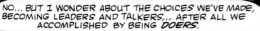

NO... BUT I WONDER ABOUT THE CHOICES WE'VE MADE, BECOMING LEADERS AND TALKERS... AFTER ALL WE ACCOMPLISHED BY BEING *DOERS*.

NOWADAYS, I LISTEN TO MYSELF SPEAKING IN CAREFUL PHRASES, AND ENGAGING IN ENDLESS DIPLOMACY, HOURS OF TALKING ABOUT NOTHING...

...TO A BUNCH OF PEOPLE WHO WANT TO HEAR IN SIX DIFFERENT WAYS WHY IT'S TO THEIR ADVANTAGE TO JOIN THE ALLIANCE NOW THAT THE HARD PART'S OVER.

I NEVER WANTED TO BE A FIGHTER, LUKE... IT'S CERTAINLY NOT WHAT I WAS RAISED FOR... BUT I DID IT WHEN I HAD TO...

NOW, I'M AFRAID I'VE GOTTEN A TASTE FOR IT... I CAN ALMOST SEE, SOMETIMES, THE THINGS WE FOUGHT FOR-- THE THINGS OUR FRIENDS DIED FOR -- BEING CASUALLY TALKED AWAY BY THE LEADERS OF WORLDS WHO BENEFITED FROM WHAT WE'VE ACCOMPLISHED.

YOU KNOW, LEIA, WHAT YOU JUST SAID IS WRONG. THE HARD PART OF OVERTHROWING THE EMPIRE HAS JUST BEGUN. IT'S RELATIVELY EASY TO DESTROY, EVEN IN A GOOD CAUSE.

WHAT COMES NOW WILL BE THE TEST. CAN WE AND THE OTHER LEADERS, ACTING FAIRLY, REALLY SET UP A SYSTEM OF GOVERNMENT THAT WILL ACTUALLY FUNCTION AND BE BETTER THAN THE EMPIRE?

7

YOU AND I BOTH HAVE TO BE VERY CAUTIOUS WITH WHAT WE DO NEXT.

MEMBERS OF OUR FAMILY ARE CAPABLE OF ACCOMPLISHING A GREAT DEAL OF GOOD... BUT WE ALSO, IF WE TAKE THE WRONG PATH...

...HAVE THE CAPACITY FOR GREAT EVIL.

OUR FATHER DIDN'T SET OUT INTENDING TO BECOME DARTH VADER...

BUT HE DID. AND THE EMPIRE MIGHT NEVER HAVE BECOME QUITE THE POWER IT WAS, OR QUITE THE HORROR, WITHOUT DARTH VADER'S INFLUENCE.

LUKE... YOU HAVEN'T TOLD ANYONE, HAVE YOU... ABOUT VADER... AND US?

NO... I DIDN'T THINK THAT TRUTH WOULD CAUSE ANYTHING BUT TROUBLE. LEIA, I'M HAPPY TO BE YOUR BROTHER, BUT I TELL NO ONE, FOR FEAR OF THE QUESTIONS IT WOULD BRING UP.

NO ONE REALLY CARES THAT VADER REFORMED AT THE END, THAT HE WAS INSTRUMENTAL IN BREAKING THE REIGN OF THE EMPEROR. THEY ONLY REMEMBER WHAT HE WAS, AND WHAT HE DID...

I WAS HORRIFIED WHEN I LEARNED THE TRUTH... AND I KNOW YOU WERE, TOO...

PEOPLE WILL PROBABLY LEARN IT, EVENTUALLY... BUT I DON'T INTEND TO GO AROUND ANNOUNCING OUR PARENTAGE IN PUBLIC JUST YET.

THAT'S ONE BIG LOAD OFF MY MIND... BUT IT STILL DOESN'T MAKE MY OTHER PROBLEM ANY EASIER...

HOW DO I RECONCILE BEING BOTH A FIGUREHEAD, AND A FIGHTER?

YOU DON'T. JUST BE WHAT YOU ARE, AND I THINK YOUR CONFLICT WILL END UP RESOLVING ITSELF.

I THINK MAYBE IT WILL, AT THAT. WANT TO SEE HOW KIRO'S DOING?

SURE.

8

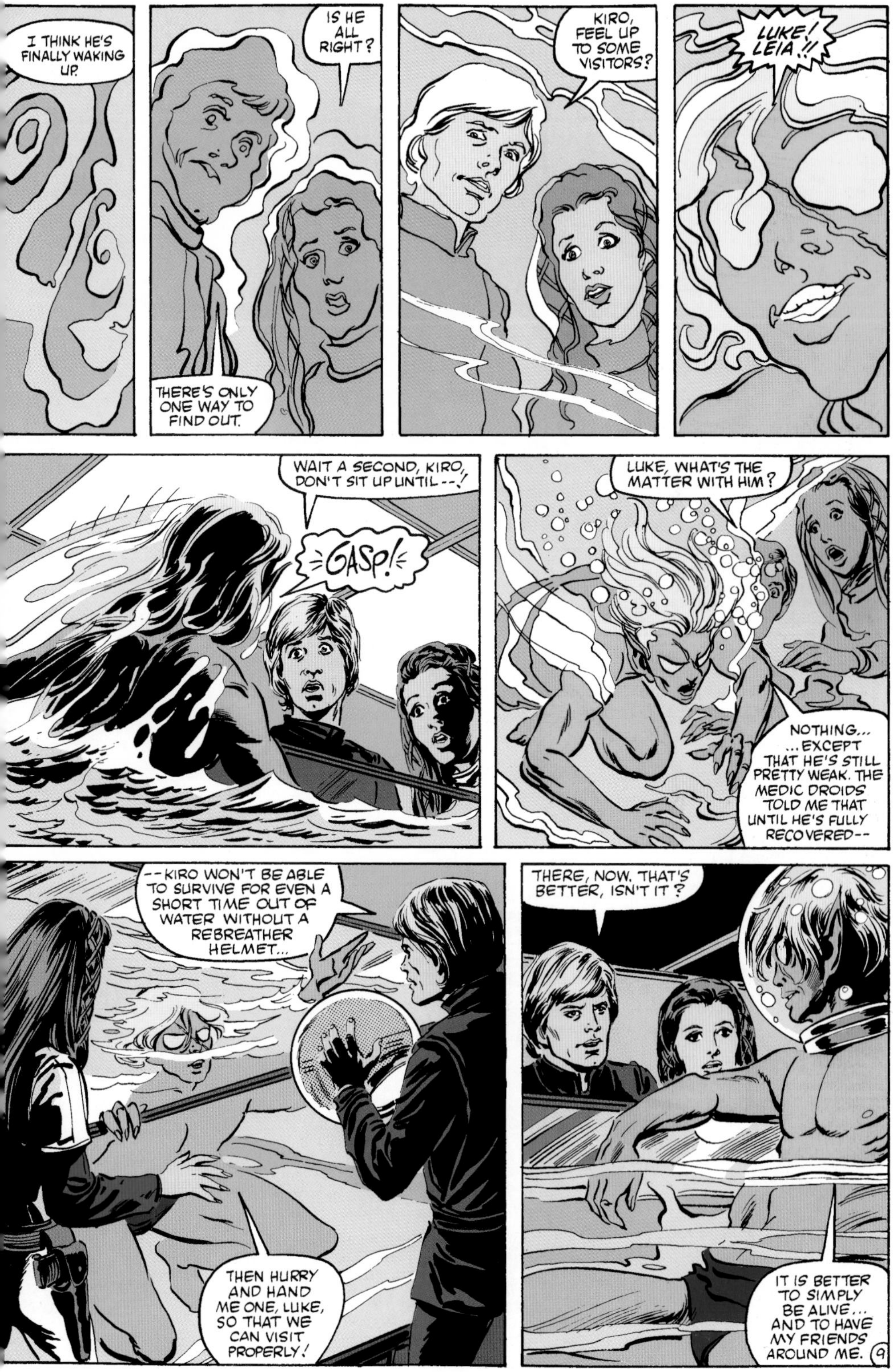
I THINK HE'S FINALLY WAKING UP.
IS HE ALL RIGHT?
THERE'S ONLY ONE WAY TO FIND OUT.
KIRO, FEEL UP TO SOME VISITORS?
LUKE! LEIA!!
WAIT A SECOND, KIRO, DON'T SIT UP UNTIL--!
GASP!
LUKE, WHAT'S THE MATTER WITH HIM?
NOTHING... ...EXCEPT THAT HE'S STILL PRETTY WEAK. THE MEDIC DROIDS TOLD ME THAT UNTIL HE'S FULLY RECOVERED--
--KIRO WON'T BE ABLE TO SURVIVE FOR EVEN A SHORT TIME OUT OF WATER WITHOUT A REBREATHER HELMET...
THEN HURRY AND HAND ME ONE, LUKE, SO THAT WE CAN VISIT PROPERLY!
THERE, NOW. THAT'S BETTER, ISN'T IT?
IT IS BETTER TO SIMPLY BE ALIVE... AND TO HAVE MY FRIENDS AROUND ME.
9

I THOUGHT I WOULD NEVER SEE THE SUNLIGHT THROUGH THE WATER, OR HEAR ANOTHER FRIENDLY VOICE AGAIN AFTER I DESTROYED THAT EVIL MACHINE, AND THE CAVERNS ON SHAWKEN EXPLODED. WHAT SAVED ME?

LUCK, MAINLY. YOU SET OFF A TIDAL WAVE, AND IT CARRIED YOU RIGHT BACK TO ME... YOU'RE ON ENDOR NOW. THE ALLIANCE'S MAIN HEADQUARTERS IS HERE.

KIRO, I'VE GOT TO ASK YOU SOMETHING VERY IMPORTANT... WE WEREN'T TOGETHER WHEN YOU DESTROYED THAT DOOMSDAY DEVICE, AND I KNOW YOU HAD NO INSTRUCTIONS ABOUT ITS WORKINGS.

HOW DID YOU KNOW WHAT TO DO?

I'M NOT SURE. THERE WAS DARKNESS ALL AROUND ME, AND MANY CARVINGS, AND MUCH CONCEALED MACHINERY, AND I WAS VERY TENSE.

WHEN, ALL AT ONCE, WITHOUT EVEN LOOKING, I KNEW WHERE THE SOURCE OF THE DANGER LAY... I COULD FEEL ITS POWER, AND ITS THREAT.

SO, WITH YOUR LIGHTSABER I DESTROYED IT, AND ENDED THE DANGER...

KIRO...DO YOU THINK IT'S POSSIBLE THAT YOU WERE GUIDED BY...*THE FORCE?*

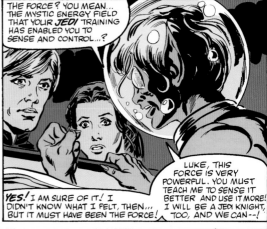

THE FORCE? YOU MEAN... THE MYSTIC ENERGY FIELD THAT YOUR *JEDI* TRAINING HAS ENABLED YOU TO SENSE AND CONTROL...?

YES! I AM SURE OF IT! I DIDN'T KNOW WHAT I FELT, THEN,... BUT IT MUST HAVE BEEN THE FORCE!

LUKE, THIS FORCE IS VERY POWERFUL. YOU MUST TEACH ME TO SENSE IT BETTER AND USE IT MORE! I WILL BE A JEDI KNIGHT, TOO, AND WE CAN--!

NO.

NO?

I'M SORRY, BUT THAT'S THE ONE THING I CAN'T DO. BELIEVE ME, IT'S FOR YOUR OWN SAFETY, AND--!

NO?!

MEAN- WHILE...

WE OF THE ALLIANCE CANNOT TELL YOU HOW GRATIFIED WE ARE THAT REPRESENTATIVES' OF SO MANY WORLDS HAVE COME HERE TO OUR FIRST CONFERENCE OF FREE PEOPLES.

WE THANK YOU ALL...YOUR SUPPORT AND CONTRIBUTIONS ARE MORE IMPORTANT NOW THAN THEY HAVE BEEN AT ANY TIME DURING THE PAST.

NOW, WE MUST DECIDE HOW BEST TO ENJOY AND PRESERVE OUR HARD WON FREEDOM.

IT IS ESSENTIAL THAT WE WORK OUT NOW, BEFORE ABUSES HAVE A CHANCE TO BEGIN, HOW ALL OF THE FREED WORLDS SHALL DEAL TOGETHER.

THERE ARE A NUMBER OF SEPARATE ASPECTS TO CONSIDER -- QUESTIONS OF TRADE, OF TAXATION, THE ADJUDICATION AND ADMINISTRATION OF A NEW BODY OF INTERPLANETARY LAWS ...

PLEASE CONSIDER THESE MATTERS CAREFULLY, FOR IN THE END, THEY SHALL BE DECIDED BY THE VOTE OF THE MAJORITY...

YOU AND YOUR PEOPLES ARE TO BE COMMENDED. WE ARE BOTH HAPPY AND RELIEVED TO SEE SO MANY REPRESENTATIVES HERE, SO SOON AFTER WE SENT OUT OUR MESSAGES TO YOU.

RECENTLY, MATTERS HAVE ARISEN WHICH UNDERLINE THE NEED FOR HASTE IN OUTLINING OUR PLANS AND SENDING ALL OF YOU HOME TO YOUR RESPECTIVE WORLDS...

AS FOR NOW, EVERYONE HAD BEST BE PRESENT,... OR WE'LL HAVE NO ALTERNATIVE BUT TO ASSUME THAT BY THEIR ABSENCE THEY FORFEIT THEIR RIGHT TO VOTE.

12

BA-REEP!

COME ALONG, ARTOO. SURELY YOU'RE USED TO THE LOCAL TERRAIN BY NOW!

STILL GETTING THE SILENT TREATMENT, HUH?

WELL, DON'T FEEL TOO BAD. KIRO'S NOT TALKING TO ME, EITHER, AND ALL I DID WAS SAY YOU WERE RIGHT AT THE WRONG MOMENT.

I DON'T FEEL BAD FOR ME, LEIA. I FEEL BAD FOR KIRO. IF HE'D JUST LET ME EXPLAIN...

INSTEAD, HE'S BEEN HANGING AROUND WITH RIK AND HIS GANG...

YEAH... PLAYING IN ONE OF THE CARD GAMES THAT'S ALWAYS GOING ON THESE DAYS.

YOU'VE NOTICED THEM, TOO? THOSE GAMES WORRY ME.

OUR LEADERS HAVE A LOT ON THEIR MINDS, WITH TRYING TO ESTABLISH THE NEW GOVERNMENT AND ALL...

I WONDER IF IT'S OCCURRED TO ANY OF THEM, YET, THAT WHAT THEY HAVE HERE IS A PLANET OF SOLDIERS...

...WHO ARE BEING THROWN TOGETHER AT CLOSE QUARTERS EVERY DAY WITH NO DISCIPLINE, NO ENEMIES, AND NO WAR.

OOH! LOOK! RIK WINS AGAIN! IT'S JUST LIKE THEY SAY ON ZELTROS... LUCKY IN CARDS, LUCKY IN LOVE!

DANI, THE EXPRESSION IS LUCKY AT CARDS, *UNLUCKY* AT LOVE.

EVERYONE ON ZELTROS IS ALWAYS LUCKY AT LOVE!

THAT'S IMPOSSIBLE!

YOU WOULDN'T SAY THAT IF YOU KNEW ANY ZELTRONS...

I MEANT THAT YOUR FRIEND HAS WON TOO MUCH.

NAH... THERE'S NO SUCH THING AS TOO MUCH WHEN IT COMES TO FREE MONEY!

IT'S NOT FREE... YOU'RE GONNA PAY FOR ALL OF IT RIGHT NOW. HOW LONG DID YOU THINK I WAS GONNA SIT HERE AND PLAY WITH A CHEAT?

13

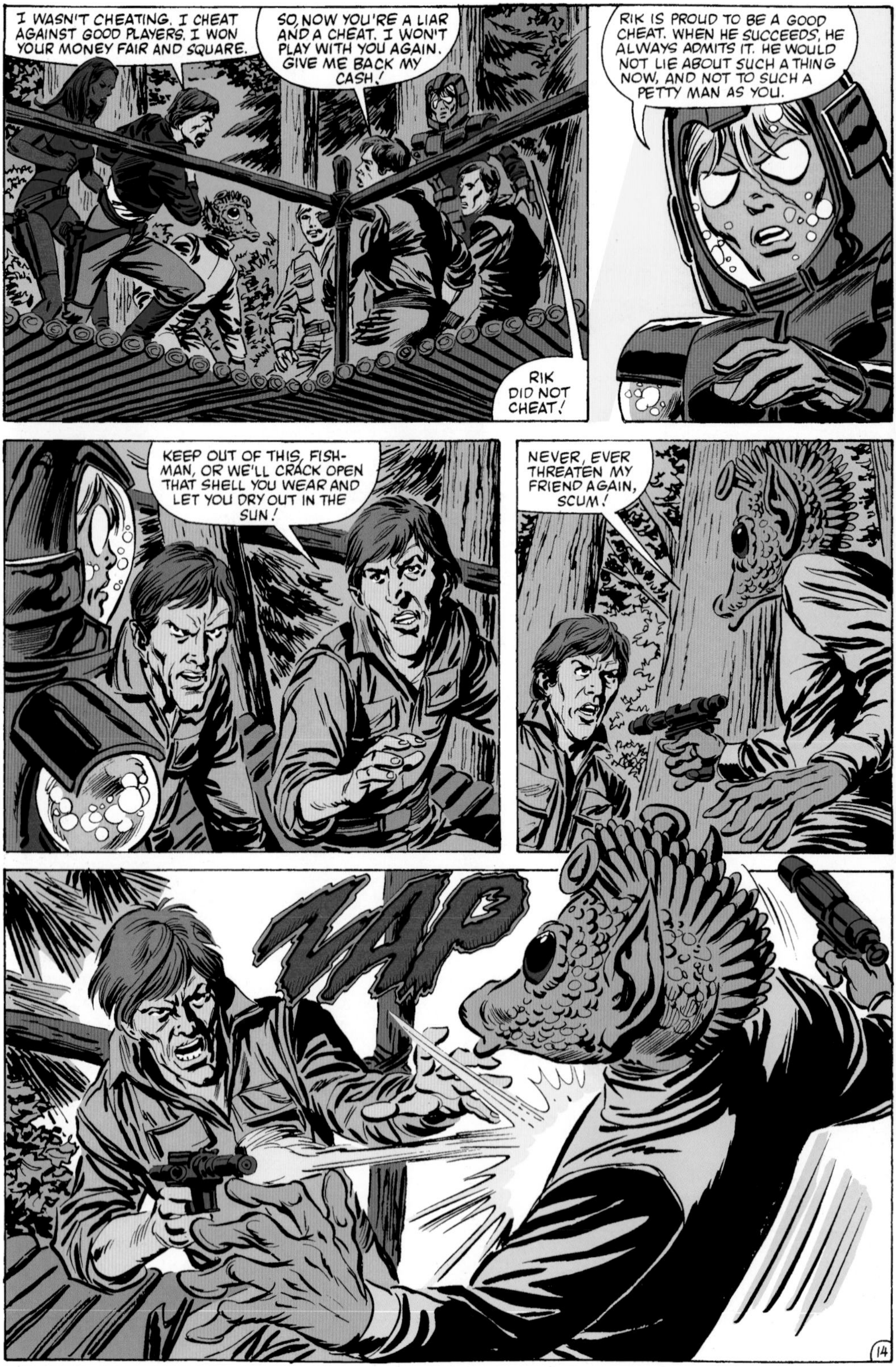

I WASN'T CHEATING. I CHEAT AGAINST GOOD PLAYERS. I WON YOUR MONEY FAIR AND SQUARE.
SO, NOW YOU'RE A LIAR AND A CHEAT. I WON'T PLAY WITH YOU AGAIN. GIVE ME BACK MY CASH!
RIK IS PROUD TO BE A GOOD CHEAT. WHEN HE SUCCEEDS, HE ALWAYS ADMITS IT. HE WOULD NOT LIE ABOUT SUCH A THING NOW, AND NOT TO SUCH A PETTY MAN AS YOU.
RIK DID NOT CHEAT!
KEEP OUT OF THIS, FISH-MAN, OR WE'LL CRACK OPEN THAT SHELL YOU WEAR AND LET YOU DRY OUT IN THE SUN!
NEVER, EVER THREATEN MY FRIEND AGAIN, SCUM!
ZAP
14

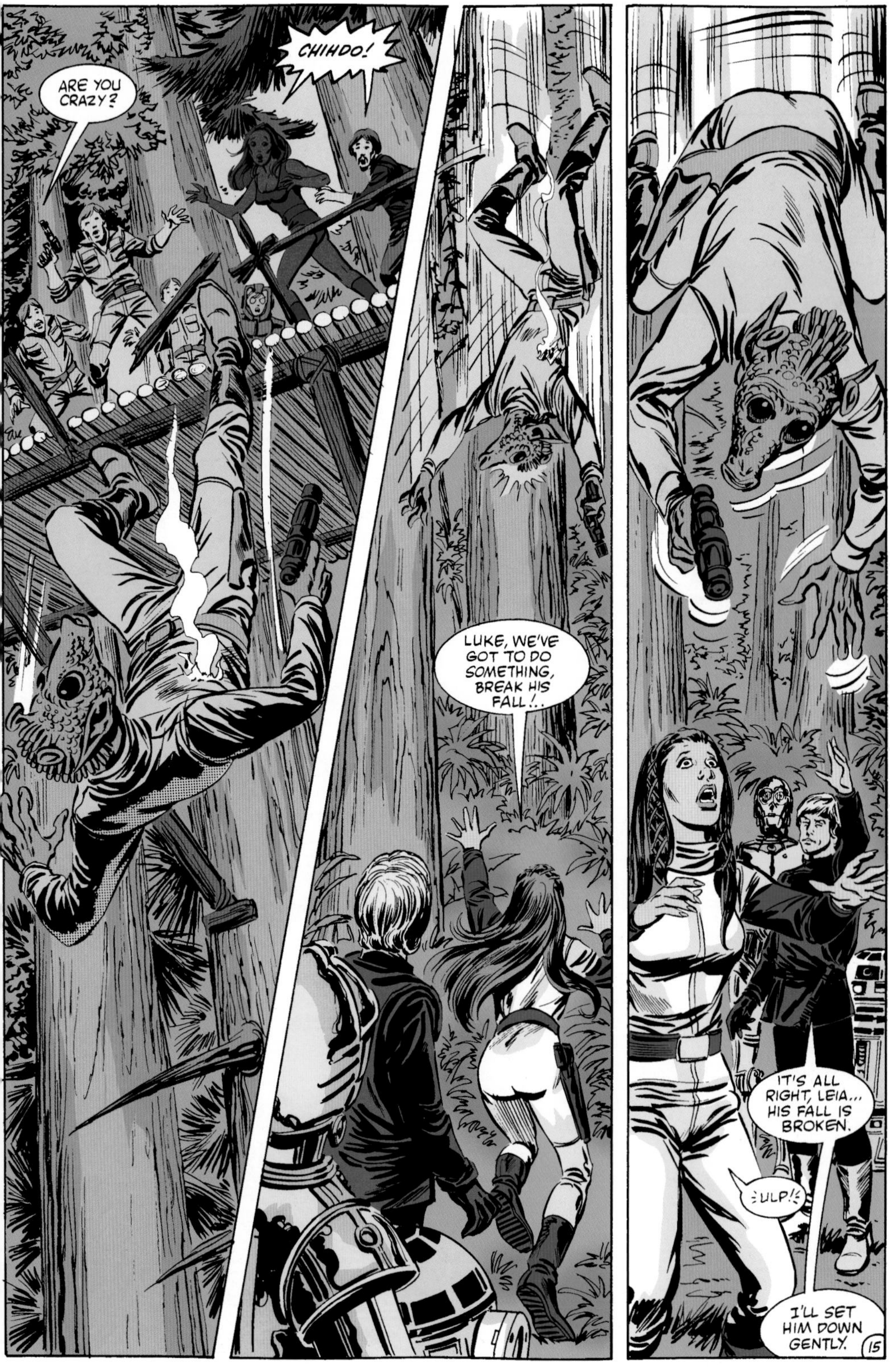
CHIHDO!
ARE YOU CRAZY?
LUKE, WE'VE GOT TO DO SOMETHING, BREAK HIS FALL!..
ULP!
IT'S ALL RIGHT, LEIA... HIS FALL IS BROKEN.
I'LL SET HIM DOWN GENTLY.
15

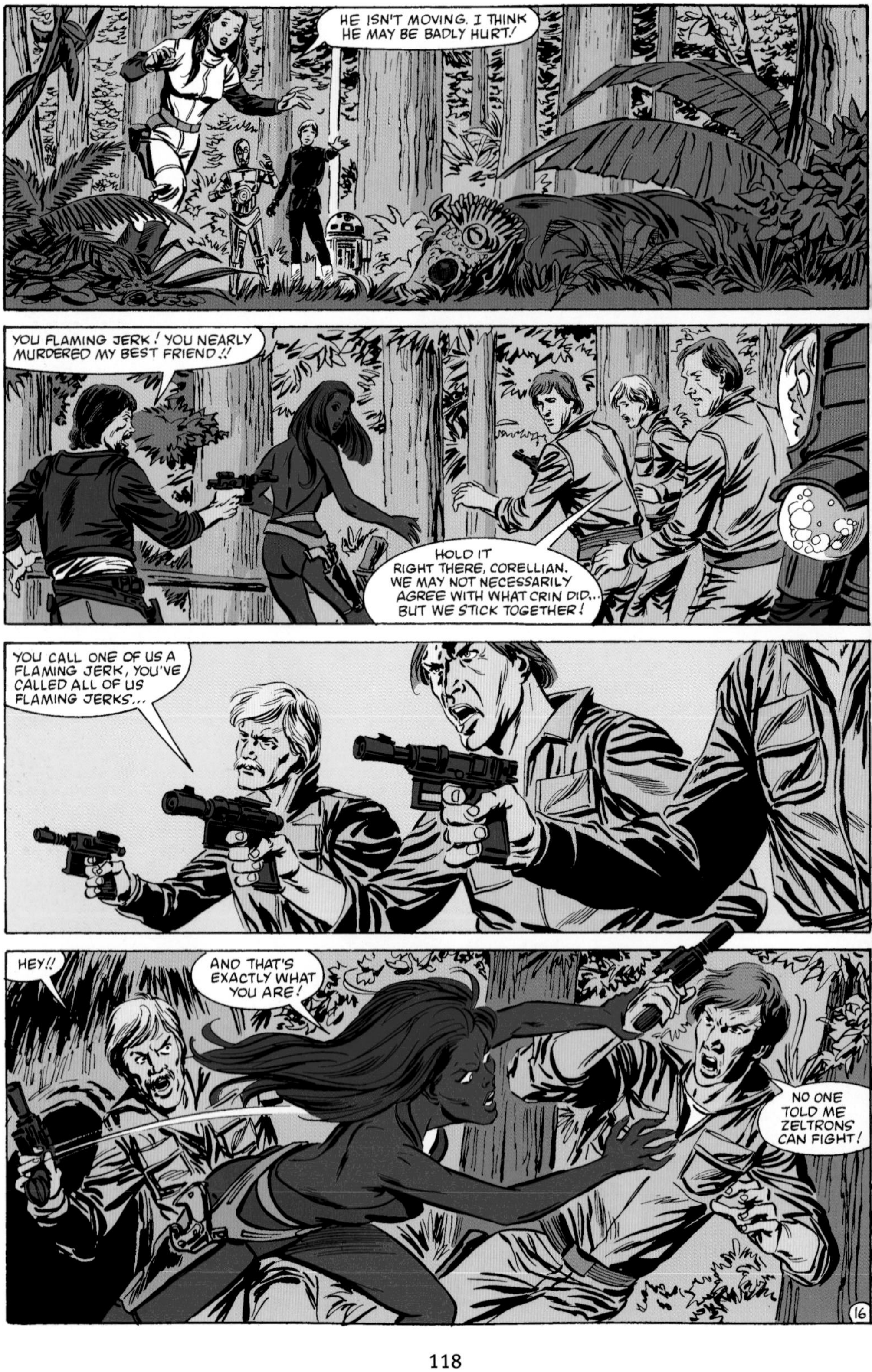
HE ISN'T MOVING. I THINK HE MAY BE BADLY HURT!
YOU FLAMING JERK! YOU NEARLY MURDERED MY BEST FRIEND!!
HOLD IT RIGHT THERE, CORELLIAN. WE MAY NOT NECESSARILY AGREE WITH WHAT CRIN DID... BUT WE STICK TOGETHER!
YOU CALL ONE OF US A FLAMING JERK, YOU'VE CALLED ALL OF US FLAMING JERKS...
HEY!!
AND THAT'S EXACTLY WHAT YOU ARE!
NO ONE TOLD ME ZELTRONS CAN FIGHT!
16

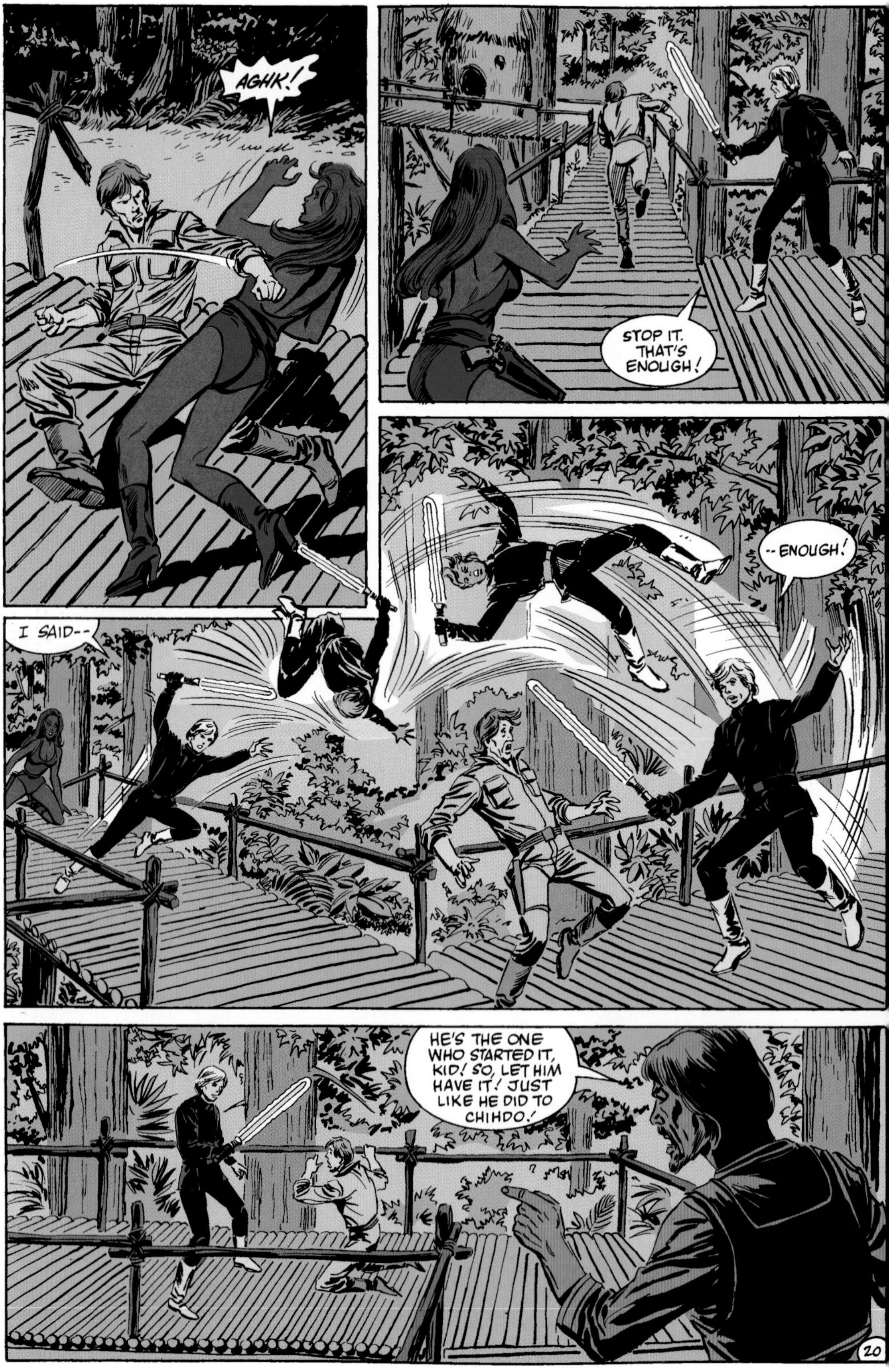
AGHK!
STOP IT. THAT'S ENOUGH!
--ENOUGH!
I SAID--
HE'S THE ONE WHO STARTED IT, KID! SO, LET HIM HAVE IT! JUST LIKE HE DID TO CHIHDO!
20

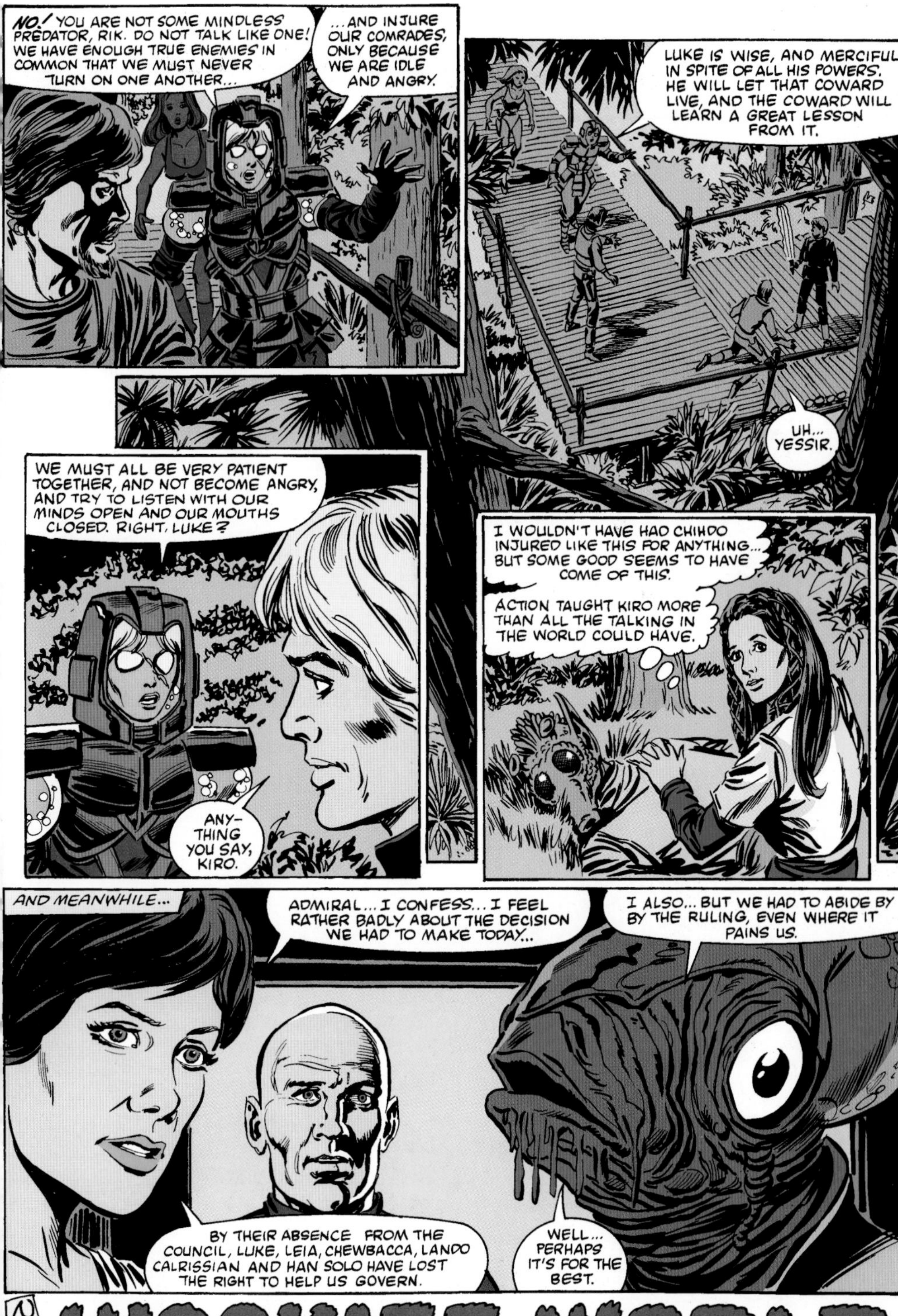
NO! YOU ARE NOT SOME MINDLESS PREDATOR, RIK. DO NOT TALK LIKE ONE! WE HAVE ENOUGH TRUE ENEMIES IN COMMON THAT WE MUST NEVER TURN ON ONE ANOTHER...
...AND INJURE OUR COMRADES, ONLY BECAUSE WE ARE IDLE AND ANGRY.
LUKE IS WISE, AND MERCIFUL IN SPITE OF ALL HIS POWERS. HE WILL LET THAT COWARD LIVE, AND THE COWARD WILL LEARN A GREAT LESSON FROM IT.
UH... YESSIR.
WE MUST ALL BE VERY PATIENT TOGETHER, AND NOT BECOME ANGRY, AND TRY TO LISTEN WITH OUR MINDS OPEN AND OUR MOUTHS CLOSED. RIGHT, LUKE?
ANYTHING YOU SAY, KIRO.
I WOULDN'T HAVE HAD CHIHDO INJURED LIKE THIS FOR ANYTHING... BUT SOME GOOD SEEMS TO HAVE COME OF THIS.
ACTION TAUGHT KIRO MORE THAN ALL THE TALKING IN THE WORLD COULD HAVE.
AND MEANWHILE...
ADMIRAL... I CONFESS... I FEEL RATHER BADLY ABOUT THE DECISION WE HAD TO MAKE TODAY...
I ALSO... BUT WE HAD TO ABIDE BY BY THE RULING, EVEN WHERE IT PAINS US.
BY THEIR ABSENCE FROM THE COUNCIL, LUKE, LEIA, CHEWBACCA, LANDO CALRISSIAN AND HAN SOLO HAVE LOST THE RIGHT TO HELP US GOVERN.
WELL... PERHAPS IT'S FOR THE BEST.
NEXT: WOOKIEE WORLD

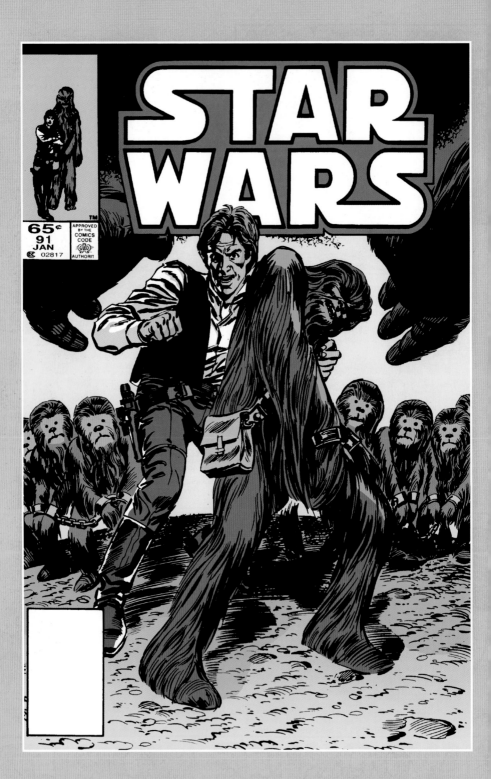

JO DUFFY ★ TONY SALMONS ★ TOM PALMER ★ KEN BRUZENAK ★ GLYNIS WEIN ★ ANN NOCENTI ★ JIM SHOOTER
SCRIPT & PLOT   PENCILLER   FINISHER   LETTERER   COLORIST   EDITOR   EDITOR-IN-CHIEF

GCRROWR!

N-NOW... CHEWBACCA, CALM DOWN... PLEASE...

IT'S NOT MY FAULT...

I'M YOUR FRIEND. YOU KNOW I WOULD NEVER DO ANYTHING TO MAKE YOU MAD--

RAHR

DON'T YOU?

COME ON, NOW... WE HAD TO FOLLOW ORDERS. I KNOW YOU WANTED TO LAND THE MILLENNIUM FALCON AND THE COBRA RIGHT IN YOUR OWN BACKYARD...

BUT WHEN WE RADIOED THE CONTROL TOWER, THEY SPECIFIED THAT OUR LANDING CLEARANCE WAS FOR THIS SPACEPORT ONLY.

KAZHYYYK IS THE WOOKIEE HOMEWORLD--YOU'RE THE NATIVE HERE.

YOU WOULDN'T WANT ME TO GO BREAKING ANY LAWS...

YORHK!

WOULD YOU...?

WHAT'S GOING ON HERE, YOU GUYS?

H-HAN! THANK GOODNESS!

SEE IF YOU CAN TALK SOME SENSE INTO HIM, WILL YOU?

2

GAROOOO

SURE, LANDO, WHAT SEEMS TO BE THE PROBLEM?

HE'S MAD AT ME BECAUSE I FOLLOWED OUR ORDERS AND SET THE COBRA DOWN HERE, AND THEN YOU FOLLOWED MY EXAMPLE.

WHURRR

WHAT...MY PARTNER AND COPILOT--OUR FRIEND--LETTING A LITTLE THING LIKE THAT UPSET HIM? NOT CHEWIE!

CHEWIE HAS TOO MUCH SENSE TO GET UPSET FOR A BONEHEADED REASON LIKE THAT!

I MEAN, NO ONE IS LIKELIER THAN HE IS TO UNDERSTAND WHY IT'S SO IMPORTANT THAT WE OBEY THE RULES HERE ON KAZHYYYK...AND WHY THE SITUATION'S SO TOUCHY HERE...

THE EMPIRE IS OVERTHROWN NOW-- THANKS TO US, AND OTHER REBELS LIKE US--

--BUT WHILE THEY WERE STILL IN POWER, NO ONE FELT HOW TOUGH THEY COULD BE MORE THAN THE WOOKIEES DID...

STORM TROOPERS WERE SENT IN AND THOUSANDS OF WOOKIEES --OLD AND YOUNG, MALE AND FEMALE ALIKE-- WERE SENT TO OTHER WORLDS AS SLAVE LABORERS...

3

SO CHEWIE HERE, OF ALL PEOPLE, HAS GOT TO APPRECIATE THE NEED FOR OBEYING LOCAL REGULATIONS, WHILE THE WOOKIEES ADJUST TO BEING FREE AGAIN...

SO...NO PROBLEM, RIGHT?

WURF

IN FACT, THIS SPACEPORT IS SO CLOSE TO WHERE CHEWIE DOES LIVE, I DON'T UNDERSTAND WHY WE'RE STANDING AROUND HERE TALKING WHEN WE COULD BE HEADING OVER TO SEE HIS WIFE, SON AND FATHER.

MRAWR!!

MY SENTIMENTS EXACTLY, PAL.

THANKS FOR DOING THAT, HAN...

YOU KNOW, FOR A MINUTE THERE, I REALLY THOUGHT HE WAS GOING TO TEAR MY HEAD OFF...

NO PROBLEM, LANDO...CHEWIE'S JUST A LITTLE EDGY, THAT'S ALL. I'VE NOTICED IT MYSELF.

HE'LL BE OKAY, ONCE HE'S SEEN THAT THINGS ARE ALL RIGHT HERE-- AND HAD SOME TIME ALONE WITH MALA,

I HOPE SO...

SAY...UH... DO THINGS HERE LOOK NORMAL TO YOU? IT'S KIND OF HARD FOR ME TO JUDGE...

SURE, EVERYTHING LOOKS FINE. WHAT...YOU'VE NEVER BEEN TO KAZHYYYK BEFORE?

UH... NO.

WELL, DON'T WORRY ABOUT IT. IT'S A NORMAL PLANET, JUST LIKE EVERY- WHERE ELSE.

SAY... HAN? IS IT MY IMAGINATION, OR DO ALL OF THE WOOKIEES HERE SEEM KIND OF... UNFRIENDLY?

NOT PARTICULAR-LY, NO...

WHEN IT COMES TO WOOKIEES, WHO CAN TELL, ANYWAY?

WHY? SOMETHING BOTHERING YOU?

NO... NOT ANYTHING THAT I CAN PUT MY FINGER ON, ANYWAY. BUT I CAN'T HELP FEELING THAT SOMETHING'S WRONG HERE...

LIKE THERE MAY BE TROUBLE.

CRURF?

AAHRR!!

OH, I DO BEG YOUR PARDON.

AM I IN YOUR WAY?

RROOWR!

REALLY? HOW ⸘ YAWN ⸘ RUDE OF ME.

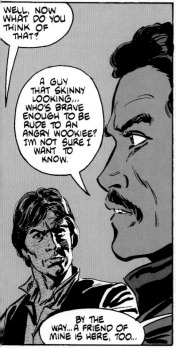

WELL, NOW WHAT DO YOU THINK OF THAT?

A GUY THAT SKINNY LOOKING... WHO'S BRAVE ENOUGH TO BE RUDE TO AN ANGRY WOOKIEE? I'M NOT SURE I WANT TO KNOW.

BY THE WAY...A FRIEND OF MINE IS HERE, TOO...

AND I DO BELIEVE THE TWO OF YOU KNOW EACH OTHER.

HHROWR!

ROO?

WELL, I'LL BE--!

HAN, MY WOOKIEE ISN'T QUITE GOOD ENOUGH TO FOLLOW ALL THAT. WHO IS THE BIG GUY?

HE SAYS HE'S MALA'S BROTHER, VARGI-- CHEWBACCA'S BROTHER-IN-LAW!

YES... IT DOES RATHER MAKE A DIFFERENCE, DOESN'T IT?

I HEARD YOU ALL MENTION THAT CHEWBACCA'S HOME WAS NEAR HERE. WOULDN'T IT BE NICE IF WE ALL ADJOURNED THERE TO- GETHER FOR REFRESHMENTS?

LOOKS LIKE YOU'RE THE HOST, BUDDY. LEAD ON.

IT'S SUCH A THRILL FOR ME TO ACTUALLY MEET THE LEGENDARY CHEWBACCA WHILE I'M HERE ON KAZHYYYK. HE IS QUITE THE LOCAL HERO, YOU KNOW.

AND, OF COURSE, YOU TWO MUST BE THE WELL-KNOWN DARE-DEVILS, HAN SOLO AND LANDO CALRISSIAN.

NATURALLY.

AND JUST WHO ARE YOU...

OH, NONE OF THE LOCALS EVER SEEM TO HAVE QUITE THE DEXTERITY OF PALATE THAT IT TAKES TO PRONOUNCE MY NAME.

THE WOOKIEES HAVE DUBBED ME SOMETHING WHICH--IN THEIR TONGUE-- ROUGHLY APPROXIMATES YOUR WORD "KNIFE" IN MEANING.

QUAINT, ISN'T IT?

AH... HERE WE ARE ALREAD

VUUHHRAAAAR

NO GOOD, PAL. LOOKS LIKE NO ONE'S HOME.

AAAHHR

HEY NOW, CALM DOWN. IT'S NOT LIKE THE END OF THE WORLD.

THEY'RE PROBABLY JUST OUT SHOPPING OR SOMETHING.

COME ON, CHEWIE. YOU CAN'T EXPECT MALA TO HAVE KNOWN YOU WERE COMING. YOU WERE THE ONE WHO INSISTED YOU WANTED TO SURPRISE YOUR FOLKS.

LOOK, WE CAN WAIT INSIDE. YOU CAN SURPRISE HER WHEN SHE GETS HOME.

WELL, LANDO, LOOKS LIKE I OWE YOU. I CAN'T QUITE PUT MY FINGER ON WHAT YET, BUT SOMETHING IS DEFINITELY WEIRD HERE.

I HAVE NO IDEA WHAT TO MAKE OF HIM. I'VE FLOWN FROM ONE SIDE OF THIS GALAXY TO THE OTHER...

YOU MEAN, LIKE THE FACT THAT CHEWIE AND VARGI DON'T SEEM TO LIKE EACH OTHER AT ALL, FOR INSTANCE? AND THAT FELLOW KNIFE... WHAT DO YOU MAKE OF HIM?

...AND NEVER SEEN ANYONE WHO LOOKS LIKE THE SAME SPECIES HE IS.

ME NEITHER.

ŞACKŞ

WHY, YOU--!

HAN! HAN, PUT YOUR BLASTER AWAY AND LOOK!

IT'S A FLAME BEETLE.

THOSE THINGS ARE POISONOUS.

UH... THANKS.

OH, ALWAYS HAPPY TO OBLIGE.

9

PAL, YOU GOT ABOUT THREE SECONDS TO GIVE US SOME EXPLANATION, OR WE'LL--!

OR NOTHING, GENERAL SOLO. IN CASE YOU HADN'T NOTICED, MY ALLIES AND I HAVE THE THREE OF YOU COVERED.

THEN, WOULD YOU DEIGN TO ANSWER ONE QUESTION FOR US?

WHY?

ISN'T IT OBVIOUS, LANDO? BUSINESS AS USUAL.

AH... YOU'RE MORE PERCEPTIVE THAN I GAVE YOU CREDIT FOR, SOLO. YOU ARE QUITE CORRECT. THE KAZHYYYK SLAVE TRADE IS ABOUT TO BE REACTIVATED.

WELL, WE SUSPECTED THERE MIGHT BE AREAS LIKE THIS... THAT THERE MIGHT BE A STRONGER IMPERIAL MACHINE THAN WE SUSPECTED STILL IN POWER IN SOME QUADRANTS...

THE EMPIRE? DO YOU TRULY BELIEVE I REPRESENT THAT PATHETIC LITTLE OUTFIT?

HAH HAH HAH HAH HAH!

FFROOR

QUIET, YOU MISERABLE BUFFOON!

11

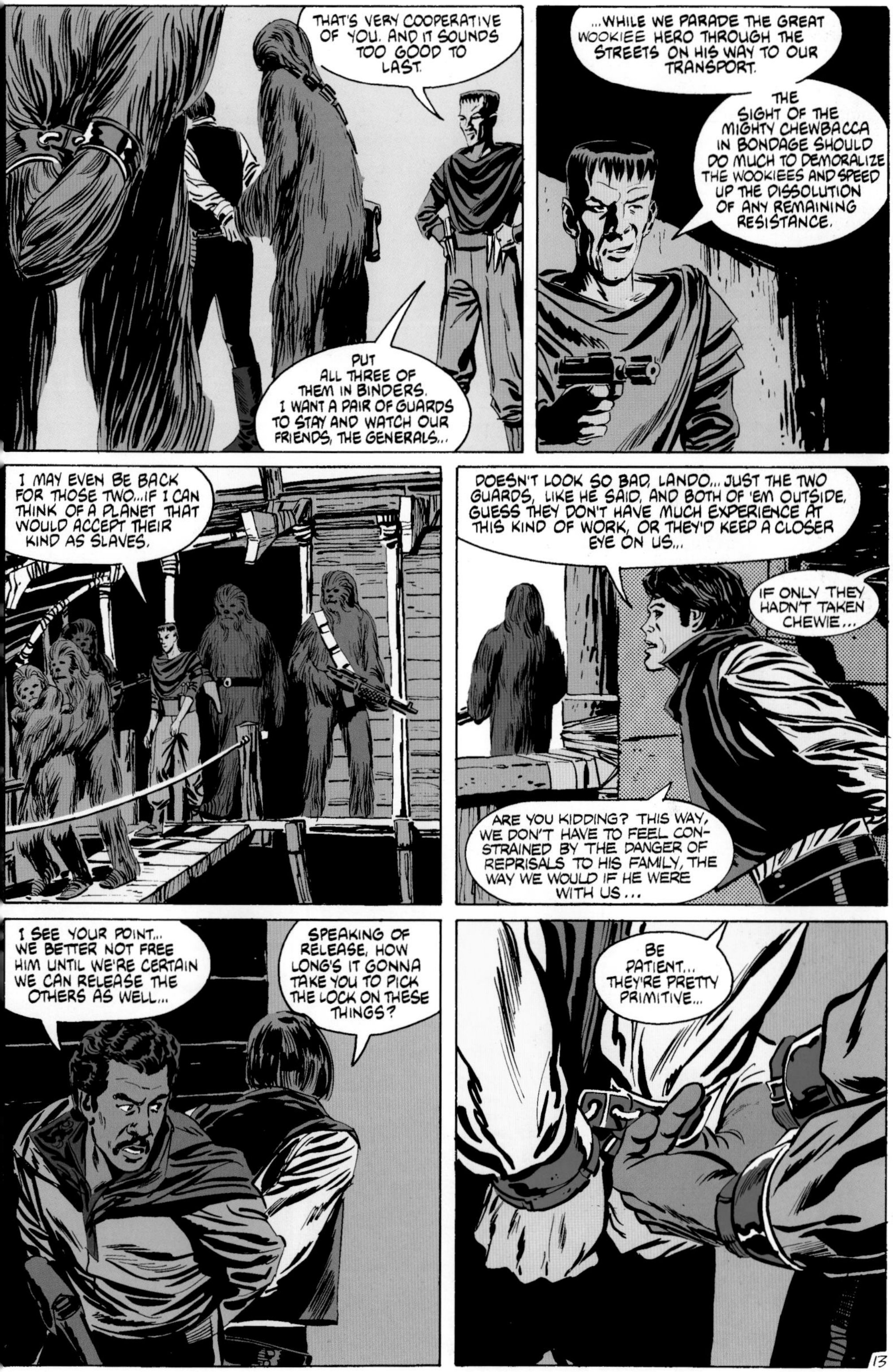

THAT'S VERY COOPERATIVE OF YOU. AND IT SOUNDS TOO GOOD TO LAST.
PUT ALL THREE OF THEM IN BINDERS. I WANT A PAIR OF GUARDS TO STAY AND WATCH OUR FRIENDS, THE GENERALS...
...WHILE WE PARADE THE GREAT WOOKIEE HERO THROUGH THE STREETS ON HIS WAY TO OUR TRANSPORT.
THE SIGHT OF THE MIGHTY CHEWBACCA IN BONDAGE SHOULD DO MUCH TO DEMORALIZE THE WOOKIEES AND SPEED UP THE DISSOLUTION OF ANY REMAINING RESISTANCE.
I MAY EVEN BE BACK FOR THOSE TWO...IF I CAN THINK OF A PLANET THAT WOULD ACCEPT THEIR KIND AS SLAVES.
DOESN'T LOOK SO BAD, LANDO... JUST THE TWO GUARDS, LIKE HE SAID, AND BOTH OF 'EM OUTSIDE. GUESS THEY DON'T HAVE MUCH EXPERIENCE AT THIS KIND OF WORK, OR THEY'D KEEP A CLOSER EYE ON US...
IF ONLY THEY HADN'T TAKEN CHEWIE...
ARE YOU KIDDING? THIS WAY, WE DON'T HAVE TO FEEL CON-STRAINED BY THE DANGER OF REPRISALS TO HIS FAMILY, THE WAY WE WOULD IF HE WERE WITH US...
I SEE YOUR POINT... WE BETTER NOT FREE HIM UNTIL WE'RE CERTAIN WE CAN RELEASE THE OTHERS AS WELL...
SPEAKING OF RELEASE, HOW LONG'S IT GONNA TAKE YOU TO PICK THE LOCK ON THESE THINGS?
BE PATIENT... THEY'RE PRETTY PRIMITIVE...
13

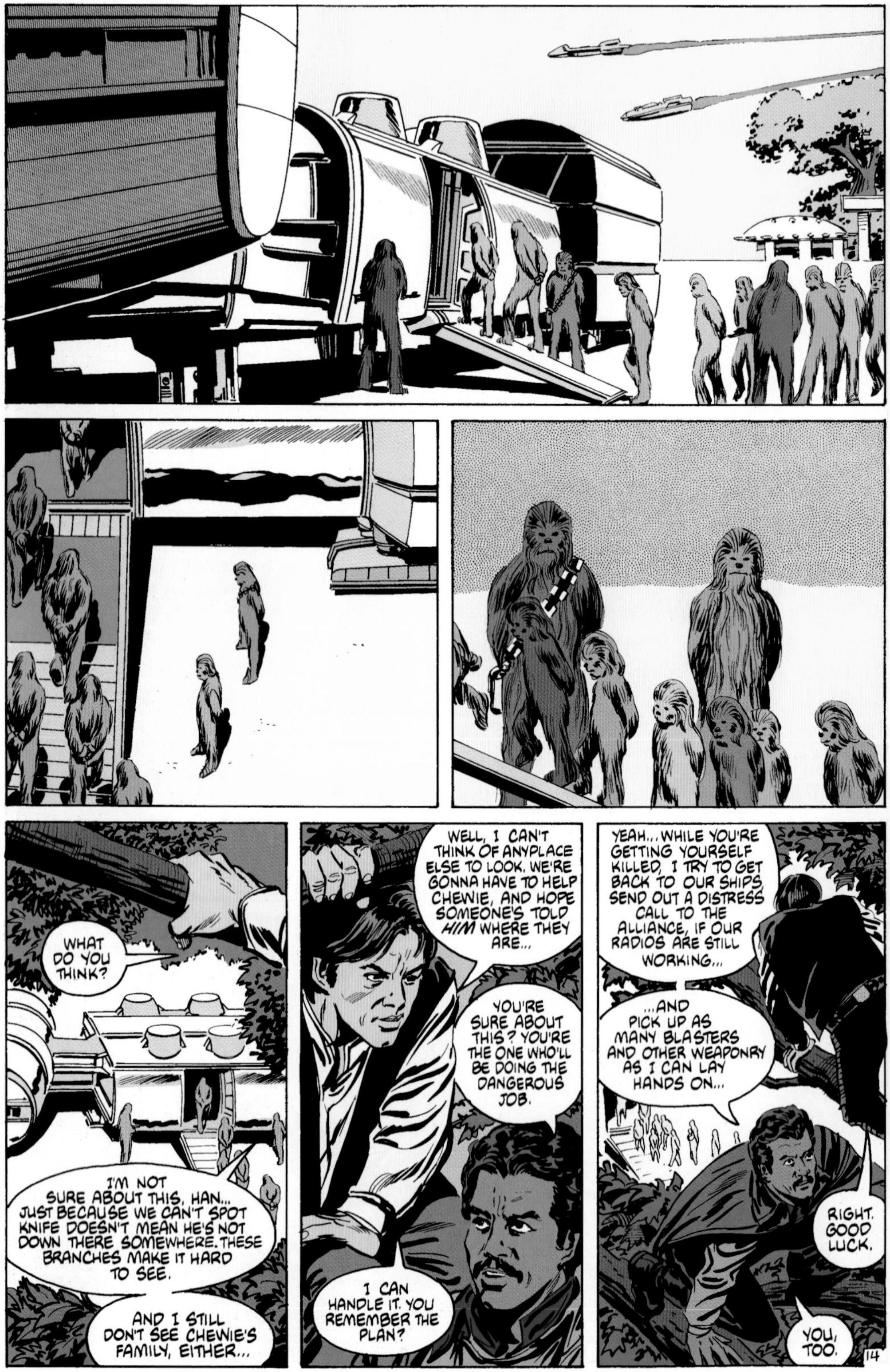
WHAT DO YOU THINK?
I'M NOT SURE ABOUT THIS, HAN... JUST BECAUSE WE CAN'T SPOT KNIFE DOESN'T MEAN HE'S NOT DOWN THERE SOMEWHERE. THESE BRANCHES MAKE IT HARD TO SEE.
AND I STILL DON'T SEE CHEWIE'S FAMILY, EITHER...
WELL, I CAN'T THINK OF ANYPLACE ELSE TO LOOK. WE'RE GONNA HAVE TO HELP CHEWIE, AND HOPE SOMEONE'S TOLD *HIM* WHERE THEY ARE...
YOU'RE SURE ABOUT THIS? YOU'RE THE ONE WHO'LL BE DOING THE DANGEROUS JOB.
I CAN HANDLE IT. YOU REMEMBER THE PLAN?
YEAH... WHILE YOU'RE GETTING YOURSELF KILLED, I TRY TO GET BACK TO OUR SHIPS, SEND OUT A DISTRESS CALL TO THE ALLIANCE, IF OUR RADIOS ARE STILL WORKING...
...AND PICK UP AS MANY BLASTERS AND OTHER WEAPONRY AS I CAN LAY HANDS ON...
RIGHT. GOOD LUCK.
YOU, TOO.
14

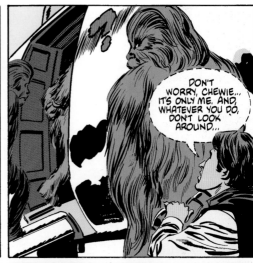

DON'T WORRY, CHEWIE... IT'S ONLY ME. AND, WHATEVER YOU DO, DON'T LOOK AROUND...

STOP SHAKING YOUR HEAD AT ME. WE'VE GOT TO GET YOU OUT OF HERE IF WE'RE GONNA HELP MALA, LUMPY AND THE OTHERS,

THIS IS GONNA WORK. TRUST ME.

CLICK!

CLICK CLICK CLICK

UH-OH.

CRAFF

15

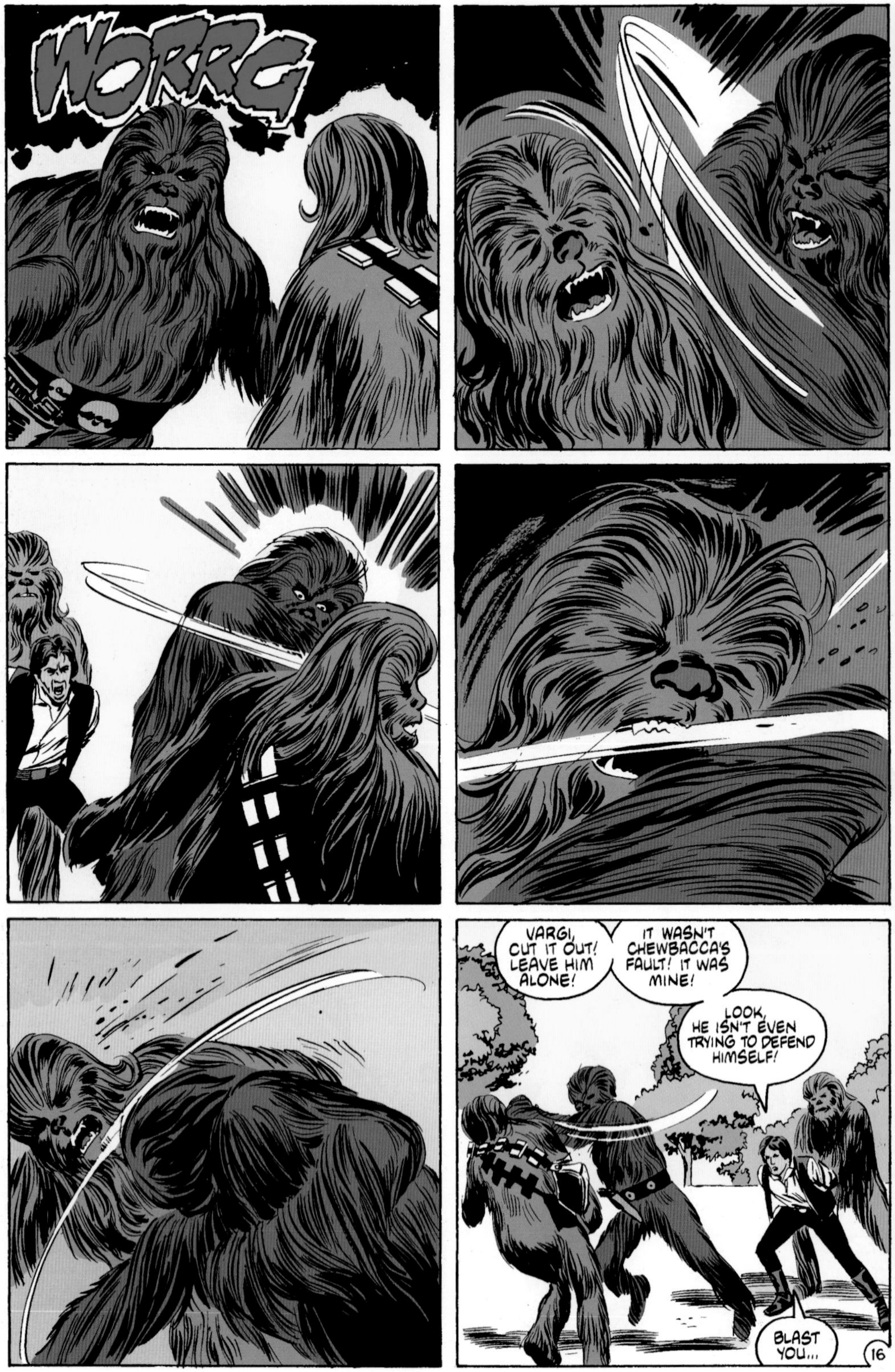
WORRG
VARGI, CUT IT OUT! LEAVE HIM ALONE!
IT WASN'T CHEWBACCA'S FAULT! IT WAS MINE!
LOOK, HE ISN'T EVEN TRYING TO DEFEND HIMSELF!
BLAST YOU...
16

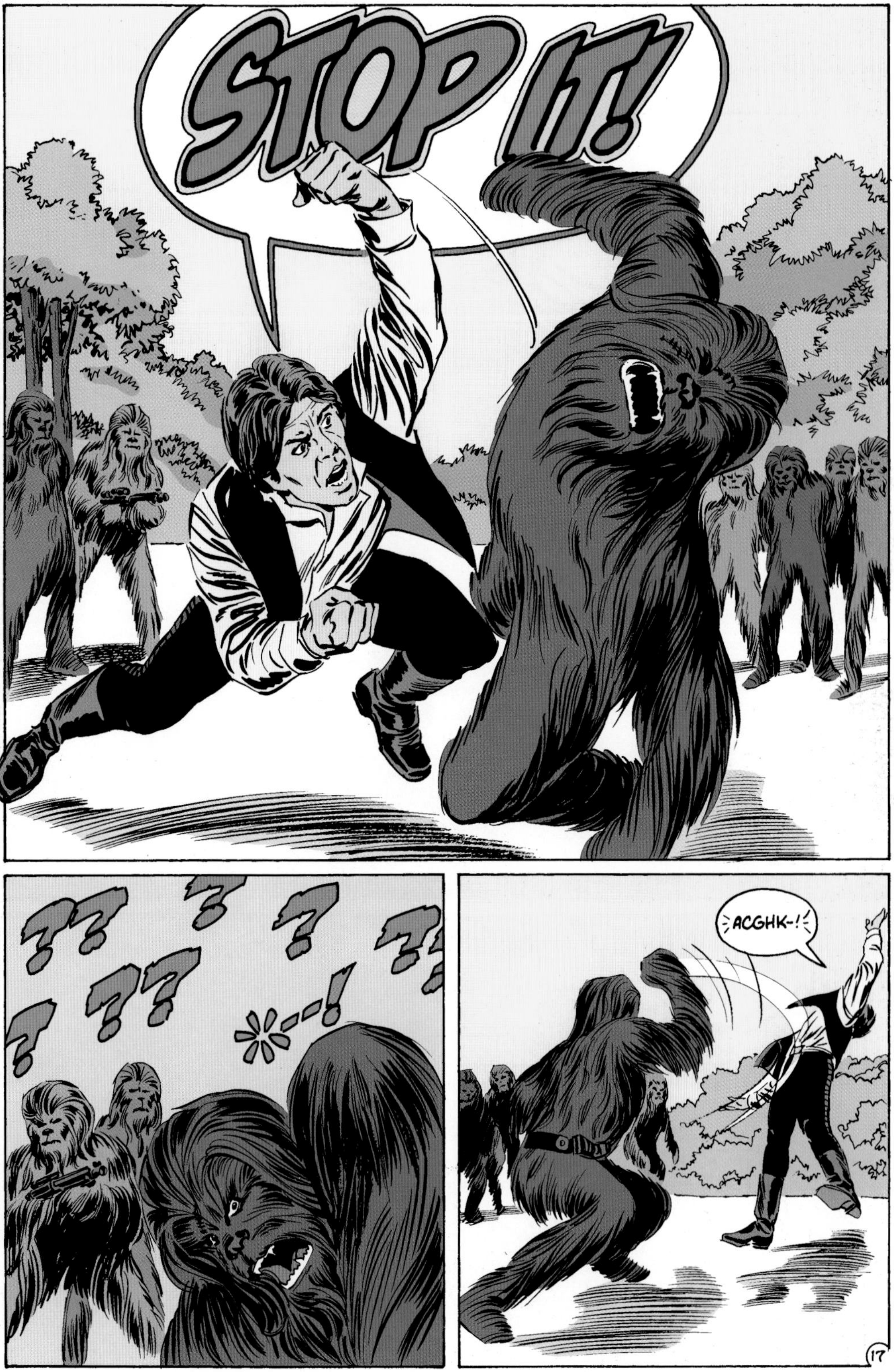
STOP IT!
??
?
??
??
??
?
*--!
ACGHK-!
17

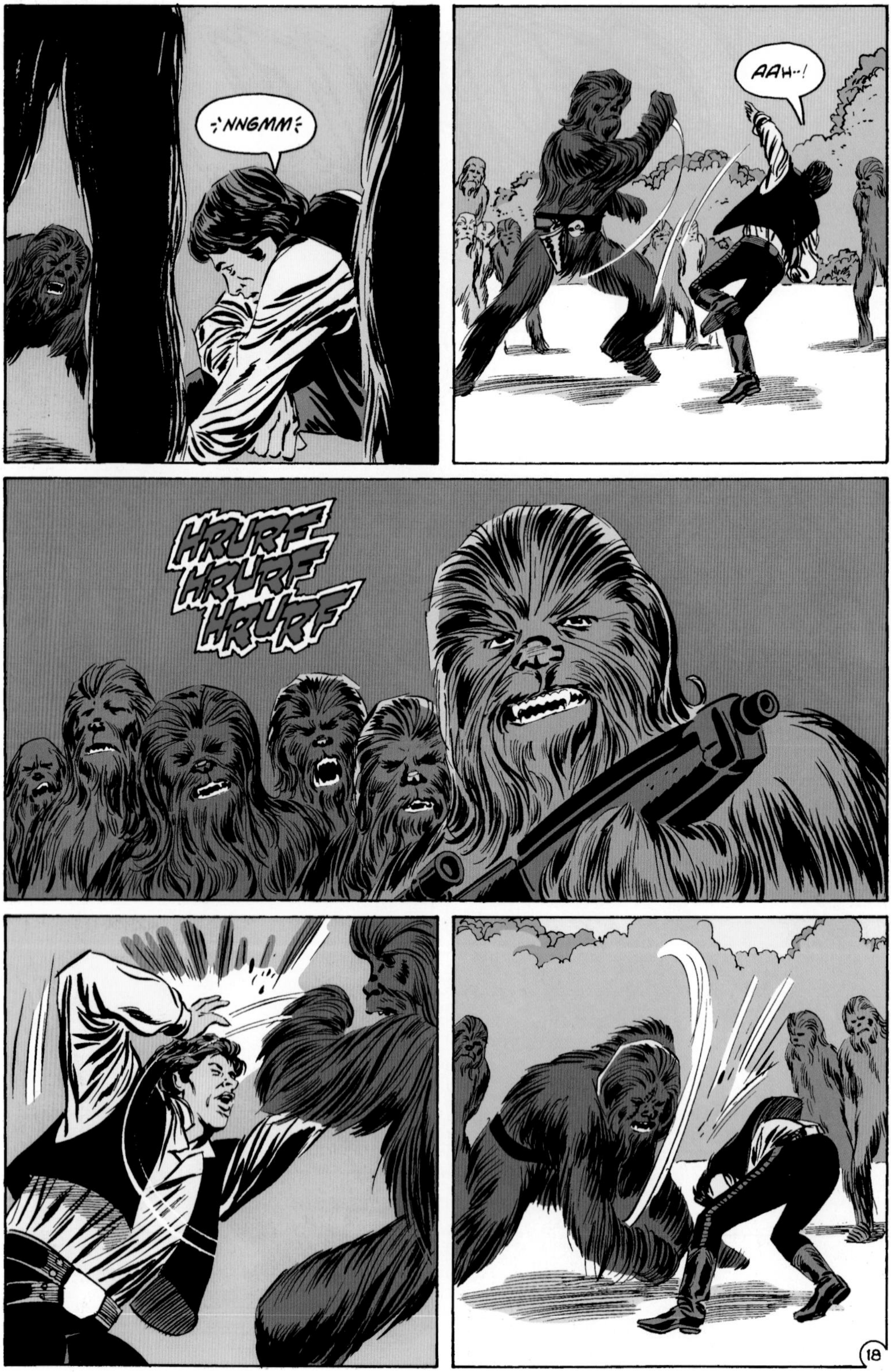
NNGMM
AAH..!
HRURF HRURF HRURF
18

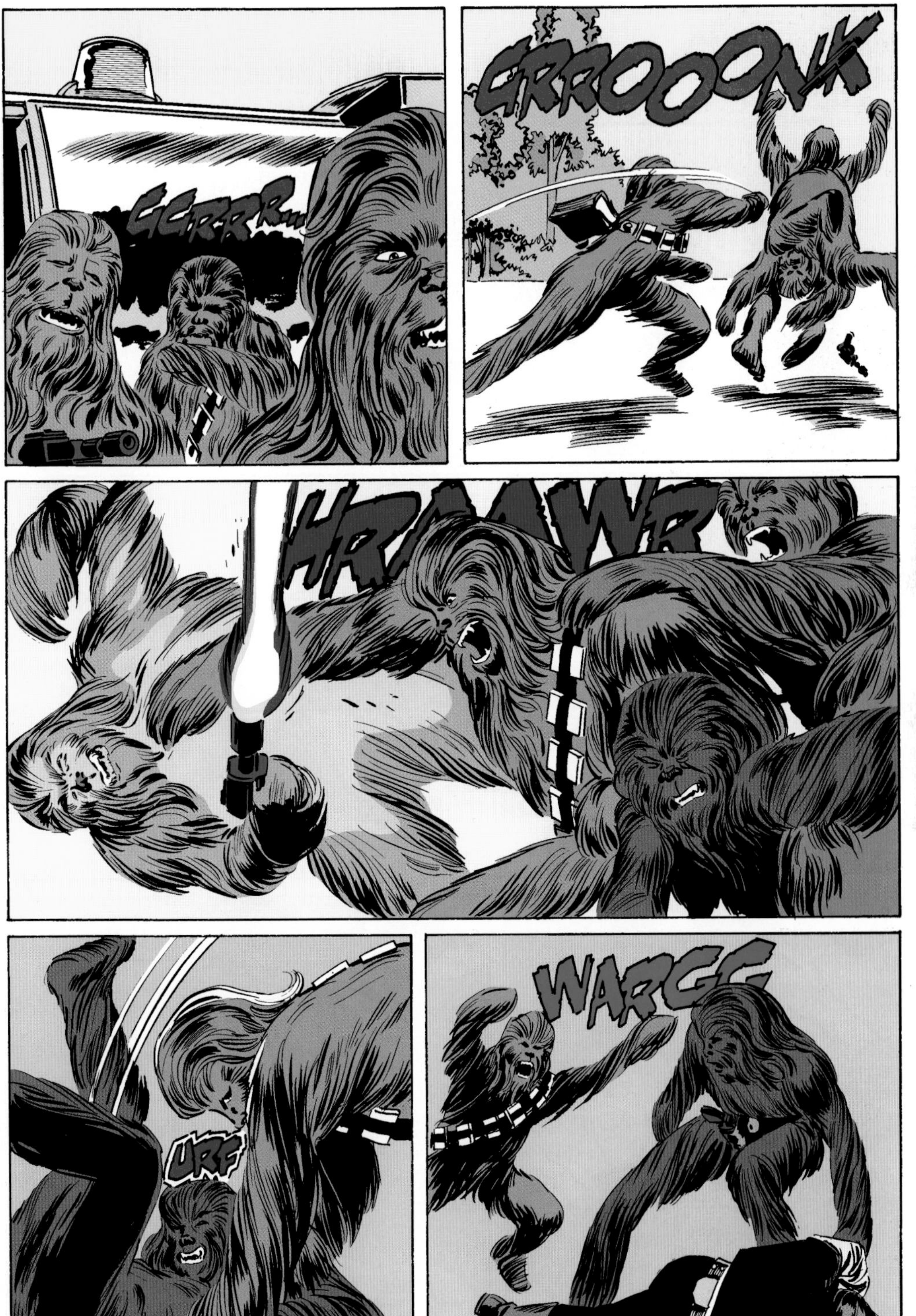
GGRRRR...
GRROOONK
HRAAWR
URF
WARGG
19

HHYYIIII~!

WHAT'S ALL THIS COMMOTION?

YOU FOOLS, YOU'VE LET HIM LOOSE!

A WASTE REALLY, BUT IT CAN'T BE HELPED!

NO!

CHEWIE, WATCH YOUR BACK!

20

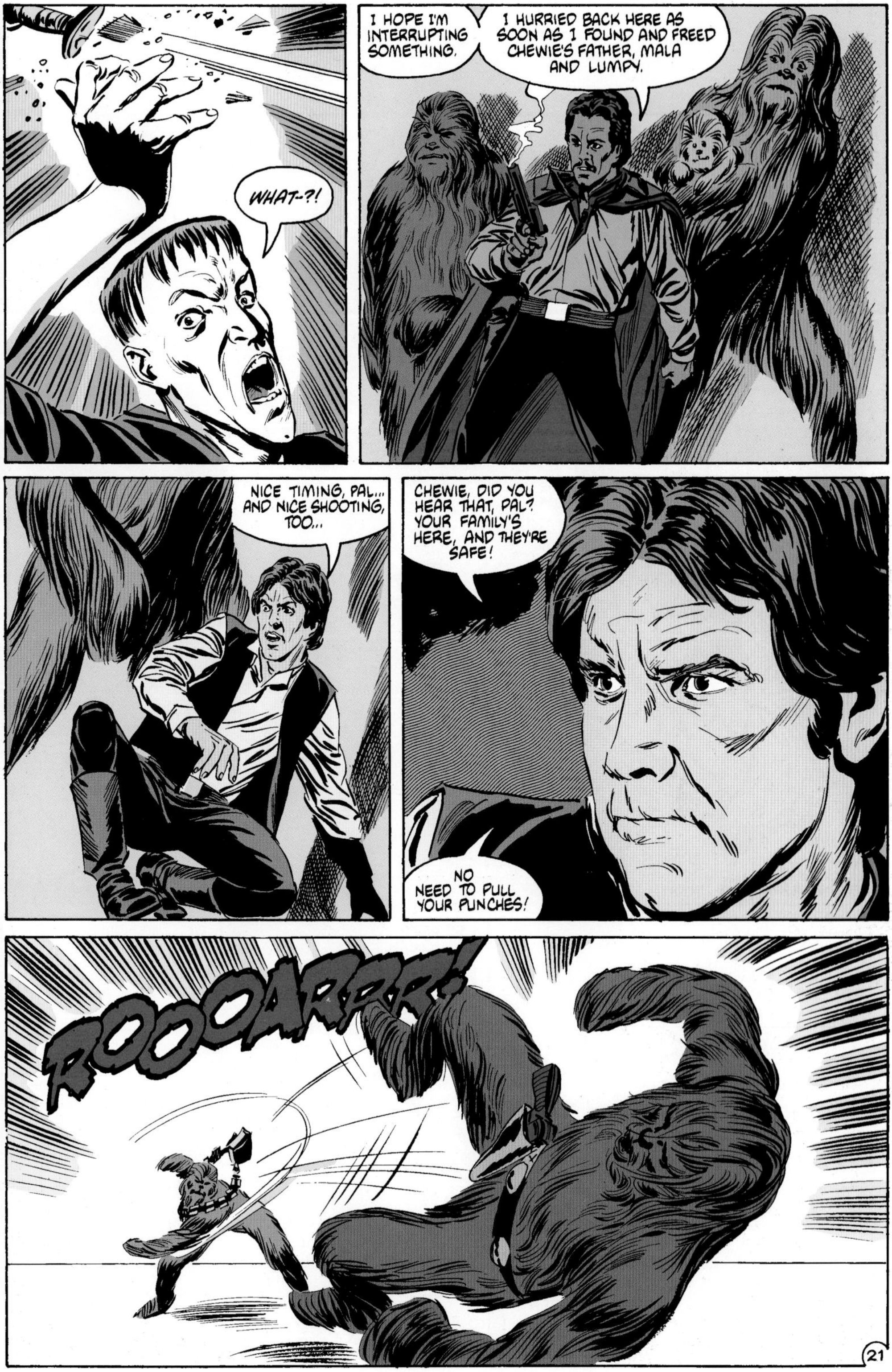
WHAT--?!
I HOPE I'M INTERRUPTING SOMETHING.
I HURRIED BACK HERE AS SOON AS I FOUND AND FREED CHEWIE'S FATHER, MALA AND LUMPY.
NICE TIMING, PAL... AND NICE SHOOTING, TOO...
CHEWIE, DID YOU HEAR THAT, PAL? YOUR FAMILY'S HERE, AND THEY'RE SAFE!
NO NEED TO PULL YOUR PUNCHES!
ROOOARRR!
21

DRAT! I APPEAR TO HAVE MISJUDGED THIS ENTIRE OPERATION.

AAAROOOOO!

YEAH, YEAH, YEAH, SURE!

NOW, WOULD YOU GUYS MIND CLEARING A PATH?

THE LEADER'S GETTING AWAY!

ROO ROO ROO

HAN, ARE YOU OKAY... IT LOOKS LIKE YOU TOOK SOME BEATING WHILE I WAS GONE!

I'LL HEAL. HEY, DO YOU HEAR A SHIP'S ENGINE?

IT SOUNDS KIND OF FAMILIAR...

IT SHOULD... I'M AFRAID I WAS IN SUCH A HURRY TO GET BACK HERE AFTER I FOUND THE PRISONERS IN THE HANGAR...

I... MAY HAVE FORGOTTEN TO RESET THE DEFENSE SYSTEMS ON THE COBRA.

SO KNIFE GOT CLEAN AWAY,... IN A FAST SHIP!

WELL, YOU CAN COUNT ON ONE THING, LANDO,... I'M GONNA TRACK HIM DOWN, AND SET UP A LITTLE REMATCH, AS SOON AS I CAN!

NEXT: The DREAM

146

$1.00
92
FEB
02817

APPROVED
BY THE
COMICS
CODE
AUTHORITY

Lucasfilm PRESENTS:
STAR WARS
THE GREATEST SPACE FANTASY OF ALL!
JO DUFFY PLOT & SCRIPT
JAN DUURSEMA PENCILS
TOM MANDRAKE INKS
R. PARKER LETTERS
G. WEIN COLORS
ANN NOCENTI EDITOR
JIM SHOOTER ED.-IN-CHIEF
THE DREAM
IT CAN'T BE!

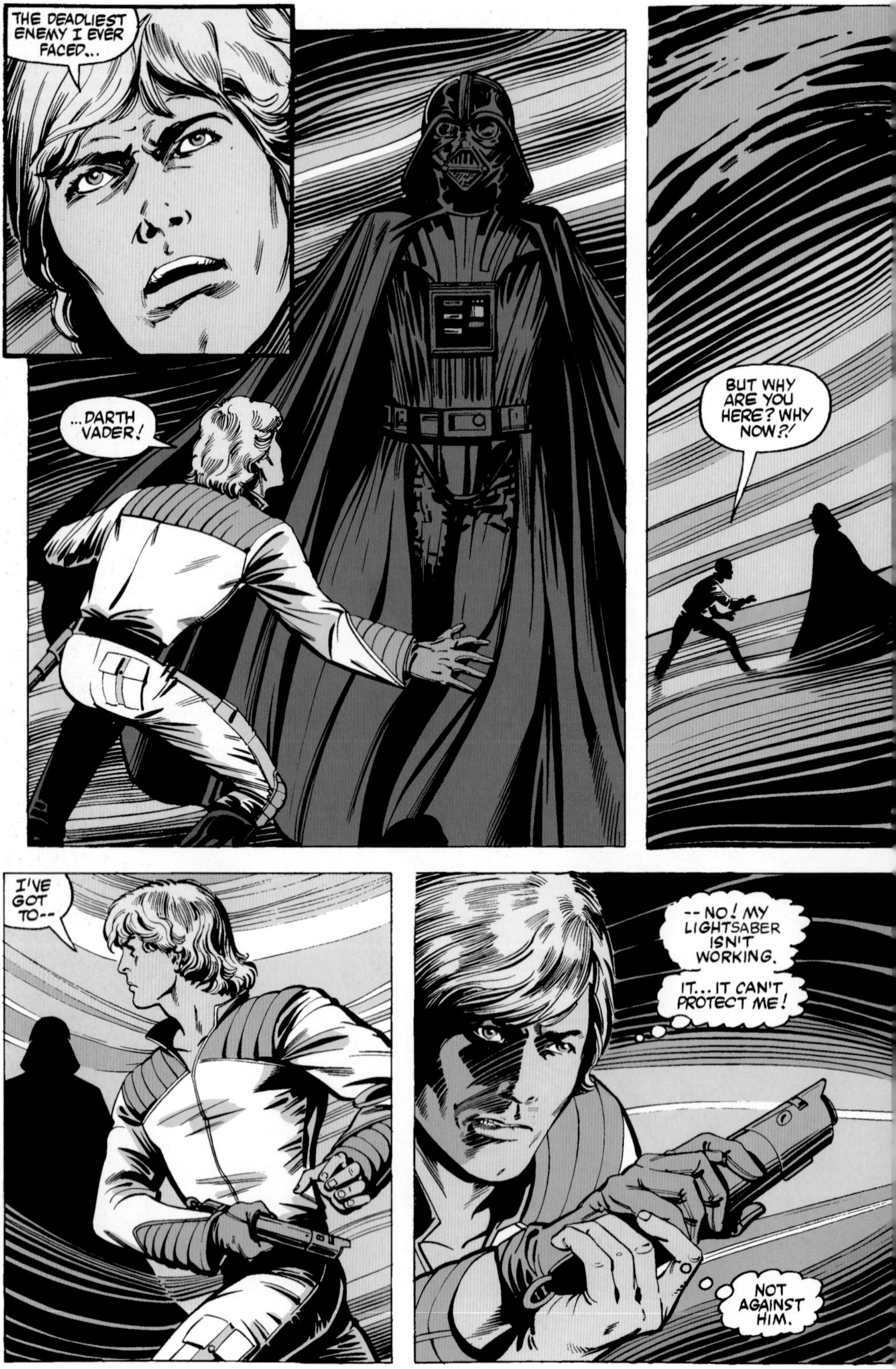
THE DEADLIEST ENEMY I EVER FACED...
...DARTH VADER!
BUT WHY ARE YOU HERE? WHY NOW?!
I'VE GOT TO--
--NO! MY LIGHTSABER ISN'T WORKING.
IT... IT CAN'T PROTECT ME!
NOT AGAINST HIM.

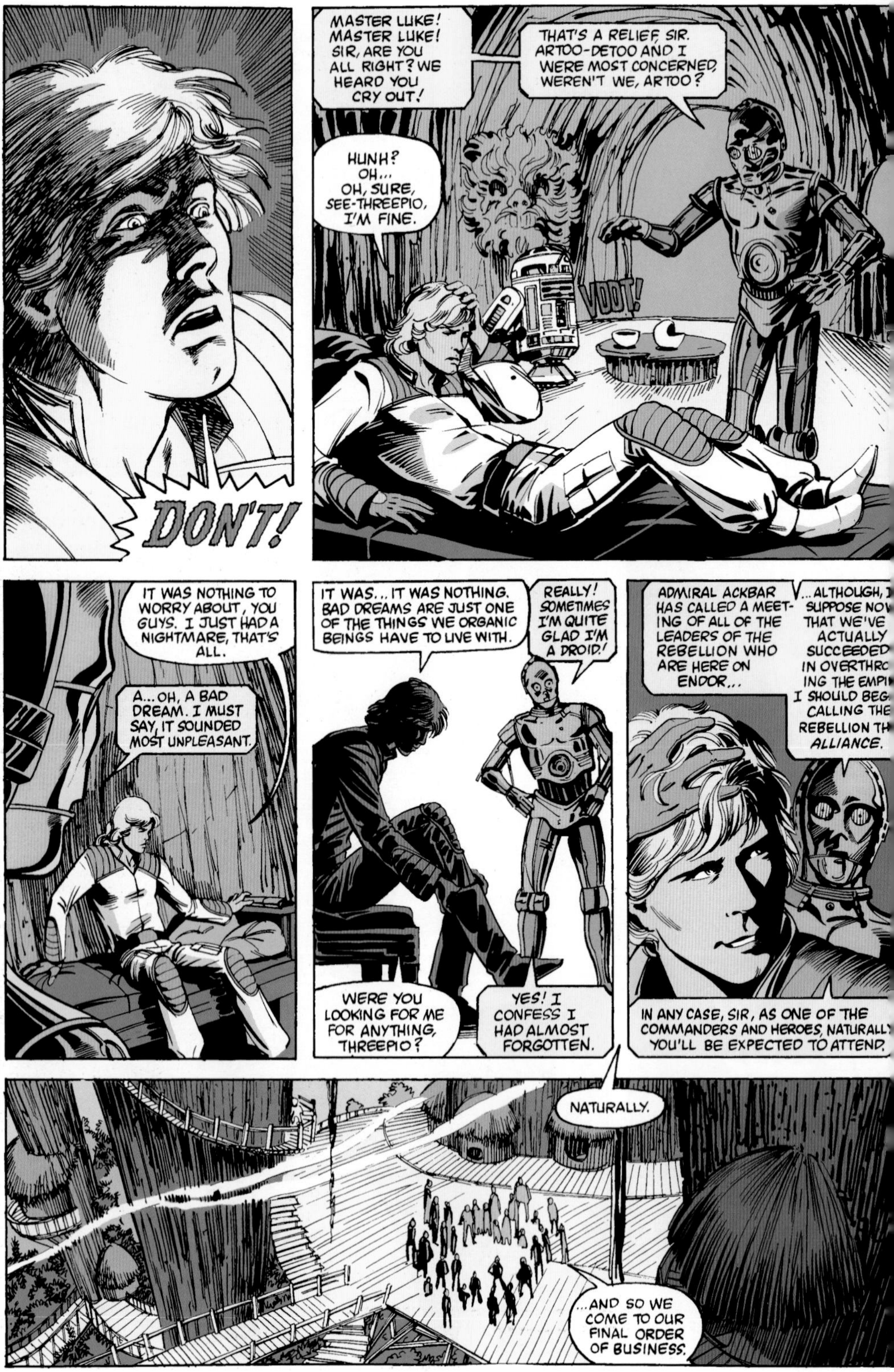

DONT!
MASTER LUKE! MASTER LUKE! SIR, ARE YOU ALL RIGHT? WE HEARD YOU CRY OUT!
HUNH? OH... OH, SURE, SEE-THREEPIO, I'M FINE.
THAT'S A RELIEF, SIR. ARTOO-DETOO AND I WERE MOST CONCERNED, WEREN'T WE, ARTOO?
VOOT!
IT WAS NOTHING TO WORRY ABOUT, YOU GUYS. I JUST HAD A NIGHTMARE, THAT'S ALL.
A...OH, A BAD DREAM. I MUST SAY, IT SOUNDED MOST UNPLEASANT.
IT WAS... IT WAS NOTHING. BAD DREAMS ARE JUST ONE OF THE THINGS WE ORGANIC BEINGS HAVE TO LIVE WITH.
REALLY! SOMETIMES I'M QUITE GLAD I'M A DROID!
WERE YOU LOOKING FOR ME FOR ANYTHING, THREEPIO?
YES! I CONFESS I HAD ALMOST FORGOTTEN.
ADMIRAL ACKBAR HAS CALLED A MEETING OF ALL OF THE LEADERS OF THE REBELLION WHO ARE HERE ON ENDOR...
...ALTHOUGH, I SUPPOSE NO THAT WE'VE ACTUALLY SUCCEEDED IN OVERTHRO ING THE EMPI I SHOULD BEG CALLING THE REBELLION TH ALLIANCE.
IN ANY CASE, SIR, AS ONE OF THE COMMANDERS AND HEROES, NATURALLY YOU'LL BE EXPECTED TO ATTEND.
NATURALLY.
...AND SO WE COME TO OUR FINAL ORDER OF BUSINESS.

AS ALL OF YOU KNOW, SINCE THE EMPIRE'S CAPITULATION TO OUR FORCES, FOLLOWING OUR DESTRUCTION OF THEIR SECOND DEATH STAR...

...WE OF THE ALLIANCE HAVE BEEN SENDING EMBASSIES TO WORLDS ALL OVER THE GALAXY, IN THE HOPE OF RE-ESTABLISH-ING PEACEFUL CONTACT, AND SETTING UP A NEW INTER-PLANETARY SYSTEM OF GOVERNMENT.

GENERAL HAN SOLO, CHEWBACCA THE WOOKIEE, AND HER HIGHNESS, PRINCESS LEIA ORGANA, HAVE ALL COME BACK FROM RECENT MISSIONS WITH INFORMATION THAT CAUSES ME GRAVE CONCERN...

HE'S RIGHT, FOLKS, CHEWIE, HERE, LANDO CALRISSIAN, AND I VISITED THE WOOKIEE HOMEWORLD RECENTLY...

CRONK!

...AND LEARNED THAT DESPITE ALL REPORTS TO THE CONTRARY, THE SLAVE TRADE WAS STARTING UP THERE AGAIN!

I FOUND SLAVERS AT WORK ON HERDESSA, AS WELL... AND THEY WERE WORKING OPENLY, WITH THE AID OF IMPERIAL STORMTROOPERS.

OOHH...

YOU SEE OUR PROBLEM? SLAVING OPERATIONS AND IMPERIAL FORCES WHERE THE EMPIRE SHOULD NO LONGER EXIST...

AND WE HAVE NO IDEA HOW WIDESPREAD, OR NUMEROUS, OR WELL-ORGANIZED THESE HOSTILE GROUPS MAY BE.

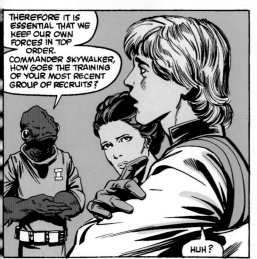

THEREFORE IT IS ESSENTIAL THAT WE KEEP OUR OWN FORCES IN TOP ORDER. COMMANDER SKYWALKER, HOW GOES THE TRAINING OF YOUR MOST RECENT GROUP OF RECRUITS?

HUH?

OH...UH, FINE, ADMIRAL. THEY'LL DO OKAY. I'M SURE OF IT.

WHAT'S WRONG WITH LUKE?!

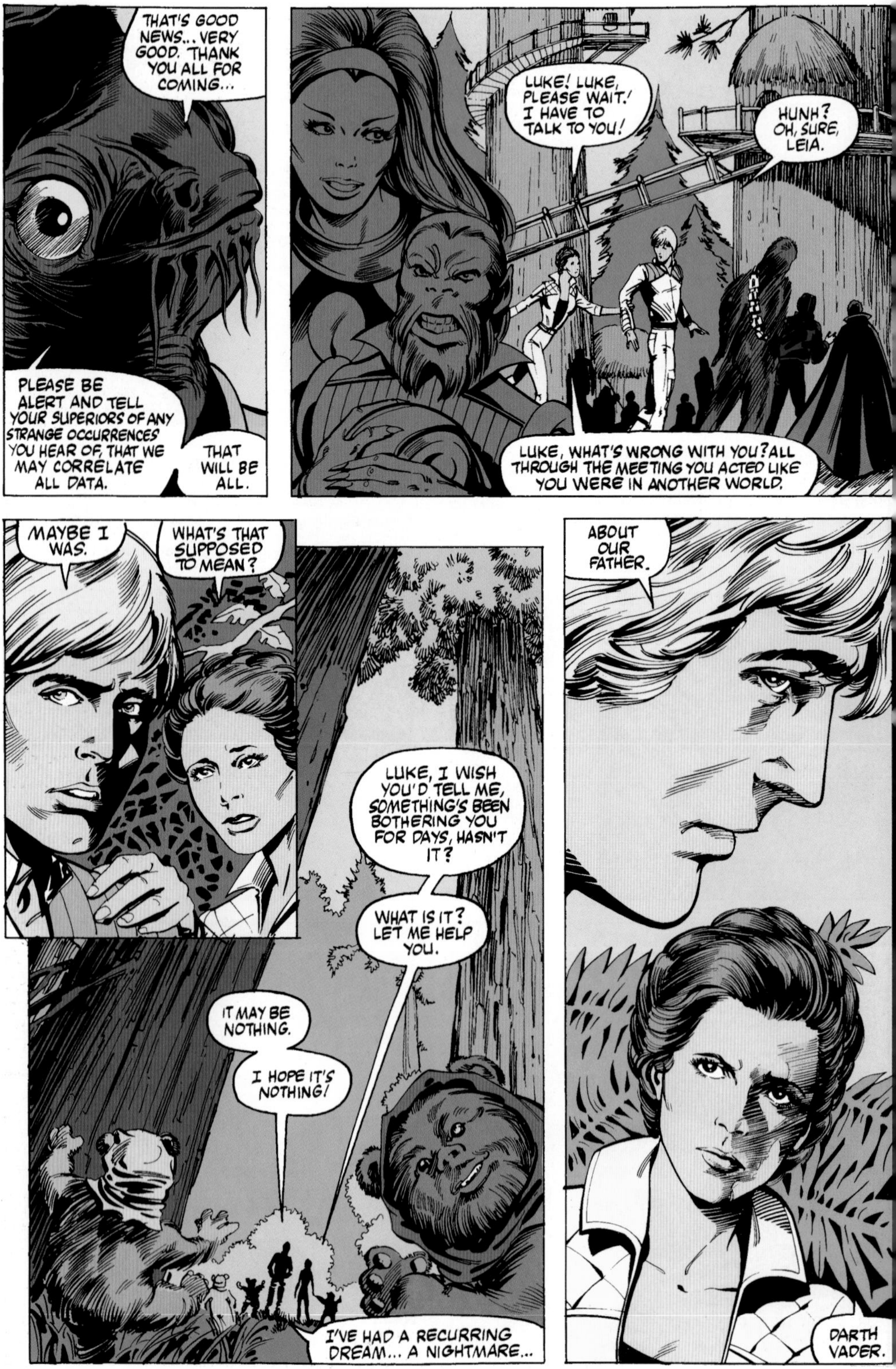

THAT'S GOOD NEWS... VERY GOOD. THANK YOU ALL FOR COMING...
PLEASE BE ALERT AND TELL YOUR SUPERIORS OF ANY STRANGE OCCURRENCES YOU HEAR OF, THAT WE MAY CORRELATE ALL DATA.
THAT WILL BE ALL.
LUKE! LUKE, PLEASE WAIT! I HAVE TO TALK TO YOU!
HUNH? OH, SURE, LEIA.
LUKE, WHAT'S WRONG WITH YOU? ALL THROUGH THE MEETING YOU ACTED LIKE YOU WERE IN ANOTHER WORLD.
MAYBE I WAS.
WHAT'S THAT SUPPOSED TO MEAN?
LUKE, I WISH YOU'D TELL ME, SOMETHING'S BEEN BOTHERING YOU FOR DAYS, HASN'T IT?
WHAT IS IT? LET ME HELP YOU.
IT MAY BE NOTHING.
I HOPE IT'S NOTHING!
I'VE HAD A RECURRING DREAM... A NIGHTMARE...
ABOUT OUR FATHER.
DARTH VADER.

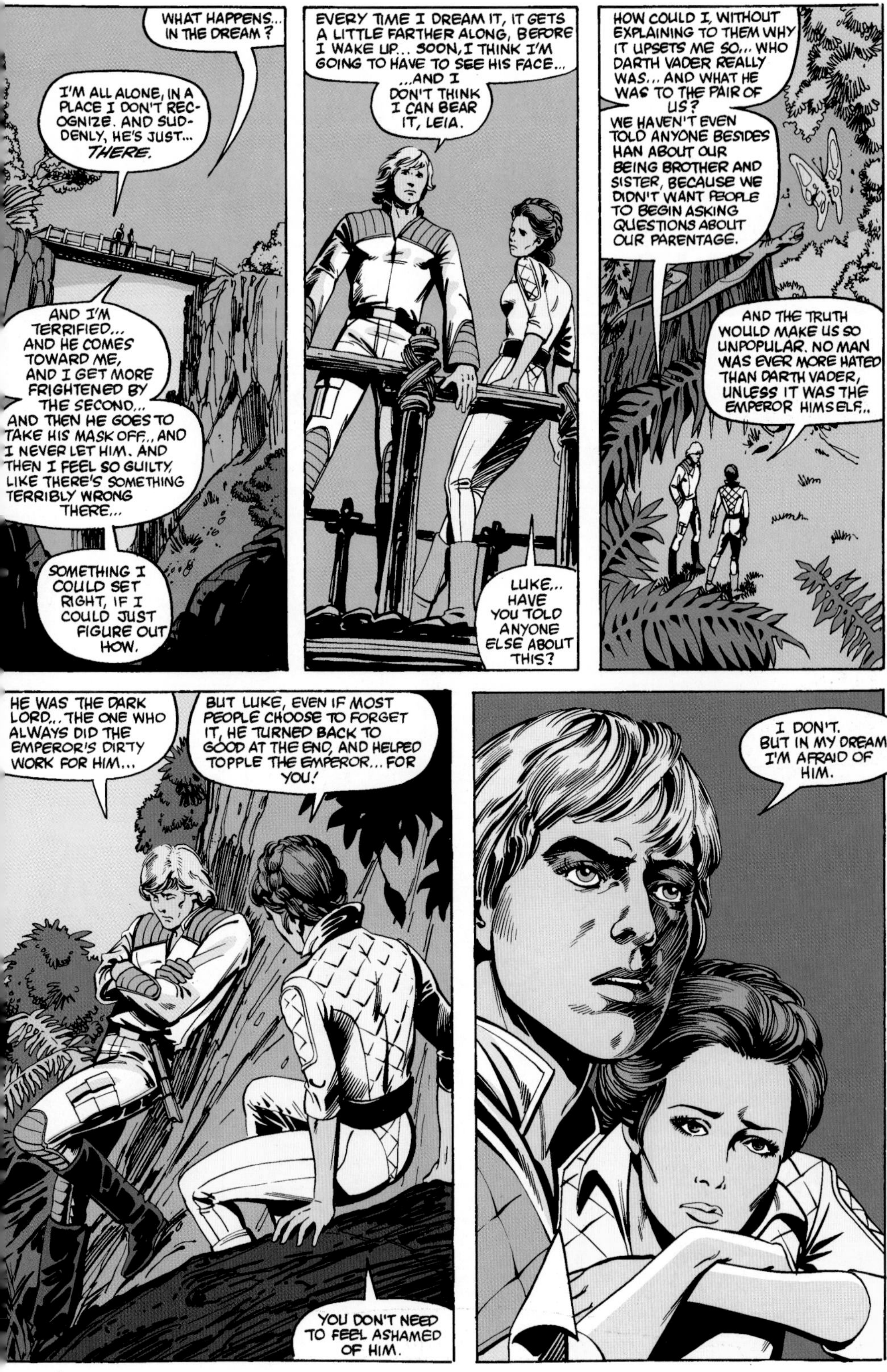

WHAT HAPPENS... IN THE DREAM?
I'M ALL ALONE, IN A PLACE I DON'T RECOGNIZE. AND SUDDENLY, HE'S JUST... THERE.
AND I'M TERRIFIED... AND HE COMES TOWARD ME, AND I GET MORE FRIGHTENED BY THE SECOND... AND THEN HE GOES TO TAKE HIS MASK OFF... AND I NEVER LET HIM. AND THEN I FEEL SO GUILTY, LIKE THERE'S SOMETHING TERRIBLY WRONG THERE...
SOMETHING I COULD SET RIGHT, IF I COULD JUST FIGURE OUT HOW.
EVERY TIME I DREAM IT, IT GETS A LITTLE FARTHER ALONG, BEFORE I WAKE UP... SOON, I THINK I'M GOING TO HAVE TO SEE HIS FACE...
...AND I DON'T THINK I CAN BEAR IT, LEIA.
LUKE... HAVE YOU TOLD ANYONE ELSE ABOUT THIS?
HOW COULD I, WITHOUT EXPLAINING TO THEM WHY IT UPSETS ME SO... WHO DARTH VADER REALLY WAS... AND WHAT HE WAS TO THE PAIR OF US?
WE HAVEN'T EVEN TOLD ANYONE BESIDES HAN ABOUT OUR BEING BROTHER AND SISTER, BECAUSE WE DIDN'T WANT PEOPLE TO BEGIN ASKING QUESTIONS ABOUT OUR PARENTAGE.
AND THE TRUTH WOULD MAKE US SO UNPOPULAR. NO MAN WAS EVER MORE HATED THAN DARTH VADER, UNLESS IT WAS THE EMPEROR HIMSELF...
HE WAS THE DARK LORD... THE ONE WHO ALWAYS DID THE EMPEROR'S DIRTY WORK FOR HIM...
BUT LUKE, EVEN IF MOST PEOPLE CHOOSE TO FORGET IT, HE TURNED BACK TO GOOD AT THE END, AND HELPED TOPPLE THE EMPEROR... FOR YOU!
YOU DON'T NEED TO FEEL ASHAMED OF HIM.
I DON'T. BUT IN MY DREAMS, I'M AFRAID OF HIM.

COMMANDER SKYWALKER...I HAVE A QUESTION. MOST OF US DO...

GO AHEAD AND ASK IT, DRACOS.

WELL...YOU'VE BEEN TRAINING US TO THE EXCLUSION OF ALMOST ALL OF YOUR OTHER DUTIES... IN SPITE OF YOUR BEING SUCH A GREAT WAR HERO.

AND WE'VE BEEN LEARNING GREAT STUFF... MEDITATION, FIGHTING SKILLS, GENERAL CONDITIONING, MARKSMANSHIP... WE REALLY APPRECIATE IT...

BUT SOME OF US ARE WONDERIN'... WHEN ARE YOU GONNA TEACH US THE REAL STUFF?

WHEN ARE WE GONNA BE JEDI KNIGHTS, LIKE YOU, WITH MAGIC?

WHEN YOU GONNA TEACH US TO USE *THE FORCE?*

I'M NOT, DRACOS. I CAN'T.

I KNOW IT'S WHAT A LOT OF YOU WERE PROBABLY EXPECTING -- AND HOPING FOR-- WHEN THE ALLIANCE LEADERS ASSIGNED ME TO BE YOUR INSTRUCTOR...

MAYBE IT'S EVEN WHAT ADMIRAL ACKBAR HAD IN MIND...

BUT I CAN'T DO IT.

156

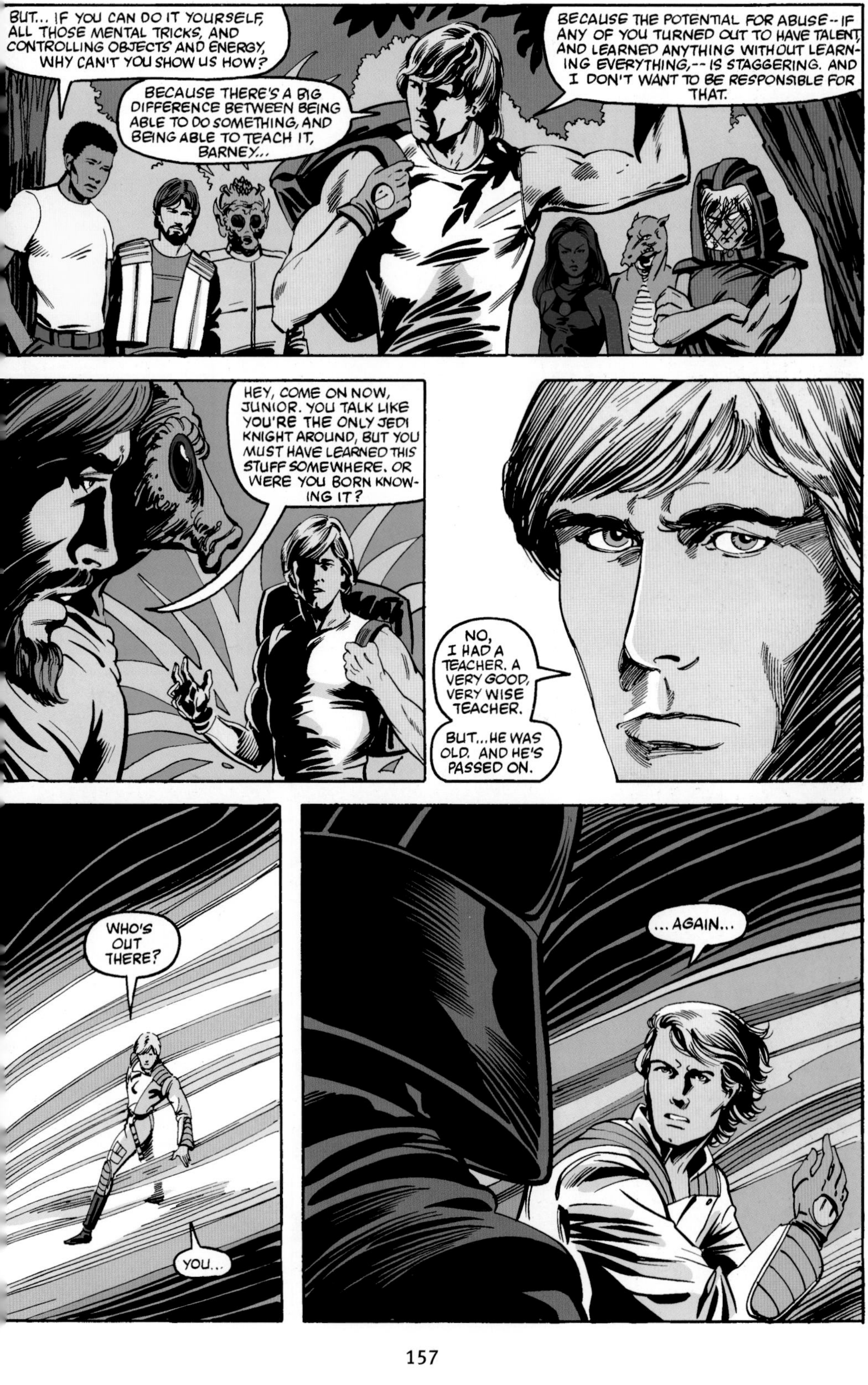

BUT... IF YOU CAN DO IT YOURSELF, ALL THOSE MENTAL TRICKS, AND CONTROLLING OBJECTS AND ENERGY, WHY CAN'T YOU SHOW US HOW?
BECAUSE THERE'S A BIG DIFFERENCE BETWEEN BEING ABLE TO DO SOMETHING, AND BEING ABLE TO TEACH IT, BARNEY...
BECAUSE THE POTENTIAL FOR ABUSE--IF ANY OF YOU TURNED OUT TO HAVE TALENT, AND LEARNED ANYTHING WITHOUT LEARNING EVERYTHING,--IS STAGGERING. AND I DON'T WANT TO BE RESPONSIBLE FOR THAT.
HEY, COME ON NOW, JUNIOR. YOU TALK LIKE YOU'RE THE ONLY JEDI KNIGHT AROUND, BUT YOU MUST HAVE LEARNED THIS STUFF SOMEWHERE. OR WERE YOU BORN KNOWING IT?
NO, I HAD A TEACHER. A VERY GOOD, VERY WISE TEACHER.
BUT...HE WAS OLD. AND HE'S PASSED ON.
WHO'S OUT THERE?
YOU...
...AGAIN...

WAIT!

PLEASE DON'T DO THAT! DON'T REMOVE YOUR MASK!

WITHOUT IT, YOU CAN'T EXIST...

FATHER!

FATHER...

...EVERY TIME I DREAM THAT DREAM, IT LASTS A LITTLE LONGER...

...COMES CLOSER TO...

...TO WHAT?

AROOO AROO

THAT'S THE GENERAL ALARM...

AROO AROOO

THE BASE IS UNDER ATTACK!

LUKE, THANK GOODNESS YOU'RE HERE!

WHAT'S WRONG?

THERE'S A SHIP COMIN' RIGHT AT US, LUKE...SMALL, VERY FAST, AND COMPLETELY UNIDENTIFIED!

HAVE YOU TRIED HAILING IT?

YES... AND GOTTEN NOTHING BUT STATIC IN RESPONSE.

WE ALSO SENT UP A WING OF SINGLE FIGHTER CRAFT TO INTERCEPT IT...

WHOEVER THAT PILOT IS, HE MANAGED TO EVADE ALL BUT ONE OF THEM.

VEET VEET

VERP!

159

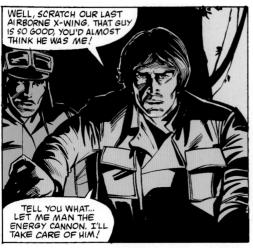

WELL, SCRATCH OUR LAST AIRBORNE X-WING. THAT GUY IS SO GOOD, YOU'D ALMOST THINK HE WAS ME!

TELL YOU WHAT... LET ME MAN THE ENERGY CANNON. I'LL TAKE CARE OF HIM!

VERY GOOD, GENERAL SOLO.

THERE'S SOMETHING... ABOUT THAT SHIP...

HAN-- WAIT!

HOLD YOUR FIRE! LET HIM LAND!

WHAT? BUT I'VE GOT HIM RIGHT IN... WHY?

BECAUSE I'VE GOT A FEELING ABOUT THIS, THAT'S WHY.

OKAY, BUT YOU'D BETTER BE RIGHT!

BE CAREFUL. HE MAY BE ARMED.

WHAT CAN ONE GUY DO TO ALL OF US?

RRRR

WHO'S IN CHARGE HERE?

HEY, HAVEN'T YOU GOT THAT BACKWARDS, PAL? YOU LANDED ON *OUR* BASE WITHOUT CLEARANCE. *WE'LL* ASK THE QUESTIONS.

IT'S HARD TO GET CLEARANCE WHEN ENEMIES HAVE SHOT OUT YOUR COMMUNICATIONS SYSTEMS...

IS THIS ENDOR? ARE THERE ANY ALLIANCE LEADERS HERE, OR ARE ALL OF YOU JUST WASTING MY TIME?

NO. THIS IS ENDOR. WHY ARE YOU HERE? AND WHAT ENEMIES MADE SUCH A WRECK OF YOUR SHIP?

THE EMPIRE... I KNOW THE ALLIANCE DEFEATED MOST OF THEM... BUT A LOT OF THEIR FORCES DIDN'T CAPITULATE. THEY REGROUPED ON MY HOMEWORLD--NALDAR!

THEY'RE SLAUGHTERING MY PEOPLE... I'M DENIN, THE--THE ONLY SURVIVING CHILD OF NALDAR'S KING.

YOU'VE GOT TO LET ME HAVE TROOPS, TAKE THEM BACK AND SAVE MY WORLD!

AND I NEED A TEACHER, TOO! EVERYONE'S HEARD THAT THERE ARE JEDI AMONG YOU.

I CAN DO MORE, FASTER, IF SOMEONE TEACHES ME TO USE THE FORCE... I KNOW I HAVE AN AFFINITY FOR IT!

YOU'RE VERY FULL OF DEMANDS, FOR SOMEONE WHO'S COME HERE AS A BEGGAR, IN A SHIP THAT'S FULL OF HOLES...

LIKE THAT STORY YOU'RE TELLING.

AND JUST WHO ARE YOU, TO SPEAK TO ME LIKE THAT?

OH, PARDON ME WHILE I MAKE INTRODUCTIONS.

YOUR ROYAL HIGHNESS PRINCE DENIN, OF THE CONQUERED PLANET NALDAR, PERMIT ME TO PRESENT HER ROYAL HIGHNESS, PRINCESS LEIA ORGANA, OF THE DESTROYED PLANET ALDERAAN.

161

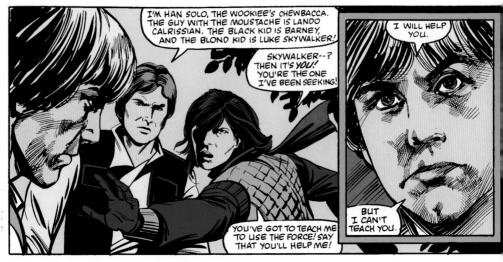

I'M HAN SOLO, THE WOOKIEE'S CHEWBACCA. THE GUY WITH THE MOUSTACHE IS LANDO CALRISSIAN, THE BLACK KID IS BARNEY, AND THE BLOND KID IS LUKE SKYWALKER!

SKYWALKER--? THEN IT'S *YOU!* YOU'RE THE ONE I'VE BEEN SEEKING!

YOU'VE GOT TO TEACH ME TO USE THE FORCE! SAY THAT YOU'LL HELP ME!

I WILL HELP YOU.

BUT I CAN'T TEACH YOU.

YOU'VE GOT TO! IT'S NALDAR'S ONLY CHANCE... OR TELL ME WHERE TO FIND SOMEONE WHO CAN! YOU WERE TRAINED BY YODA, WEREN'T YOU--THE LEGENDARY TEACHER?!

WHERE IS HE? YOU'VE GOT TO TELL ME HOW TO GET TO HIM!

MASTER YODA HAS GONE BEYOND WHERE ANYONE CAN REACH HIM, DENIN...

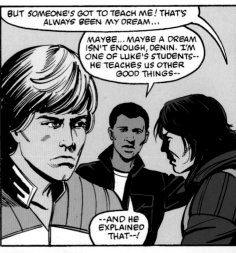

BUT SOMEONE'S GOT TO TEACH ME! THAT'S ALWAYS BEEN MY DREAM...

MAYBE... MAYBE A DREAM ISN'T ENOUGH, DENIN. I'M ONE OF LUKE'S STUDENTS-- HE TEACHES US OTHER GOOD THINGS--

--AND HE EXPLAINED THAT--!

I'M NOT GOING TO GIVE UP!

I'M WARNING YOU, I'M GOING TO STICK WITH YOU UNTIL YOU HAVE TO TEACH ME SOMETHING!

WONDERFUL. AND WERE YOU EXPECTING TO USE THAT SAME BRAND OF PERSUASIVE DIPLOMACY TO CONVINCE ADMIRAL ACKBAR TO SEND AID TO YOUR WORLD?

IF SO, MAYBE YOU'D BETTER LET US MAKE THE REQUEST.

WE'LL SEE TO IT THAT YOU GET A FAIRER HEARING THAN YOU JUST GAVE LUKE.

SO THE ADMIRAL DIDN'T GO FOR IT, HUNH?

IT WAS JUST WHAT WE WERE AFRAID OF...HE'S SO CONCERNED WITH THE TROUBLES THAT HAVE ERUPTED RECENTLY, CLOSE TO THE HEART OF THE ALLIANCE...

...HE JUST ISN'T WILLING TO RISK SENDING A LARGE MILITARY FORCE TO ONE OF THE OUTER PLANETS.

I TRIED TO CONVINCE HIM... BUT LATELY, HE DOESN'T LISTEN TO ME OR LUKE ANYMORE...TREATS US LIKE WE'RE RETAINERS, INSTEAD OF LEADERS...

YOU'RE NOT THE ONLY ONES, SWEETHEART. SOMETIMES, I THINK HE'S GIVING MORE RESPECT TO ARTOO AND THREEPIO THAN ME, LANDO AND CHEWIE GET.

÷SIGH÷

SWELL. DON'T EXPECT HIM TO LISTEN TO ME. I'M JUST A FIRST-YEAR CADET.

LEIA... WE WERE AFRAID HE MIGHT NOT LISTEN...

DID YOU PROPOSE OUR ALTERNATE PLAN TO HIM?

YES... AND HE AGREED TO THAT.

POOR DENIN... I FEEL SO SORRY FOR HIM... FOR EVERYONE ON HIS PLANET.

WHAT'S HAPPENING ON NALDAR SOUNDS A LOT LIKE WHAT HAPPENED TO MY HOMEWORLD-- BELDERONE-- RIGHT BEFORE I JOINED THE ALLIANCE.

THE TWO PLANETS ARE EVEN CLOSE TOGETHER...I HEAR A LOT OF BELDERONES TOOK REFUGE ON NALDAR... I WONDER IF ANY OF MY FRIENDS ARE THERE...

THE EMPIRE DID SUCH A GREAT JOB OF RUINING PEOPLE'S LIVES...

LIKE MY FRIEND, FLINT. HE AND I GREW UP WANTING TO BE JEDI, JUST LIKE DENIN...

AND THEN HIS MOTHER WAS KILLED IN THAT ATTACK, AND HE CHANGED...HE WANTED POWER-- ANY KIND OF POWER-- RIGHT AWAY. *

HE JOINED UP WITH THAT DARK LORD-- THAT DARTH VADER --

*SEE STAR WARS ANNUAL #3.

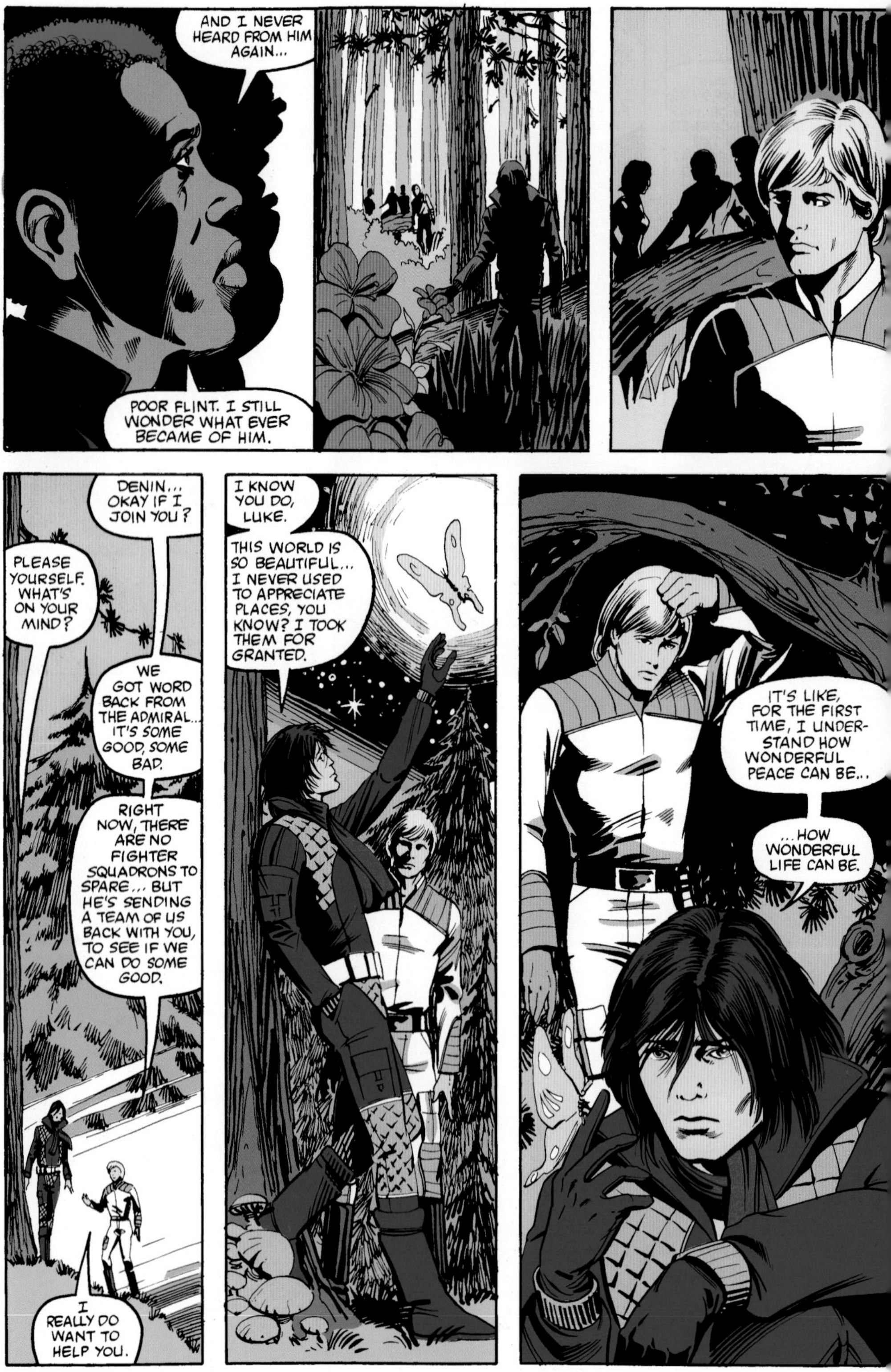

AND I NEVER HEARD FROM HIM AGAIN...
POOR FLINT. I STILL WONDER WHAT EVER BECAME OF HIM.
DENIN... OKAY IF I JOIN YOU?
PLEASE YOURSELF. WHAT'S ON YOUR MIND?
WE GOT WORD BACK FROM THE ADMIRAL... IT'S SOME GOOD, SOME BAD.
RIGHT NOW, THERE ARE NO FIGHTER SQUADRONS TO SPARE... BUT HE'S SENDING A TEAM OF US BACK WITH YOU, TO SEE IF WE CAN DO SOME GOOD.
I REALLY DO WANT TO HELP YOU.
I KNOW YOU DO, LUKE.
THIS WORLD IS SO BEAUTIFUL... I NEVER USED TO APPRECIATE PLACES, YOU KNOW? I TOOK THEM FOR GRANTED.
IT'S LIKE, FOR THE FIRST TIME, I UNDERSTAND HOW WONDERFUL PEACE CAN BE...
...HOW WONDERFUL LIFE CAN BE.

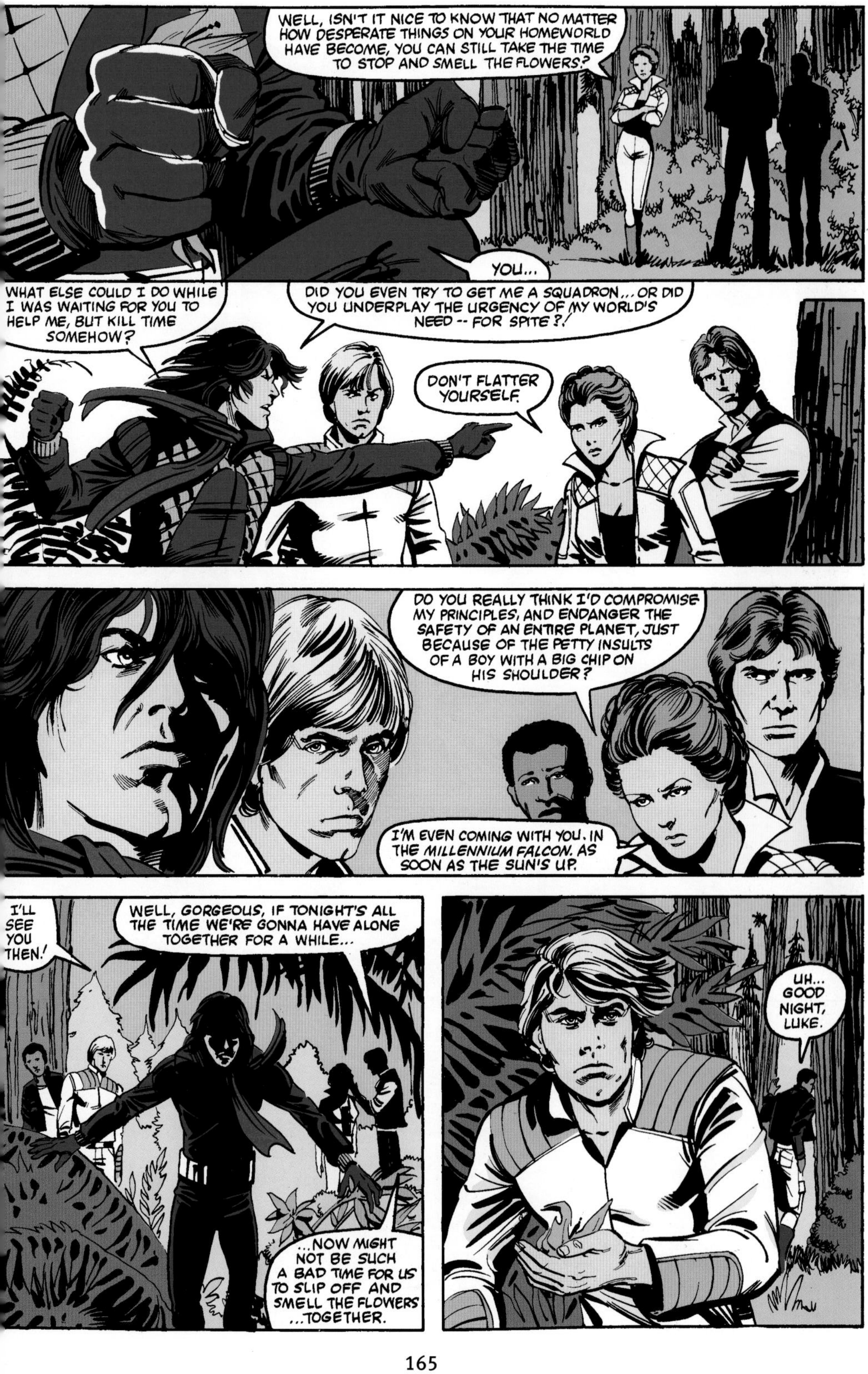
WELL, ISN'T IT NICE TO KNOW THAT NO MATTER HOW DESPERATE THINGS ON YOUR HOMEWORLD HAVE BECOME, YOU CAN STILL TAKE THE TIME TO STOP AND SMELL THE FLOWERS?
YOU...
WHAT ELSE COULD I DO WHILE I WAS WAITING FOR YOU TO HELP ME, BUT KILL TIME SOMEHOW?
DID YOU EVEN TRY TO GET ME A SQUADRON... OR DID YOU UNDERPLAY THE URGENCY OF MY WORLD'S NEED -- FOR SPITE?!
DON'T FLATTER YOURSELF.
DO YOU REALLY THINK I'D COMPROMISE MY PRINCIPLES, AND ENDANGER THE SAFETY OF AN ENTIRE PLANET, JUST BECAUSE OF THE PETTY INSULTS OF A BOY WITH A BIG CHIP ON HIS SHOULDER?
I'M EVEN COMING WITH YOU. IN THE *MILLENNIUM FALCON*. AS SOON AS THE SUN'S UP.
I'LL SEE YOU THEN!
WELL, *GORGEOUS*, IF TONIGHT'S ALL THE TIME WE'RE GONNA HAVE ALONE TOGETHER FOR A WHILE...
...NOW MIGHT NOT BE SUCH A BAD TIME FOR US TO SLIP OFF AND SMELL THE FLOWERS ...TOGETHER.
UH... GOOD NIGHT, LUKE.

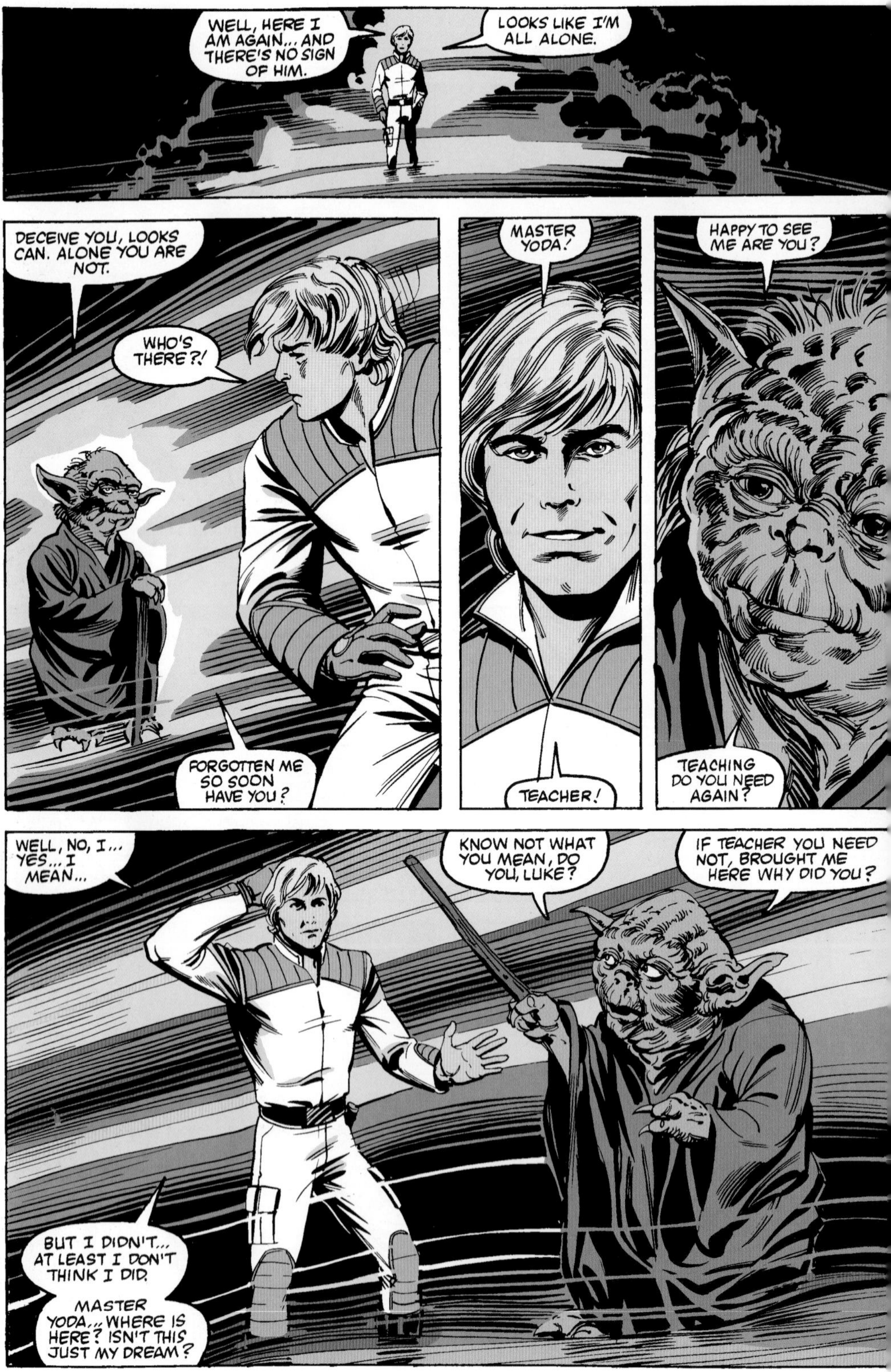
WELL, HERE I AM AGAIN... AND THERE'S NO SIGN OF HIM.
LOOKS LIKE I'M ALL ALONE.
DECEIVE YOU, LOOKS CAN. ALONE YOU ARE NOT.
WHO'S THERE?!
FORGOTTEN ME SO SOON HAVE YOU?
MASTER YODA!
TEACHER!
HAPPY TO SEE ME ARE YOU?
TEACHING DO YOU NEED AGAIN?
WELL, NO, I... YES... I MEAN...
KNOW NOT WHAT YOU MEAN, DO YOU, LUKE?
IF TEACHER YOU NEED NOT, BROUGHT ME HERE WHY DID YOU?
BUT I DIDN'T... AT LEAST I DON'T THINK I DID.
MASTER YODA... WHERE IS HERE? ISN'T THIS JUST MY DREAM?

IF DREAM THIS IS, WHAT DOES IT MATTER? REAL TO YOU IS IT, AND FRIGHTENING.

OF THE FORCE... OF BECOMING A JEDI DO MANY DREAM. POWERFUL THE FORCE IS, AND EVIL IT CAN BE, TOO.

JEDI ARE PART OF IT. PART OF IT AM I. AND PART OF IT, TOO, IS THE FORCE.

WHEN THE DARK SIDE THERE IS, A NIGHTMARE DOES THE DREAM BECOME.

WHAT YODA'S TRYING TO SAY, LUKE--

BEN KENOBI-- OBI-WAN!

--IS THAT IT DOESN'T MATTER WHETHER THIS PLACE IS REAL, AND IT, AND WE WITHIN IT, PHYSICALLY EXIST SOMEWHERE, OR IF IT IS JUST A PRODUCT OF YOUR OWN MIND.

YOU ARE HERE FOR A REASON, AND WE, YOUR TWO TEACHERS, ARE HERE TO HELP YOU LEARN WHAT THAT REASON IS.

YOU ARE HERE BECAUSE THIS IS THE PLACE WHERE THE PAST AND THE FUTURE COME TOGETHER. YOU HAVE BEEN GRANTED A CHANCE TO RIGHT A GREAT WRONG.

I SEE IT NOW.

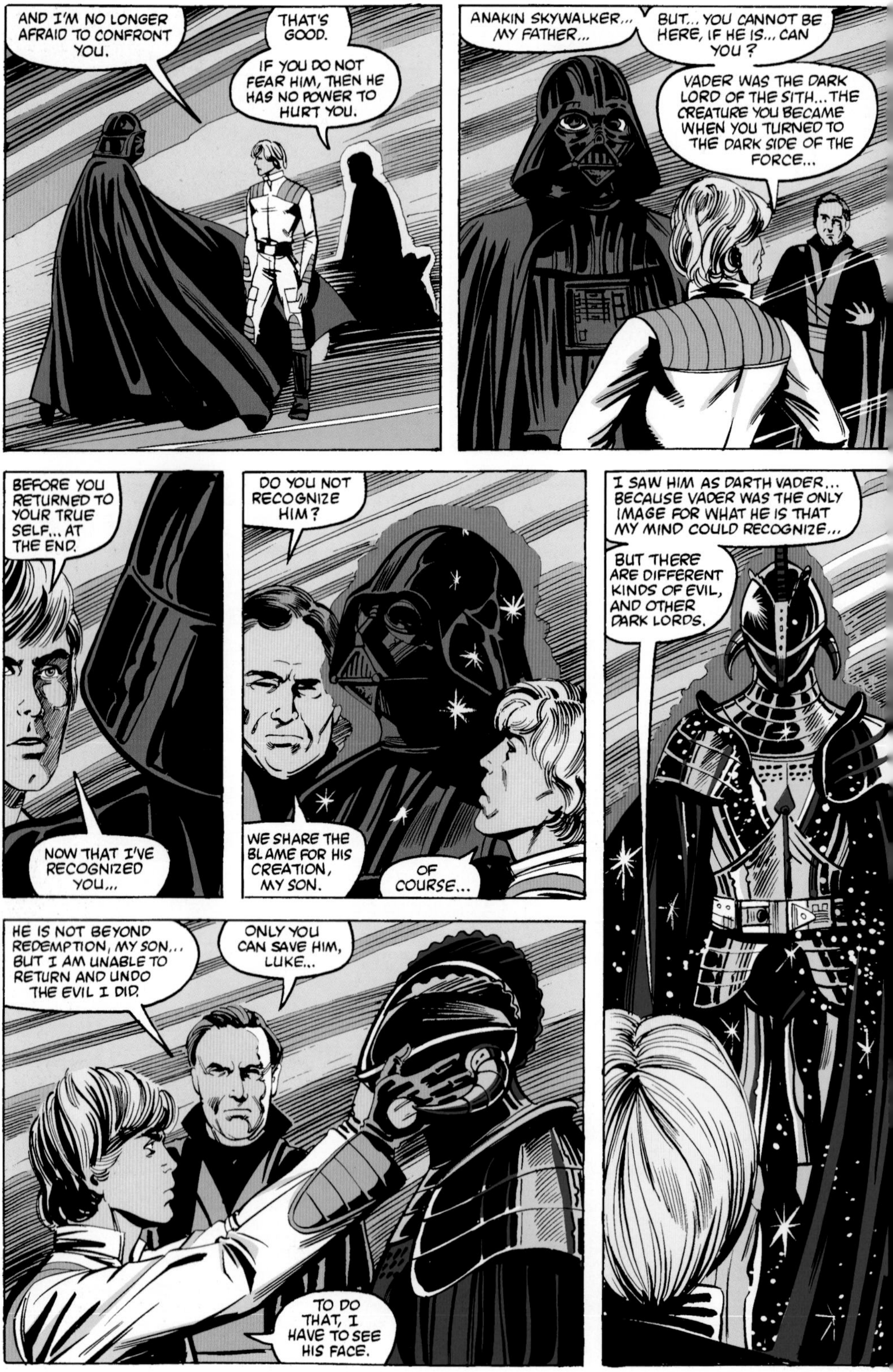

AND I'M NO LONGER AFRAID TO CONFRONT YOU.
THAT'S GOOD.
IF YOU DO NOT FEAR HIM, THEN HE HAS NO POWER TO HURT YOU.
ANAKIN SKYWALKER... MY FATHER...
BUT... YOU CANNOT BE HERE, IF HE IS... CAN YOU?
VADER WAS THE DARK LORD OF THE SITH... THE CREATURE YOU BECAME WHEN YOU TURNED TO THE DARK SIDE OF THE FORCE...
BEFORE YOU RETURNED TO YOUR TRUE SELF... AT THE END.
NOW THAT I'VE RECOGNIZED YOU...
DO YOU NOT RECOGNIZE HIM?
WE SHARE THE BLAME FOR HIS CREATION, MY SON.
OF COURSE...
I SAW HIM AS DARTH VADER... BECAUSE VADER WAS THE ONLY IMAGE FOR WHAT HE IS THAT MY MIND COULD RECOGNIZE...
BUT THERE ARE DIFFERENT KINDS OF EVIL, AND OTHER DARK LORDS.
HE IS NOT BEYOND REDEMPTION, MY SON... BUT I AM UNABLE TO RETURN AND UNDO THE EVIL I DID.
ONLY YOU CAN SAVE HIM, LUKE...
TO DO THAT, I HAVE TO SEE HIS FACE.

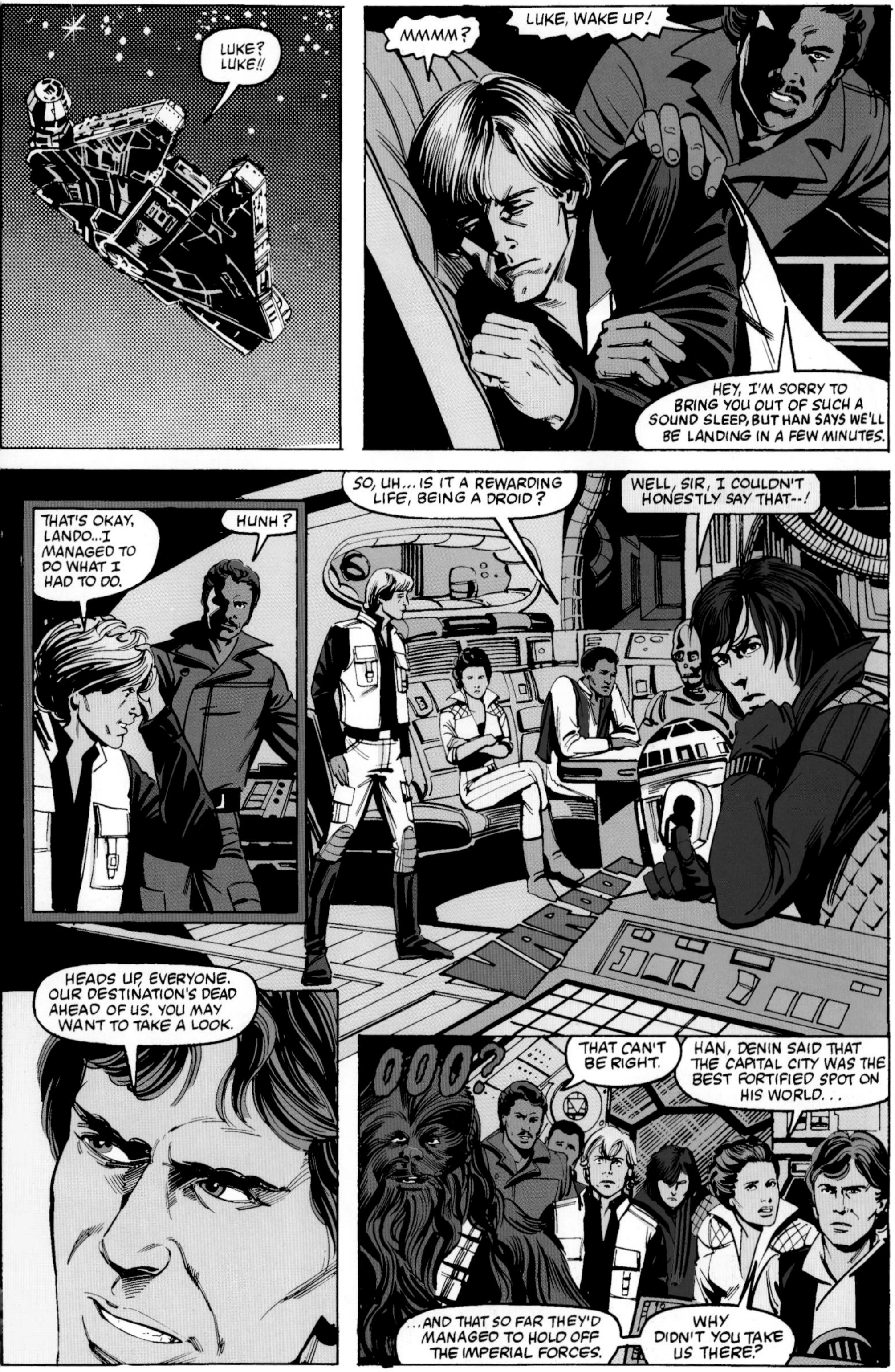
LUKE? LUKE!!
LUKE, WAKE UP!
MMMM?
HEY, I'M SORRY TO BRING YOU OUT OF SUCH A SOUND SLEEP, BUT HAN SAYS WE'LL BE LANDING IN A FEW MINUTES.
THAT'S OKAY, LANDO...I MANAGED TO DO WHAT I HAD TO DO.
HUNH?
SO, UH... IS IT A REWARDING LIFE, BEING A DROID?
WELL, SIR, I COULDN'T HONESTLY SAY THAT--!
HEADS UP, EVERYONE. OUR DESTINATION'S DEAD AHEAD OF US. YOU MAY WANT TO TAKE A LOOK.
OOO?
THAT CAN'T BE RIGHT.
HAN, DENIN SAID THAT THE CAPITAL CITY WAS THE BEST FORTIFIED SPOT ON HIS WORLD...
...AND THAT SO FAR THEY'D MANAGED TO HOLD OFF THE IMPERIAL FORCES.
WHY DIDN'T YOU TAKE US THERE?

I GOT BAD NEWS FOR YOU, LEIA. I DID TAKE US THERE.

YOU'RE LOOKING AT ALL THAT'S LEFT OF THE CAPITAL.

HAS THERE REALLY BEEN SO MUCH DESTRUCTION IN SUCH A SHORT TIME?

YES...

WURF

HE'S RIGHT, LUKE. YOU AND DENIN BETTER GET TO THE GUN TURRETS.

WE'VE STARTED SCANNING ENERGY SOURCES THAT INDICATE THERE'S A RECEPTION COMMITTEE WARMING UP FOR US!

DENIN WAS TELLING THE TRUTH-- THE EMPIRE'S HERE, ALL RIGHT.

LOOK AT THAT-- *TIE* FIGHTERS.

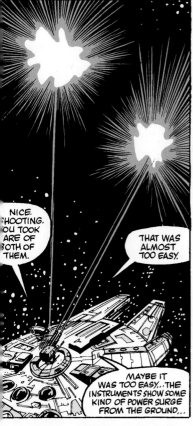

NICE SHOOTING. YOU TOOK CARE OF BOTH OF THEM.

THAT WAS ALMOST TOO EASY.

MAYBE IT WAS TOO EASY... THE INSTRUMENTS SHOW SOME KIND OF POWER SURGE FROM THE GROUND...

IT'S AN ENERGY CANNON!

HANG ON, EVERYONE... IT'S WINGED US!

WILL YOU BE ABLE TO LAND THE SHIP?

I DON'T KNOW!

WHRUMMP!

I'M AFRAID YOU'RE RIGHT, BARNEY... THE CRASH DAMAGED THOSE HALPITON CIRCUITS TOO BADLY FOR US TO REPAIR THEM.

THEY'LL HAVE TO BE REPLACED.

I THOUGHT YOU WERE SUPPOSED TO BE SUCH A GREAT PILOT.

WHEN SOMEONE SHOOTS AT YOU, YOU'RE SUPPOSED TO TAKE EVASIVE ACTION. I FLEW BETTER THAN THAT IN A CRIPPLED SHIP!

OH, YEAH? I SUPPOSE YOU'RE OVERLOOKING A LITTLE DETAIL LIKE LUKE, DOWN ON THE SURFACE YELLING "DON'T SHOOT!" AT THE CRUCIAL MOMENT.

NO ONE DID ME THAT LITTLE FAVOR!

GRONNK!

KNOCK IT OFF, CHEWIE. I ALREADY TOLD YOU, IT'S NOT MY FAULT.

BAOOP!

YOU'RE RIGHT, ARTOO. IT IS DESOLATE. IT MUST BE VERY SAD FOR THE PEOPLE WHO LIVED HERE.

I JUST HOPE WE CAN FIND SOME FUNCTIONAL HALPITON CIRCUITS.

NO SWEAT, LEIA. I'VE NEVER SEEN A MAJOR CITY WHOSE COMPUTERS WEREN'T RUN ON 'EM. JUST MAKE SURE THE IMPERIALS DON'T FIND YOU.

BARNEY, IF ANY IMPERIALS FIND THE SHIP WHILE YOU, HAN AND CHEWBACCA ARE MAKING REPAIRS, TALK THEM INTO TAKING OFF, EVEN IF WE'RE NOT BACK YET.

HEYY--!

DENIN!

BE CAREFUL. DON'T HURT YOURSELF.

LUKE, HE WAS WALKING AROUND ON HIS OWN FOR YEARS BEFORE HE HAD YOU TO LOOK AFTER HIM.

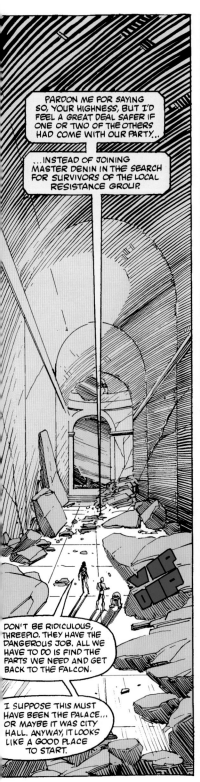

PARDON ME FOR SAYING SO, YOUR HIGHNESS, BUT I'D FEEL A GREAT DEAL SAFER IF ONE OR TWO OF THE OTHERS HAD COME WITH OUR PARTY...

...INSTEAD OF JOINING MASTER DENIN IN THE SEARCH FOR SURVIVORS OF THE LOCAL RESISTANCE GROUP.

DON'T BE RIDICULOUS, THREEPIO. THEY HAVE THE DANGEROUS JOB. ALL WE HAVE TO DO IS FIND THE PARTS WE NEED AND GET BACK TO THE FALCON.

I SUPPOSE THIS MUST HAVE BEEN THE PALACE... OR MAYBE IT WAS CITY HALL. ANYWAY, IT LOOKS LIKE A GOOD PLACE TO START.

I GIVE UP... IT'S SUCH A SHAMBLES, WE'LL NEVER FIND WHAT WE'RE AFTER, UNLESS WE KNOW WHERE TO LOOK. ARTOO, PLUG INTO THAT COMPUTER TERMINAL. SEE IF YOU CAN TURN UP A FLOOR PLAN OR SOMETHING.

PUH WHEET

YOUR HIGHNESS, THIS IS MOST INTERESTING!

ARTOO SAYS HE HAS INDEED LOCATED THE HALPITON CIRCUITRY WE NEED...

AND WHILE HE WAS PLUGGED INTO THE COMPUTER, HE ALSO FOUND RECORDS CONCERNING THE RECENT HISTORY OF THE RULERS HERE--MASTER DENIN'S FAMILY.

WHAT DOES IT SAY THAT HAS HIM SO,...

OH. OH, MY...

BUT IT'S SIMPLY NOT...

WE'VE GOT TO GET BACK TO THE FALCON... WARN HAN, AND LUKE!

YOU'RE RIGHT, ARTOO. IT IS A RELIEF TO BE BACK.

HAN? HAN! I HAVE TO TALK TO YOU!

TAKE IT EASY, LEIA. WHAT'S WRONG? YOU'RE ACTING LIKE YOU'VE SEEN A--!

ARE LUKE AND THE OTHERS BACK YET?

NO. SAY, WHAT'S THIS ALL A--?

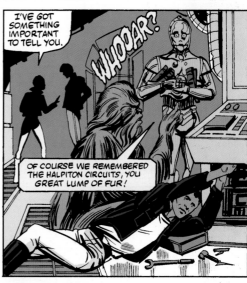

I'VE GOT SOMETHING IMPORTANT TO TELL YOU.

WHOOAR?

OF COURSE WE REMEMBERED THE HALPITON CIRCUITS, YOU GREAT LUMP OF FUR!

WE FOUND THEM IN THE LIBRARY. WHILE WE WERE LOOKING FOR THEM, ARTOO TURNED UP THE MOST RECENT HISTORICAL DATA...

THERE WAS A GREAT DEAL OF INFORMATION ON IT ABOUT THE ROYAL FAMILY.

..STORED HOLOGRAPHICALLY BEFORE THE WAR GOT SO BAD, PEOPLE STOPPED KEEPING RECORDS.

LIKE WHAT?

TWO YEARS AGO, WHILE DEFENDING THE REST OF HIS FAMILY DURING THE EMPIRE'S INITIAL ASSAULT HERE, PRINCE DENIN OF NALDAR WAS KILLED.

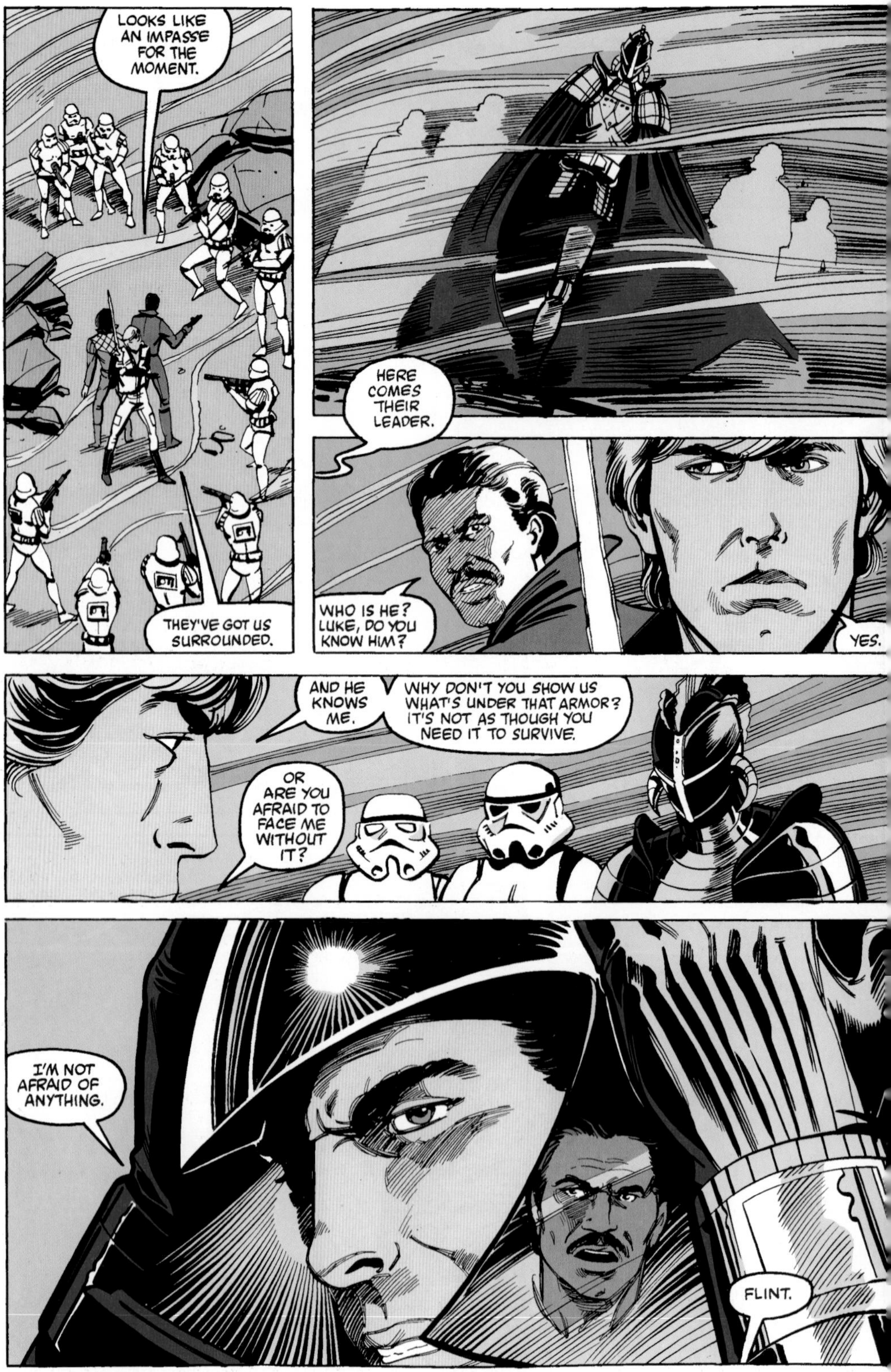

LOOKS LIKE AN IMPASSE FOR THE MOMENT.
THEY'VE GOT US SURROUNDED.
HERE COMES THEIR LEADER.
WHO IS HE? LUKE, DO YOU KNOW HIM?
YES.
AND HE KNOWS ME.
WHY DON'T YOU SHOW US WHAT'S UNDER THAT ARMOR? IT'S NOT AS THOUGH YOU NEED IT TO SURVIVE.
OR ARE YOU AFRAID TO FACE ME WITHOUT IT?
I'M NOT AFRAID OF ANYTHING.
FLINT.

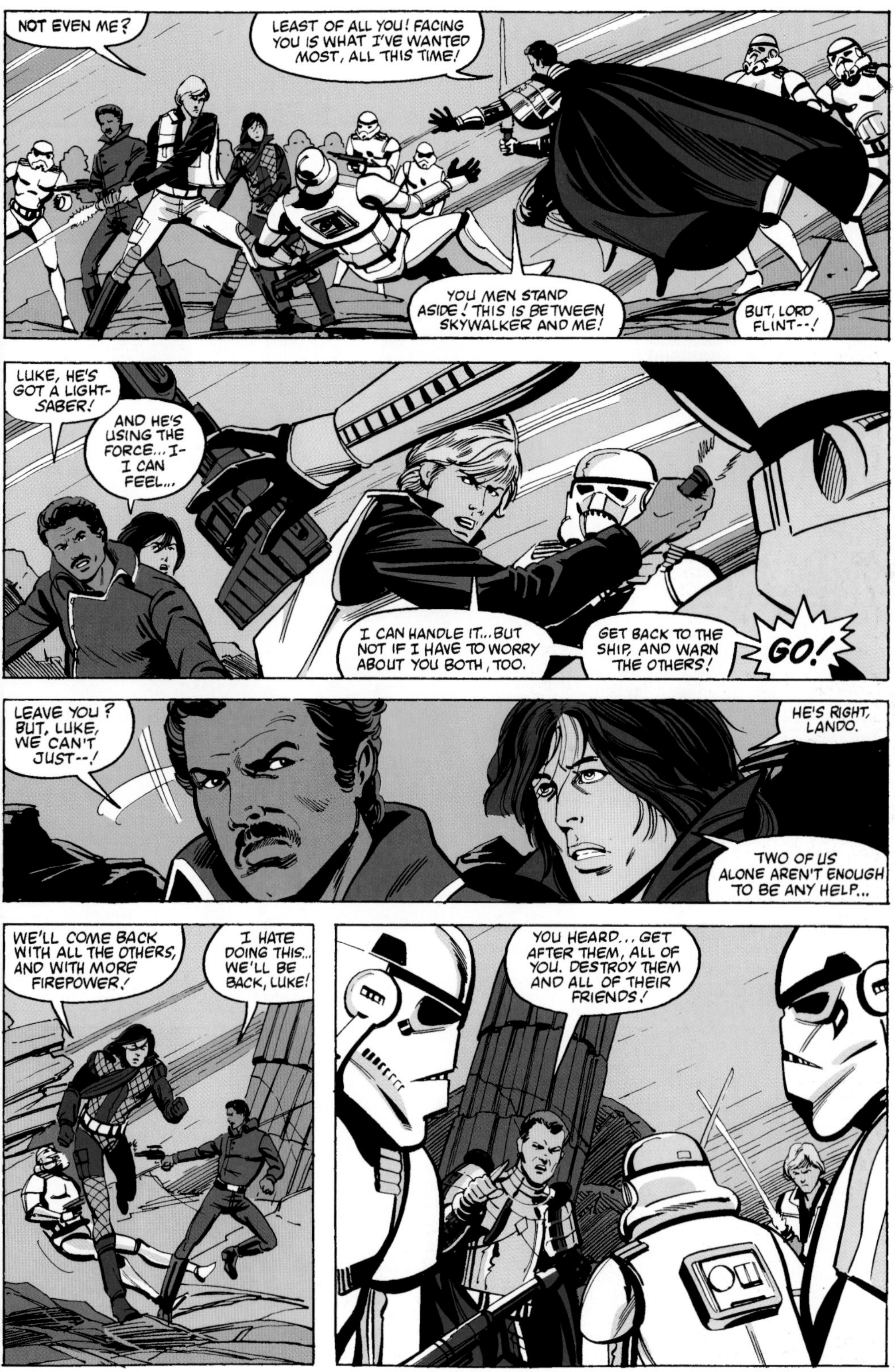
NOT EVEN ME?
LEAST OF ALL YOU! FACING YOU IS WHAT I'VE WANTED MOST, ALL THIS TIME!
YOU MEN STAND ASIDE! THIS IS BETWEEN SKYWALKER AND ME!
BUT, LORD FLINT--!
LUKE, HE'S GOT A LIGHT-SABER!
AND HE'S USING THE FORCE... I-I CAN FEEL...
I CAN HANDLE IT... BUT NOT IF I HAVE TO WORRY ABOUT YOU BOTH, TOO.
GET BACK TO THE SHIP, AND WARN THE OTHERS!
GO!
LEAVE YOU? BUT, LUKE, WE CAN'T JUST--!
HE'S RIGHT, LANDO.
TWO OF US ALONE AREN'T ENOUGH TO BE ANY HELP...
WE'LL COME BACK WITH ALL THE OTHERS, AND WITH MORE FIREPOWER!
I HATE DOING THIS... WE'LL BE BACK, LUKE!
YOU HEARD... GET AFTER THEM, ALL OF YOU. DESTROY THEM AND ALL OF THEIR FRIENDS!

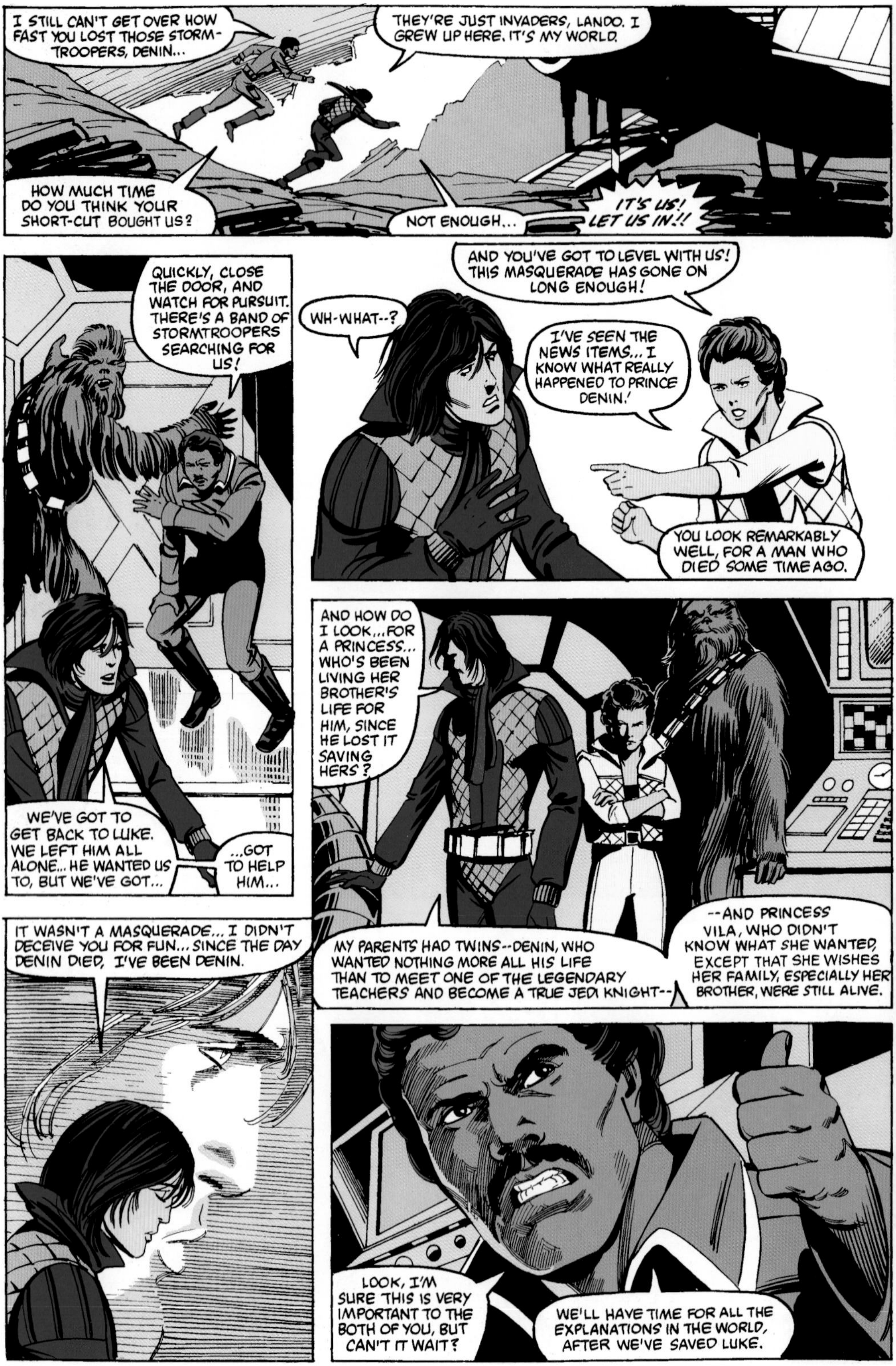
I STILL CAN'T GET OVER HOW FAST YOU LOST THOSE STORM-TROOPERS, DENIN...
THEY'RE JUST INVADERS, LANDO. I GREW UP HERE. IT'S MY WORLD.
HOW MUCH TIME DO YOU THINK YOUR SHORT-CUT BOUGHT US?
NOT ENOUGH...
IT'S US! LET US IN!!
QUICKLY, CLOSE THE DOOR, AND WATCH FOR PURSUIT. THERE'S A BAND OF STORMTROOPERS SEARCHING FOR US!
WE'VE GOT TO GET BACK TO LUKE. WE LEFT HIM ALL ALONE... HE WANTED US TO, BUT WE'VE GOT...
...GOT TO HELP HIM...
AND YOU'VE GOT TO LEVEL WITH US! THIS MASQUERADE HAS GONE ON LONG ENOUGH!
WH-WHAT--?
I'VE SEEN THE NEWS ITEMS... I KNOW WHAT REALLY HAPPENED TO PRINCE DENIN.'
YOU LOOK REMARKABLY WELL, FOR A MAN WHO DIED SOME TIME AGO.
AND HOW DO I LOOK... FOR A PRINCESS... WHO'S BEEN LIVING HER BROTHER'S LIFE FOR HIM, SINCE HE LOST IT SAVING HERS?
IT WASN'T A MASQUERADE... I DIDN'T DECEIVE YOU FOR FUN... SINCE THE DAY DENIN DIED, I'VE BEEN DENIN.
MY PARENTS HAD TWINS--DENIN, WHO WANTED NOTHING MORE ALL HIS LIFE THAN TO MEET ONE OF THE LEGENDARY TEACHERS AND BECOME A TRUE JEDI KNIGHT--
--AND PRINCESS VILA, WHO DIDN'T KNOW WHAT SHE WANTED, EXCEPT THAT SHE WISHES HER FAMILY, ESPECIALLY HER BROTHER, WERE STILL ALIVE.
LOOK, I'M SURE THIS IS VERY IMPORTANT TO THE BOTH OF YOU, BUT CAN'T IT WAIT?
WE'LL HAVE TIME FOR ALL THE EXPLANATIONS IN THE WORLD, AFTER WE'VE SAVED LUKE.

ALL I EVER WANTED, MY WHOLE LIFE, WAS TO BECOME A JEDI KNIGHT, AND YOU... YOU--!

I WENT TO YOU, I WANTED TRAINING. YOU DIDN'T JUST SPURN ME, I WAS BENEATH YOUR NOTICE.

AND YOU TOOK THAT AWAY FROM ME, TOO!

AND FINALLY, I FOUND A MASTER. HE WAS TEACHING ME... HE CARED ABOUT ME!

FLINT, YOU HAVE IT ALL WRONG. DARTH VADER WAS A CREATURE OF THE DARK SIDE OF THE FORCE, BUT HE TURNED FROM THE DARK SIDE AT THE END.

HE WAS NEVER REALLY MY ENEMY.

HE WAS MY FATHER.

DO YOU THINK HE NEVER MENTIONED YOU TO ME...? HE TOLD ME THAT HIS GREATEST CHALLENGE WAS TO COME ON THE DAY THAT HE FACED YOU! HE TOLD ME ALL THAT.

AND WHEN MY MASTER DIED, AND THE EMPEROR WITH HIM, EVERYONE KNEW WHO'D KILLED HIM --

--HIS GREAT ENEMY, YOU... LUKE SKYWALKER!

LIAR! LIAR! I'LL KILL YOU!!!

FLINT... I KNOW I WRONGED YOU...

I WAS WRONG TO IGNORE YOU AND YOUR NEED TO BE TAUGHT, WHEN I MET YOU...

BUT EVEN IF I HAD ACKNOWLEDGED IT, MY ANSWER WOULD HAVE BEEN THE SAME...

I CAN'T TEACH YOU, BECAUSE I'M NOT GOOD ENOUGH...

AND THE FORCE IN THE WRONG HANDS IS A TERRIBLE WEAPON... LOOK AT HOW YOU'RE WIELDING IT NOW!

181

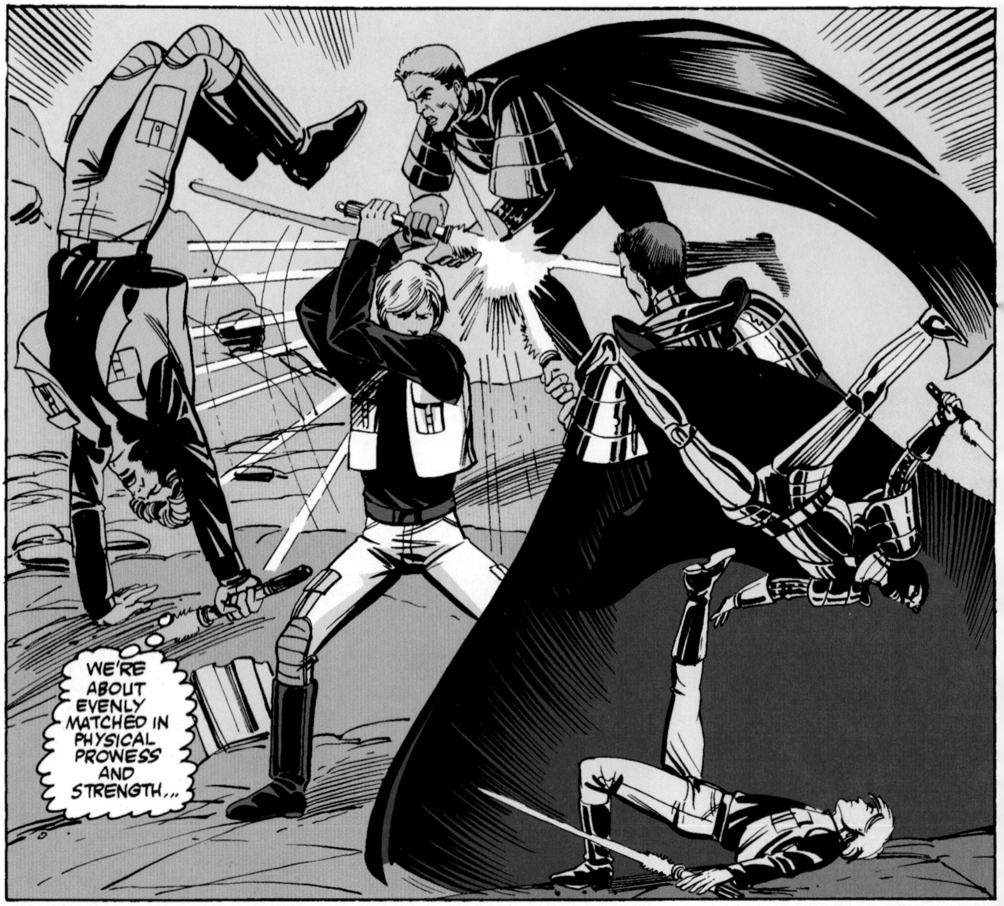
WE'RE ABOUT EVENLY MATCHED IN PHYSICAL PROWESS AND STRENGTH...

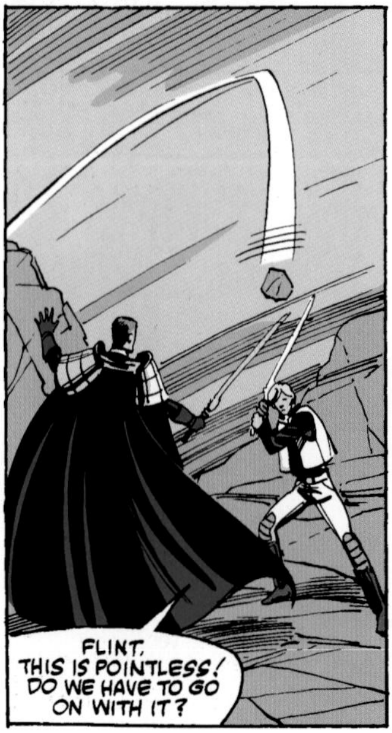
FLINT, THIS IS POINTLESS! DO WE HAVE TO GO ON WITH IT?

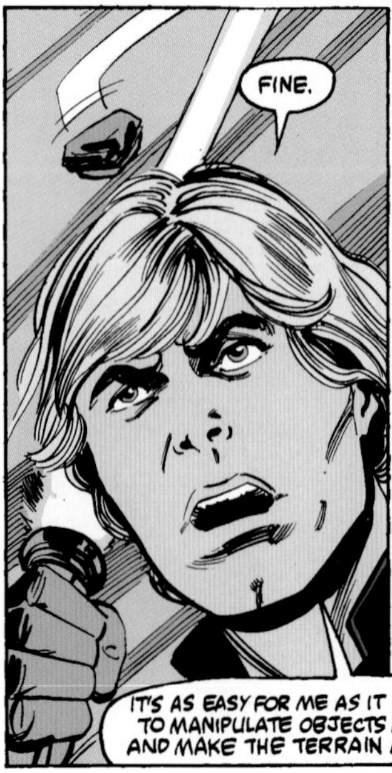
FINE.
IT'S AS EASY FOR ME AS IT IS FOR YOU TO MANIPULATE OBJECTS AROUND US AND MAKE THE TERRAIN A WEAPON...

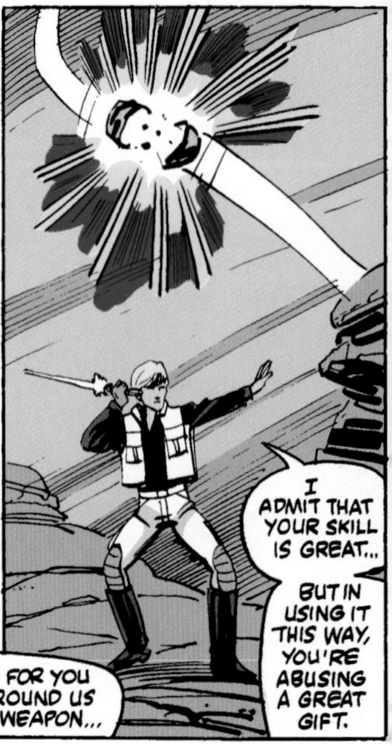
I ADMIT THAT YOUR SKILL IS GREAT...
BUT IN USING IT THIS WAY, YOU'RE ABUSING A GREAT GIFT.

LOOKS LIKE I GOT BACK HERE JUST IN TIME... THE STRANGER MUST BE BETTER THAN WE DREAMED TO BE GIVING LORD FLINT SUCH A HARD TIME OF IT...

MY FATHER ABANDONED THE DARK PATH BEFORE HE DIED. HE WANTED YOU TO, AS WELL.

THAT'S WHY I'M HERE.

LIAR!

THEY'RE SO OCCUPIED WITH ONE ANOTHER... IF I CAN JUST GET A CLEAR SHOT...

VREEP

≡AUGH≡

THAT WASN'T NECESSARY!

VREEP

LUKE! LUKE, ARE YOU ALL RIGHT?!

ARE WE HERE IN TIME?

NO, YOU AREN'T!

IT WAS TOO LATE FOR ALL OF YOU, BEFORE YOU EVEN LEFT YOUR SHIP!

THIS ENTIRE WORLD'S POWER SOURCES ARE ALL UNITED, POWERING ONE ENORMOUS ENERGY CANNON... MY TROOPS AWAIT MY SIGNAL TO TURN IT ON THIS SECTOR OF THE CITY...AND THEY'LL GET THAT SIGNAL ONCE WE'RE SAFELY OUT OF RANGE.

I'M ONLY SORRY YOU WON'T ALL BE AROUND TO SEE WHAT HAPPENS THEN, AS WE MOVE TO ALL THE OTHER ALLIANCE WORLDS IN THIS SECTOR!

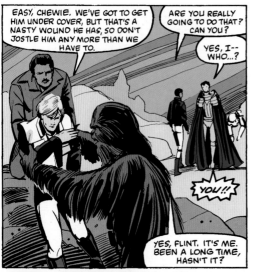

EASY, CHEWIE. WE'VE GOT TO GET HIM UNDER COVER, BUT THAT'S A NASTY WOUND HE HAS, SO DON'T JOSTLE HIM ANY MORE THAN WE HAVE TO.

ARE YOU REALLY GOING TO DO THAT? CAN YOU?

YES, I-- WHO...?

YOU!!

YES, FLINT. IT'S ME. BEEN A LONG TIME, HASN'T IT?

OR DOES IT JUST SEEM THAT WAY?

WHAT DO YOU --?

HEY, YOU WANT TO KILL US ALL? GO AHEAD... BUT LISTEN TO YOURSELF.

YOU'RE TALKING ABOUT KILLING US, RAZING THE CITY, AND THEN MOVING ON TO DESTROY OTHER ALLIANCE WORLDS?

DO YOU HEAR THAT? THE ALLIANCE? THE PEOPLE YOU WANTED TO JOIN...THE PEOPLE YOU WANTED TO BE LIKE.

THE PEOPLE WHO TRIED TO SAVE BELDERONE.

TRIED? SURE THEY TRIED! AND THEY FAILED! MY MOTHER WAS KILLED DURING THE ALLIANCE'S LAST STAND ON BELDERONE!

WAS IT AN ALLIANCE BOMB THAT KILLED HER? NO, IT WAS THE EMPIRE.

AND YOU COULDN'T SAVE HER...SO NOW YOU'RE GONNA PUNISH THE WHOLE UNIVERSE, AND KILL A WHOLE LOT OF MOTHERS AND SONS AND INNOCENT PEOPLE?

THAT MAKES A LOT OF SENSE! FRANKLY, I DON'T THINK YOU CAN. BUT I'VE BEEN WRONG BEFORE.

SO, PROVE IT TO ME, FOR OLD TIMES'S SAKE, SEE THE FACE OF ONE OF YOUR VICTIMS. KILL ME FIRST, FLINT.

I...CAN'T!

DENIN!!!

VILA!

OH, DENIN...

NOT DENIN, LUKE... PRINCESS VILA...

DENIN... WE NEVER REALLY KNEW DENIN. HE WAS A MAN WHO DIED WITH HIS DREAM UNFULFILLED...

AND HIS TWIN SISTER'S BEEN TRYING TO FULFILL IT FOR HIM.

I... SEE...

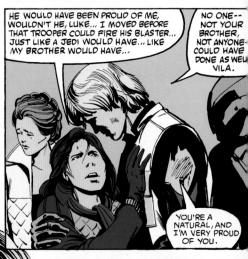

HE WOULD HAVE BEEN PROUD OF ME, WOULDN'T HE, LUKE... I MOVED BEFORE THAT TROOPER COULD FIRE HIS BLASTER... JUST LIKE A JEDI WOULD HAVE... LIKE MY BROTHER WOULD HAVE...

NO ONE-- NOT YOUR BROTHER, NOT ANYONE-- COULD HAVE DONE AS WELL VILA.

YOU'RE A NATURAL, AND I'M VERY PROUD OF YOU.

YOU'RE GOING TO MAKE A FINE JEDI KNIGHT.

I'M GLAD, LUKE... IT'S WHAT I WANT.

I KNOW THAT NOW... I DON'T JUST WANT IT FOR DENIN.

I WANT TO BE A JEDI KNIGHT, MORE THAN ANYTHING...

WHAT'S GOING ON THERE? LORD FLINT, DO YOU COPY? WHAT ARE OUR ORDERS?

SHALL WE PROCEED WITH THE BOMBARD- MENT?

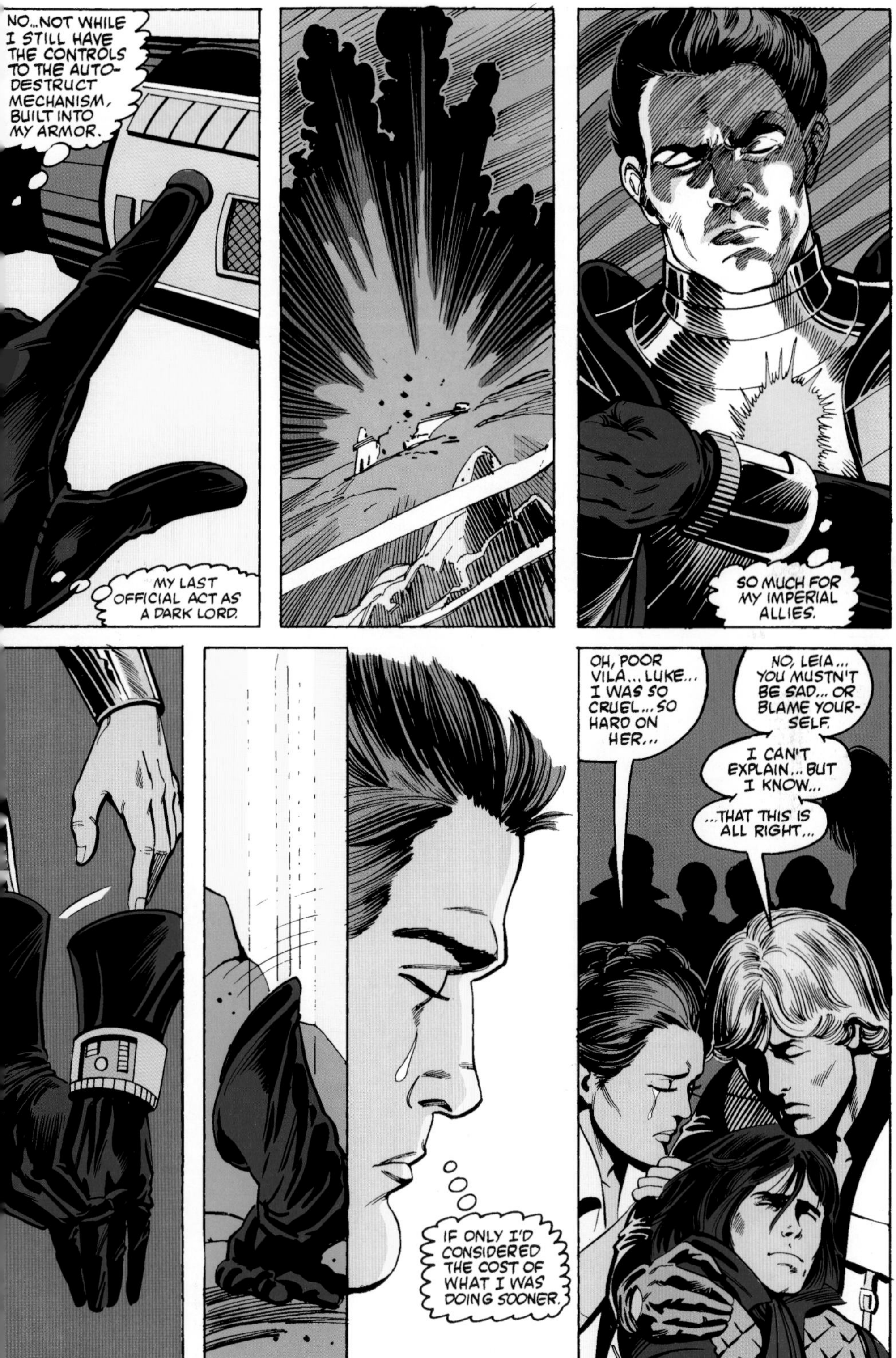
NO...NOT WHILE I STILL HAVE THE CONTROLS TO THE AUTO-DESTRUCT MECHANISM, BUILT INTO MY ARMOR.
MY LAST OFFICIAL ACT AS A DARK LORD.
SO MUCH FOR MY IMPERIAL ALLIES.
IF ONLY I'D CONSIDERED THE COST OF WHAT I WAS DOING SOONER.
OH, POOR VILA... LUKE... I WAS SO CRUEL... SO HARD ON HER...
NO, LEIA... YOU MUSTN'T BE SAD... OR BLAME YOUR-SELF.
I CAN'T EXPLAIN... BUT I KNOW...
...THAT THIS IS ALL RIGHT...

IT'S ALL RIGHT.

I WONDER WHERE I AM...

VILA VILA!

VILA!

WHO'S THERE?

ME, OF COURSE!

DENIN! OH, I'VE MISSED YOU!

AND I'VE MISSED YOU, TOO.

I'VE BEEN WAITING FOR YOU.

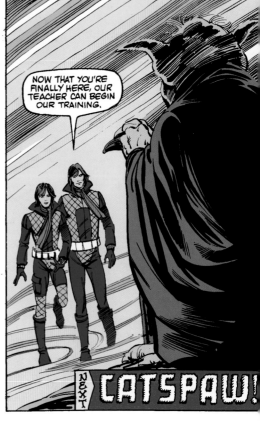

NOW THAT YOU'RE FINALLY HERE, OUR TEACHER CAN BEGIN OUR TRAINING.

NEXT CATSPAW!

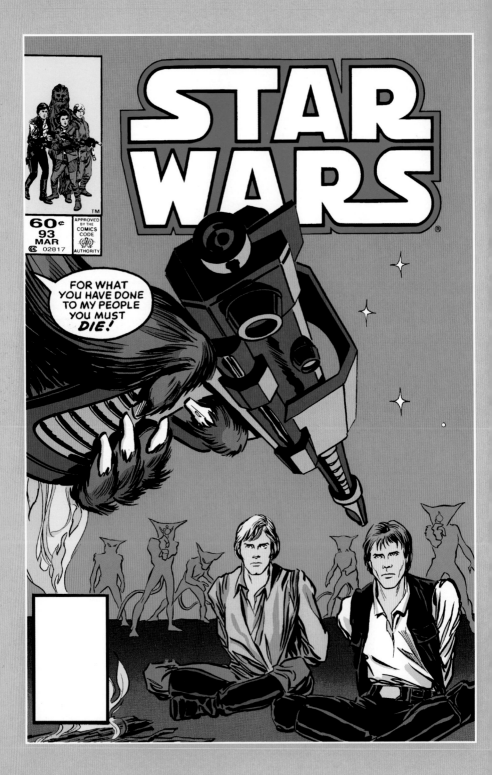

Y'KNOW, LUKE, LEIA, I GOTTA TELL YOU, WHEN THE BRASS ASKED US TO COME HERE ON THAT DIPLOMATIC MISSION, I NEVER EXPECTED TO GET THE KIND OF HOSPITALITY WE'VE HAD SINCE WE LANDED...

I KNOW WHAT YOU MEAN, HAN...IT'S A SIDE-EFFECT OF THE REBELLION'S SUCCESS THAT I NEVER LOOKED FOR...

BUT, IT DOES MAKE A KIND OF SENSE, LUKE, AFTER ALL, THE BACKWATER PLANETS LIKE THIS ONE WERE USUALLY THE HARD-EST HIT BY THE EMPIRE'S TYRANNY, WHILE IT EXISTED...

AND THE PEOPLE HERE WERE SO FAR FROM THE CENTER OF THE ACTION. YOU KNOW HOW STORIES CAN GROW AND BE DISTORTED...

YEAH...BUT IT STILL MADE ME FEEL WEIRD... HEARING THEM TALK LIKE WE WERE SOME KIND OF IMMORTAL HEROES... WRITING SONGS ABOUT US...

EVEN SAYING OUR NAMES LIKE THEY WERE HOLY INCAN- TATIONS...

PRINCESS LEIA ORGANA, WHO FORSOOK HER PLACE IN THE IMPERIAL SENATE TO AVENGE HER DESTROYED WORLD.

LUKE SKYWALKER, LAST OF THE JEDI KNIGHTS, WHO FELLED THE EM- PEROR AND THE MOST DREADED OF HIS MINIONS...

AND ME, OF COURSE.

OF COURSE. WHERE WOULD ANY OF US BE WITHOUT THE BRAVERY OF CAPTAIN HAN SOLO?

LOST, PROBABLY, BUT EVEN I COULDN'T DO ALL THE THINGS THESE PEOPLE BELIEVE I'VE DONE.

MAYBE NOT...BUT I'LL BET YOU'LL TAKE CREDIT FOR THEM ANYWAY...

HAN! LEIA! LOOK UP THERE!

AN X-WING SHIP... IN REAL TROUBLE.

BUT LOOK WHAT'S PURSUING IT.

THREE Y-WINGS!

BUT... BOTH THOSE DESIGNATIONS ARE FOR SHIPS WE USED IN THE REBELLION.

WHO'S OUR ALLY, AND WHO'S OUR ENEMY...?

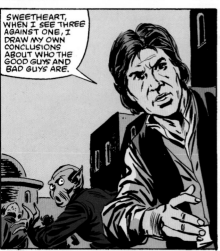

SWEETHEART, WHEN I SEE THREE AGAINST ONE, I DRAW MY OWN CONCLUSIONS ABOUT WHO THE GOOD GUYS AND BAD GUYS ARE.

THIS WOULDN'T BE THE FIRST TIME THAT ONE SIDE OR THE OTHER USED HARDWARE THEY CAPTURED.

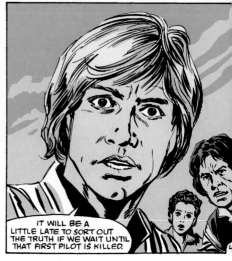

IT WILL BE A LITTLE LATE TO SORT OUT THE TRUTH IF WE WAIT UNTIL THAT FIRST PILOT IS KILLED.

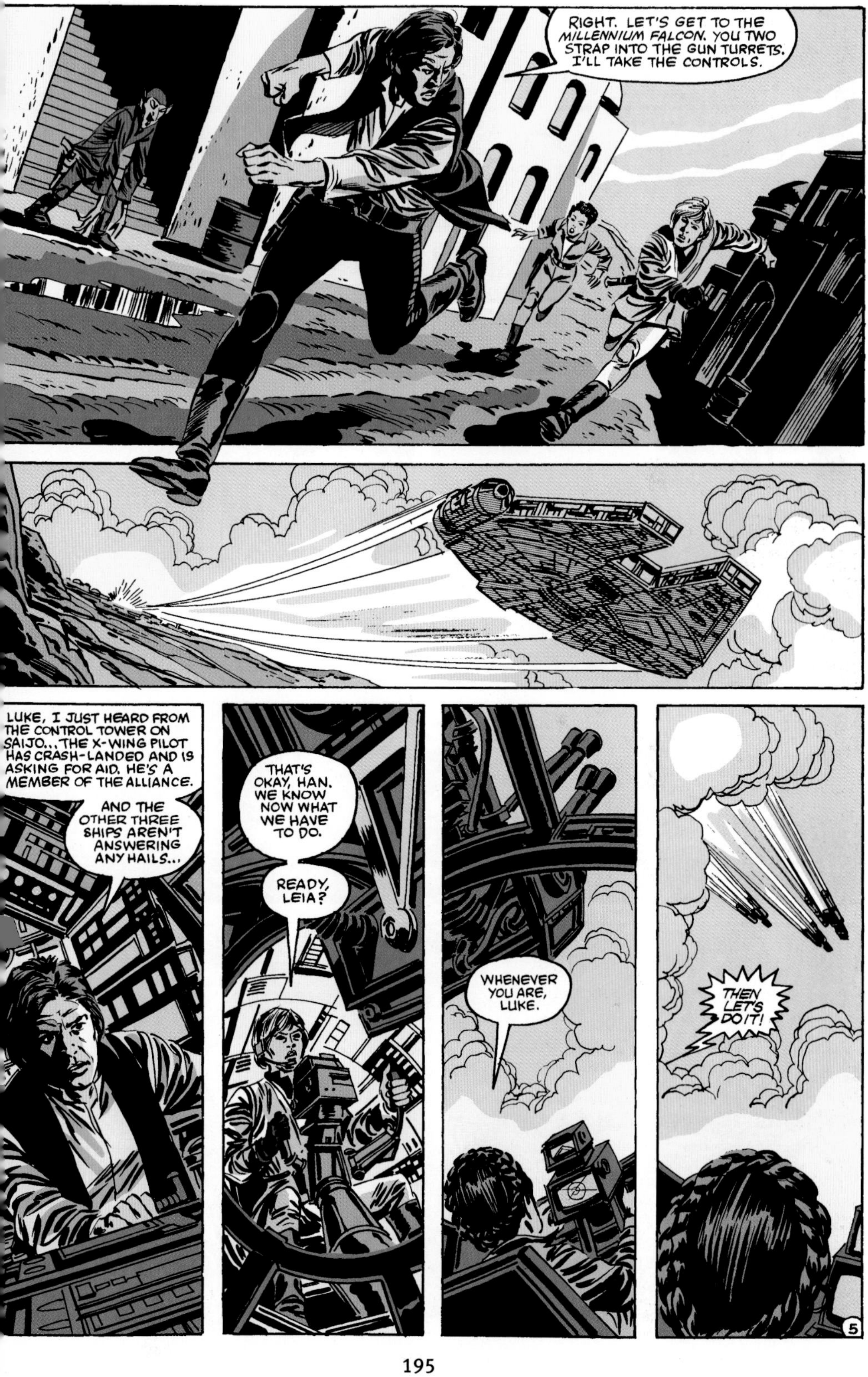
RIGHT. LET'S GET TO THE MILLENNIUM FALCON. YOU TWO STRAP INTO THE GUN TURRETS. I'LL TAKE THE CONTROLS.
LUKE, I JUST HEARD FROM THE CONTROL TOWER ON SAIJO... THE X-WING PILOT HAS CRASH-LANDED AND IS ASKING FOR AID. HE'S A MEMBER OF THE ALLIANCE.
AND THE OTHER THREE SHIPS AREN'T ANSWERING ANY HAILS...
THAT'S OKAY, HAN. WE KNOW NOW WHAT WE HAVE TO DO.
READY, LEIA?
WHENEVER YOU ARE, LUKE.
THEN LET'S DO IT!
5

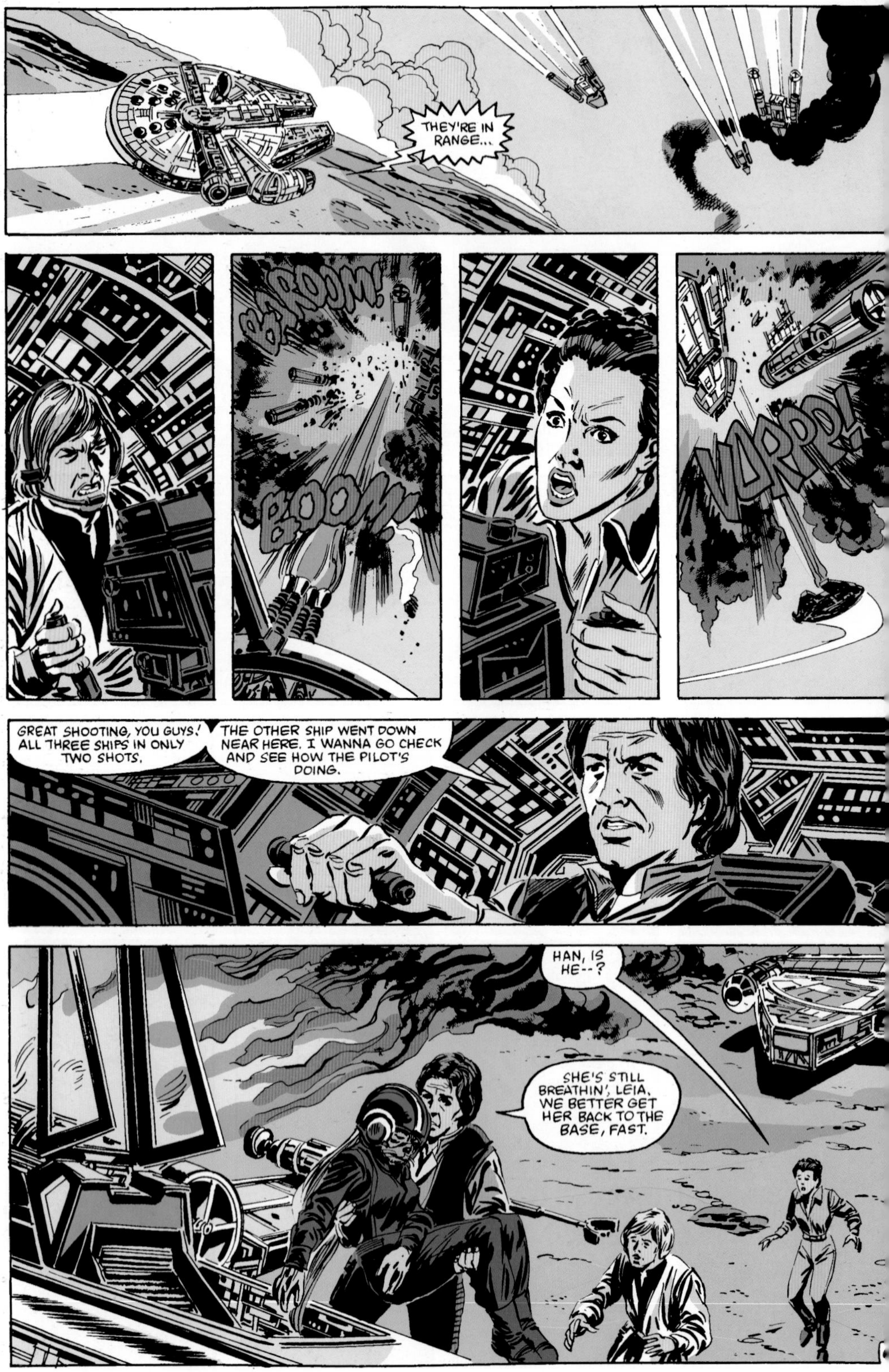
THEY'RE IN RANGE...
BA-BOOM!
BOOM!
VARRP!
GREAT SHOOTING, YOU GUYS! ALL THREE SHIPS IN ONLY TWO SHOTS.
THE OTHER SHIP WENT DOWN NEAR HERE. I WANNA GO CHECK AND SEE HOW THE PILOT'S DOING.
HAN, IS HE--?
SHE'S STILL BREATHIN', LEIA. WE BETTER GET HER BACK TO THE BASE, FAST.

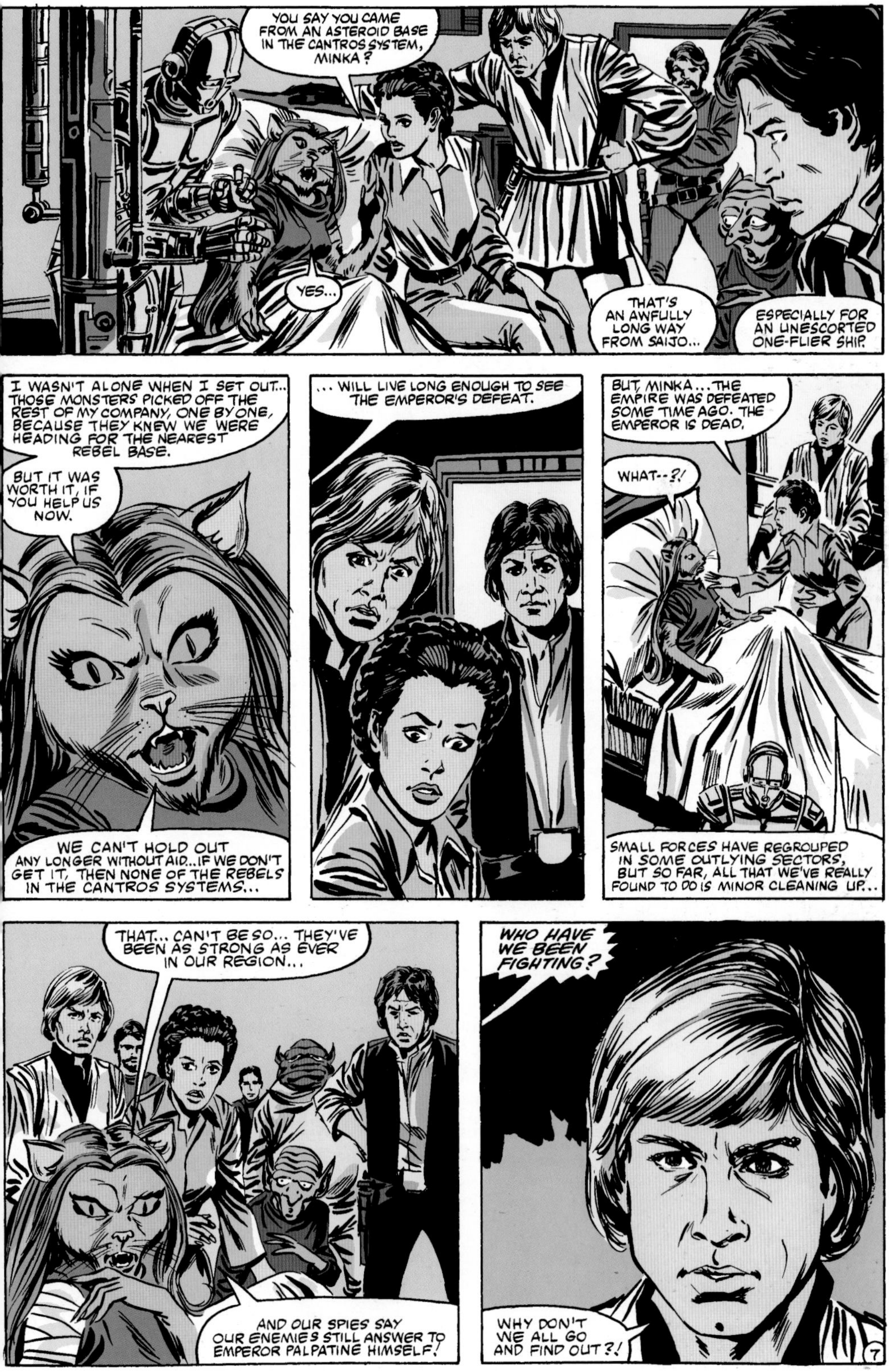
YOU SAY YOU CAME FROM AN ASTEROID BASE IN THE CANTROS SYSTEM, MINKA?
YES...
THAT'S AN AWFULLY LONG WAY FROM SAIJO...
ESPECIALLY FOR AN UNESCORTED ONE-FLIER SHIP.
I WASN'T ALONE WHEN I SET OUT... THOSE MONSTERS PICKED OFF THE REST OF MY COMPANY, ONE BY ONE, BECAUSE THEY KNEW WE WERE HEADING FOR THE NEAREST REBEL BASE.
BUT IT WAS WORTH IT, IF YOU HELP US NOW.
WE CAN'T HOLD OUT ANY LONGER WITHOUT AID...IF WE DON'T GET IT, THEN NONE OF THE REBELS IN THE CANTROS SYSTEMS...
... WILL LIVE LONG ENOUGH TO SEE THE EMPEROR'S DEFEAT.
BUT, MINKA... THE EMPIRE WAS DEFEATED SOME TIME AGO. THE EMPEROR IS DEAD.
WHAT--?!
SMALL FORCES HAVE REGROUPED IN SOME OUTLYING SECTORS, BUT SO FAR, ALL THAT WE'VE REALLY FOUND TO DO IS MINOR CLEANING UP...
THAT... CAN'T BE SO... THEY'VE BEEN AS STRONG AS EVER IN OUR REGION...
AND OUR SPIES SAY OUR ENEMIES STILL ANSWER TO EMPEROR PALPATINE HIMSELF!
WHO HAVE WE BEEN FIGHTING?
WHY DON'T WE ALL GO AND FIND OUT?!
7

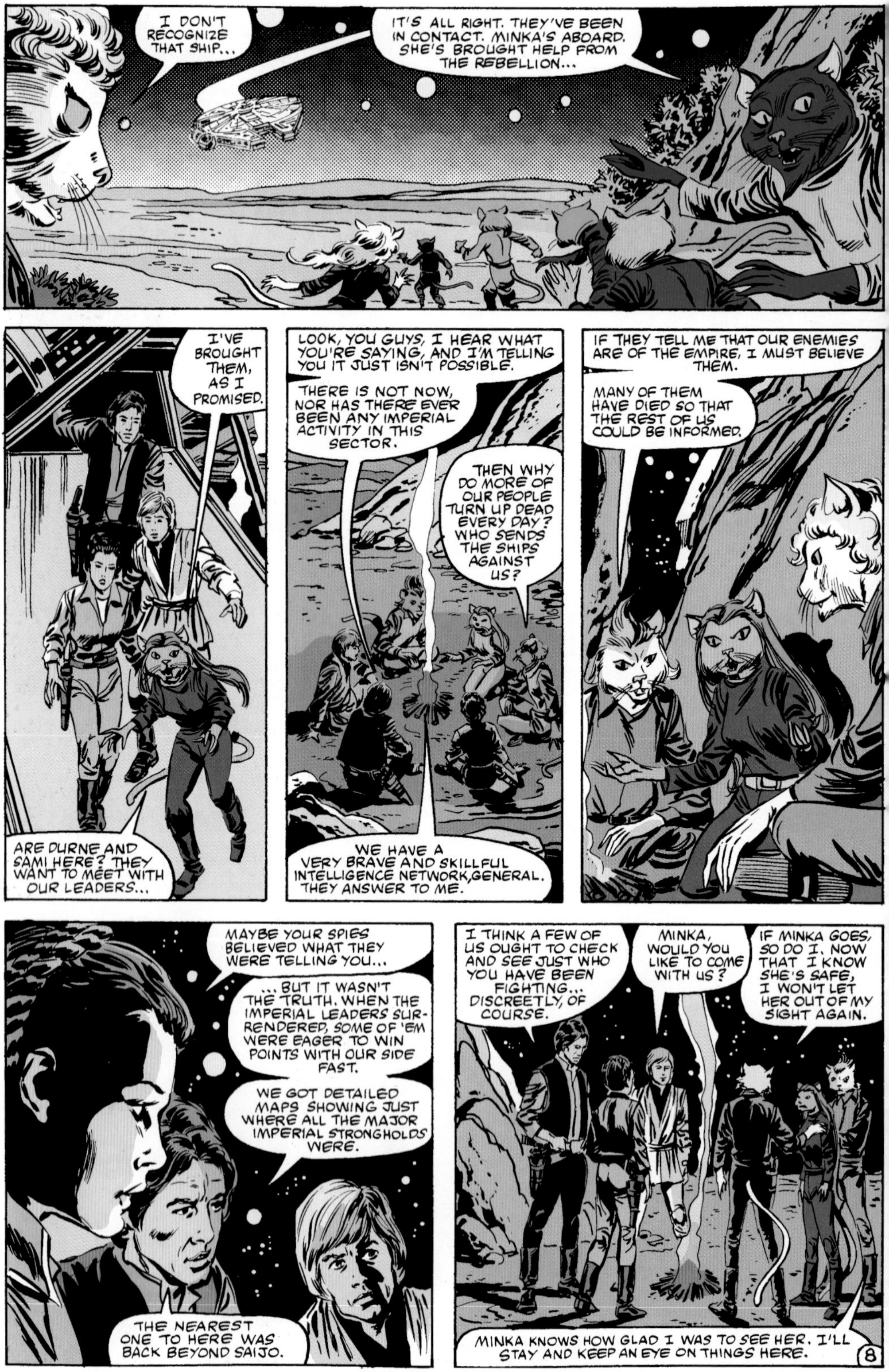
I DON'T RECOGNIZE THAT SHIP...
IT'S ALL RIGHT. THEY'VE BEEN IN CONTACT. MINKA'S ABOARD. SHE'S BROUGHT HELP FROM THE REBELLION...
I'VE BROUGHT THEM, AS I PROMISED.
ARE DURNE AND SAMI HERE? THEY WANT TO MEET WITH OUR LEADERS...
LOOK, YOU GUYS, I HEAR WHAT YOU'RE SAYING, AND I'M TELLING YOU IT JUST ISN'T POSSIBLE.
THERE IS NOT NOW, NOR HAS THERE EVER BEEN ANY IMPERIAL ACTIVITY IN THIS SECTOR.
THEN WHY DO MORE OF OUR PEOPLE TURN UP DEAD EVERY DAY? WHO SENDS THE SHIPS AGAINST US?
WE HAVE A VERY BRAVE AND SKILLFUL INTELLIGENCE NETWORK, GENERAL. THEY ANSWER TO ME.
IF THEY TELL ME THAT OUR ENEMIES ARE OF THE EMPIRE, I MUST BELIEVE THEM.
MANY OF THEM HAVE DIED SO THAT THE REST OF US COULD BE INFORMED.
MAYBE YOUR SPIES BELIEVED WHAT THEY WERE TELLING YOU...
...BUT IT WASN'T THE TRUTH. WHEN THE IMPERIAL LEADERS SURRENDERED, SOME OF 'EM WERE EAGER TO WIN POINTS WITH OUR SIDE FAST.
WE GOT DETAILED MAPS SHOWING JUST WHERE ALL THE MAJOR IMPERIAL STRONGHOLDS WERE.
THE NEAREST ONE TO HERE WAS BACK BEYOND SAIJO.
I THINK A FEW OF US OUGHT TO CHECK AND SEE JUST WHO YOU HAVE BEEN FIGHTING... DISCREETLY, OF COURSE.
MINKA, WOULD YOU LIKE TO COME WITH US?
IF MINKA GOES, SO DO I. NOW THAT I KNOW SHE'S SAFE, I WON'T LET HER OUT OF MY SIGHT AGAIN.
MINKA KNOWS HOW GLAD I WAS TO SEE HER. I'LL STAY AND KEEP AN EYE ON THINGS HERE.
8

THE THREE OF YOU SEEM TO KNOW SO MUCH 'BOUT HOW THE FINAL BATTLES WITH THE EMPIRE WENT...

WERE YOU STATIONED VERY CLOSE TO THE HEART OF THE ACTION?

YOU COULD SAY WE *WERE* THE ACTION, SAMI.

AS A MATTER OF FACT, THE THREE OF US ARE THE ONES WHO--!

WE'RE THE ONES WHO THE LEADERS SEND OUT...

...WHEN IMPORTANT MEMBERS OF THE REBELLION ARE ELSEWHERE.

YOU KNOW SOME OF THE 'MPORTANT MEMBERS OF THE REBELLION? THE HEROES? WE'VE HEARD TALES OF HOW THE EARLIER, DECISIVE BATTLES WERE WON, AND--!

SAMI, EVERYONE WHO'S WILLING TO RISK HIS LIFE FOR FREEDOM IS A HERO, NO MATTER WHO GETS TALKED ABOUT!

LUKE, WE'RE COMING IN ON THAT SO-CALLED IMPERIAL BASE NOW, AND IT LOOKS LIKE THEY WERE EXPECTING US...

BLAST!! WHOEVER THEY ARE, THEY AREN'T FRIENDLY!

HAN, PRETEND THAT THEY'VE HIT US...MAKE IT LOOK LIKE WE'RE CRASH-LANDING.

THAT SHOULDN'T BE TOO HARD, KID.

THEY *HAVE* HIT US!

9

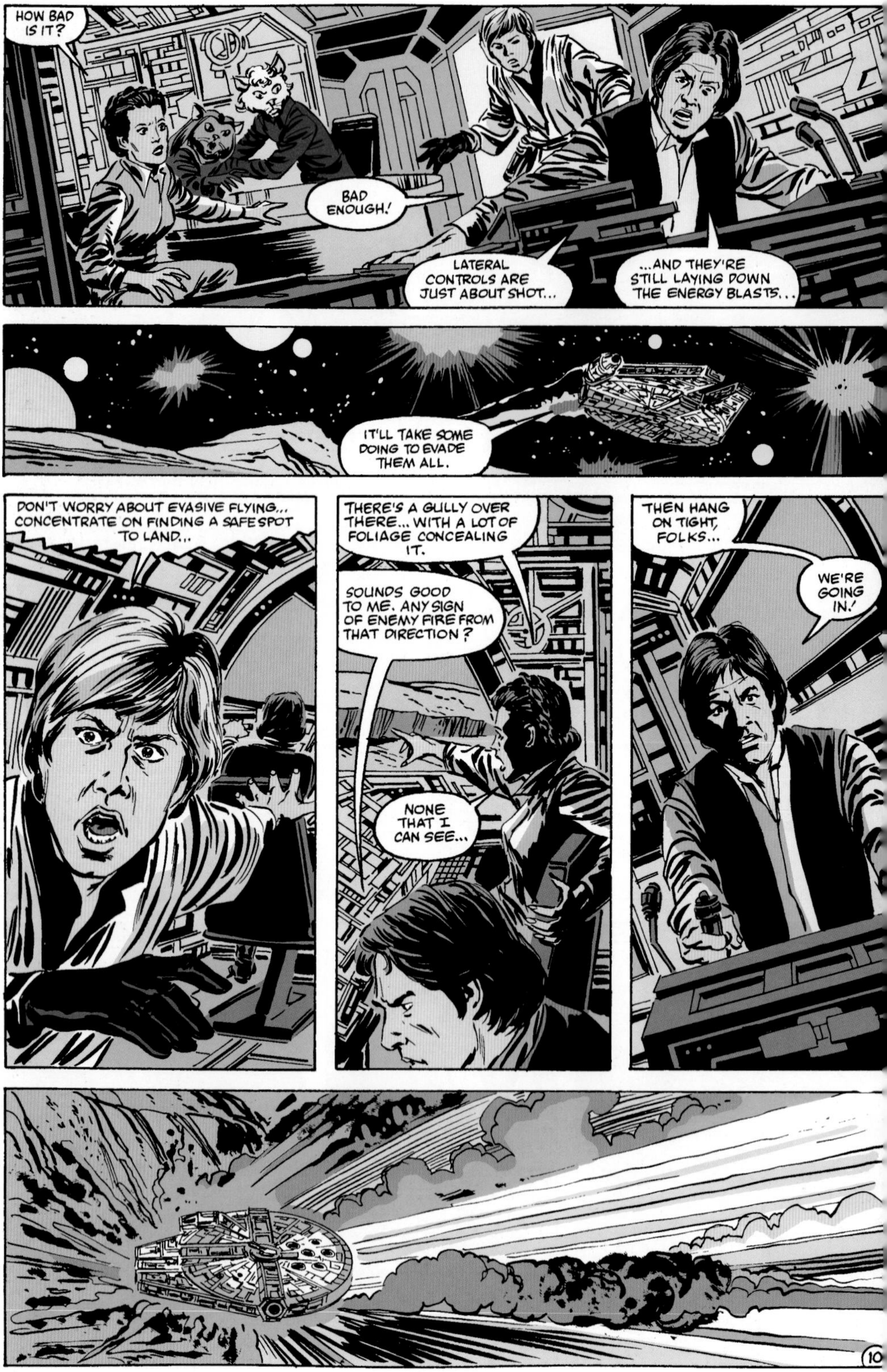
HOW BAD IS IT?
BAD ENOUGH!
LATERAL CONTROLS ARE JUST ABOUT SHOT...
...AND THEY'RE STILL LAYING DOWN THE ENERGY BLASTS...
IT'LL TAKE SOME DOING TO EVADE THEM ALL.
DON'T WORRY ABOUT EVASIVE FLYING... CONCENTRATE ON FINDING A SAFE SPOT TO LAND...
THERE'S A GULLY OVER THERE... WITH A LOT OF FOLIAGE CONCEALING IT.
SOUNDS GOOD TO ME. ANY SIGN OF ENEMY FIRE FROM THAT DIRECTION?
NONE THAT I CAN SEE...
THEN HANG ON TIGHT, FOLKS...
WE'RE GOING IN!
10

IS EVERYONE IN ONE PIECE?

WITH ME AT THE CONTROLS-- NATURALLY.

HAN-- CAN YOU REPAIR THE DAMAGE?

NO SWEAT. BUT FIRST I WANT TO LOOK AROUND AND MAKE SURE THERE'S NO ONE COMING TO PUT MORE HOLES IN THE FALCON...

...OR IN ANY OF US.

THERE'S NO SIGN OF ANYONE, SO FAR...

THAT DOESN'T SURPRISE ME, LUKE... LOOK.

IT'S MUCH TOO STEEP TO CLIMB OUT OF THE GULLEY.

SWELL.

I'M SURE LUKE CAN TAKE CARE OF THAT.

I THINK I CAN...

IF YOU'LL JUST RELAX...

...AND LET ME USE THE FORCE.

11

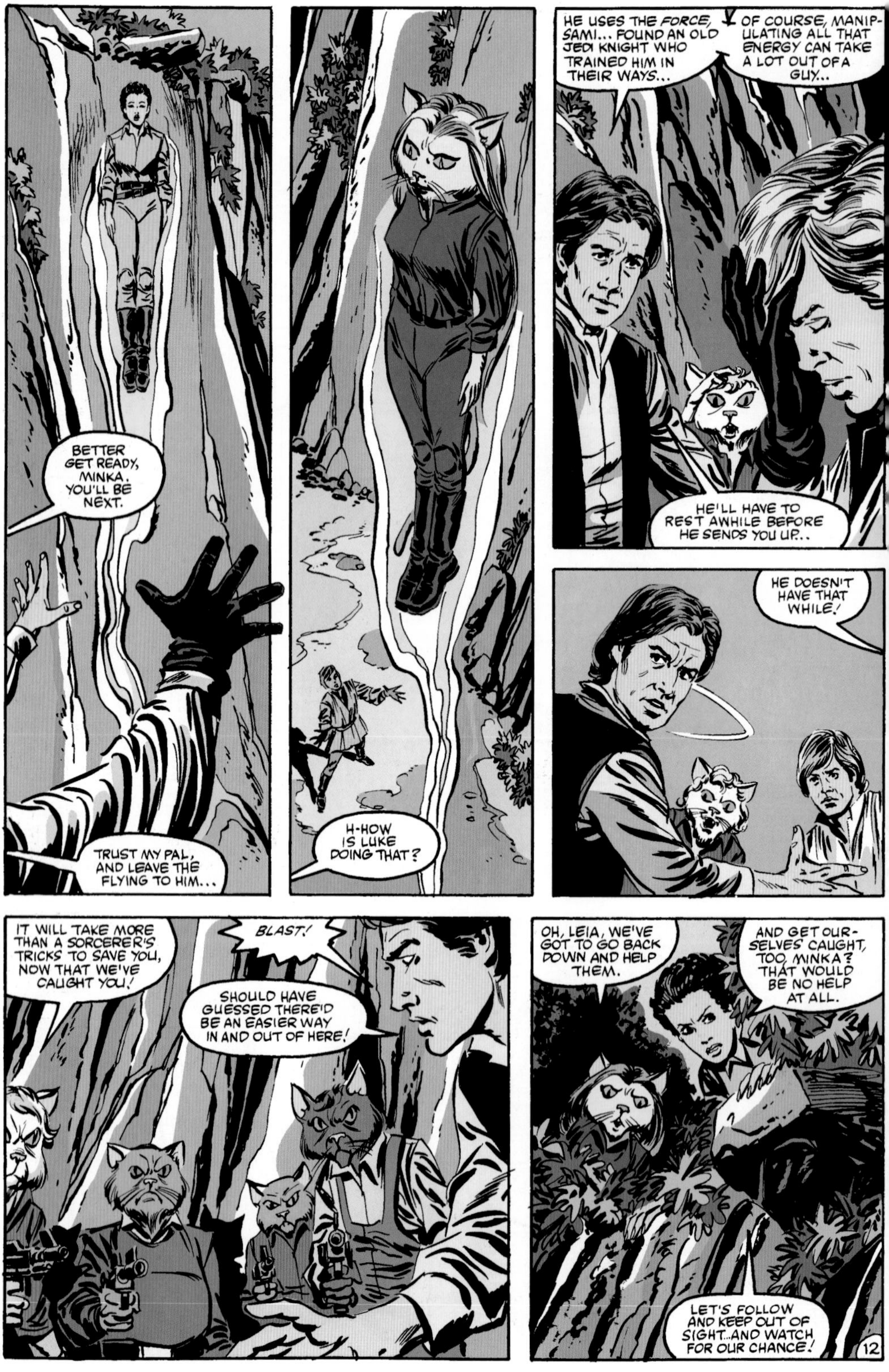

BETTER GET READY, MINKA. YOU'LL BE NEXT.
TRUST MY PAL, AND LEAVE THE FLYING TO HIM...
H-HOW IS LUKE DOING THAT?
HE USES THE FORCE, SAMI... FOUND AN OLD JEDI KNIGHT WHO TRAINED HIM IN THEIR WAYS...
OF COURSE, MANIPULATING ALL THAT ENERGY CAN TAKE A LOT OUT OF A GUY...
HE'LL HAVE TO REST AWHILE BEFORE HE SENDS YOU UP..
HE DOESN'T HAVE THAT WHILE!
IT WILL TAKE MORE THAN A SORCERER'S TRICKS TO SAVE YOU, NOW THAT WE'VE CAUGHT YOU!
BLAST!
SHOULD HAVE GUESSED THERE'D BE AN EASIER WAY IN AND OUT OF HERE!
OH, LEIA, WE'VE GOT TO GO BACK DOWN AND HELP THEM.
AND GET OURSELVES CAUGHT, TOO, MINKA? THAT WOULD BE NO HELP AT ALL.
LET'S FOLLOW AND KEEP OUT OF SIGHT...AND WATCH FOR OUR CHANCE!
12

UH...LUKE, DON'T YOU THINK YOU'VE LISTENED LONG ENOUGH?

COME ON...YOU SAID YOU HAD A PLAN. LET'S HEAR IT.

NOT YET, HAN. BE PATIENT. THIS IS GETTING INTERESTING.

INTERESTING?

÷SIGH÷

BLAST! I HATE BEING TORTURED...!

WHICH ONE YOU WANT TO START WITH?

THE STUPID-LOOKING ONE.

WHA--?!

NIRU, WHAT ARE YOU DOING?

I CAN'T LET YOU DO THIS!

TORTURING THE HELPLESS IS THE WAY OF THE EMPIRE! IF WE DO IT, WE BETRAY EVERYTHING THE REBELLION STANDS FOR!

14

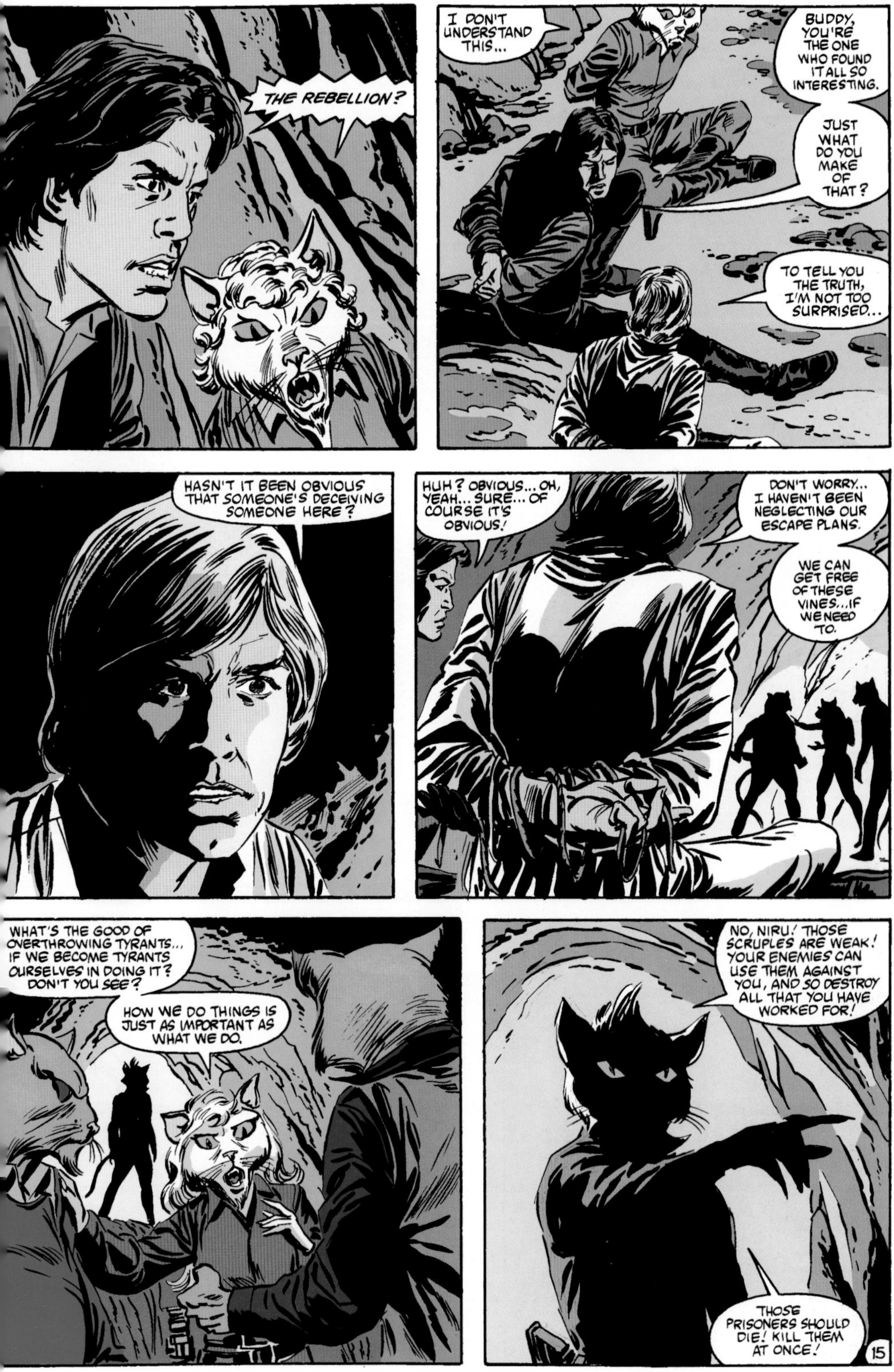
THE REBELLION?
I DON'T UNDERSTAND THIS...
BUDDY, YOU'RE THE ONE WHO FOUND IT ALL SO INTERESTING.
JUST WHAT DO YOU MAKE OF THAT?
TO TELL YOU THE TRUTH, I'M NOT TOO SURPRISED...
HASN'T IT BEEN OBVIOUS THAT SOMEONE'S DECEIVING SOMEONE HERE?
HUH? OBVIOUS... OH, YEAH... SURE... OF COURSE IT'S OBVIOUS!
DON'T WORRY... I HAVEN'T BEEN NEGLECTING OUR ESCAPE PLANS.
WE CAN GET FREE OF THESE VINES... IF WE NEED TO.
WHAT'S THE GOOD OF OVERTHROWING TYRANTS... IF WE BECOME TYRANTS OURSELVES IN DOING IT? DON'T YOU SEE?
HOW WE DO THINGS IS JUST AS IMPORTANT AS WHAT WE DO.
NO, NIRU! THOSE SCRUPLES ARE WEAK! YOUR ENEMIES CAN USE THEM AGAINST YOU, AND SO DESTROY ALL THAT YOU HAVE WORKED FOR!
THOSE PRISONERS SHOULD DIE! KILL THEM AT ONCE!
15

207

18

I HATE FIRING ON FELLOW REBELS...

BUT BELIEVE ME, YOU'LL THANK US FOR THIS WHEN YOU WAKE UP AND WE SORT THE MESS OUT!

I WAS ALMOST LOOSE, YOU KNOW.

OF COURSE YOU WERE.

KEEP YOUR BLASTER SET TO STUN. NO MATTER HOW MISGUIDED THEY MAY BE, THESE PEOPLE ARE OUR ALLIES!

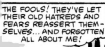

THE FOOLS! THEY'VE LET THEIR OLD HATREDS AND FEARS REASSERT THEM-SELVES... AND FORGOTTEN ALL ABOUT ME!

NIRU HAS BEEN THE VOICE OF REASON. THEY LISTEN TO HER...

ONE TRAGIC SHOT FROM AN UNIDENTIFIED SOURCE...

...AND THINGS SHOULD BE BACK UNDER MY CONTROL IN NO TIME!

STOP! ALL OF YOU! PLEASE LISTEN TO ME!

DURNE--!

19

209

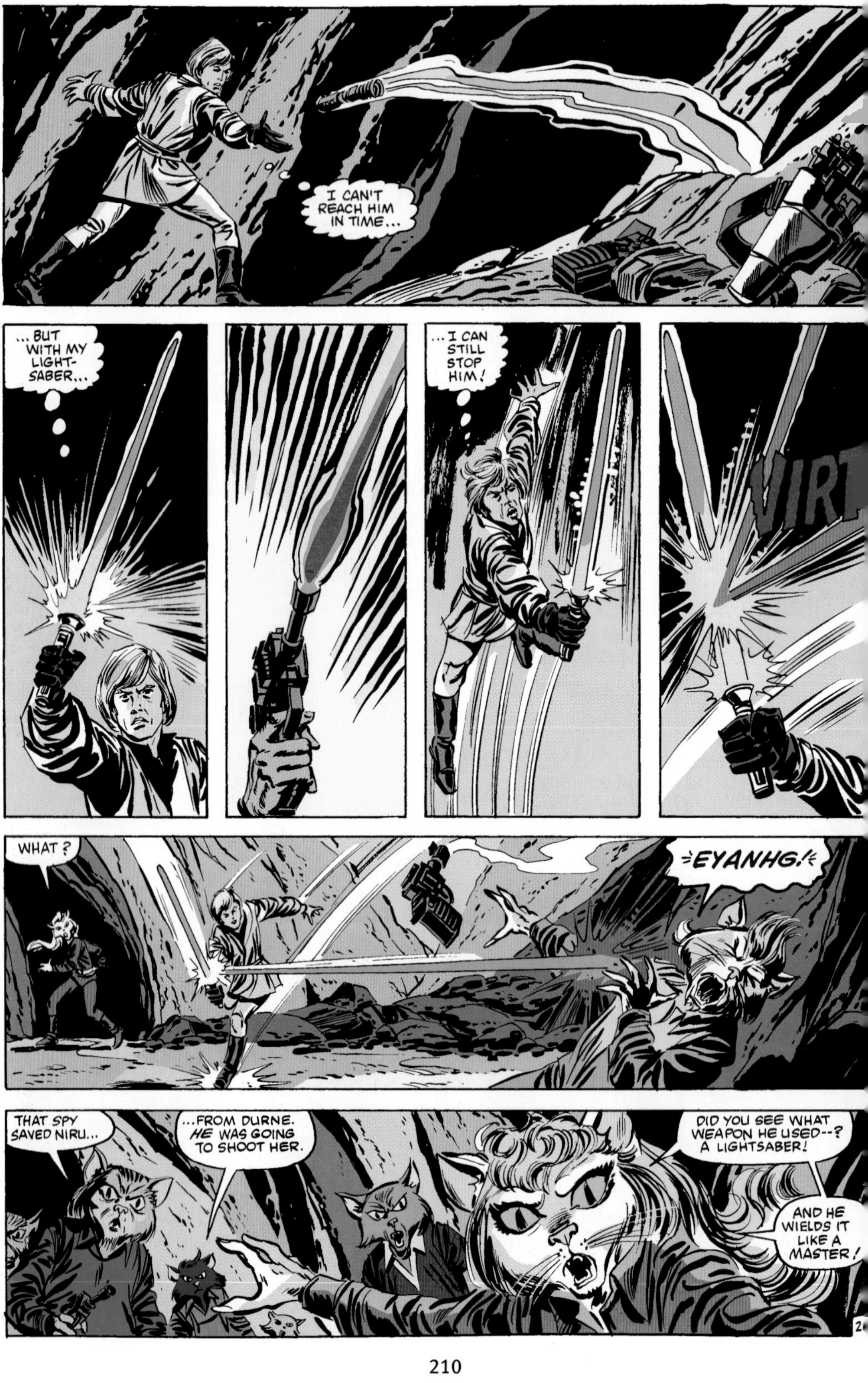
I CAN'T REACH HIM IN TIME...
...BUT WITH MY LIGHT-SABER...
...I CAN STILL STOP HIM!
WHAT?
EYANHG!
THAT SPY SAVED NIRU...
...FROM DURNE. HE WAS GOING TO SHOOT HER.
DID YOU SEE WHAT WEAPON HE USED--? A LIGHTSABER!
AND HE WIELDS IT LIKE A MASTER!

ARE YOU... WHAT YOU APPEAR TO BE? THE EMPIRE DESTROYED MOST OF THE JEDI KNIGHTS...

BUT WE'VE HEARD OF ONE... WHO SERVES THE CAUSE OF FREEDOM...

AN' NOW YOU'VE MET HIM.

KID'S NOT TOO BAD, IS HE?

YOU MEAN HE'S REALLY... TRULY...

...LUKE SKYWALKER?

AND YOU'RE HAN SOLO... AND PRINCESS LEIA ORGANA?

OUR HEROES!?

WELL, SINCE YOU PRIED IT OUT OF US...

WE'RE JUST PEOPLE, LIKE ALL OF YOU.

DURNE'S GETTING AWAY!

OH, NO HE'S NOT!

NOT TILL HE ANSWERS A LOT OF QUESTIONS.

LUCKY FOR HIM WE REBELS ARE ABOVE THINGS LIKE KILLING OR TORTURING PRISONERS!

21

211

SO... ALL THESE MONTHS, YOU'VE BEEN KILLING US, AND HATING US...

AND WE'VE BEEN DOING THE SAME TO YOU...

AND THERE NEVER REALLY WAS AN IMPERIAL BASE HERE AT ALL.

THEN... I GUESS WE WIN... SORT OF...

AND LOSE... SORT OF.

MINKA AND I ARE FROM THE CAPITAL OF CANTROS SEVEN. HOW ABOUT YOU?

I'LL BET WE WERE NEIGHBORS ONCE... IT'S A BIG TOWN.

IT'S GOING TO BE NICE... HAVING NEW ALLIES AND NO ENEMIES.

HARD TO BELIEVE ONE GUY COULD CAUSE ALL THAT TROUBLE, ISN'T IT, LEIA?

IT ISN'T HARD TO MAKE PEOPLE PARANOID, HAN... WHEN THERE REALLY IS SOMEONE OUT TO GET THEM.

LUKE, WHAT'S THE MATTER? IT'S OVER. WE'VE WON.

WHY ARE YOU SO SAD?

I KNOW... BUT IT WON'T BRING BACK ALL OF THE DEAD... REBELS KILLED BY REBELS.

WE KILLED A FEW OF THEM, OURSELVES, YOU KNOW.

WE ALSO SAVED A LOT OF LIVES. THE KILLING IS OVER NOW.

IS IT? I HOPE SO.

BUT I'LL FEEL A LOT BETTER IF WE CAN JUST FIND OUT WHO DURNE WAS REALLY WORKING FOR.

WHAT'S GOING ON IN THIS GALAXY?

NEXT: THERE'S TROUBLE BREWING AMONG THE FORCES OF THE ALLIANCE, AND DISASTER LOOMS...

SMALL WARS

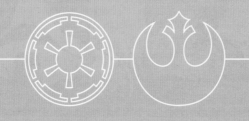

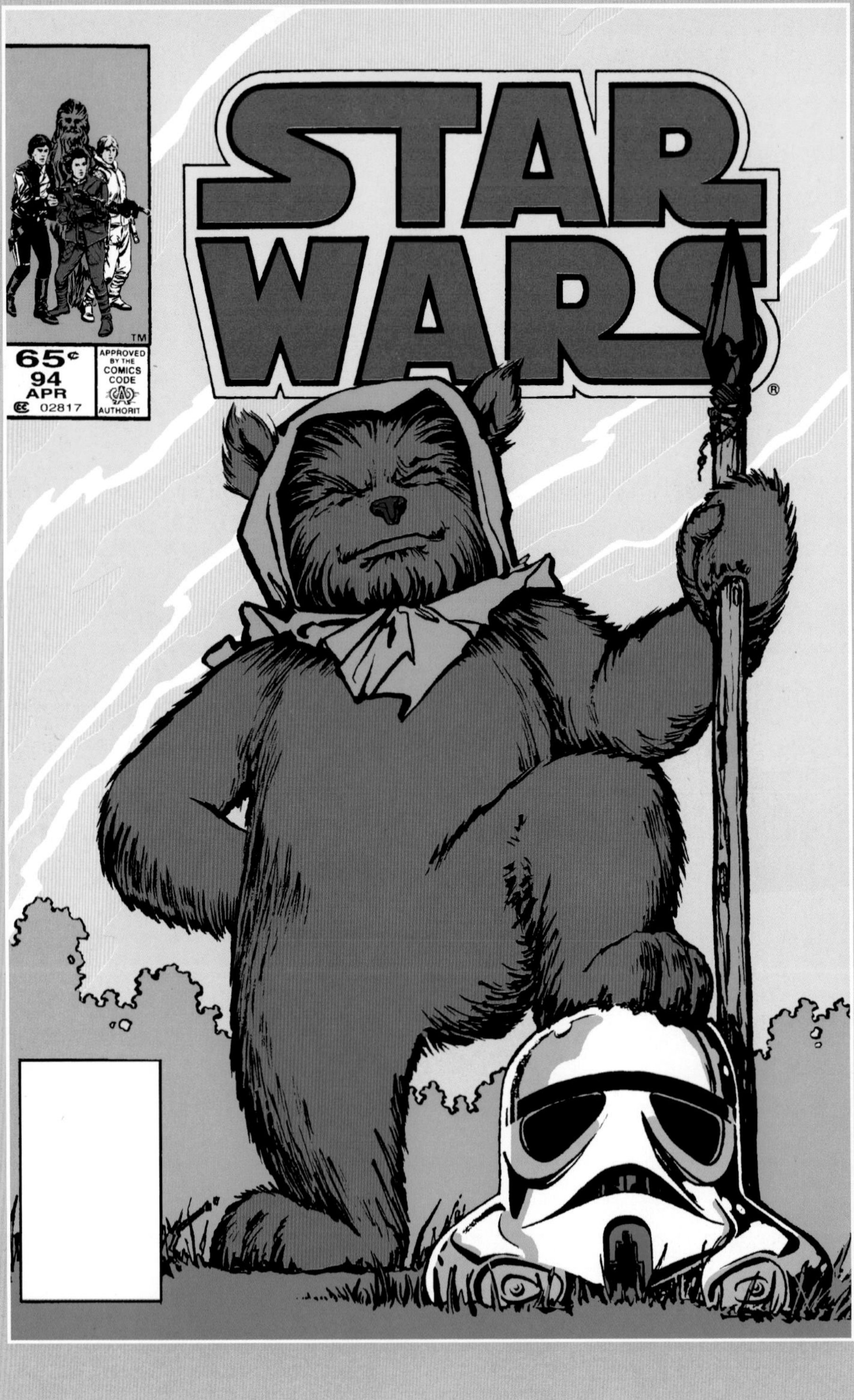
STAR WARS
TM
®
65¢
94
APR
02817
APPROVED BY THE COMICS CODE AUTHORITY

Lucasfilm PRESENTS: STAR WARS™ THE GREATEST SPACE FANTASY OF ALL!
SMALL WARS
OH, ARTOO-DETOO, I FEEL JUST TERRIBLE ABOUT THIS! THE ALLIANCE OF FREE PLANETS IS CRUMBLING...
...AND IT'S ALL MY FAULT!
VROOT?
OH, WOE...
JO DUFFY......SCRIPT/PLOT
CYNTHIA MARTIN....PENCILS
TOM PALMER........INKS
RICK PARKER.....LETTERS
GLYNIS WEIN......COLORS
ANN NOCENTI.....EDITOR
JIM SHOOTER..........
EDITOR IN CHIEF

SEE-THREEPIO SURE IS TAKING IT HARD, ISN'T HE, HAN?

YEP. HE SURE IS, LUKE.

NOT THAT I BLAME HIM. THINGS ARE PRETTY BLEAK.

I NEVER THOUGHT IT COULD HAPPEN.

NO ONE DID.

IT WASN'T SO LONG AGO WE WERE ALL FIGHTING A REBELLION AGAINST THE TYRANNY OF THE EMPIRE. AFTER WE WON, EVERYONE THOUGHT OUR TROUBLES WOULD BE OVER. NOW, INSTEAD, BEFORE WE'VE EVEN SET UP A NEW, FAIR SYSTEM OF INTERPLANETARY GOVERNMENT, TWO OF THE ALLIED WORLDS ARE ABOUT TO GO TO WAR AGAIN-- WITH EACH OTHER.

SURE IS A SHAME.

ALL I WAS DOING WAS REPEATING WHAT I'D SEEN...

I CONSIDERED IT PART OF MY DUTY AS A TRANSLATOR AND PROTOCOL DROID.

I HAD NO IDEA WHAT I'D SET IN MOTION...

AND WHEN I THINK OF HOW THEY LOOK UP TO ME, AND HOW BENEFICIAL MY INFLUENCE MIGHT HAVE BEEN...

YOU KNOW, BEFORE YOU BROUGHT SEE-THREEPIO ABOARD MY SHIP, I WAS IN THE HABIT OF THINKING OF DROIDS AS COOL AND UNEMOTIONAL.

MOST DROIDS ARE. BUT NOT HIM.

NOPE.

HERE COMES HER ROYAL HIGHNESS. SHE, LANDO AND CHEWIE HAVE BEEN CONFERRING WITH ADMIRAL ACKBAR AND HIS AIDE HIROG, SEEING IF THEY COULD MEDIATE OUR WAY OUT OF THIS DISASTER.

HEY, LEIA, DID YOU HAVE ANY LUCK?

I'M SORRY, HAN, BUT NO. WHEN THE LEADERS FOUND OUT WHY WE WANTED TO TALK TO THEM, THEY ACTUALLY STARTED BRANDISHING THEIR WEAPONS AT US. WHAT IT COMES DOWN TO IS THAT UNLESS YOU SIDE WITH THEM UNCRITICALLY AND COMPLETELY, THEY'RE GOING TO REGARD YOU AS AN ENEMY.

GRONK

YEAH, CHEWBACCA'S RIGHT. WE HAD TO CLEAR OUT OF THERE... WHEN THE FOLKS YOU'RE TALKING TO GET MAD ENOUGH TO START THREATENING A WOOKIEE LIKE HIM, THE TIME FOR WORDS HAS PASSED...

TOO TRUE, LANDO. TOO TRUE.

ADMIRAL ACKBAR, ARE YOU SURE?

I'M AFRAID SO, COMMANDER SKYWALKER. THE LEADERS HAD DETERMINED THEIR COURSE OF ACTION BEFORE THEY AGREED TO SPEAK WITH US.

SO IT'S WAR, HUNH?

YES, GENERAL SOLO. IT'S WAR.

OH, NO! ARTOO, DID YOU HEAR THAT? WAR!!

COME ALONG, HIROG. WE HAVE MUCH TO DO IN PREPARATION FOR THIS.

YES, ADMIRAL.

WE MUST DRAFT RESOLUTIONS, MOBILIZE OUR FORCES, APPRISE THE OTHER ALLIANCE RULERS OF THE SITUATION, AND URGE THEIR NEUTRALITY...

...IF SUCH A THING IS STILL POSSIBLE.

IT'S A DARK DAY FOR THE FREE PLANETS IN THIS SYSTEM,

A VERY DARK DAY.

≥HHRRUPH≥

3

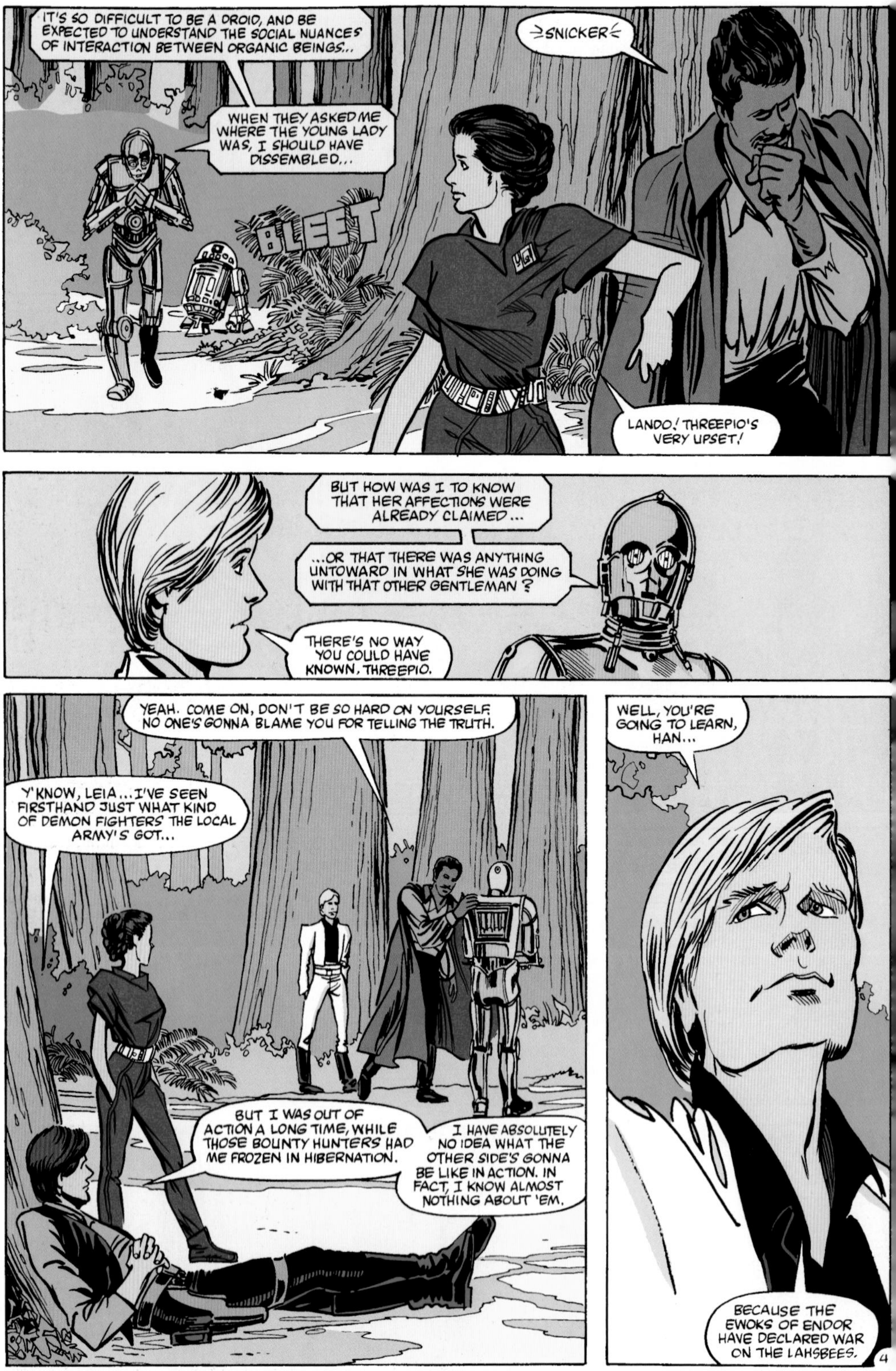
IT'S SO DIFFICULT TO BE A DROID, AND BE EXPECTED TO UNDERSTAND THE SOCIAL NUANCES OF INTERACTION BETWEEN ORGANIC BEINGS...
WHEN THEY ASKED ME WHERE THE YOUNG LADY WAS, I SHOULD HAVE DISSEMBLED...
BLEET
⇉SNICKER⇇
LANDO! THREEPIO'S VERY UPSET!
BUT HOW WAS I TO KNOW THAT HER AFFECTIONS WERE ALREADY CLAIMED...
...OR THAT THERE WAS ANYTHING UNTOWARD IN WHAT SHE WAS DOING WITH THAT OTHER GENTLEMAN?
THERE'S NO WAY YOU COULD HAVE KNOWN, THREEPIO.
YEAH. COME ON, DON'T BE SO HARD ON YOURSELF. NO ONE'S GONNA BLAME YOU FOR TELLING THE TRUTH.
Y'KNOW, LEIA...I'VE SEEN FIRSTHAND JUST WHAT KIND OF DEMON FIGHTERS THE LOCAL ARMY'S GOT...
BUT I WAS OUT OF ACTION A LONG TIME, WHILE THOSE BOUNTY HUNTERS HAD ME FROZEN IN HIBERNATION.
I HAVE ABSOLUTELY NO IDEA WHAT THE OTHER SIDE'S GONNA BE LIKE IN ACTION. IN FACT, I KNOW ALMOST NOTHING ABOUT 'EM.
WELL, YOU'RE GOING TO LEARN, HAN...
BECAUSE THE EWOKS OF ENDOR HAVE DECLARED WAR ON THE LAHSBEES.
4

TEE HEE HEE HEE

TEE HEE HEE HEE

TEE HEE

THIS ISN'T GOING TO BE A VERY EVEN FIGHT.

GRRRRR!

GRRUF!

HEY, WICKET, I WAS JUST ABOUT TO BEGIN MY LIGHTSABER PRACTICE FOR THE DAY. DO YOU OR ANY OF THE OTHER EWOKS WANT TO JOIN IN?

RRRRRR!!

BAH!

NO, HUNH?

ANYBODY ELSE?

OOF!

I GUESS THAT MEANS YES...?

HIROG TO THE HIROMI MOTHER SHIP... HIROG TO THE HIROMI MOTHER SHIP... DO YOU COPY?

DO NOT, REPEAT, DO NOT BE AFRAID TO RESPOND. IT IS PERFECTLY SAFE FOR US TO CONVERSE. I HAVE USED MY POSITION AS AIDE TO ADMIRAL ACKBAR--

--TO MAKE CERTAIN THAT NO ALLIANCE PERSONNEL WILL MONITOR THIS FREQUENCY.

I AM PLEASED TO REPORT THAT ALL IS PROCEEDING ACCORDING TO PLAN. AFTER OVER TWO MILLENNIA OF WATCHING AND PLANNING, IT IS TIME FOR US -- THE HIROMI-- TO ACHIEVE OUR GLORIOUS DESTINY.

WE ARE GOING TO CONQUER THIS GALAXY!

I HAVE ARRANGED IT ALL... BY A SERIES OF MYSTERIOUS, UNSIGNED MESSAGES, AN APPEAL TO CHIVALRY, AND A SWIFT, MASTERFUL STRIKE IN A LONELY SPOT, AT AN AUSPICIOUS TIME...

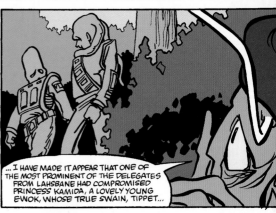

... I HAVE MADE IT APPEAR THAT ONE OF THE MOST PROMINENT OF THE DELEGATES FROM LAHSBANE HAD COMPROMISED PRINCESS KAMIDA, A LOVELY YOUNG EWOK, WHOSE TRUE SWAIN, TIPPET...

...IS A PILLAR OF BOTH HIS OWN RACE AND OF THE ALLIANCE. AND I ARRANGED FOR AN IMPARTIAL, UTTERLY TRUSTWORTHY BLABBERMOUTH TO SEE THE MOST INCRIMINATING MOMENT OF THE WHOLE!

TIPPET IS SO JEALOUS, HE WON'T HEAR REASON, AND SO HIS ENTIRE RACE HAVE DECLARED WAR ON THE TREACHEROUS, LASCIVIOUS LAHSBEES!

THESE ARE TWO OF THE SILLIEST, MOST INCONSEQUENTIAL PEOPLES I HAVE EVER ENCOUNTERED. OF COURSE, OTHER ALLIANCE RACES WILL HAVE TO TAKE SIDES!

AND, AS THEIR UNITY CRUMBLES, WE CAN MOVE IN!

IT SIMPLY CAN'T FAIL!

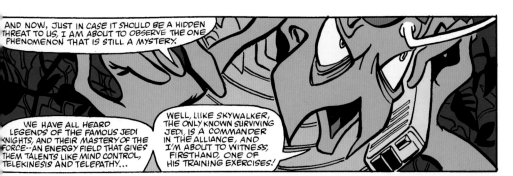

AND NOW, JUST IN CASE IT SHOULD BE A HIDDEN THREAT TO US, I AM ABOUT TO OBSERVE THE ONE PHENOMENON THAT IS STILL A MYSTERY.

WE HAVE ALL HEARD LEGENDS OF THE FAMOUS JEDI KNIGHTS, AND THEIR MASTERY OF THE FORCE--AN ENERGY FIELD THAT GIVES THEM TALENTS LIKE MIND CONTROL, TELEKINESIS AND TELEPATHY...

WELL, LIIKE SKYWALKER, THE ONLY KNOWN SURVIVING JEDI, IS A COMMANDER IN THE ALLIANCE, AND I'M ABOUT TO WITNESS, FIRSTHAND, ONE OF HIS TRAINING EXERCISES!

YOU GUYS SURE YOU'VE GOT IT?

I'M GOING TO WAIT, WITH MY BACK TO YOU, AND MY EYES CLOSED. I WON'T EVEN HAVE MY LIGHTSABER ACTIVATED. YOU BE AS QUIET AS YOU CAN, AND ATTACK ME FROM AS MANY DIFFERENT DIRECTIONS AS YOU WANT.

GOOD.

OKAY. READY WHENEVER YOU ARE.

			-TEE-HEE-HEE-HEE-			
					-HEE HEE-					

⑦

221

HHHMMMMMMMM

||||| SSHHH |||||

NOW!

!

ZOOM

ZOOM

ZOOM

ZOOM

HEY!

|||||||||||

GEE, DO YOU THINK I SCARED THEM?

LOOKS THAT WAY, DOESN'T IT, KID?

THIS WHOLE THING IS RIDICULOUS. THOSE LITTLE GUYS AREN'T ANY THREAT TO ANYBODY. HOW COULD TIPPET WANT TO GO TO WAR WITH THEM, NO MATTER WHAT HE THINKS ONE OF 'EM DID?

GROOOO

LAHSBEES, DANGEROUS? COME OFF IT, PAL! YOU'RE NEVER GONNA CONVINCE ME YOU WERE EVER SCARED OF ONE OF 'EM.

THIS WHOLE THING IS A JOKE, RIGHT?

NO, HAN. CHEWIE'S SERIOUS. THERE'S A WHOLE SIDE TO THE LAHSBEES THAT YOU HAVEN'T SEEN YET.

GRURF

I DON'T BELIEVE IT!

WHAT DO YOU MEAN THEY GET THAT BIG?

WELL... THEY'RE DIFFERENT AFTER THEY HIT PUBERTY. THE ONES HERE ARE ALL YOUNG, BUT ONCE THEY'RE ADOLES-CENT... YOU'LL SEE.

HE'LL ALSO SEE IF ONE OF THEM GETS OVER-EXCITED...

DO YOU REMEMBER WHAT YOU STARTED THAT TIME ON KABRAY, PRINCESS LEIA?

TRUST A ZELTRON TO REMEMBER THAT...

OH, I DON'T THINK ANYONE WHO WAS THERE THAT NIGHT IS EVER GOING TO FORGET IT... OR YOU.

GENERAL SOLO DOESN'T WANT TO HEAR ABOUT THIS!

WHY NOT? EVERYONE ON ZELTROS DID.

9

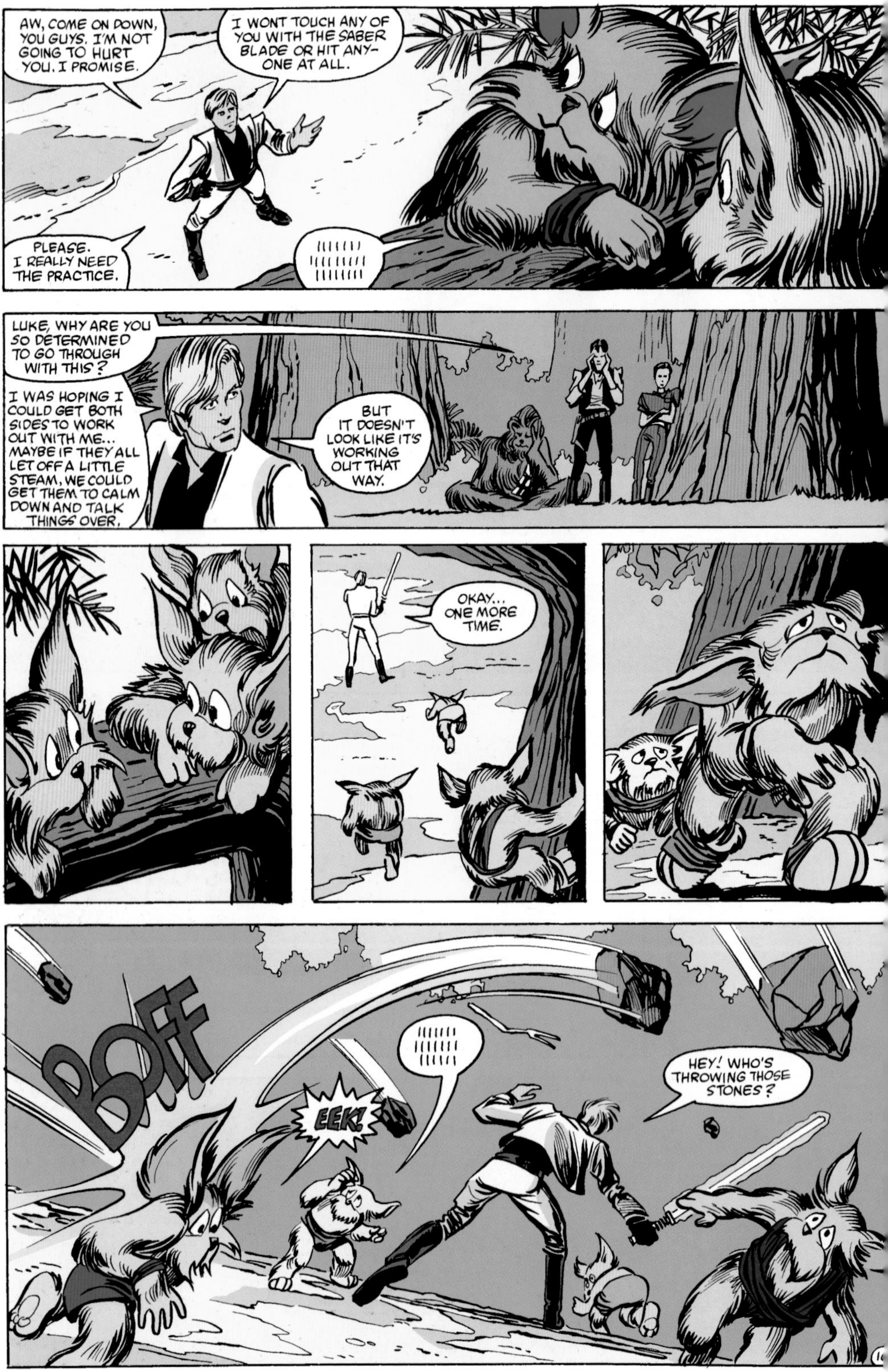
AW, COME ON DOWN, YOU GUYS. I'M NOT GOING TO HURT YOU. I PROMISE.
I WONT TOUCH ANY OF YOU WITH THE SABER BLADE OR HIT ANY-ONE AT ALL.
PLEASE. I REALLY NEED THE PRACTICE.
!!!!!! !!!!!!!! !!!!!!!!
LUKE, WHY ARE YOU SO DETERMINED TO GO THROUGH WITH THIS?
I WAS HOPING I COULD GET BOTH SIDES TO WORK OUT WITH ME... MAYBE IF THEY ALL LET OFF A LITTLE STEAM, WE COULD GET THEM TO CALM DOWN AND TALK THINGS OVER.
BUT IT DOESN'T LOOK LIKE IT'S WORKING OUT THAT WAY.
OKAY... ONE MORE TIME.
BOFF
!!!!!!! !!!!!!!! !!!!!!!
EEK!
HEY! WHO'S THROWING THOSE STONES?

IT'S THE EWOKS! THEY'RE REALLY ANGRY I'M HAVING ANYTHING AT ALL TO DO WITH THE LAHSBEES!

THEY MUST HAVE USED ONE OF THEIR CATAPULTS TO FLING THIS ROCK. IT'S HUGE...

IT'S A GOOD THING I CAN USE THE FORCE TO CHANGE ITS DIRECTION...

BASH

...OR IT MIGHT HURT SOMEONE.

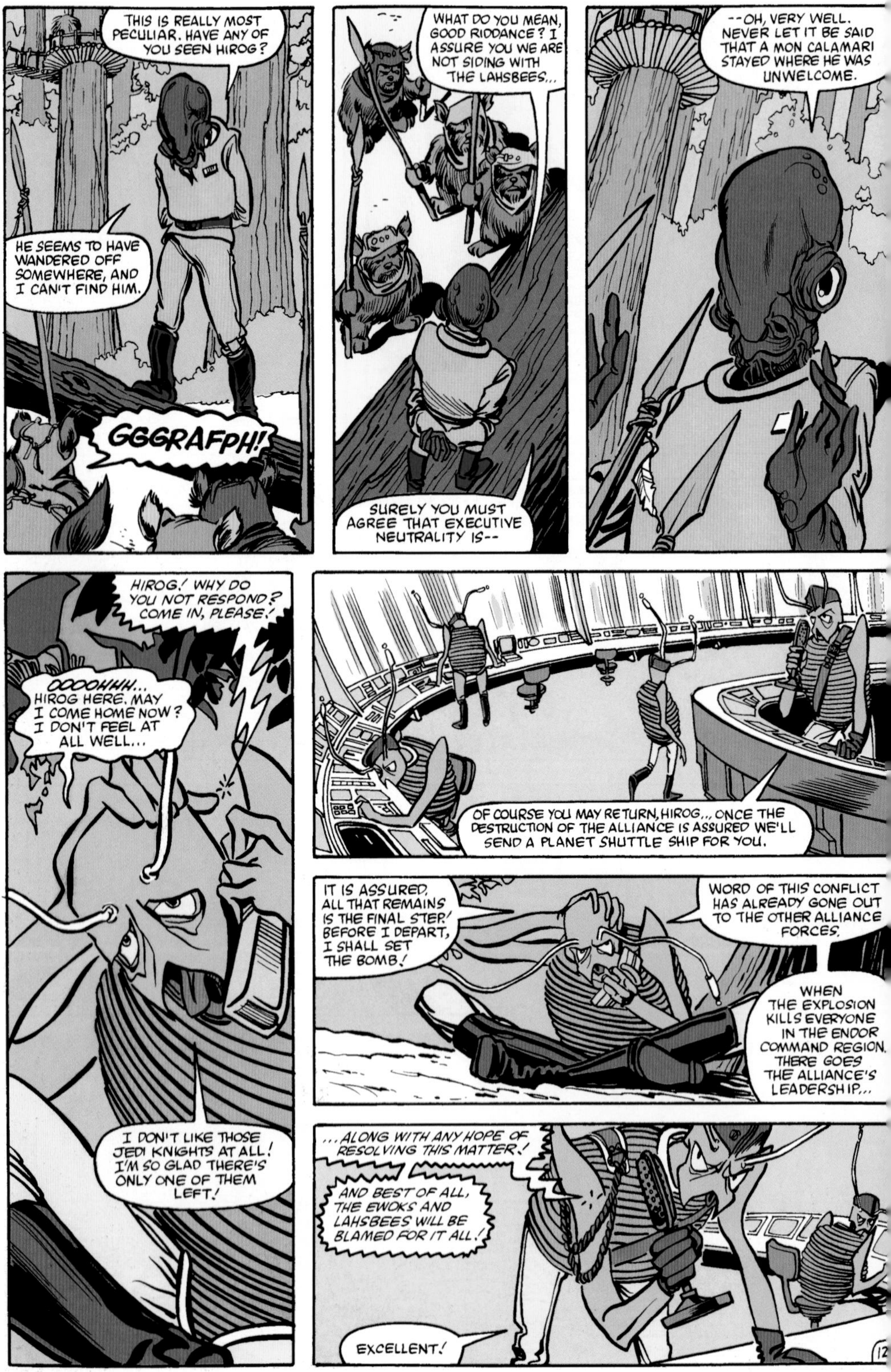
THIS IS REALLY MOST PECULIAR. HAVE ANY OF YOU SEEN HIROG?
HE SEEMS TO HAVE WANDERED OFF SOMEWHERE, AND I CAN'T FIND HIM.
GGGRAFPH!
WHAT DO YOU MEAN, GOOD RIDDANCE? I ASSURE YOU WE ARE NOT SIDING WITH THE LAHSBEES...
SURELY YOU MUST AGREE THAT EXECUTIVE NEUTRALITY IS--
--OH, VERY WELL. NEVER LET IT BE SAID THAT A MON CALAMARI STAYED WHERE HE WAS UNWELCOME.
HIROG! WHY DO YOU NOT RESPOND? COME IN, PLEASE!
OOOOHHH... HIROG HERE. MAY I COME HOME NOW? I DON'T FEEL AT ALL WELL...
I DON'T LIKE THOSE JEDI KNIGHTS AT ALL! I'M SO GLAD THERE'S ONLY ONE OF THEM LEFT!
OF COURSE YOU MAY RETURN, HIROG... ONCE THE DESTRUCTION OF THE ALLIANCE IS ASSURED WE'LL SEND A PLANET SHUTTLE SHIP FOR YOU.
IT IS ASSURED. ALL THAT REMAINS IS THE FINAL STEP! BEFORE I DEPART, I SHALL SET THE BOMB!
WORD OF THIS CONFLICT HAS ALREADY GONE OUT TO THE OTHER ALLIANCE FORCES.
WHEN THE EXPLOSION KILLS EVERYONE IN THE ENDOR COMMAND REGION, THERE GOES THE ALLIANCE'S LEADERSHIP...
...ALONG WITH ANY HOPE OF RESOLVING THIS MATTER!
AND BEST OF ALL, THE EWOKS AND LAHSBEES WILL BE BLAMED FOR IT ALL!
EXCELLENT!
12

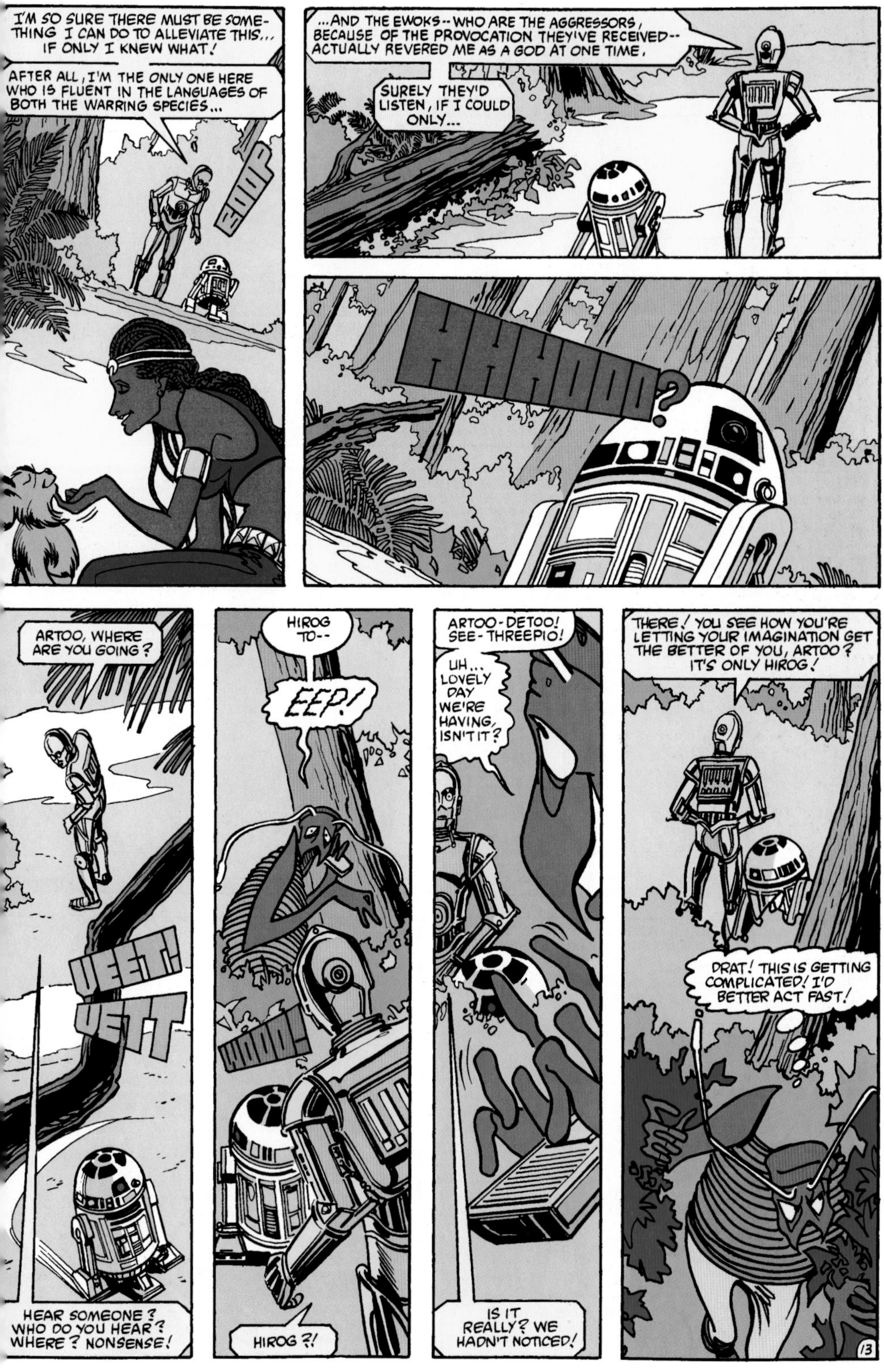
I'M SO SURE THERE MUST BE SOMETHING I CAN DO TO ALLEVIATE THIS... IF ONLY I KNEW WHAT!
AFTER ALL, I'M THE ONLY ONE HERE WHO IS FLUENT IN THE LANGUAGES OF BOTH THE WARRING SPECIES...
SOOP
...AND THE EWOKS--WHO ARE THE AGGRESSORS, BECAUSE OF THE PROVOCATION THEY'VE RECEIVED--ACTUALLY REVERED ME AS A GOD AT ONE TIME.
SURELY THEY'D LISTEN, IF I COULD ONLY...
HHHOOO?
ARTOO, WHERE ARE YOU GOING?
VEET! VETT
HEAR SOMEONE? WHO DO YOU HEAR? WHERE? NONSENSE!
HIROG TO--
EEP!
WHOO!
HIROG?!
ARTOO-DETOO! SEE-THREEPIO!
UH... LOVELY DAY WE'RE HAVING, ISN'T IT?
IS IT REALLY? WE HADN'T NOTICED!
THERE! YOU SEE HOW YOU'RE LETTING YOUR IMAGINATION GET THE BETTER OF YOU, ARTOO? IT'S ONLY HIROG!
DRAT! THIS IS GETTING COMPLICATED! I'D BETTER ACT FAST!
13

OH, YOU ARE JUST THE CUTEST LITTLE THING!

STOP WHAT YOU ARE DOING AND PUT THAT LAHSBEE DOWN!

| | | | | | | | | | | | | | | | | | | | | |

BUT ADMIRAL ACKBAR, HE LIKES IT!

AND THAT IS PRECISELY WHY IT MUST STOP! SOME OF THOSE LAHSBEES HAVE REACHED A DANGEROUSLY ADVANCED AGE, YOU KNOW. DOES'N'T THE TERM "HUHK" MEAN ANYTHING TO YOU?

SURE... I WAS ONE OF THE ZELTRONS ON KABRAY, BUT...

...OH, WELL...

| | | | | | | | | | | | | | | | | | | | | |

≥ SIGH ≤

WELL, THAT WAS A COMPLETE WASHOUT.

THE LAHSBEES DON'T WANT TO FIGHT. BUT THEY DIDN'T WANT TO FIGHT IN THE FIRST PLACE.

ALL I'VE DONE IS MAKE TIPPET AND HIS FRIENDS THINK WE'RE GANGING UP ON THEM...

THEY WON'T BELIEVE THAT PRINCESS KAMIDA AND THAT LAHSBEE WERE FRAMED SOMEHOW...

...AND THEY'RE MORE DETERMINED TO FIGHT THAN EVER.

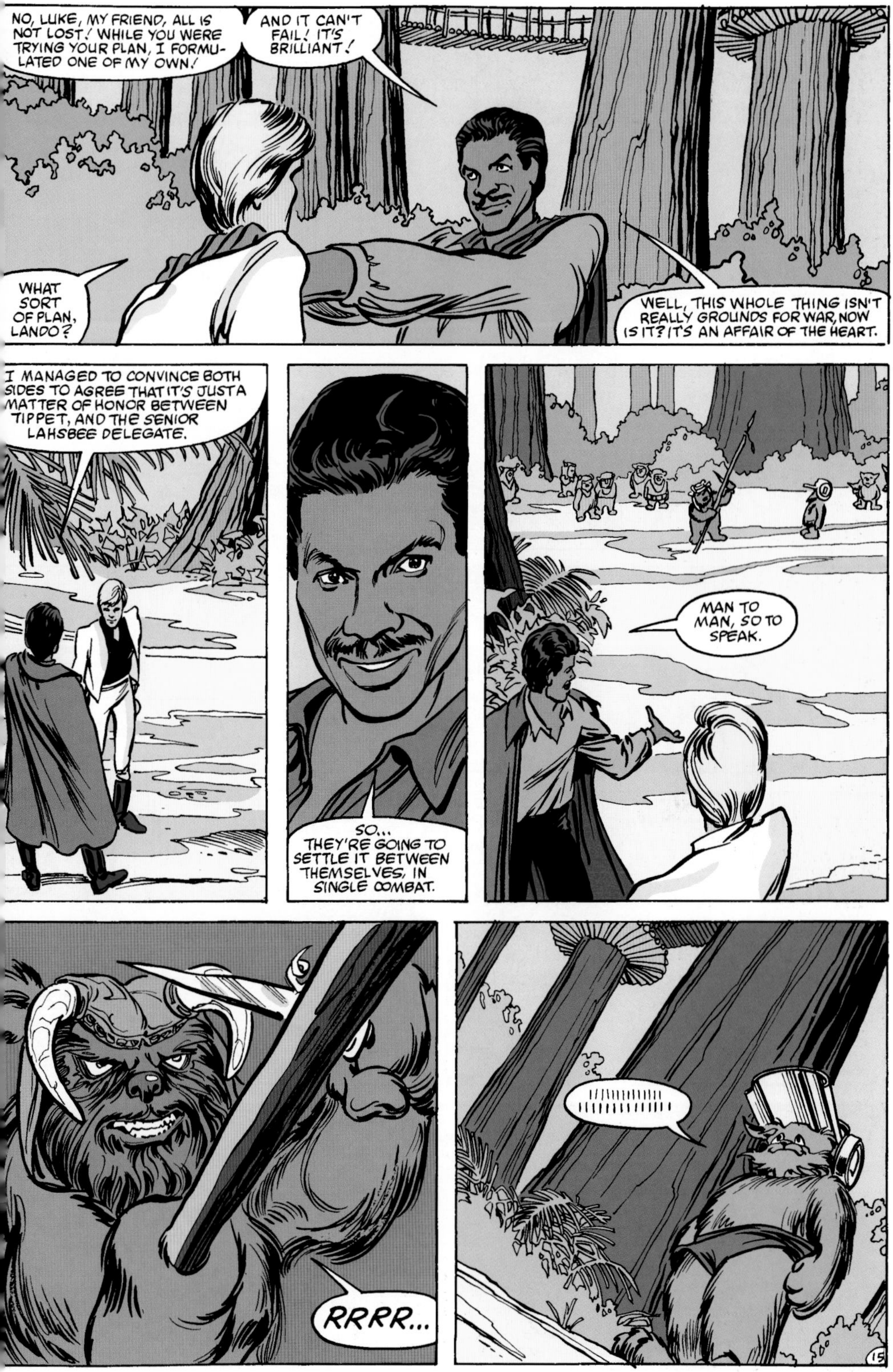
NO, LUKE, MY FRIEND, ALL IS NOT LOST! WHILE YOU WERE TRYING YOUR PLAN, I FORMULATED ONE OF MY OWN!
AND IT CAN'T FAIL! IT'S BRILLIANT!
WHAT SORT OF PLAN, LANDO?
WELL, THIS WHOLE THING ISN'T REALLY GROUNDS FOR WAR, NOW IS IT? IT'S AN AFFAIR OF THE HEART.
I MANAGED TO CONVINCE BOTH SIDES TO AGREE THAT IT'S JUST A MATTER OF HONOR BETWEEN TIPPET, AND THE SENIOR LAHSBEE DELEGATE.
SO... THEY'RE GOING TO SETTLE IT BETWEEN THEMSELVES, IN SINGLE COMBAT.
MAN TO MAN, SO TO SPEAK.
RRRR...
15

WHAT'S GOTTEN INTO THAT LITTLE FLUFFBALL? HAS HE GONE CRAZY? YOU'D THINK HE'D NEVER SEEN A BLASTER BEFORE!

HE HASN'T! THEY'VE OUTLAWED BLASTERS ON LAHSBANE, BECAUSE--!

TELL ME LATER!

YEEK!

!!!!!
!!!!!

MMMM!

ROWR!

OH, FINE!!

SOMEBODY'S GONE AND RUINED MY BEAUTIFUL, BEAUTIFUL BOMB!

THEY'VE SPOILED IT!

THE TIMING MECHANISM IS COMPLETELY DESTROYED!

AND WITHOUT THE TIMER, THERE'S ABSOLUTELY NO WAY TO CONTROL WHEN IT'S GOING TO--!

TIC

TIC TIC TIC

RROOOO!

NICE GOING, HAN! YOU HAD TO GIVE HIM THAT BLASTER, DIDN'T YOU?

IT'S NOT MY FAULT!

I DIDN'T KNOW WHAT WOULD HAPPEN IF HE GOT UPSET. BESIDES, THE DUEL WAS YOUR IDEA...

THOSE EWOKS ARE PRETTY BRAVE, SUPPORTING TIPPET LIKE THAT, BUT THEY'RE GONNA GET SLAUGHTERED.

THINK WE OUGHT TO HELP THEM?

YEAH. YOU FIRST.

LUKE, SOMEONE'S REALLY GOING TO GET HURT HERE.

I AGREE. WE HAVE TO PUT A STOP TO THIS.

HUHK

TIPPET HUHK

19

HAN BLASTER

TIPPET

HUHK HAN

VORP

MMRR?

||||||||||||

RUN! RUN FOR YOUR LIVES! EVERYONE RUN! WE ARE ALL GOING TO DIE!

MY BOMB IS GOING TO EXPLODE AND KILL US ALL, AND I CAN'T CONTROL IT! WE ARE ALL DOOMED!

?

?

!

HELP! OH, HELP! PLEASE HELP!!!

HE-HE-HE-E-E-E-LP!!

||||||||||
||||||||||

COMMANDER! WE'VE LOST THE SIGNAL FROM OUR BOMB! IT HAS CEASED TO FUNCTION!

WHAT DO YOU HEAR FROM HIROG?

NOTHING BUT CRIES OF TERROR AND SCREAMS OF PAIN... PLUS THE ROARS OF SOME CREATURE I CAN'T IDENTIFY...

HHHMMM... AND HE ASSURED US THAT HE WAS DEALING WITH THE *LEAST* DANGEROUS OF THE ALLIANCE CIVILIZATIONS...? PERHAPS THE GLORIOUS DESTINY OF THE HIROMI WOULD BEST BE SERVED IF WE WERE TO STRATE- GICALLY WITHDRAW... AT ONCE!

VERY GOOD, SIR... BUT WHAT ABOUT HIROG?

HIROG WHO?

WELL, I GUESS THAT SETTLES THAT.

YEP. SETTING UP THAT DUEL WAS PRETTY CLEVER OF ME, WASN'T IT?

CLEVER OF YOU? I'M THE ONE WHO GAVE THEM THE BLASTER.

I KNOW THAT STUFF HIROG SPOUTED OFF ABOUT A BOMB SOUNDED PRETTY SUS- PICIOUS... BUT DON'T YOU THINK WE OUGHT TO AT LEAST TRY TO HELP HIM?

MASTER LUKE, SIR... I AM HAPPY TO REPORT THAT THESE TWO MIGHTY WARRIORS, HAVING SETTLED THEIR DIFFERENCES... FEEL THAT THEY ARE MORE THAN ABLE TO COPE WITH THAT LITTLE PROBLEM FOR US!

NEXT NO ZELTRONS!

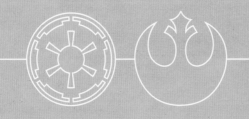

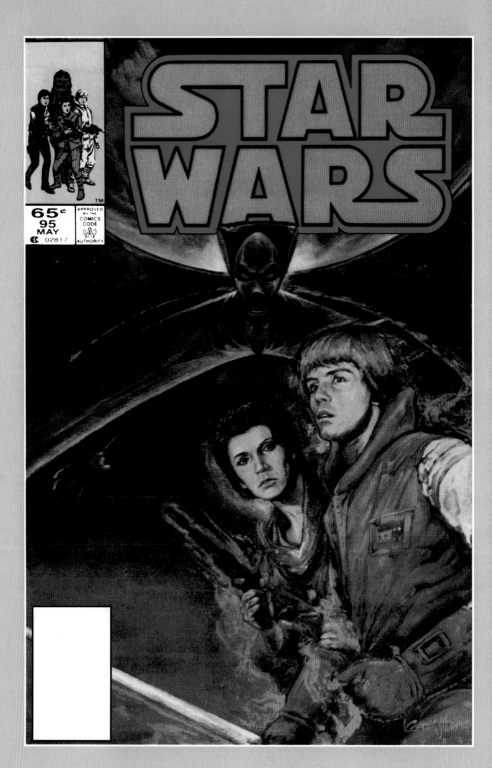

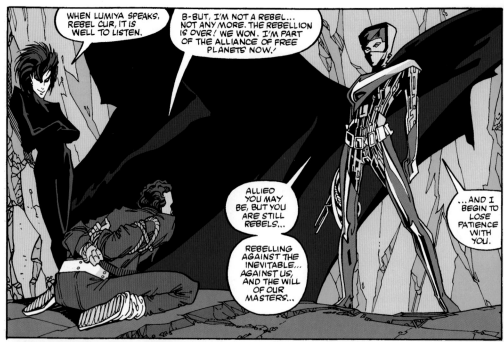

WHEN LUMIYA SPEAKS, REBEL CUR, IT IS WELL TO LISTEN.

B-BUT, I'M NOT A REBEL... NOT ANY MORE. THE REBELLION IS OVER! WE WON. I'M PART OF THE ALLIANCE OF FREE PLANETS NOW!

ALLIED YOU MAY BE, BUT YOU ARE STILL REBELS...

REBELLING AGAINST THE INEVITABLE... AGAINST US... AND THE WILL OF OUR MASTERS...

...AND I BEGIN TO LOSE PATIENCE WITH YOU.

I'M NOT AFRAID.

THEN YOU ARE A FOOL. THINK.

THERE WERE TWENTY IN YOUR PARTY WHEN WE CAPTURED YOU.

NOW, YOU ARE ALONE. YOU KNOW WHAT I CAN DO WITH THIS.

BUT, IF YOU ARE A FOOL, THEN YOU SHALL DIE A FOOL'S DEATH--

SLOWLY, AND ALONE.

W-WAIT--!

2

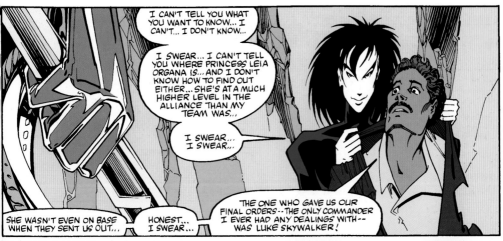

I CAN'T TELL YOU WHAT YOU WANT TO KNOW... I CAN'T... I DON'T KNOW...

I SWEAR... I CAN'T TELL YOU WHERE PRINCESS LEIA ORGANA IS... AND I DON'T KNOW HOW TO FIND OUT EITHER... SHE'S AT A MUCH HIGHER LEVEL IN THE ALLIANCE THAN MY TEAM WAS...

I SWEAR... I SWEAR...

SHE WASN'T EVEN ON BASE WHEN THEY SENT US OUT...

HONEST... I SWEAR...

THE ONE WHO GAVE US OUR FINAL ORDERS--THE ONLY COMMANDER I EVER HAD ANY DEALINGS WITH-- WAS LUKE SKYWALKER!

SKYWALKER.

NO.

OH, NO! NOT THAT! ANYTHING BUT THAT!

TAKE IT EASY, LEIA. YOU ACT LIKE THIS IS THE END OF THE UNIVERSE, OR SOMETHING.

IT MIGHT AS WELL BE, HAN...

ADMIRAL ACKBAR... I KNOW THAT EVERYONE HAS TO MAKE SOME SAC- RIFICES FOR THE GOOD OF THE ALLIANCE ...BUT DOES IT HAVE TO BE THIS?

ISN'T THERE SOME OTHER WAY, SIR?

I'M AFRAID NOT, GENERAL SOLO.

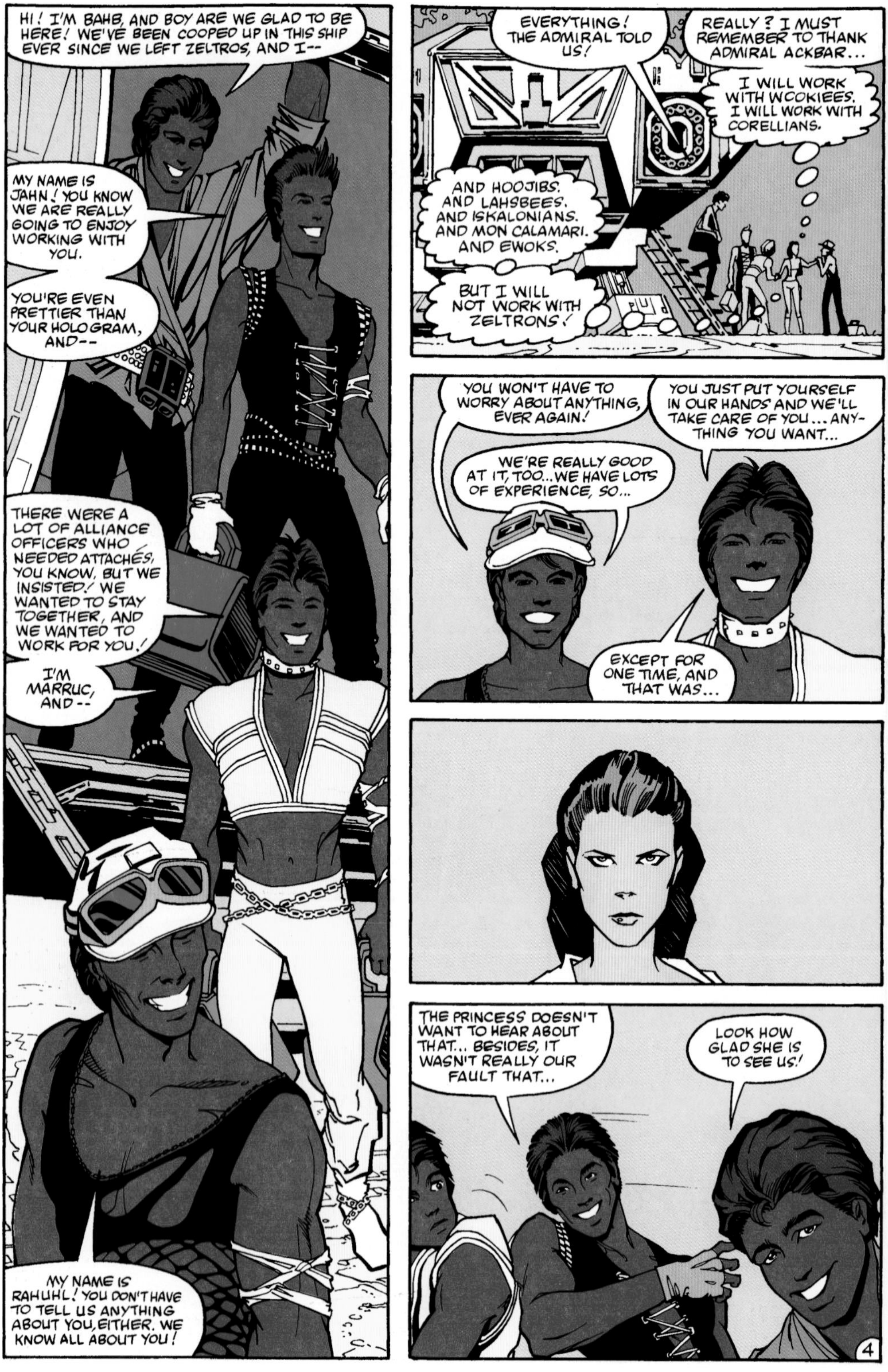
HI! I'M BAHB, AND BOY ARE WE GLAD TO BE HERE! WE'VE BEEN COOPED UP IN THIS SHIP EVER SINCE WE LEFT ZELTROS, AND I--
MY NAME IS JAHN! YOU KNOW WE ARE REALLY GOING TO ENJOY WORKING WITH YOU.
YOU'RE EVEN PRETTIER THAN YOUR HOLOGRAM, AND--
THERE WERE A LOT OF ALLIANCE OFFICERS WHO NEEDED ATTACHÉS, YOU KNOW, BUT WE INSISTED! WE WANTED TO STAY TOGETHER, AND WE WANTED TO WORK FOR YOU!
I'M MARRUC, AND--
MY NAME IS RAHUHL! YOU DON'T HAVE TO TELL US ANYTHING ABOUT YOU, EITHER. WE KNOW ALL ABOUT YOU!
EVERYTHING! THE ADMIRAL TOLD US!
REALLY? I MUST REMEMBER TO THANK ADMIRAL ACKBAR...
I WILL WORK WITH WOOKIEES. I WILL WORK WITH CORELLIANS.
AND HOOJIBS. AND LAHSBEES. AND ISKALONIANS. AND MON CALAMARI. AND EWOKS.
BUT I WILL NOT WORK WITH ZELTRONS!
YOU WON'T HAVE TO WORRY ABOUT ANYTHING, EVER AGAIN!
WE'RE REALLY GOOD AT IT, TOO...WE HAVE LOTS OF EXPERIENCE, SO...
YOU JUST PUT YOURSELF IN OUR HANDS AND WE'LL TAKE CARE OF YOU...ANYTHING YOU WANT...
EXCEPT FOR ONE TIME, AND THAT WAS...
THE PRINCESS DOESN'T WANT TO HEAR ABOUT THAT... BESIDES, IT WASN'T REALLY OUR FAULT THAT...
LOOK HOW GLAD SHE IS TO SEE US!
4

ADMIRAL...DID YOU REALLY HAVE TO ASSIGN THEM TO HER?

I'M AFRAID IT WAS INEVITABLE, GENERAL SOLO... FOR VERY DELICATE REASONS-- WHICH I AM NOT AT LIBERTY TO DIVULGE --PLACING THOSE YOUNG MEN IN HER HIGHNESS' CARE...

...IS ESSENTIAL, IF THE ALLIANCE WISHES TO RETAIN ITS DIPLO- MATIC TIES WITH THEIR HOMEWORLD...

TOO BAD, CONSIDERING HOW LEIA FEELS ABOUT ZELTRONS...

BUT MAYBE I CAN GET HER TO SEE REASON...

AND WE'RE REALLY GLAD TO MEET YOU, TOO!

ME? BUT I--!

OH, SURE! YOU'RE OUR HERO! EVERY- ONE ON ZELTRON WISHES THEY COULD MEET YOU!

ESPECIALLY THE GIRLS!

WHY...YOU'RE THE PILOT OF THE *MILLENNIUM FALCON!* CHEWBACCA THE WOOKIEE IS YOUR PARTNER!

THAT'S TRUE, BUT...

A LEGENDARY PILOT AND SMUGGLER...AND WHAT A NAVIGATOR!

...BLEW UP THE DEATH STAR! WHY, THEY NEVER COULD HAVE DEFEATED THE GALACTIC EMPIRE, WITHOUT YOUR HELP!

WELL, YEAH, BUT...

AND YOU'RE MODEST, AND EVERYTHING!

MAYBE WORKING WITH THESE KIDS ISN'T GOING TO BE SO BAD...

WAIT TILL WE TELL ALL OUR FRIENDS WE ACTUALLY GOT TO MEET THE FAMOUS GENERAL--

LANDO CALRISSIAN!

5

SHE'S RIGHT. THOSE LITTLE MENACES HAVE GOT TO GO!

ALL RIGHT, ADMIRAL. GIVEN THAT I'VE ACCEPTED THE SITUATION...

...WHAT IS OUR ASSIGNMENT?

CERTAIN WORLDS WITHIN THE ALLIANCE HAVE GIVEN VOICE, RECENTLY, TO CERTAIN RUMBLINGS...

THEY HINT THAT THOSE OF US WHO ACTUALLY OVERTHREW THE EMPIRE ARE PERHAPS, TOO ROUGH AND READY IN OUR METHODS TO ACTUALLY GOVERN NOW...

...THERE IS A PARTY, OF SORTS, BEING HELD ON KABRAY. THE LEADERS OF THE DISCONTENTS WILL ALL BE THERE.

YOU ARE TO GO... AND ENJOY YOURSELVES... AND BY BOTH WORD AND EXAMPLE, DO ALL YOU CAN TO LAY THEIR FEARS TO REST.

SEE-THREEPIO... HAVE YOU AND THE OTHER DROIDS FINISHED PREPARING EVERYONE'S GEAR AND LOADING IT ALL INTO THE PROPER SHIPS?

YES, ADMIRAL... ARTOO-DETOO AND I OVERSAW THE ENTIRE OPERATION OURSELVES...

IT WAS A JOB OF SOME COMPLEXITY, SEEING THAT THE MILITARY EXPEDITIONS HAD THE RIGHT WEAPONS, THE EXPLORATORY PARTIES THE RIGHT SURVIVAL GEAR, AND THE DIPLOMATS THE TOOLS OF THEIR TRADE...

BUT, I ASSURE YOU, NO OTHER DROIDS COULD HAVE DONE BETTER WITH SO MANY TEAMS DEPARTING AT ONE TIME!

I HOPE DANI, KIRO, AND I CAN COUNT ON THAT, THREEPIO.

WHERE YOU THREE OFF TO, LUKE?

WELL, BE GOOD...

PROBABLY TO FIND A BURNED OUT TRANSCEIVER... THERE'S A SCOUTING PARTY ON KINOOINE WHO HAVEN'T REPORTED IN LATELY. WE'RE GOING TO CHECK IT OUT...

HAVE FUN.

BETWEEN THE THREE OF US, WE SHOULD MANAGE BOTH.

YOU TWO DO THE SAME. SEE YOU WHEN WE GET BACK.

6

I DON'T BELIEVE IT. I SIMPLY DON'T BELIEVE IT. AS IF THINGS WEREN'T BAD ENOUGH ALREADY!

AND DISPUTE OUR FITNESS TO ADMINISTER THE FREEDOMS WE FOUGHT FOR...

BUT NOW I'M EXPECTED TO DO IT WITHOUT SO MUCH AS A DRESS TO WEAR!

NO, IT'S NOT ENOUGH THAT I HAVE TO COME BACK TO KABRAY, IN THE COMPANY OF FOUR ZELTRONS...

NOT BAD ENOUGH THAT I HAVE TO GO TO A PARTY, AND LISTEN TO A BUNCH OF PEOPLE WHO NEVER LIFTED A FINGER AGAINST THE EMPIRE YAWN AND MINCE...

I DON'T KNOW WHY YOU'RE SURPRISED. I EXPECTED SOMETHING LIKE THIS THE MINUTE I HEARD THREEPIO WAS IN CHARGE OF PACKING OUR GEAR.

I DIDN'T HEAR YOU SAY ANYTHING WHILE WE WERE STILL BACK ON ENDOR.

CHEER UP. THINK OF THE LOOK ON LUKE'S FACE, WHEN HE GOES LOOKING FOR HIS COLD WEATHER SURVIVAL SUIT... AND COMES UP WITH HALF A DOZEN PARTY DRESSES INSTEAD.

HA-HA.

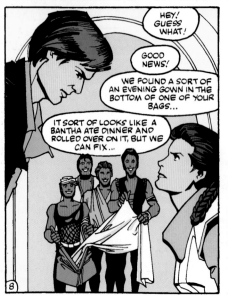

HEY! GUESS WHAT!

GOOD NEWS!

WE FOUND A SORT OF AN EVENING GOWN IN THE BOTTOM OF ONE OF YOUR BAGS...

IT SORT OF LOOKS LIKE A BANTHA ATE DINNER AND ROLLED OVER ON IT, BUT WE CAN FIX...

UM... I HAVE TO GET DRESSED. I'M SUPPOSED TO GO TO THIS PARTY TOO, YOU KNOW...

SURE, YOU JUST SLEEP, AND LEAVE EVERYTHING TO

COULD LOOK GREAT WITH A LITTLE

NOT THAT DRESS...I MEANT TO BURN IT, AFTER THAT BANQUET...THE AMBASSADOR UPSET HIS ENTIRE PLATE ON... I NEED A REST...

UNLESS THOSE ARE WINE STAINS

ALL IT NEEDS IS SOME

8

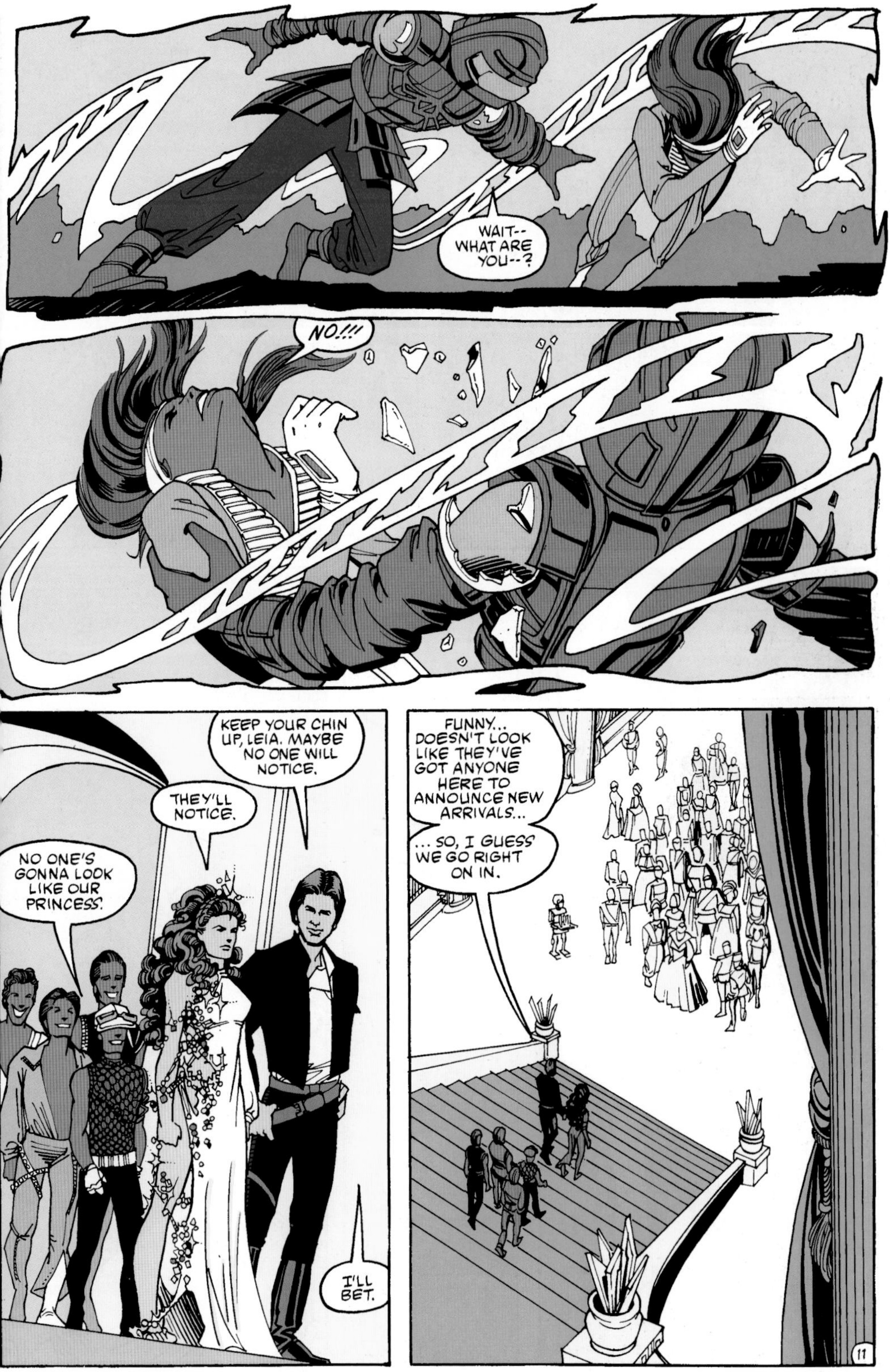
WAIT-- WHAT ARE YOU--?
NO.!!!
KEEP YOUR CHIN UP, LEIA. MAYBE NO ONE WILL NOTICE.
THEY'LL NOTICE.
NO ONE'S GONNA LOOK LIKE OUR PRINCESS.
I'LL BET.
FUNNY... DOESN'T LOOK LIKE THEY'VE GOT ANYONE HERE TO ANNOUNCE NEW ARRIVALS...
... SO, I GUESS WE GO RIGHT ON IN.
11

HONESTLY... THE WAY THESE PEOPLE ARE ALL STANDING AROUND STARING...

YOU'D THINK THEY'D NEVER SEEN ZELTRONS BEFORE.

YOUR HIGHNESS... WELCOME BACK TO KABRAY.

THANK YOU GOVERNOR. IT'S A PLEASURE TO BE BACK.

AND MAY I SAY THAT IT'S A PLEASURE TO WELCOME YOU...

...TO OUR DISTINGUISHED BAND OF PRISONERS?

HEY, NOW, WHOEVER YOU ARE, DON'T YOU THINK YOU'RE BEING A LITTLE OVERCONFIDENT, THROWING AROUND A WORD LIKE "PRISONERS" TO A MAN WHO HAS A BLASTER ON YOU?

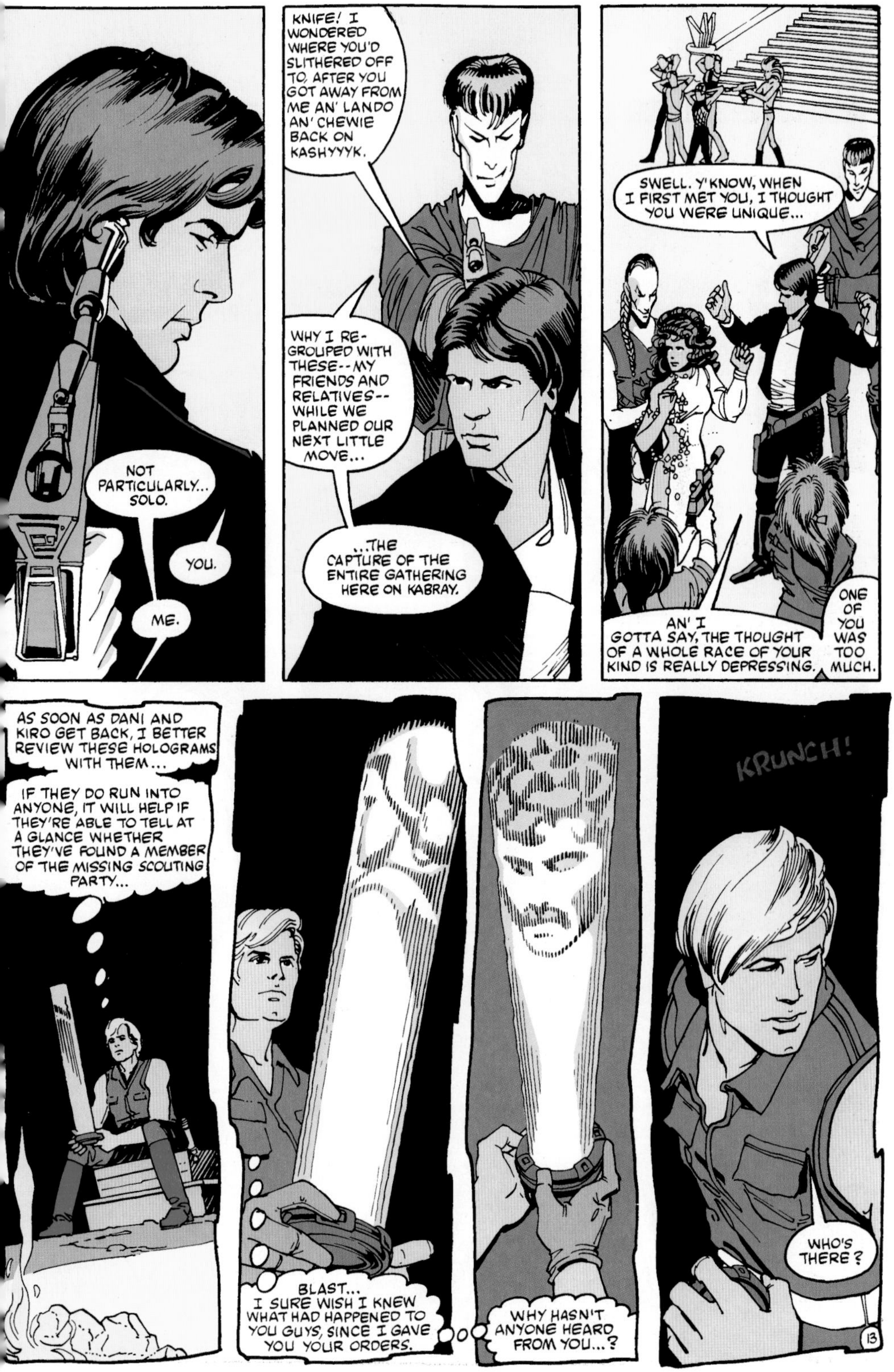
NOT PARTICULARLY... SOLO.
YOU.
ME.
KNIFE! I WONDERED WHERE YOU'D SLITHERED OFF TO, AFTER YOU GOT AWAY FROM ME AN' LANDO AN' CHEWIE BACK ON KASHYYYK.
WHY I RE-GROUPED WITH THESE--MY FRIENDS AND RELATIVES--WHILE WE PLANNED OUR NEXT LITTLE MOVE...
...THE CAPTURE OF THE ENTIRE GATHERING HERE ON KABRAY.
SWELL. Y'KNOW, WHEN I FIRST MET YOU, I THOUGHT YOU WERE UNIQUE...
AN' I GOTTA SAY, THE THOUGHT OF A WHOLE RACE OF YOUR KIND IS REALLY DEPRESSING.
ONE OF YOU WAS TOO MUCH.
AS SOON AS DANI AND KIRO GET BACK, I BETTER REVIEW THESE HOLOGRAMS WITH THEM...
IF THEY DO RUN INTO ANYONE, IT WILL HELP IF THEY'RE ABLE TO TELL AT A GLANCE WHETHER THEY'VE FOUND A MEMBER OF THE MISSING SCOUTING PARTY...
BLAST... I SURE WISH I KNEW WHAT HAD HAPPENED TO YOU GUYS, SINCE I GAVE YOU YOUR ORDERS.
WHY HASN'T ANYONE HEARD FROM YOU...?
KRUNCH!
WHO'S THERE?
13

WE'VE GOT NO BLASTERS, NO ALLIES, NO DROIDS...

THE ROOM IS OUTER-LOCKED, TOTALLY SEALED, WINDOWLESS...

≈ACHOO≈

AND COLD.

AH, CHEER UP, SWEETHEART. ONE OF 'EM'S BOUND TO COME IN HERE TO GLOAT SOONER OR LATER. I FIGURE THAT'S WHEN WE MAKE OUR MOVE.

I DON'T NEED CHEERING UP. I WANT TO KNOW WHO THOSE PEOPLE ARE AND WHAT THEY WANT.

I THINK THEY HAVE WHAT THEY WANT.

SHUT UP, RAHUHL.

LAST TIME I RAN INTO KNIFE, HE WAS LEADING ONE OF THOSE SLAVING OPERATIONS THAT THE ALLIANCE HAS BEEN SO CONCERNED ABOUT, SINCE OUR VICTORY.

THAT'S INTERESTING... I RAN INTO A SLAVING OPERATION MYSELF... THERE WERE NO KNIVES ON THE SCENE...

BUT THE PEOPLE RUNNING THAT ONE HAD THE SUPPORT OF A LOT OF THE EMPIRE'S OLD STORM TROOPERS.

I WONDER IF THE TWO ARE CONNECTED.

BEATS ME. LET'S ASK 'EM, WHEN WE GET OUT OF THIS.

254

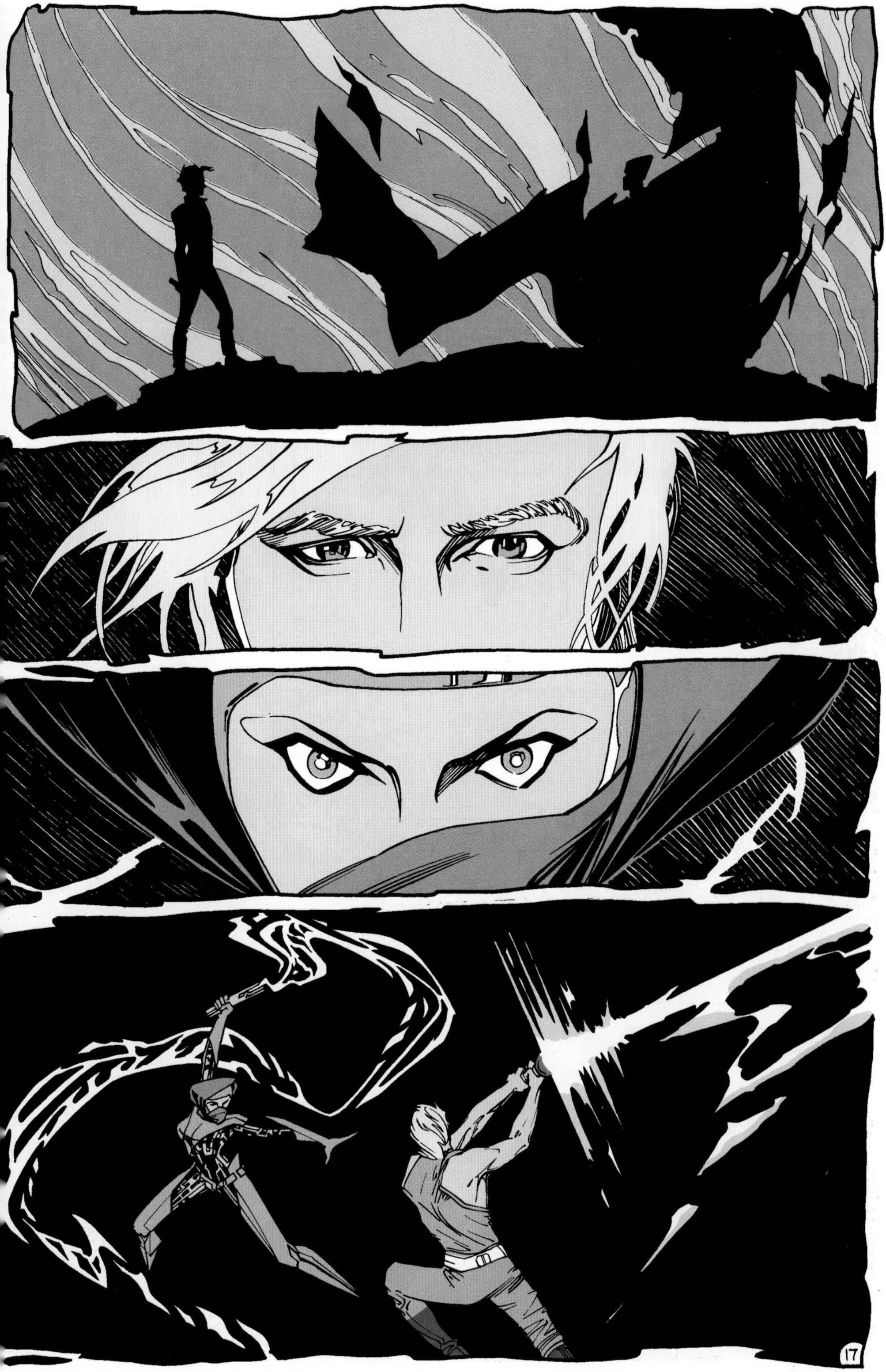
17

OH, NO, YOUR HIGHNESS. WHATEVER YOU HAVE TO SAY, BY WAY OF TREATY, YOU MAY SAY TO MY LEADERS... AFTER WE'VE TRANSPORTED YOU TO OUR BASE...

AND ANYTHING YOU HAVE TO SAY TO ME HAD BEST BE SAID FROM ACROSS THE ROOM...

NOT THAT I DON'T TRUST YOU, BUT--

YAAAA!!

--EH?

BASH

VORPP

LET'S GET 'EM!

GOOD WORK, JAHN!

OW!

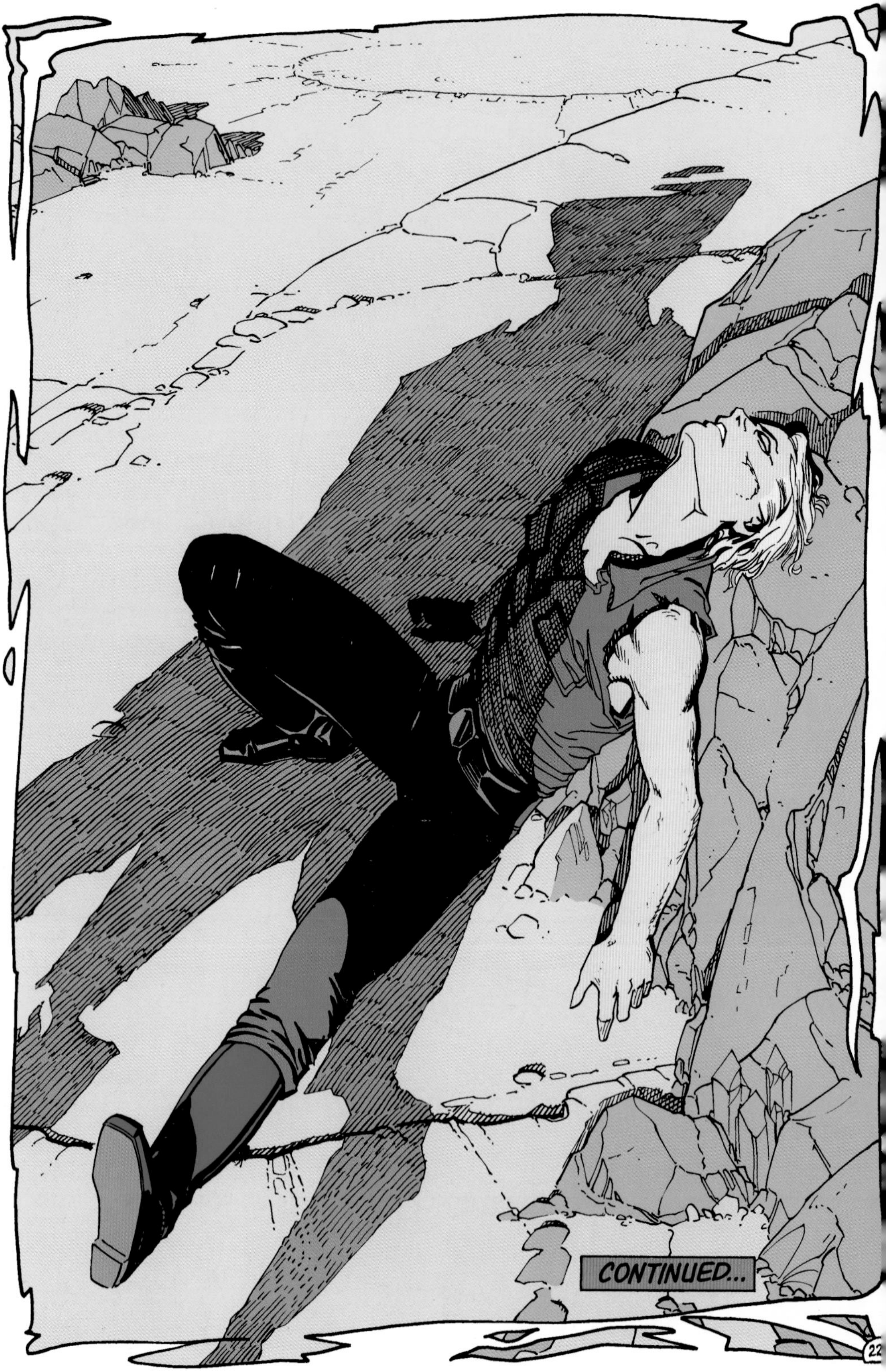
CONTINUED...
22

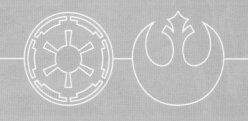

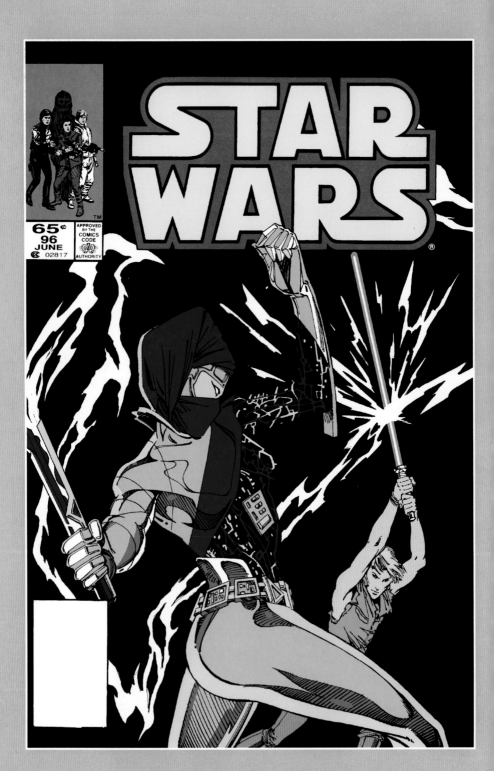

STAR WARS

65¢
96
JUNE
02817

TM

APPROVED
BY THE
COMICS
CODE
AUTHORITY

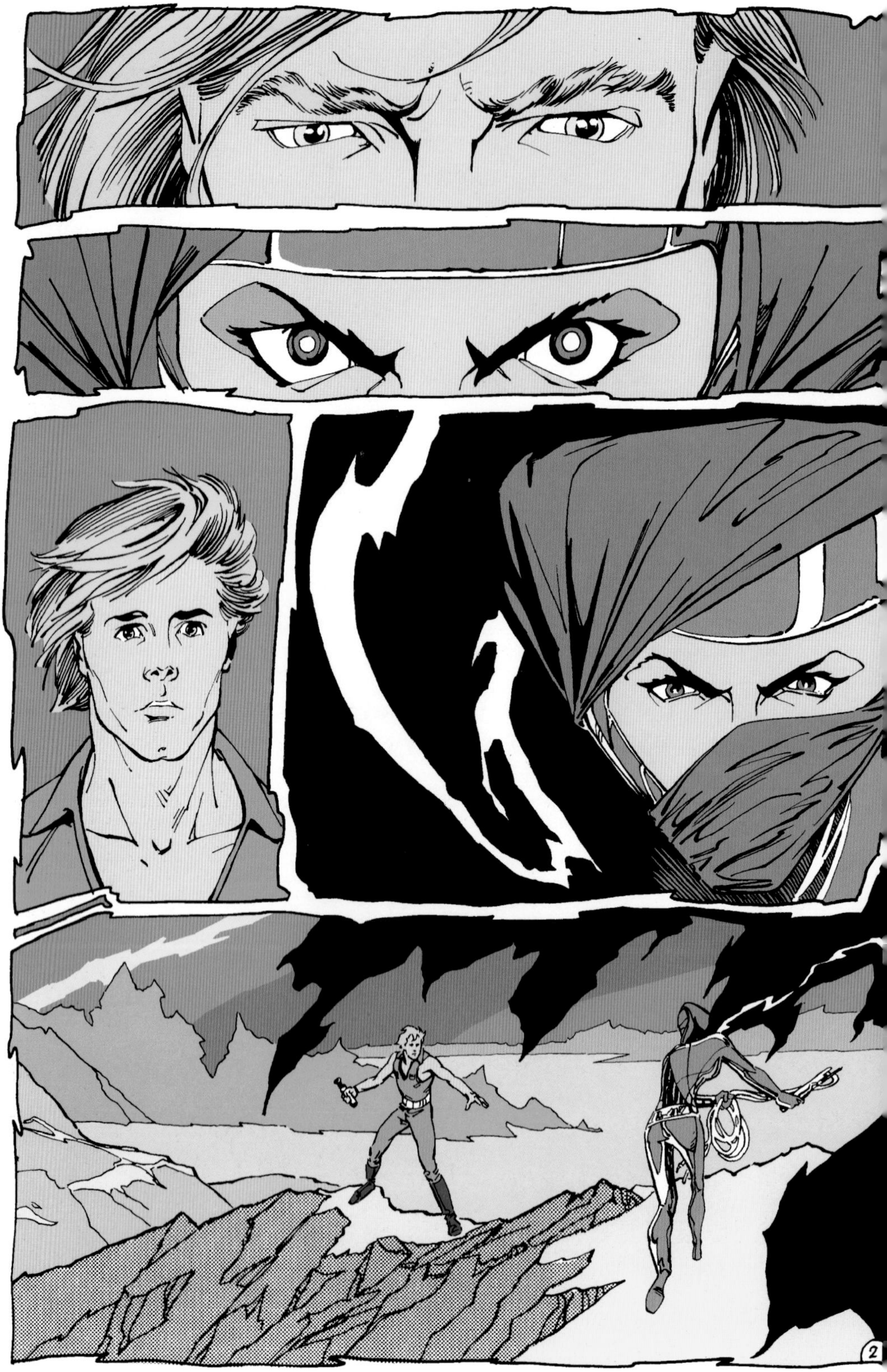
2

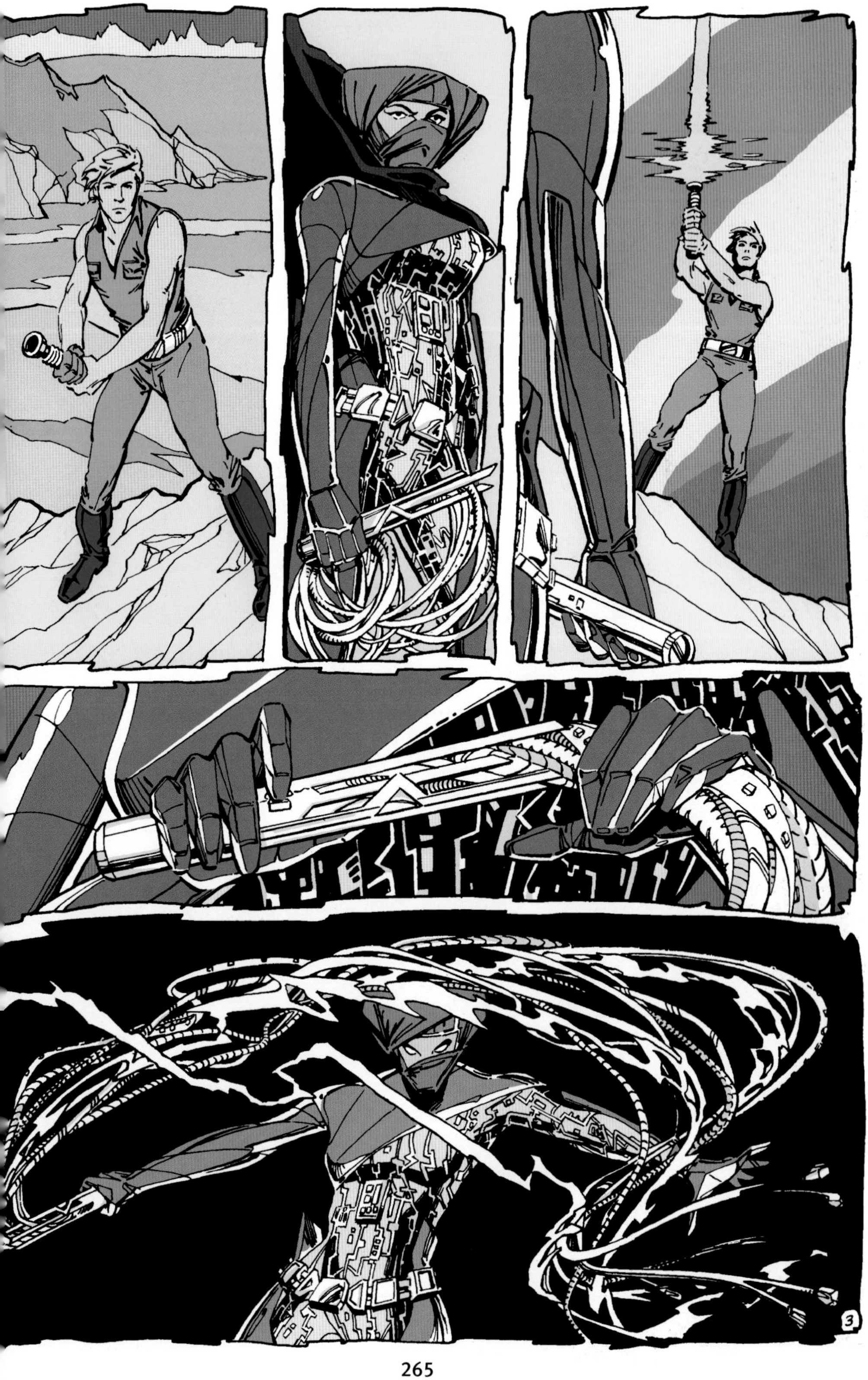
3

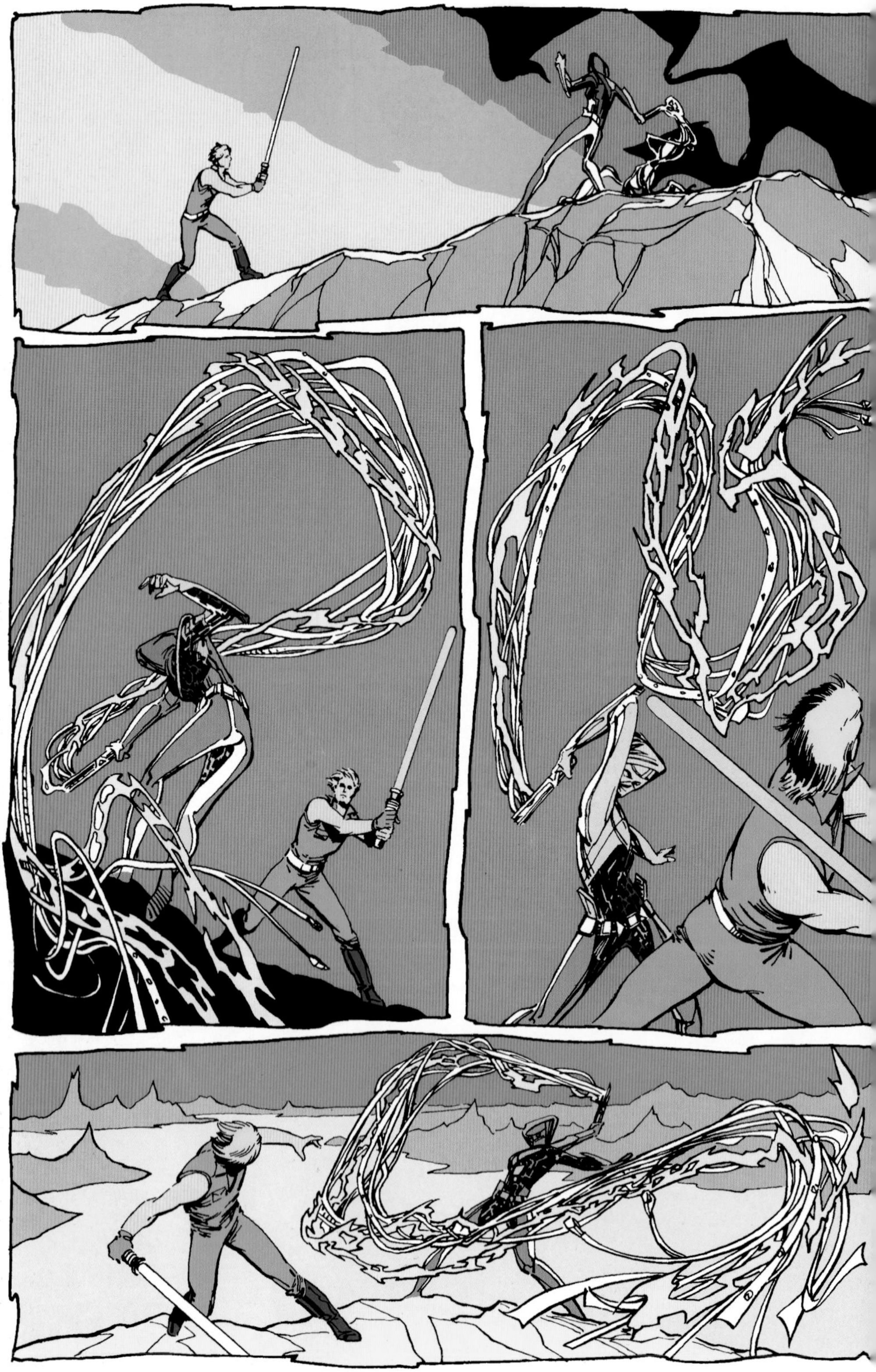

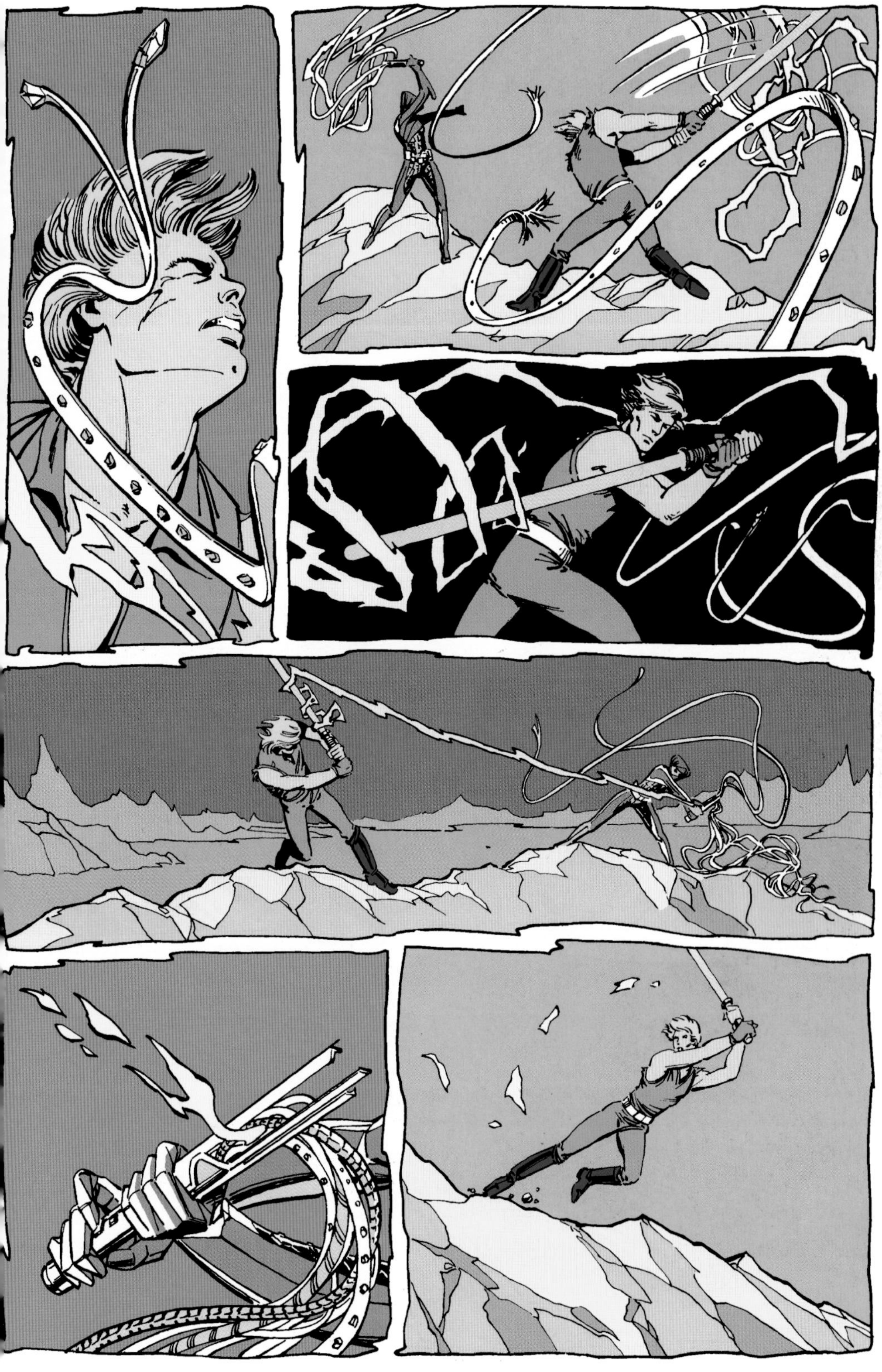

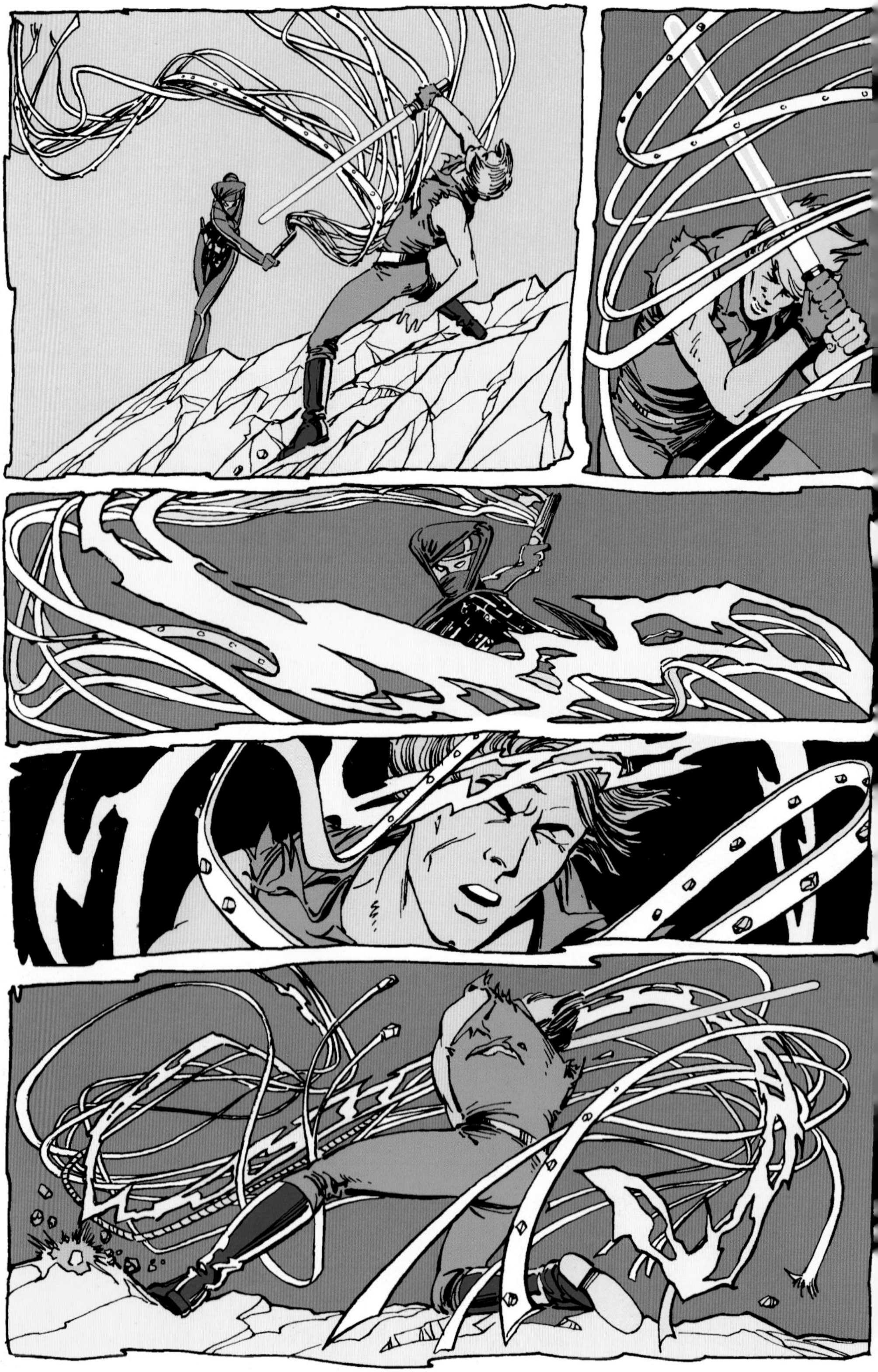

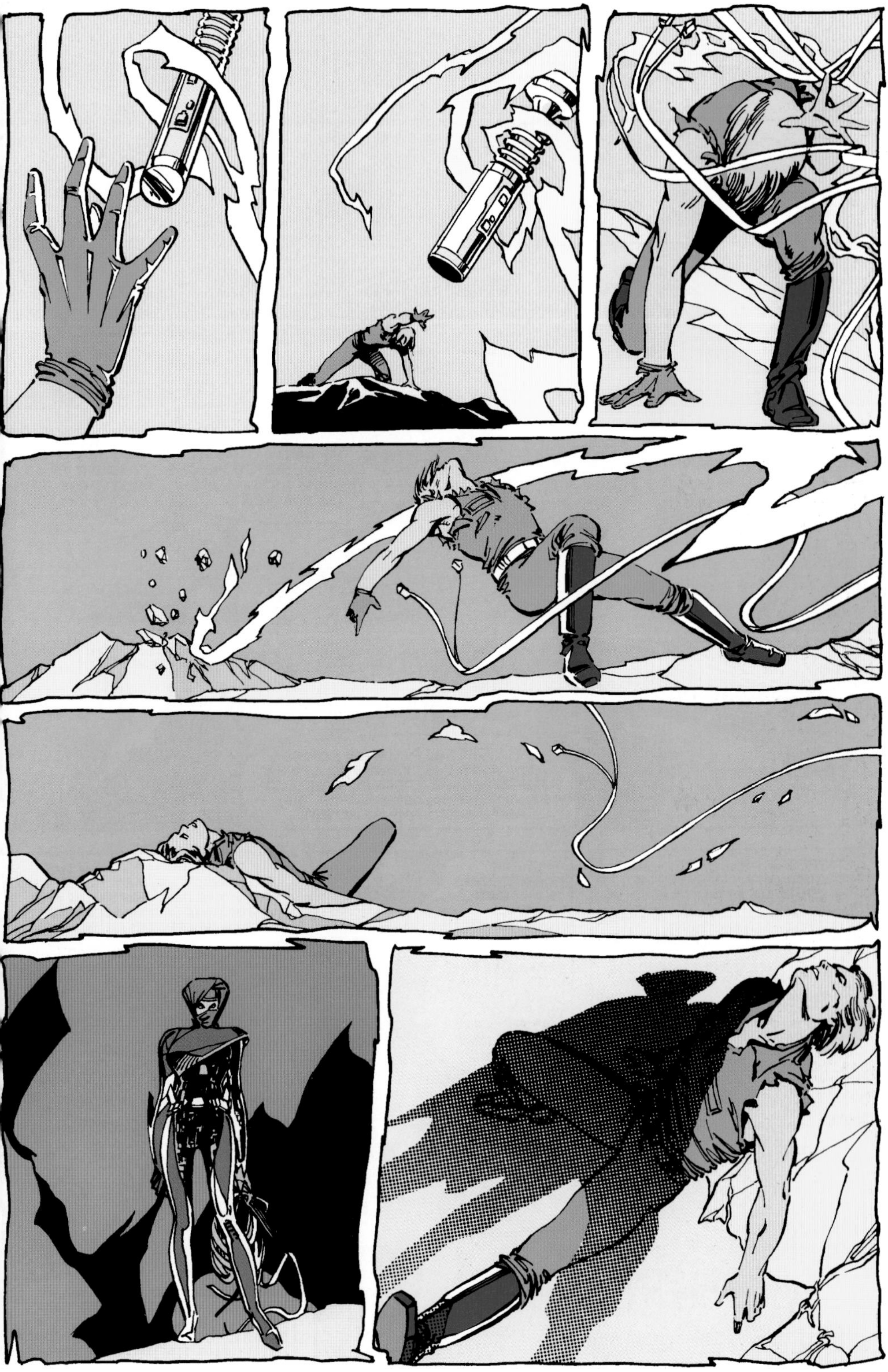

| JO DUFFY | CYNTHIA MARTIN | BOB WIACEK | RICK PARKER | GLYNIS OLIVER | ANN NOCENTI | JIM SHOOTER |
| WRITER | PENCILER | INKER | LETTERER | COLORIST | EDITOR | EDITOR IN CHIEF |

SO, LUMIYA, YOU'VE DONE IT AT LAST.

THAT'S RIGHT, DEN. I'VE DONE IT.

DEFEATED YOUR GREATEST ENEMY, THE MAN WHO HAS HAUNTED YOUR NIGHTMARES FOR AS LONG AS I'VE KNOWN YOU-- LUKE SKYWALKER.

NOW ALL THAT REMAINS IS TO CONQUER THOSE HE SERVED, YOUR ORIGINAL ENEMIES-- THE ALLIANCE OF FREE PLANETS.

I FOUGHT THE ALLIANCE BEFORE-- BACK WHEN THEY WERE STILL IN WHAT APPEARED TO BE A DOOMED REBELLION AGAINST THE GALACTIC EMPIRE. THEY ARE A HARD FOE TO DEFEAT...

...OVERCONFIDENCE, COUNTING TOO MUCH ON AN EASY VICTORY, COULD BE FATAL TO US.

BEATING SKYWALKER IS ENOUGH FOR ME.

THEN WHY DID YOU STOP SHORT OF KILLING HIM, IF THIS IS ALL THE SATISFACTION YOU EXPECT TO HAVE?

THERE ARE WORSE THINGS THAN DEATH, DEN.

I KNOW.

THAT IS WHY SKYWALKER STILL LIVES. IF I BE- LIEVED OTHER- WISE, THEN NO MATTER WHAT OUR MASTERS COMMANDED...

...I WOULD NOT HAVE SPARED HIM AT THE LAST MINUTE, ON THAT CLIFFSIDE.

AND THIS IS HIS WEAPON-- THE LIGHTSABER, USED BY THOSE WHO STUDY THE FIGHTING SKILLS AND MYSTIC ARTS OF THE JEDI KNIGHTS WHO ONCE KEPT PEACE IN THIS GALAXY?

TELL ME... HOW DOES IT WORK?

ON THE SAME PRINCIPLE AS MY WHIP...WHEN YOU ACTIVATE THAT STUD ON THE HILT, IT RELEASES A BEAM OF COHERENT ENERGY WHICH FORMS THE SWORD BLADE.

8

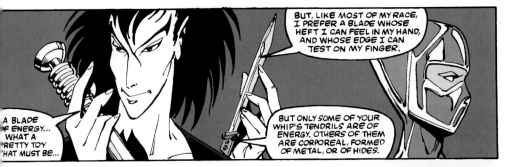

BUT, LIKE MOST OF MY RACE, I PREFER A BLADE WHOSE HEFT I CAN FEEL IN MY HAND, AND WHOSE EDGE I CAN TEST ON MY FINGER.

A BLADE OF ENERGY... WHAT A PRETTY TOY THAT MUST BE...

BUT ONLY SOME OF YOUR WHIP'S TENDRILS ARE OF ENERGY. OTHERS OF THEM ARE CORPOREAL, FORMED OF METAL, OR OF HIDES.

THAT COMBINATION IS WHAT DEFEATED HIM. HIS JEDI TRAINING HAD PREPARED HIM FOR AN ENERGY WEAPON, OR A SOLID ONE. NOT ONE THAT WAS BOTH AT ONCE.

WELL, LIVE AND LEARN. HE'LL KNOW BETTER NEXT TIME.

THERE WILL BE NO NEXT TIME.

WHAT DO YOU HEAR FROM THE MAIN FLEET?

WORD IS GOOD. WE RECEIVED A TRANSMISSION JUST BEFORE THEY MADE THEIR LAST DROP INTO HYPERSPACE.

THEY WERE PLEASED TO HEAR THAT WE HAD THE UNDERGROUND BASE READY HERE, AND POINTS OF POWER THROUGHOUT THIS GALAXY ALREADY ESTABLISHED.

THEIR VICTORY IS IMPORTANT TO ME, AND TO ALL OF MY ALLIES. I WOULDN'T LEAVE ANYTHING TO CHANCE.

NEITHER, DEAR LUMIYA, DO THE NAGAI.

9

BEFORE THE OTHERS ARRIVE, I WANT TO TEST THE VERACITY OF THAT EXTRAORDINARY REPORT WE RECEIVED LAST NIGHT-- --THAT A BAND OF THIRTEEN NAGAI, WHO HAD CAPTURED A MAJOR DIPLOMATIC BASE OF THE ALLIANCE--

--WERE DEFEATED AND CAPTURED BY FOUR UNARMED TEENAGED BOYS ?!

THERE'S NOTHING EXTRAORDINARY IN THAT. THE BOYS WERE ZELTRONS. IF YOUR PEOPLE WISH TO CONQUER HERE, THEY'D BEST LEARN TO ALLOW FOR THAT...

ALL ZELTRONS ARE OBSESSED WITH ROMANCE. WHEN THEY CANNOT LOVE, THEY FIGHT. BOTH ARE SPORTS TO THEM.

COUPLED WITH THEIR LOVE OF GAMBLING, IT MAKES ONE ZELTRON IN THE GRIP OF ENTHU-SIASM A FORMIDABLE ENEMY. A PACK OF ADOLESCENTS IS VIRTUALLY A FORCE OF NATURE.

AND THIS GIRL-- THIS DANI --SHE IS FROM ZELTROS?

LOOK AT HER HAIR AND SKIN. THEY MARK HER UNMISTAKABLY.

LUMIYA, LET ME HAVE HER. THERE IS MUCH I NEED TO LEARN FROM HER, TO ENSURE MY PEOPLE'S VICTORY...

AND PERHAPS, BEFORE I AM THROUGH, SHE MIGHT LEARN A LITTLE FROM ME, AS WELL.

I HAVE SKYWALKER. NONE OF THE REST THAT WE'VE CAPTURED OR KILLED ARE OF THE SLIGHTEST INTEREST TO ME. TAKE BOTH OF THESE IF YOU WISH...

YOU HEARD THE DARK LADY. BRING THE ZELTRON AND FOLLOW ME... AND TREAT HER KINDLY. REMEMBER, SHE HADN'T THE GOOD FORTUNE YOU DID, IN BEING OFFERED A CHANCE TO SERVE US.

Y-YES, MASTER DEN... LADY LUMIYA...

L-LUKE...

DANI... YOU HAVE... TO SAVE HER...

10

272

OOOHHHH...

UUHMMM

I... SWIM! I BREATHE. I HURT AS I HAVE NEVER HURT BEFORE!

BUT I LIVE!

THANKS TO LUKE-- THANKS TO THE SPIRIT THAT MAKES ALL THAT LIVE CARE FOR THOSE WHO BELONG WITH THEM --

I LIVE!!

LUKE? LUKE, MY FRIEND, ARE YOU HERE? DANI?

DANI?

NO ANSWER... AND JUDGING BY THE LIGHT, IT'S BEEN HOURS SINCE I STUMBLED BACK HERE.

THEY ARE MY FRIENDS. THEY NEED ME. I MUST FIND THEM.

BUT FIRST, I MUST OUTFIT MYSELF.

THAT WOMAN'S WHIP DESTROYED MY REBREATHER GARB... UNLESS I CAN FIND SOME KIND OF CLOTHING THAT WILL CONTAIN ENOUGH MOISTURE TO KEEP MY SKIN WARM...

AND A HELMET THAT WILL HOLD WATER FOR ME TO BREATHE, I CANNOT LIVE FOR LONG.

I'VE CARRIED THIS BLADE WITH ME SINCE BEFORE I LEFT MY HOMEWORLD, ISKALON. WELL, BY THE SCHOOL, LET IT SERVE ME WELL TODAY.

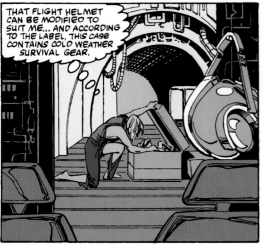

THAT FLIGHT HELMET CAN BE MODIFIED TO SUIT ME... AND ACCORDING TO THE LABEL, THIS CASE CONTAINS COLD WEATHER SURVIVAL GEAR.

PARTY DRESSES? I MUST HAVE THE WRONG BOX!

11

PLINK

EH?

REI? TARU, IS THAT YOU?

NO!

ERK

IT IS ONE YOUR LEADER LEFT FOR DEAD...

...AN ISKALONIAN GHOST WHO WANTS A LOT OF COMPANY!

WE SEARCHED ALL AFTERNOON, AND STILL NO SIGN OF THE INVADERS' BASE. NOR THEIR SHIP. LUMIYA WON'T BE PLEASED. SHE DOESN'T TAKE FAILURE WELL.

THEN TELL HER TO SEARCH. THERE ARE A LOT OF HIDING PLACES ON THIS FORSAKEN BALL OF ROCK.

I WONDER WHERE MENDO GOT TO...

HE BETTER BE INSIDE. OTHERWISE, HE'LL BE IN REAL TROUBLE.

HE IS.

AND NOW, SO ARE YOU. AND SO IS ANY-ONE ELSE WHO TRIES TO STOP ME!

12

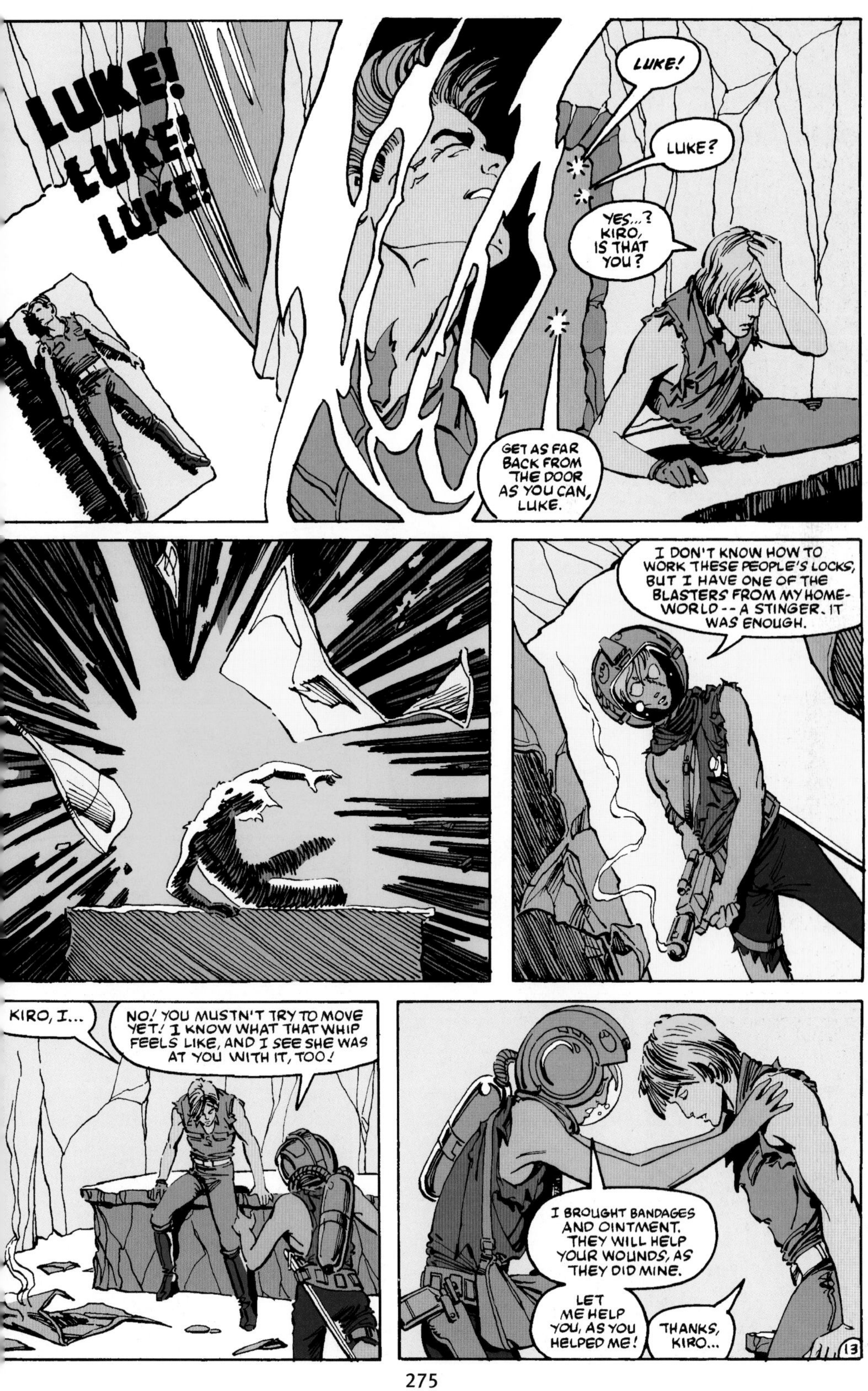
LUKE!
LUKE!
LUKE!
LUKE!
LUKE?
YES...? KIRO, IS THAT YOU?
GET AS FAR BACK FROM THE DOOR AS YOU CAN, LUKE.
I DON'T KNOW HOW TO WORK THESE PEOPLE'S LOCKS, BUT I HAVE ONE OF THE BLASTERS FROM MY HOME-WORLD -- A STINGER. IT WAS ENOUGH.
KIRO, I...
NO! YOU MUSTN'T TRY TO MOVE YET! I KNOW WHAT THAT WHIP FEELS LIKE, AND I SEE SHE WAS AT YOU WITH IT, TOO!
I BROUGHT BANDAGES AND OINTMENT. THEY WILL HELP YOUR WOUNDS, AS THEY DID MINE.
LET ME HELP YOU, AS YOU HELPED ME!
THANKS, KIRO...
13

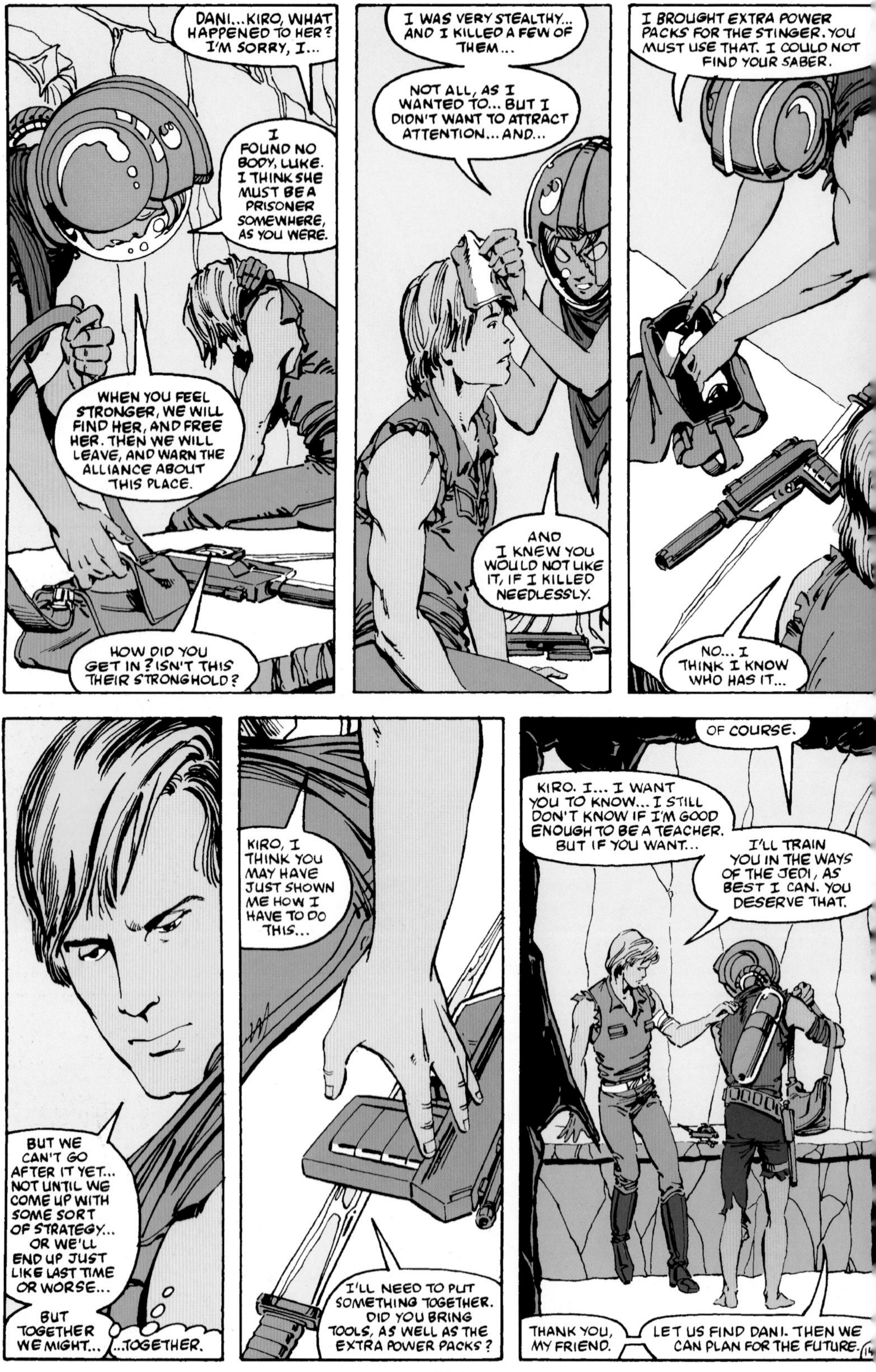
DANI...KIRO, WHAT HAPPENED TO HER? I'M SORRY, I...
I FOUND NO BODY, LUKE. I THINK SHE MUST BE A PRISONER SOMEWHERE, AS YOU WERE.
WHEN YOU FEEL STRONGER, WE WILL FIND HER, AND FREE HER. THEN WE WILL LEAVE, AND WARN THE ALLIANCE ABOUT THIS PLACE.
HOW DID YOU GET IN? ISN'T THIS THEIR STRONGHOLD?
I WAS VERY STEALTHY... AND I KILLED A FEW OF THEM...
NOT ALL, AS I WANTED TO... BUT I DIDN'T WANT TO ATTRACT ATTENTION... AND...
AND I KNEW YOU WOULD NOT LIKE IT, IF I KILLED NEEDLESSLY.
I BROUGHT EXTRA POWER PACKS FOR THE STINGER. YOU MUST USE THAT. I COULD NOT FIND YOUR SABER.
NO... I THINK I KNOW WHO HAS IT...
BUT WE CAN'T GO AFTER IT YET... NOT UNTIL WE COME UP WITH SOME SORT OF STRATEGY... OR WE'LL END UP JUST LIKE LAST TIME OR WORSE...
BUT TOGETHER WE MIGHT...
...TOGETHER.
KIRO, I THINK YOU MAY HAVE JUST SHOWN ME HOW I HAVE TO DO THIS...
I'LL NEED TO PUT SOMETHING TOGETHER. DID YOU BRING TOOLS, AS WELL AS THE EXTRA POWER PACKS?
OF COURSE.
KIRO. I... I WANT YOU TO KNOW... I STILL DON'T KNOW IF I'M GOOD ENOUGH TO BE A TEACHER. BUT IF YOU WANT...
I'LL TRAIN YOU IN THE WAYS OF THE JEDI, AS BEST I CAN. YOU DESERVE THAT.
THANK YOU, MY FRIEND.
LET US FIND DANI. THEN WE CAN PLAN FOR THE FUTURE.

I BELIEVE YOU HAVE SOMETHING THAT BELONGS TO ME.

YOU!

HELLO, LUMIYA.

NO!!

CURSE YOU, USING THE *FORCE*-- TELEKINESIS.

THE POWER OF ENERGY OVER MATTER... AND MIND OVER BOTH.

YOU DIDN'T THINK I'D FACE YOU UNPREPARED A SECOND TIME, DID YOU?

THEN I HOPE YOU'VE COME PREPARED TO DIE!

15

LIKE ALL OF THE OTHERS FROM THE ALLIANCE WHO MET YOU HERE?

I WANTED YOU ALIVE-- ALIVE AND WITHOUT HOPE! BUT I'LL KILL YOU MYSELF SOONER THAN SEE YOU GO FREE!

WILL YOU?

COME ON, THEN.

AGAINST THE TWO NATURES OF YOUR WEAPON.

TWO BLADES-- ONE LONG AND ONE SHORT--?

278

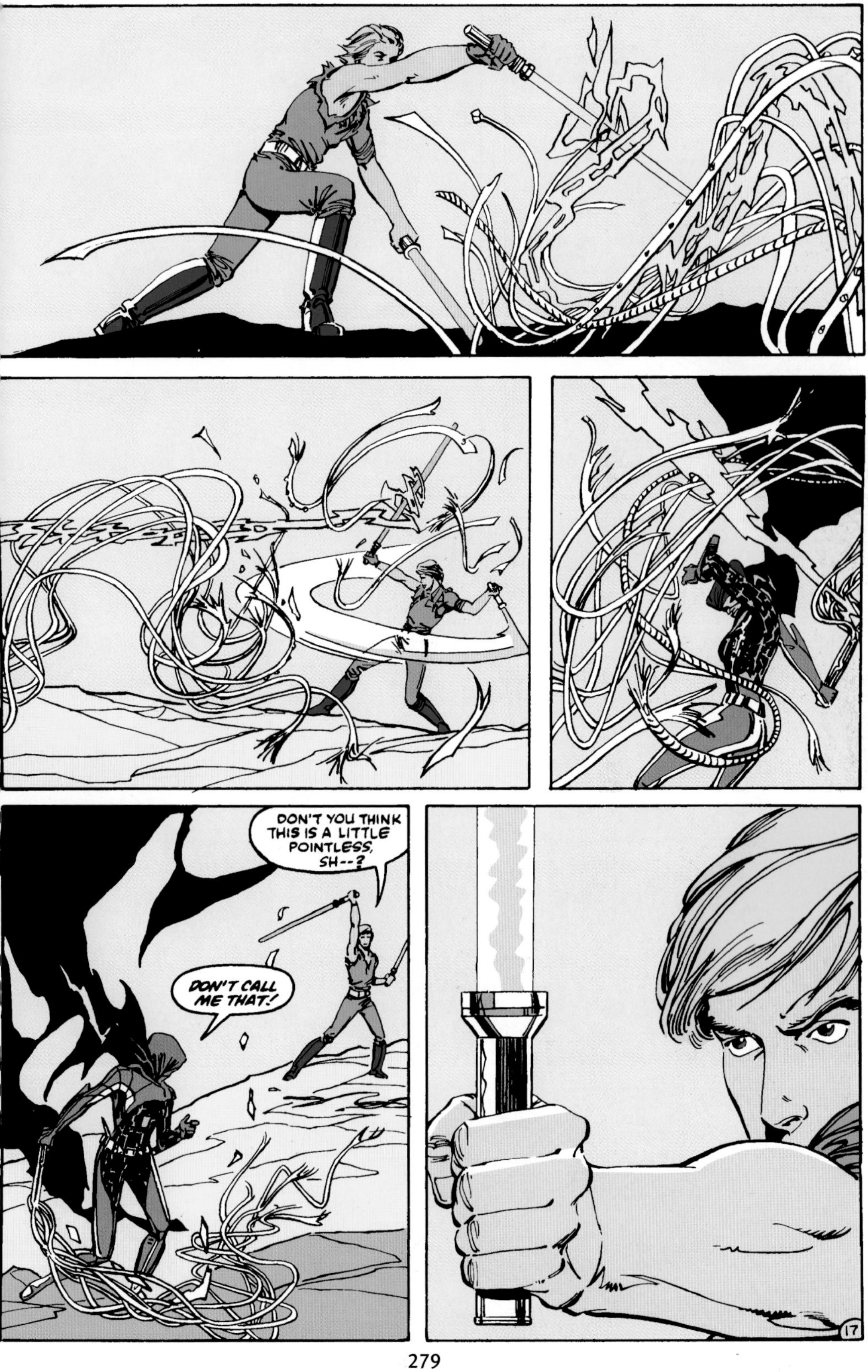
DON'T YOU THINK THIS IS A LITTLE POINTLESS, SH--?
DON'T CALL ME THAT!
17

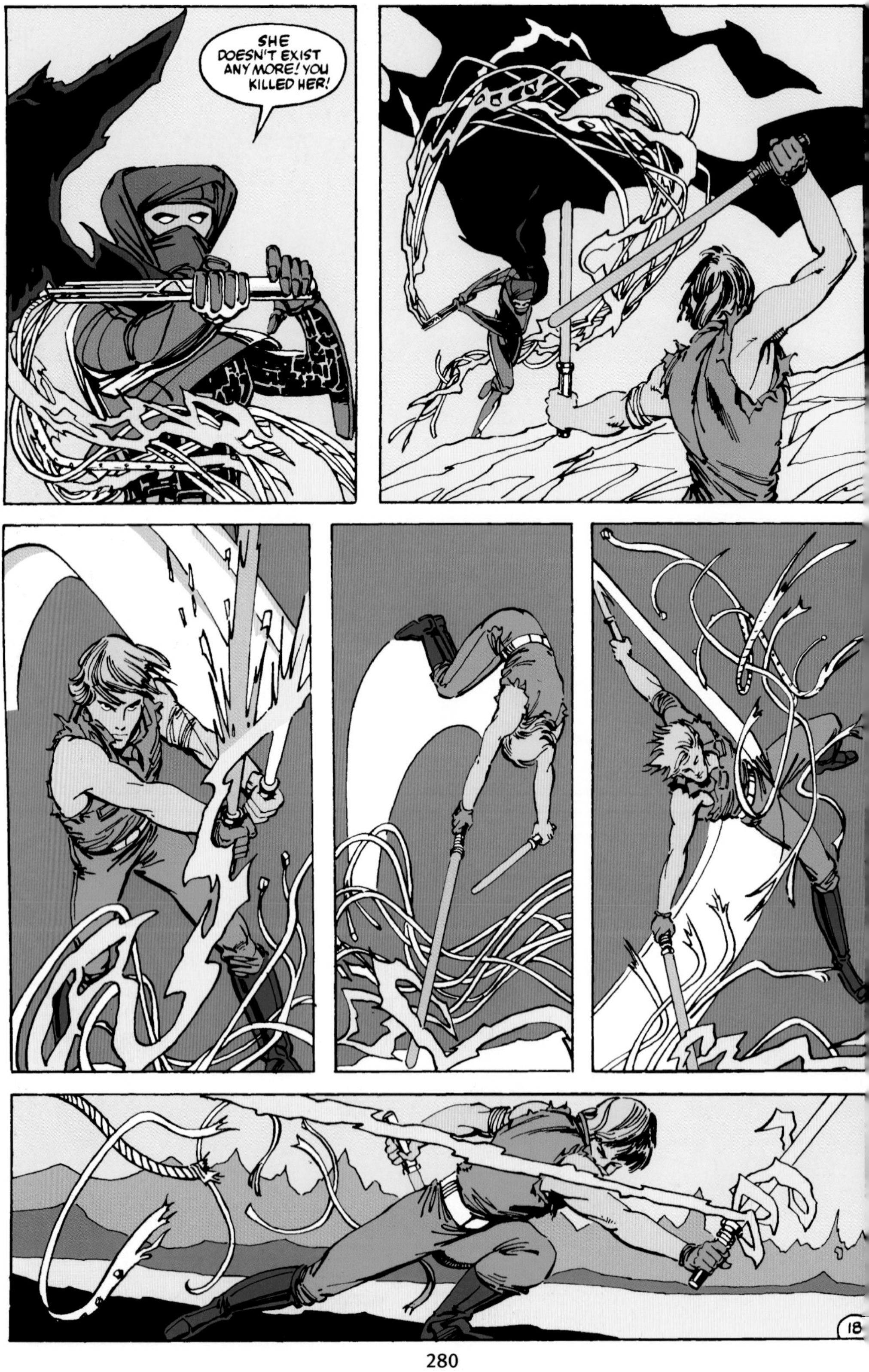
SHE DOESN'T EXIST ANY MORE! YOU KILLED HER!
18

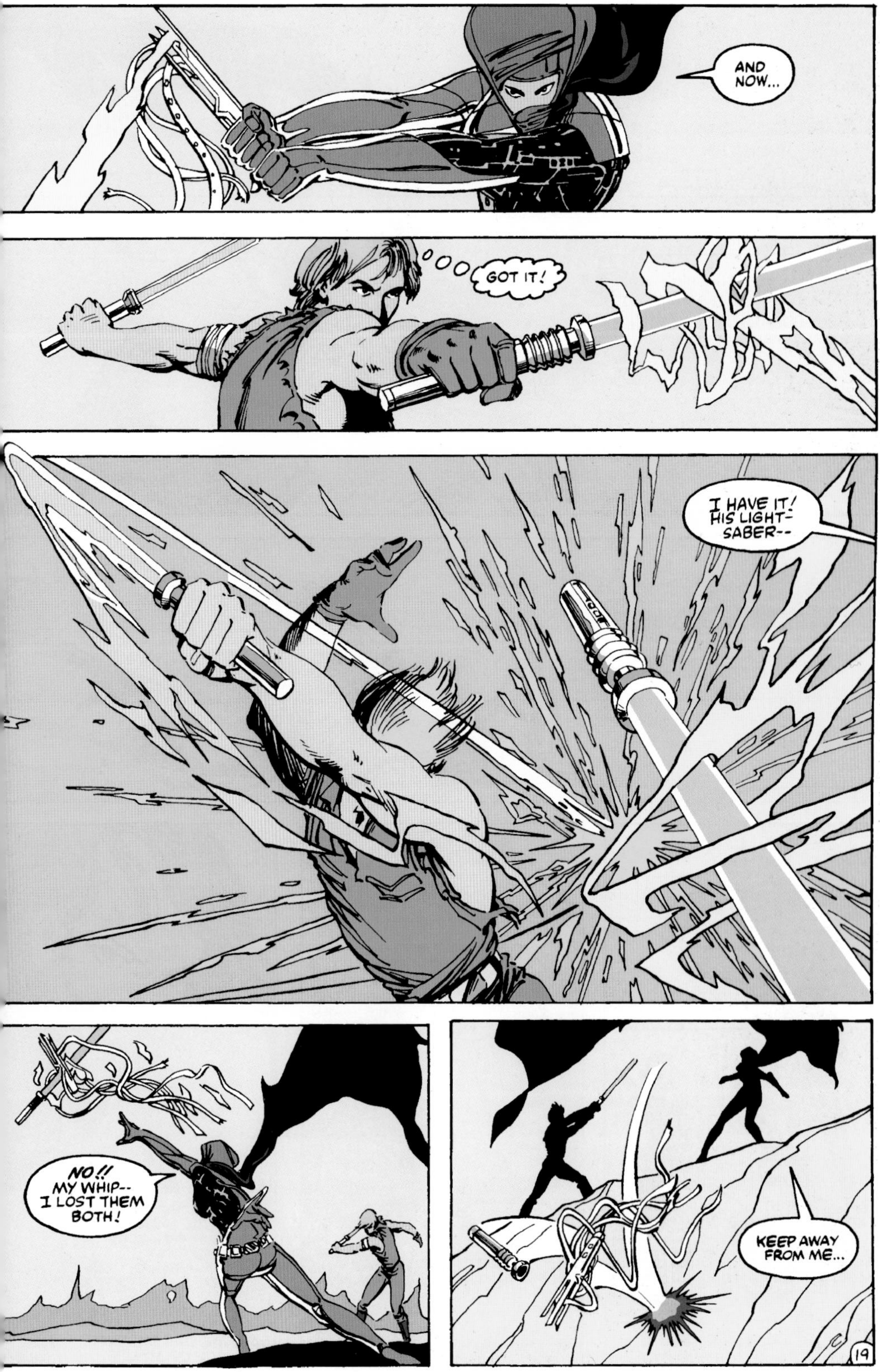
AND NOW...
GOT IT!
I HAVE IT! HIS LIGHT-SABER--
NO!! MY WHIP-- I LOST THEM BOTH!
KEEP AWAY FROM ME...
19

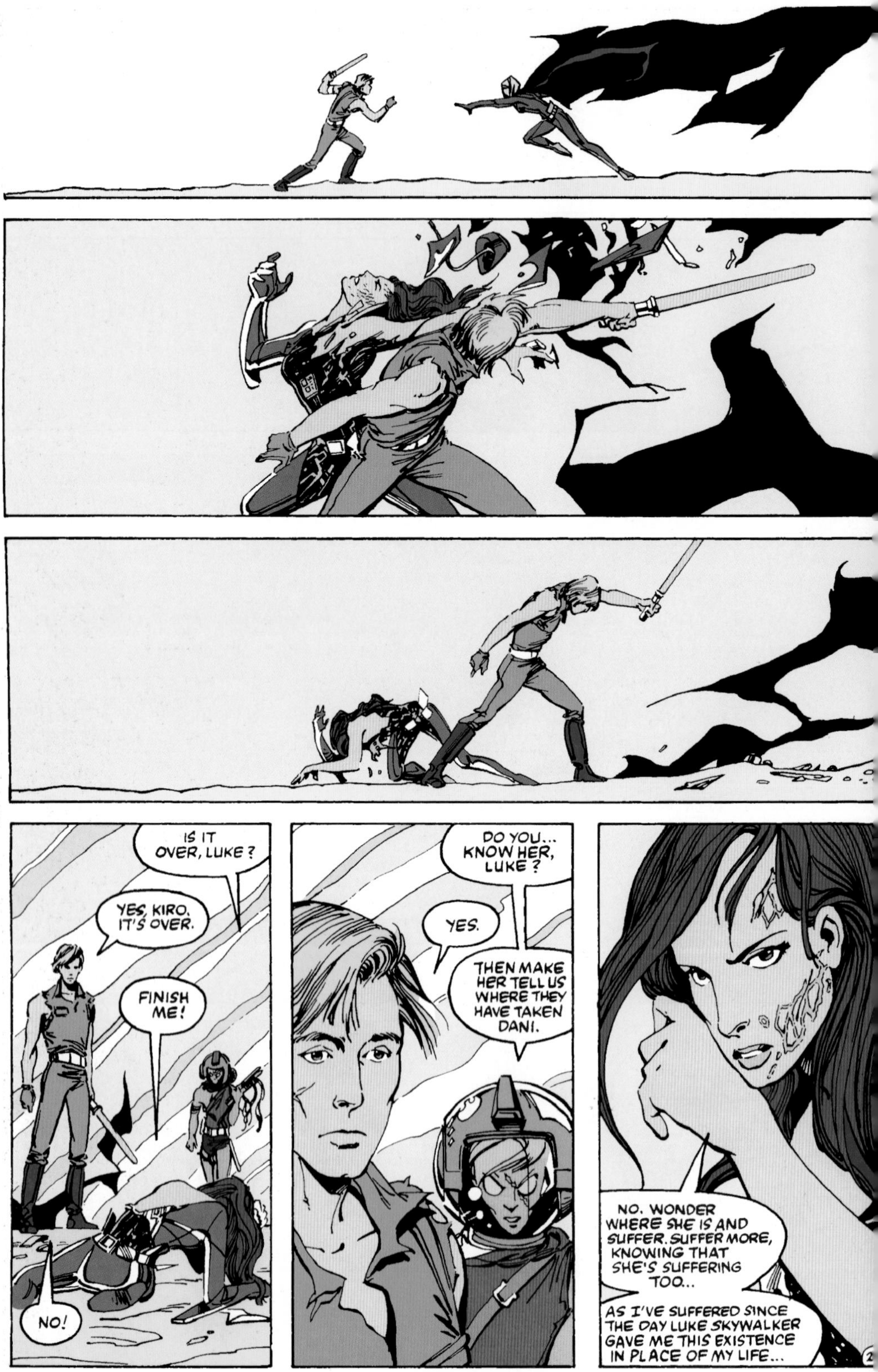
IS IT
OVER, LUKE?
YES, KIRO.
IT'S OVER.
FINISH
ME!
NO!
DO YOU...
KNOW HER,
LUKE?
YES.
THEN MAKE
HER TELL US
WHERE THEY
HAVE TAKEN
DANI.
NO. WONDER
WHERE SHE IS AND
SUFFER. SUFFER MORE,
KNOWING THAT
SHE'S SUFFERING
TOO...
AS I'VE SUFFERED SINCE
THE DAY LUKE SKYWALKER
GAVE ME THIS EXISTENCE
IN PLACE OF MY LIFE...

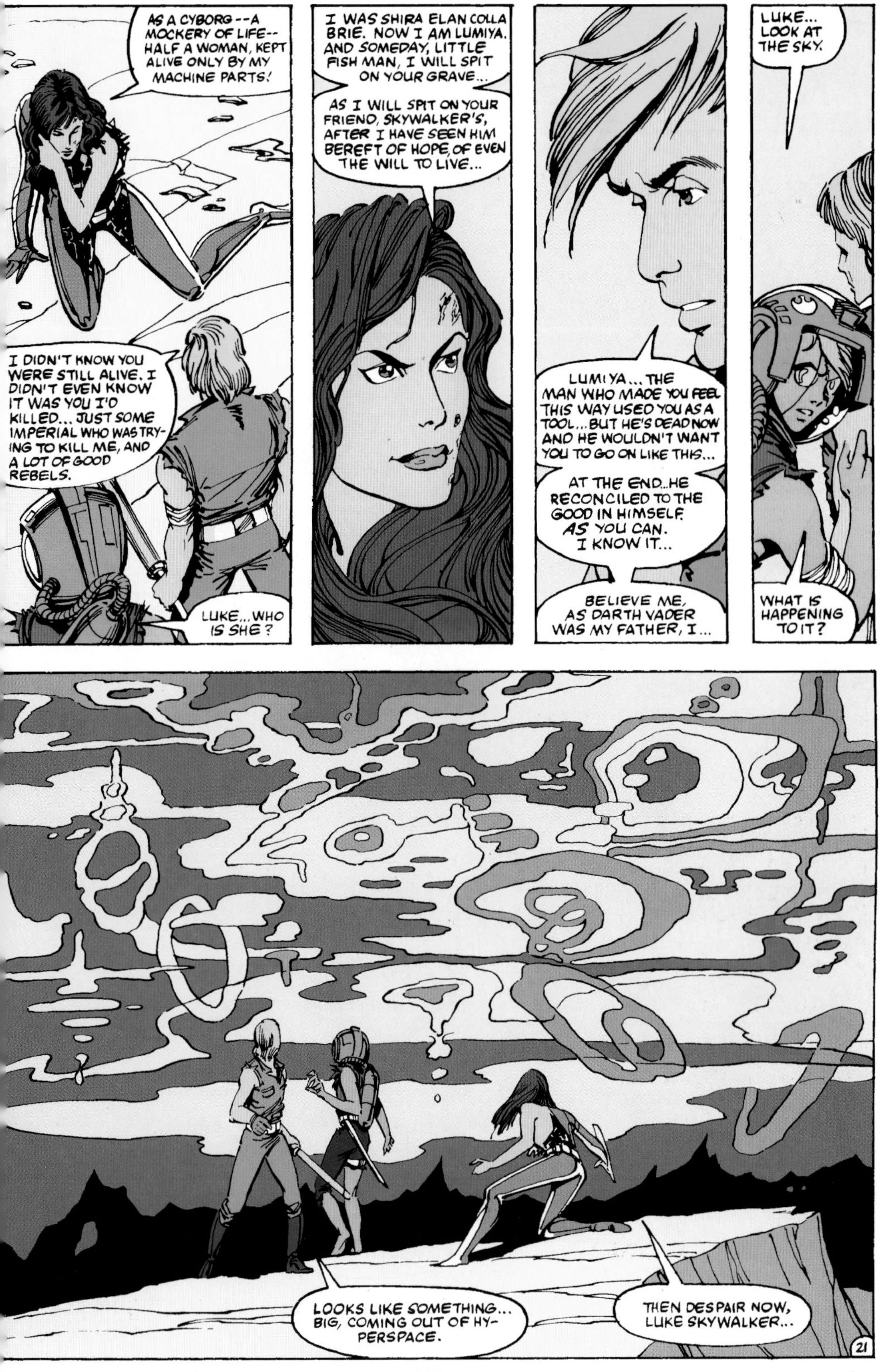
AS A CYBORG--A MOCKERY OF LIFE--HALF A WOMAN, KEPT ALIVE ONLY BY MY MACHINE PARTS!
I DIDN'T KNOW YOU WERE STILL ALIVE. I DIDN'T EVEN KNOW IT WAS YOU I'D KILLED... JUST SOME IMPERIAL WHO WAS TRYING TO KILL ME, AND A LOT OF GOOD REBELS.
LUKE... WHO IS SHE?
I WAS SHIRA ELAN COLLA BRIE. NOW I AM LUMIYA. AND SOMEDAY, LITTLE FISH MAN, I WILL SPIT ON YOUR GRAVE...
AS I WILL SPIT ON YOUR FRIEND, SKYWALKER'S, AFTER I HAVE SEEN HIM BEREFT OF HOPE, OF EVEN THE WILL TO LIVE...
LUMIYA... THE MAN WHO MADE YOU FEEL THIS WAY USED YOU AS A TOOL... BUT HE'S DEAD NOW AND HE WOULDN'T WANT YOU TO GO ON LIKE THIS...
AT THE END..HE RECONCILED TO THE GOOD IN HIMSELF. AS YOU CAN. I KNOW IT...
BELIEVE ME, AS DARTH VADER WAS MY FATHER, I...
LUKE... LOOK AT THE SKY.
WHAT IS HAPPENING TO IT?
LOOKS LIKE SOMETHING... BIG, COMING OUT OF HYPERSPACE.
THEN DESPAIR NOW, LUKE SKYWALKER...
21

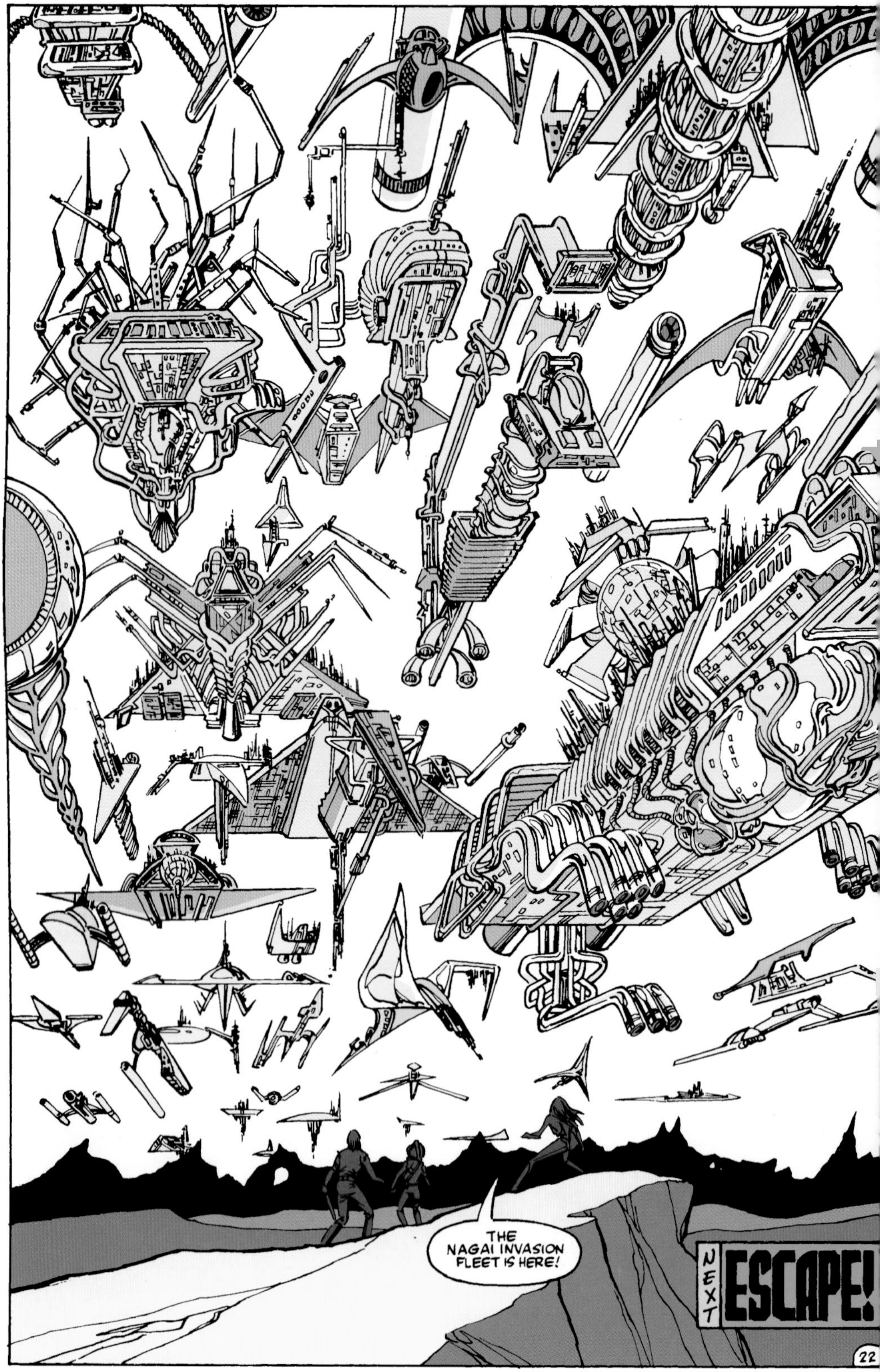
THE NAGAI INVASION FLEET IS HERE!
NEXT
ESCAPE!
22

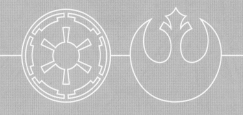

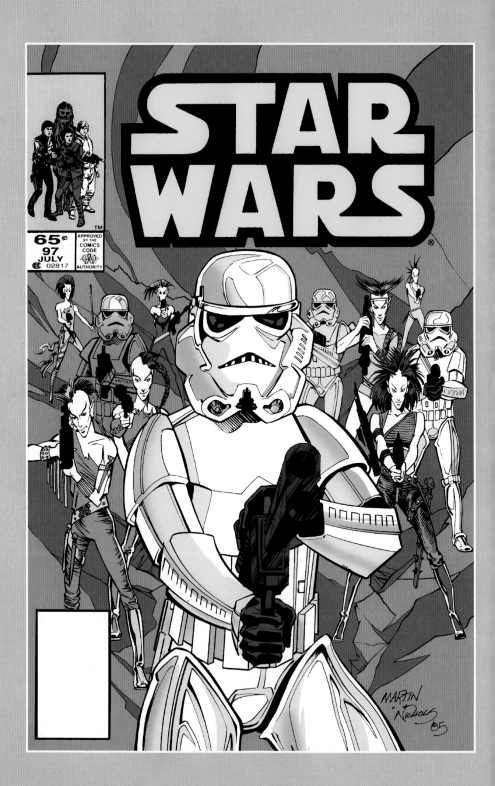

ucasfilm PRESENTS: STAR WARS™ THE GREATEST SPACE FANTASY OF ALL!
O DUFFY WRITER
CYNTHIA MARTIN PENCILER
ART NICHOLS INKER
RICK PARKER LETTERING
PETRA SCOTESE COLORING
ANN NOCENTI EDITOR
JIM SHOOTER EDITOR IN CHIEF
ESCAPE
IMPERIAL STORM-TROOPERS--FORCES OF THE NAGAI--MOVE OUT!

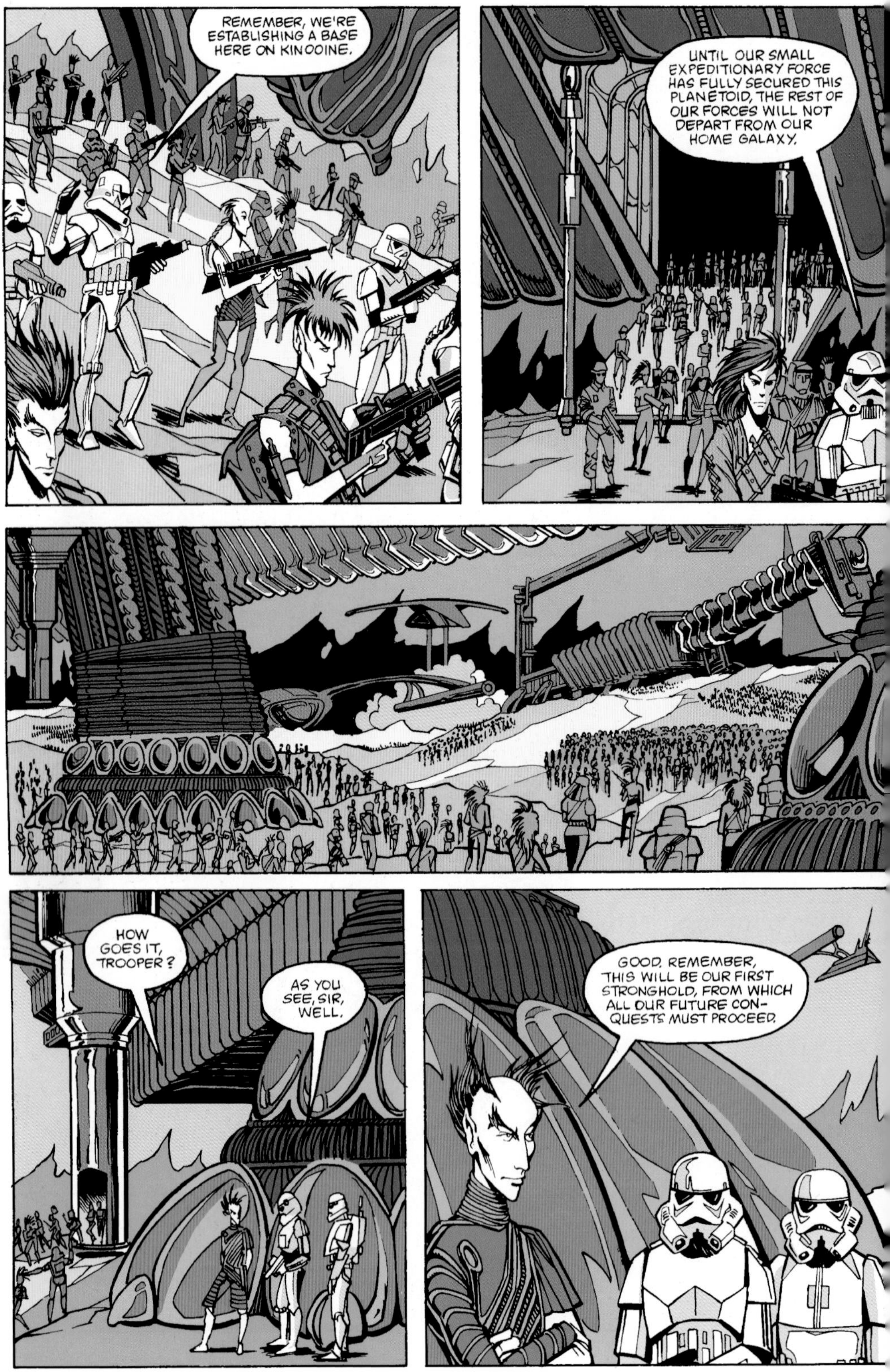
REMEMBER, WE'RE ESTABLISHING A BASE HERE ON KINOOINE.
UNTIL OUR SMALL EXPEDITIONARY FORCE HAS FULLY SECURED THIS PLANETOID, THE REST OF OUR FORCES WILL NOT DEPART FROM OUR HOME GALAXY.
HOW GOES IT, TROOPER?
AS YOU SEE, SIR, WELL.
GOOD. REMEMBER, THIS WILL BE OUR FIRST STRONGHOLD, FROM WHICH ALL OUR FUTURE CON-QUESTS MUST PROCEED.

AND THAT'S IMPORTANT TO ALL OF US. WE NEED NEW TERRITORIES, IF OUR RACE IS TO CONTINUE TO GROW...

AND YOU ARE EAGER TO HAVE REVENGE AGAINST THE SELF-STYLED "ALLIANCE OF FREE PLANETS," WHOSE REBELLION ACTUALLY SUCCEEDED IN TOPPLING YOUR EMPIRE.

ANY WORD FROM THE OFFICERS WE LEFT HERE-- DEN SIVA AND THE DARK LADY, LUMIYA?

DEN SIVA IS IN ONE OF OUR UNDERGROUND INSTALLATIONS ON THE DARK SIDE OF THIS WORLD, CONDUCTING EXPERIMENTS...

...WHICH HE SAYS MAY HAVE GREAT BEARING ON OUR WORK IN THIS GALAXY.

NO ONE HAS HEARD FROM LUMIYA IN SOME TIME... BUT AT HER LAST REPORT, SHE HAD SUC-CEEDED IN BESTING HER ENEMY-- LUKE SKYWALKER.

GOOD. OUR LEADERS WOULD LEARN MORE OF THIS SKYWALKER.

OUR INTELLIGENCE STATES QUITE CLEARLY THAT HE WAS INSTRUMENTAL IN THE OVERTHROW OF THE EMPIRE...

AND THAT HE WAS PRESENT AT THE DEATH OF EMPEROR PALPATINE HIMSELF.

THEY SAY SKYWALKER HAS EXTRAORDINARY ABILITIES... THAT HE IS THE LAST OF THE LEGENDARY JEDI KNIGHTS...

...AND THAT HE IS A MASTER OF THE MYSTIC ENERGY FIELD THAT THOSE OF THIS GALAXY CALL THE FORCE.

WE MUST LEARN WHAT THREAT HIS KIND COULD POSE TO US.

COME ON... WE'VE HEARD ENOUGH...

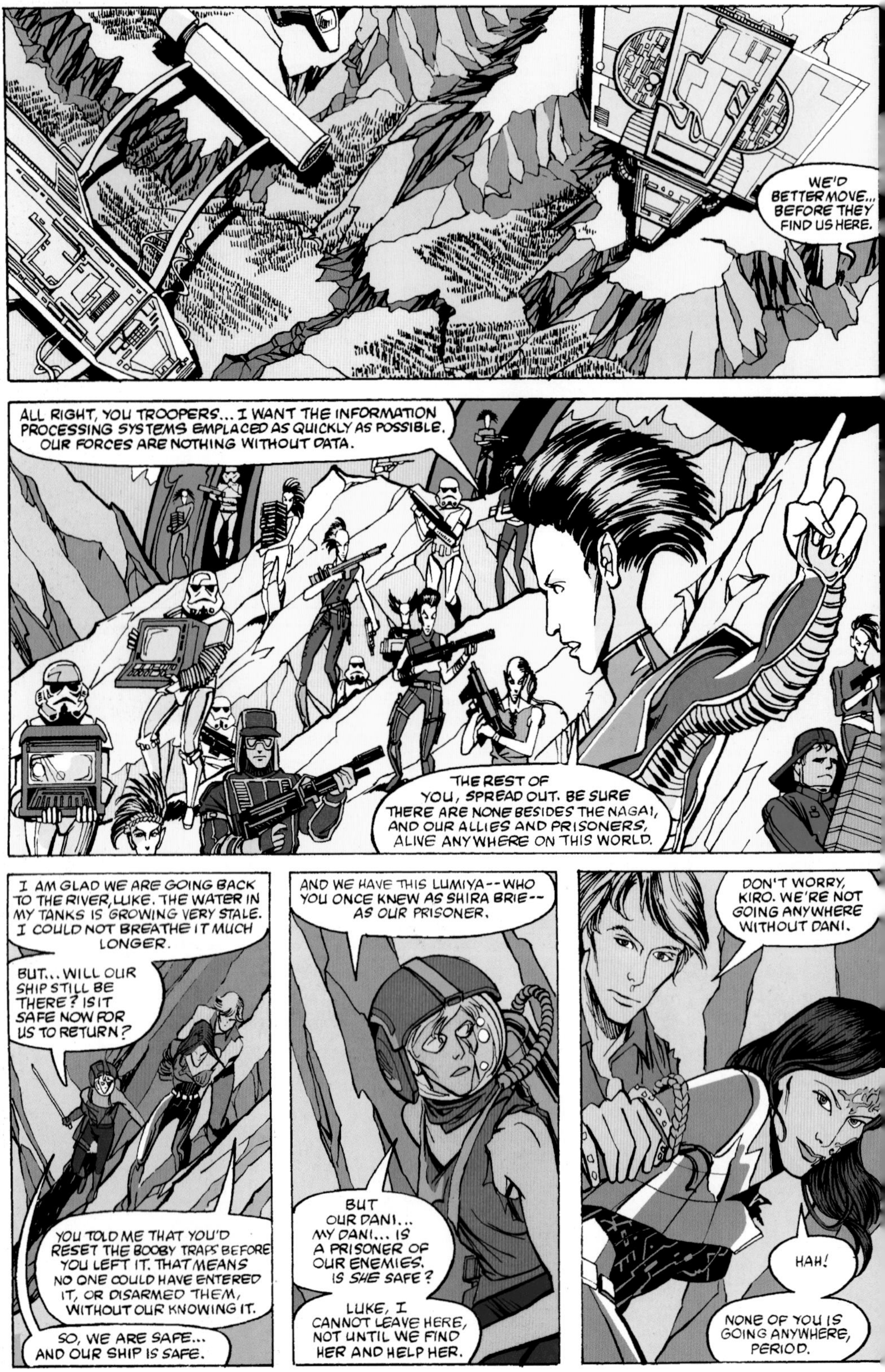
WE'D BETTER MOVE... BEFORE THEY FIND US HERE.
ALL RIGHT, YOU TROOPERS... I WANT THE INFORMATION PROCESSING SYSTEMS EMPLACED AS QUICKLY AS POSSIBLE. OUR FORCES ARE NOTHING WITHOUT DATA.
THE REST OF YOU, SPREAD OUT. BE SURE THERE ARE NONE BESIDES THE NAGAI, AND OUR ALLIES AND PRISONERS, ALIVE ANYWHERE ON THIS WORLD.
I AM GLAD WE ARE GOING BACK TO THE RIVER, LUKE. THE WATER IN MY TANKS IS GROWING VERY STALE. I COULD NOT BREATHE IT MUCH LONGER.
BUT... WILL OUR SHIP STILL BE THERE? IS IT SAFE NOW FOR US TO RETURN?
YOU TOLD ME THAT YOU'D RESET THE BOOBY TRAPS BEFORE YOU LEFT IT. THAT MEANS NO ONE COULD HAVE ENTERED IT, OR DISARMED THEM, WITHOUT OUR KNOWING IT.
SO, WE ARE SAFE... AND OUR SHIP IS SAFE.
AND WE HAVE THIS LUMIYA--WHO YOU ONCE KNEW AS SHIRA BRIE--AS OUR PRISONER.
BUT OUR DANI... MY DANI... IS A PRISONER OF OUR ENEMIES. IS SHE SAFE?
LUKE, I CANNOT LEAVE HERE, NOT UNTIL WE FIND HER AND HELP HER.
DON'T WORRY, KIRO. WE'RE NOT GOING ANYWHERE WITHOUT DANI.
HAH!
NONE OF YOU IS GOING ANYWHERE, PERIOD.

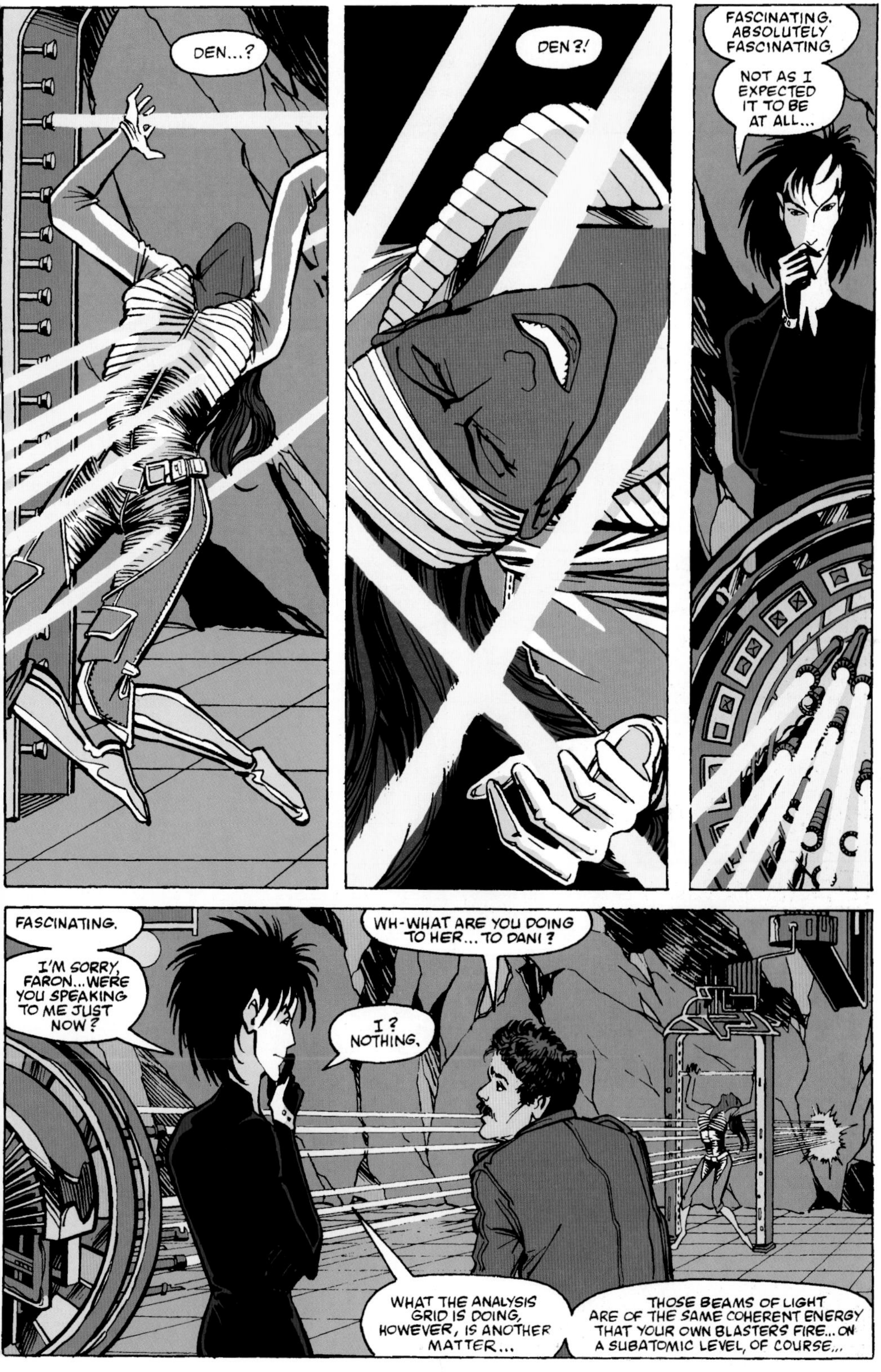
DEN...?
DEN?!
FASCINATING. ABSOLUTELY FASCINATING.
NOT AS I EXPECTED IT TO BE AT ALL...
FASCINATING.
I'M SORRY, FARON...WERE YOU SPEAKING TO ME JUST NOW?
WH-WHAT ARE YOU DOING TO HER... TO DANI?
I? NOTHING.
WHAT THE ANALYSIS GRID IS DOING, HOWEVER, IS ANOTHER MATTER...
THOSE BEAMS OF LIGHT ARE OF THE SAME COHERENT ENERGY THAT YOUR OWN BLASTERS FIRE... ON A SUBATOMIC LEVEL, OF COURSE...

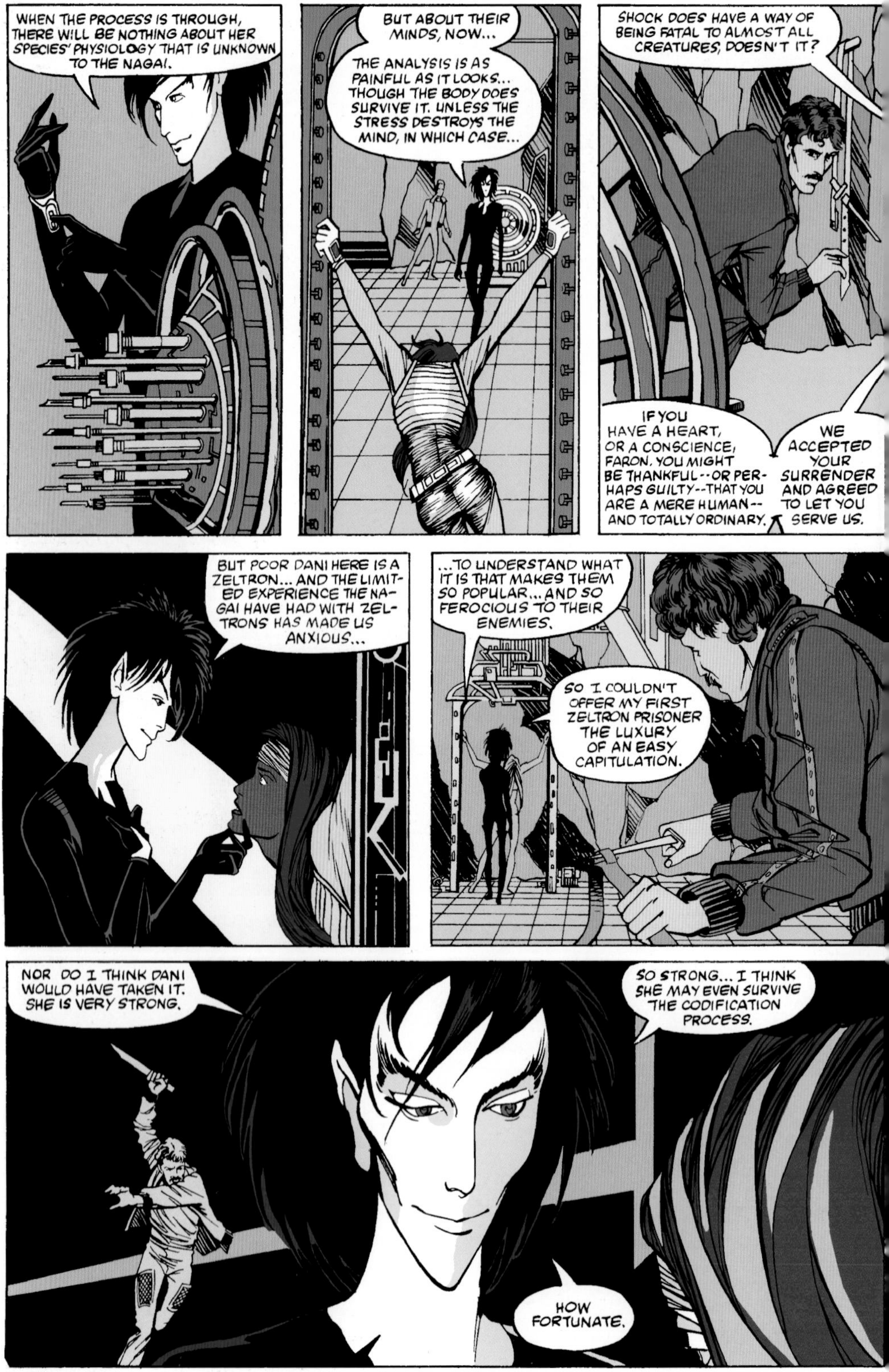
WHEN THE PROCESS IS THROUGH, THERE WILL BE NOTHING ABOUT HER SPECIES' PHYSIOLOGY THAT IS UNKNOWN TO THE NAGAI.
BUT ABOUT THEIR MINDS, NOW...
THE ANALYSIS IS AS PAINFUL AS IT LOOKS... THOUGH THE BODY DOES SURVIVE IT. UNLESS THE STRESS DESTROYS THE MIND, IN WHICH CASE...
SHOCK DOES HAVE A WAY OF BEING FATAL TO ALMOST ALL CREATURES, DOESN'T IT?
IF YOU HAVE A HEART, OR A CONSCIENCE, FARON, YOU MIGHT BE THANKFUL--OR PERHAPS GUILTY--THAT YOU ARE A MERE HUMAN--AND TOTALLY ORDINARY.
WE ACCEPTED YOUR SURRENDER AND AGREED TO LET YOU SERVE US.
BUT POOR DANI HERE IS A ZELTRON... AND THE LIMITED EXPERIENCE THE NAGAI HAVE HAD WITH ZELTRONS HAS MADE US ANXIOUS...
...TO UNDERSTAND WHAT IT IS THAT MAKES THEM SO POPULAR... AND SO FEROCIOUS TO THEIR ENEMIES.
SO I COULDN'T OFFER MY FIRST ZELTRON PRISONER THE LUXURY OF AN EASY CAPITULATION.
NOR DO I THINK DANI WOULD HAVE TAKEN IT. SHE IS VERY STRONG.
SO STRONG... I THINK SHE MAY EVEN SURVIVE THE CODIFICATION PROCESS.
HOW FORTUNATE.

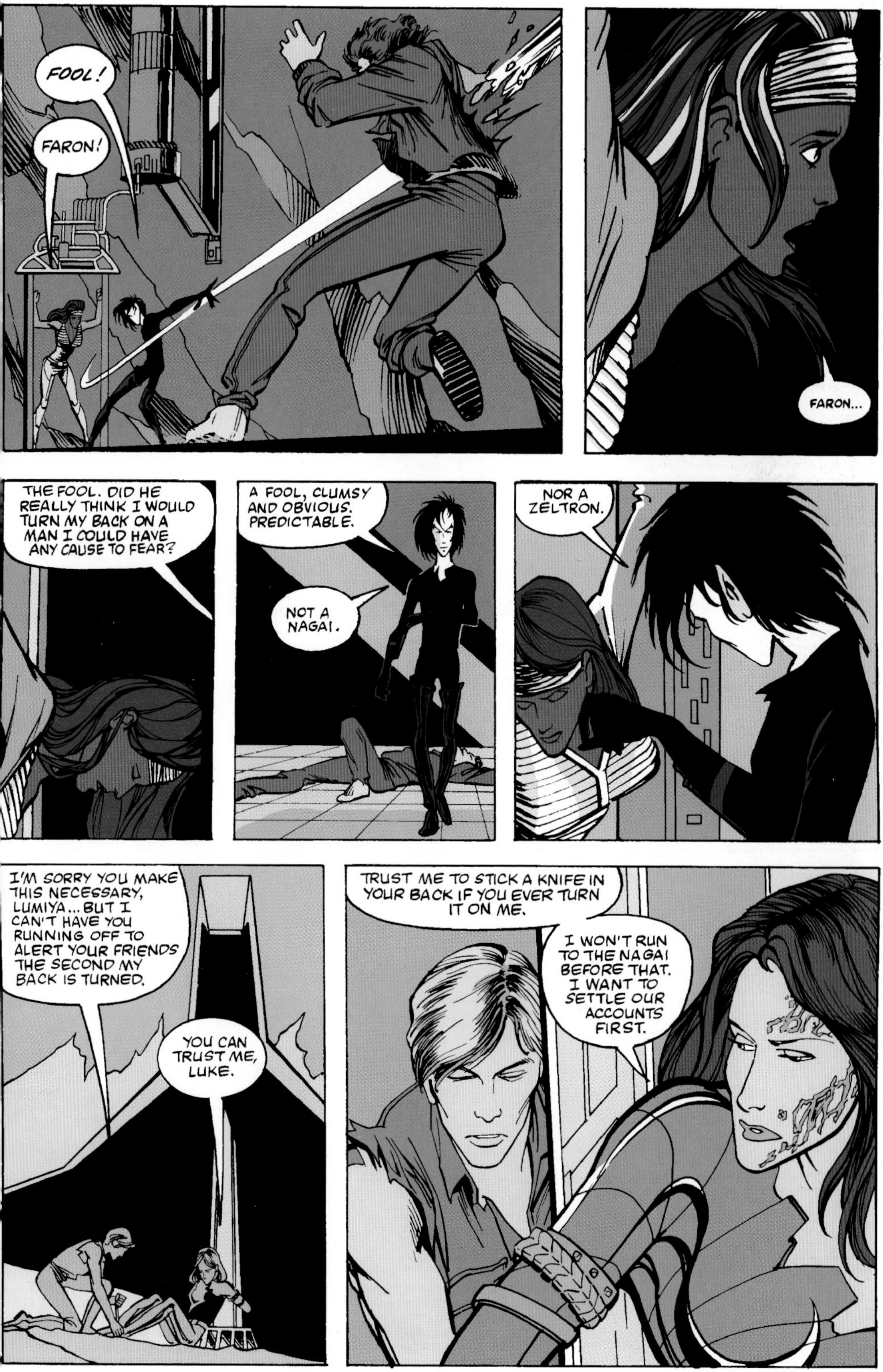
FOOL!
FARON!
FARON...
THE FOOL. DID HE REALLY THINK I WOULD TURN MY BACK ON A MAN I COULD HAVE ANY CAUSE TO FEAR?
A FOOL, CLUMSY AND OBVIOUS. PREDICTABLE.
NOT A NAGAI.
NOR A ZELTRON.
I'M SORRY YOU MAKE THIS NECESSARY, LUMIYA... BUT I CAN'T HAVE YOU RUNNING OFF TO ALERT YOUR FRIENDS THE SECOND MY BACK IS TURNED.
YOU CAN TRUST ME, LUKE.
TRUST ME TO STICK A KNIFE IN YOUR BACK IF YOU EVER TURN IT ON ME.
I WON'T RUN TO THE NAGAI BEFORE THAT. I WANT TO SETTLE OUR ACCOUNTS FIRST.

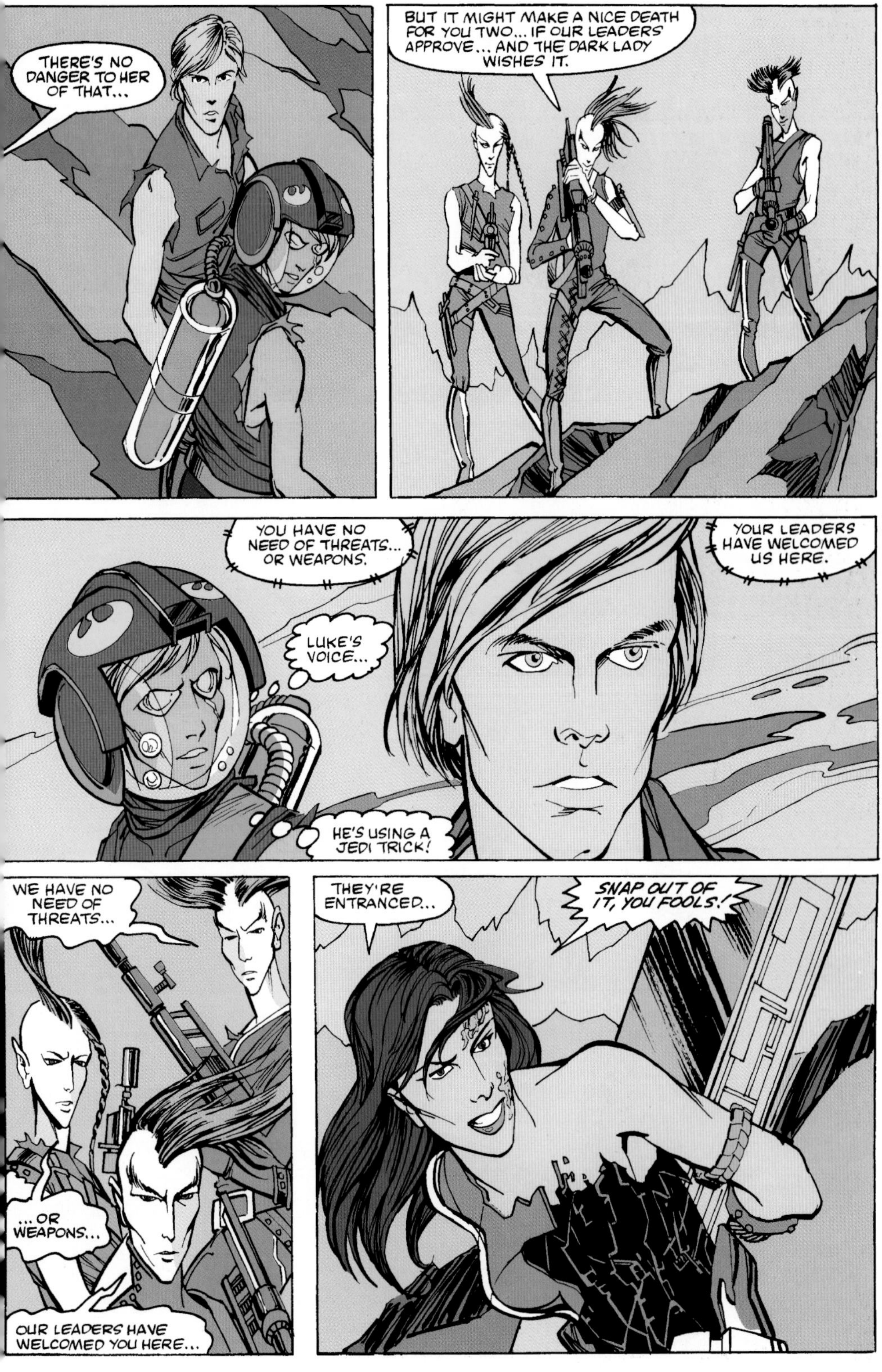
THERE'S NO DANGER TO HER OF THAT...
BUT IT MIGHT MAKE A NICE DEATH FOR YOU TWO... IF OUR LEADERS APPROVE... AND THE DARK LADY WISHES IT.
YOU HAVE NO NEED OF THREATS... OR WEAPONS.
YOUR LEADERS HAVE WELCOMED US HERE.
LUKE'S VOICE...
HE'S USING A JEDI TRICK!
WE HAVE NO NEED OF THREATS...
...OR WEAPONS...
OUR LEADERS HAVE WELCOMED YOU HERE...
THEY'RE ENTRANCED...
SNAP OUT OF IT, YOU FOOLS!

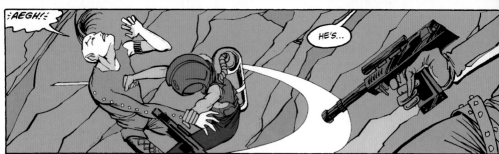

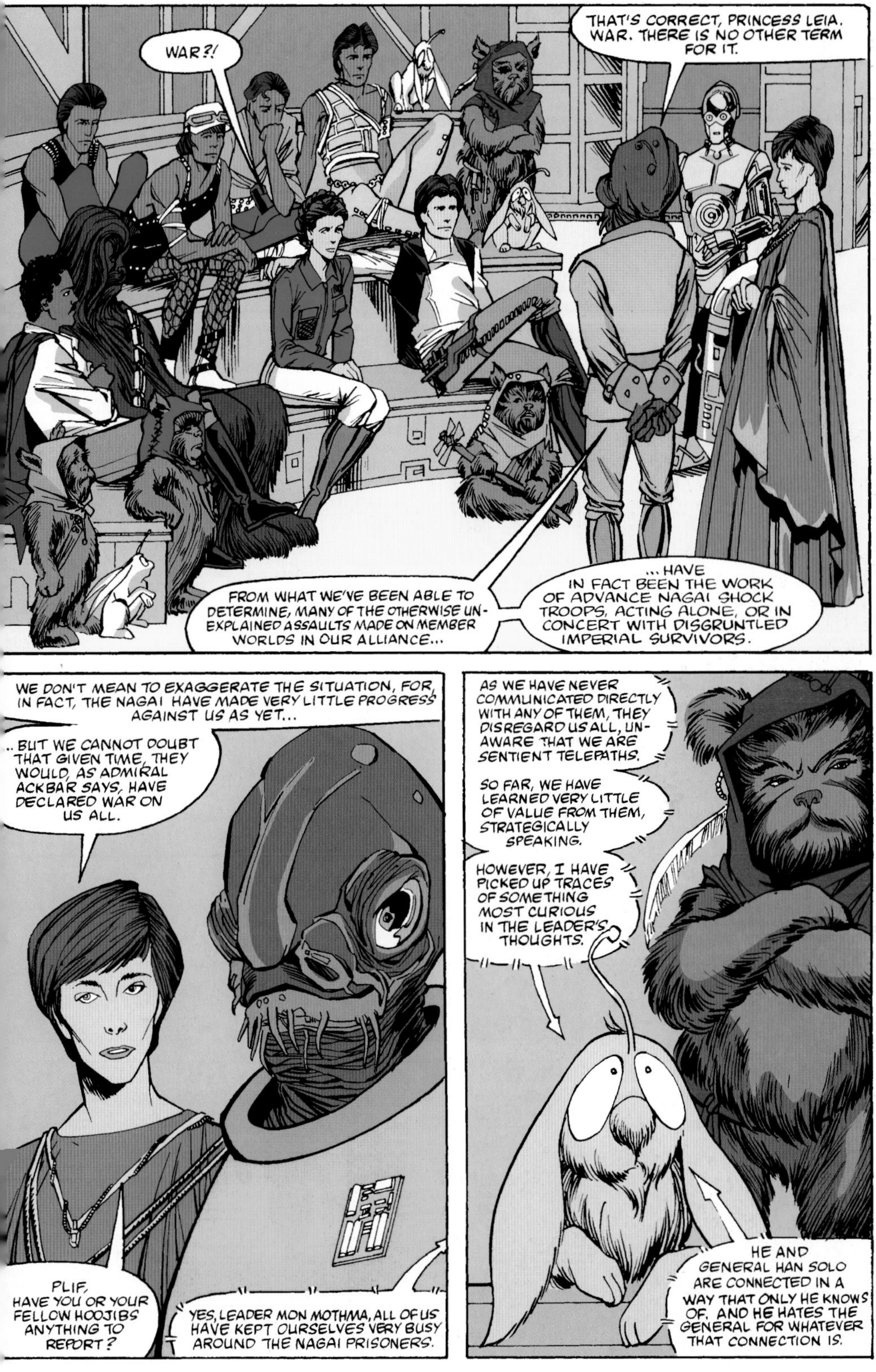
WAR?!
THAT'S CORRECT, PRINCESS LEIA. WAR. THERE IS NO OTHER TERM FOR IT.
FROM WHAT WE'VE BEEN ABLE TO DETERMINE, MANY OF THE OTHERWISE UN-EXPLAINED ASSAULTS MADE ON MEMBER WORLDS IN OUR ALLIANCE...
...HAVE IN FACT BEEN THE WORK OF ADVANCE NAGAI SHOCK TROOPS, ACTING ALONE, OR IN CONCERT WITH DISGRUNTLED IMPERIAL SURVIVORS.
WE DON'T MEAN TO EXAGGERATE THE SITUATION, FOR, IN FACT, THE NAGAI HAVE MADE VERY LITTLE PROGRESS AGAINST US AS YET...
.. BUT WE CANNOT DOUBT THAT GIVEN TIME, THEY WOULD, AS ADMIRAL ACKBAR SAYS, HAVE DECLARED WAR ON US ALL.
PLIF, HAVE YOU OR YOUR FELLOW HOOJIBS ANYTHING TO REPORT?
YES, LEADER MON MOTHMA, ALL OF US HAVE KEPT OURSELVES VERY BUSY AROUND THE NAGAI PRISONERS.
AS WE HAVE NEVER COMMUNICATED DIRECTLY WITH ANY OF THEM, THEY DISREGARD US ALL, UN-AWARE THAT WE ARE SENTIENT TELEPATHS.
SO FAR, WE HAVE LEARNED VERY LITTLE OF VALUE FROM THEM, STRATEGICALLY SPEAKING.
HOWEVER, I HAVE PICKED UP TRACES OF SOMETHING MOST CURIOUS IN THE LEADER'S THOUGHTS.
HE AND GENERAL HAN SOLO ARE CONNECTED IN A WAY THAT ONLY HE KNOWS OF. AND HE HATES THE GENERAL FOR WHATEVER THAT CONNECTION IS.

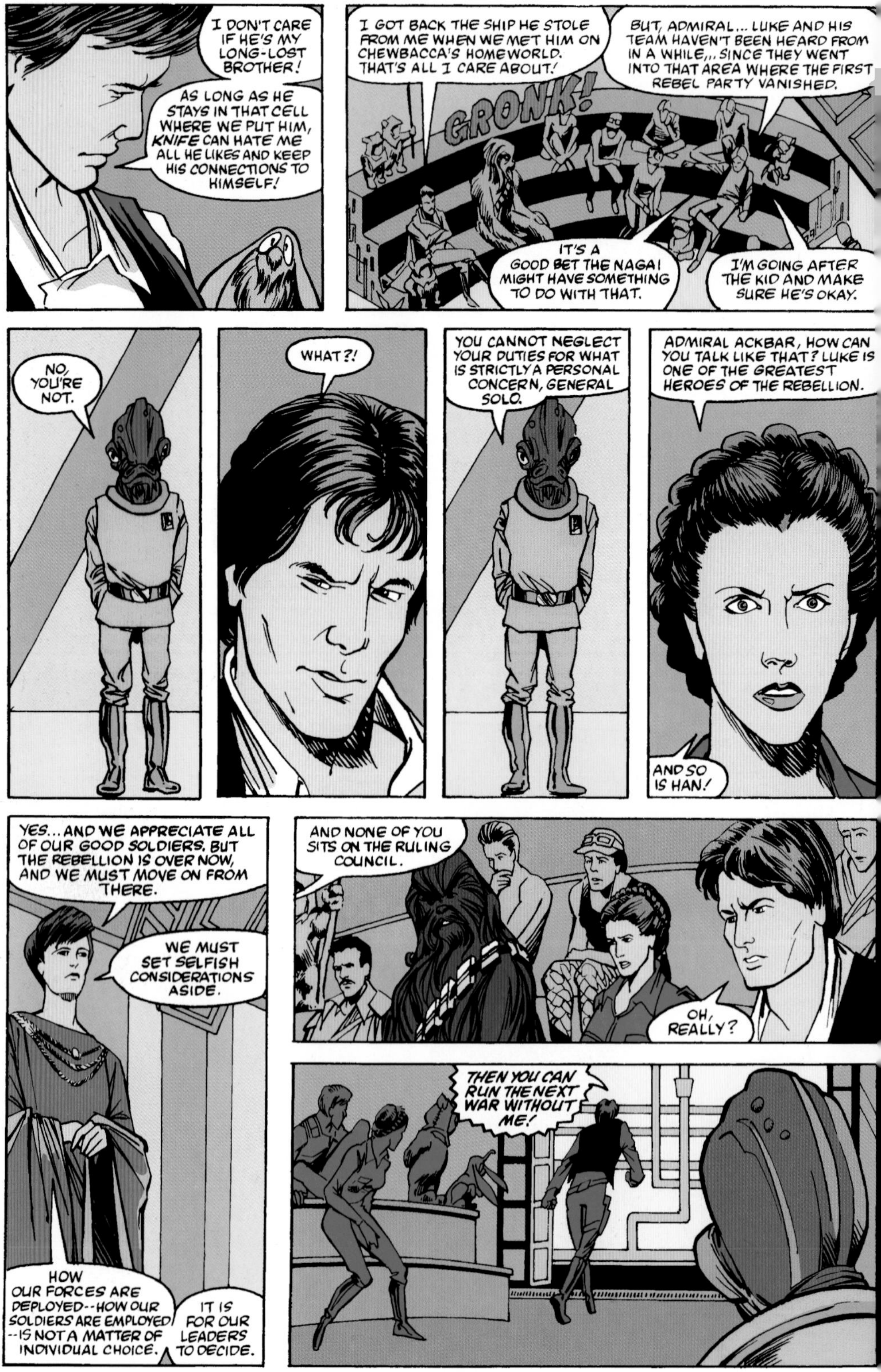
I DON'T CARE IF HE'S MY LONG-LOST BROTHER!
AS LONG AS HE STAYS IN THAT CELL WHERE WE PUT HIM, KNIFE CAN HATE ME ALL HE LIKES AND KEEP HIS CONNECTIONS TO HIMSELF!
I GOT BACK THE SHIP HE STOLE FROM ME WHEN WE MET HIM ON CHEWBACCA'S HOMEWORLD. THAT'S ALL I CARE ABOUT!
BUT, ADMIRAL... LUKE AND HIS TEAM HAVEN'T BEEN HEARD FROM IN A WHILE... SINCE THEY WENT INTO THAT AREA WHERE THE FIRST REBEL PARTY VANISHED.
GRONK!
IT'S A GOOD BET THE NAGAI MIGHT HAVE SOMETHING TO DO WITH THAT.
I'M GOING AFTER THE KID AND MAKE SURE HE'S OKAY.
NO, YOU'RE NOT.
WHAT?!
YOU CANNOT NEGLECT YOUR DUTIES FOR WHAT IS STRICTLY A PERSONAL CONCERN, GENERAL SOLO.
ADMIRAL ACKBAR, HOW CAN YOU TALK LIKE THAT? LUKE IS ONE OF THE GREATEST HEROES OF THE REBELLION.
AND SO IS HAN!
YES... AND WE APPRECIATE ALL OF OUR GOOD SOLDIERS. BUT THE REBELLION IS OVER NOW, AND WE MUST MOVE ON FROM THERE.
WE MUST SET SELFISH CONSIDERATIONS ASIDE.
HOW OUR FORCES ARE DEPLOYED--HOW OUR SOLDIERS ARE EMPLOYED --IS NOT A MATTER OF INDIVIDUAL CHOICE.
IT IS FOR OUR LEADERS TO DECIDE.
AND NONE OF YOU SITS ON THE RULING COUNCIL.
OH, REALLY?
THEN YOU CAN RUN THE NEXT WAR WITHOUT ME!

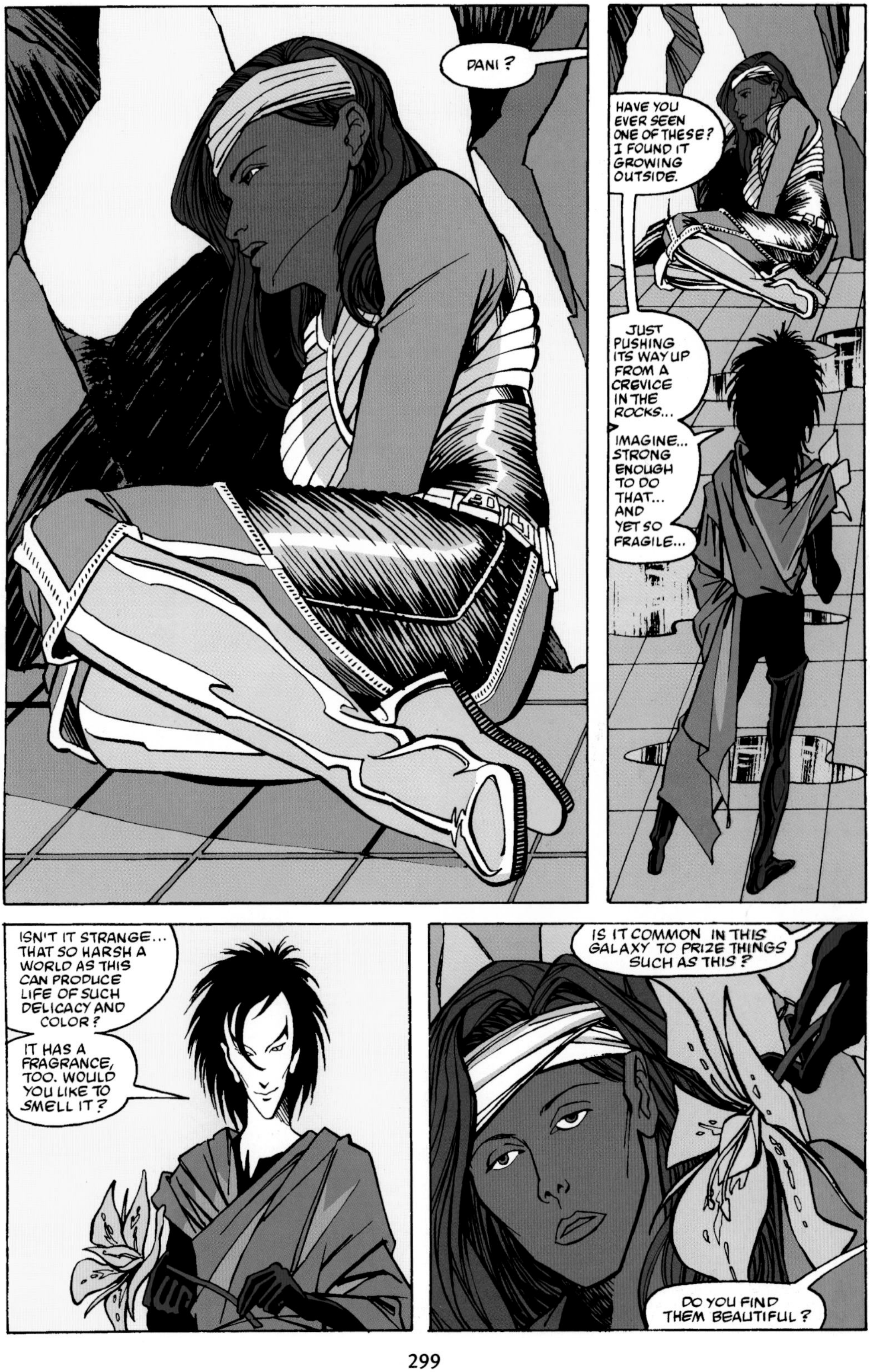
DANI?
HAVE YOU EVER SEEN ONE OF THESE? I FOUND IT GROWING OUTSIDE.
JUST PUSHING ITS WAY UP FROM A CREVICE IN THE ROCKS...
IMAGINE... STRONG ENOUGH TO DO THAT... AND YET SO FRAGILE...
ISN'T IT STRANGE... THAT SO HARSH A WORLD AS THIS CAN PRODUCE LIFE OF SUCH DELICACY AND COLOR?
IT HAS A FRAGRANCE, TOO. WOULD YOU LIKE TO SMELL IT?
IS IT COMMON IN THIS GALAXY TO PRIZE THINGS SUCH AS THIS?
DO YOU FIND THEM BEAUTIFUL?

YES, I RATHER THOUGHT YOU MIGHT.

ON NAGI, THERE ARE THINGS WE FIND BEAUTIFUL...

WE PRIZE THINGS FOR THEIR STRENGTH... OR THEIR WORKMANSHIP... OR THEIR ELEGANCE.

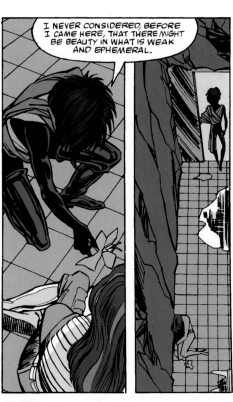

I NEVER CONSIDERED, BEFORE I CAME HERE, THAT THERE MIGHT BE BEAUTY IN WHAT IS WEAK AND EPHEMERAL.

KIRO...

DANI.

KIRO.

KIRO...

OH, KIRO!!

IT'S ALL RIGHT, DANI.

I AM HERE, AND YOU ARE SAFE, AND I WILL NOT LET ANYONE HURT YOU AGAIN.

NOW, WE WILL ESCAPE, AND WE MUST BE VERY QUIET.

LUKE IS ABOUT, SOMEWHERE... HE IS GOING TO DO SOMETHING TO OUR ENEMIES' COMPUTERS, SO THAT THEY CANNOT FIND US.

AND HE WILL STEAL WHAT DATA HE CAN FOR THE ALLIANCE. THEN WE MAY LEAVE.

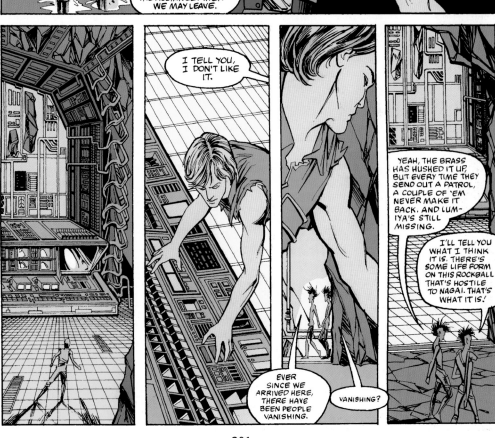

I TELL YOU, I DON'T LIKE IT.

YEAH, THE BRASS HAS HUSHED IT UP, BUT EVERY TIME THEY SEND OUT A PATROL, A COUPLE OF 'EM NEVER MAKE IT BACK, AND LUMIYA'S STILL MISSING.

I'LL TELL YOU WHAT I THINK IT IS. THERE'S SOME LIFE FORM ON THIS ROCKBALL THAT'S HOSTILE TO NAGAI. THAT'S WHAT IT IS!

EVER SINCE WE ARRIVED HERE, THERE HAVE BEEN PEOPLE VANISHING.

VANISHING?

301

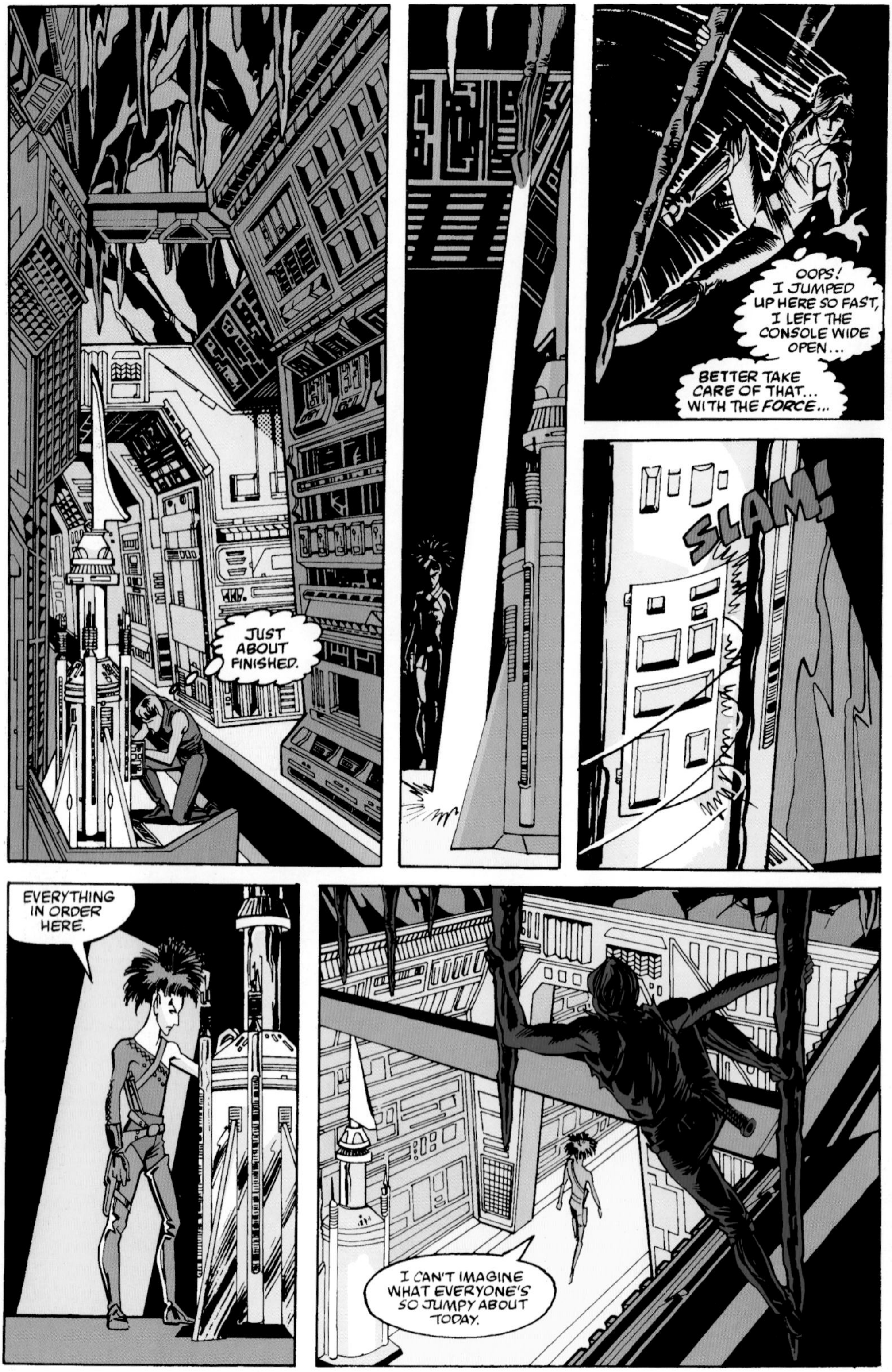
JUST ABOUT FINISHED.
OOPS! I JUMPED UP HERE SO FAST, I LEFT THE CONSOLE WIDE OPEN...
BETTER TAKE CARE OF THAT... WITH THE *FORCE*...
SLAM!
EVERYTHING IN ORDER HERE.
I CAN'T IMAGINE WHAT EVERYONE'S SO JUMPY ABOUT TODAY.

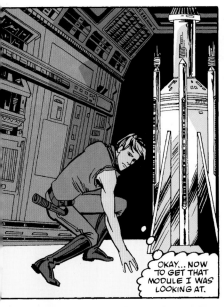

OKAY... NOW TO GET THAT MODULE I WAS LOOKING AT.

YES...THIS IS THE ONE...IF I CAN JUST GET IT SAFELY BACK TO THE ALLIANCE...

WHOOPS... CAN'T GO RUNNING INTO STORM-TROOPERS...

BETTER ARRANGE A LITTLE DIVERSION... ON THE FAR END OF THE CORRIDOR.

RRUMMBLE

WHAT WAS THAT?

I DON'T KNOW, BUT IT SOUNDED LIKE IT CAME FROM DOWN THERE. WE BETTER GO CHECK IT OUT.

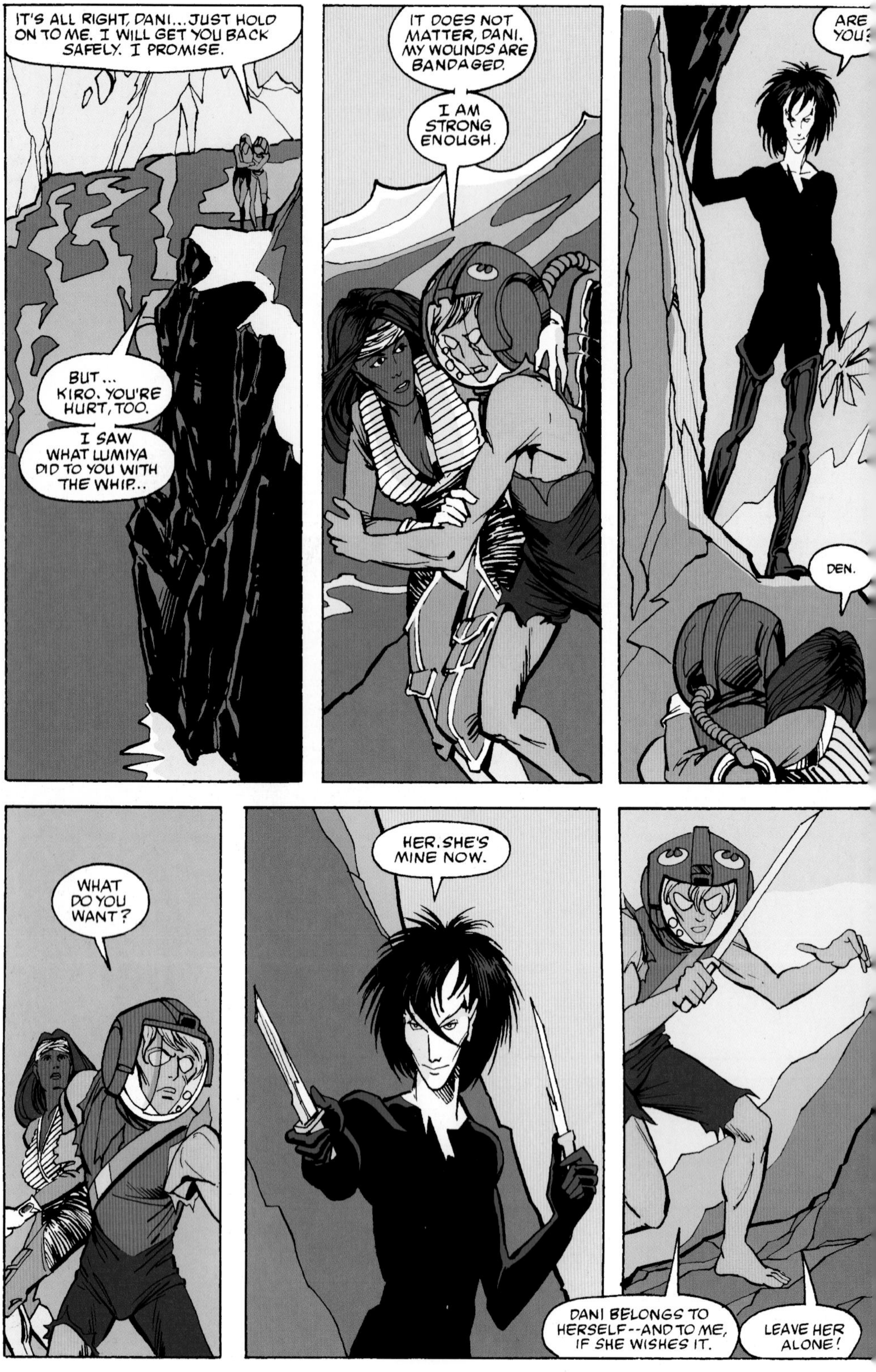
IT'S ALL RIGHT, DANI... JUST HOLD ON TO ME. I WILL GET YOU BACK SAFELY. I PROMISE.
BUT... KIRO. YOU'RE HURT, TOO.
I SAW WHAT LUMIYA DID TO YOU WITH THE WHIP...
IT DOES NOT MATTER, DANI. MY WOUNDS ARE BANDAGED.
I AM STRONG ENOUGH.
ARE YOU?
DEN.
WHAT DO YOU WANT?
HER. SHE'S MINE NOW.
DANI BELONGS TO HERSELF--AND TO ME, IF SHE WISHES IT.
LEAVE HER ALONE!

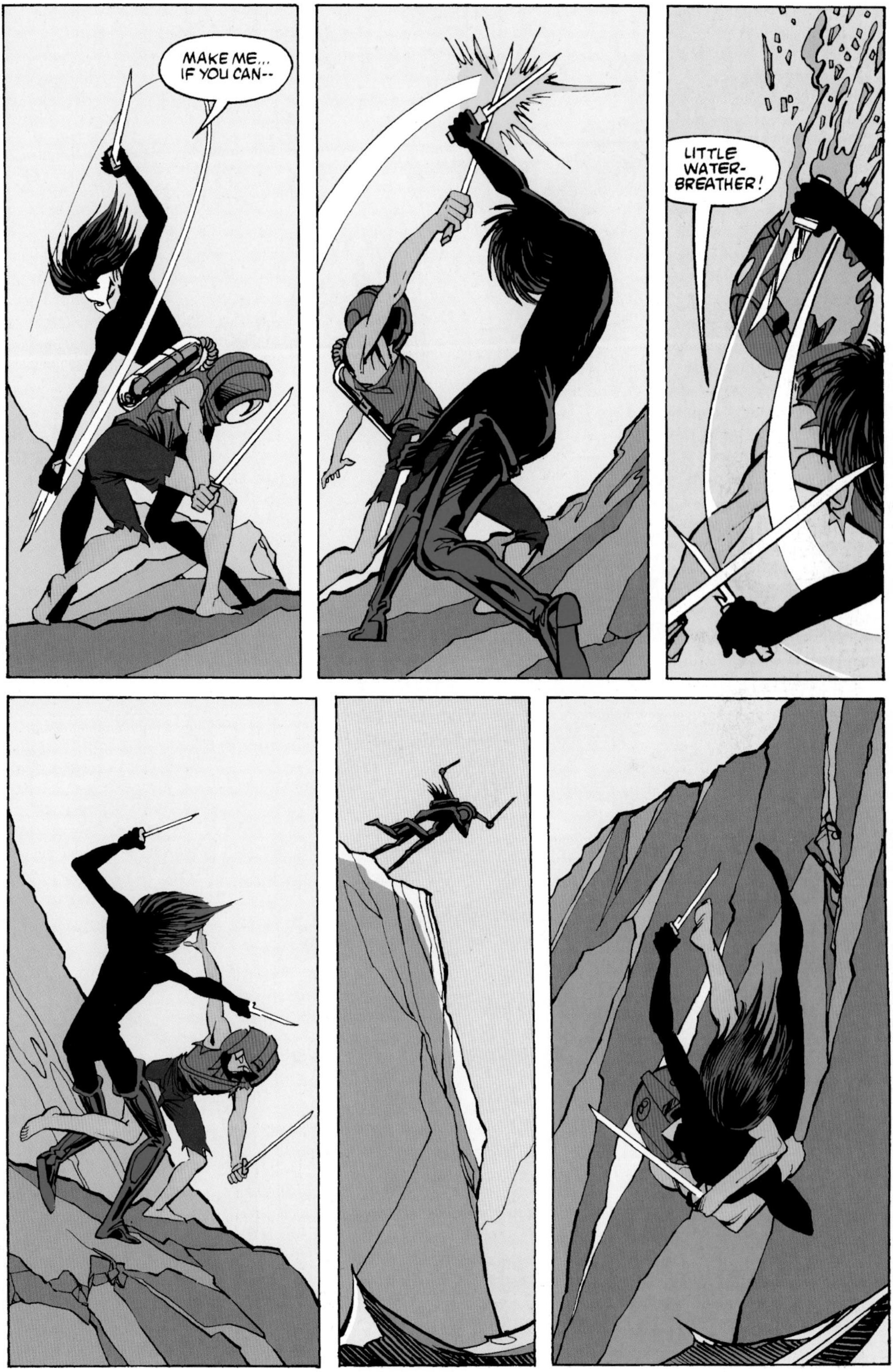
MAKE ME...
IF YOU CAN--
LITTLE
WATER-
BREATHER!

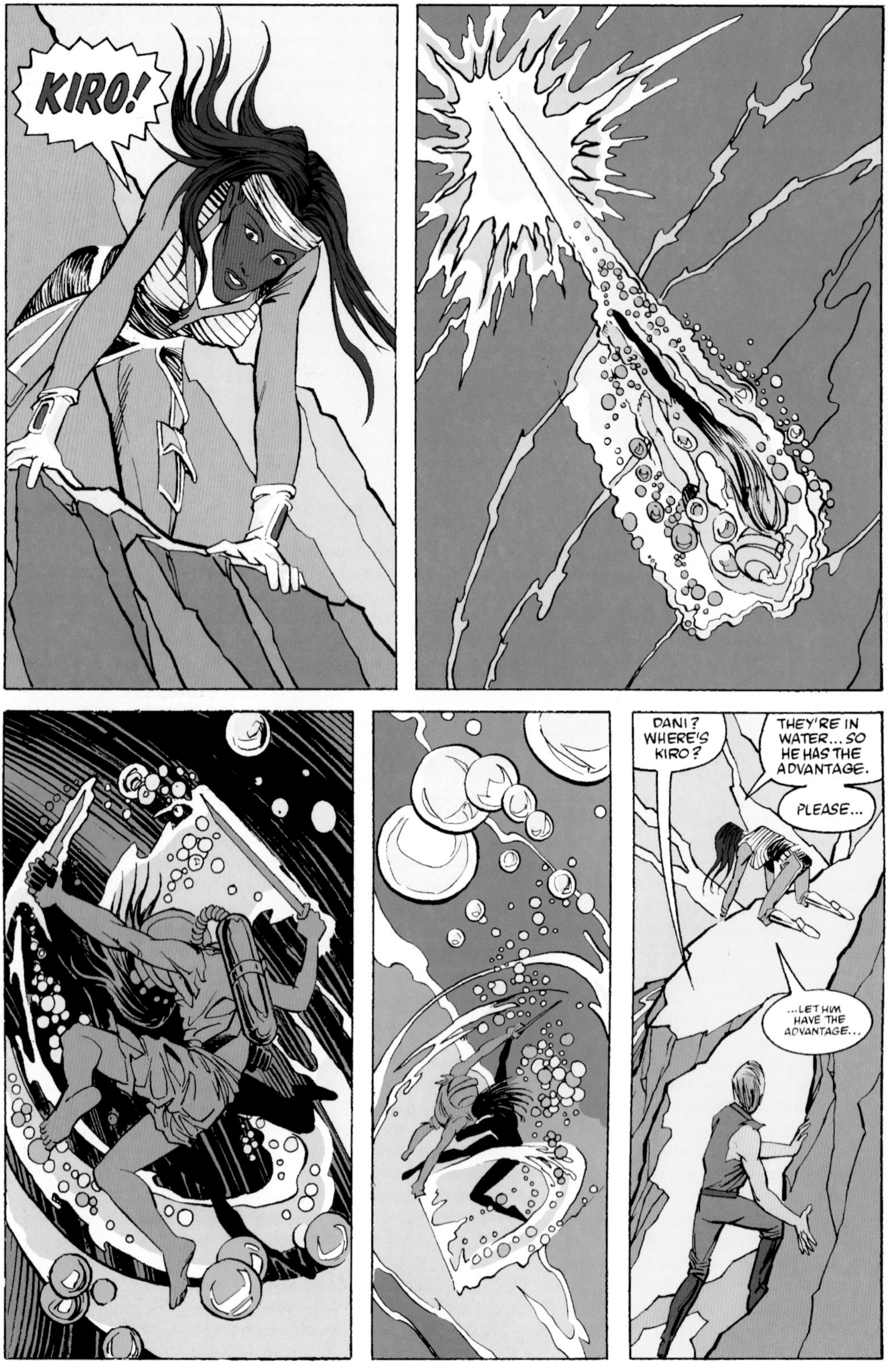
KIRO!
DANI? WHERE'S KIRO?
THEY'RE IN WATER... SO HE HAS THE ADVANTAGE.
PLEASE...
...LET HIM HAVE THE ADVANTAGE...

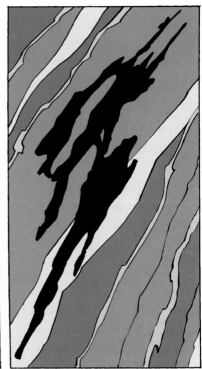

KIRO.

OH, LUKE--!

DANI, IT...

IT MIGHT NOT BE HIS BLOOD.

IT IS! YOU KNOW IT IS!

HE MAY ONLY BE WOUNDED. WE'LL LOOK. MAYBE WE CAN STILL HELP HIM...

...NO SIGN OF A BODY... OF EITHER BODY.

HE MIGHT-- ONE OF THEM MIGHT HAVE MADE IT.

THEN HE'D HAVE CALLED OUT TO US FOR HELP.

OR HE'D HAVE BEEN THERE, NEEDING US.

WELL... IF HE MADE IT, HE'D HAVE FOUND SOME WAY OF GETTING BACK TO THE CAMP WHERE WE LEFT LUMIYA.

WE'VE GOT TO GO NOW.

I KNOW. SOMEONE HAS TO WARN THE ALLIANCE...ABOUT THE NAGAI.

IF THEY CATCH US... KIRO WILL HAVE DIED FOR NOTHING.

DANI...

...ONE OF THEM...

...DID MAKE IT.

NEXT

FAR, FAR AWAY

22

308

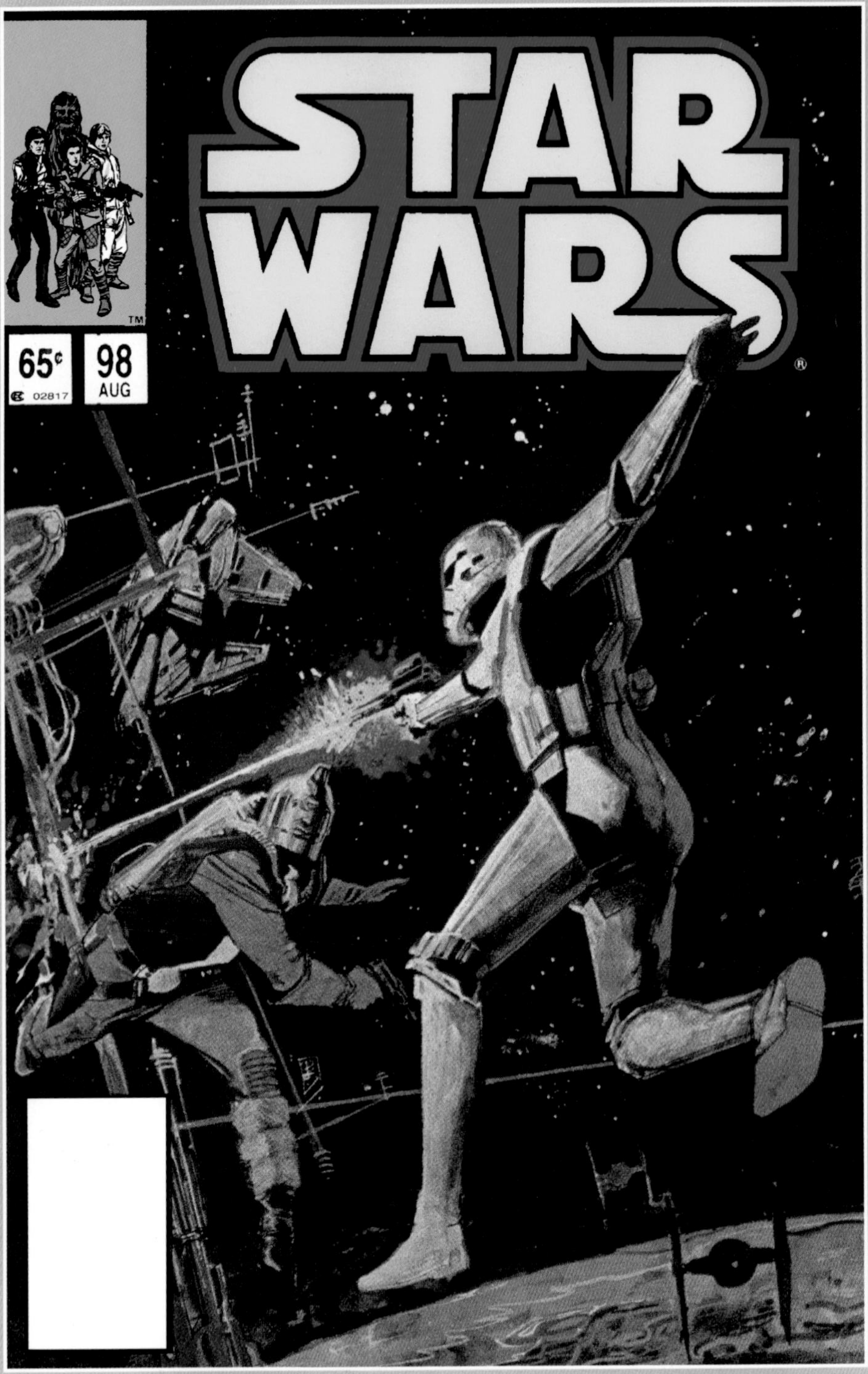
STAR WARS
65¢
02817
98
AUG

THE STARSHIP YARDS OF FONDOR. HERE, OVER THE CENTURIES, MOST OF THE GALAXY'S FINEST SPACECRAFT HAVE BEEN BUILT. FOR THE OLD REPUBLIC. FOR THE DARK EMPIRE WHICH REPLACED IT. AND NOW, FOR THE REBEL ALLIANCE. EXCEPT, THAT IS, WHEN THERE ARE OCCASIONAL PROBLEMS OF...

SUPPLY AN

SOME *SABOTEUR* IS TRYIN' TO *DESTROY* MY *SHIP!*

BUT GENERAL SOLO...! I MUST POINT OUT--

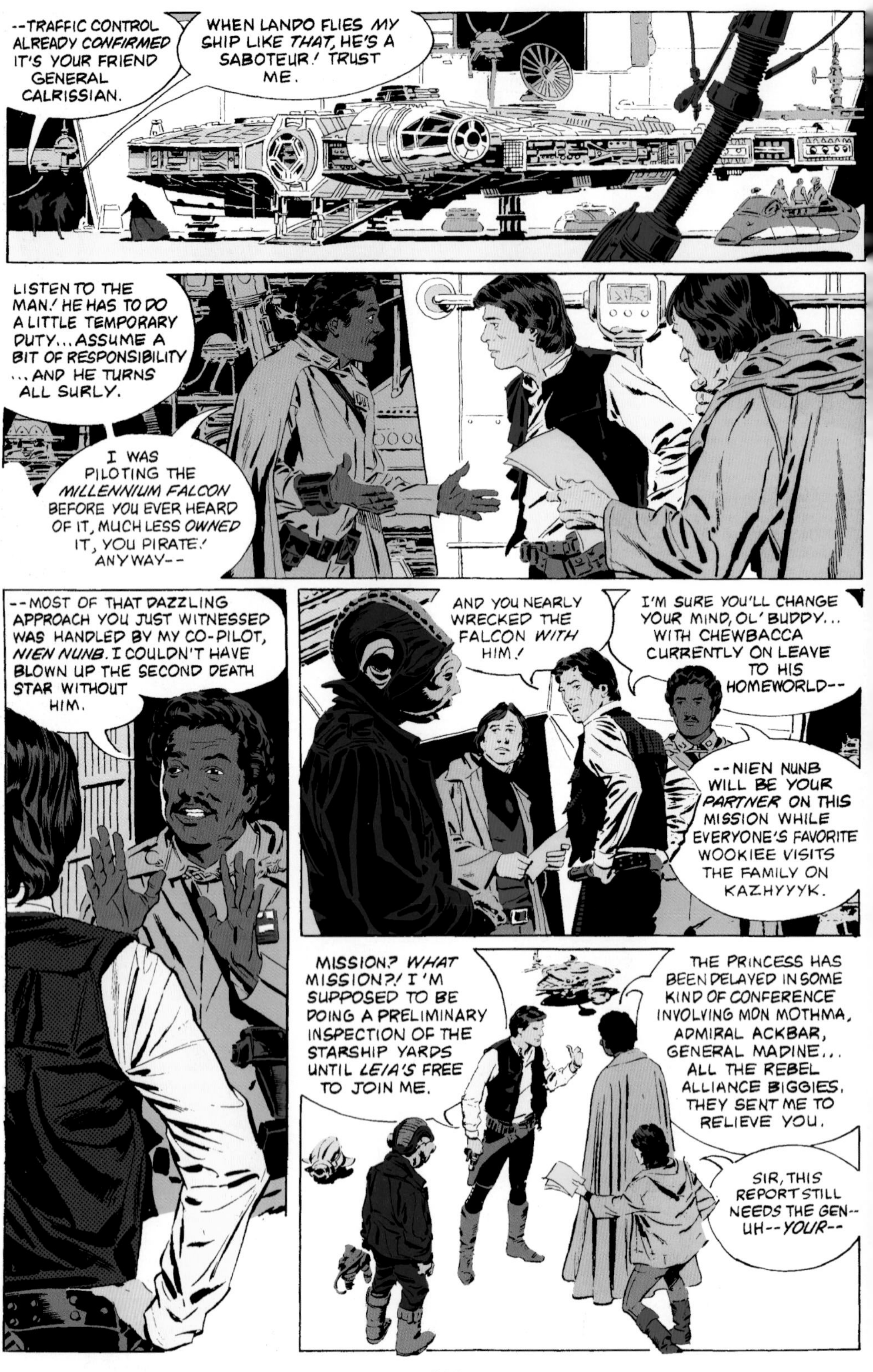
--TRAFFIC CONTROL ALREADY *CONFIRMED* IT'S YOUR FRIEND GENERAL CALRISSIAN.
WHEN LANDO FLIES *MY* SHIP LIKE *THAT*, HE'S A SABOTEUR! TRUST ME.
LISTEN TO THE MAN! HE HAS TO DO A LITTLE TEMPORARY DUTY... ASSUME A BIT OF RESPONSIBILITY ...AND HE TURNS ALL SURLY.
I WAS PILOTING THE *MILLENNIUM FALCON* BEFORE YOU EVER HEARD OF IT, MUCH LESS *OWNED* IT, YOU PIRATE! ANYWAY--
--MOST OF THAT DAZZLING APPROACH YOU JUST WITNESSED WAS HANDLED BY MY CO-PILOT, *NIEN NUNB*. I COULDN'T HAVE BLOWN UP THE SECOND DEATH STAR WITHOUT HIM.
AND YOU NEARLY WRECKED THE FALCON *WITH* HIM!
I'M SURE YOU'LL CHANGE YOUR MIND, OL' BUDDY... WITH CHEWBACCA CURRENTLY ON LEAVE TO HIS HOMEWORLD--
--NIEN NUNB WILL BE YOUR *PARTNER* ON THIS MISSION WHILE EVERYONE'S FAVORITE WOOKIEE VISITS THE FAMILY ON KAZHYYYK.
MISSION? *WHAT* MISSION?! I'M SUPPOSED TO BE DOING A PRELIMINARY INSPECTION OF THE STARSHIP YARDS UNTIL *LEIA'S* FREE TO JOIN ME.
THE PRINCESS HAS BEEN DELAYED IN SOME KIND OF CONFERENCE INVOLVING MON MOTHMA, ADMIRAL ACKBAR, GENERAL MADINE... ALL THE REBEL ALLIANCE BIGGIES. THEY SENT ME TO RELIEVE YOU.
SIR, THIS REPORT STILL NEEDS THE GEN-- UH--*YOUR*--

LET'S *SEE* THIS. UH HUH... WE ALREADY KNOW PRODUCTION IS AT AN ALL-TIME *LOW*... UH HUH...CONFIRMING FIGURES, FLOW CHARTS AND--*RIGHT!* IT'S A *SUPPLY* PROBLEM ON...*VANDELHELM.*

DON'T GAPE, SON. I DIDN'T TURN *CLOUD CITY* INTO A *PROFIT-MAKER* BY BEING SLOW. AND DON'T WORRY ABOUT THE PROBLEM--

"--MY PAL HAN IS ON HIS WAY TO *SOLVE* IT."

...NOT SO *HEAVY* WITH THE TRIM...! *WATCH* THE THRUST... FLIP THAT TOGGLE NOW, NIEN NUNB, OR YOU'LL *NEVER* MAKE THE LEAP TO --

YOU'VE DONE THIS *BEFORE*, RIGHT?

WELL...DON'T GET COCKY! JUST KEEP AN EYE ON THINGS WHILE I GO--UH-- MAKE PLANS.

BEGINNIN' TO FEEL KIND'A USELESS! WITH THE EMPIRE GONE, SEEMS LIKE *ANYONE* CAN HANDLE THE KIND OF STUFF THAT POPS UP NOW... A LOT OF 'EM *BETTER* THAN I DO.

STILL, ACCORDIN' TO LANDO...*THIS* JOB WAS MADE FOR ME.

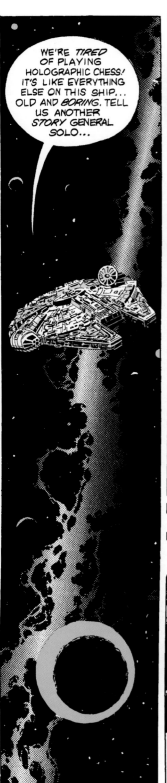

WE'RE *TIRED* OF PLAYING HOLOGRAPHIC CHESS! IT'S LIKE EVERYTHING ELSE ON THIS SHIP... OLD AND *BORING.* TELL US ANOTHER *STORY* GENERAL SOLO...

WE *LIKED* THAT ONE ABOUT DARTH VADER COVERING YOU WITH ALL THAT FREEZING, ICKY STUFF!

SNIF

CARBONITE. AND DON'T CALL ME GENERAL. HAVE YOU WIPED THAT KID'S NOSE LATELY? WE'LL BE HITTIN' YOUR SYSTEM SOON AND I DON'T WANT--

--*NIEN NUMB!* WHAT ARE YOU DOING *NOW?!*

THE RESPONSE FROM THE TEMPORARY CO-PILOT IS NOT ENCOURAGING...

WE DROPPED OUT OF HYPERSPACE INTO THE MIDDLE OF AN ASTEROID SWARM?!

ASTEROIDS DON'T EXPLODE! LEMME AT THOSE CONTROLS!

THOSE THINGS ARE *MINED!* OUR *SHIELD* SYSTEM IS SETTIN''EM OFF! IT'S AN OLD TRICK IMPERIAL ANTI-SMUGGLING PATROLS USED TO PULL!

THEY PLANT A *DISRUPTER* IN A SPOT LIKE THIS. THAT BREAKS AN INCOMING SHIP'S HYPERDRIVE SETTINGS, SO... *BOOM!* YOU POP DOWN IN THE CENTER OF A TRAP!

RELUCTANTLY, NIEN NUNB ASKS THE OBVIOUS QUESTION, AND...

HOW DO YOU GET *OUT?* SWITCH OFF YOUR SHIELDS AND GO THROUGH *UNPROTECTED,* HOW ELSE?

WHAT'S *WRONG* MORDUR?! YOU ASSURED ME THE CRAFT WITH THE *VENERATED* ONES WOULD BE *VAPORIZED* INSTANTLY!

THE REBELS SENT A *SMALL FREIGHTER...!* FAR MORE MANEUVERABLE THAN THE BATTLE CRUISER OR LUXURY TRANSPORT YOU'D *EXPECT* TO CARRY SUCH DIGNITARIES.

BUT IT WOULD REQUIRE AN *UNBELIEVABLE PILOT* TO GET ANYTHING THROUGH THOSE ASTEROIDS...EVEN IF THEY *WEREN'T* MINED!

NO DOUBT SOMETHING SIMILAR WAS SAID ABOARD BOTH YOUR *DEATH STARS!* I'M TAKING PART OF YOUR CREW... TO SETTLE THIS MY WAY IF NECESSARY.

CLEAR SPACE AHEAD, NIEN NUNB! SEEMED PRETTY HAIRY FOR A WHILE BUT WE MADE IT!

I BETTER CHECK ON THOSE KIDS. A COUPLE OF MY MORE INSPIRED MOVES PROBABLY SCARED 'EM SILLY.

321

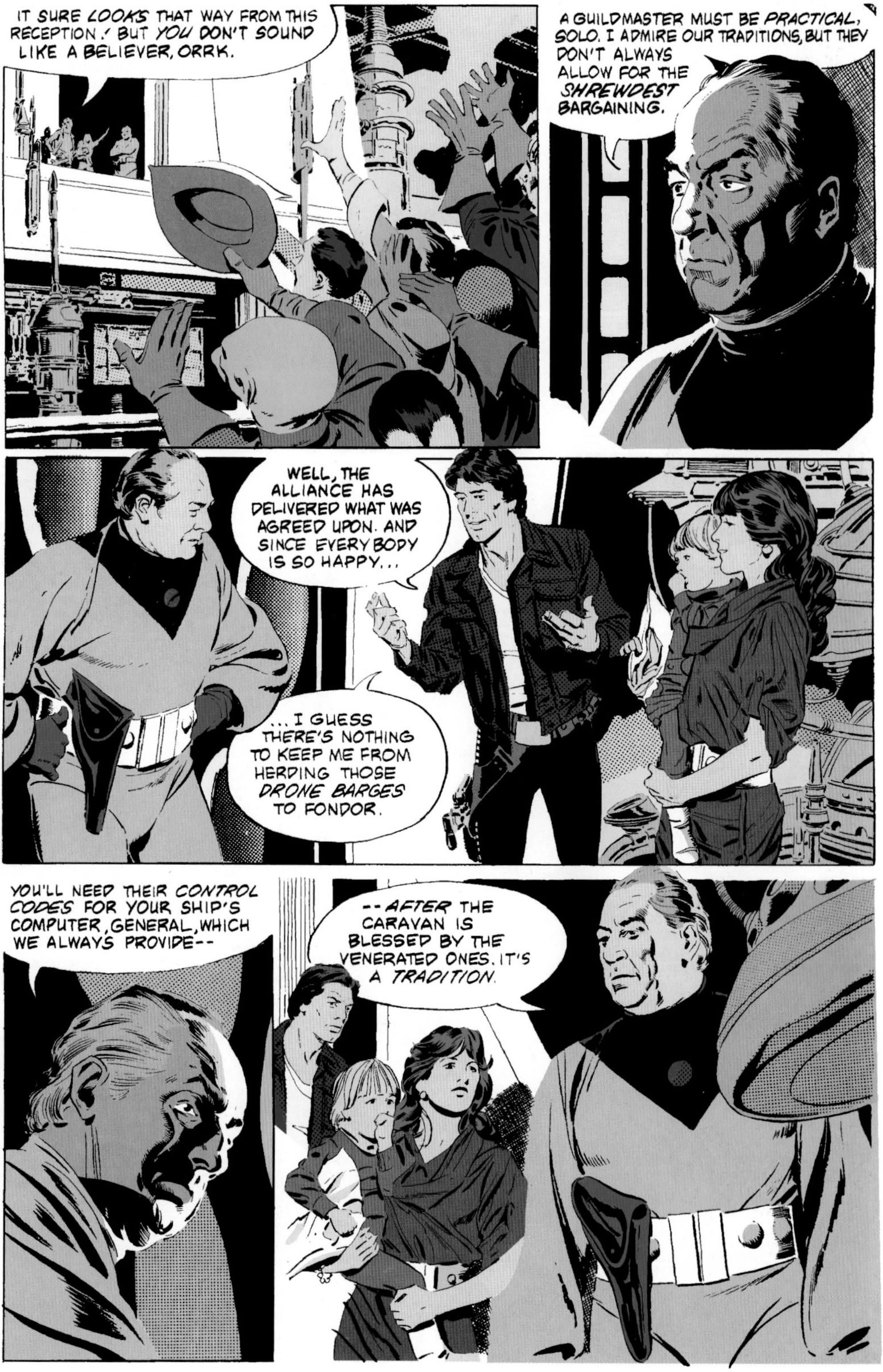
IT SURE LOOKS THAT WAY FROM THIS RECEPTION! BUT YOU DON'T SOUND LIKE A BELIEVER, ORRK.
A GUILDMASTER MUST BE PRACTICAL, SOLO. I ADMIRE OUR TRADITIONS, BUT THEY DON'T ALWAYS ALLOW FOR THE SHREWDEST BARGAINING.
WELL, THE ALLIANCE HAS DELIVERED WHAT WAS AGREED UPON. AND SINCE EVERYBODY IS SO HAPPY...
...I GUESS THERE'S NOTHING TO KEEP ME FROM HERDING THOSE DRONE BARGES TO FONDOR.
YOU'LL NEED THEIR CONTROL CODES FOR YOUR SHIP'S COMPUTER, GENERAL, WHICH WE ALWAYS PROVIDE--
--AFTER THE CARAVAN IS BLESSED BY THE VENERATED ONES. IT'S A TRADITION.

--BUT WITH WHAT MORDUR AND I WILL BE ABLE TO *DEMAND*, WE CAN PROBABLY FINANCE OUR OWN LITTLE EMPIRE SOMEWH-- YEEAAARRGHHHH.!

WHAT'S PAIN FOR ONE MAN IS OPPORTUNITY FOR ANOTHER...

...IF HE'S FAST ON THE DRAW AS HAN SOLO!

BUT...

KIDS ARE TOO CLOSE TO RISK A *SHOT* AT ORRK--

AND IN THE WILD TUMBLE THAT FOLLOWS THE INITIAL IMPACT...

...THE *GUILDMASTER'S* SIZE AND WEIGHT BECOME A FATAL ADVANTAGE!

--BLAST IT.!

DON'T BOTHER HANGING ON, SOLO... YOU'RE ALREADY DEAD!

N-NO....!

WHAT....?! YOU MISERABLE LITTLE WITCH, I'LL

GUILDMASTER... YOU'VE DONE ENOUGH!

HEY, YOU TWO WEREN'T BAD... FOR A COUPLE OF BRATS. BUT YOU CAN RELAX NOW, THE WORST IS --

WE'VE FOUND WHAT *DELAYED* GUILDMASTER ORRK, ADMIRAL.

YOU CAN PROCEED WITH THE DRONE BARGES WHILE WE *ELIMINATE* THE PROBLEM.

A CHILL TOUCHES HAN SOLO. THEN, ABOVE THE CRACKLE OF THE IMPERIALS' COM-LINK, HE CATCHES ANOTHER, MORE FAMILIAR SOUND...

...AND KNOWS WHAT HE HAS TO DO!

DOWN, KIDS!

GOOD *MOVE*, NIEN NUNB... GRABBIN' *CHEWIE'S* OLD BLASTER FROM OUR WEAPONS LOCKER! THE SOUND OF IT'S SAFETY CLICKIN' OFF ALERTED *ME*--

-- BUT *NOT* THOSE TWO STORMTROOPERS!

OKAY, ONTO THE *FALCON*, KIDS! WITHOUT KNOWIN' HOW MANY *OTHER* IMPERIAL HELPERS ORRK HAS AROUND, THAT'LL BE *SAFEST* FOR YOU!

BUT KEEP *QUIET* AND STAY OUT OF MY WAY--

"-- THE WORST ISN'T QUITE AS OVER AS I THOUGHT."

SHIP COMING UP, ADMIRAL MORDUR... THE *FREIGHTER* THAT *ESCAPED* OUR TRAP! APPEARS BENT ON *STOPPING* US.

THAT *CONFIRMS* GUILDMASTER ORRK FAILED. IT WON'T AFFECT OUR OWN *SUCCESS.*

SIR, WE CONVERTED THIS BARGE INTO A COMMAND SHIP... BUT IT'S HARDLY A *COMBAT* VESSEL.

IT CAN LEAD THE CARAVAN *WHEREVER* WE WANT... AND CARGO LIKE THIS IS *ALWAYS* IN DEMAND! WE'LL HAVE A *FORTUNE!* TO REBUILD...TO *START AGAIN....!*

AS FOR *FIGHTING*...WE'LL SOON HAVE OUR VERY OWN *REBEL ESCORT* TO EASE ANY ALLIANCE INTERVENTION...THE SHIP OF A RENOWNED *HERO!*

SWITCH TO THE *EMERGENCY COURSE* I PLOTTED!

WHAT...? EVERY DRONE BARGE IS *LOCKED* ON THAT LEAD SHIP, NIEN NUNB...AN' IT'S HEADIN' 'EM INTO THE *SUN!*

SNEAKY! THIS ADMIRAL *MORDUR* KNOWS WE DON'T DARE BLOW *HIS* CRAFT AWAY--

--BECAUSE THE DRONES WILL JUST KEEP *LUMBERIN'* ON THAT COURSE! WITHOUT THE CONTROL CODE, *WE* CAN'T TURN 'EM!

SEEMS TO COME DOWN TO EITHER *BARGAINING* OR BEING WILLING TO LOSE IT *ALL!* UNLESS--

--WE TAKE OVER THAT LEAD BARGE *OURSELVES!*

THERE! TRUST A HERO TO ATTEMPT A BOLD SOLUTION, BOARDING US LIKE A PIRATE...AS I PREDICTED! THE MOMENT THEIR RAMP COMES DOWN--

AND

--THAT SHIP'S OURS. SO MUCH FOR THE FAMOUS GENERAL SOLO!

DON'T CALL ME GENERAL! NOT AS LONG AS I'M ENOUGH OF A PIRATE TO SMELL A SET-UP WHEN I'M ENTERING ONE!

YOU ALREADY IMPRESSED ME AS SNEAKY, MORDUR... THAT'S WHY I SLIPPED OUT OF THE FALCON JUST BEFORE MY CO-PILOT BROUGHT HER IN!

BUT IF THE IMPERIAL ADMIRAL IS LISTENING, HE IS ALSO MOVING...

...INTO THE COMMAND BARGE, SEALING THE HATCH BEHIND HIM.

MY LAST TWO *MEN*...! *BLASTED* REBEL! BUT IT WILL TAKE HIM *TIME* TO BURN HIS WAY IN--

HE MAY HAVE HELPED BRING DOWN THE *EMPEROR*... BUT I WON'T LET HIM DRAW A *VICTORY* OUT OF THIS!

IF *I* CAN'T HAVE THE MATERIALS FROM VANDELHELM...THEY'RE *NOT* GOING TO END UP REFITTING THE ALLIANCE FLEET!

THE DRONE BARGES' *CONTROL CODE* IS IN OUR COMPUTER. WITH *THAT* DESTROYED...*NOTHING* CAN PREVENT THE ENTIRE CONVOY PLUNGING INTO THE SUN!

PIRATES DON'T *BOTHER* BURNIN' THROUGH HATCHES, ADMIRAL... NOT WHEN IT'S *FASTER* TO BLAST A WEAKLY-SHIELDED SHIP'S *VIEWPORT!*

BUT NOW...

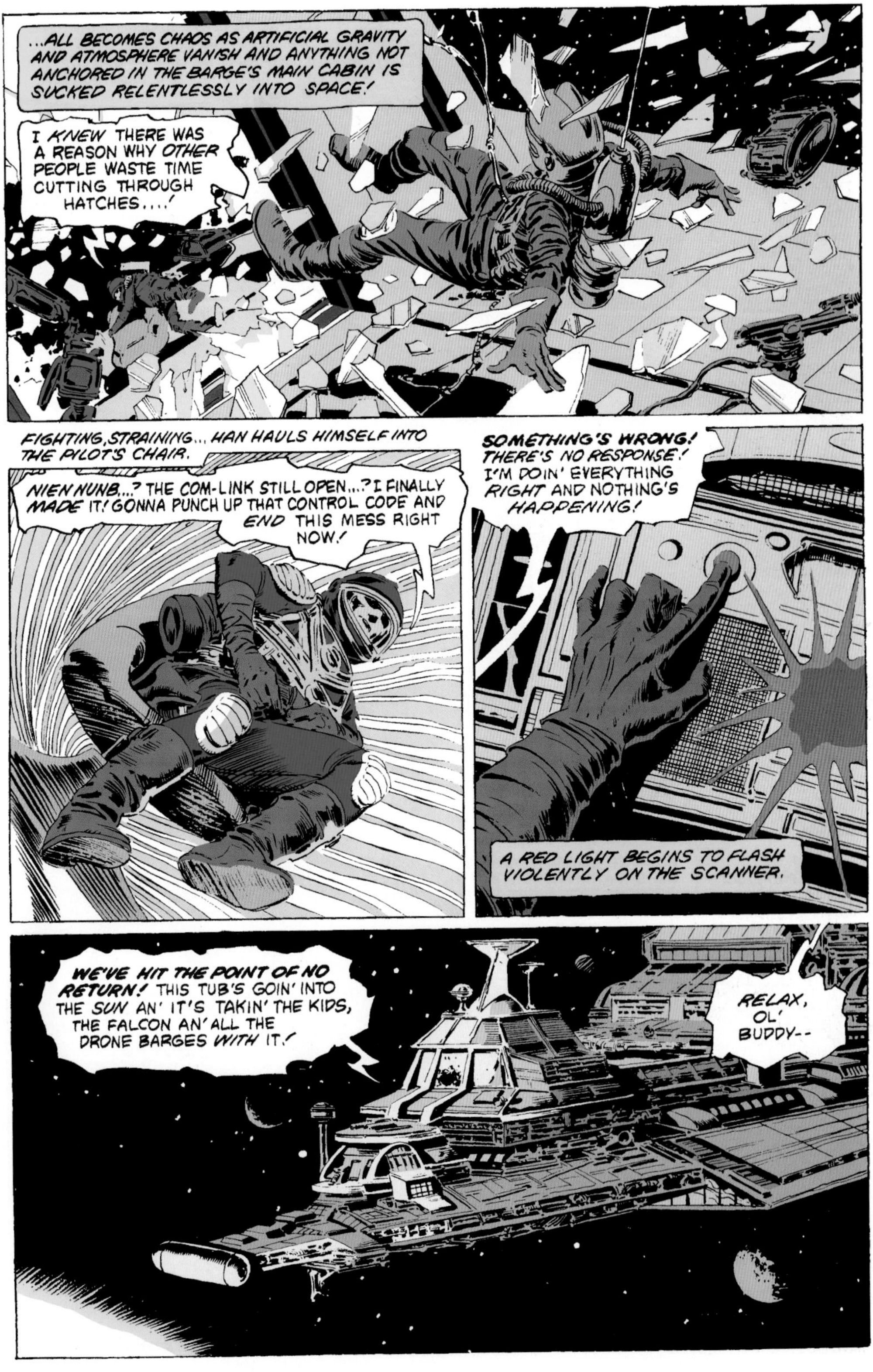
...ALL BECOMES CHAOS AS ARTIFICIAL GRAVITY AND ATMOSPHERE VANISH AND ANYTHING NOT ANCHORED IN THE BARGE'S MAIN CABIN IS SUCKED RELENTLESSLY INTO SPACE!
I KNEW THERE WAS A REASON WHY OTHER PEOPLE WASTE TIME CUTTING THROUGH HATCHES....!
FIGHTING, STRAINING... HAN HAULS HIMSELF INTO THE PILOT'S CHAIR.
NIEN NUNB...? THE COM-LINK STILL OPEN...? I FINALLY MADE IT! GONNA PUNCH UP THAT CONTROL CODE AND END THIS MESS RIGHT NOW!
SOMETHING'S WRONG! THERE'S NO RESPONSE! I'M DOIN' EVERYTHING RIGHT AND NOTHING'S HAPPENING!
A RED LIGHT BEGINS TO FLASH VIOLENTLY ON THE SCANNER.
WE'VE HIT THE POINT OF NO RETURN! THIS TUB'S GOIN' INTO THE SUN AN' IT'S TAKIN' THE KIDS, THE FALCON AN' ALL THE DRONE BARGES WITH IT!
RELAX, OL' BUDDY--

--YOU'RE IN SAFE HANDS.

THEY'RE ALREADY TURNING AWAY, HAN. WE USED THE COMMAND CODE TO *OVERRIDE* THE LEAD BARGE'S COMPUTER... THAT'S WHY *YOU* HAD TROUBLE.

THE *COMMAND CODE...?!* HOW DID *YOU* GET IT?

LANDO...?! I'M IN YOUR TRACTOR BEAM...?! B-BUT...ALL THE *OTHER* BARGES! THEY'RE--

A QUESTION SOON ANSWERED...ON VANDELHELM.

YOU *KIDS* KNEW THE CODE? AND YOU HAD NIEN NUNB TRANSMIT IT TO THE *CRUISER* WHEN IT APPEARED? *WHY* DIDN'T YOU TELL *ME?!*

YOU ORDERED US TO KEEP QUIET--

--AND IF WE DIDN'T *OBEY*, YOU MIGHT NOT BRING US ON ANY MORE *FUN* ADVENTURES.

ALLIANCE COMMAND WAS *SUSPICIOUS* OF THE SITUATION HERE...BUT ANY DIRECT INTERFERENCE MIGHT HAVE ALIENATED THE GUILD. *SOMETHING* WAS NEEDED TO MAKE THE PLOTTERS *REVEAL* THEMSELVES --

-- AND *YOU'RE* THE MOST USEFUL GUY WE HAVE FOR STIRRING THINGS UP!

YEAH, WELL, I'VE BEEN *WONDERIN'* ABOUT A REAL *PURPOSE* LATELY. ONLY NEXT TIME...*DON'T* BE AFRAID TO *FILL ME IN* A LITTLE. I MEAN,...I'M *HAN SOLO.* TRUST ME.

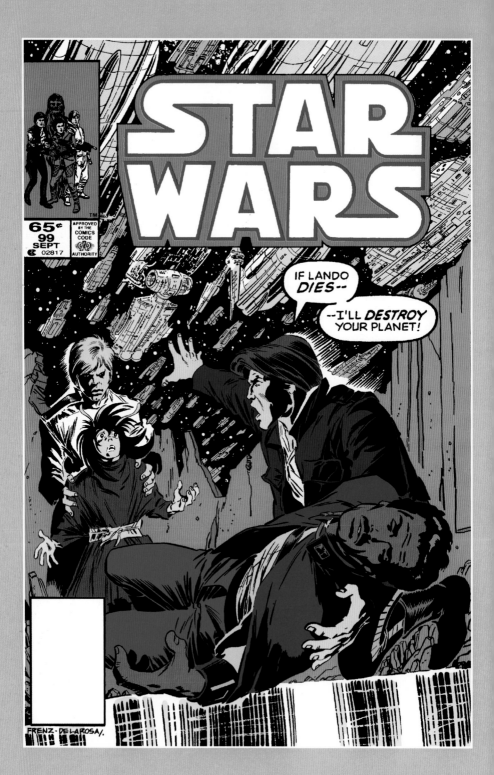

TOUCH OF THE GODDESS

JO DUFFY
WRITER

RON FRENZ
PENCILS

SAM DE LA ROSA
INKS

RICK PARKER
LETTERING

GLYNIS OLIVER
COLORS

ANN NOCENTI
EDITOR

JIM SHOOTER, EDITOR IN CHIEF

LUKE...WHAT ARE YOU THINKING ABOUT?

ABOUT LIFE...AND FRIENDSHIP.

ABOUT KIRO.

ARE YOU BLAMING YOURSELF... FOR HIS DEATH?

WHY NOT?

LANDO, I AM RESPONSIBLE.

IT'S NOT LIKE YOU'RE THE ONE WHO KILLED HIM.

NO, BUT HE LEFT HIS HOME, AND HIS PEOPLE, AND DIED IN THE WATERS OF AN ASTEROID LIGHT YEARS FROM WHERE HE BELONGED...

BECAUSE OF ME.

A LOT OF PEOPLE HAVE DIED SINCE THE REBELLION BEGAN.

THIS IS DIFFERENT. KIRO DIDN'T JOIN US UNTIL AFTER THE REBELLION AGAINST THE EMPIRE HAD SUCCEEDED.

HE JOINED THE ALLIANCE OF FREE PLANETS BECAUSE HE WANTED TO BE A *JEDI KNIGHT*-- TO BE TRAINED IN MASTERY OF THE *FORCE*... AND TO HAVE LESS MYSTICAL, MORE PRACTICAL PHYSICAL TRAINING AS WELL.

BUT YOU TOLD ME YOURSELF... HE DIDN'T DIE FOR NOTHING. HE SAVED DANI FROM ONE OF THE *NAGAI* INVADERS.

YEAH... AND JUST LOOK AT DANI NOW...

SHE LOVED HIM, LANDO... REALLY LOVED HIM. AND NOW SHE'S HURTING SO MUCH, NOT EVEN HER CLOSEST FRIENDS CAN REACH HER.

CAN YOU BELIEVE IT? A *ZELTRON* WHO CAN'T BE TOUCHED.

SHE'S NOT THE ONLY UNHAPPY ZELTRON WE HAVE AROUND THE ALLIANCE THESE DAYS.

PRINCESS LEIA'S ATTACHÉS ARE GLUMMER THAN I EVER THOUGHT THEY COULD BE.

SO... THE NAGAI HAVE OPENLY ATTACKED PLANETS IN YOUR SYSTEM... AND EVEN ESTABLISHED BASES THERE, FENN?

THAT'S RIGHT, PRINCESS LEIA.

WELL... MAYBE HE KNOWS THINGS THAT ARE IMPORTANT... SHE HAS TO LISTEN TO HIM.

BUT GENERAL SOLO DOESN'T LIKE IT...

YOU'RE RIGHT... THEY'RE NOT HAPPY, BUT I THINK IT'S BECAUSE THEY'RE JEALOUS.

ON THEIR OWN BEHALF... OR HAN'S?

MAYBE A LITTLE OF EACH. AFTER ALL, SHE'S THEIR PRINCESS... BUT HAN'S THEIR HERO, AND THEY KNOW HOW HE AND LEIA FELT ABOUT EACH OTHER.

IF WE HADN'T HAD THE HELP OF OUTSIDERS LIKE BEY IN SETTING UP RESISTANCE GROUPS, WELL...

TRUE. HAN CERTAINLY HASN'T BEEN TOO THRILLED SINCE FENN SHOWED UP AT OUR BASE HERE...

WHY IS HER HIGHNESS ALWAYS WITH THAT FENN SHYSA?

ALTHOUGH HE SEEMED KIND OF GLAD WHEN HE FOUND OUT THAT FENN BROUGHT BEY WITH HIM.*

*THE STORY OF FENN AND BEY'S ARRIVAL WILL BE TOLD IN ISSUE #101 -- ANN.

HOW ABOUT YOU, LUKE? DID IT SURPRISE YOU AT ALL, TO FIND OUT THAT THE FAMOUS BEY IS A HALF-BREED COR- ELLIAN, AND THAT HE AND HAN WERE FRIENDS WHILE THEY WERE GROWING UP?

SURE.

YOU KNOW, EVEN IF HE DOESN'T SAY SO, HAN WAS SO GLAD TO SEE BEY, THAT HE ACTUALLY VOLUN- TEERED TO ACCOMPANY ADMIRAL ACKBAR AND HIM ON A MISSION.

OH? IS HE HELPING WITH THE TRANSPORT OF WEAPONS TO PLANETS THE NAGAI ARE ATTACKING?

NO, THIS IS A MERCY MISSION.

3

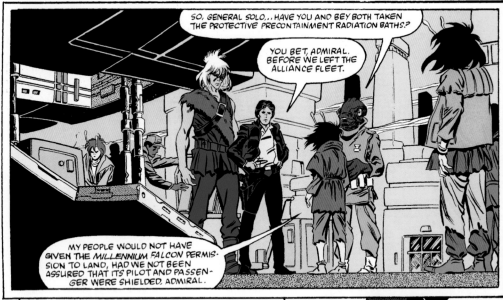

SO, GENERAL SOLO... HAVE YOU AND BEY BOTH TAKEN THE PROTECTIVE PRECONTAINMENT RADIATION BATHS?

YOU BET, ADMIRAL. BEFORE WE LEFT THE ALLIANCE FLEET.

MY PEOPLE WOULD NOT HAVE GIVEN THE *MILLENNIUM FALCON* PERMISSION TO LAND, HAD WE NOT BEEN ASSURED THAT ITS PILOT AND PASSENGER WERE SHIELDED, ADMIRAL.

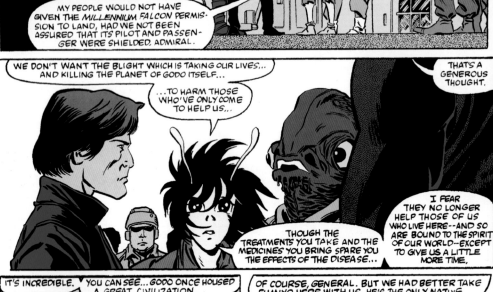

WE DON'T WANT THE BLIGHT WHICH IS TAKING OUR LIVES... AND KILLING THE PLANET OF GODO ITSELF...

...TO HARM THOSE WHO'VE ONLY COME TO HELP US...

THAT'S A GENEROUS THOUGHT.

THOUGH THE TREATMENTS YOU TAKE AND THE MEDICINES YOU BRING SPARE YOU THE EFFECTS OF THE DISEASE...

I FEAR THEY NO LONGER HELP THOSE OF US WHO LIVE HERE--AND SO ARE BOUND TO THE SPIRIT OF OUR WORLD--EXCEPT TO GIVE US A LITTLE MORE TIME.

IT'S INCREDIBLE. YOU CAN SEE... GODO ONCE HOUSED A GREAT CIVILIZATION...

BUT NOW... IT'S LIKE THE PLANET ITSELF ISN'T FIT TO SUPPORT LIFE.

IT'S MORE THAN THAT, HAN... IT SEEMS TO BE POISONING ALL THE LIFE THAT WALKS UPON IT.

ADMIRAL... CAN WE WALK AROUND HERE... CHECK THINGS OUT... TALK TO SOME PEOPLE?

OF COURSE, GENERAL. BUT WE HAD BETTER TAKE FUMIYO, HERE, WITH US. HE'S THE ONLY NATIVE GODOAN WHO HAS MASTERED GALACTIC STANDARD SPEECH.

THAT IS... IF YOU FEEL UP TO IT?

I AM BETTER THAN MOST, ADMIRAL ACKBAR. I WILL DO WHAT I CAN FOR THOSE WHO ARE GOOD ENOUGH TO CARE ABOUT US.

4

I MUST RETURN TO THE FLEET SHORTLY... I AM NEEDED IN OVERSEEING THE SHIPMENT OF WEAPONS TO OUR OTHER WORLDS...

...THOSE WHO ARE BELEAGUERED BY WAR AND NOT BY NATURE.

AT THE SAME TIME I'LL SEE HOW THE DOCTORS ARE PROGRESSING WITH TRYING TO ISOLATE THE CAUSE OF ALL THIS...

SO, BEY, YOU GOT ANY BRIGHT IDEAS?

YOU'RE THE BIG HERO OF SONG AND LEGEND.

SO... WHAT DO WE DO, SADDLED WITH RESPONSIBILITY FOR A BUNCH OF ALIENS WHO LOOK AND ACT LIKE SICK KIDS?

AND, DON'T GO LOOKIN' AT ME! I HATE KIDS.

I KNOW. I HATE SEEING THEM LIKE THIS, TOO.

HEY...

AM I SEEING THINGS? THESE LITTLE HOLLOWS...

THERE'S ONE BESIDE THE DOOR OF EVERY BUILDING... AND UNLESS I'M CRAZY, EVERY ONE OF THEM IS FILLED WITH...

THEY ARE! WITH FLAME GEMS. LYING AROUND IN THE OPEN.

DO YOU KNOW WHAT THESE THINGS ARE WORTH?

OF COURSE... BUT THEY HAVE A GREATER WORTH TO US...WHICH IS WHY WE NEVER TOUCH THEM.

EACH HOME IS PROTECTED BY A CACHE OF GEMS... LEFT THERE IN TRIBUTE TO OUR GODDESS, SO THAT SHE WILL SMILE ON US.

BUT, ALREADY WE HAVE FAILED HER... AND SHE FROWNS ON US...

AND THAT IS WHY THE ILLNESS CAME.

UH... YEAH.

DON'T WORRY. I WAS GONNA PUT THEM BACK.

5

339

LET ME TAKE YOU TO THE HOUSE OF THE GODDESS. IT IS THE HEART OF OUR PLANET, AND THE CENTER OF OUR WORSHIP?

YOU ARE HERE TO HELP HER PEOPLE, SO I KNOW YOU WILL BE WELCOME THERE.

A TRULY BEAUTIFUL STRUCTURE.

YES... AND, DO YOU NOTICE, IT HAS BEEN AFFECTED BY THE GENERAL PLANETARY DECAY LESS THAN ANY PLACE WE'VE YET SEEN?

FUNNY... THERE'S SOMETHING FAMILIAR ABOUT ALL THIS...

AND ABOUT SOME OF THESE LITTLE DOODADS BACK HERE ON THE WALL...

...ALMOST LIKE...

BEY, CAN'T YOU SEE IT?

MM?

OH, MOST GRACIOUS LADY, WELCOME THESE GUESTS WHO HAVE COME TO HELP US.

WHAT IS IT?

I'M NOT...

HEY!

YES, I AM SURE. IT'S OBVIOUS. HOW COULD YOU GUYS HAVE MISSED IT, ALL THIS TIME?

THIS ISN'T JUST A TEMPLE. THIS WHOLE PLACE IS A MACHINE!

FUMI, GO BACK TO THE FALCON. IF CHEWBACCAS HAD HIS PROTECTIVE INNOCULATION, TELL HIM TO COME HERE, AND BRING ARTOO-DETOO AND SEE-THREEPIO! (6)

REMARKABLE THAT NO ONE HAS EVER NOTICED IT BEFORE, GENERAL SOLO. THE ENTIRE STRUCTURE IS, INDEED, A TECHNO-ORGANIC CONSTRUCT.

WELL, NOT EVERYONE HAS HAN'S MASTERFUL GRASP OF THE OBVIOUS.

THANKS, I--HEY!

MAKE YOURSELF USEFUL, WISE GUY. YOU'RE TALL ENOUGH. IF IT'S OKAY WITH YOU AND YOUR FRIENDS, FUMI, I'D LIKE BEY TO UNVEIL THAT BIG SHAPE.

OF COURSE. ALL ARE WELCOME TO GAZE UPON OUR LADY AS SHE DANCES.

SHE IS LOVELY.

AAARROOOOOO

YEAH, YOU'RE RIGHT, CHEWIE.

GRONK!

YOU HAVE SEEN THAT SHAPE BEFORE, AND SO HAVE I!

THIS IS SO EXCITING. THE ENTIRE BUILDING IS A MACHINE...

WHAT'S MORE, ARTOO SAYS THAT IT IS IN NEAR PERFECT WORKING ORDER... EXCEPT THAT TWO OF ITS COMPONENTS-- WHICH WOULD APPEAR MERELY DECORATIVE TO THE UNTRAINED EYE--

BLEEP

--ARE MISSING.

WELL, I THINK I KNOW WHERE TO FIND THEM.

COME ON. WE GOTTA GET BACK TO ENDOR, PRONTO, AND TALK TO LANDO.

7

341

THERE'S NO MISTAKE, LANDO. CHEWIE AN' ME BOTH SPOTTED IT-- THE LITTLE STATUES THAT ARE MISSING ARE THE SAME ONES YOU USED TO HAVE-- THE DANCING GODDESS AND THE MINSTREL

GROOF

WELL, I'LL BE... I WON THOSE THINGS IN A CARD GAME A LONG TIME AGO...

TOOK THEM BECAUSE THE MAN I WAS PLAYING HAD STAKED EVERYTHING ELSE HE HAD, AND MY HAND WAS TOO GOOD NOT TO RAISE THE ANTE.

HE SWORE THEY WERE IMMENSELY VALUABLE... BUT WHEN I PRESSED HIM, HE ADMITTED HE DIDN'T KNOW WHY.

IN A SENSE HE WAS RIGHT--THOSE TWO STATUETTES ARE PRICELESS-- BECAUSE THE SURVIVAL OF AN EN- TIRE PEOPLE DEPENDS ON THEM.

IT SEEMS PRETTY OBVIOUS... SOMEWHERE ALONG THE LINE, GODO BECAME UNFIT TO SUPPORT ITS NATIVE LIFE FORMS, AND SOMEONE DEVISED A MACHINE THAT COULD CORRECT THAT...

AND THEN BASED A RELIGION UPON THE WHOLE THING. THE GODDESS LITERALLY DOES GIVE THEM LIFE. OR DID.

MEANWHILE, EVERY TREASURE HUNTER AND PIRATE IN THE SECTOR HAS BEEN AFTER THOSE COMPONENTS, WITHOUT KNOWING THEIR REAL NATURE...

...OR THE FACT THAT THEIR ONLY REAL VALUE IS TO THE GODOANS.

WHERE ARE THEY NOW LANDO?

ONE WAS TAKEN FROM ME BY LEMO AND SANDA'S GANG...

AND I GAVE THE OTHER TO THAT OLD ENEMY OF MINE, DREBBLE, TELLING HIM IT WAS AN AWARD FOR HIS HEROISM...

ME AN' LUKE'LL SEE YOU GUYS BACK ON GODO, AFTER WE GET THE STATUES. GOOD LUCK.

WELL, WE KNOW WHERE DREBBLE IS --SO HE'S ALL YOURS AN' CHEWIE'S-- AND WE CAN TRACK DOWN LEMO AND SANDA EASILY ENOUGH...

BOUNTY HUNTERS FINALLY CAUGHT UP WITH THEM IN THE KEYORIN SYSTEM. THEY'RE PROBABLY STILL ON THE PRISON ASTEROID IN THAT SECTOR.

8

HEY, LEMO, HAVEN'T YOU AT LEAST GOT A FRIENDLY WORD FOR AN OLD FRIEND? YOU AN' SANDA AREN'T EXACTLY EASY TO SEE THESE DAYS.

ME AN' THE KID HADDA LAY DOWN A LOT OF GREASE TO GET IN HERE.

MY HEART BLEEDS, SOLO.

ESPECIALLY SINCE WE OWE IT TO YOU, CALRISSIAN, AN' THE WOOKIEE, THAT WE'RE IN HERE IN THE FIRST PLACE.

NOW, BE NICE. YOU COOPERATE WITH US, GIVE US SOME INFORMATION, AND WE'RE WILLING TO LAY DOWN ENOUGH GREASE TO GET YOU BOTH BACK OUT OF HERE -- PERMANENTLY.

KEEP TALKING.

I WANT THE MINSTREL BACK.

I DON'T SUPPOSE IT WOULD MAKE ANY DIFFERENCE TO EITHER OF YOU TO KNOW THAT BILLIONS OF INNOCENT LIVES DEPEND ON THAT STATUE BEING RECOVERED QUICKLY...?

YOU SUPPOSE RIGHT.

FORGET IT. IT WOULD TAKE A LOT MORE THAN JUST WALKING OUT OF HERE TO MAKE LOSING THAT WORTH OUR WHILE.

BE A BUSINESSMAN, LEMO, DREBBLE'S GOT THE GODDESS NOW, AN' WITHOUT THAT, THE MINSTREL'S NO GOOD TO ANYONE.

HAN KNOWS OUR OLD HIDE-OUT, ON ARCAN IV... NOW, WHEN YOU GET THERE, YOU...

BUT, I KNOW WHERE I COULD LAY MY HANDS ON A LOT OF FLAME JEWELS -- OR AN EQUIVALENT AMOUNT, IN STANDARD CREDITS -- SAY TWENTY THOUSAND'S WORTH.

OKAY... DEAL. WE'LL TAKE IT IN CREDITS, AFTER WE'RE OUT OF HERE.

THE STATUE?

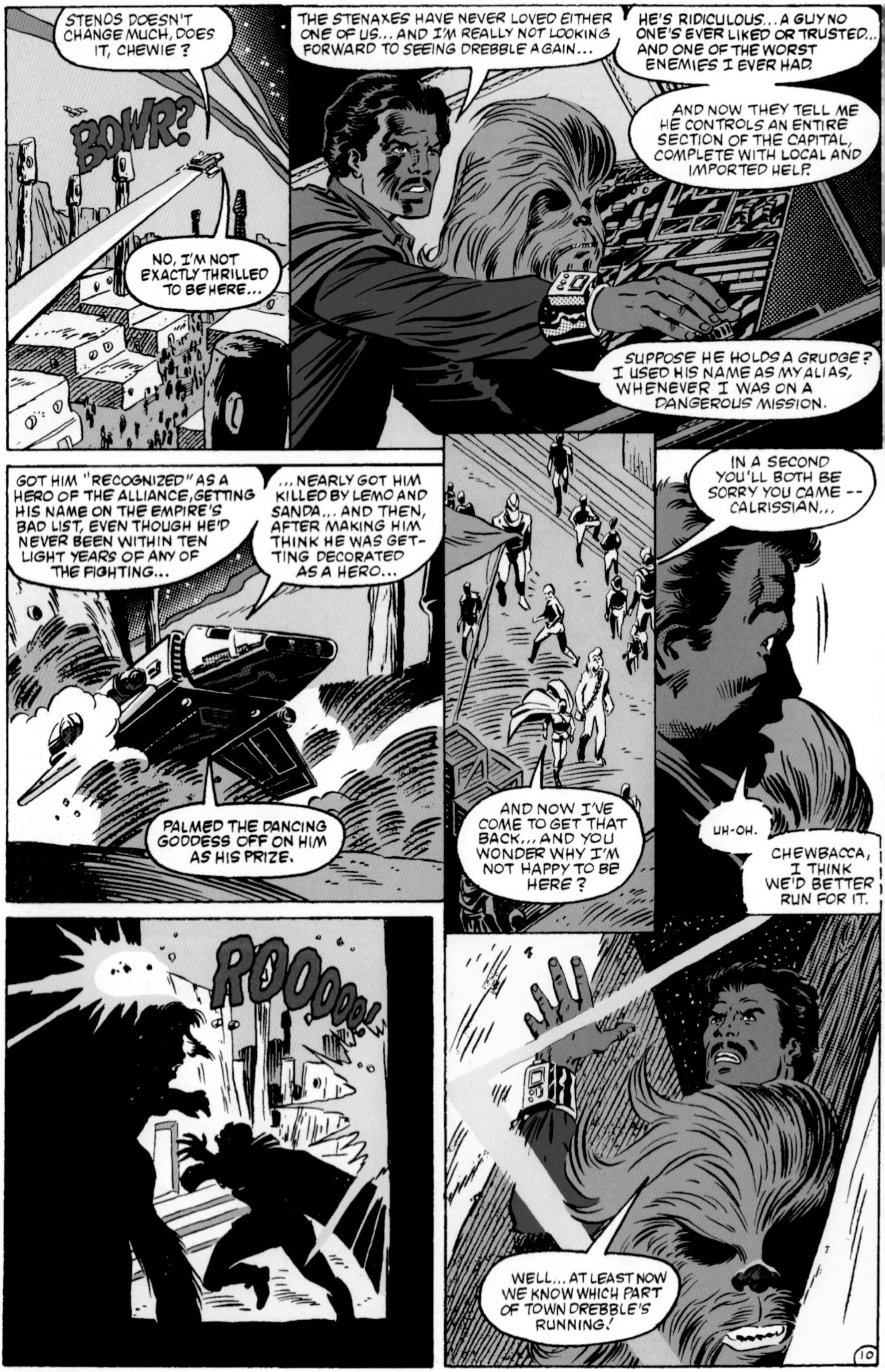
STENOS DOESN'T CHANGE MUCH, DOES IT, CHEWIE?
BOWR?
NO, I'M NOT EXACTLY THRILLED TO BE HERE...
THE STENAXES HAVE NEVER LOVED EITHER ONE OF US... AND I'M REALLY NOT LOOKING FORWARD TO SEEING DREBBLE AGAIN...
HE'S RIDICULOUS... A GUY NO ONE'S EVER LIKED OR TRUSTED... AND ONE OF THE WORST ENEMIES I EVER HAD.
AND NOW THEY TELL ME HE CONTROLS AN ENTIRE SECTION OF THE CAPITAL, COMPLETE WITH LOCAL AND IMPORTED HELP.
SUPPOSE HE HOLDS A GRUDGE? I USED HIS NAME AS MY ALIAS, WHENEVER I WAS ON A DANGEROUS MISSION.
GOT HIM "RECOGNIZED" AS A HERO OF THE ALLIANCE, GETTING HIS NAME ON THE EMPIRE'S BAD LIST, EVEN THOUGH HE'D NEVER BEEN WITHIN TEN LIGHT YEARS OF ANY OF THE FIGHTING...
...NEARLY GOT HIM KILLED BY LEMO AND SANDA... AND THEN, AFTER MAKING HIM THINK HE WAS GETTING DECORATED AS A HERO...
PALMED THE DANCING GODDESS OFF ON HIM AS HIS PRIZE.
AND NOW I'VE COME TO GET THAT BACK... AND YOU WONDER WHY I'M NOT HAPPY TO BE HERE?
IN A SECOND YOU'LL BOTH BE SORRY YOU CAME -- CALRISSIAN...
UH-OH.
CHEWBACCA, I THINK WE'D BETTER RUN FOR IT.
ROOOOOO!
WELL... AT LEAST NOW WE KNOW WHICH PART OF TOWN DREBBLE'S RUNNING!
10

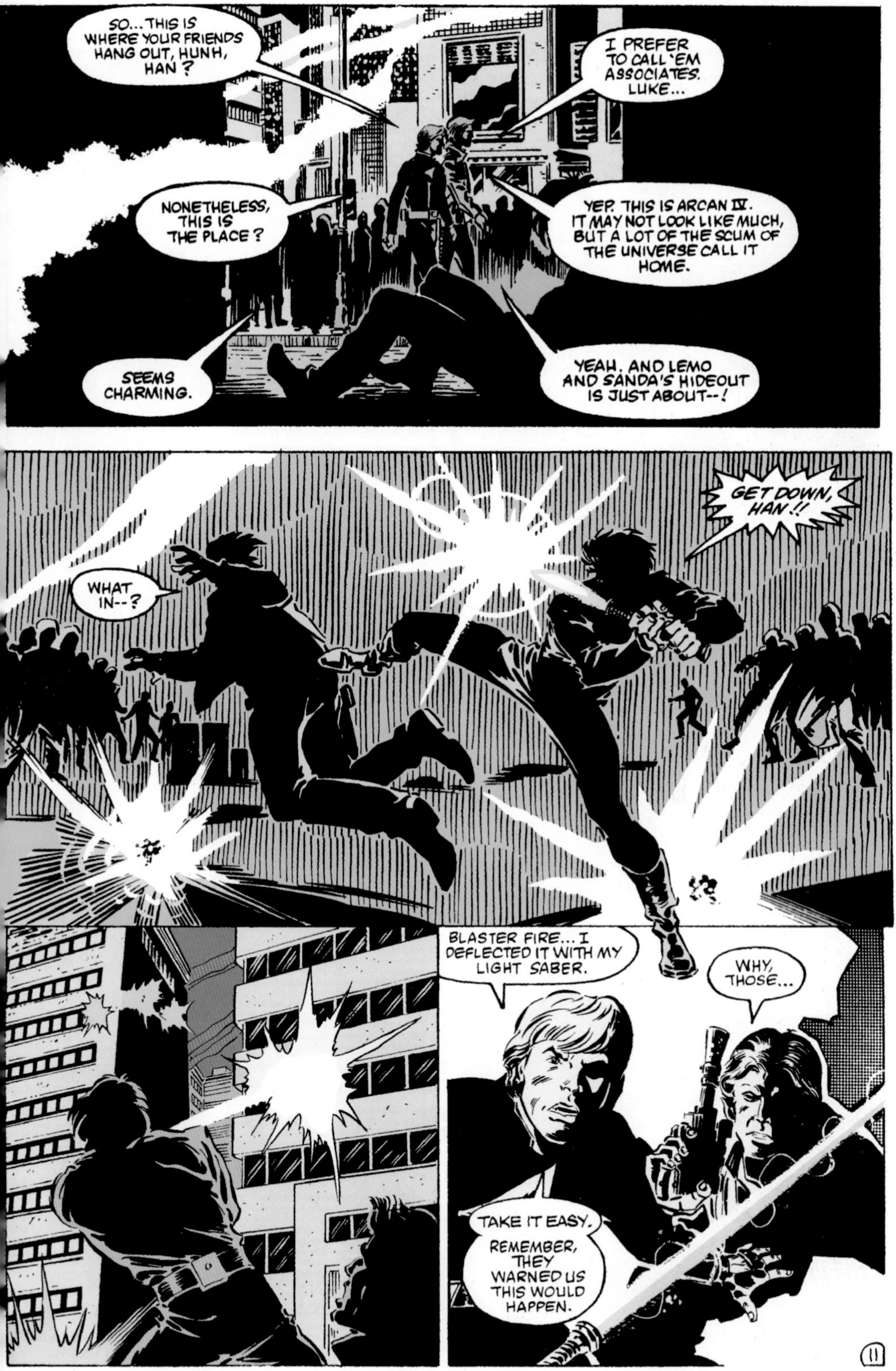
SO... THIS IS WHERE YOUR FRIENDS HANG OUT, HUNH, HAN?
I PREFER TO CALL 'EM ASSOCIATES. LUKE...
NONETHELESS, THIS IS THE PLACE?
YEP. THIS IS ARCAN IV. IT MAY NOT LOOK LIKE MUCH, BUT A LOT OF THE SCUM OF THE UNIVERSE CALL IT HOME.
SEEMS CHARMING.
YEAH. AND LEMO AND SANDA'S HIDEOUT IS JUST ABOUT--!
GET DOWN, HAN!!
WHAT IN--?
BLASTER FIRE... I DEFLECTED IT WITH MY LIGHT SABER.
WHY, THOSE...
TAKE IT EASY.
REMEMBER, THEY WARNED US THIS WOULD HAPPEN.
11

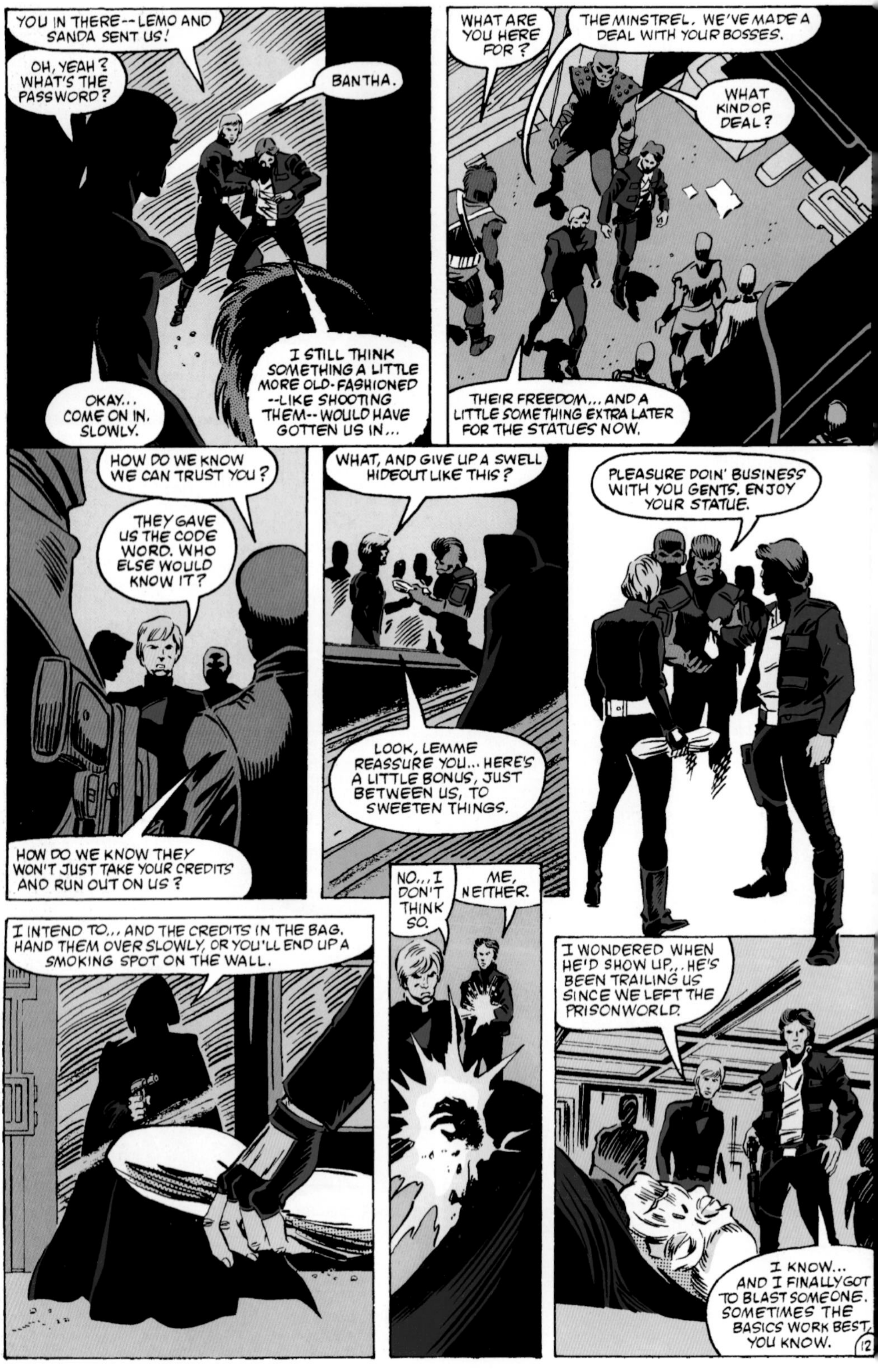

YOU IN THERE--LEMO AND SANDA SENT US!
OH, YEAH? WHAT'S THE PASSWORD?
BANTHA.
OKAY... COME ON IN. SLOWLY.
I STILL THINK SOMETHING A LITTLE MORE OLD-FASHIONED --LIKE SHOOTING THEM--WOULD HAVE GOTTEN US IN...
WHAT ARE YOU HERE FOR?
THE MINSTREL. WE'VE MADE A DEAL WITH YOUR BOSSES.
WHAT KIND OF DEAL?
THEIR FREEDOM... AND A LITTLE SOMETHING EXTRA LATER FOR THE STATUES NOW.
HOW DO WE KNOW WE CAN TRUST YOU?
THEY GAVE US THE CODE WORD. WHO ELSE WOULD KNOW IT?
HOW DO WE KNOW THEY WON'T JUST TAKE YOUR CREDITS AND RUN OUT ON US?
WHAT, AND GIVE UP A SWELL HIDEOUT LIKE THIS?
LOOK, LEMME REASSURE YOU... HERE'S A LITTLE BONUS, JUST BETWEEN US, TO SWEETEN THINGS.
PLEASURE DOIN' BUSINESS WITH YOU GENTS. ENJOY YOUR STATUE.
I INTEND TO... AND THE CREDITS IN THE BAG. HAND THEM OVER SLOWLY, OR YOU'LL END UP A SMOKING SPOT ON THE WALL.
NO... I DON'T THINK SO.
ME, NEITHER.
I WONDERED WHEN HE'D SHOW UP... HE'S BEEN TRAILING US SINCE WE LEFT THE PRISONWORLD.
I KNOW... AND I FINALLY GOT TO BLAST SOMEONE. SOMETIMES THE BASICS WORK BEST, YOU KNOW.
12

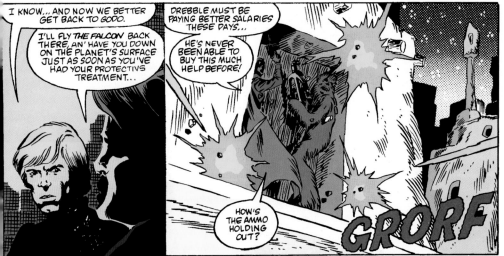

I KNOW... AND NOW WE BETTER GET BACK TO GODO.

I'LL FLY *THE FALCON* BACK THERE, AN' HAVE YOU DOWN ON THE PLANET'S SURFACE JUST AS SOON AS YOU'VE HAD YOUR PROTECTIVE TREATMENT...

DREBBLE MUST BE PAYING BETTER SALARIES THESE DAYS...

HE'S NEVER BEEN ABLE TO BUY THIS MUCH HELP BEFORE!

HOW'S THE AMMO HOLDING OUT?

GRORF

WELL, MAKE THE MOST OF IT.

I'M BEGINNING TO GET THE IDEA THAT PROTECTING OL' DREBBLE-- AND TAKING CARE OF US-- IS MORE THAN JUST A JOB TO THESE GUYS.

I DOUBT ANYTHING COULD CONVINCE THEM TO--!

STOP!

WHA--?

RARP?

WHAT IN...

...YOU!

13

YOU KNOW, LANDO...THE DAY YOU GAVE ME THAT AWARD FOR BRAVERY WAS THE DAY MY LIFE CHANGED...

I KNOW IT SOUNDS SILLY... BUT THERE WAS A TIME WHEN I THOUGHT NO ONE LIKED ME... NO ONE NEEDED ME... NO ONE CARED...

UH... YOUR AWARD. I NEED IT BACK.

BACK?

ONCE I REALIZED... I HAD TANGIBLE PROOF THAT THEY LIKED ME, AND CARED...

NOW, I KNOW WHAT I WAS MISSING. PEOPLE I COULD DEPEND ON... WHO KNOW THEY CAN DEPEND ON ME... SELF-RESPECT... FRIENDS...

BY THE WAY... WHAT BRINGS YOU HERE?

ARE YOU TIRED OF LIVING, "FRIEND"?

I... I CAN'T LIE TO YOU, DREBBLE. I THOUGHT OF TRYING TO CHEAT YOU... OR STEALING IT...

BUT I CAN'T. I OWE YOU THE TRUTH.

BACK?

LANDO, FRIENDS SHOULD NEVER RESORT TO CHEATING AND STEALING FROM ONE ANOTHER.

IF YOU NEED THE DANCING GODDESS THAT BADLY...

THAT STATUE, PHYSICALLY MEANS LIFE OR DEATH TO A WORLD FULL OF DESPERATE, INNOCENT PEOPLE.

YOU MUST SIMPLY... TAKE IT.

DREBBLE... CHEWIE AND I ARE TAKING THIS... BECAUSE WE HAVE TO... BUT NO ONE CAN TAKE AWAY THE FACT THAT YOU EARNED IT.

YOU'VE STILL GOT WHAT IT TAKES.

NOW YOU'RE A HERO OF THE ALLIANCE'S PEACE... AS WELL AS THE WAR.

TILL WE MEET AGAIN, MY FRIEND.

I SUPPOSE... IN LIGHT OF WHAT YOU'VE TOLD ME... IF I WERE TO INSIST ON KEEPING IT... I WOULD NO LONGER DESERVE IT.

⑮

WELL, WE'RE OFF TO DELIVER THE BOMBS AND ENERGY CANNONS, FUMIYO...

THAT'S IF YOU'RE SURE THINGS ARE OKAY WITH YOUR PEOPLE...

OH, YES, HAN SOLO... AND WE THANK YOU FOR IT. ALREADY, OUR PLANET BEGINS TO BLOOM AGAIN... AND WE VOW NO ONE WILL EVER AGAIN PROFANE OUR LADY OR HER PEOPLE, AS THEY MAKE THE MUSIC IN THE TEMPLE...

THEN WE CAN BE ON OUR WAY.

AN' KNOW THERE'LL BE AT LEAST ONE PLACE WE'RE WELCOME FOR A WHILE, HUNH, LANDO?

LANDO?

UUHGHH

LANDO!!

HEY, PAL, WHAT'S WRONG?

DON'T KNOW... FEEL ALL KIND OF... HOT AND COLD... AND FLOATY... ...AND DRY... ...ALL AT ONCE... ...STRANGE...

HAN... THOSE SOUND LIKE THE SYMPTOMS OF THE GODOAN'S DISEASE. FUMIYO WAS LIKE THAT... RIGHT BEFORE HE COLLAPSED.

THAT'S STUPID. THE RADIOACTIVE INNOCULATIONS PROTECTED ALL OF THE REST OF US. WHY WOULDN'T IT WORK FOR LANDO?

WH-WHAT INNOCULATIONS...

ROWNK!

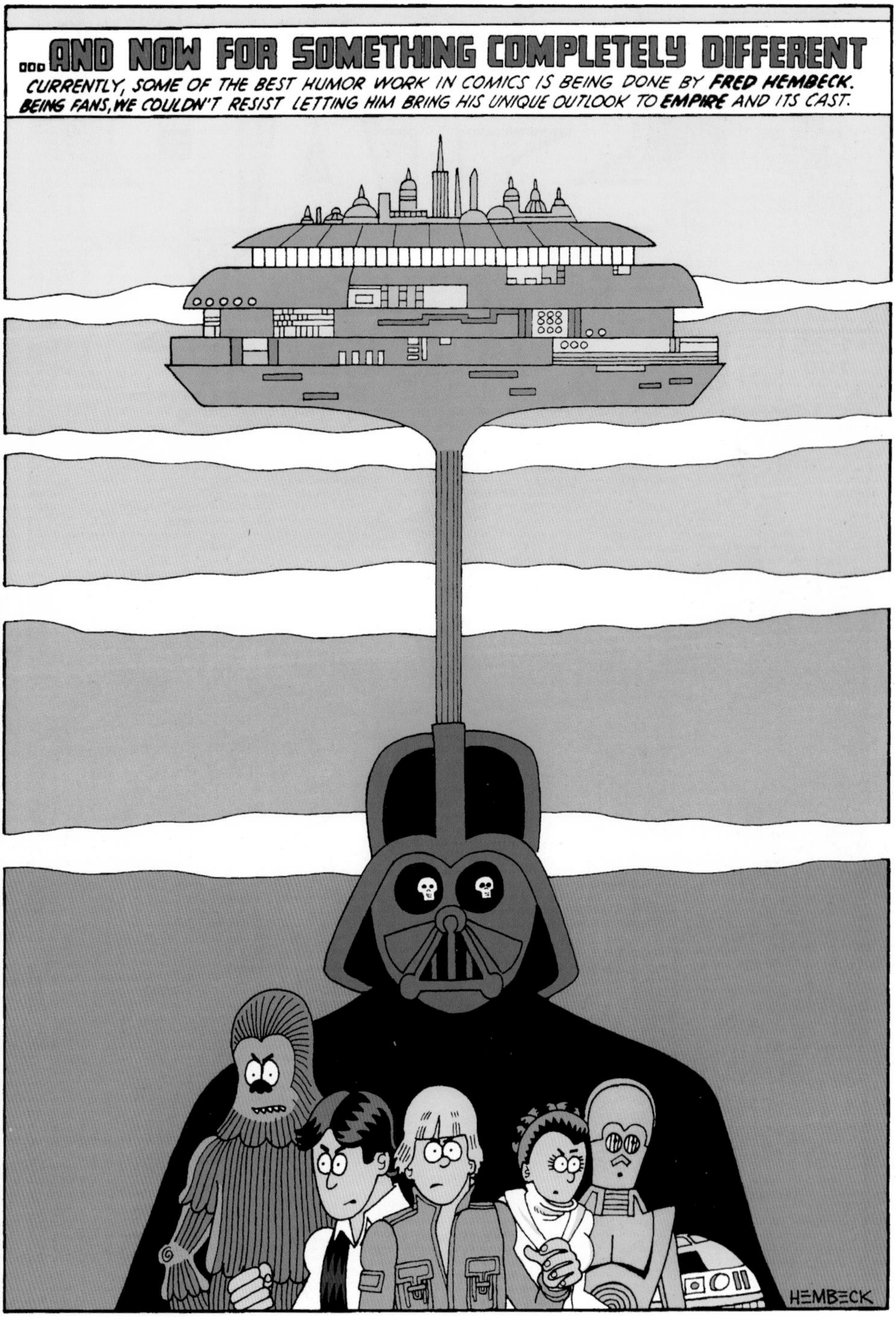
...AND NOW FOR SOMETHING COMPLETELY DIFFERENT
CURRENTLY, SOME OF THE BEST HUMOR WORK IN COMICS IS BEING DONE BY FRED HEMBECK. BEING FANS, WE COULDN'T RESIST LETTING HIM BRING HIS UNIQUE OUTLOOK TO EMPIRE AND ITS CAST.
HEMBECK

FIRST STRIKE

--THE ENEMY *TIE* FIGHTERS AND BATTLE CRUISERS, THE RADIATION BELTS AND ASTEROID FIELDS YOU MUST FLY THROUGH, AND THE FIRE YOU MUST EVADE--

--FROM THE ENERGY CANNONS PLACED ON THE SURFACE OF THE PLANET YOU ARE FLYING OVER.

AS YOU ARE ALSO AWARE THERE IS A VERY VITAL TIME ELEMENT INVOLVED.

SPEED IS OF THE ESSENCE HERE--SPEED AND SAFETY.

OH, COME *ON!*

NOW, MAN YOUR FLIGHT COMPUTERS. *GOOD LUCK* --

--AND MAY *THE FORCE* BE WITH YOU.

2

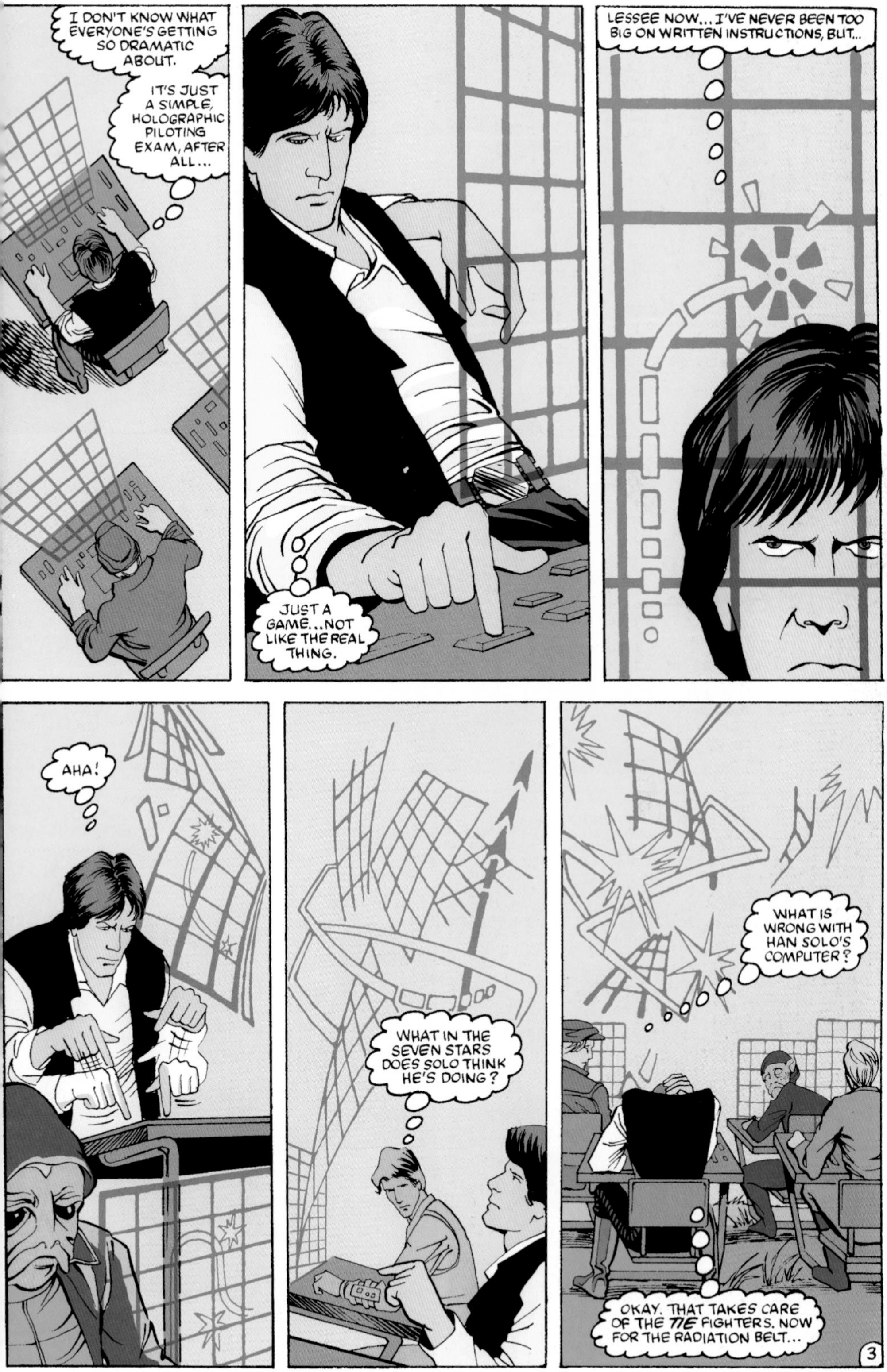
I DON'T KNOW WHAT EVERYONE'S GETTING SO DRAMATIC ABOUT.
IT'S JUST A SIMPLE, HOLOGRAPHIC PILOTING EXAM, AFTER ALL...
JUST A GAME...NOT LIKE THE REAL THING.
LESSEE NOW... I'VE NEVER BEEN TOO BIG ON WRITTEN INSTRUCTIONS, BUT...
AHA!
WHAT IN THE SEVEN STARS DOES SOLO THINK HE'S DOING?
WHAT IS WRONG WITH HAN SOLO'S COMPUTER?
OKAY. THAT TAKES CARE OF THE TIE FIGHTERS. NOW FOR THE RADIATION BELT...
3

LUKE, LANDO, I CAN TELL YOU ONE THING. IF ANYONE BESIDES ADMIRAL ACKBAR HAD ORDERED ME TO TAKE THAT TEST, I WOULDN'T HAVE STOOD FOR IT.

WHY NOT? YOU PASSED, DIDN'T YOU?

'COURSE I DID, BUT... THERE'S A BIG DIFFERENCE BETWEEN BEING ABLE TO HANDLE A DANGEROUS SET-UP AND BEING ABLE TO TELL A COMPUTER HOW TO DO IT, IN TERMS IT CAN UN-DERSTAND.

HERE COMES HER ROYAL HIGHNESS. MAYBE SHE CAN EXPLAIN WHAT THE TESTING WAS ALL ABOUT IN THE FIRST PLACE...

LEIA?

LEIA, I--!

AH, PRINCESS LEIA. YOU LOOK AS LOVELY AS EVER TODAY.

FENN SHYSA-- AGAIN!

THANK YOU, FENN...

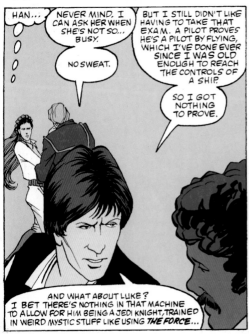

HAN...

NEVER MIND. I CAN ASK HER WHEN SHE'S NOT SO... BUSY.

NO SWEAT.

BUT I STILL DIDN'T LIKE HAVING TO TAKE THAT EXAM. A PILOT PROVES HE'S A PILOT BY FLYING, WHICH I'VE DONE EVER SINCE I WAS OLD ENOUGH TO REACH THE CONTROLS OF A SHIP?

SO I GOT NOTHING TO PROVE.

AND WHAT ABOUT LUKE? I BET THERE'S NOTHING IN THAT MACHINE TO ALLOW FOR HIM BEING A JEDI KNIGHT, TRAINED IN WEIRD MYSTIC STUFF LIKE USING *THE FORCE*...

HE DOESN'T EVEN USE A TARGETTING COMPUTER WHEN HE FLIES.

SO, WHO CAME UP WITH THE DUMB IDEA OF TESTING US?

UH, HAN... I DIDN'T SEE YOUR FRIEND, BEY, SIGNED UP FOR ANY OF THE TESTING SESSIONS.

HE'S NOT.

SPEAKING OF BEY, ISN'T THAT HIM OVER THERE, TALKING TO FENN AND LEIA?

4

YEP, NO ONE ELSE EXCEPT A WOOKIEE--LIKE CHEWBACCA-- IS THAT TALL.

WHY DIDN'T HE TAKE THE EXAM, THOUGH?

BECAUSE HE'S NEVER BEEN MUCH OF A FLIER, HE LIKES HIS ACTION ON THE GROUND, HAND TO HAND AND PERSONAL. ALWAYS HAS.

GRONK

OH, HI, CHEWIE.

Y'KNOW, HAN...EVEN WHEN I WAS A KID ON TATOOINE, WE'D HEAR STORIES ABOUT BEY, THE WAY HE TRAVELLED AROUND, THE GREAT THINGS HE DID FOR PEOPLE.

IT GOT SO I DIDN'T BELIEVE HE WAS EVEN A REAL PERSON.

I WAS PRETTY SURPRISED TO FIND THAT YOU HAD EVEN MET HIM...

WE PRACTICALLY GREW UP TOGETHER...MY WHOLE LIFE, WHEREVER I WENT, IT SEEMED LIKE BEY WAS AROUND, AT LEAST PART OF THE TIME, COMING AND GOING...

BUT... HE DOESN'T LOOK MUCH LIKE A CORELLIAN.

WELL, LUKE... HIS FATHER WAS A CORELLIAN... BUT HIS MOTHER WAS LONG GONE BEFORE I WAS EVEN BORN.

I DON'T THINK BEY EVER KNEW ANYTHING ABOUT HER... EXCEPT THAT HIS FATHER HATED HER FOR LEAVING AND TOOK IT OUT ON HIM.

MOST PEOPLE TREATED HIM LIKE HE WAS LESS THAN A PERSON, BUT...

5

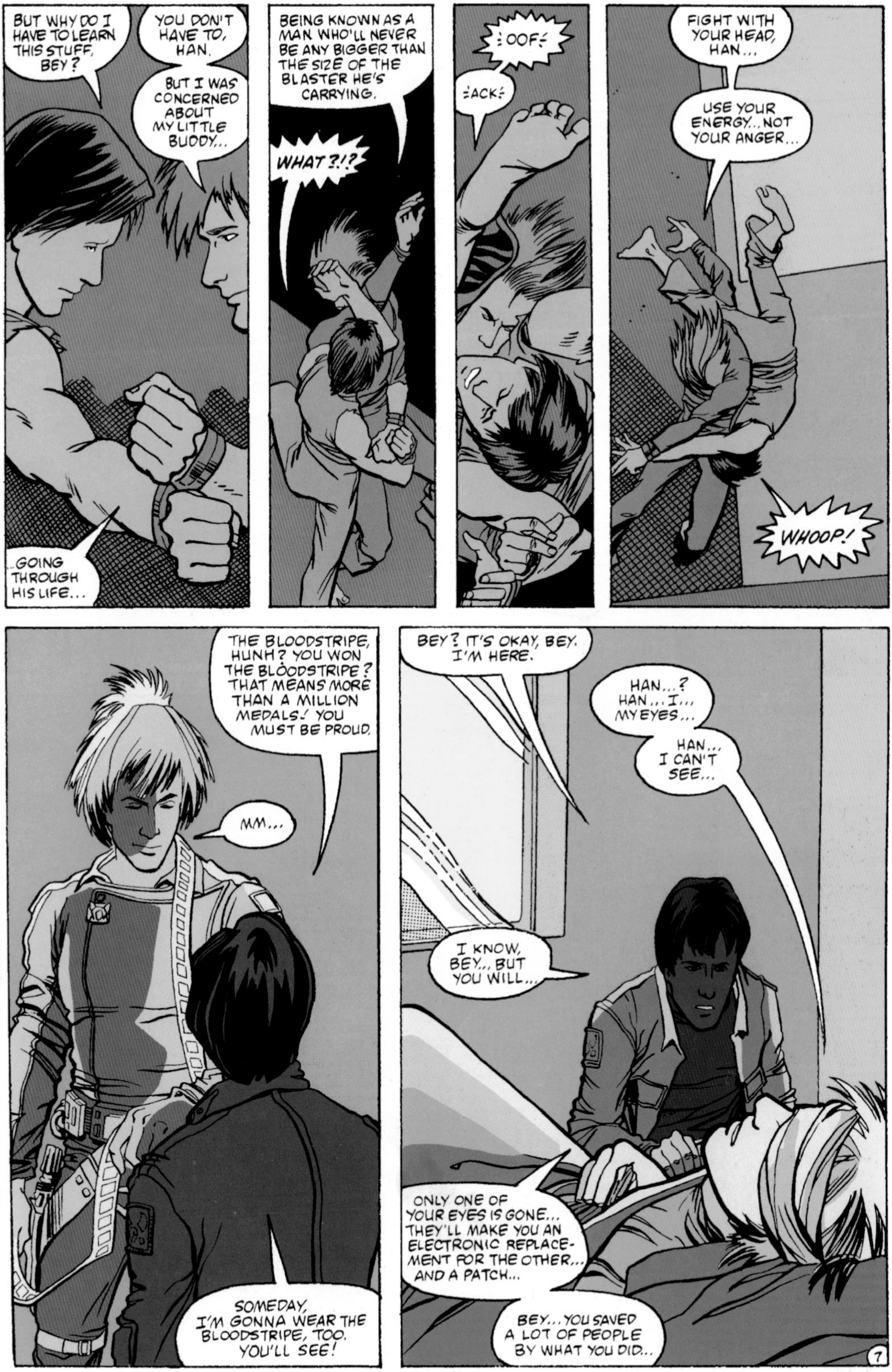

BUT WHY DO I HAVE TO LEARN THIS STUFF, BEY?
YOU DON'T HAVE TO, HAN.
BUT I WAS CONCERNED ABOUT MY LITTLE BUDDY...
...GOING THROUGH HIS LIFE...
BEING KNOWN AS A MAN WHO'LL NEVER BE ANY BIGGER THAN THE SIZE OF THE BLASTER HE'S CARRYING.
WHAT?!?
OOF
ACK
FIGHT WITH YOUR HEAD, HAN...
USE YOUR ENERGY... NOT YOUR ANGER...
WHOOP!
THE BLOODSTRIPE, HUNH? YOU WON THE BLOODSTRIPE? THAT MEANS MORE THAN A MILLION MEDALS! YOU MUST BE PROUD.
MM...
SOMEDAY, I'M GONNA WEAR THE BLOODSTRIPE, TOO. YOU'LL SEE!
BEY? IT'S OKAY, BEY. I'M HERE.
HAN...? HAN... I... MY EYES...
HAN... I CAN'T SEE...
I KNOW, BEY... BUT YOU WILL...
ONLY ONE OF YOUR EYES IS GONE... THEY'LL MAKE YOU AN ELECTRONIC REPLACEMENT FOR THE OTHER... AND A PATCH...
BEY... YOU SAVED A LOT OF PEOPLE BY WHAT YOU DID...
7

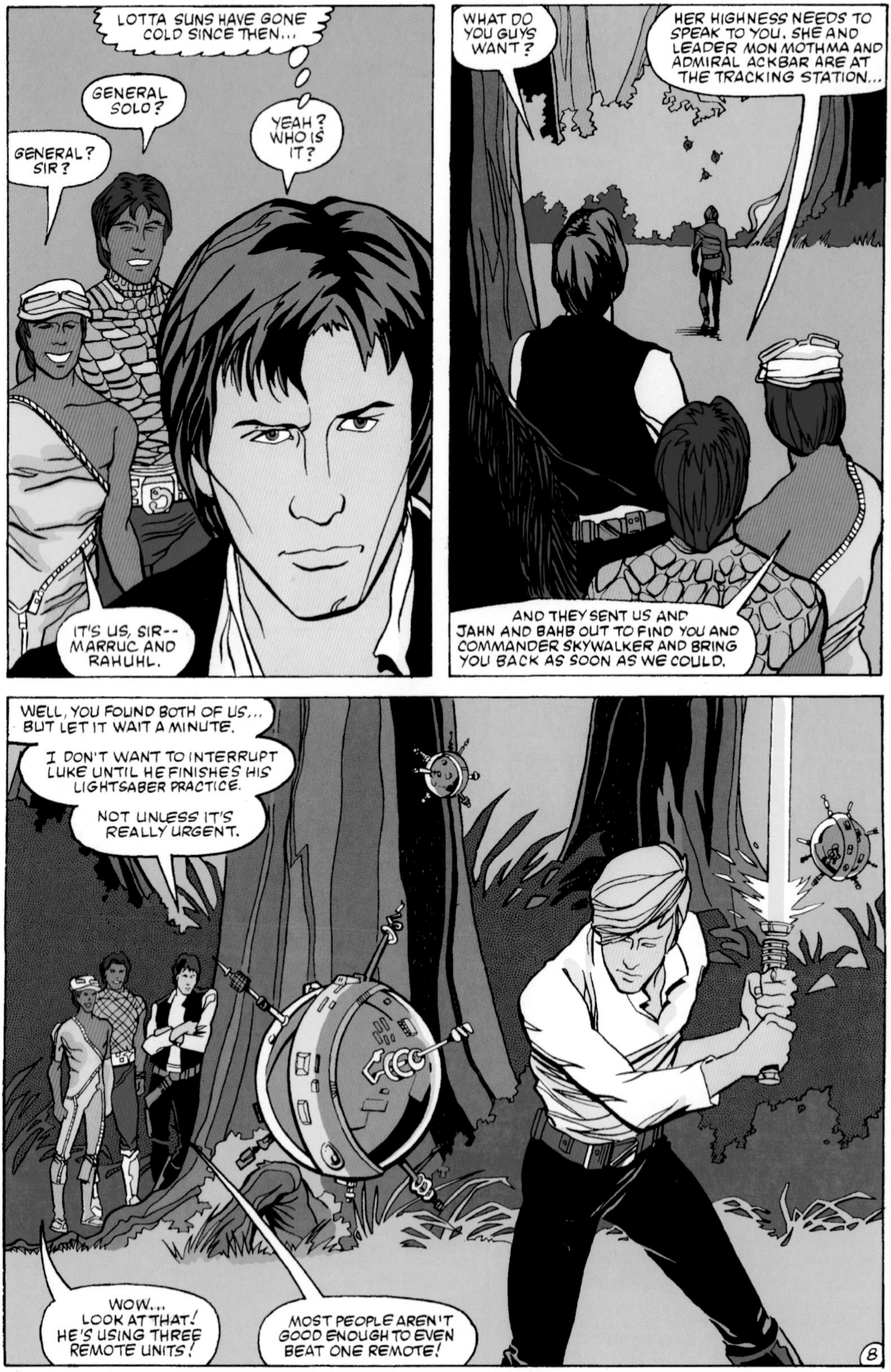

LOTTA SUNS HAVE GONE COLD SINCE THEN...
GENERAL SOLO?
GENERAL? SIR?
YEAH? WHO IS IT?
IT'S US, SIR-- MARRUC AND RAHUHL.
WHAT DO YOU GUYS WANT?
HER HIGHNESS NEEDS TO SPEAK TO YOU. SHE AND LEADER MON MOTHMA AND ADMIRAL ACKBAR ARE AT THE TRACKING STATION...
AND THEY SENT US AND JAHN AND BAHB OUT TO FIND YOU AND COMMANDER SKYWALKER AND BRING YOU BACK AS SOON AS WE COULD.
WELL, YOU FOUND BOTH OF US... BUT LET IT WAIT A MINUTE.
I DON'T WANT TO INTERRUPT LUKE UNTIL HE FINISHES HIS LIGHTSABER PRACTICE.
NOT UNLESS IT'S REALLY URGENT.
WOW... LOOK AT THAT! HE'S USING THREE REMOTE UNITS!
MOST PEOPLE AREN'T GOOD ENOUGH TO EVEN BEAT ONE REMOTE!
8

COMMANDER SKYWALKER! SIR? HER HIGHNESS' NEEDS TO SEE YOU!

BUT I'M NOT JAHN, GENERAL. I'M BAHB.

S'OKAY, JAHN, HE ALREADY KNOWS.

WHICHEVER. I KNEW IT WAS ONE OF YOU ZELTRONS.

COME ON, HAN. WE BETTER GET OVER TO THE MONITOR TOWER AND SEE WHAT'S UP.

WHILE I WAS ON KINOOINE, FIGHTING THAT ADVANCE NAGAI SQUADRON, I RAN AFOUL OF AN OLD IMPERIAL COLLABORATOR-- SHIRA BRIE, SHE WAS CALLED--

--THOUGH NOW SHE GOES BY THE NAME OF LUMIYA. ANYWAY, SHE HAD A WEAPON THAT WAS HALF COHERENT ENERGY, LIKE A SABER, AND HALF SOLID MATTER.

MY SABER COULD ONLY TAKE ON ONE PART OR THE OTHER OF IT AT A TIME, SO I DECIDED TO BUILD ANOTHER SABER, TO INCREASE MY OPTIONS, AND BEAT HER.

SO... WHERE'D YOU PICK UP THE EXTRA LIGHTSABER?

SOUNDS PRETTY TOUGH. YOU KNOW, THE MORE I HEAR ABOUT THESE NAGAI AND THEIR ALLIES, AND THE MORE OF THEIR HANDIWORK I SEE--

--THE LESS I LIKE IT.

ME, TOO.

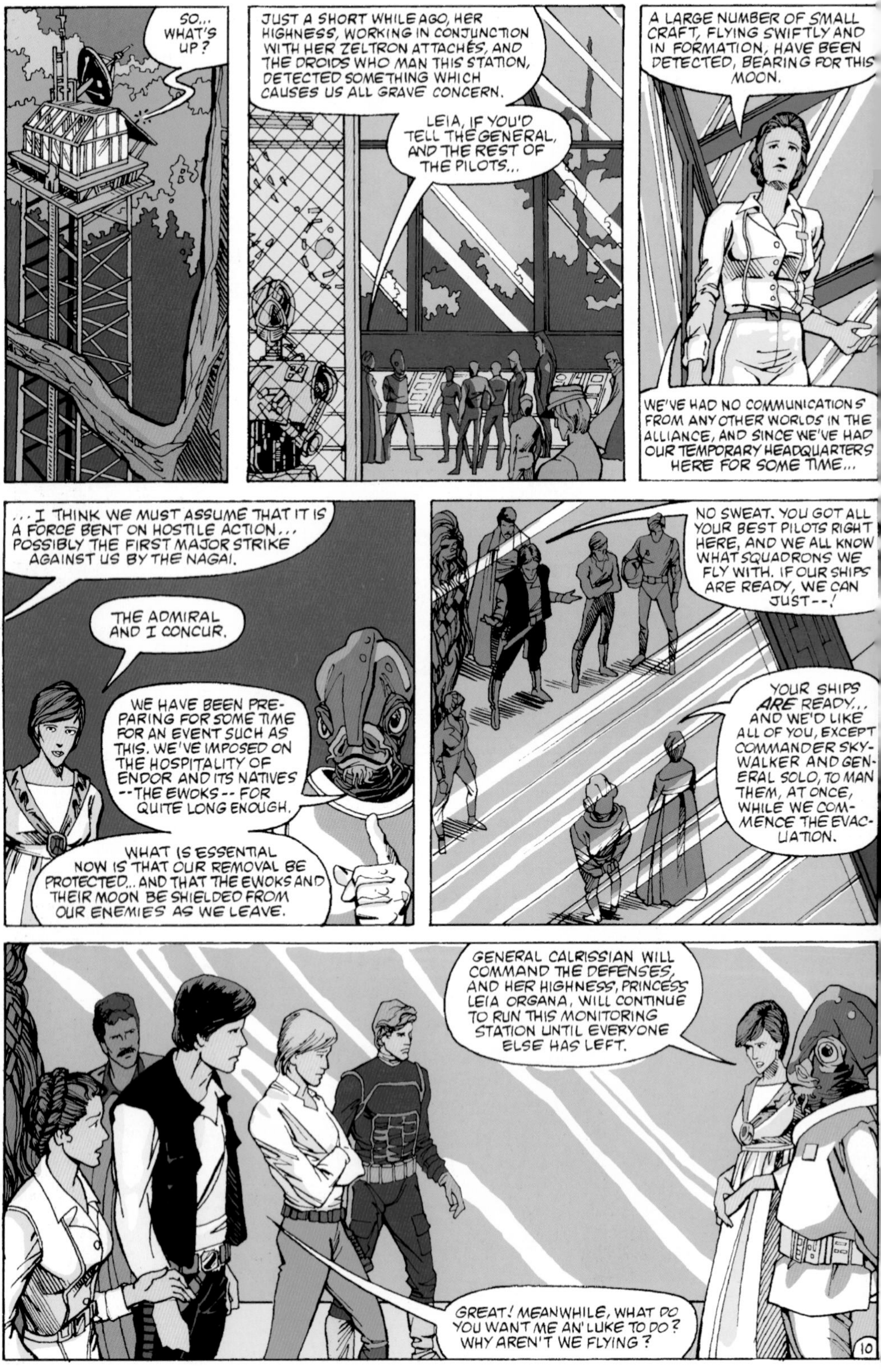
SO... WHAT'S UP?
JUST A SHORT WHILE AGO, HER HIGHNESS, WORKING IN CONJUNCTION WITH HER ZELTRON ATTACHÉS, AND THE DROIDS WHO MAN THIS STATION, DETECTED SOMETHING WHICH CAUSES US ALL GRAVE CONCERN.
LEIA, IF YOU'D TELL THE GENERAL, AND THE REST OF THE PILOTS...
A LARGE NUMBER OF SMALL CRAFT, FLYING SWIFTLY AND IN FORMATION, HAVE BEEN DETECTED, BEARING FOR THIS MOON.
WE'VE HAD NO COMMUNICATIONS FROM ANY OTHER WORLDS IN THE ALLIANCE, AND SINCE WE'VE HAD OUR TEMPORARY HEADQUARTERS HERE FOR SOME TIME...
...I THINK WE MUST ASSUME THAT IT IS A FORCE BENT ON HOSTILE ACTION... POSSIBLY THE FIRST MAJOR STRIKE AGAINST US BY THE NAGAI.
THE ADMIRAL AND I CONCUR.
WE HAVE BEEN PRE-PARING FOR SOME TIME FOR AN EVENT SUCH AS THIS. WE'VE IMPOSED ON THE HOSPITALITY OF ENDOR AND ITS NATIVES --THE EWOKS-- FOR QUITE LONG ENOUGH.
WHAT IS ESSENTIAL NOW IS THAT OUR REMOVAL BE PROTECTED... AND THAT THE EWOKS AND THEIR MOON BE SHIELDED FROM OUR ENEMIES AS WE LEAVE.
NO SWEAT. YOU GOT ALL YOUR BEST PILOTS RIGHT HERE, AND WE ALL KNOW WHAT SQUADRONS WE FLY WITH. IF OUR SHIPS ARE READY, WE CAN JUST--!
YOUR SHIPS ARE READY... AND WE'D LIKE ALL OF YOU, EXCEPT COMMANDER SKY-WALKER AND GEN-ERAL SOLO, TO MAN THEM, AT ONCE, WHILE WE COM-MENCE THE EVAC-UATION.
GENERAL CALRISSIAN WILL COMMAND THE DEFENSES, AND HER HIGHNESS, PRINCESS LEIA ORGANA, WILL CONTINUE TO RUN THIS MONITORING STATION UNTIL EVERYONE ELSE HAS LEFT.
GREAT! MEANWHILE, WHAT DO YOU WANT ME AN' LUKE TO DO? WHY AREN'T WE FLYING?
10

YOU... CAN'T. THERE'S BEEN SOME SORT OF COMPUTER ERROR... AND UNTIL WE CAN STRAIGHTEN OUT WHERE THE PROBLEM LIES... NEITHER OF YOU WILL BE CLEARED TO PILOT ANY SHIP.

ERR... THE ALLIANCE DID... WHEN IT GAVE THE FLIGHT EXAMS.

THE EXAMS...

OH, NO...

COMPUTER ERROR?! WHO ASKED A COMPUTER'S OPINION?

ACCORDING TO YOUR TEST SCORES BOTH OF YOU FLY YOUR SHIPS IN WAYS NO SANE PILOT WOULD ATTEMPT.

SANITY HAS NOTHING TO DO WITH IT! I WAS A SMUGGLER. THAT'S HOW WE ALL FLY. AND LUKE'S SUPPOSED TO BE CRAZY, TOO. HE'S GOT THE FORCE.

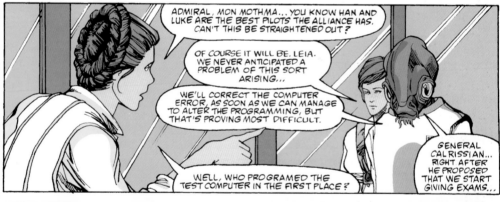

ADMIRAL, MON MOTHMA... YOU KNOW HAN AND LUKE ARE THE BEST PILOTS THE ALLIANCE HAS. CAN'T THIS BE STRAIGHTENED OUT?

OF COURSE IT WILL BE, LEIA. WE NEVER ANTICIPATED A PROBLEM OF THIS SORT ARISING...

WE'LL CORRECT THE COMPUTER ERROR, AS SOON AS WE CAN MANAGE TO ALTER THE PROGRAMMING, BUT THAT'S PROVING MOST DIFFICULT.

WELL, WHO PROGRAMED THE TEST COMPUTER IN THE FIRST PLACE?

GENERAL CALRISSIAN... RIGHT AFTER HE PROPOSED THAT WE START GIVING EXAMS...

LANDO?!!

HAN, I SWEAR TO YOU I DIDN'T KNOW...

I'LL FIGURE OUT SOME WAY OF FIXING THIS, AS SOON AS WE TAKE CARE OF THOSE INCOMING SHIPS...

I DON'T WANT TO HEAR IT!!!

11

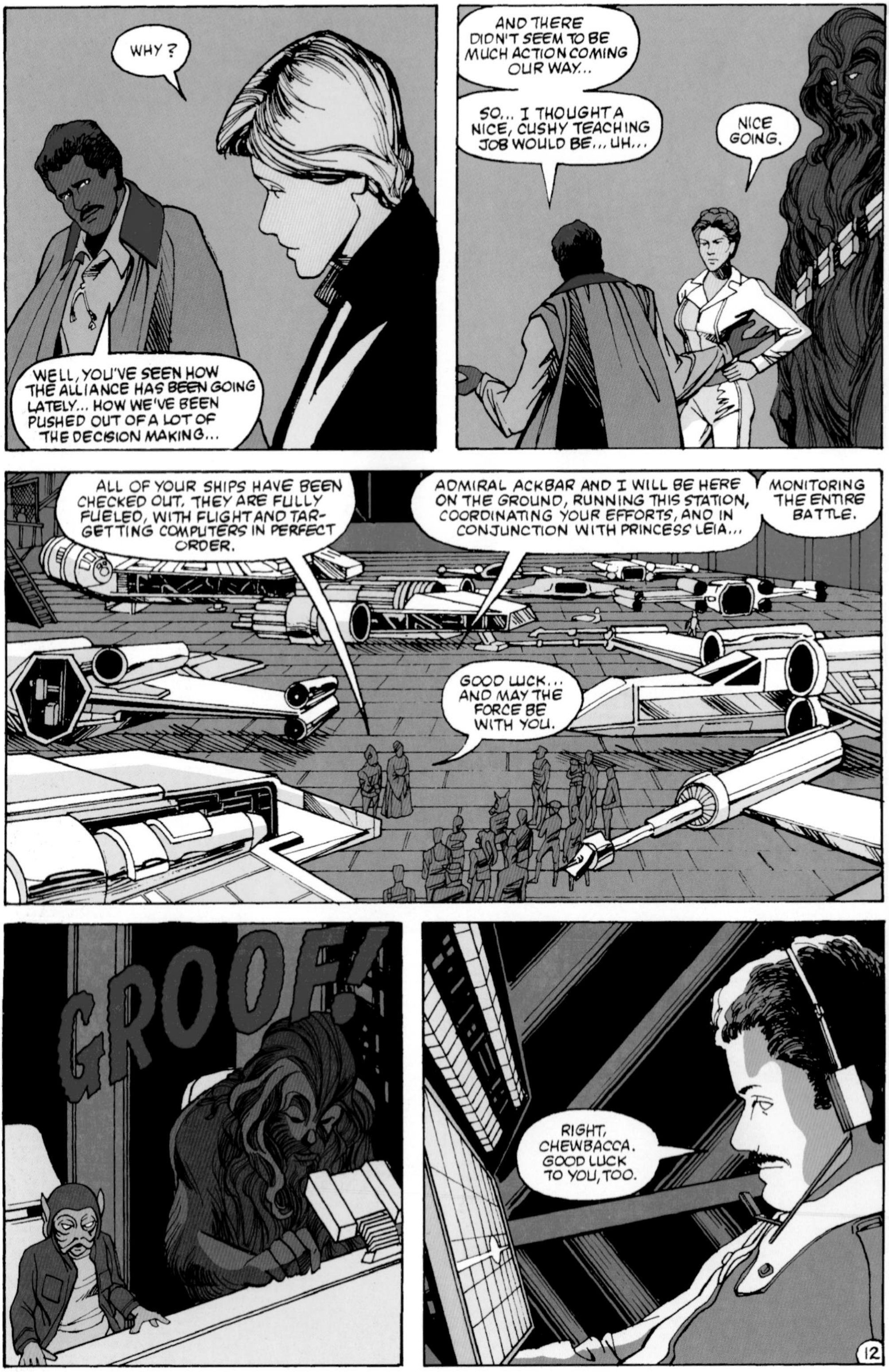
WHY?
WELL, YOU'VE SEEN HOW THE ALLIANCE HAS BEEN GOING LATELY... HOW WE'VE BEEN PUSHED OUT OF A LOT OF THE DECISION MAKING...
AND THERE DIDN'T SEEM TO BE MUCH ACTION COMING OUR WAY...
SO... I THOUGHT A NICE, CUSHY TEACHING JOB WOULD BE... UH...
NICE GOING.
ALL OF YOUR SHIPS HAVE BEEN CHECKED OUT. THEY ARE FULLY FUELED, WITH FLIGHT AND TAR-GETTING COMPUTERS IN PERFECT ORDER.
ADMIRAL ACKBAR AND I WILL BE HERE ON THE GROUND, RUNNING THIS STATION, COORDINATING YOUR EFFORTS, AND IN CONJUNCTION WITH PRINCESS LEIA...
MONITORING THE ENTIRE BATTLE.
GOOD LUCK... AND MAY THE FORCE BE WITH YOU.
GROOF!
RIGHT, CHEWBACCA. GOOD LUCK TO YOU, TOO.
12

SO, HAN... YOU FEELING ANY BETTER?

NO. WORSE. I TRIED TO TAKE OFF IN THE MILLENNIUM FALCON, BLOW OFF SOME STEAM BY FLYING.... AND THE GROUND COMPUTER LOCKED US IN A TRACTOR BEAM....

THAT DIDN'T RELEASE, UNTIL CHEWIE AND NIEN NUNB SIGNALED THAT THEY WERE GONNA TAKE OFF IN HER.

MY OWN SHIP...

I SURE HATE BEIN' LEFT OUT OF WHATEVER ACTION THERE'S GONNA BE.

WELL, WE MAY NOT HAVE TO MISS IT ENTIRELY.

TIPPET WAS TELLING ME HE AND SOME OF THE OTHER EWOKS SPOTTED SOMETHING STRANGE EARLIER TODAY, BUT THEY COULDN'T REALLY DESCRIBE IT.

WANT TO GRAB A COUPLE OF SPEEDER BIKES AND CHECK IT OUT?

SURE.

THERE'S TIPPET NOW.

LET'S LEAVE THE BIKES OVER HERE, SO WE CAN SNEAK UP ON WHATEVER'S GOT THE LITTLE FUZZBALLS SO NERVOUS...

RIGHT...

WELL... I'LL...

13

371

IN WHICH CASE, THEY'LL HAVE BEEN IN CLOSE CONTACT WITH THE SURVIVORS OF THE EMPIRE. IN FACT, THERE MAY BE SOME IMPERIALS AMONG THEM.

AS YOU ALL KNOW, THE FORCES WE ARE FACING ARE PROBABLY PILOTS FROM THE NAGAI!...

THEREFORE, WE'LL BE USING THE NEW FLIGHT FORMATIONS WE'VE WORKED OUT IN RECENT WEEKS, PATTERNS THE EMPIRE NEVER SAW AND THEREFORE CAN'T HAVE LEARNED.

DOES EVERYBODY COPY?

GRUFF

ROGER, GOLD LEADER.

FENN, HOW ABOUT YOU AND YOUR SQUADRON?

YOU CAN COUNT ON US, LANDO.

A LOT OF US HAVE PERSONAL SCORES TO SETTLE WITH THESE NAGAI FOR WHAT THEY'VE DONE TO OUR HOMEWORLD.

OKAY, EVERYONE... ACCORDING TO THE COMPUTERS, WE SHOULD HAVE VISUAL AND PHYSICAL CONTACT WITH THE ENEMY IN JUST A FEW MORE MINUTES.

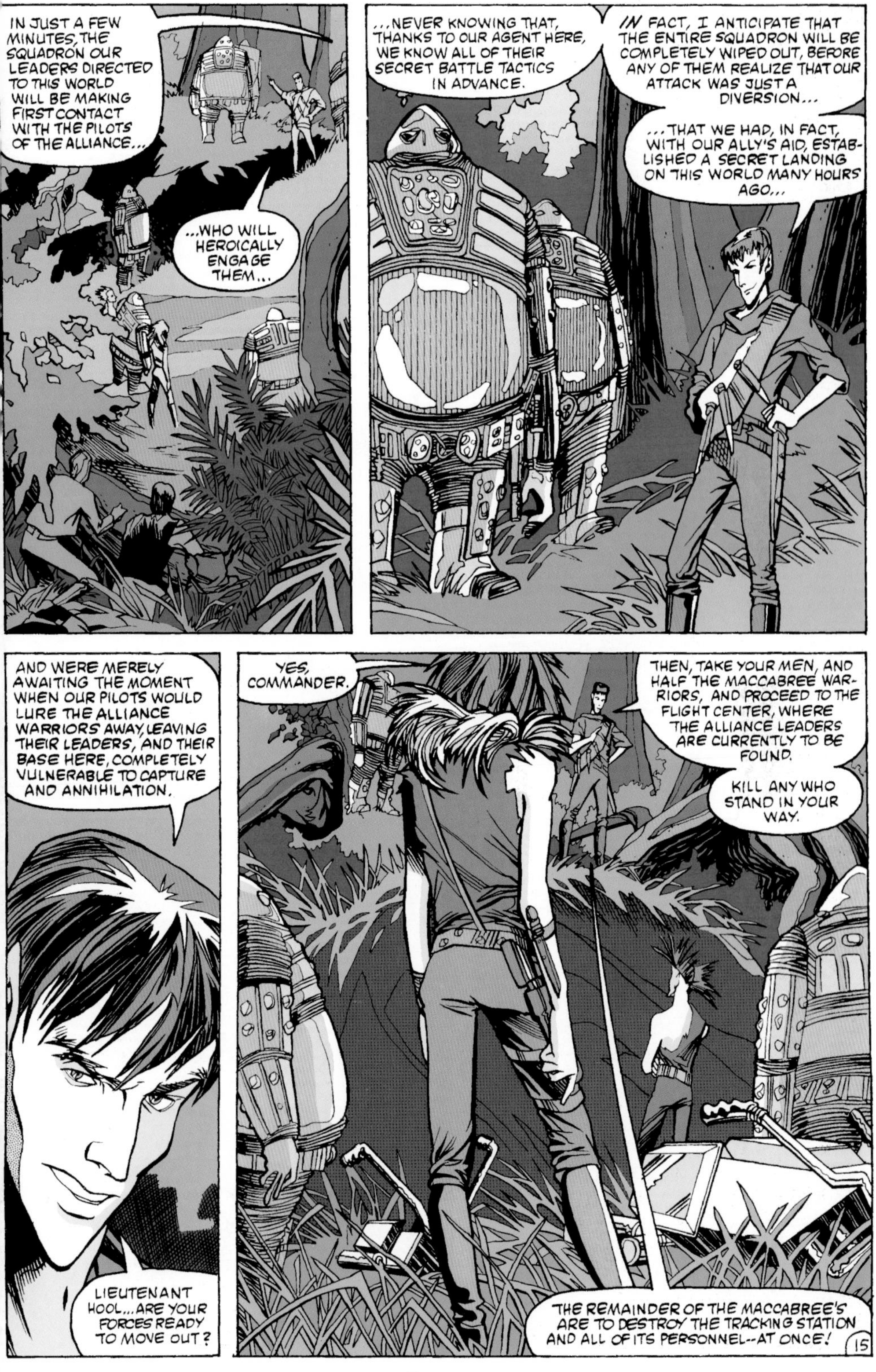

IN JUST A FEW MINUTES, THE SQUADRON OUR LEADERS DIRECTED TO THIS WORLD WILL BE MAKING FIRST CONTACT WITH THE PILOTS OF THE ALLIANCE...
...WHO WILL HEROICALLY ENGAGE THEM...
...NEVER KNOWING THAT, THANKS TO OUR AGENT HERE, WE KNOW ALL OF THEIR SECRET BATTLE TACTICS IN ADVANCE.
IN FACT, I ANTICIPATE THAT THE ENTIRE SQUADRON WILL BE COMPLETELY WIPED OUT, BEFORE ANY OF THEM REALIZE THAT OUR ATTACK WAS JUST A DIVERSION...
...THAT WE HAD, IN FACT, WITH OUR ALLY'S AID, ESTABLISHED A SECRET LANDING ON THIS WORLD MANY HOURS AGO...
AND WERE MERELY AWAITING THE MOMENT WHEN OUR PILOTS WOULD LURE THE ALLIANCE WARRIORS AWAY, LEAVING THEIR LEADERS, AND THEIR BASE HERE, COMPLETELY VULNERABLE TO CAPTURE AND ANNIHILATION.
LIEUTENANT HOOL...ARE YOUR FORCES READY TO MOVE OUT?
YES, COMMANDER.
THEN, TAKE YOUR MEN, AND HALF THE MACCABREE WARRIORS, AND PROCEED TO THE FLIGHT CENTER, WHERE THE ALLIANCE LEADERS ARE CURRENTLY TO BE FOUND.
KILL ANY WHO STAND IN YOUR WAY.
THE REMAINDER OF THE MACCABREE'S ARE TO DESTROY THE TRACKING STATION AND ALL OF ITS PERSONNEL--AT ONCE!
15

MON MOTHMA WAS RIGHT, HAN. THOSE SOLDIERS ARE NAGAI.

THAT'S THE LEAST OF OUR CONCERNS, BUDDY... THEIR LEADER IS THE ONE WHO HATES ME SO MUCH, WITHOUT HAVIN' ANY REASON I KNOW OF-- *KNIFE.*

BUT... I THOUGHT KNIFE WAS AN ALLIANCE PRISONER.

YOU HEARD WHAT THE MAN SAID... HE'S GOT A FRIEND IN OUR CAMP.

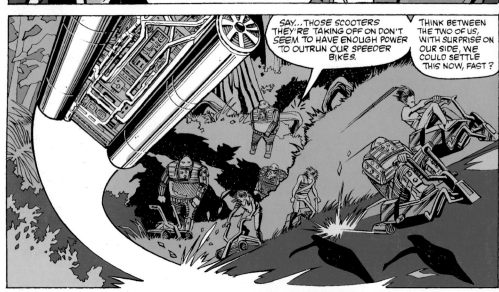

SAY...THOSE SCOOTERS THEY'RE TAKING OFF ON DON'T SEEM TO HAVE ENOUGH POWER TO OUTRUN OUR SPEEDER BIKES.

THINK BETWEEN THE TWO OF US, WITH SURPRISE ON OUR SIDE, WE COULD SETTLE THIS NOW, FAST?

MAYBE... BUT WHY TAKE CHANCES?

OUR FIRST PRIORITY HAS TO BE TO WARN LEIA-- AND THE ADMIRAL AND MON MOTHMA. WE HAVE ENOUGH ALLIES BACK AT THE BASE TO MAKE WIN-NING A SURE THING.

GUESS YOU'RE RIGHT.

WE'LL SPLIT UP... I'LL WARN LEIA AND THOSE KIDS OF--!

LOOK--

16

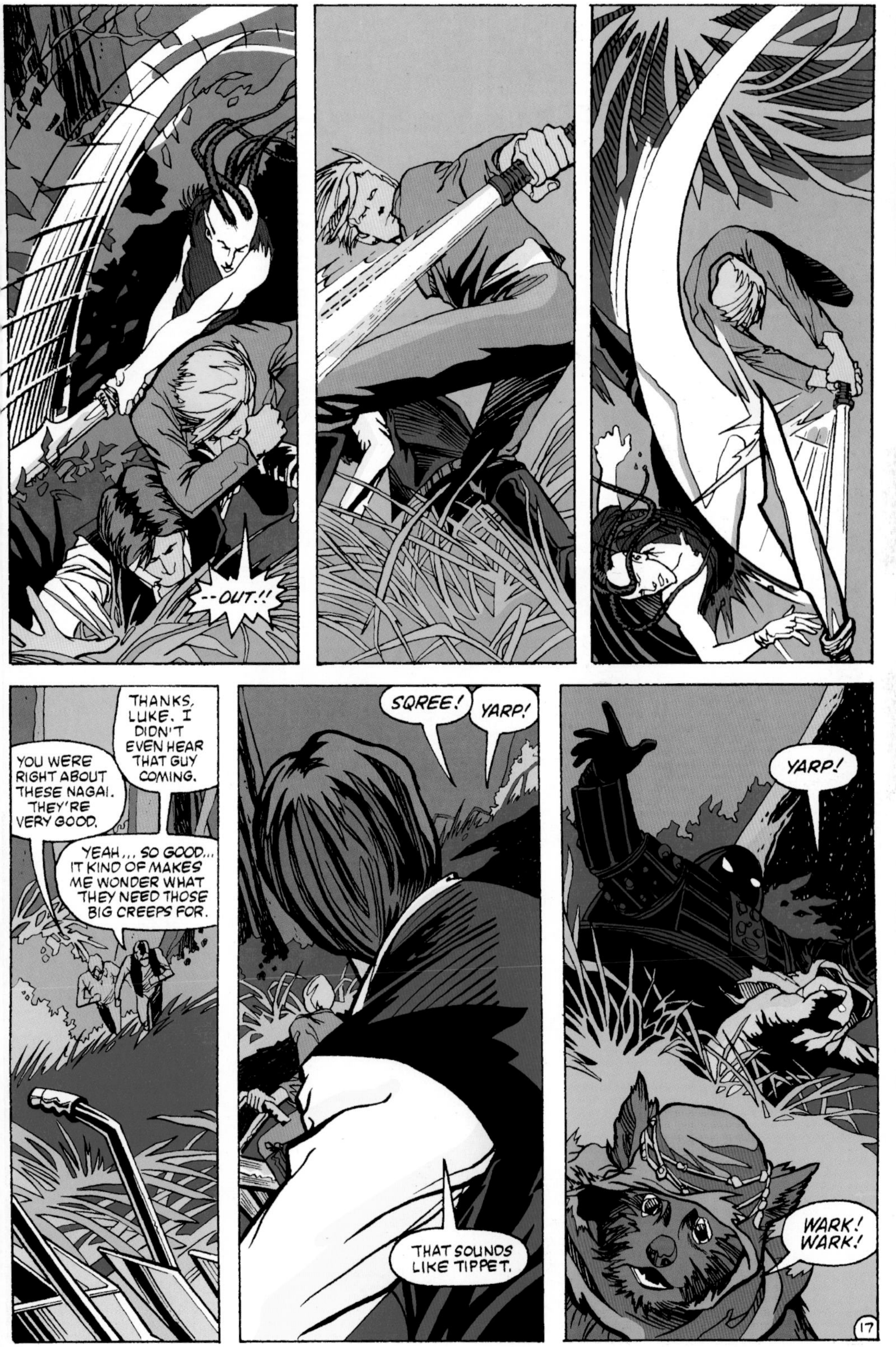
--OUT!!
YOU WERE RIGHT ABOUT THESE NAGAI. THEY'RE VERY GOOD.
THANKS, LUKE. I DIDN'T EVEN HEAR THAT GUY COMING.
YEAH... SO GOOD... IT KIND OF MAKES ME WONDER WHAT THEY NEED THOSE BIG CREEPS FOR.
SQREE!
YARP!
THAT SOUNDS LIKE TIPPET.
YARP!
WARK! WARK!
17

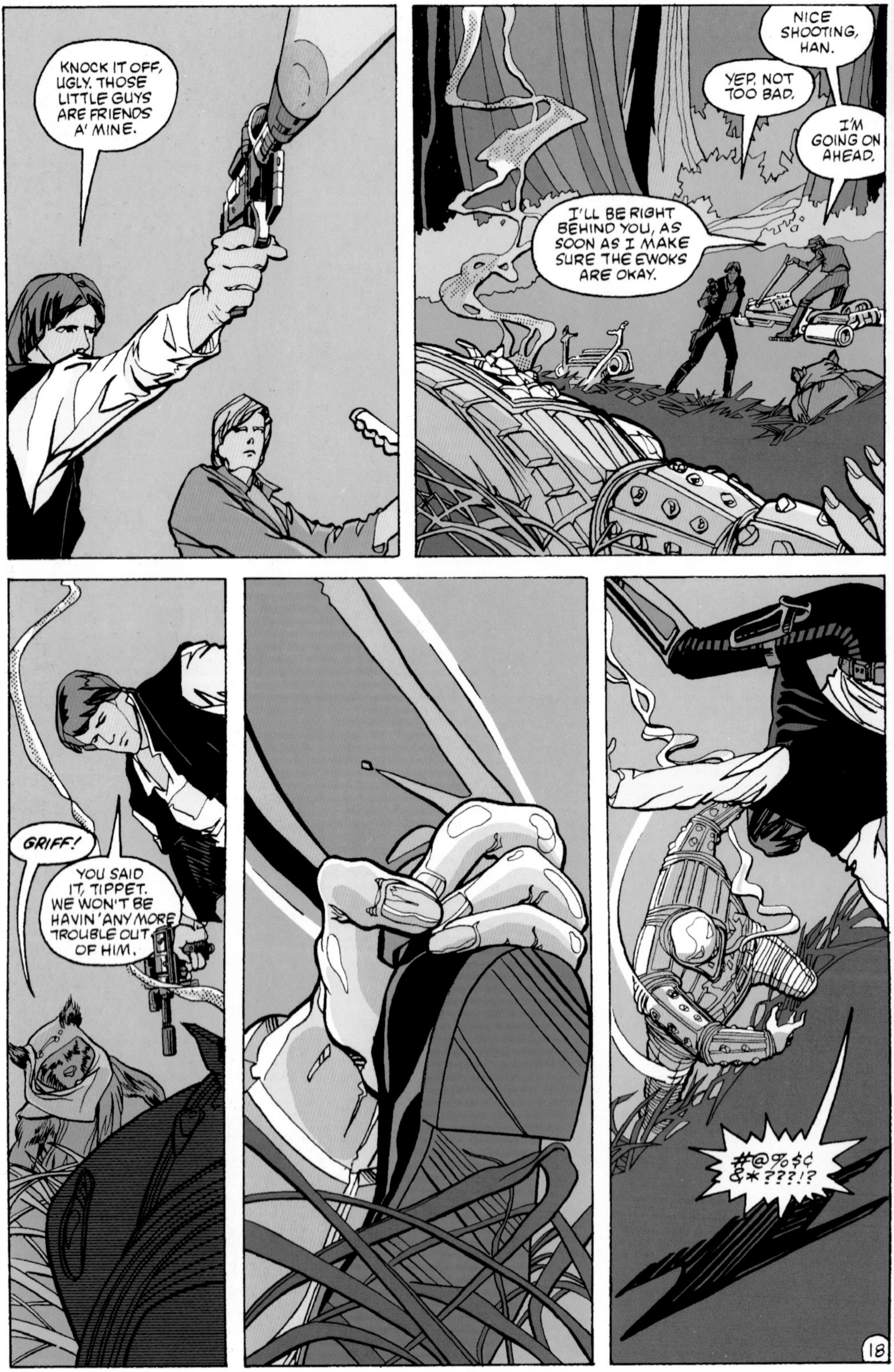
KNOCK IT OFF, UGLY. THOSE LITTLE GUYS ARE FRIENDS A' MINE.
NICE SHOOTING, HAN.
YEP. NOT TOO BAD.
I'M GOING ON AHEAD.
I'LL BE RIGHT BEHIND YOU, AS SOON AS I MAKE SURE THE EWOKS ARE OKAY.
GRIFF!
YOU SAID IT, TIPPET. WE WON'T BE HAVIN' ANY MORE TROUBLE OUT OF HIM.
#@%$¢ &*???!?
18

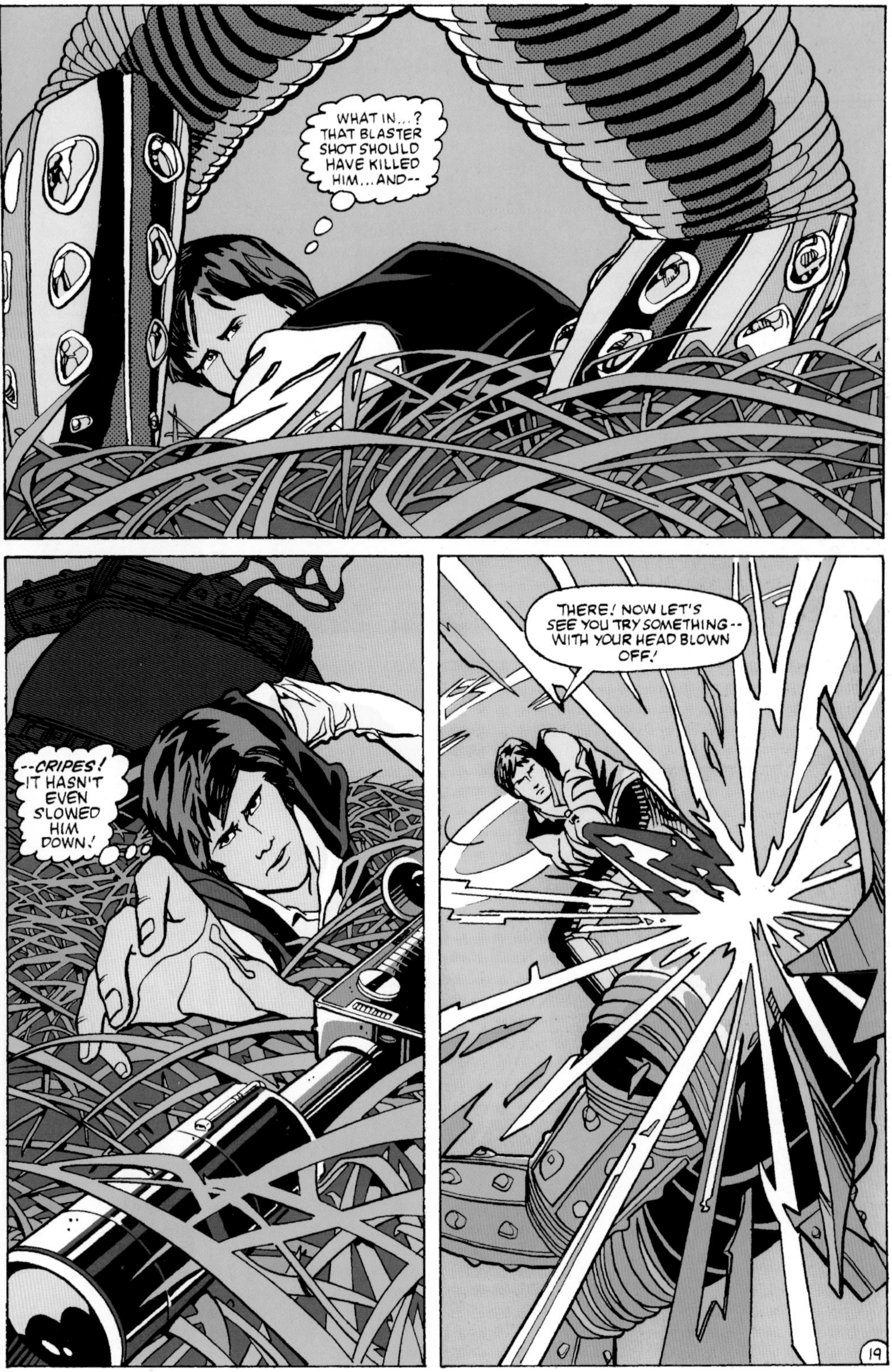
WHAT IN...? THAT BLASTER SHOT SHOULD HAVE KILLED HIM... AND--
--CRIPES! IT HASN'T EVEN SLOWED HIM DOWN!
THERE! NOW LET'S SEE YOU TRY SOMETHING -- WITH YOUR HEAD BLOWN OFF!
19

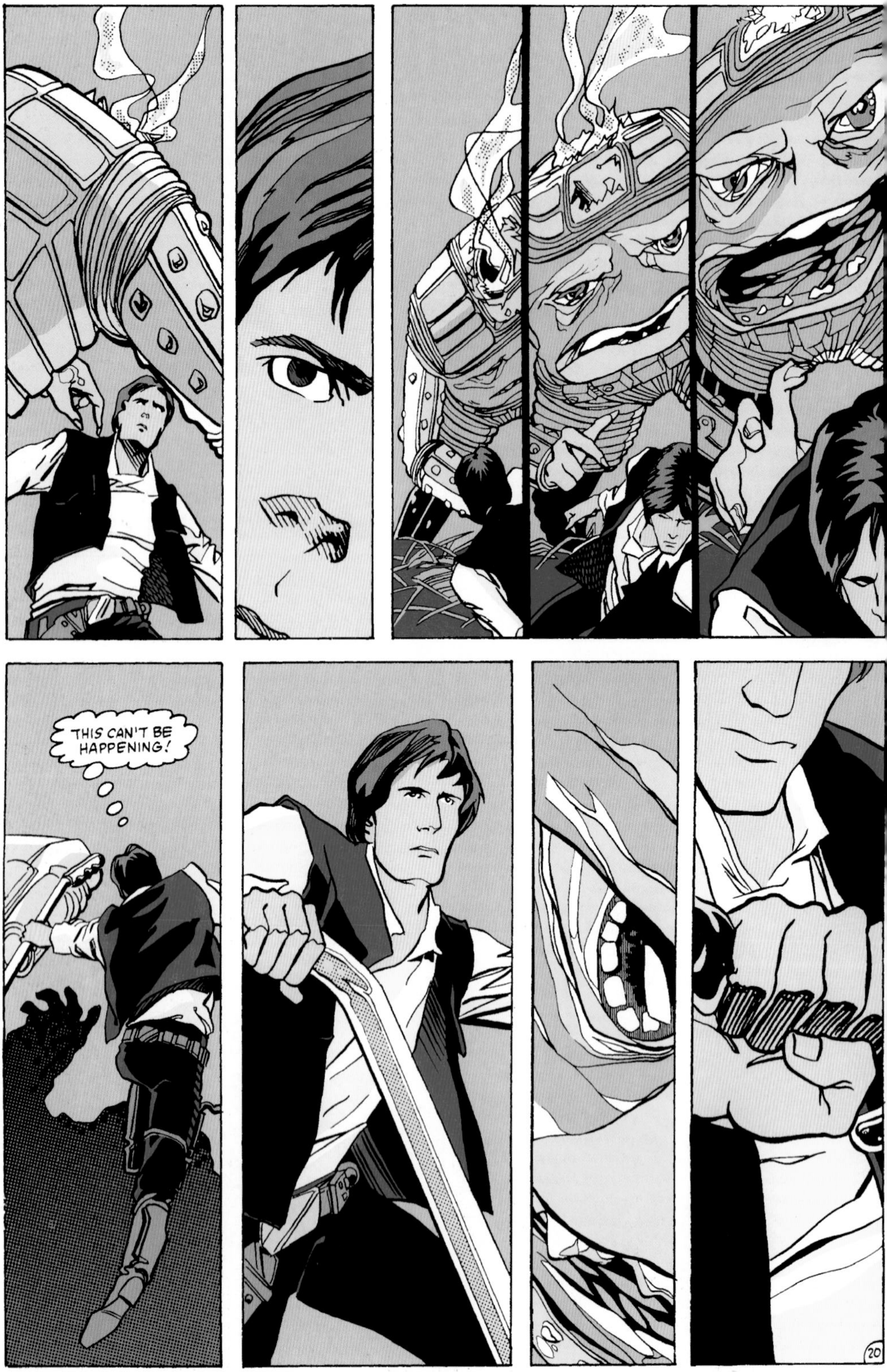
THIS CAN'T BE HAPPENING!
20

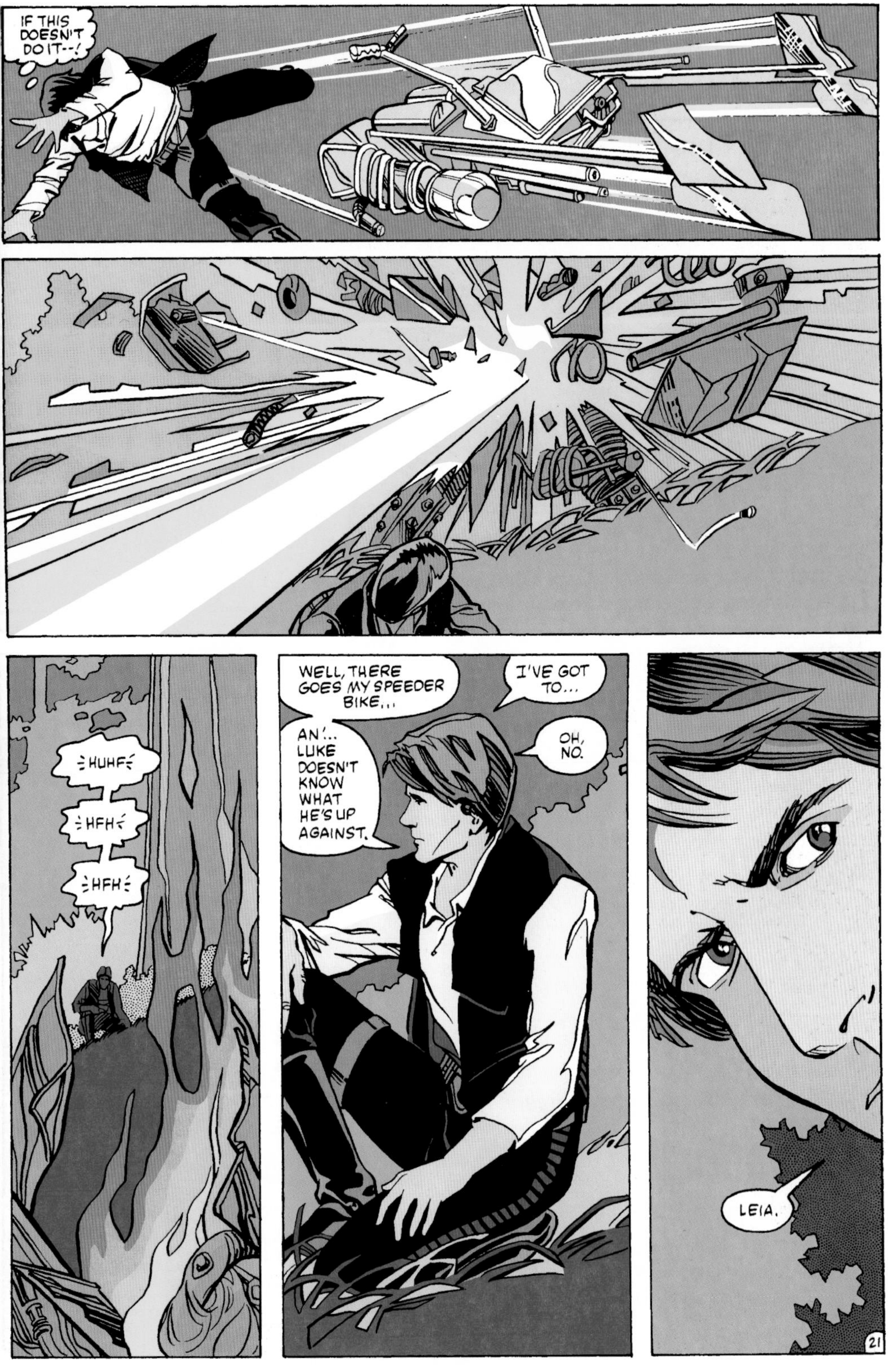
IF THIS DOESN'T DO IT--!
HUHF
HFH
HFH
WELL, THERE GOES MY SPEEDER BIKE...
I'VE GOT TO...
AN'... LUKE DOESN'T KNOW WHAT HE'S UP AGAINST.
OH, NO.
LEIA.
21

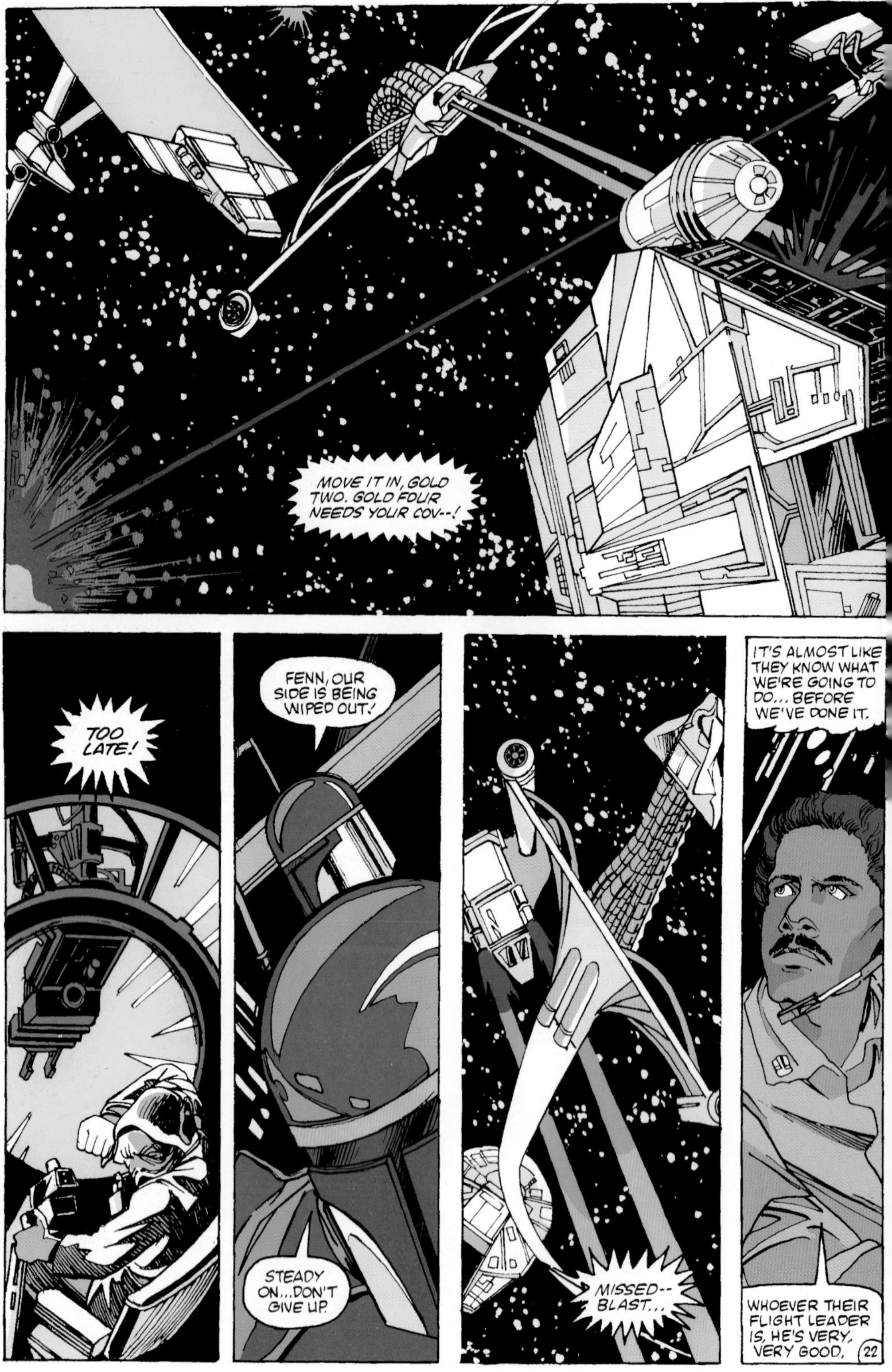
MOVE IT IN, GOLD TWO. GOLD FOUR NEEDS YOUR COV--!
TOO LATE!
FENN, OUR SIDE IS BEING WIPED OUT!
STEADY ON... DON'T GIVE UP.
MISSED-- BLAST...
IT'S ALMOST LIKE THEY KNOW WHAT WE'RE GOING TO DO... BEFORE WE'VE DONE IT.
WHOEVER THEIR FLIGHT LEADER IS, HE'S VERY, VERY GOOD.
22

...HE'S VERY VERY GOOD.

AH, REVENGE IS SWEET! I WONDER HOW MANY OF THOSE FOOLS WILL DIE BEFORE THEY REALIZE THE TRUTH--THAT THEY WERE BETRAYED BEFORE WE EVER ARRIVED HERE.

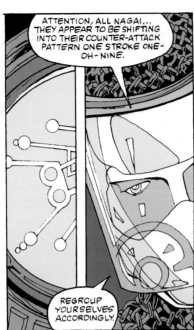

ATTENTION, ALL NAGAI... THEY APPEAR TO BE SHIFTING INTO THEIR COUNTER-ATTACK PATTERN ONE STROKE ONE-OH-NINE.

REGROUP YOURSELVES ACCORDINGLY.

YES, LADY LUMIYA...

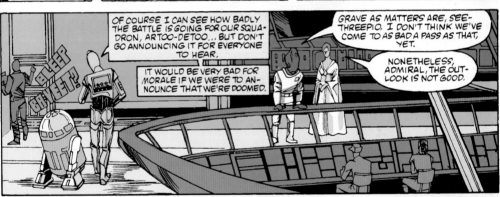

OF COURSE I CAN SEE HOW BADLY THE BATTLE IS GOING FOR OUR SQUADRON, ARTOO-DETOO... BUT DON'T GO ANNOUNCING IT FOR EVERYONE TO HEAR.

IT WOULD BE VERY BAD FOR MORALE IF WE WERE TO ANNOUNCE THAT WE'RE DOOMED.

BLEEP BRVEEP?

GRAVE AS MATTERS ARE, SEE-THREEPIO, I DON'T THINK WE'VE COME TO AS BAD A PASS AS THAT, YET.

NONETHELESS, ADMIRAL, THE OUTLOOK IS NOT GOOD.

OUR EVACUATION...?

WOULD BE SUICIDE, WITH AN ENEMY AS FORMIDABLE AND WELL PREPARED AS THAT SQUADRON, WAITING ABOVE US.

23

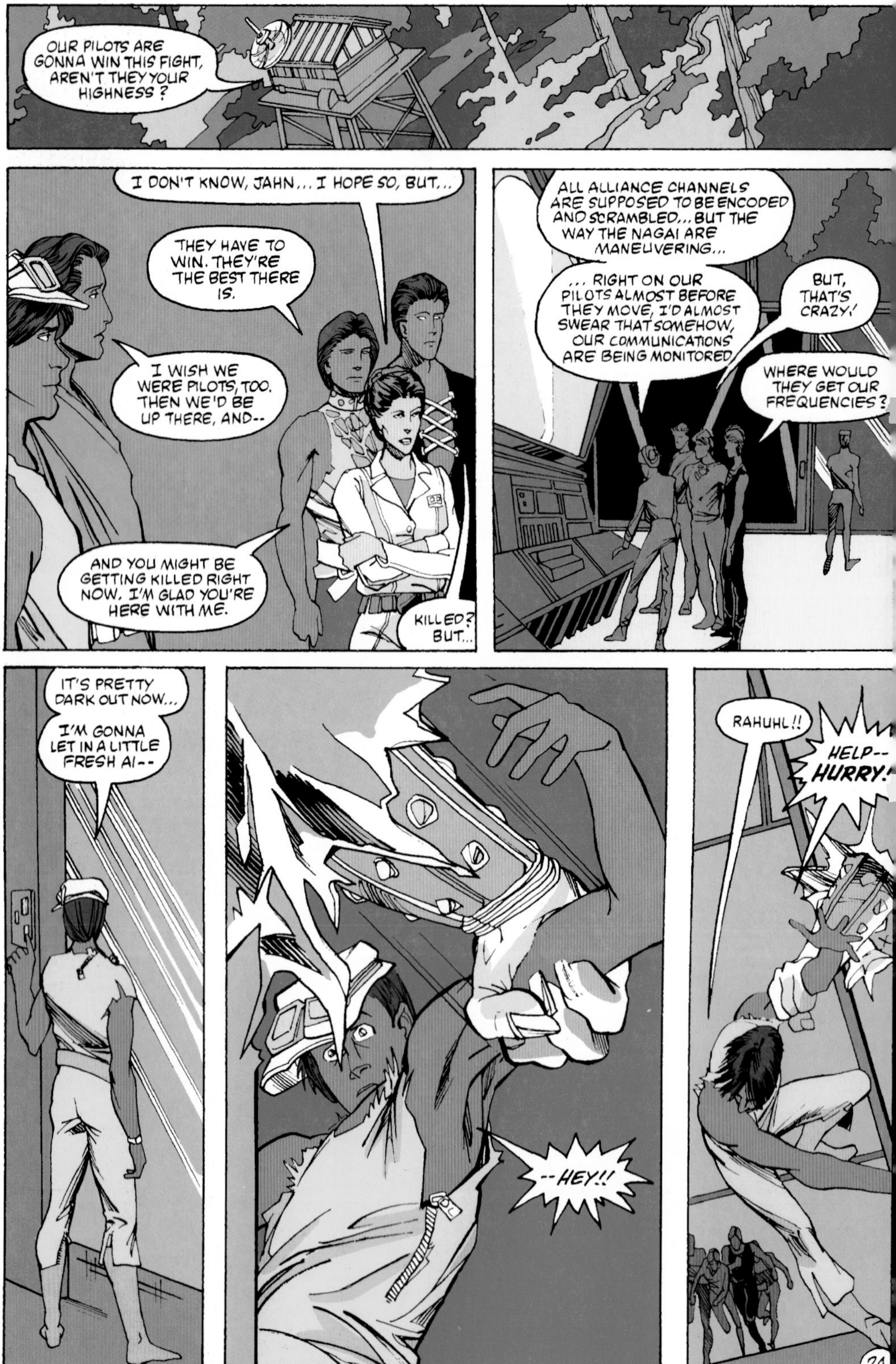
OUR PILOTS ARE GONNA WIN THIS FIGHT, AREN'T THEY YOUR HIGHNESS?
I DON'T KNOW, JAHN... I HOPE SO, BUT...
THEY HAVE TO WIN. THEY'RE THE BEST THERE IS.
I WISH WE WERE PILOTS, TOO. THEN WE'D BE UP THERE, AND--
AND YOU MIGHT BE GETTING KILLED RIGHT NOW. I'M GLAD YOU'RE HERE WITH ME.
KILLED? BUT...
ALL ALLIANCE CHANNELS ARE SUPPOSED TO BE ENCODED AND SCRAMBLED... BUT THE WAY THE NAGAI ARE MANEUVERING...
... RIGHT ON OUR PILOTS ALMOST BEFORE THEY MOVE, I'D ALMOST SWEAR THAT SOMEHOW, OUR COMMUNICATIONS ARE BEING MONITORED.
BUT, THAT'S CRAZY!
WHERE WOULD THEY GET OUR FREQUENCIES?
IT'S PRETTY DARK OUT NOW...
I'M GONNA LET IN A LITTLE FRESH AI--
--HEY!!
RAHUHL!!
HELP-- HURRY!
24

H-HURRY... IT HURTS...

C'MON... IT'S NOT GETTIN' YOU UNLESS IT GETS ALL OF US...

BUT WHAT IF IT DOES?

NOTHING'S THAT STRONG... IS IT?

MY ARM ISN'T THAT STRONG...IT FEELS LIKE YOU'RE PULLING IT OFF.

BOP

WHAT WAS THAT THING?

ARE YOU ALL RIGHT, RAHUHL?

NO.

LUCKY HER HIGHNESS FIGURED OUT HOW TO HURT THE MONSTER.

I'M NOT SURE I DID. I THINK IT LET GO BECAUSE OF--

-- SURPRISE.

COMMANDER SKYWALKER!

WHAT'S WRONG?

IT'S THE NAGAI-- THEY'VE HAD AN INFORMANT ON ENDOR FOR SOME TIME...

THERE'S A PARTY OF THEM ON THEIR WAY HERE NOW, TO DESTROY THIS STATION AND EVERYONE IN IT...

YOU'D BETTER ALERT ALL PERSONNEL, AND THEN GET READY TO EVACUATE.

ARE YOU CERTAIN?

KNIFE IS FREE, SIR. HAN AND I HEARD HIM GIVE THE COMMANDS TO ATTACK.

HAN'S PROBABLY WARNING LEIA AND THE ZELTRONS RIGHT NOW.

25

≶PUFF≶

≶HUFF≶

≶HUFF≶

NOT EVEN HALFWAY THERE...

AND WITHOUT A SPEEDER BIKE, I'LL NEVER...

LEIA....

STOP!

WHAT?!

WHO IN--?!

BEY!

WHEN I SAW YOU UP THERE, FOR A SECOND I IMAGINED--! BROTHER, AM I GLAD TO SEE YOU!

THIS WHOLE NIGHT HAS BEEN LIKE ONE LONG BAD DREAM!

HAN...

WE—WE'VE GOT TO WARN... LUKE AN' LEIA...

THERE'RE NAGAI HERE... A WHOLE MESS OF 'EM...

AN' SOME OTHER WEIRD GUYS, TOO...

IF WE RUN, WE CAN STILL...

NO, HAN.

LOOK,... I DON'T HAVE TIME TO ARGUE WITH YOU. IF YOU REALLY DON'T WANNA HELP ME, THEN FINE, BUT I--!

I SAID NO.

HEY, WHAT ARE YOU--?

I CAN'T LET YOU STOP THE NAGAI.

I'M THE ONE WHO BROUGHT THEM HERE.

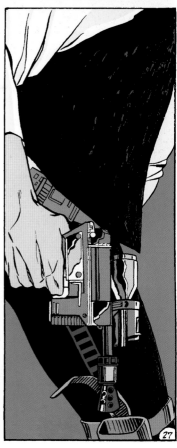

27

385

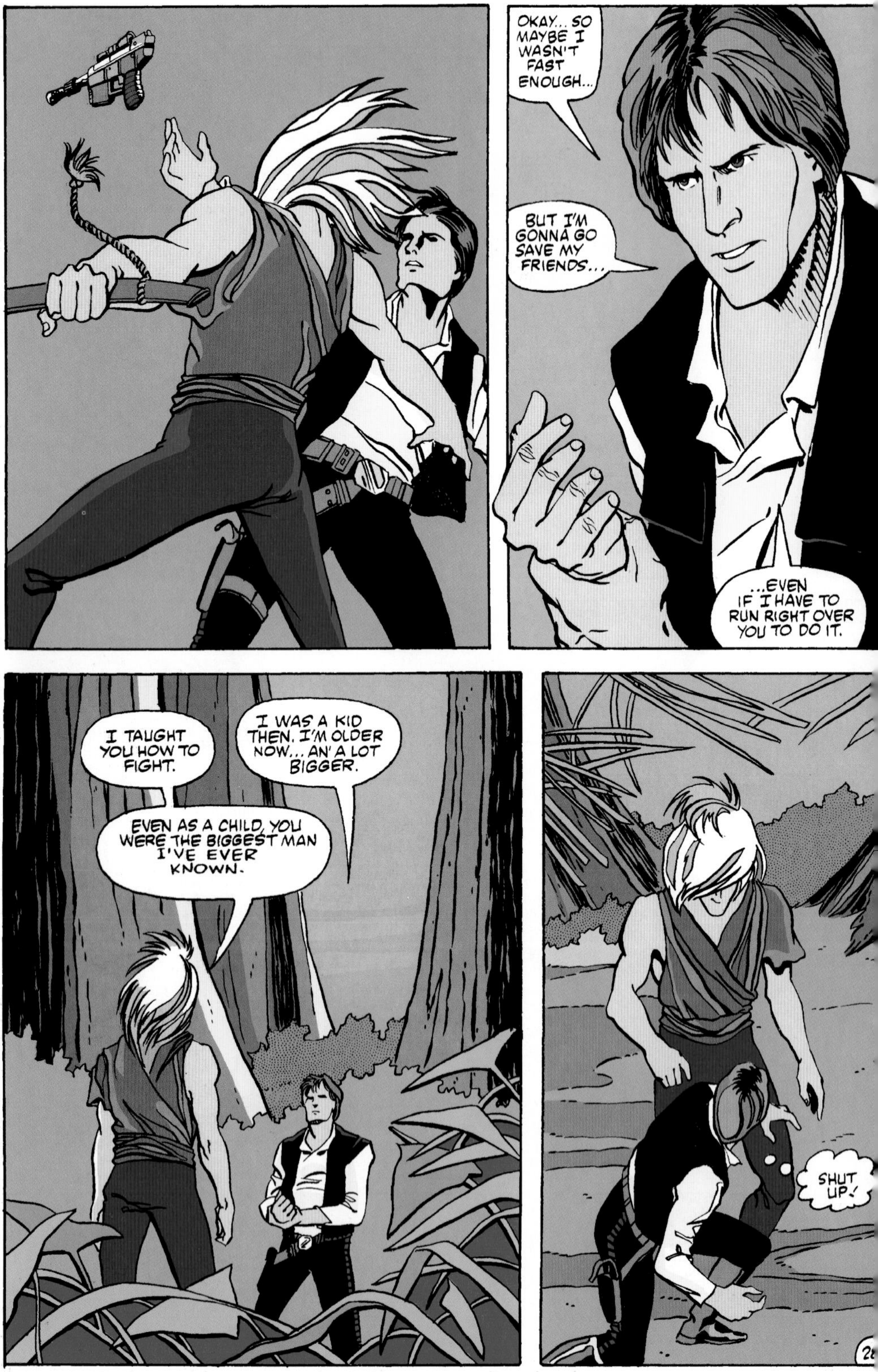
OKAY... SO MAYBE I WASN'T FAST ENOUGH...
BUT I'M GONNA GO SAVE MY FRIENDS...
...EVEN IF I HAVE TO RUN RIGHT OVER YOU TO DO IT.
I TAUGHT YOU HOW TO FIGHT.
I WAS A KID THEN. I'M OLDER NOW... AN' A LOT BIGGER.
EVEN AS A CHILD, YOU WERE THE BIGGEST MAN I'VE EVER KNOWN.
SHUT UP!

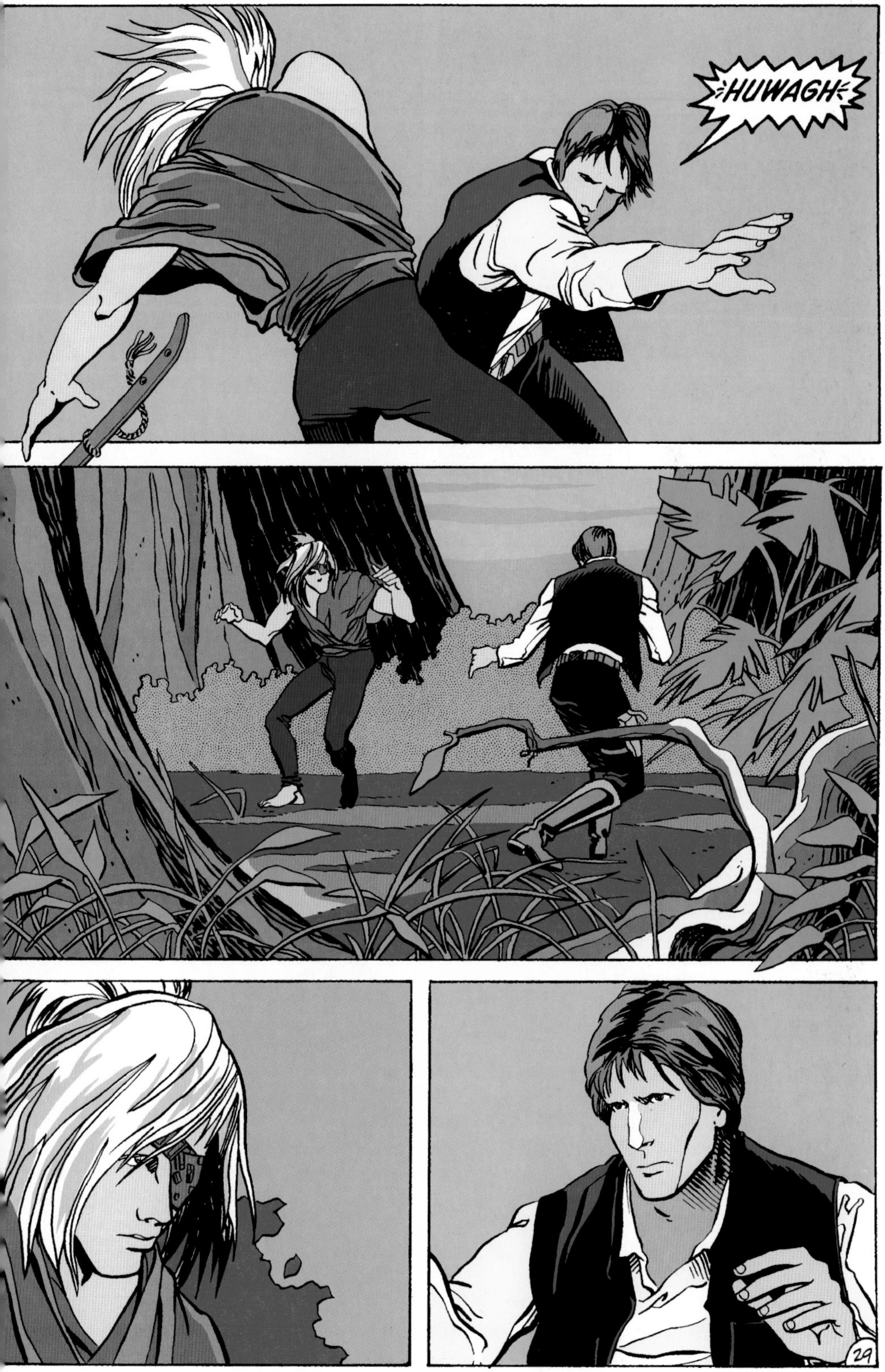
HUWAGH
29

STAY DOWN, HAN. I DON'T WANT TO HURT YOU, SO DON'T MAKE ME.

WHY?! BEY, WHY ARE YOU DOING THIS? WHY ARE YOU SIDING WITH THE NAGAI AGAINST US, AGAINST YOUR OWN PEOPLE?

MY PEOPLE, HAN? THE NAGAI ARE MY PEOPLE... MORE THAN THE ALLIANCE... MORE THAN ANYONE BUT YOU... CERTAINLY MORE THAN THE CORRELLIANS.

WHAT ARE YOU TALKING ABOUT?

ALL THOSE TRIPS I TOOK, RAMBLING AROUND FROM PLANET TO PLANET, LEARNING WHAT I COULD, MAKING FRIENDS WHERE I COULD...

THE DAY FINALLY CAME WHEN GOOD LUCK AND BAD INSTRUMENTS FORCED ME TO WHERE NONE OF US HAD EVER BEEN -- BEYOND THE GALACTIC PERIMETER.

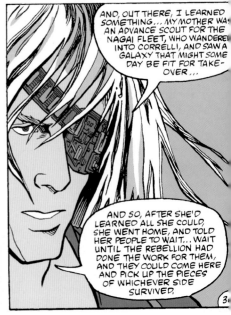

AND, OUT THERE, I LEARNED SOMETHING... MY MOTHER WAS AN ADVANCE SCOUT FOR THE NAGAI FLEET, WHO WANDERED INTO CORRELLI, AND SAW A GALAXY THAT MIGHT SOME DAY BE FIT FOR TAKE-OVER...

AND SO, AFTER SHE'D LEARNED ALL SHE COULD, SHE WENT HOME, AND TOLD HER PEOPLE TO WAIT... WAIT UNTIL THE REBELLION HAD DONE THE WORK FOR THEM, AND THEY COULD COME HERE AND PICK UP THE PIECES OF WHICHEVER SIDE SURVIVED.

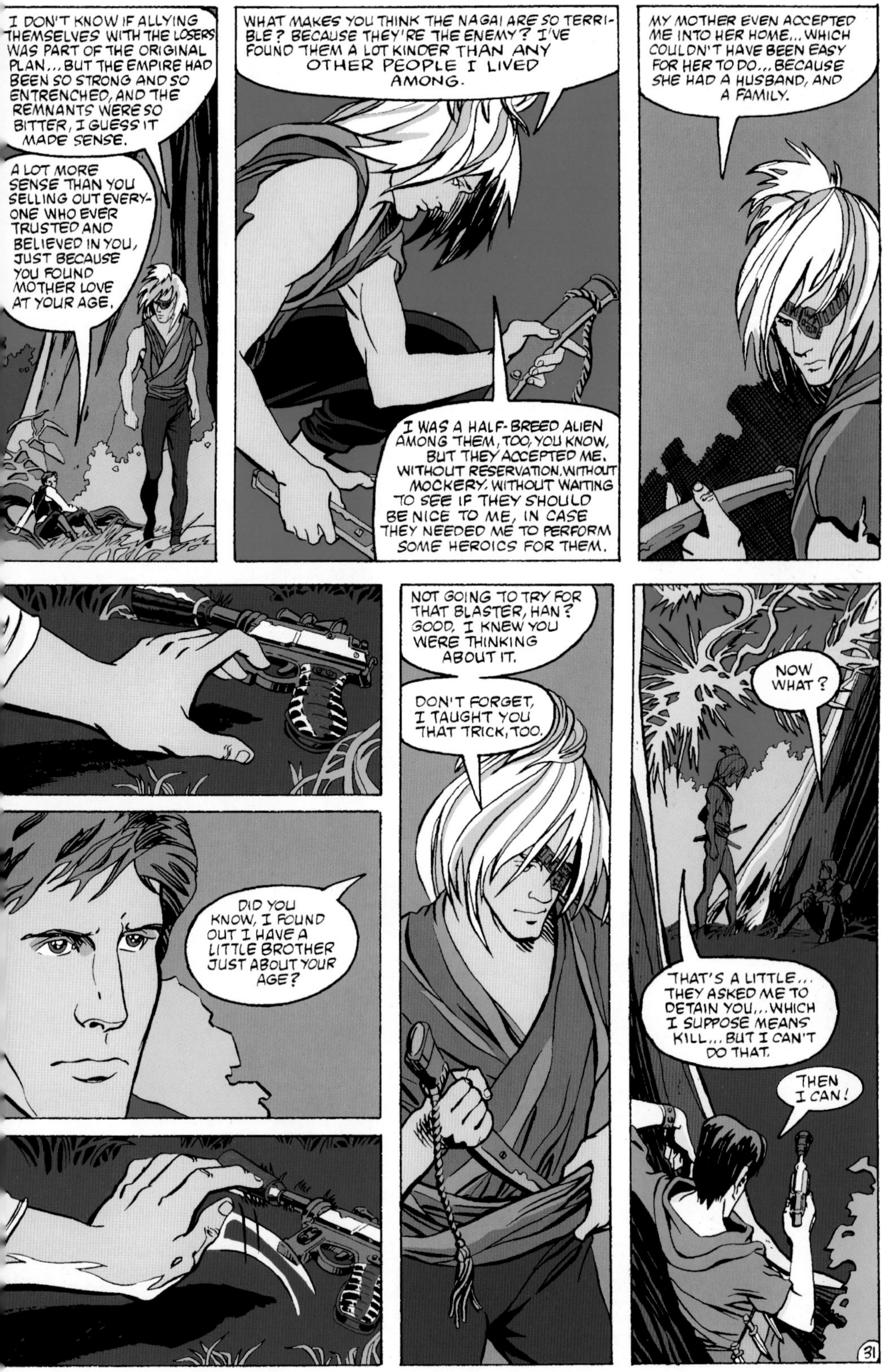
I DON'T KNOW IF ALLYING THEMSELVES WITH THE LOSERS WAS PART OF THE ORIGINAL PLAN... BUT THE EMPIRE HAD BEEN SO STRONG AND SO ENTRENCHED, AND THE REMNANTS WERE SO BITTER, I GUESS IT MADE SENSE.
A LOT MORE SENSE THAN YOU SELLING OUT EVERY-ONE WHO EVER TRUSTED AND BELIEVED IN YOU, JUST BECAUSE YOU FOUND MOTHER LOVE AT YOUR AGE.
WHAT MAKES YOU THINK THE NAGAI ARE SO TERRI-BLE? BECAUSE THEY'RE THE ENEMY? I'VE FOUND THEM A LOT KINDER THAN ANY OTHER PEOPLE I LIVED AMONG.
I WAS A HALF-BREED ALIEN AMONG THEM, TOO, YOU KNOW, BUT THEY ACCEPTED ME. WITHOUT RESERVATION. WITHOUT MOCKERY. WITHOUT WAITING TO SEE IF THEY SHOULD BE NICE TO ME, IN CASE THEY NEEDED ME TO PERFORM SOME HEROICS FOR THEM.
MY MOTHER EVEN ACCEPTED ME INTO HER HOME... WHICH COULDN'T HAVE BEEN EASY FOR HER TO DO... BECAUSE SHE HAD A HUSBAND, AND A FAMILY.
DID YOU KNOW, I FOUND OUT I HAVE A LITTLE BROTHER JUST ABOUT YOUR AGE?
NOT GOING TO TRY FOR THAT BLASTER, HAN? GOOD, I KNEW YOU WERE THINKING ABOUT IT.
DON'T FORGET, I TAUGHT YOU THAT TRICK, TOO.
NOW WHAT?
THAT'S A LITTLE... THEY ASKED ME TO DETAIN YOU... WHICH I SUPPOSE MEANS KILL... BUT I CAN'T DO THAT.
THEN I CAN!
31

MERCY TO THE ENEMY ISN'T OUR WAY, BEY. I THOUGHT YOU UNDERSTOOD THAT.

NO!

KNIFE, I CAN'T LET YOU...

KNIFE...

TRAITOR...

≠AUGNH≠

KNIFE!!

32

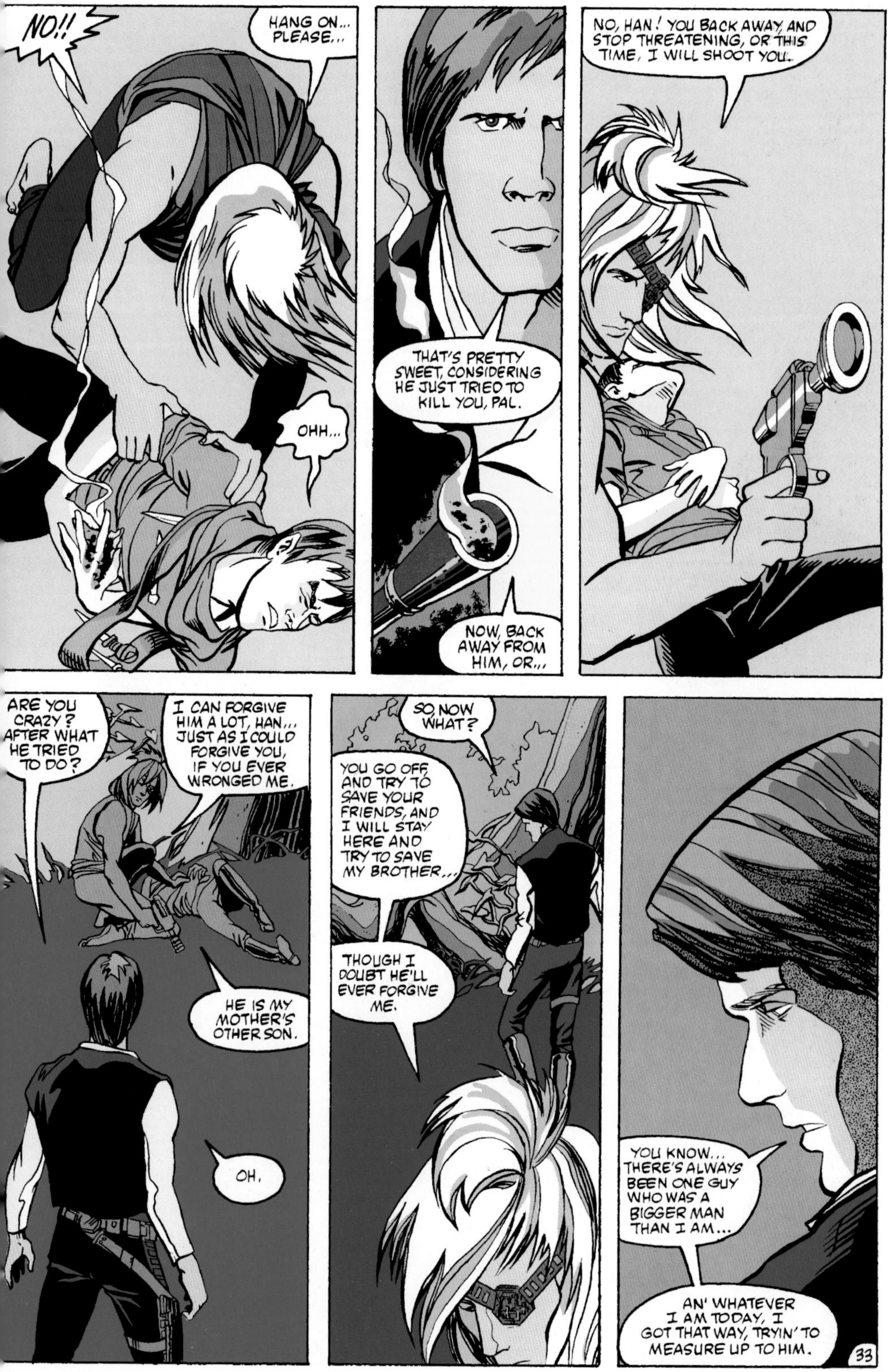
NO!!
HANG ON... PLEASE...
OHH...
THAT'S PRETTY SWEET, CONSIDERING HE JUST TRIED TO KILL YOU, PAL.
NOW, BACK AWAY FROM HIM, OR...
NO, HAN! YOU BACK AWAY, AND STOP THREATENING, OR THIS TIME, I WILL SHOOT YOU.
ARE YOU CRAZY? AFTER WHAT HE TRIED TO DO?
I CAN FORGIVE HIM A LOT, HAN... JUST AS I COULD FORGIVE YOU, IF YOU EVER WRONGED ME.
HE IS MY MOTHER'S OTHER SON.
OH.
SO, NOW WHAT?
YOU GO OFF, AND TRY TO SAVE YOUR FRIENDS, AND I WILL STAY HERE AND TRY TO SAVE MY BROTHER...
THOUGH I DOUBT HE'LL EVER FORGIVE ME.
YOU KNOW... THERE'S ALWAYS BEEN ONE GUY WHO WAS A BIGGER MAN THAN I AM...
AN' WHATEVER I AM TODAY, I GOT THAT WAY, TRYIN' TO MEASURE UP TO HIM.
33

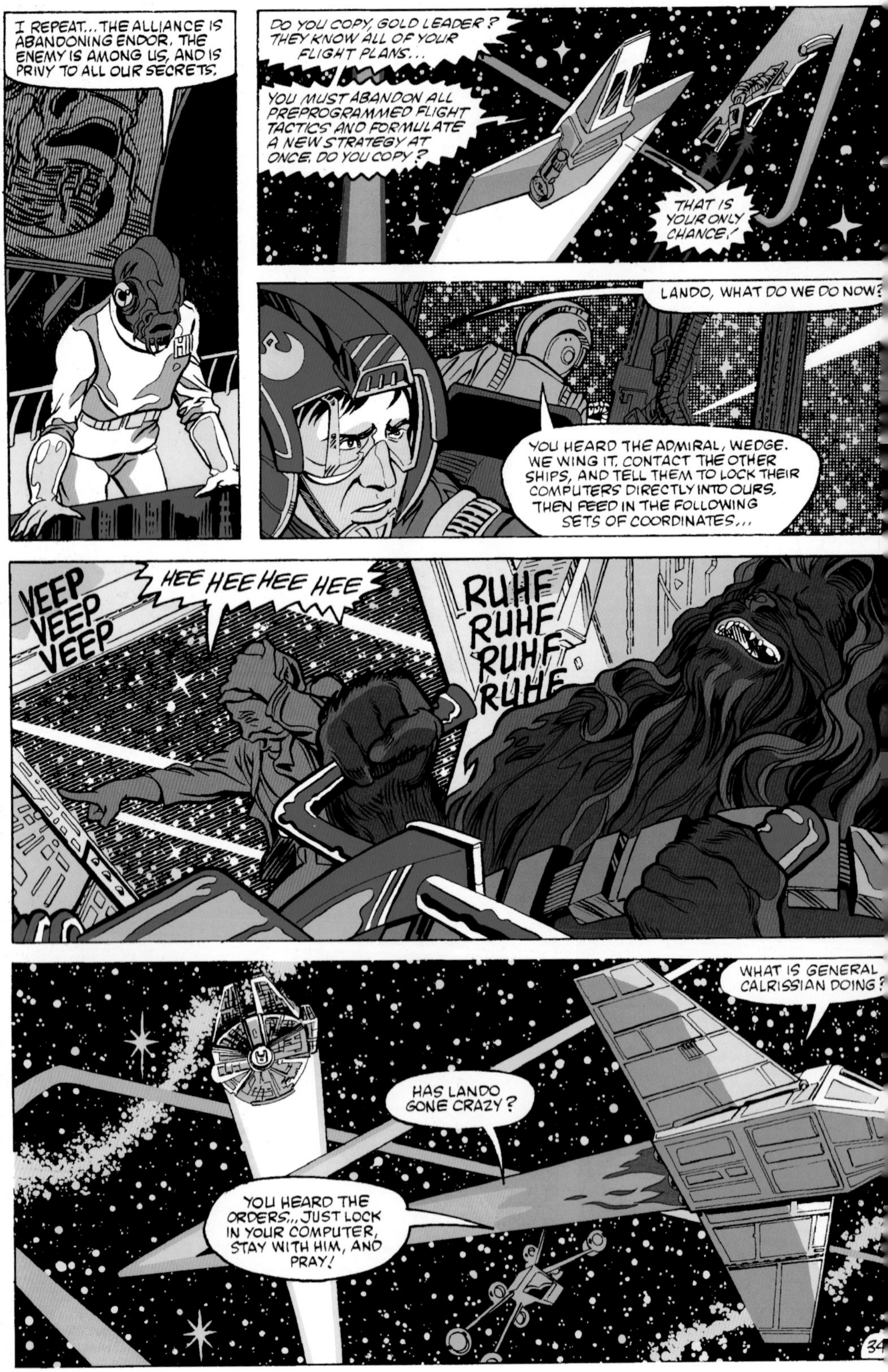
I REPEAT... THE ALLIANCE IS ABANDONING ENDOR. THE ENEMY IS AMONG US, AND IS PRIVY TO ALL OUR SECRETS.
DO YOU COPY, GOLD LEADER? THEY KNOW ALL OF YOUR FLIGHT PLANS...
YOU MUST ABANDON ALL PREPROGRAMMED FLIGHT TACTICS AND FORMULATE A NEW STRATEGY AT ONCE. DO YOU COPY?
THAT IS YOUR ONLY CHANCE!
LANDO, WHAT DO WE DO NOW?
YOU HEARD THE ADMIRAL, WEDGE. WE WING IT. CONTACT THE OTHER SHIPS, AND TELL THEM TO LOCK THEIR COMPUTERS DIRECTLY INTO OURS, THEN FEED IN THE FOLLOWING SETS OF COORDINATES...
VEEP VEEP VEEP
HEE HEE HEE HEE
RUHF RUHF RUHF RUHF
WHAT IS GENERAL CALRISSIAN DOING?
HAS LANDO GONE CRAZY?
YOU HEARD THE ORDERS... JUST LOCK IN YOUR COMPUTER, STAY WITH HIM, AND PRAY!
34

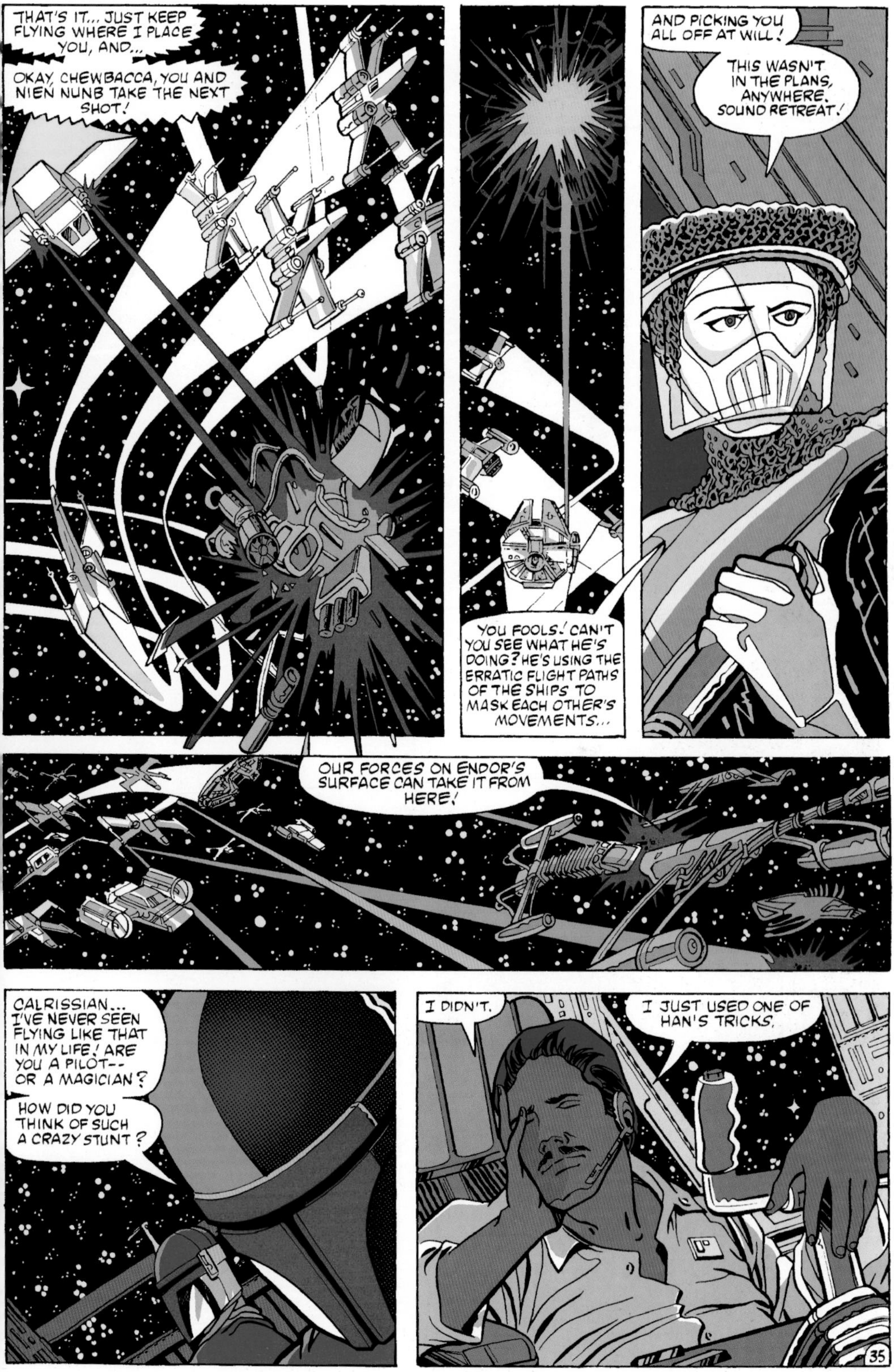
THAT'S IT... JUST KEEP FLYING WHERE I PLACE YOU, AND...
OKAY, CHEWBACCA, YOU AND NIEN NUNB TAKE THE NEXT SHOT!
YOU FOOLS! CAN'T YOU SEE WHAT HE'S DOING? HE'S USING THE ERRATIC FLIGHT PATHS OF THE SHIPS TO MASK EACH OTHER'S MOVEMENTS...
AND PICKING YOU ALL OFF AT WILL!
THIS WASN'T IN THE PLANS, ANYWHERE. SOUND RETREAT!
OUR FORCES ON ENDOR'S SURFACE CAN TAKE IT FROM HERE!
CALRISSIAN... I'VE NEVER SEEN FLYING LIKE THAT IN MY LIFE! ARE YOU A PILOT-- OR A MAGICIAN?
HOW DID YOU THINK OF SUCH A CRAZY STUNT?
I DIDN'T.
I JUST USED ONE OF HAN'S TRICKS.
35

THE OTHER PARTS ARE JUST FOR SHOW!

SO, THAT'S IT! THEIR BODIES ARE VULNERABLE, BECAUSE THAT'S WHERE THEY HOUSE THEIR BRAINS AND CENTRAL NERVOUS SYSTEMS!

J...JUST IN TIME, LUKE. THANK YOU.

COULDN'T LET ANYTHING HAPPEN TO MY SISTER, COULD I?

HOW DID YOU GUESS...ABOUT HOW TO KILL THOSE MONSTERS?

I DIDN'T... BUT I COULD FEEL THE FORCE WARNING ME, SO I LET IT GUIDE ME.

WOW,..I WISH I COULD BE A JEDI KNIGHT, TOO.

UH-OH...

ARE THEY LINING UP TO FIGHT?

OR RUN?

38

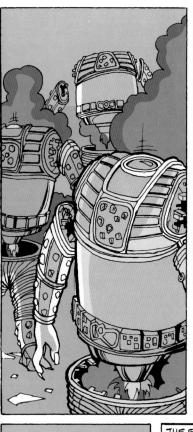

LOOKIT WHAT THEY'RE DOING! THEIR ARMS AND LEGS ARE--!

I DON'T THINK THOSE WERE "THEIR" ARMS AND LEGS, MARRUC...

THEY MUST HAVE GOTTEN THEM ON LOAN FROM THE NAGAI.

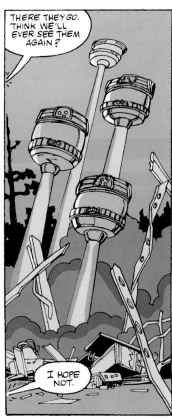

THERE THEY GO. THINK WE'LL EVER SEE THEM AGAIN?

I HOPE NOT.

≷PUFF≷

≷HFH≷

≷HFPH≷

≷HFPH≷

LEIA...

THE ELEVATOR... WAS OUT...HADDA...

HAN!

WHEN I SAW THE BUILDING WRECKED, I THOUGHT...

I THOUGHT THEY'D...

THOUGHT YOU WERE...

OH, HAN...

39

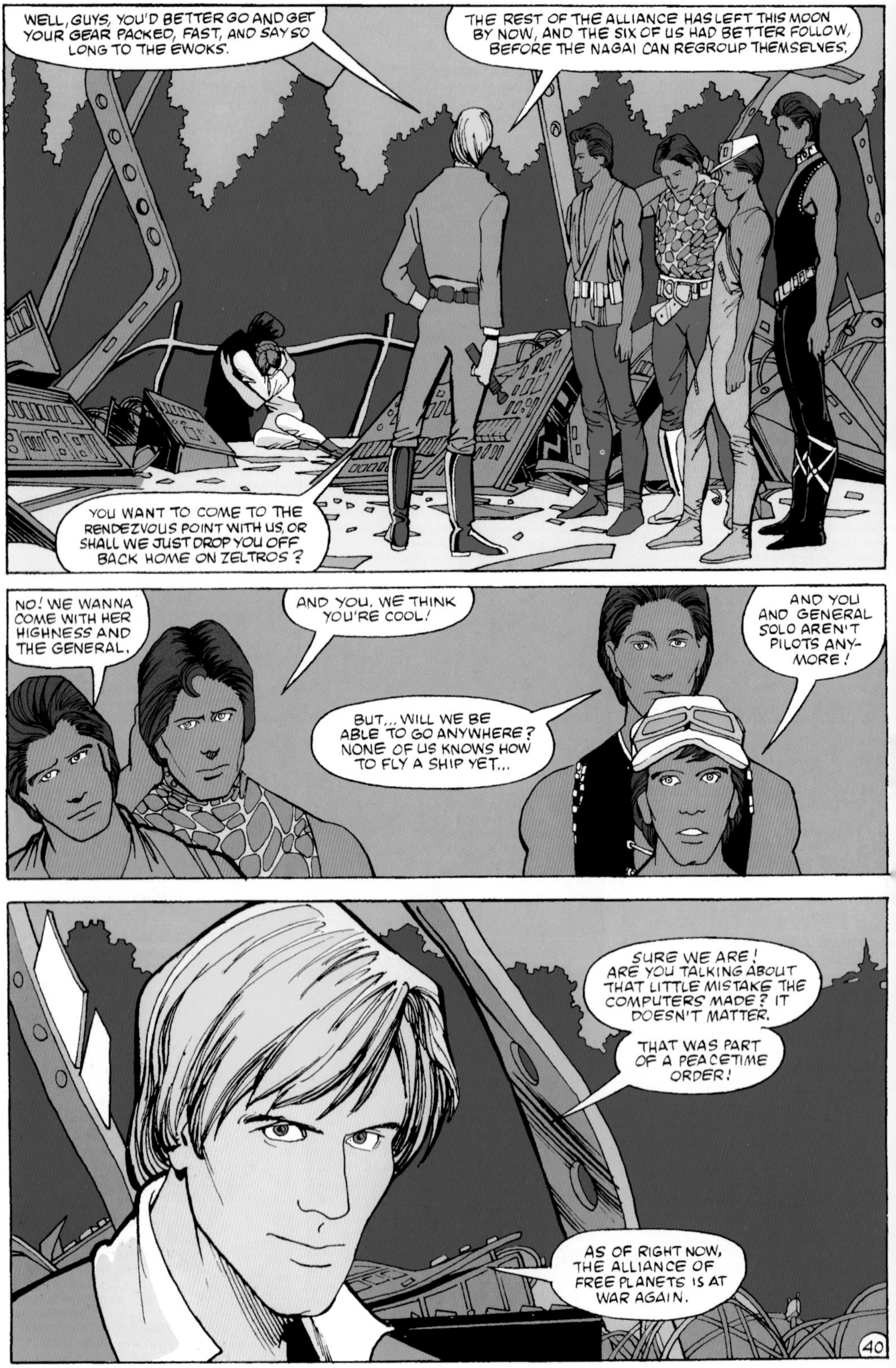
WELL, GUYS, YOU'D BETTER GO AND GET YOUR GEAR PACKED, FAST, AND SAY SO LONG TO THE EWOKS.
THE REST OF THE ALLIANCE HAS LEFT THIS MOON BY NOW, AND THE SIX OF US HAD BETTER FOLLOW, BEFORE THE NAGAI CAN REGROUP THEMSELVES.
YOU WANT TO COME TO THE RENDEZVOUS POINT WITH US, OR SHALL WE JUST DROP YOU OFF BACK HOME ON ZELTROS?
NO! WE WANNA COME WITH HER HIGHNESS AND THE GENERAL,
AND YOU. WE THINK YOU'RE COOL!
BUT... WILL WE BE ABLE TO GO ANYWHERE? NONE OF US KNOWS HOW TO FLY A SHIP YET...
AND YOU AND GENERAL SOLO AREN'T PILOTS ANYMORE!
SURE WE ARE! ARE YOU TALKING ABOUT THAT LITTLE MISTAKE THE COMPUTERS MADE? IT DOESN'T MATTER.
THAT WAS PART OF A PEACETIME ORDER!
AS OF RIGHT NOW, THE ALLIANCE OF FREE PLANETS IS AT WAR AGAIN.
40

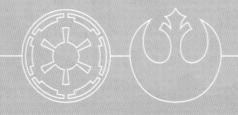

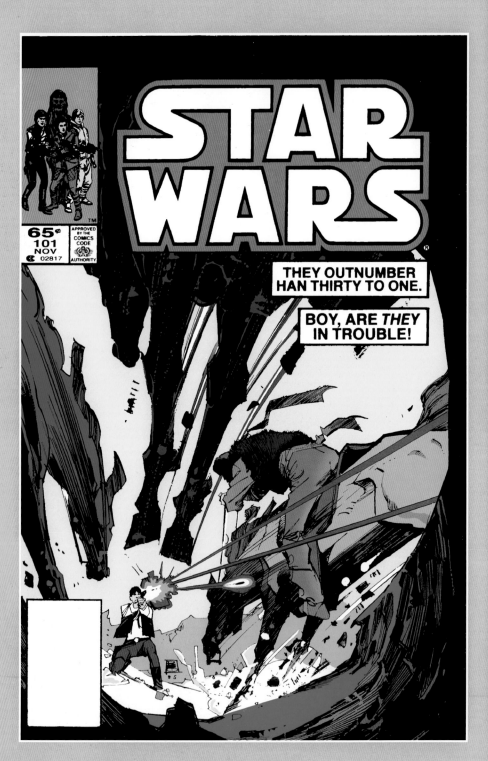

STAR WARS

65¢
101
NOV

APPROVED
BY THE
COMICS
CODE
AUTHORITY

02817

THEY OUTNUMBER
HAN THIRTY TO ONE.

BOY, ARE *THEY*
IN TROUBLE!

THEN WHY AREN'T YOU WILLING TO DO ONE SIMPLE LITTLE JOB FOR THE ALLIANCE?

BECAUSE I DIDN'T SIGN ON TO WORK FOR ANY "ALLIANCE," LEIA! I SIGNED ON TO WORK FOR THE *REBELLION!*

AND SINCE THE REBELLION *SUCCEEDED,* THEY'VE BEEN TREATING US LIKE *FLUNKIES!*

THE EVENTS IN THIS ISSUE'S STORY TAKE PLACE *BEFORE* STAR WARS #99.

NO ONE ORDERS ME TO TAKE VERMIN ABOARD THE *MILLENNIUM FALCON!*

NOT ABOARD MY SHIP!

HAN... THE HOOJIBS AREN'T VERMIN. THEY ARE CIVILIZED TELEPATHIC EATERS, AND THEY AREN'T GOING TO HURT YOUR PRECIOUS...

THAT'S NOT THE POINT!

HUNH--?

DON'T--!

YOU...

UHNGH!

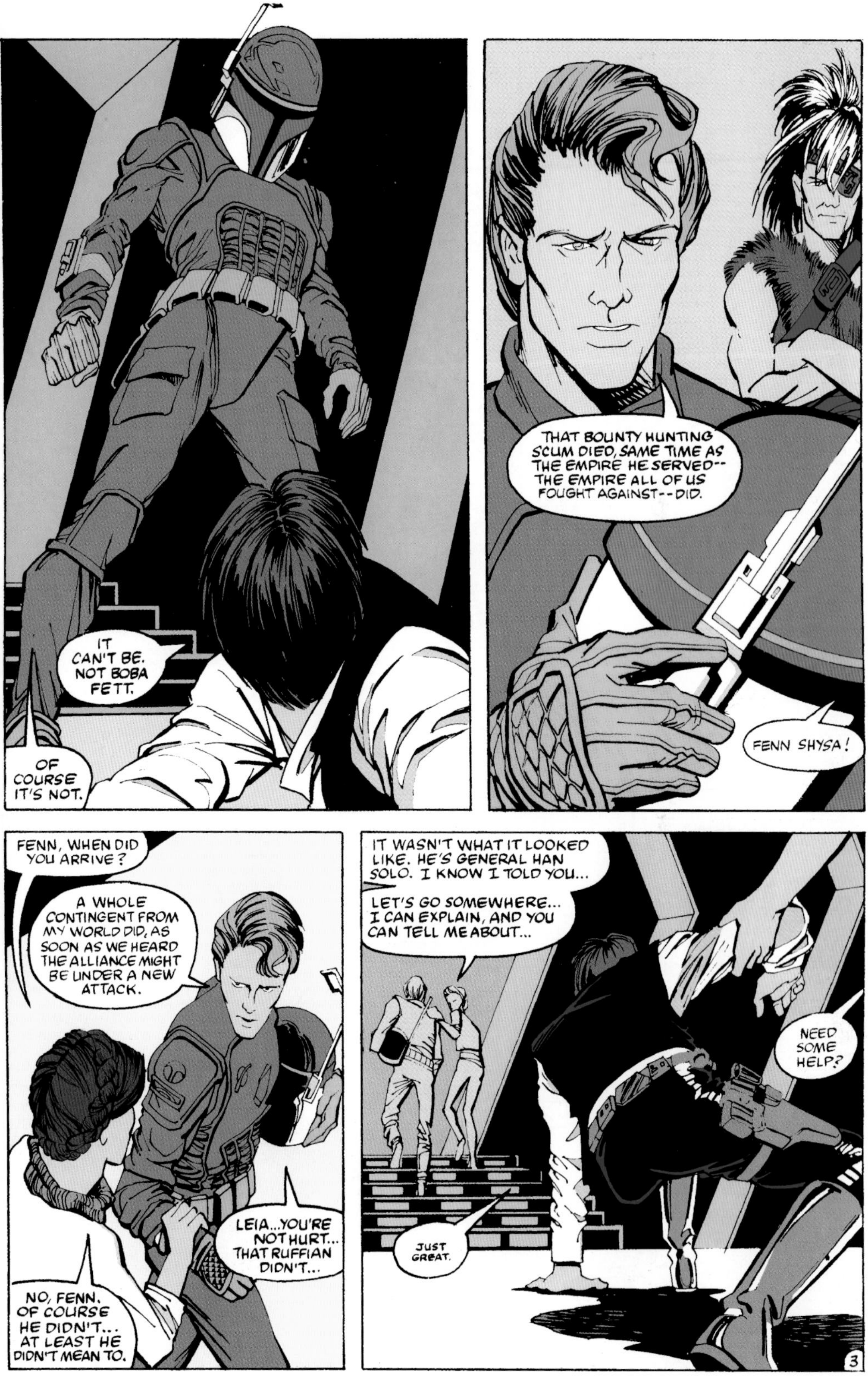
IT CAN'T BE. NOT BOBA FETT.
OF COURSE IT'S NOT.
THAT BOUNTY HUNTING SCUM DIED, SAME TIME AS THE EMPIRE HE SERVED-- THE EMPIRE ALL OF US FOUGHT AGAINST--DID.
FENN SHYSA!
FENN, WHEN DID YOU ARRIVE?
A WHOLE CONTINGENT FROM MY WORLD DID, AS SOON AS WE HEARD THE ALLIANCE MIGHT BE UNDER A NEW ATTACK.
LEIA...YOU'RE NOT HURT... THAT RUFFIAN DIDN'T...
NO, FENN. OF COURSE HE DIDN'T... AT LEAST HE DIDN'T MEAN TO.
IT WASN'T WHAT IT LOOKED LIKE. HE'S GENERAL HAN SOLO. I KNOW I TOLD YOU...
LET'S GO SOMEWHERE... I CAN EXPLAIN, AND YOU CAN TELL ME ABOUT...
NEED SOME HELP?
JUST GREAT.
3

BEY??!? WHEN DID YOU COME IN? WHERE DID YOU COME FROM?

I'VE BEEN HERE AND THERE. I WAS ON FENN'S HOMEWORLD, WHEN THE CALL FROM YOUR ADMIRAL ACKBAR CAME IN.

IT SOUNDED LIKE IT MIGHT BE AMUSING, SO I CAME WITH HIM.

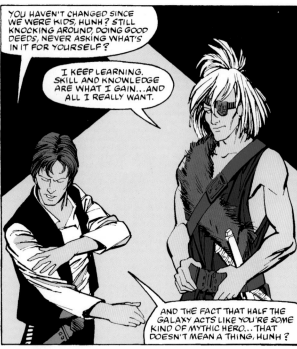

YOU HAVEN'T CHANGED SINCE WE WERE KIDS, HUNH? STILL KNOCKING AROUND, DOING GOOD DEEDS, NEVER ASKING WHAT'S IN IT FOR YOURSELF?

I KEEP LEARNING. SKILL AND KNOWLEDGE ARE WHAT I GAIN...AND ALL I REALLY WANT.

AND THE FACT THAT HALF THE GALAXY ACTS LIKE YOU'RE SOME KIND OF MYTHIC HERO...THAT DOESN'T MEAN A THING, HUNH?

AND YOU...ARE YOU STILL IN IT FOR THE MONEY... OR HAVE YOU FINALLY FOUND ANYTHING ELSE THAT MEANS MORE TO YOU?

I DON'T KNOW WHAT YOU'RE TALKING ABOUT. THE MONEY'S GOOD.

THAT GIRL... THE PRINCESS? SHE'S RESPECTED THROUGHOUT THE ALLIANCE...SHE MEANS SOMETHING TO YOU?

IS IT MUTUAL?

NONE OF YOUR BUSINESS.

YOU'RE STILL YOUR USUAL SELF, HAN. HAVEN'T YOU LEARNED YET?

IF YOU CARE FOR SOMEONE, TREAT HER WELL. TELL HER THAT YOU CARE.

I DON'T HAVE TO TELL LEIA! SHE KNOWS HOW I FEEL!

MMM?

THAT'S ENOUGH!

4

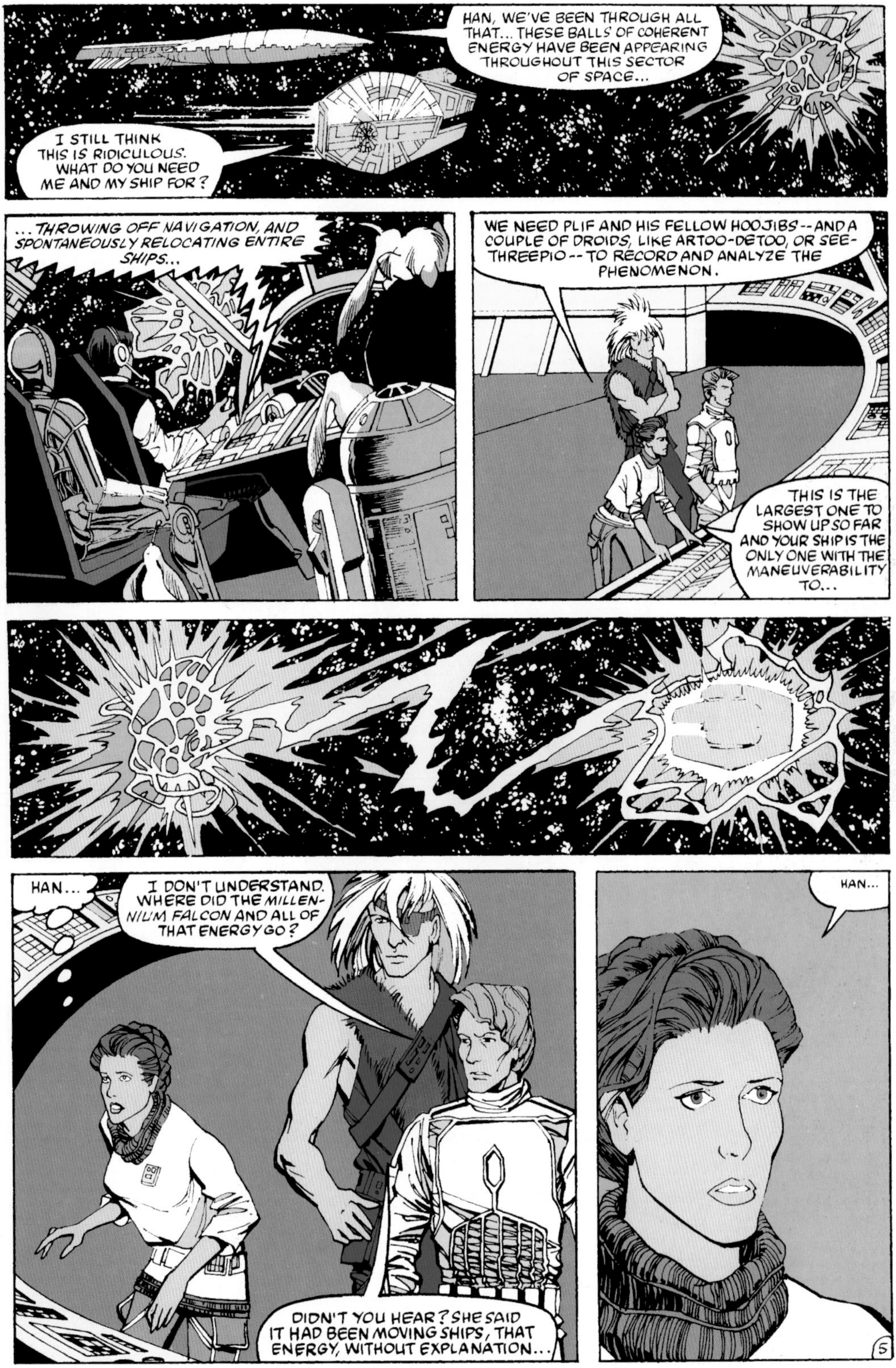
HAN, WE'VE BEEN THROUGH ALL THAT... THESE BALLS OF COHERENT ENERGY HAVE BEEN APPEARING THROUGHOUT THIS SECTOR OF SPACE...
I STILL THINK THIS IS RIDICULOUS. WHAT DO YOU NEED ME AND MY SHIP FOR?
...THROWING OFF NAVIGATION, AND SPONTANEOUSLY RELOCATING ENTIRE SHIPS...
WE NEED PLIF AND HIS FELLOW HOOJIBS--AND A COUPLE OF DROIDS, LIKE ARTOO-DETOO, OR SEE-THREEPIO--TO RECORD AND ANALYZE THE PHENOMENON.
THIS IS THE LARGEST ONE TO SHOW UP SO FAR AND YOUR SHIP IS THE ONLY ONE WITH THE MANEUVERABILITY TO...
HAN...
I DON'T UNDERSTAND. WHERE DID THE MILLENNIUM FALCON AND ALL OF THAT ENERGY GO?
DIDN'T YOU HEAR? SHE SAID IT HAD BEEN MOVING SHIPS, THAT ENERGY, WITHOUT EXPLANATION...
HAN...
5

WHAT'S HAPPENING?

I DON'T KNOW... JUST HANG ON, AND LET ME NAVIGATE THROUGH IT.

BLEEP!

I AGREE WITH ARTOO, GENERAL SOLO! I WANT TO KNOW WHERE WE ARE!

BEATS ME, THREEPIO!

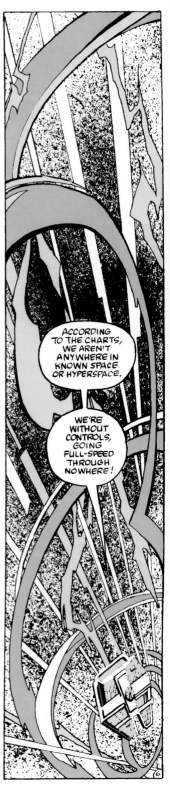

ACCORDING TO THE CHARTS, WE AREN'T ANYWHERE IN KNOWN SPACE OR HYPERSPACE.

WE'RE WITHOUT CONTROLS, GOING FULL-SPEED THROUGH NOWHERE!

AFTER THEM! DON'T LET THEM GET AWAY.

HURRY, RISA, THEY'RE GAINING ON US!

OH, GIL--!

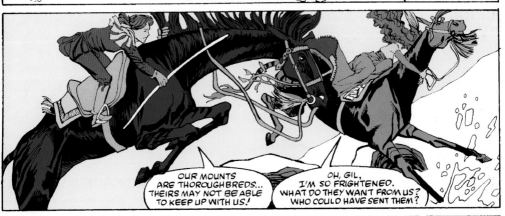

OUR MOUNTS ARE THOROUGHBREDS... THEIRS MAY NOT BE ABLE TO KEEP UP WITH US!

OH, GIL, I'M SO FRIGHTENED. WHAT DO THEY WANT FROM US? WHO COULD HAVE SENT THEM?

STOP FIRING, YOU IDIOTS! OUR ORDERS WERE TO CAPTURE THE PRINCE AND PRINCESS ALIVE IF WE COULD.

I'D LIKE TO KNOW WHERE THOSE BRIGANDS GOT SUCH FANTASTIC WEAPONS...

I...I'M ALMOST OUT OF ARROWS, YOU KNOW.

OH, NO...

AND... IT LOOKS TO ME LIKE THE CANYON CLOSES OFF UP AHEAD.

LOOK OUT, STUPID!

IF THEY WERE RIDING TALLER HORSES...

...THEY'D HAVE US BY NOW!

7

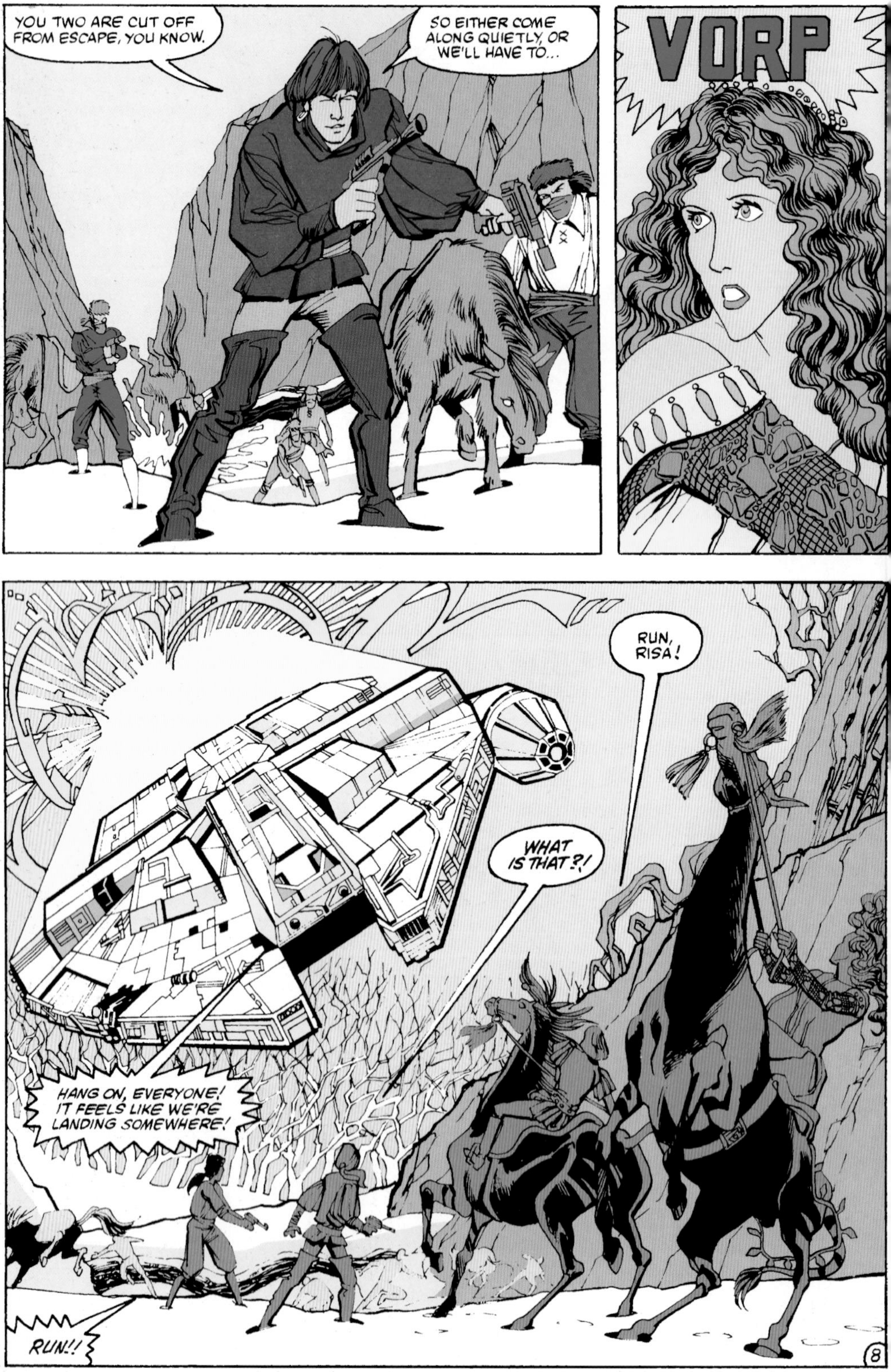
YOU TWO ARE CUT OFF FROM ESCAPE, YOU KNOW.
SO EITHER COME ALONG QUIETLY, OR WE'LL HAVE TO...
VORP
RUN, RISA!
WHAT IS THAT?!
HANG ON, EVERYONE! IT FEELS LIKE WE'RE LANDING SOMEWHERE!
RUN!!
8

NOBODY SHOOTS AT ME IN MY OWN SHIP!

WHOOP--

‡OOF!‡

*#✱!!6 SNOW! I HATE SNOW!

ZEEP!

ZIP!

AND WHAT KIND OF TOY WEAPONS ARE THOSE GUYS PACKING, ANY- WAY?

THEY PACK A REAL CHARGE, BUT THEY'RE TOO PRIMITIVE AND INACCURATE TO BE STANDARD BLASTERS!

ZIPP

ZIPP

KILL THE INTRUDER!

BUT THAT DOESN'T MEAN I'LL TAKE CHANCES ON LETTING ONE OF THEM LAND A SHOT ON ME!

‡AGH‡

10

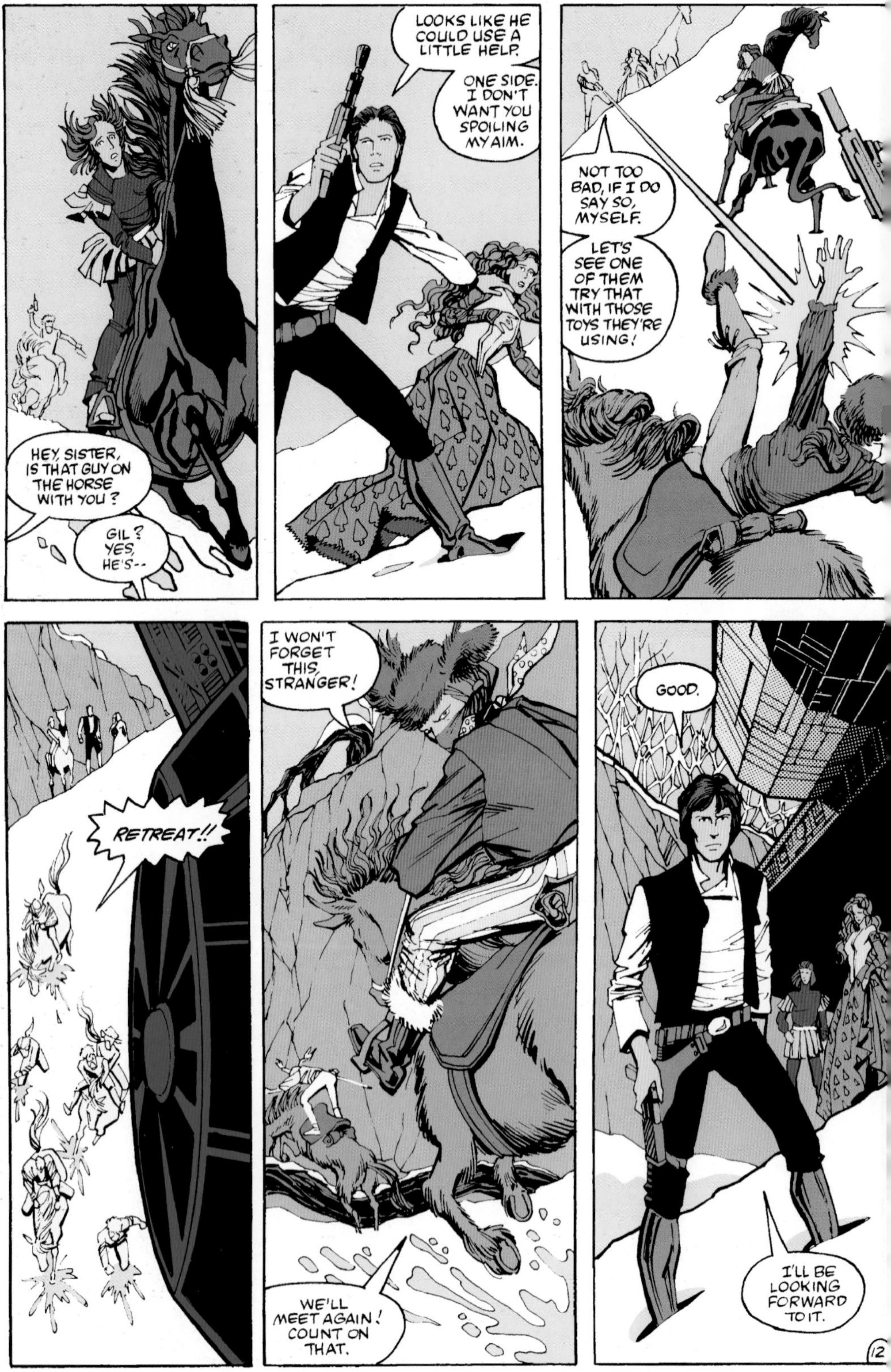
HEY, SISTER, IS THAT GUY ON THE HORSE WITH YOU?
GIL? YES, HE'S--
LOOKS LIKE HE COULD USE A LITTLE HELP.
ONE SIDE. I DON'T WANT YOU SPOILING MY AIM.
NOT TOO BAD, IF I DO SAY SO, MYSELF.
LET'S SEE ONE OF THEM TRY THAT WITH THOSE TOYS THEY'RE USING!
RETREAT!!
I WON'T FORGET THIS, STRANGER!
WE'LL MEET AGAIN! COUNT ON THAT.
GOOD.
I'LL BE LOOKING FORWARD TO IT.
12

COME ON, YOU TWO. WE BETTER GET INSIDE MY SHIP... FROM THE WAY THOSE GUYS' WERE TALKING, THEY'LL BE BACK AS SOON AS THEY FIND ENOUGH FRIENDS.

YOU CAN LEAVE THE LIVESTOCK OUT HERE.

BLEE!

GENERAL SOLO! ARTOO AND I WERE SO WORRIED WHEN WE HEARD ALL THE SHOOTING. AS SOON AS IT STOPPED, OF COURSE WE...

YOU MEAN YOU'RE A... A GENERAL? HOW WONDERFUL!

NOW... LET ME GET THIS STRAIGHT... YOUR FAMILIES, BETWEEN THE TWO OF THEM, RULE THIS ENTIRE WORLD?

THAT'S RIGHT. MY FATHER IS THE KING OF THE SIDE THAT IS CLOSEST TO THE SUN.

MY FAMILY HAS ALWAYS RULED THE SIDE CLOSEST TO THE NIGHT.

THERE WAS WAR BETWEEN THEM, FOR MANY GENE-RATIONS, AND BANDITS LIKE THE ONES WE MET ONCE HAUNTED THE SHADOWED LANDS BETWEEN ALL, ATTACKING LONE TRAVELLERS.

BUT, WHEN GIL AND I WERE CHILDREN, OUR FATHERS FINALLY STRUCK A TRUCE... AND LAID DOWN TENTATIVE PLANS FOR AN ALLIANCE.

THAT'S WHY WE'RE HERE NOW, SIR. YOU SEE, WE'RE IN THE SECTION RISA'S FATHER RULES, AND WHEN SHE AND I MARRY...

I'M SURE THE GENERAL DOESN'T WANT TO HEAR ABOUT THAT, GIL.

SURELY NO ONE NEED DRAW ANY CON-CLUSIONS, JUST BECAUSE YOU, MY OLD CHILDHOOD PLAYMATE CAME VISITING...

BESIDES, NOTHING'S SETTLED YET.

13

413

BUH-WHEET-

NO... I'VE NEVER SEEN ANY ENERGY FORM QUITE LIKE IT, EITHER... COHERENT... BUT ONLY BRIEFLY POWERFUL, AND AT SHORT RANGE.

DO BE CAREFUL WITH IT, OLD CHAP!

YAAA

OH, DEAR! IF WE CAN'T FIND **SOME** WAY OF DRAINING IT FROM THE SHIP'S SYSTEMS, WE'LL NEVER BE ABLE TO RETURN HOME.

AND YOU SAY, MASTER GIL, THAT THESE ENERGY BALLS HAVE ALWAYS BEEN A NATURAL PHENOMENON OF YOUR WORLD...?

WELL... SORT OF THEY COME AND GO AT RANDOM...

BUT LATELY, THEY'VE BEEN... DIFFERENT. KIND OF DANGER-OUS... STRIKING THINGS, MAKING OBJECTS APPEAR AND DISAPPEAR...

IT'S LIKE SOME-THING HAS CHANGED THEM, SOMEHOW.

SO... WE COULD END UP STUCK HERE, HUNH?

SWELL. REALLY TERRIFIC.

BUT... DON'T YOU LIKE IT HERE? WOULDN'T YOU ENJOY STAYING FOR A WHILE?

YEAH, I THINK IT WOULD BE JUST GREAT, SWEETHEART...

...EXCEPT THAT THERE'S... SOMETHING AT HOME I LEFT BEHIND, UNFINISHED... SOMETHING I'D REALLY LIKE TO GET BACK TO.

OH, THAT'S TOO BAD. COULD YOU... COULD YOU TELL ME ABOUT IT?

I'M A VERY GOOD LISTENER.

14

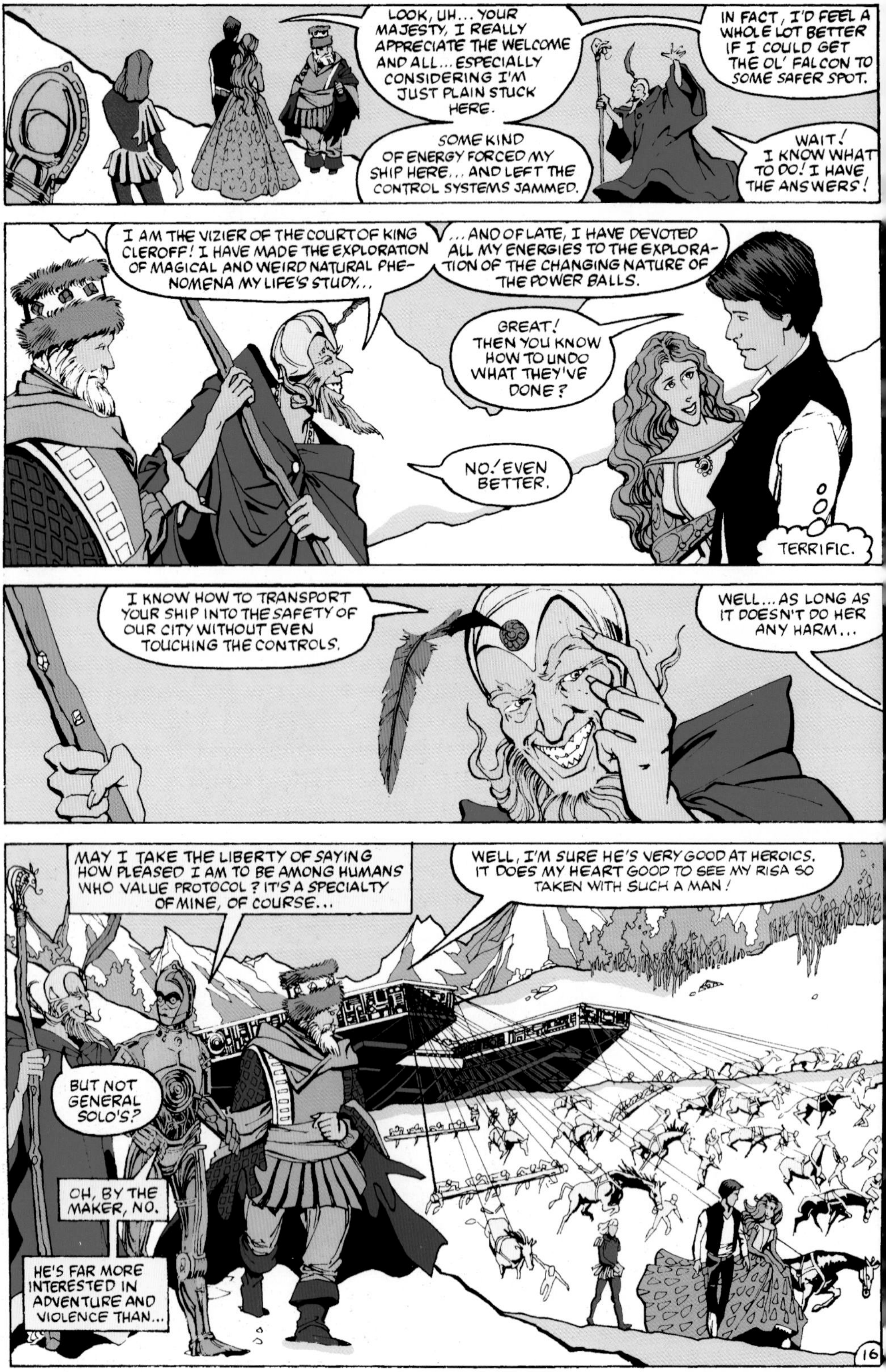
LOOK, UH... YOUR MAJESTY, I REALLY APPRECIATE THE WELCOME AND ALL... ESPECIALLY CONSIDERING I'M JUST PLAIN STUCK HERE.
SOME KIND OF ENERGY FORCED MY SHIP HERE... AND LEFT THE CONTROL SYSTEMS JAMMED.
IN FACT, I'D FEEL A WHOLE LOT BETTER IF I COULD GET THE OL' FALCON TO SOME SAFER SPOT.
WAIT! I KNOW WHAT TO DO! I HAVE THE ANSWERS!
I AM THE VIZIER OF THE COURT OF KING CLEROFF! I HAVE MADE THE EXPLORATION OF MAGICAL AND WEIRD NATURAL PHENOMENA MY LIFE'S STUDY...
...AND OF LATE, I HAVE DEVOTED ALL MY ENERGIES TO THE EXPLORATION OF THE CHANGING NATURE OF THE POWER BALLS.
GREAT! THEN YOU KNOW HOW TO UNDO WHAT THEY'VE DONE?
NO! EVEN BETTER.
TERRIFIC.
I KNOW HOW TO TRANSPORT YOUR SHIP INTO THE SAFETY OF OUR CITY WITHOUT EVEN TOUCHING THE CONTROLS.
WELL... AS LONG AS IT DOESN'T DO HER ANY HARM...
MAY I TAKE THE LIBERTY OF SAYING HOW PLEASED I AM TO BE AMONG HUMANS WHO VALUE PROTOCOL? IT'S A SPECIALTY OF MINE, OF COURSE...
WELL, I'M SURE HE'S VERY GOOD AT HEROICS. IT DOES MY HEART GOOD TO SEE MY RISA SO TAKEN WITH SUCH A MAN!
BUT NOT GENERAL SOLO'S?
OH, BY THE MAKER, NO.
HE'S FAR MORE INTERESTED IN ADVENTURE AND VIOLENCE THAN...
16

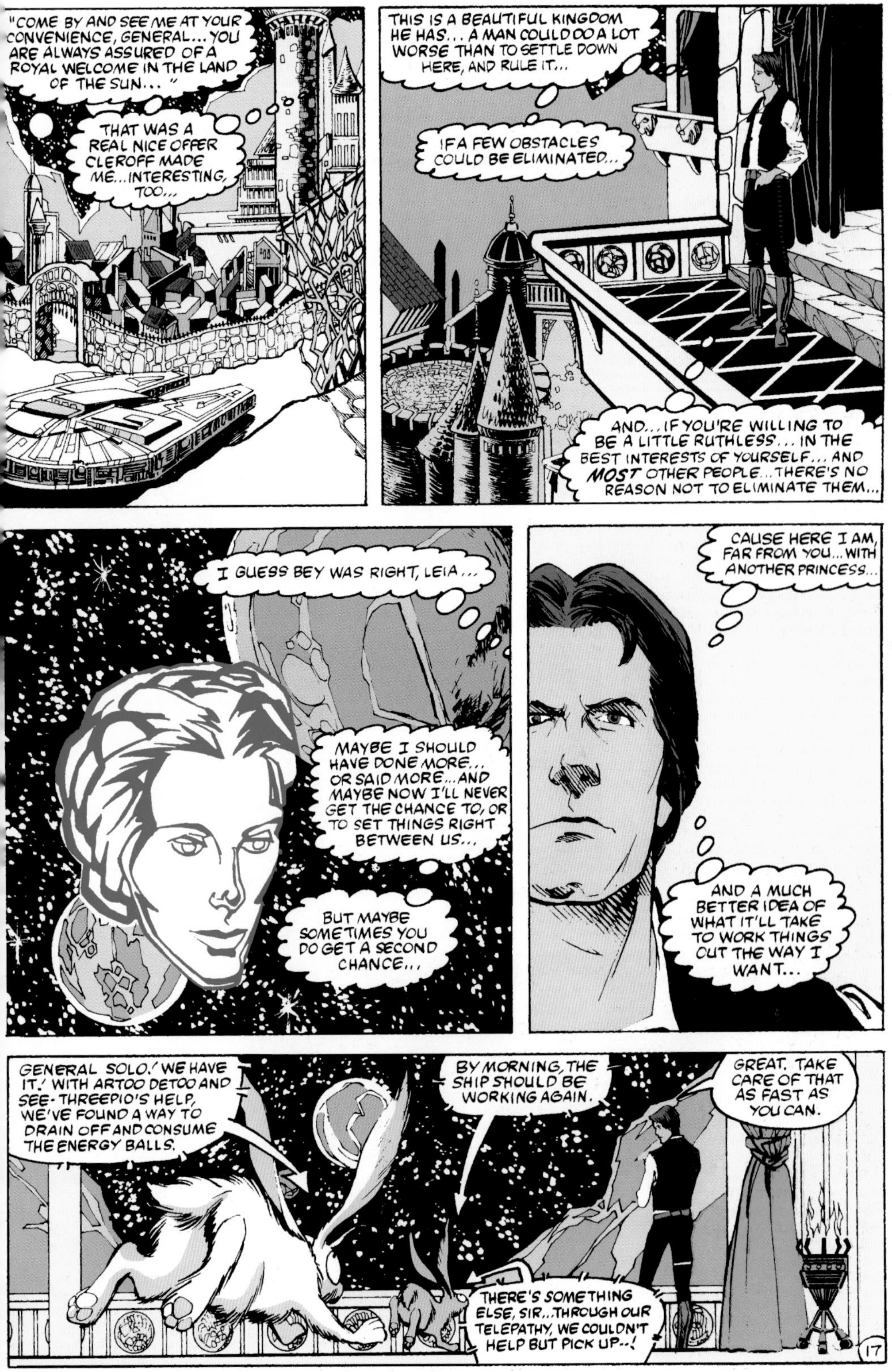
"COME BY AND SEE ME AT YOUR CONVENIENCE, GENERAL... YOU ARE ALWAYS ASSURED OF A ROYAL WELCOME IN THE LAND OF THE SUN..."
THAT WAS A REAL NICE OFFER CLEROFF MADE ME... INTERESTING, TOO...
THIS IS A BEAUTIFUL KINGDOM HE HAS... A MAN COULD DO A LOT WORSE THAN TO SETTLE DOWN HERE, AND RULE IT...
IF A FEW OBSTACLES COULD BE ELIMINATED...
AND... IF YOU'RE WILLING TO BE A LITTLE RUTHLESS... IN THE BEST INTERESTS OF YOURSELF... AND MOST OTHER PEOPLE... THERE'S NO REASON NOT TO ELIMINATE THEM...
I GUESS BEY WAS RIGHT, LEIA...
MAYBE I SHOULD HAVE DONE MORE... OR SAID MORE... AND MAYBE NOW I'LL NEVER GET THE CHANCE TO, OR TO SET THINGS RIGHT BETWEEN US...
BUT MAYBE SOMETIMES YOU DO GET A SECOND CHANCE...
CAUSE HERE I AM, FAR FROM YOU... WITH ANOTHER PRINCESS...
AND A MUCH BETTER IDEA OF WHAT IT'LL TAKE TO WORK THINGS OUT THE WAY I WANT...
GENERAL SOLO! WE HAVE IT! WITH ARTOO DETOO AND SEE-THREEPIO'S HELP, WE'VE FOUND A WAY TO DRAIN OFF AND CONSUME THE ENERGY BALLS.
BY MORNING, THE SHIP SHOULD BE WORKING AGAIN.
GREAT. TAKE CARE OF THAT AS FAST AS YOU CAN.
THERE'S SOMETHING ELSE, SIR... THROUGH OUR TELEPATHY, WE COULDN'T HELP BUT PICK UP--!
17

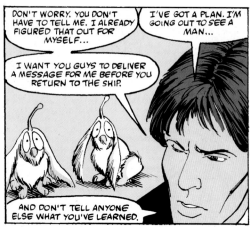

DON'T WORRY. YOU DON'T HAVE TO TELL ME. I ALREADY FIGURED THAT OUT FOR MYSELF...

I'VE GOT A PLAN. I'M GOING OUT TO SEE A MAN...

I WANT YOU GUYS TO DELIVER A MESSAGE FOR ME BEFORE YOU RETURN TO THE SHIP.

AND DON'T TELL ANYONE ELSE WHAT YOU'VE LEARNED.

THIS SHOULDN'T BE *TOO* HARD... KIND OF PEOPLE I'M LOOKING FOR TEND TO HANG OUT IN THE SAME KINDS OF PLACES ON EVERY WORLD...

...YEAH... TELL HIM I'M LOOKING FOR HIM.

HE'LL KNOW WHO I AM...

...RIGHT, DOLL. IT'S TO HIS BEST ADVANTAGE TO HEAR ME OUT...

...IT CAN'T FAIL ...BELIEVE ME, I'VE SET THIS UP VERY CAREFULLY.

YOU JUST DO LIKE I TELL YOU, AND WE BOTH WIN OUT

THE GENERAL WANTS TO SEE ME?

THAT'S RIGHT!

HE'S BEEN OUT CHECKING AROUND... AND LEARNED SOMETHING THAT COULD HAVE A VERY DRAMATIC EFFECT ON YOUR FUTURE!

HE'S MOST CONCERNED THAT YOU MEET HIM, AND FIND OUT ABOUT IT AT ONCE!

WE'LL DIRECT YOU. AND YOU MUSTN'T TELL ANYONE ELSE.

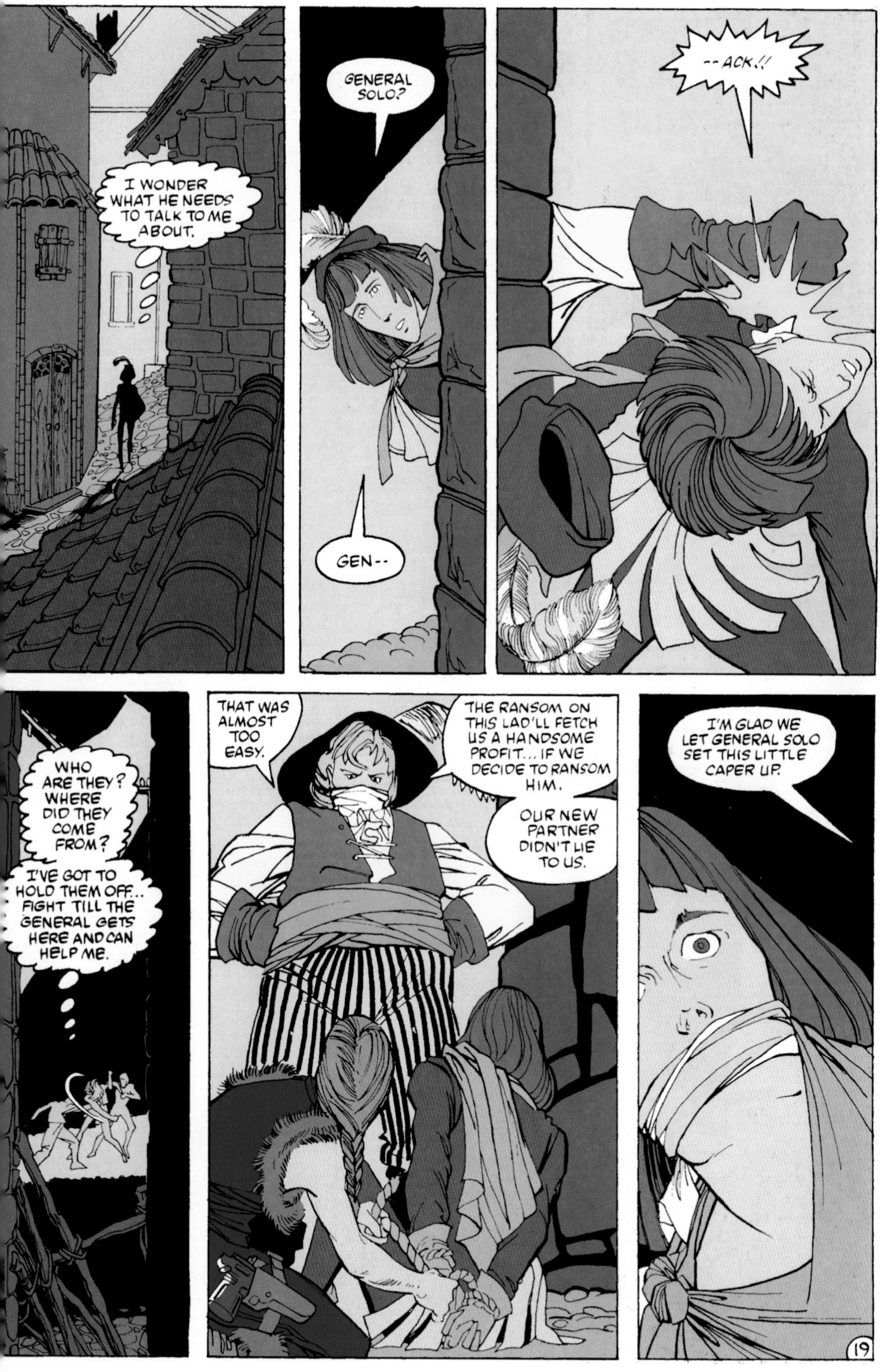
I WONDER WHAT HE NEEDS TO TALK TO ME ABOUT.
GENERAL SOLO?
GEN--
--ACK!!
WHO ARE THEY? WHERE DID THEY COME FROM?
I'VE GOT TO HOLD THEM OFF... FIGHT TILL THE GENERAL GETS HERE AND CAN HELP ME.
THAT WAS ALMOST TOO EASY.
THE RANSOM ON THIS LAD'LL FETCH US A HANDSOME PROFIT... IF WE DECIDE TO RANSOM HIM.
OUR NEW PARTNER DIDN'T LIE TO US.
I'M GLAD WE LET GENERAL SOLO SET THIS LITTLE CAPER UP.
19

THEY'LL PLAY THE GAME MY WAY, 'CAUSE THEY FIGURE I CAN MAKE 'EM RICH...

...AND I FIGURE YOU CAN DICTATE YOUR OWN TERMS TO HIS PARENTS, IF THEY EVER HOPE TO SEE THEIR BOY AGAIN...

I SEE...

...AND THAT REALLY DOES ELIMINATE ANY NEED I MIGHT HAVE TO CONSIDER... ¿AHEM¿ WORLD POLITICS WHEN I SELECT MY SON-IN-LAW...

NO!

NO! THAT'S HORRIBLE! YOU'RE HORRIBLE!

YOU'RE A HORRIBLE, EVIL, NASTY, CORRUPT... OLD...

...MAN, YOU!

YOU GET MY GIL BACK, DO YOU HEAR?

I HATE YOU!! I HATE YOU!! I HATE YOU!!

TAKE IT EASY, SISTER.

DADDY, YOU PAY THOSE BANDITS WHATEVER RANSOM THEY WANT, AND GET MY BOYFRIEND BACK, OR I SWEAR I'LL...

...I'LL... ...I'LL...

NOW, NOW, MY DEAR. YOU MUSTN'T BELIEVE EVERYTHING WE MEN SAY... A LOT OF IT IS JUST TALK AND... PROTOCOL.

WE'LL GET HIM BACK, MY PRECIOUS, TRULY...

...WON'T WE?

I KINDA FIGURED YOU'D SAY THAT. BUT IT'S OKAY. THAT'S ALL PART OF MY *REAL* PLAN.

WE GO, WE GET GIL BACK, HIS FAMILY'S GRATEFUL, THE BANDITS WON'T BE EXPECTING A DOUBLE-CROSS, WE TAKE CARE OF THEM, EVERYBODY'S HAPPY!

WONDERFUL! HOW DO WE TAKE CARE OF THEM?

JUST LEAVE THAT TO ME... BUT WE GOTTA LULL 'EM INTO A FALSE SENSE OF SECURITY. SO YOU TWO COME ALONG... AN' WE'LL ALL BE UNARMED.

21

ARE YOU CERTAIN THIS IS THE BEST WAY TO HANDLE THINGS, GENERAL?

OF COURSE. I TOLD YOU I'D TAKE CARE OF THINGS

THIS PLAN HAS ANGLES SO SHARP THAT WHEN I THOUGHT OF 'EM... I EVEN SURPRISED MYSELF!

SURPRISE!!!

HEY! I....UH....I THOUGHT I TOLD YOU GUYS TO WAIT FOR MY SIGNAL.

MAYBE YOU DID. MAYBE WE DECIDED, WITH THREE ROYAL HOSTAGES, WE DON'T NEED ANY SIGNALS. OR PARTNERS.

WE'VE BEEN MAKING PLANS OF OUR OWN.

R-RISA...?

GIL!!

22

422

... GOTTA GIVE THE FALCON CREDIT... SHE MIGHT NOT HAVE KNOWN WHERE WE WERE GOING... BUT HER COMPUTERS KEPT A RECORD OF HOW WE GOT THERE...

AND GOT US BACK. ENDOR AHEAD, FOLKS!

AND YOU MEAN TO SAY YOU HOOJIBS KNEW WHAT GENERAL SOLO WAS UP TO ALL ALONG, AND YOU COOPERATED WITH HIM?

DEAR BOY, WE ENCOURAGED HIM. IT IS RATHER SWEET, WHEN YOU THINK OF IT...

RISA REMINDED HIM SO MUCH OF HIS OWN PRINCESS LEIA, HE WAS DETERMINED TO ENGINEER HER HAPPINESS FOR HER...

...WITH OR WITHOUT HER COOPERATION, WHICH IS QUITE A TRIBUTE TO HER HIGHNESS, AND THE PLACE SHE HOLDS IN HIS HEART.

REALLY? I DON'T THINK I'LL EVER UNDERSTAND ORGANIC BEINGS!

LATER...

IT'S ALMOST TOO GOOD TO BE TRUE, HAVING YOU BACK.

HAN, I WAS AFRAID I'D NEVER SEE YOU AGAIN.

THAT'S TOO BAD. YOU SHOULD HAVE KEPT BUSY, LIKE I DID, IT WOULD HAVE TAKEN YOUR MIND OFF THINGS...SWEETHEART.

NEXT ▷ SCHOOL SPIRIT!

24

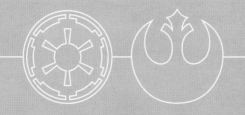

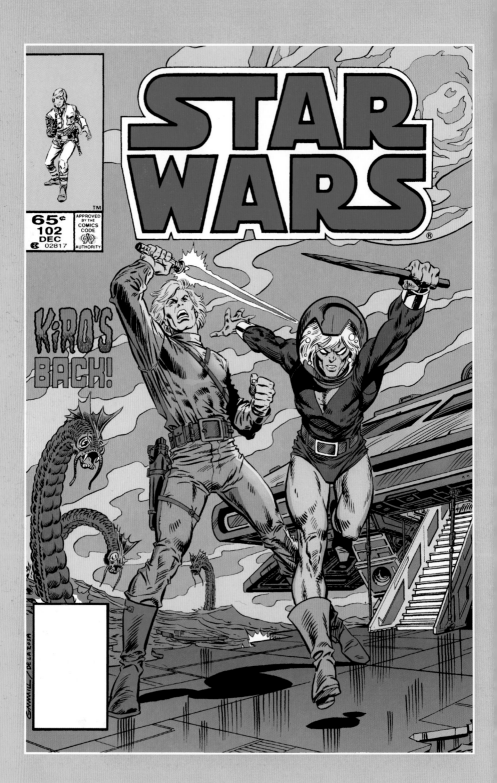

JO DUFFY / SAL BUSCEMA / SAM DE LA ROSA / RICK PARKER / PETRA SCOTESE / ANN NOCENTI / JIM SHOOTER
WRITER / BREAKDOWNS / FINISHES / LETTERING / COLORING / EDITOR / EDITOR IN CHIEF

SCHOOL SPIRIT!

IT'S UNBELIEVABLE!

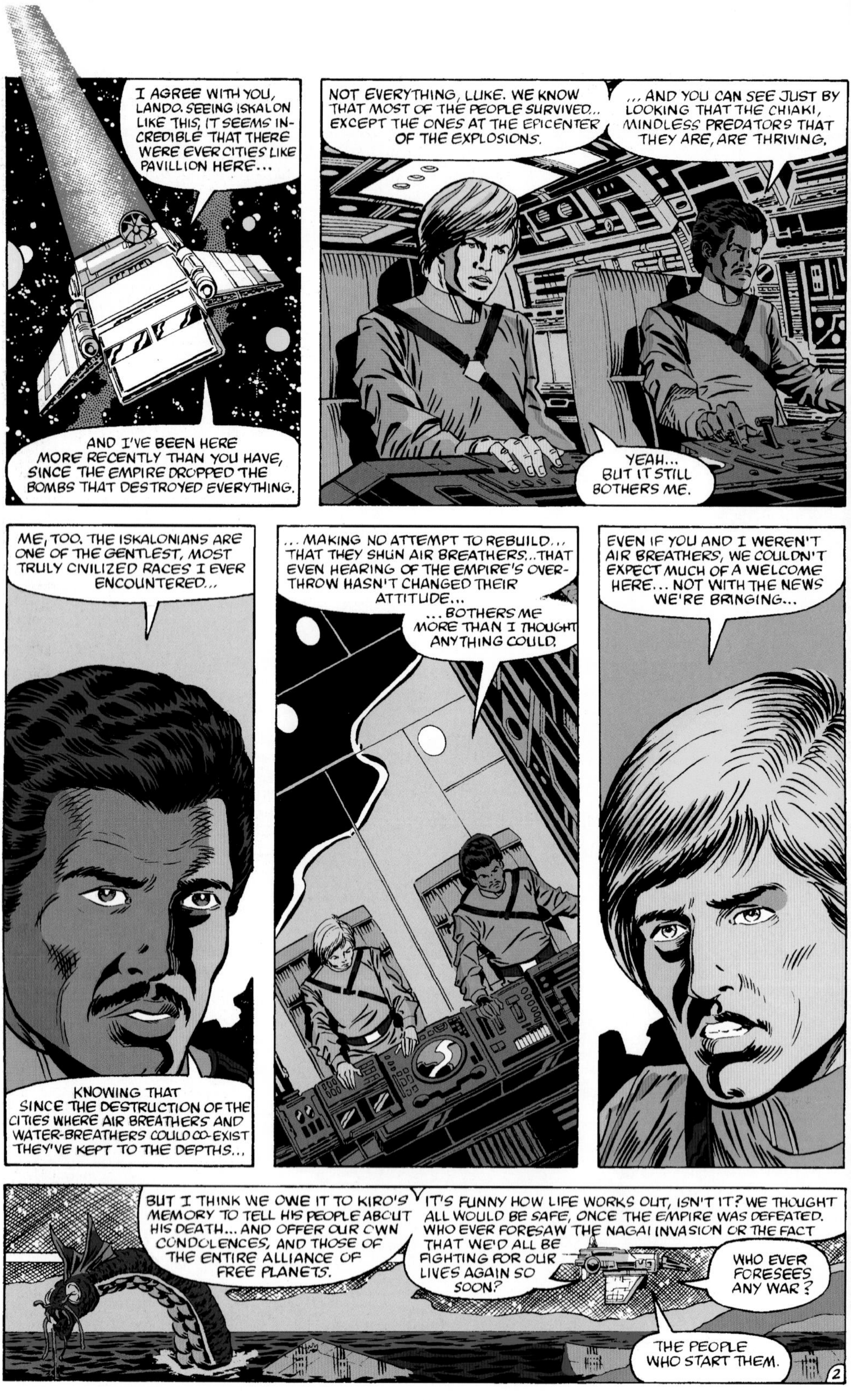
I AGREE WITH YOU, LANDO. SEEING ISKALON LIKE THIS, IT SEEMS INCREDIBLE THAT THERE WERE EVER CITIES LIKE PAVILLION HERE...
AND I'VE BEEN HERE MORE RECENTLY THAN YOU HAVE, SINCE THE EMPIRE DROPPED THE BOMBS THAT DESTROYED EVERYTHING.
NOT EVERYTHING, LUKE. WE KNOW THAT MOST OF THE PEOPLE SURVIVED... EXCEPT THE ONES AT THE EPICENTER OF THE EXPLOSIONS.
...AND YOU CAN SEE JUST BY LOOKING THAT THE CHIAKI, MINDLESS PREDATORS THAT THEY ARE, ARE THRIVING.
YEAH... BUT IT STILL BOTHERS ME.
ME, TOO. THE ISKALONIANS ARE ONE OF THE GENTLEST, MOST TRULY CIVILIZED RACES I EVER ENCOUNTERED...
KNOWING THAT SINCE THE DESTRUCTION OF THE CITIES WHERE AIR BREATHERS AND WATER-BREATHERS COULD CO-EXIST THEY'VE KEPT TO THE DEPTHS...
...MAKING NO ATTEMPT TO REBUILD... THAT THEY SHUN AIR BREATHERS...THAT EVEN HEARING OF THE EMPIRE'S OVERTHROW HASN'T CHANGED THEIR ATTITUDE...
...BOTHERS ME MORE THAN I THOUGHT ANYTHING COULD.
EVEN IF YOU AND I WEREN'T AIR BREATHERS, WE COULDN'T EXPECT MUCH OF A WELCOME HERE... NOT WITH THE NEWS WE'RE BRINGING...
BUT I THINK WE OWE IT TO KIRO'S MEMORY TO TELL HIS PEOPLE ABOUT HIS DEATH... AND OFFER OUR OWN CONDOLENCES, AND THOSE OF THE ENTIRE ALLIANCE OF FREE PLANETS.
IT'S FUNNY HOW LIFE WORKS OUT, ISN'T IT? WE THOUGHT ALL WOULD BE SAFE, ONCE THE EMPIRE WAS DEFEATED. WHO EVER FORESAW THE NAGAI INVASION OR THE FACT THAT WE'D ALL BE FIGHTING FOR OUR LIVES AGAIN SO SOON?
WHO EVER FORESEES ANY WAR?
THE PEOPLE WHO START THEM.
2

SOME OF THE WRECKAGE OF WHAT USED TO BE PAVILLION IS UP AHEAD.

WE CAN LAND THE COBRA THERE, AND THEN FIGURE OUT HOW TO CONTACT MONE AND HIS PEOPLE.

BEATS ME HOW YOU CAN SEE THROUGH THIS FOG TO...

NO, WAIT A MINUTE. I FIGURED IT OUT. YOUR SKILLS AS A JEDI KNIGHT, RIGHT?

USE OF THE *FORCE?* EXTRAORDINARY TRAINING?

YEP.

DID YOU HEAR SOMETHING? A SHIP, PERHAPS?

I'M NOT CERTAIN. I'M STILL NOT ACCUSTOMED TO THE MANNER IN WHICH ALL THE WATER HERE DISTORTS AND MAGNIFIES SOUND.

IT DOESN'T MATTER. THE TRACKING INSTRUMENTS AT THE BASE WILL HAVE RECORDED AND IDENTIFIED IT, WHATEVER IT IS...

AND IT MUST HAVE BEEN ONE OF OURS.

IT COULD HARDLY HAVE BEEN ONE OF THEIR S.

REMARKABLE, THE FIGHT THEY PUT UP.

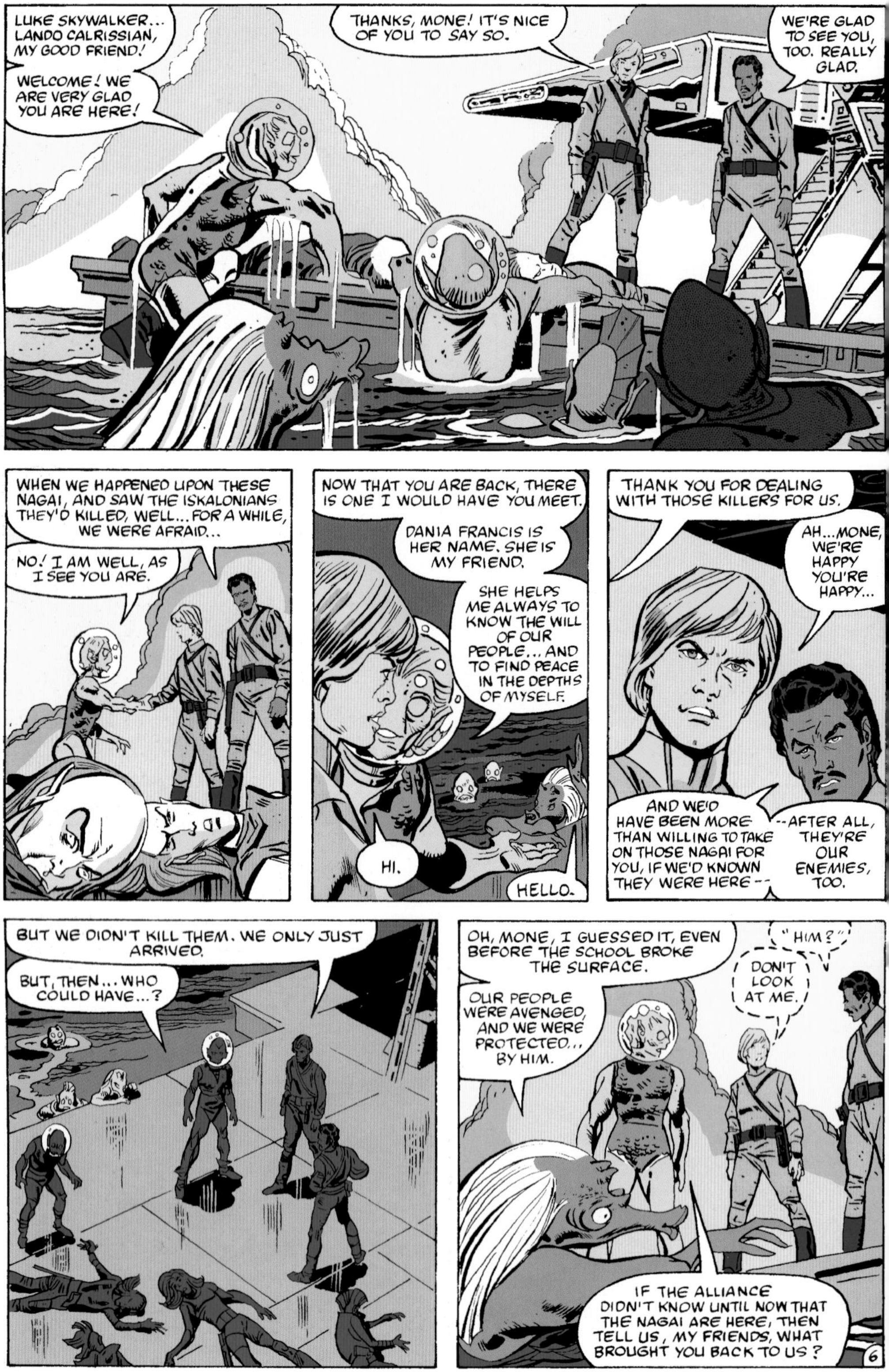
LUKE SKYWALKER... LANDO CALRISSIAN, MY GOOD FRIEND!
WELCOME! WE ARE VERY GLAD YOU ARE HERE!
THANKS, MONE! IT'S NICE OF YOU TO SAY SO.
WE'RE GLAD TO SEE YOU, TOO. REALLY GLAD.
WHEN WE HAPPENED UPON THESE NAGAI, AND SAW THE ISKALONIANS THEY'D KILLED, WELL... FOR A WHILE, WE WERE AFRAID...
NO! I AM WELL, AS I SEE YOU ARE.
NOW THAT YOU ARE BACK, THERE IS ONE I WOULD HAVE YOU MEET.
DANIA FRANCIS IS HER NAME. SHE IS MY FRIEND.
SHE HELPS ME ALWAYS TO KNOW THE WILL OF OUR PEOPLE... AND TO FIND PEACE IN THE DEPTHS OF MYSELF.
HI.
HELLO.
THANK YOU FOR DEALING WITH THOSE KILLERS FOR US.
AH...MONE, WE'RE HAPPY YOU'RE HAPPY...
AND WE'D HAVE BEEN MORE THAN WILLING TO TAKE ON THOSE NAGAI FOR YOU, IF WE'D KNOWN THEY WERE HERE --
--AFTER ALL, THEY'RE OUR ENEMIES, TOO.
BUT WE DIDN'T KILL THEM. WE ONLY JUST ARRIVED.
BUT, THEN... WHO COULD HAVE...?
OH, MONE, I GUESSED IT, EVEN BEFORE THE SCHOOL BROKE THE SURFACE.
OUR PEOPLE WERE AVENGED, AND WE WERE PROTECTED... BY HIM.
"HIM?"
DON'T LOOK AT ME.
IF THE ALLIANCE DIDN'T KNOW UNTIL NOW THAT THE NAGAI ARE HERE, THEN TELL US, MY FRIENDS, WHAT BROUGHT YOU BACK TO US?
6

MONE... I'M AFRAID IT'S BAD NEWS...

IT'S NOT SOMETHING ANYONE COULD HAVE FORESEEN...

YOU SEE... ISKALON ISN'T THE ONLY WORLD THE NAGAI HAVE INVADED... THEY'RE ALL OVER THE GALAXY NOW.

KIRO AND I WERE PART OF A SMALL SCOUTING PARTY ON THE GALACTIC PERIMETER WHEN THE MAIN FORCE ARRIVED.

HE... KIRO... MET AND ENGAGED ONE OF THEIR LEADERS, ALONE.

I'M SORRY THERE ISN'T ANY EASY WAY TO SAY THIS...

HE WAS KILLED IN THAT FLIGHT.

LUKE, WHAT ARE YOU TALKING ABOUT? KIRO IS NOT DEAD!

MONE... WE KNOW HOW HARD IT MUST BE FOR YOU TO ACCEPT... KIRO WAS YOUR BEST FRIEND, AND ONE OF YOUR PEOPLE'S GREATEST HEROES, BUT...

LANDO, DO NOT DISTRESS YOURSELF, WE *KNOW* KIRO IS NOT DEAD, BECAUSE HE IS BACK ON ISKALON. WE HAVE SEEN HIM.

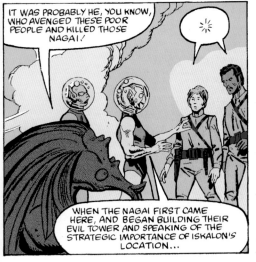

IT WAS PROBABLY HE, YOU KNOW, WHO AVENGED THESE POOR PEOPLE AND KILLED THOSE NAGAI!

WHEN THE NAGAI FIRST CAME HERE, AND BEGAN BUILDING THEIR EVIL TOWER AND SPEAKING OF THE STRATEGIC IMPORTANCE OF ISKALON'S LOCATION...

... AND ENSLAVING OUR PEOPLE... THAT WAS WHEN WE NEEDED OUR EXILED HERO MOST...

AND THAT IS WHEN KIRO CAME BACK.

7

IT WAS A TWO-PASSENGER CRAFT, NOT ANY KNOWN CLASS OF MILITARY CRAFT, SO IT MAY BE PRIVATELY OWNED.

ANY WORD AS YET ON THAT SHIP THAT CAME IN?

DEFINITELY NOT ONE OF OURS, SIR.

THEY MADE NO ATTEMPT TO IDENTIFY THEMSELVES, AND OBTAINED NO CLEARANCES WHATSOEVER.

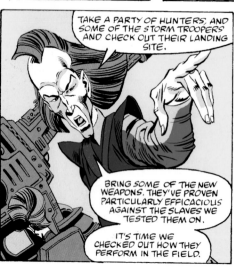

TAKE A PARTY OF HUNTERS, AND SOME OF THE STORM TROOPERS AND CHECK OUT THEIR LANDING SITE.

BRING SOME OF THE NEW WEAPONS. THEY'VE PROVEN PARTICULARLY EFFICACIOUS AGAINST THE SLAVES WE TESTED THEM ON.

IT'S TIME WE CHECKED OUT HOW THEY PERFORM IN THE FIELD.

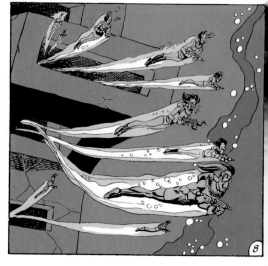

8

NOW THAT YOU'RE HERE... YOU'LL HELP US TO FREE THOSE WHO ARE ENSLAVED?

YOU'LL HELP US DRIVE BACK THE NAGAI?

OF COURSE, WE'D HAVE BEEN HERE SOONER, IF ONLY WE'D KNOWN.

YOU SHOULD HAVE CONTACTED US!

OUTWORLDERS! WATER BREATHERS! SURRENDER TO US OR DIE!

WE ARE YOUR SUPERIORS! WE ARE NAGAI!

SLAVERY? NEVER! TOO MANY OF OUR PEOPLE HAVE FELT YOUR OPPRESSION ALREADY!

DANIA! TAKE THEM TO THE DEEPS AND FLEE!

LUKE AND I ARE ARMED, SO LET US COVER YOUR RETREAT.

HURRY, EVERYONE!

LOOK AT THEIR ARMS... THEY MUST BE FROM THE ALLIANCE OF FREE PLANETS. ONE OF THEM HAS A BLASTER AND THE OTHER...

THIS IS A LIGHT-SABER.

YOU ALL KEEP BACK, OR YOU CAN FIND OUT FIRST-HAND WHAT THAT THING FEELS LIKE!

9

435

OH, REALLY?

AND DO YOU THINK IT FEELS AS UNPLEASANT...

...AS THIS?

≡AUGHN≡

OOHH...!

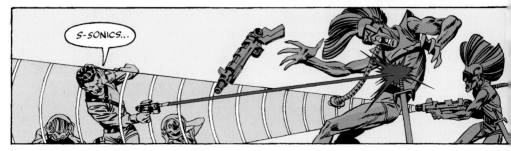

S-SONICS...

USING SONICS... MAKING IT HARD TO...

NO... HEARING IS JUST A... SENSE...

SENSES CAN... DECEIVE... BETRAY...

GOT TO...

...TO...

10

436

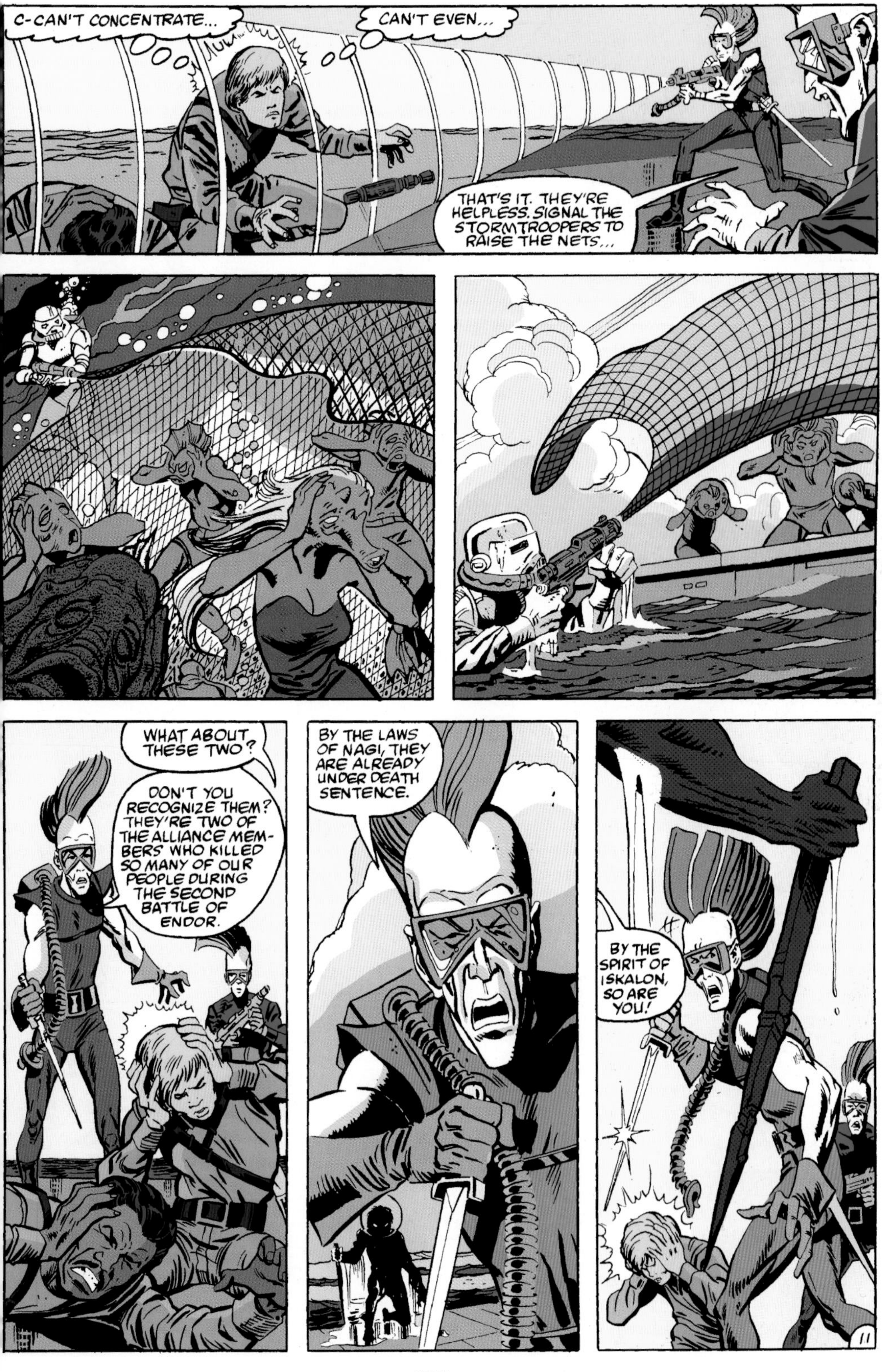
C-CAN'T CONCENTRATE...
CAN'T EVEN...
THAT'S IT. THEY'RE HELPLESS. SIGNAL THE STORMTROOPERS TO RAISE THE NETS...
WHAT ABOUT THESE TWO?
DON'T YOU RECOGNIZE THEM? THEY'RE TWO OF THE ALLIANCE MEMBERS WHO KILLED SO MANY OF OUR PEOPLE DURING THE SECOND BATTLE OF ENDOR.
BY THE LAWS OF NAGI, THEY ARE ALREADY UNDER DEATH SENTENCE.
BY THE SPIRIT OF ISKALON, SO ARE YOU!
11

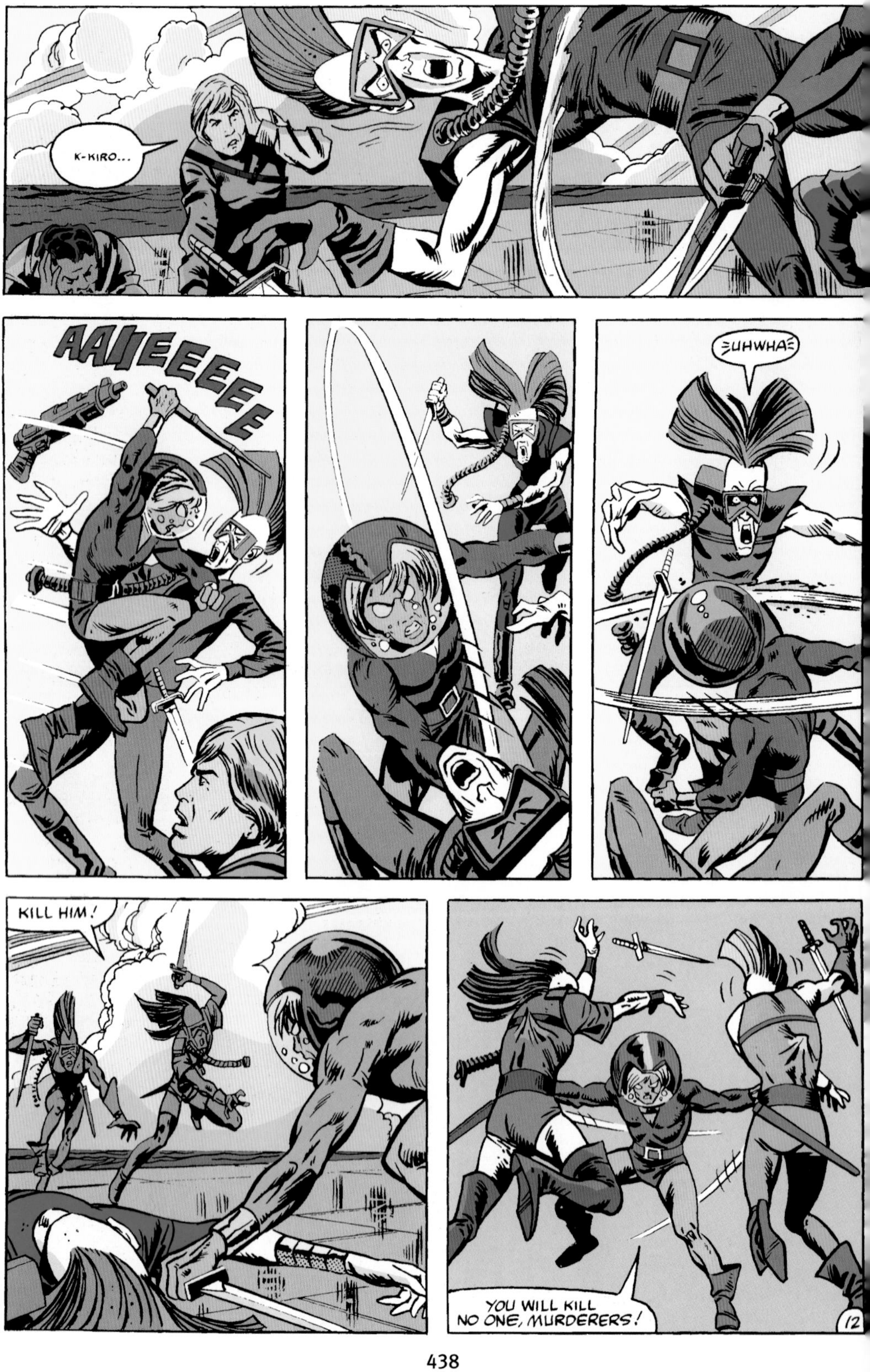
K-KIRO...
AAIIEEEEEE
UHWHA
KILL HIM!
YOU WILL KILL NO ONE, MURDERERS!
12

KIRO--?!

WAIT! DON'T RUN OFF YET!

≶OOWGHN≶

LANDO... HOW ARE YOU FEELING?

ALIVE... BETTER THAN I EXPECTED TO BE.

TAKE IT EASY. THOSE SONIC BLASTERS OF THEIRS ARE PRETTY DEBILITATING.

IT'S PROBABLY GONNA BE A FEW MINUTES BEFORE WE SHAKE OFF THE EFFECTS.

LUKE... I THOUGHT I SAW... I HEARD YOU CALL...

IS IT REALLY HIM?

YEAH, LANDO. YOU WEREN'T DREAMING.

I COULD SWEAR I SAW HIM DIE, BUT KIRO'S HERE, AND HE'S ALIVE.

I WISH HE'D STUCK AROUND.

ME, TOO. I'D LIKE SOME ANSWERS.

ANSWERS CAN WAIT. WHAT WE NEED NOW IS HELP.

I'M... NOT SURE I FOLLOW YOU.

MONE'S GONE. HE WAS TAKEN BY THE NAGAI, WASN'T HE?

THEY ALL WERE, WITH THOSE WEAPONS THEY HAD IT'S A GOOD BET THE NAGAI GOT DANIA AND THE OTHERS AS WELL.

WELL, WE'D BETTER RESCUE THEM, AND QUICKLY...

OR IT COULD MEAN THE DEATH OF EVERY MAN, WOMAN, AND CHILD ON ISKALON.

WHAT--?!

13

439

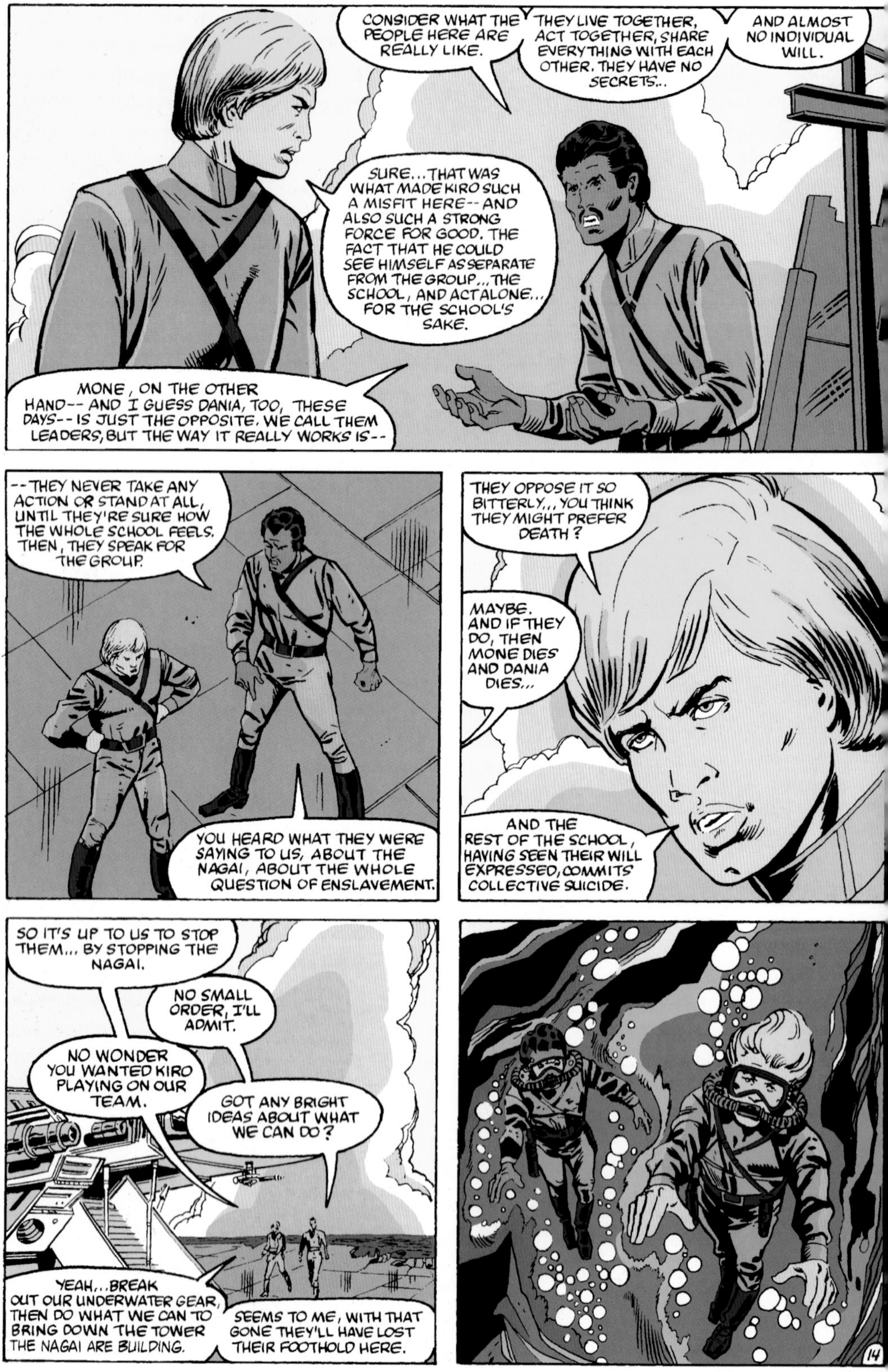
CONSIDER WHAT THE PEOPLE HERE ARE REALLY LIKE.
THEY LIVE TOGETHER, ACT TOGETHER, SHARE EVERYTHING WITH EACH OTHER. THEY HAVE NO SECRETS..
AND ALMOST NO INDIVIDUAL WILL.
SURE... THAT WAS WHAT MADE KIRO SUCH A MISFIT HERE-- AND ALSO SUCH A STRONG FORCE FOR GOOD. THE FACT THAT HE COULD SEE HIMSELF AS SEPARATE FROM THE GROUP... THE SCHOOL, AND ACT ALONE... FOR THE SCHOOL'S SAKE.
MONE, ON THE OTHER HAND-- AND I GUESS DANIA, TOO, THESE DAYS-- IS JUST THE OPPOSITE. WE CALL THEM LEADERS, BUT THE WAY IT REALLY WORKS IS--
--THEY NEVER TAKE ANY ACTION OR STAND AT ALL, UNTIL THEY'RE SURE HOW THE WHOLE SCHOOL FEELS. THEN, THEY SPEAK FOR THE GROUP.
YOU HEARD WHAT THEY WERE SAYING TO US, ABOUT THE NAGAI, ABOUT THE WHOLE QUESTION OF ENSLAVEMENT.
THEY OPPOSE IT SO BITTERLY,,, YOU THINK THEY MIGHT PREFER DEATH?
MAYBE. AND IF THEY DO, THEN MONE DIES AND DANIA DIES...
AND THE REST OF THE SCHOOL, HAVING SEEN THEIR WILL EXPRESSED, COMMITS COLLECTIVE SUICIDE.
SO IT'S UP TO US TO STOP THEM... BY STOPPING THE NAGAI.
NO SMALL ORDER, I'LL ADMIT.
NO WONDER YOU WANTED KIRO PLAYING ON OUR TEAM.
GOT ANY BRIGHT IDEAS ABOUT WHAT WE CAN DO?
YEAH... BREAK OUT OUR UNDERWATER GEAR, THEN DO WHAT WE CAN TO BRING DOWN THE TOWER THE NAGAI ARE BUILDING.
SEEMS TO ME, WITH THAT GONE THEY'LL HAVE LOST THEIR FOOTHOLD HERE.
14

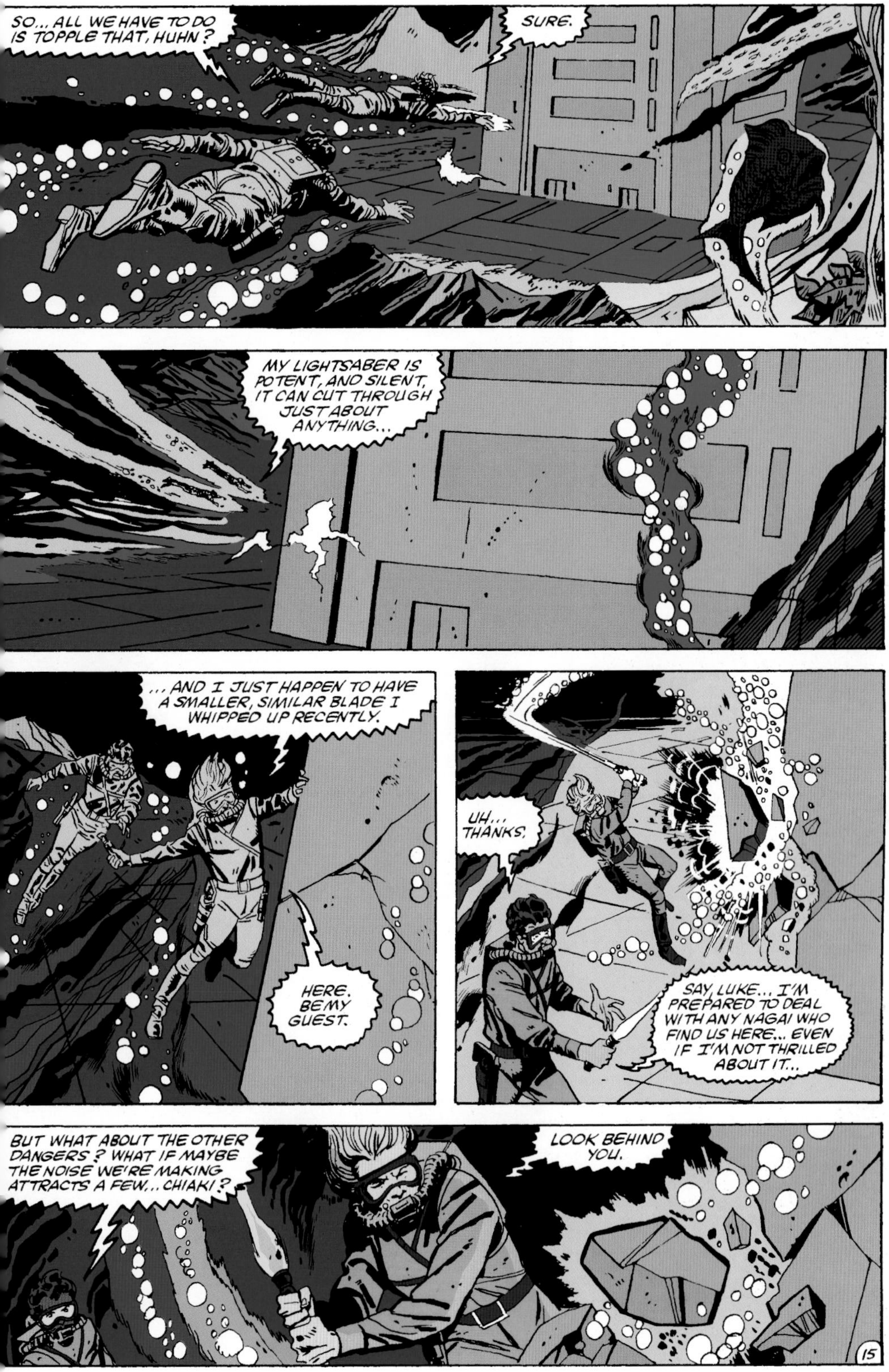
SO... ALL WE HAVE TO DO IS TOPPLE THAT, HUHN?
SURE.
MY LIGHTSABER IS POTENT, AND SILENT. IT CAN CUT THROUGH JUST ABOUT ANYTHING...
...AND I JUST HAPPEN TO HAVE A SMALLER, SIMILAR BLADE I WHIPPED UP RECENTLY.
HERE. BE MY GUEST.
UH... THANKS.
SAY, LUKE... I'M PREPARED TO DEAL WITH ANY NAGAI WHO FIND US HERE... EVEN IF I'M NOT THRILLED ABOUT IT...
BUT WHAT ABOUT THE OTHER DANGERS? WHAT IF MAYBE THE NOISE WE'RE MAKING ATTRACTS A FEW... CHIAKI?
LOOK BEHIND YOU.
15

WITH ALL THE VIOLENCE HERE LATELY, I THINK THEY'RE PRETTY MUCH SATED.

OH.

THEY'RE CURIOUS NOW, THAT'S ALL. IF NOTHING HAPPENS TO PROVOKE THEM, I DON'T THINK WE WILL HAVE A PROBLEM.

PROVOKE 'EM? WOULDN'T DREAM OF IT!

WAIT A SECOND. I FEEL... LANDO, SOMETHING'S...

NAGAI!

AND IT LOOKS LIKE THEY'VE PROVOKED A PREDATOR OF THEIR OWN.

I HAVE TOLD YOU BEFORE TO LEAVE MY FRIENDS ALONE!

16

442

YOU HAVE TAKEN MUCH FROM THE CREATURES OF THIS WORLD.

NOW...YOU MUST GIVE SOMETHING BACK!

KIRO!

KIRO! IT'S GREAT TO SEE YOU, GUY, I...

I AM GLAD TO SEE YOU BOTH... BUT THERE IS NO TIME FOR TALK OR JOY NOW.

WE MUST HELP MY BEST OF FRIENDS, AND HIS DANIA, OR ALL OF MY PEOPLE WILL BE IN PERIL.

KIRO, ARE YOU SURE? WE SUSPECTED THAT, BUT...

YES,..YES, I AM SURE!

I KNOW!

WHAT YOU ARE DOING HERE IS GOOD AND IMPORTANT. KEEP IT UP. THERE SHOULD BE NO MORE GUARDS UNTIL THE LATE CYCLE.

I WILL RESCUE MONE AND THE OTHERS, BEFORE IT IS TOO LATE.

I WILL FIND WHERE THEY ARE.

I... WILL KNOW.

17

443

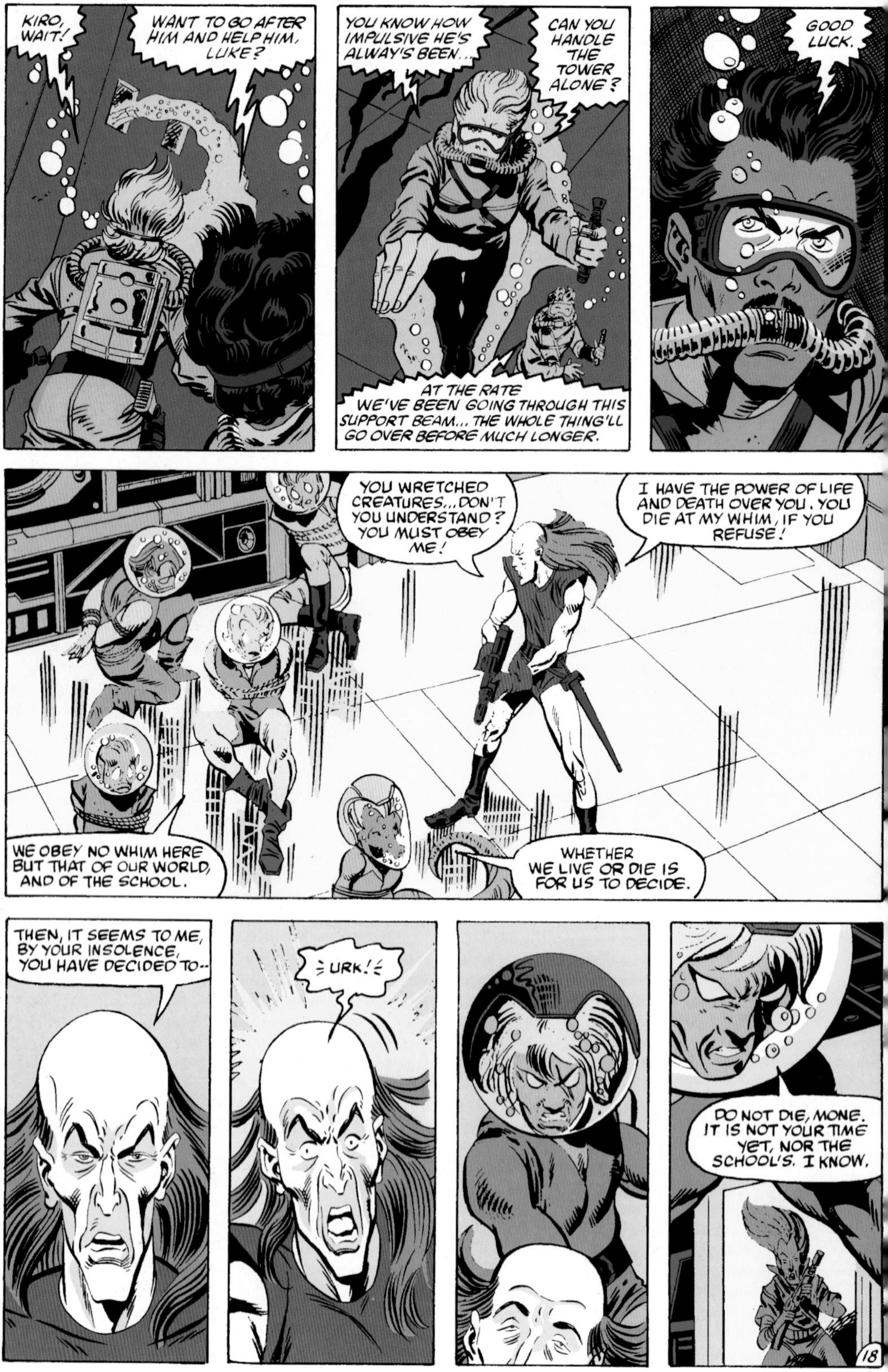
KIRO, WAIT!
WANT TO GO AFTER HIM AND HELP HIM, LUKE?
YOU KNOW HOW IMPULSIVE HE'S ALWAY'S BEEN...
CAN YOU HANDLE THE TOWER ALONE?
AT THE RATE WE'VE BEEN GOING THROUGH THIS SUPPORT BEAM... THE WHOLE THING'LL GO OVER BEFORE MUCH LONGER.
GOOD LUCK.
YOU WRETCHED CREATURES... DON'T YOU UNDERSTAND? YOU MUST OBEY ME!
I HAVE THE POWER OF LIFE AND DEATH OVER YOU. YOU DIE AT MY WHIM, IF YOU REFUSE!
WE OBEY NO WHIM HERE BUT THAT OF OUR WORLD, AND OF THE SCHOOL.
WHETHER WE LIVE OR DIE IS FOR US TO DECIDE.
THEN, IT SEEMS TO ME, BY YOUR INSOLENCE, YOU HAVE DECIDED TO--
URK!
DO NOT DIE, MONE. IT IS NOT YOUR TIME YET, NOR THE SCHOOL'S. I KNOW.
18

THAT'S IT, THEN. THE NAGAI HOLD IS BROKEN HERE, FOR NOW.

... BUT REMEMBER, THEY MAY NOT HAVE GONE FAR.

IF THINGS GET TO BE TOO MUCH FOR YOU, SEND WORD AND THE ALLIANCE WILL SEND AS MUCH HELP AS OUR RE-SOURCES ALLOW.

THERE ARE OTHER FORTIFIED WORLDS THAT ONCE SERVED THE EMPIRE, RIGHT HERE IN THIS SYSTEM.

LET THEM COME AGAIN. THEY WILL NOT FIND US UNPREPARED, THIS TIME.

WE ARE FREE, LUKE. THE EVIL IS FALLEN.

WHY ARE YOU SO SAD?

BECAUSE THERE'S BEEN NO SIGN OF KIRO SINCE THE TOWER FELL.

I HOPED I WAS WRONG,,, THAT MAYBE MY EYES HAD DECEIVED ME...

BUT THEY DIDN'T. THAT NAGAI OFFICER SHOT HIM RIGHT IN THE HEART.

HE COULDN'T HAVE SURVIVED.

POOR KIRO...

20

LUKE...

THAT NAGAI DIDN'T SHOOT MY HEART... I FELL ASIDE, SO THAT HE WOULD BE FOOLED, AND NOT FIRE AT ME AGAIN.

ALIVE... YOU'RE ALIVE... REALLY ALIVE...

IT IS GOOD TO SEE YOU AGAIN, MY FRIEND. I AM GLAD YOU CAME HERE, SO THAT WE COULD TALK.

KIRO... WHAT HAPPENED TO YOU... BACK ON KINOOINE?

WHEN DANI AND I SAW THE STAIN IN THE WATER... WHEN DEN SIVA SURVIVED YOUR DUEL... WE BOTH ASSUMED...

LUKE... LET DANI ...LET ALL OF THEM GO ON AS- SUMING. I LOVE HER... BUT I CAN- NOT GO BACK... NOT WHILE MY PEOPLE NEED ME. IT WOULD BE BET- TER IF NO ONE KNEW...

BECAUSE I... LOVE DANI, I HAD TO LET HER GO. DO NOT... STOP HER FROM... LETTING GO OF ME.

BUT...

DEN WOUNDED ME, LUKE... I WAS BADLY HURT... AND I DON'T REMEMBER MUCH OF WHAT HAPPENED AFTER THAT...

BUT... WHEN THE NAGAI CAME HERE, THE SAME NAGAI WHO HAD DONE THOSE TERRIBLE THINGS TO US ON KINOOINE...

I HAD TO PROTECT MY PEOPLE.

YOU HAVE BEEN MY TRUEST OF FRIENDS, LUKE... CLOSER TO ME EVEN THAN MONE IN MANY WAYS.

PLEASE... KEEP MY SECRET...

REMEMBER ME.

21

KIRO?

KIRO, I...

...I...

I'LL REMEMBER YOU. AND I'LL KEEP YOUR SECRET FOR YOU... FROM EVERYONE...

AND I'LL SEE TO IT LANDO DOES THE SAME.

SO THEY DIDN'T GET THE LITTLE GUY AFTER ALL, HUNH?

NOPE. THEY DIDN'T.

AND HE'S GOING TO BE RIGHT HERE, PROTECTING HIS WORLD AND HIS PEOPLE, AS LONG AS THEY WANT HIM TO.

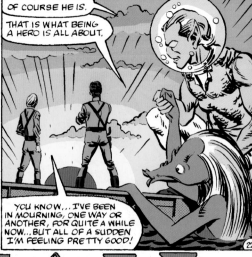

OF COURSE HE IS.

THAT IS WHAT BEING A HERO IS ALL ABOUT.

YOU KNOW... I'VE BEEN IN MOURNING, ONE WAY OR ANOTHER, FOR QUITE A WHILE NOW...BUT ALL OF A SUDDEN I'M FEELING PRETTY GOOD!

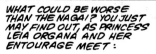

NEXT WHAT COULD BE WORSE THAN THE NAGAI? YOU JUST MAY FIND OUT, AS PRINCESS LEIA ORGANA AND HER ENTOURAGE MEET:

TAI!

LASER FIRE AT THE LANDING PLATFORM!

*LEIA, LANDO, CHEWBACCA AND THE DROIDS BATTLE THEIR WAY ABOARD THE **MILLENNIUM FALCON**, AS SEEN BY **MARSHALL ROGERS**.*

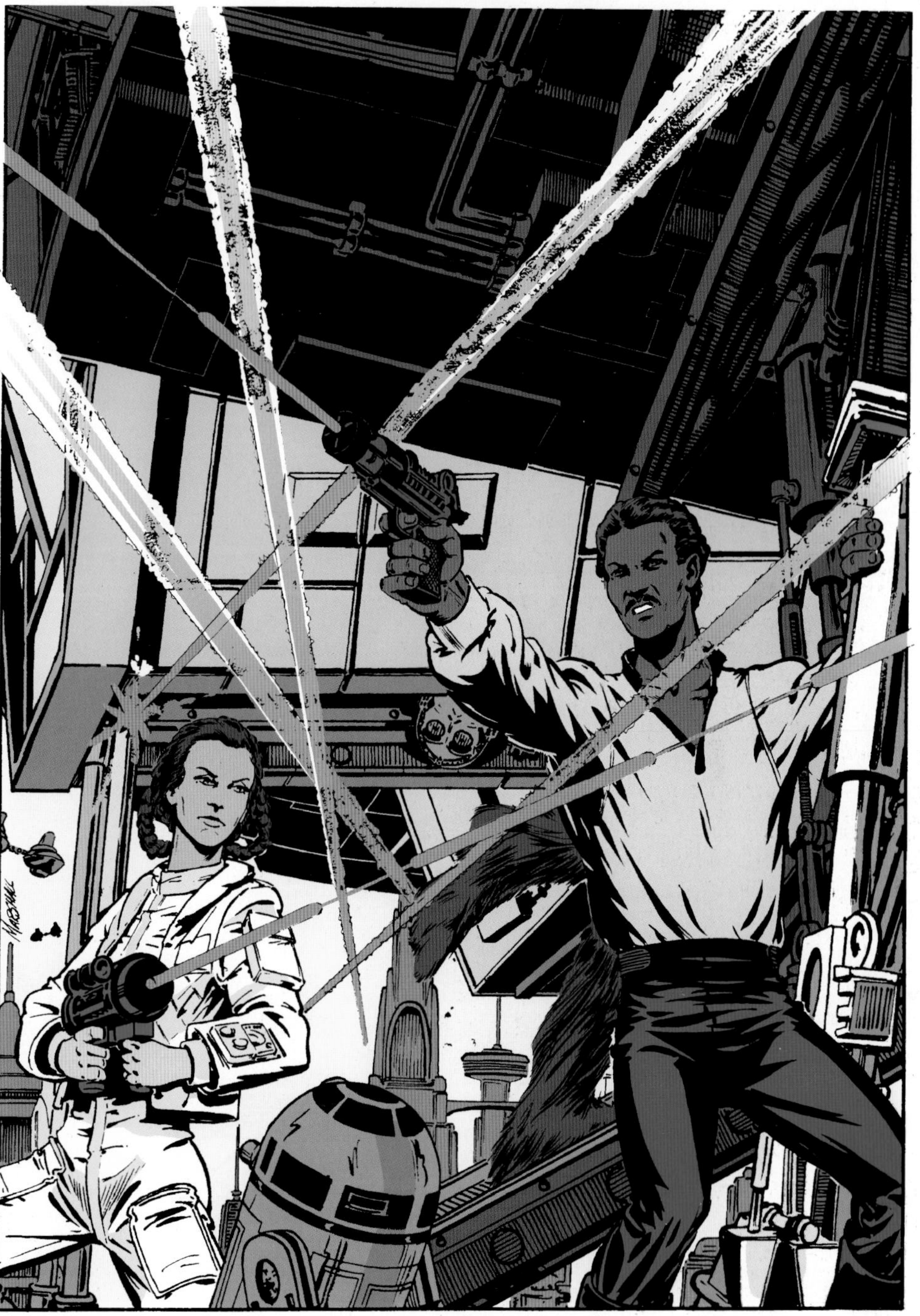

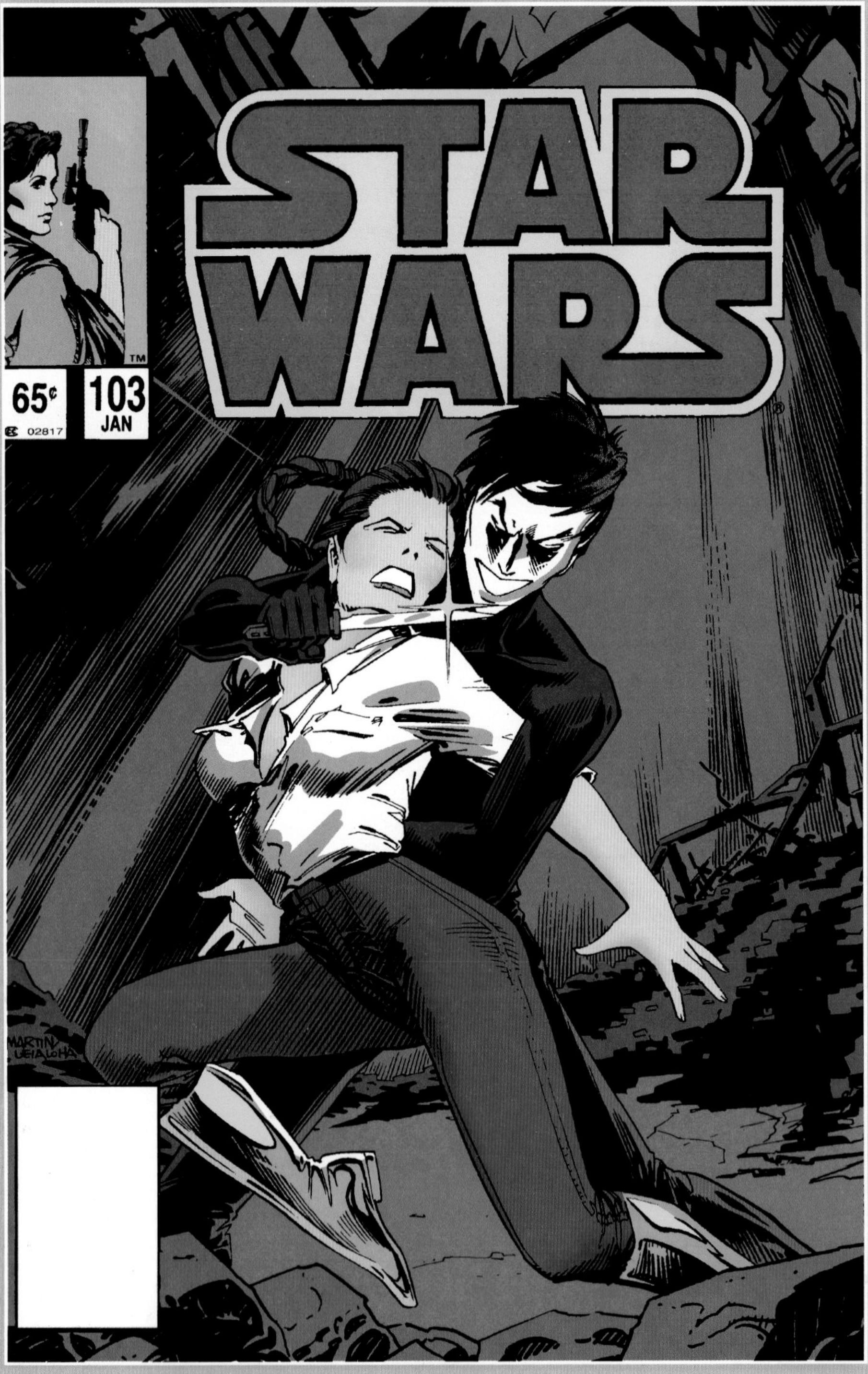
STAR WARS
65¢
103
JAN
02817
TM
MARTIN/
WEIALOHA

DUFFY WRITER **CYNTHIA MARTIN** PENCILER **ART NICHOLS** INKER **RICK PARKER** LETTERING **M. WRIGHTSON** COLORING **ANN NOCENTI** EDITOR **JIM SHOOTER** EDITOR IN CHIEF

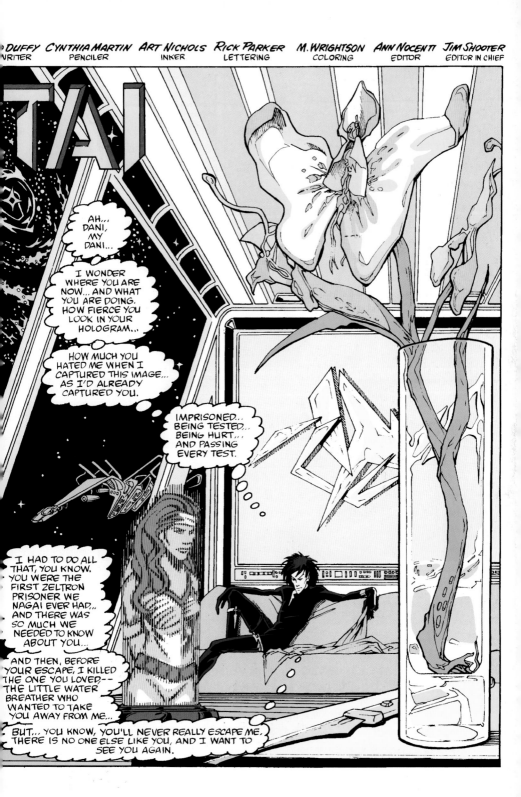

AH... DANI, MY DANI...

I WONDER WHERE YOU ARE NOW... AND WHAT YOU ARE DOING. HOW FIERCE YOU LOOK IN YOUR HOLOGRAM...

HOW MUCH YOU HATED ME WHEN I CAPTURED THIS IMAGE... AS I'D ALREADY CAPTURED YOU.

IMPRISONED... BEING TESTED... BEING HURT... AND PASSING EVERY TEST.

I HAD TO DO ALL THAT, YOU KNOW. YOU WERE THE FIRST ZELTRON PRISONER WE NAGAI EVER HAD... AND THERE WAS SO MUCH WE NEEDED TO KNOW ABOUT YOU...

AND THEN, BEFORE YOUR ESCAPE, I KILLED THE ONE YOU LOVED-- THE LITTLE WATER BREATHER WHO WANTED TO TAKE YOU AWAY FROM ME...

BUT... YOU KNOW, YOU'LL NEVER REALLY ESCAPE ME. THERE IS NO ONE ELSE LIKE YOU, AND I WANT TO SEE YOU AGAIN.

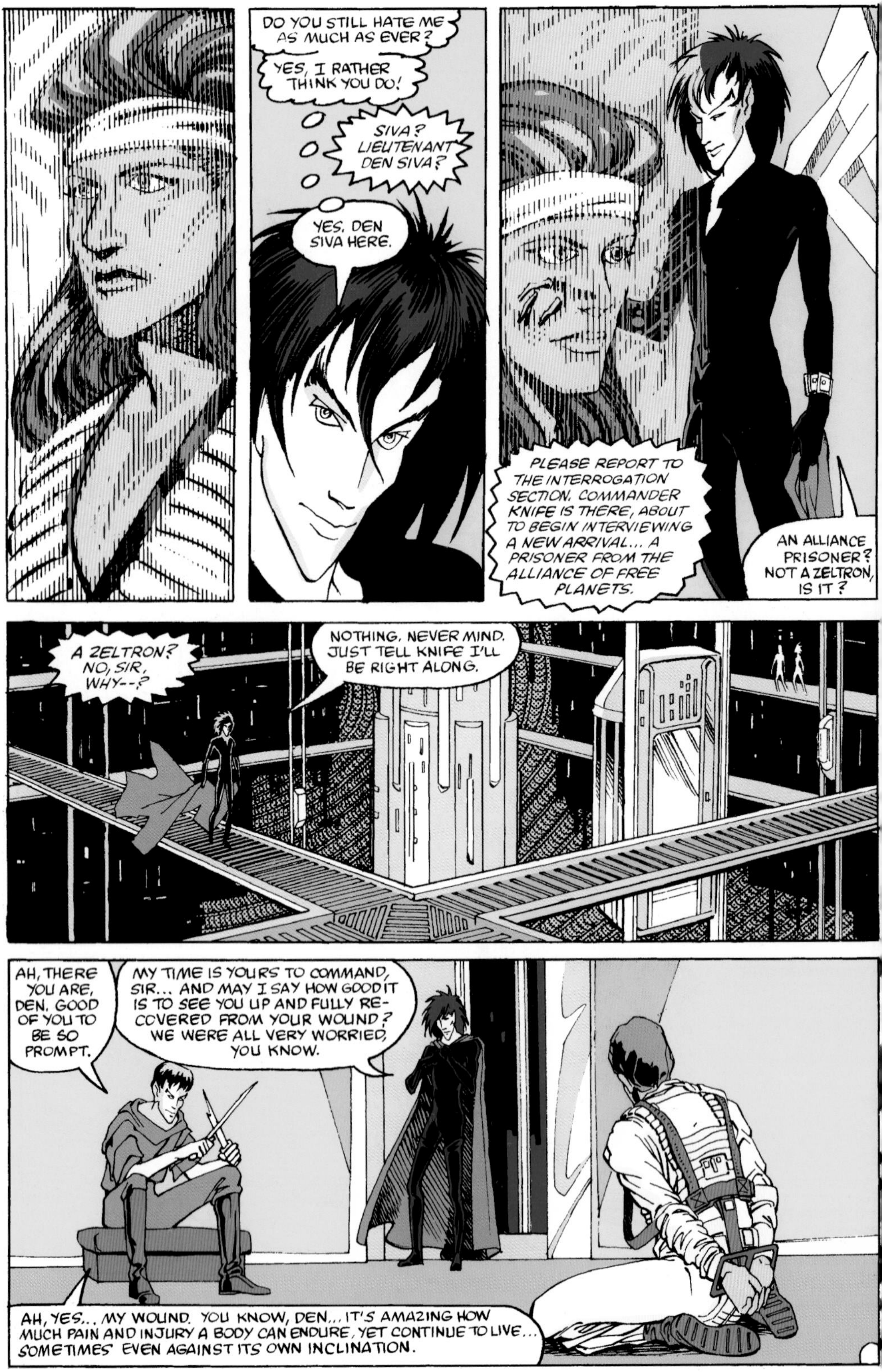

DO YOU STILL HATE ME AS MUCH AS EVER?
YES, I RATHER THINK YOU DO!
SIVA? LIEUTENANT DEN SIVA?
YES. DEN SIVA HERE.
PLEASE REPORT TO THE INTERROGATION SECTION. COMMANDER KNIFE IS THERE, ABOUT TO BEGIN INTERVIEWING A NEW ARRIVAL... A PRISONER FROM THE ALLIANCE OF FREE PLANETS.
AN ALLIANCE PRISONER? NOT A ZELTRON, IS IT?
A ZELTRON? NO, SIR, WHY--?
NOTHING. NEVER MIND. JUST TELL KNIFE I'LL BE RIGHT ALONG.
AH, THERE YOU ARE, DEN. GOOD OF YOU TO BE SO PROMPT.
MY TIME IS YOURS TO COMMAND, SIR... AND MAY I SAY HOW GOOD IT IS TO SEE YOU UP AND FULLY RECOVERED FROM YOUR WOUND? WE WERE ALL VERY WORRIED, YOU KNOW.
AH, YES... MY WOUND. YOU KNOW, DEN... IT'S AMAZING HOW MUCH PAIN AND INJURY A BODY CAN ENDURE, YET CONTINUE TO LIVE... SOMETIMES EVEN AGAINST ITS OWN INCLINATION.

AH... JUST SO, SIR. IT WILL BE GOOD TO HAVE YOU IN COMMAND AGAIN.

I LOOK FORWARD TO IT MYSELF... BUT YOU SEEM TO HAVE DONE AN EXCELLENT JOB DURING MY ABSENCE.

I NOTICED ON YOUR LAST COMPLETED LOG ENTRY THAT THERE HAD BEEN NO WORD OF THE SQUADRON FROM THE TWELFTH SECTOR IN SOME TIME. HOW DOES THAT SITUATION STAND?

TWO DAYS AGO, WE RECEIVED WORD ON WHAT WAS BELIEVED TO BE A DEAD WORLD IN AN ALLIANCE SYSTEM. THEY WERE ABOUT TO ENGAGE AN ENEMY WHO HAD UNEXPECTEDLY APPEARED, STRONGLY ENTRENCHED ON THAT WORLD AND FAR SUPERIOR TO THEM IN NUMBERS AND FIREPOWER.

THERE WAS NEVER A SECOND MESSAGE, SIR.

THE ENEMY THIS TRANSMISSION DESCRIBED... WERE THEY ALLIANCE MEMBERS?

NO, SIR. THEY WERE... THE OLD ENEMY, SIR.

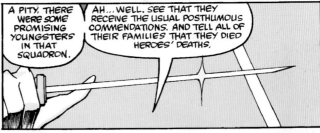

A PITY. THERE WERE SOME PROMISING YOUNGSTERS IN THAT SQUADRON.

AH... WELL. SEE THAT THEY RECEIVE THE USUAL POSTHUMOUS COMMENDATIONS. AND TELL ALL OF THEIR FAMILIES THAT THEY DIED HEROES' DEATHS.

AND NOW... TO NEWER BUSINESS... AND OUR NEWER ENEMY.

JUST GREAT... WE FLY THROUGH THE TRENWYTH SYSTEM, KNOWING THAT ALL THE WORLDS HERE ARE DEAD, AND THAT IT'S THE SAFEST, MOST DIRECT WAY TO GET YOU FOUR BOYS HOME TO ZELTROS...

AND WE STILL MANAGE TO COME OUT OF HYPERSPACE RIGHT INTO THE MIDDLE OF A PITCHED BATTLE, AND CATCH A STRAY BURST FROM AN ENERGY CANNON...

AH... YOUR HIGHNESS? PRINCESS LEIA?

...THAT TAKES OUT ONE OF OUR STABILIZERS AND ASSURES THAT WE WON'T BE GOING ANYWHERE FOR AS MANY DAYS AS IT TAKES US TO FIX IT.

WE... RECOGNIZED SOME OF THE SHIPS AS BEING FROM NAGI... BUT WHAT ABOUT THE ENEMY? WERE THEY ALLIANCE SHIPS? WERE THEY FROM TRENWYTH?

TRENWYTH'S BEEN DEAD FOR TOO LONG TO BE SENDING UP ANYTHING BUT MEMORIES AND HISTORY LESSONS. LOOKS LIKE THE NAGAI BROUGHT A FEW ENEMIES OF THEIR OWN INTO THIS SYSTEM...

THOSE ARE PROBABLY SOME OF THEIR BODIES DOWN THERE, AMONG ALL THE NAGAI...

SO MAYBE EVERYONE HERE DIED IN THE BATTLE. BUT LET'S NOT COUNT ON IT.

LOOK FOR A LARGE SHELTERED AREA TO SET DOWN, AND WE'LL ALL STAY UNDER COVER UNTIL WE'RE SURE OF THE SITUATION HERE... OR READY TO LEAVE.

STANDARD, VERY CAUTIOUS EXPLORATION FOR PARTS TO FIX THE SHIP WITH, OR SURVIVORS WHO CAN TELL US WHAT HAPPENED HERE ONLY. NOTHING MORE.

YES, MA'AM.

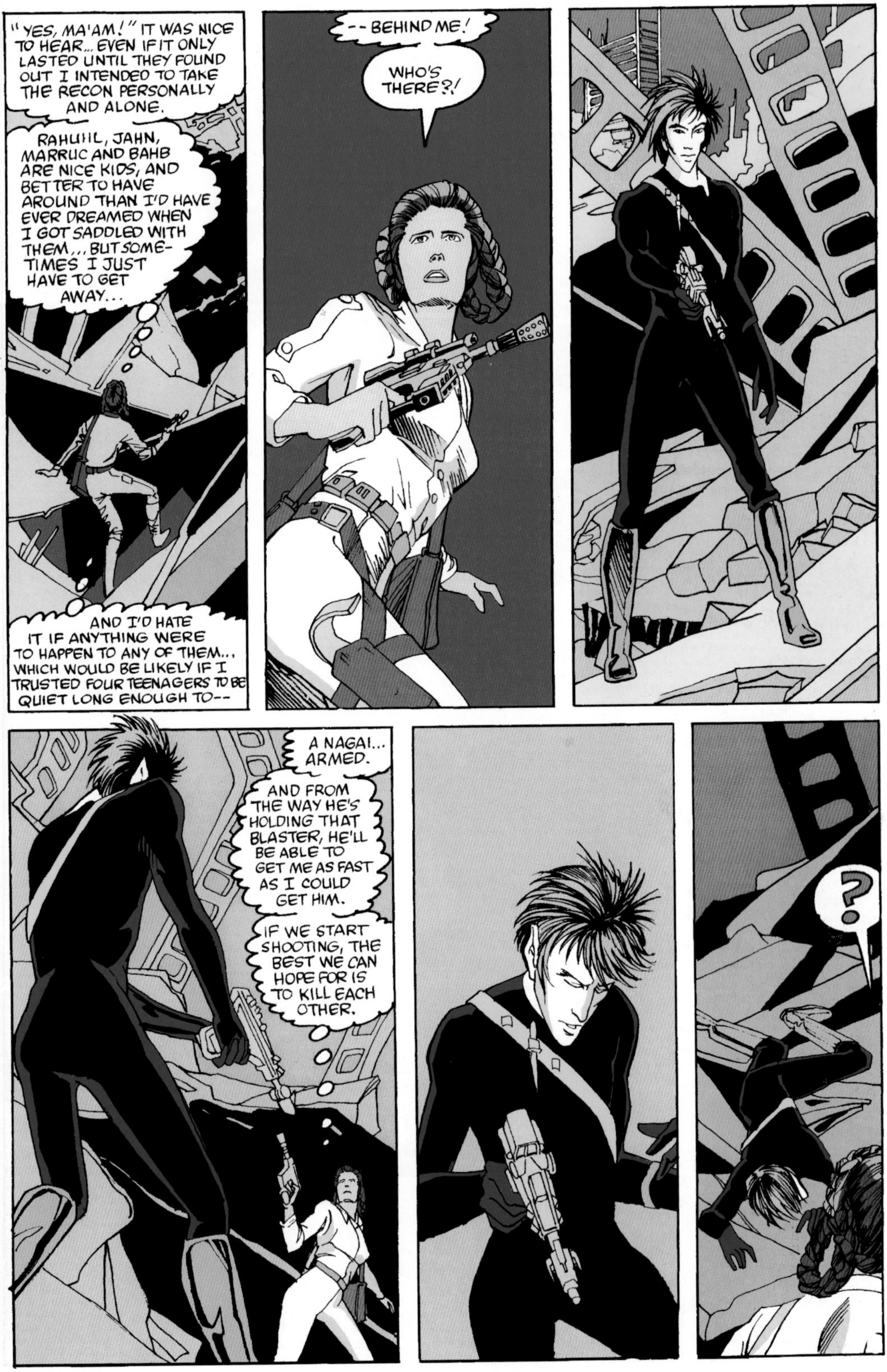

"YES, MA'AM!" IT WAS NICE TO HEAR... EVEN IF IT ONLY LASTED UNTIL THEY FOUND OUT I INTENDED TO TAKE THE RECON PERSONALLY AND ALONE.
RAHUHL, JAHN, MARRUC AND BAHB ARE NICE KIDS, AND BETTER TO HAVE AROUND THAN I'D HAVE EVER DREAMED WHEN I GOT SADDLED WITH THEM... BUT SOMETIMES I JUST HAVE TO GET AWAY...
AND I'D HATE IT IF ANYTHING WERE TO HAPPEN TO ANY OF THEM... WHICH WOULD BE LIKELY IF I TRUSTED FOUR TEENAGERS TO BE QUIET LONG ENOUGH TO--
--BEHIND ME!
WHO'S THERE?!
A NAGAI... ARMED.
AND FROM THE WAY HE'S HOLDING THAT BLASTER, HE'LL BE ABLE TO GET ME AS FAST AS I COULD GET HIM.
IF WE START SHOOTING, THE BEST WE CAN HOPE FOR IS TO KILL EACH OTHER.
?

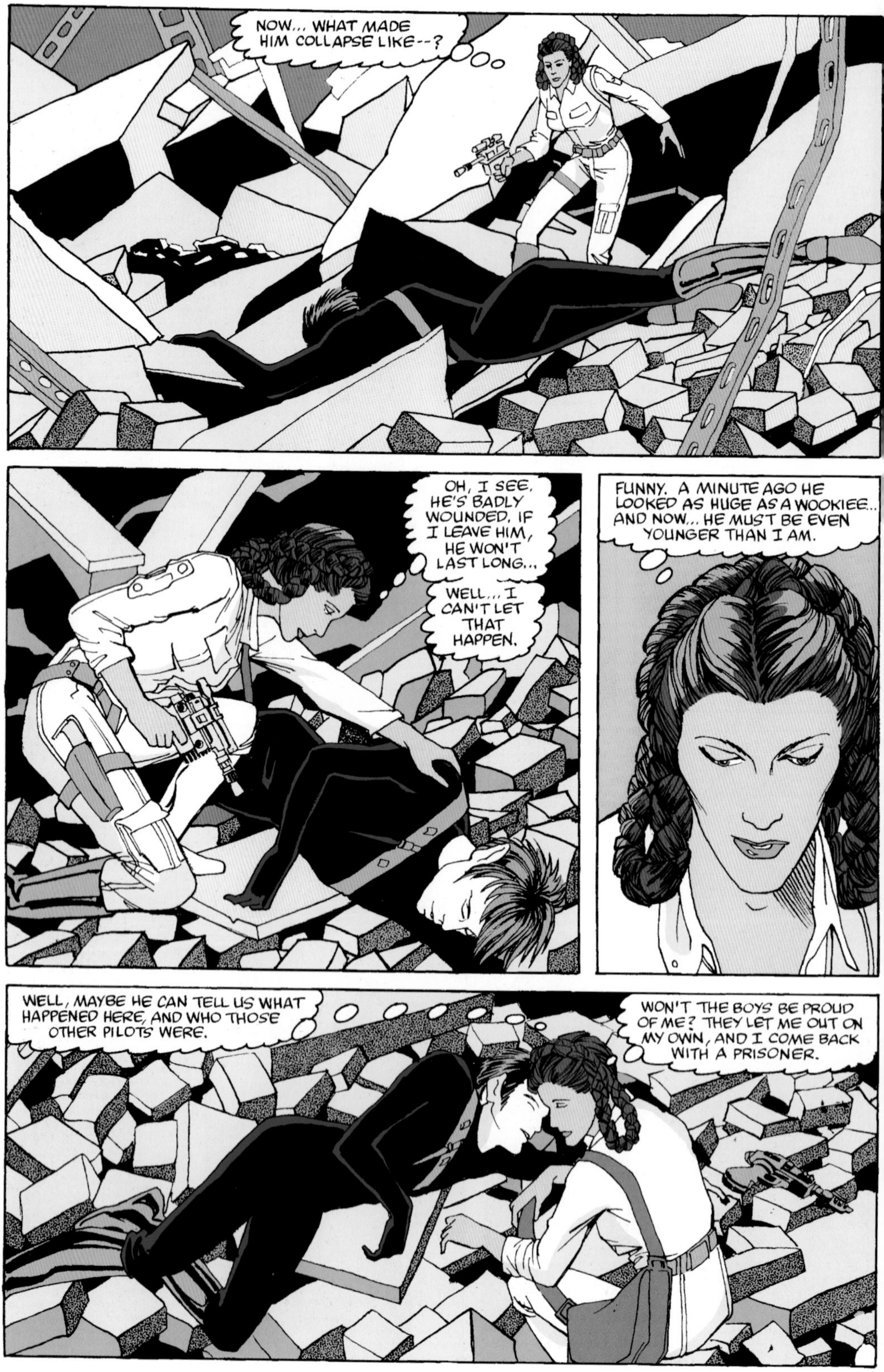

NOW... WHAT MADE HIM COLLAPSE LIKE--?
OH, I SEE. HE'S BADLY WOUNDED. IF I LEAVE HIM, HE WON'T LAST LONG...
WELL... I CAN'T LET THAT HAPPEN.
FUNNY. A MINUTE AGO HE LOOKED AS HUGE AS A WOOKIEE... AND NOW... HE MUST BE EVEN YOUNGER THAN I AM.
WELL, MAYBE HE CAN TELL US WHAT HAPPENED HERE, AND WHO THOSE OTHER PILOTS WERE.
WON'T THE BOYS BE PROUD OF ME? THEY LET ME OUT ON MY OWN, AND I COME BACK WITH A PRISONER.

I THINK HE'S WAKING UP.

ABOUT TIME.

HE DOESN'T LOOK SO TOUGH.

NOT MANY PEOPLE WOULD RAHUHL, IN HIS SITUATION.

BUT WE THOUGHT NAGAI WERE SOME KIND OF SUPERHUMAN MONSTERS...AFTER WHAT ONE OF THEM DID TO DANI...

AND ONE OF THEM KILLED KIRO.

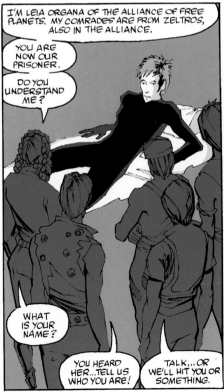

I'M LEIA ORGANA OF THE ALLIANCE OF FREE PLANETS. MY COMRADES ARE FROM ZELTROS, ALSO IN THE ALLIANCE.

YOU ARE NOW OUR PRISONER.

DO YOU UNDERSTAND ME?

WHAT IS YOUR NAME?

YOU HEARD HER...TELL US WHO YOU ARE!

TALK...OR WE'LL HIT YOU OR SOMETHING.

UH...I DON'T THINK HE CAN UNDERSTAND US.

HAH! NAGAI CAN SPEAK GALACTIC STANDARD! KNIFE SPOKE IT!

BUT KNIFE WAS AN OFFICER. THIS ONE'S PROBABLY JUST A RANK AND FILE TROOPER.

AND HE'S PROBABLY EXTREMELY HOSTILE. HE'S THE ONLY LIVE NAGAI-- AND BARELY LIVING WHEN I FOUND HIM-- WE'VE SEEN ON TRENWYTH.

THINK OF HOW MANY OF THE OTHER SPECIES WE'VE SEEN MOVING AROUND OUTSIDE SINCE I BROUGHT OUR FRIEND HERE.

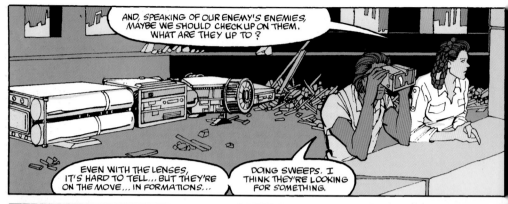

AND, SPEAKING OF OUR ENEMY'S ENEMIES, MAYBE WE SHOULD CHECK UP ON THEM. WHAT ARE THEY UP TO?

EVEN WITH THE LENSES, IT'S HARD TO TELL... BUT THEY'RE ON THE MOVE... IN FORMATIONS...

DOING SWEEPS. I THINK THEY'RE LOOKING FOR SOMETHING.

PROBABLY NAGAI SURVIVORS.

LITTLE AS OUR FRIEND APPRECIATES IT, HE'S PROBABLY EXTREMELY LUCKY TO BE HIDDEN HERE WITH US.

458

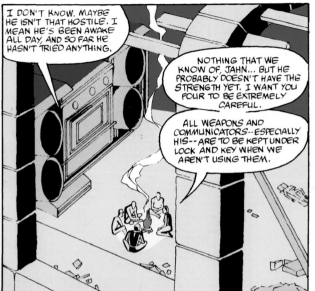

I DON'T KNOW. MAYBE HE ISN'T THAT HOSTILE. I MEAN HE'S BEEN AWAKE ALL DAY, AND SO FAR HE HASN'T TRIED ANYTHING.

NOTHING THAT WE KNOW OF, JAHN... BUT HE PROBABLY DOESN'T HAVE THE STRENGTH YET. I WANT YOU FOUR TO BE EXTREMELY CAREFUL.

ALL WEAPONS AND COMMUNICATORS--ESPECIALLY HIS--ARE TO BE KEPT UNDER LOCK AND KEY WHEN WE AREN'T USING THEM.

HEY! YOUR HIGHNESS! WHERE ARE YOU GOING?

WHERE YOU THINK, BAHB?

HE MAY BE AN ENEMY... BUT HE'S ALSO SICK AND HURT. WE CAN'T VERY WELL STARVE HIM.

I'VE BROUGHT YOU SOME DINNER. NOTHING FANCY, BUT IT'S GOOD AND THERE'S PLENTY OF IT. IT'S WHAT WE'RE HAVING.

REALLY. NO STRINGS ATTACHED. NO DRUGS IN IT, AND I WON'T TRY TO INTERROGATE YOU OR ANYTHING IN RETURN FOR IT.

STOP SCOWLING AT ME. I KNOW YOU CAN'T UNDERSTAND MY SPEECH... BUT SURELY YOU CAN UNDERSTAND A CONCEPT LIKE FOOD.

I KNOW YOU NAGAI HAVE TO EAT-- KNIFE ALWAYS DID, AND YOU'LL NEVER GET YOUR STRENGTH BACK IF YOU DON'T.

LOOK, IF YOU'RE TOO PROUD TO EAT WITH ME WATCHING, FINE. I WANT TO FINISH MY OWN DINNER ANYWAY.

BUT WE'RE GOING TO COUNT THE DISHES WHEN WE GET THEM BACK FROM YOU...

459

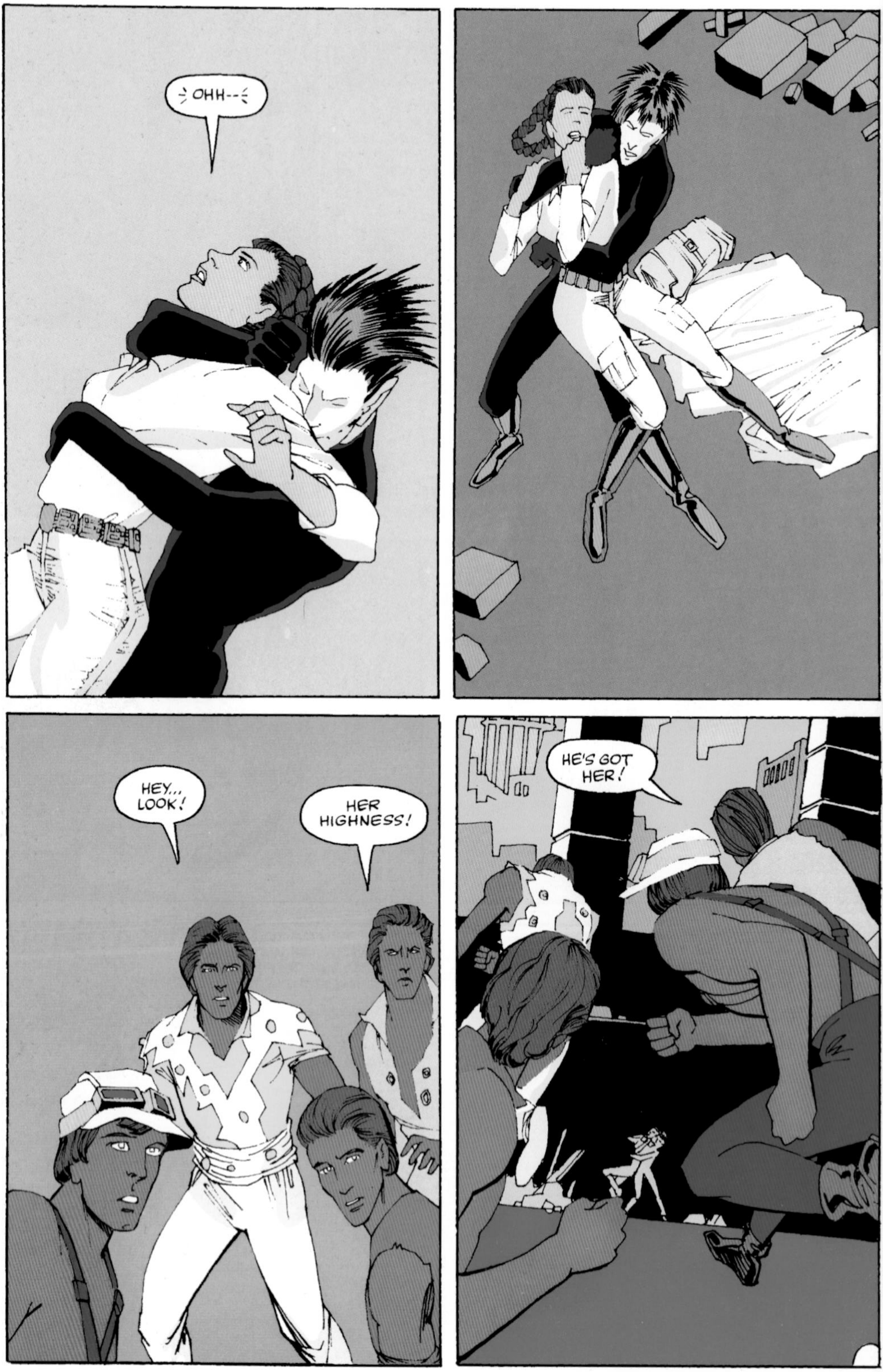
OHH--
HEY... LOOK!
HER HIGHNESS!
HE'S GOT HER!

LET GO OF HER‚!!

HELP ME, YOU GUYS! HE'S TOO STRONG--!

≥MMMPH≥

THIS IS CRAZY! HE LOST SO MUCH BLOOD! HOW CAN HE BE THIS STRONG?

JAHN... NO ONE'S EVER REALLY... TESTED NAGAI... FOR STRENGTH BEFORE, Y'KNOW...

≥GASP≥

ARE YOU OKAY, YOUR HIGHNESS?

I...WILL BE...AS SOON AS I... GET MY BREATH BACK... RAHUHL...

OKAY, BAHB... MARRUC AN' ME HAVE HIS ARMS, NOW YOU GET HIS--!

≥OOGKH≥

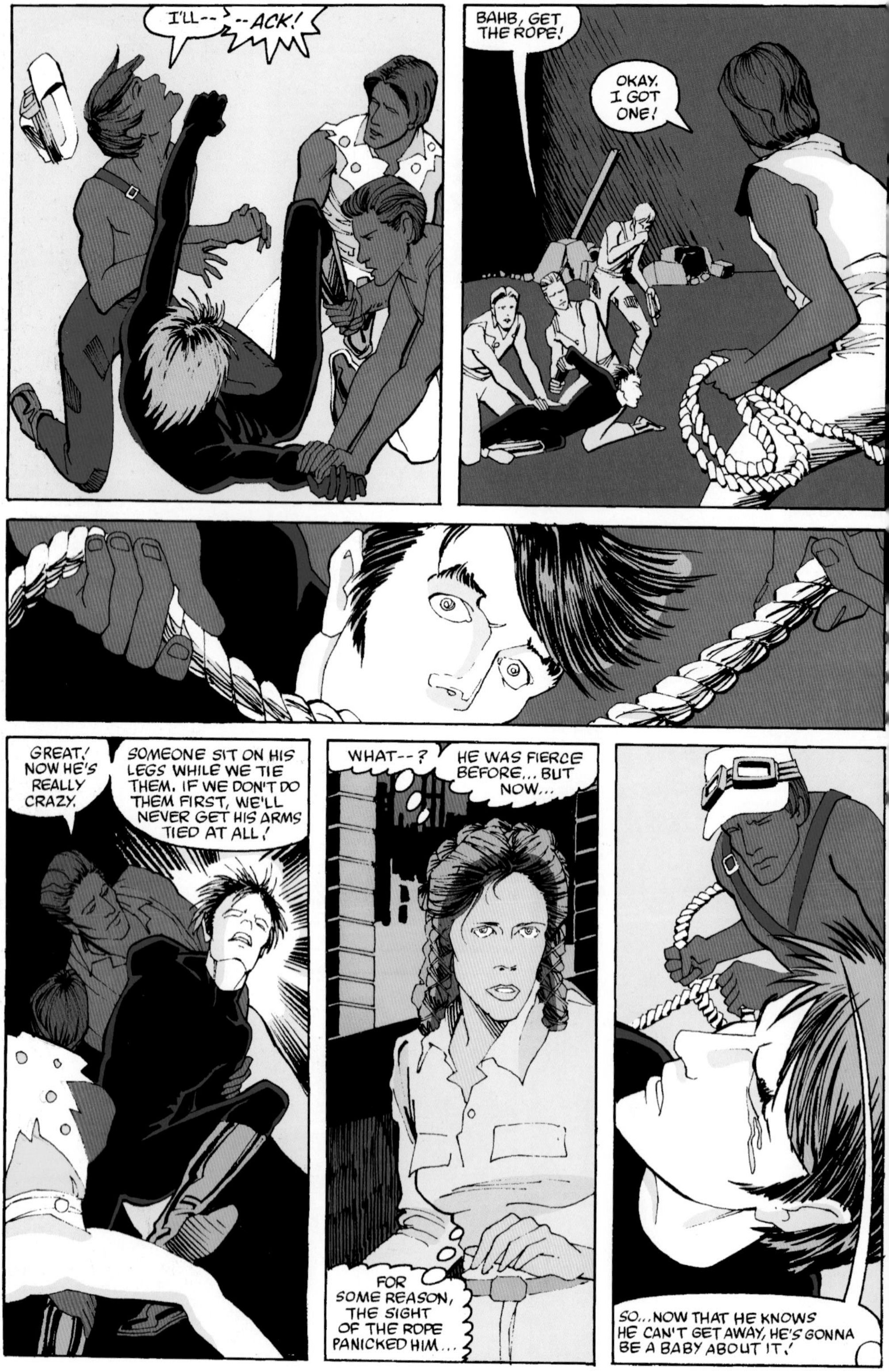
I'LL--
--ACK!
BAHB, GET THE ROPE!
OKAY. I GOT ONE!
GREAT! NOW HE'S REALLY CRAZY.
SOMEONE SIT ON HIS LEGS WHILE WE TIE THEM. IF WE DON'T DO THEM FIRST, WE'LL NEVER GET HIS ARMS TIED AT ALL!
WHAT--?
HE WAS FIERCE BEFORE... BUT NOW...
FOR SOME REASON, THE SIGHT OF THE ROPE PANICKED HIM...
SO... NOW THAT HE KNOWS HE CAN'T GET AWAY, HE'S GONNA BE A BABY ABOUT IT!

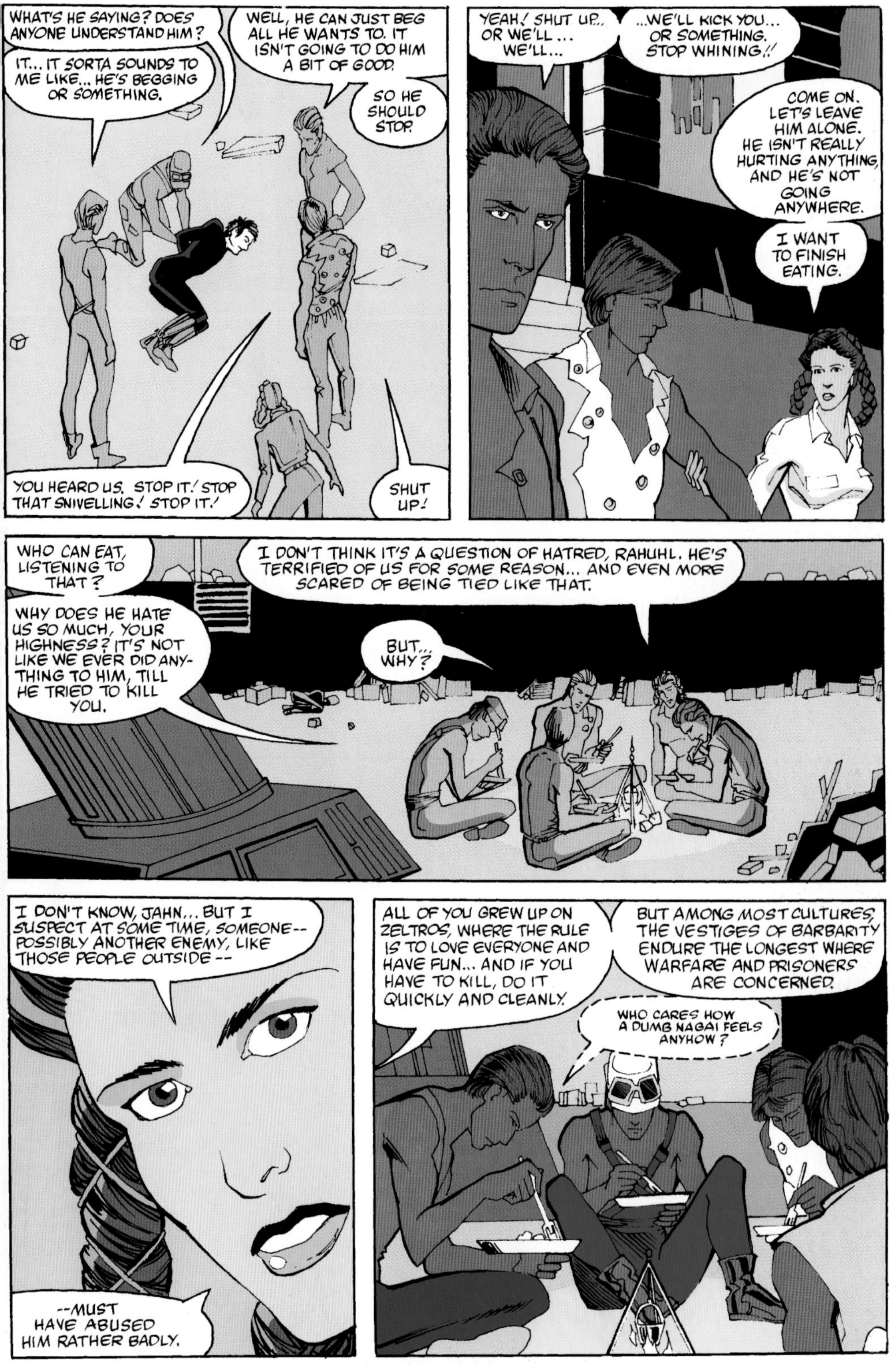

WHAT'S HE SAYING? DOES ANYONE UNDERSTAND HIM?
IT... IT SORTA SOUNDS TO ME LIKE... HE'S BEGGING OR SOMETHING.
WELL, HE CAN JUST BEG ALL HE WANTS TO. IT ISN'T GOING TO DO HIM A BIT OF GOOD.
SO HE SHOULD STOP.
YOU HEARD US. STOP IT! STOP THAT SNIVELLING! STOP IT!
SHUT UP!
YEAH! SHUT UP.. OR WE'LL ... WE'LL...
...WE'LL KICK YOU... OR SOMETHING. STOP WHINING!!
COME ON. LET'S LEAVE HIM ALONE. HE ISN'T REALLY HURTING ANYTHING, AND HE'S NOT GOING ANYWHERE.
I WANT TO FINISH EATING.
WHO CAN EAT, LISTENING TO THAT?
WHY DOES HE HATE US SO MUCH, YOUR HIGHNESS? IT'S NOT LIKE WE EVER DID ANYTHING TO HIM, TILL HE TRIED TO KILL YOU.
I DON'T THINK IT'S A QUESTION OF HATRED, RAHUHL. HE'S TERRIFIED OF US FOR SOME REASON... AND EVEN MORE SCARED OF BEING TIED LIKE THAT.
BUT... WHY?
I DON'T KNOW, JAHN... BUT I SUSPECT AT SOME TIME, SOMEONE-- POSSIBLY ANOTHER ENEMY, LIKE THOSE PEOPLE OUTSIDE --
--MUST HAVE ABUSED HIM RATHER BADLY.
ALL OF YOU GREW UP ON ZELTROS, WHERE THE RULE IS TO LOVE EVERYONE AND HAVE FUN... AND IF YOU HAVE TO KILL, DO IT QUICKLY AND CLEANLY.
BUT AMONG MOST CULTURES, THE VESTIGES OF BARBARITY ENDURE THE LONGEST WHERE WARFARE AND PRISONERS ARE CONCERNED.
WHO CARES HOW A DUMB NAGAI FEELS ANYHOW?

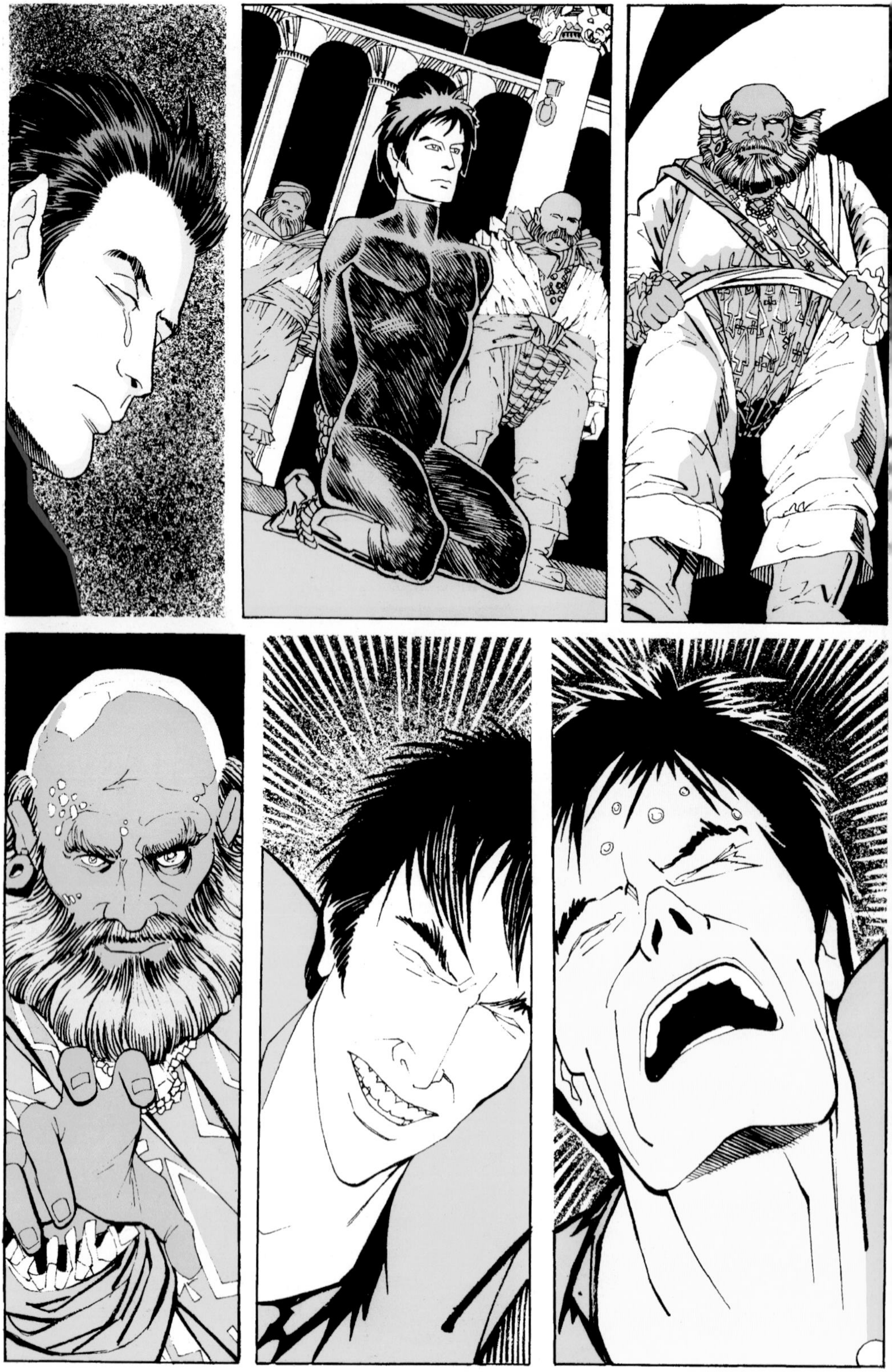

I CANNOT STAND LISTENING TO THAT FOR ANOTHER *SECOND.*

IT'S GONE ON LONG ENOUGH.

YOU BOYS CAN SAY YOU TOLD ME SO, IF ANYTHING GOES WRONG, BUT--!

WHERE ARE YOU GOING?

I AM GOING, MARRUC, TO PUT A STOP TO THAT CRYING!

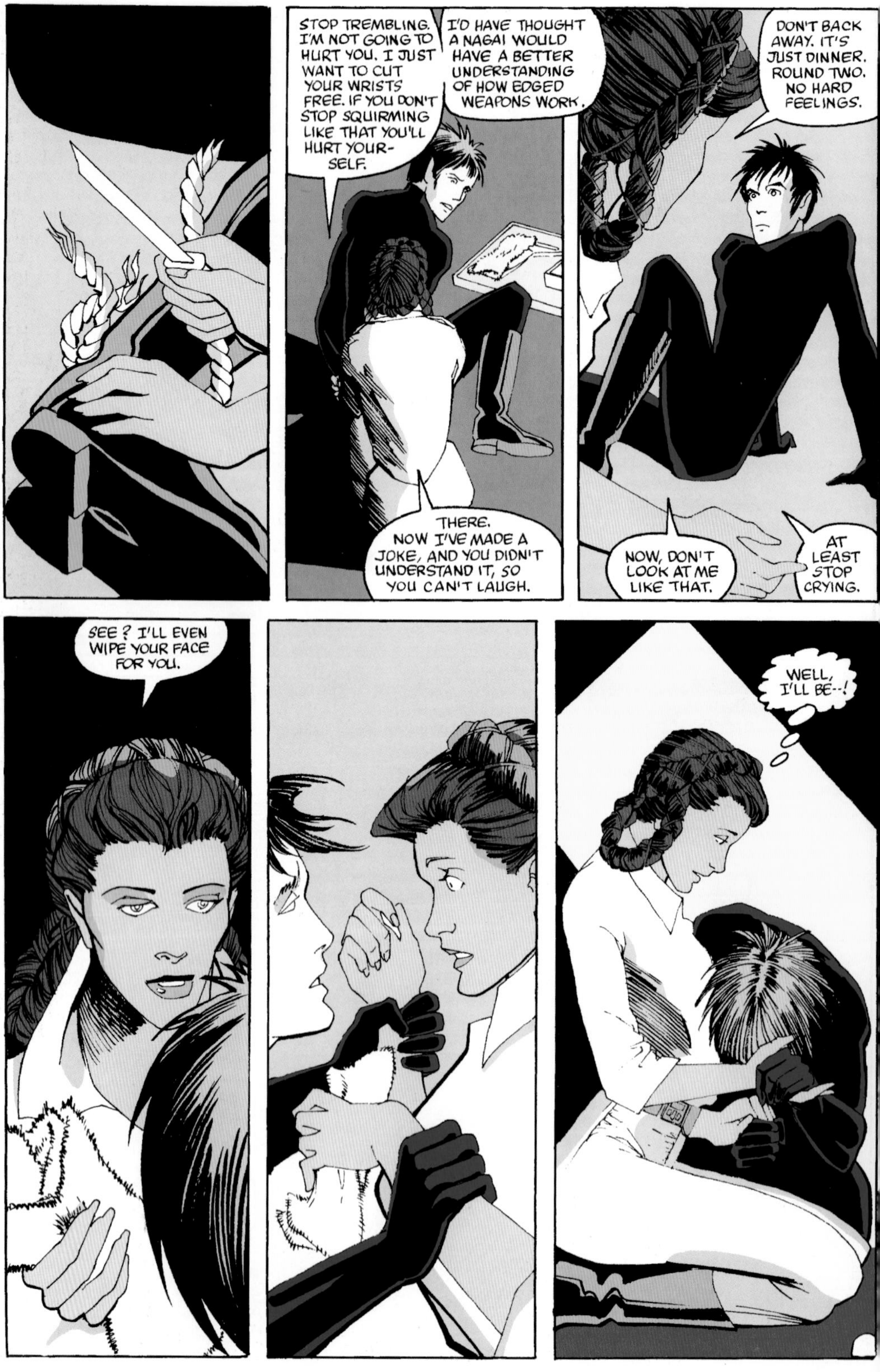
STOP TREMBLING. I'M NOT GOING TO HURT YOU. I JUST WANT TO CUT YOUR WRISTS FREE. IF YOU DON'T STOP SQUIRMING LIKE THAT YOU'LL HURT YOURSELF.
I'D HAVE THOUGHT A NAGAI WOULD HAVE A BETTER UNDERSTANDING OF HOW EDGED WEAPONS WORK.
THERE. NOW I'VE MADE A JOKE, AND YOU DIDN'T UNDERSTAND IT, SO YOU CAN'T LAUGH.
DON'T BACK AWAY. IT'S JUST DINNER. ROUND TWO. NO HARD FEELINGS.
NOW, DON'T LOOK AT ME LIKE THAT.
AT LEAST STOP CRYING.
SEE? I'LL EVEN WIPE YOUR FACE FOR YOU.
WELL, I'LL BE--!

467

LOOK, YOUR HIGHNESS! SOME OF THE NAGAI *DID* SURVIVE!

SEE, THE OTHER GUYS HAVE THEM AS PRISONERS AND THEY--!

LET ME SEE.

US, TOO!

I'M GLAD...HE'S SLEEPING THROUGH THIS.

THOSE WERE PROBABLY FRIENDS OF HIS.

SO...THERE ARE WORSE PEOPLE THAN NAGAI OUT THERE!

LISTEN TO THOSE GUYS... THEY'RE LAUGHING!

POOR NAGAI.

SO, THERE WE WERE... WITH FOUR HIROMI, A STENAX, TWO LAHSBEES, AND HALF A DOZEN HOOJIBS... PLUS THE GOVERNOR'S FIVE DAUGHTERS... AND ALL SO DRUNK THAT...

HEY, JAHN, HER HIGHNESS SAID NO TORTURING THE PRISONER. THAT INCLUDES NO BORING HIM TO DEATH.

IT'S NOT LIKE HE UNDERSTANDS A WORD YOU'RE SAYING, YOU KNOW.

LUCKY HIM.

SO, WHEN IT TURNED OUT THAT THE GUY IN THE *STORE* REMEMBERED WHO'D BOUGHT THE WINE, AND THEN THE GOVERNOR CAME LOOKING FOR US...

...WELL, IT SEEMED LIKE AS GOOD A TIME AS ANY TO FIND OUT WHAT LIFE ON OTHER PLANETS WAS LIKE.

DON'T YOU THINK SO?

YEAH, I KNEW YOU'D AGREE WITH ME.

BUT, REALLY, ZELTROS IS THE MOST FUN OF ANYPLACE. YOU OUGHTTA VISIT THERE, WHEN YOU GET THE CHANCE.

TELL 'EM YOU KNOW ME, AN' YOU'LL HAVE A GREAT TIME. EVEN THE GOVERNOR CAN'T HOLD A GRUDGE FOREVER.

HEY, THEY GOT ANY NICE GIRLS OR GOOD DRINKS WHERE YOU COME FROM?

... CHECKS OUT JUST FINE. AND SINCE THOSE OTHER PEOPLE REALLY DO SEEM TO HAVE LEFT TRENWYTH, WE CAN BE ON OUR WAY JUST AS SOON AS YOU FOUR GET THE GEAR PACKED.

RIGHT.

WHICH LEAVES ME JUST ONE MORE LITTLE THING TO TAKE CARE OF.

LOOK... WE'RE GOING NOW. CAN YOU UNDERSTAND ME?

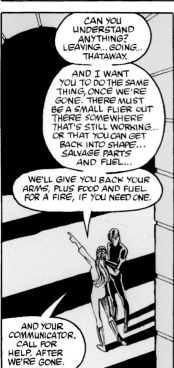

CAN YOU UNDERSTAND ANYTHING? LEAVING... GOING... THATAWAY.

AND I WANT YOU TO DO THE SAME THING, ONCE WE'RE GONE. THERE MUST BE A SMALL FLIER OUT THERE SOMEWHERE THAT'S STILL WORKING... OR THAT YOU CAN GET BACK INTO SHAPE... SALVAGE PARTS AND FUEL...

WE'LL GIVE YOU BACK YOUR ARMS, PLUS FOOD AND FUEL FOR A FIRE, IF YOU NEED ONE.

AND YOUR COMMUNICATOR. CALL FOR HELP, AFTER WE'RE GONE.

LISTEN... I'M AN ALLIANCE OFFICER. WE SHOULD TAKE YOU BACK WITH US, AS A PRISONER... BUT AFTER ALL WE'VE BEEN THROUGH, I JUST CAN'T!

AREN'T YOU GETTING ANY OF THIS? SHOO! SCRAM! GO!

WHAT ARE YOU WAITING FOR?

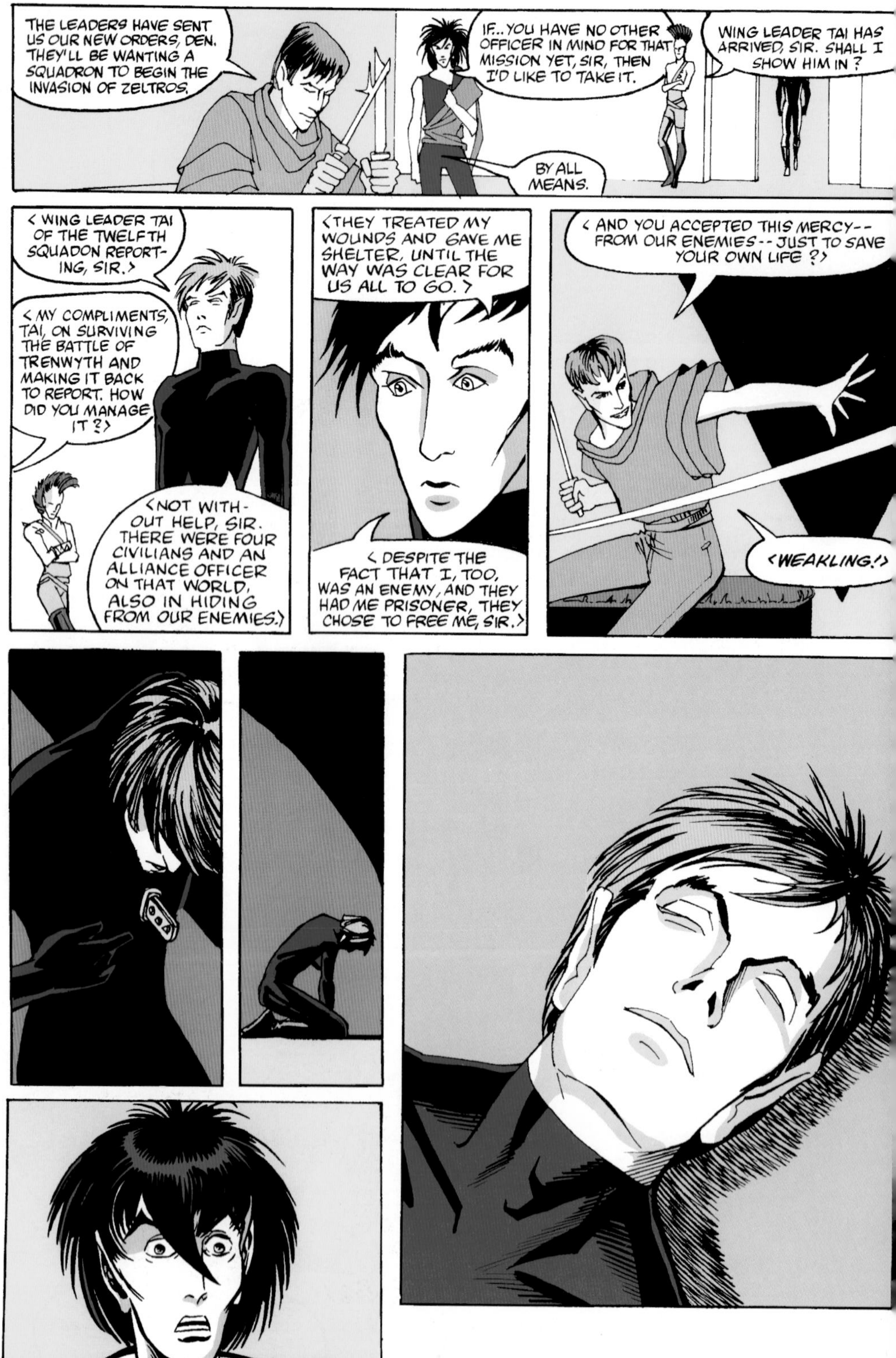
THE LEADERS HAVE SENT US OUR NEW ORDERS, DEN. THEY'LL BE WANTING A SQUADRON TO BEGIN THE INVASION OF ZELTROS.
IF.. YOU HAVE NO OTHER OFFICER IN MIND FOR THAT MISSION YET, SIR, THEN I'D LIKE TO TAKE IT.
BY ALL MEANS.
WING LEADER TAI HAS ARRIVED, SIR. SHALL I SHOW HIM IN ?
< WING LEADER TAI OF THE TWELFTH SQUADON REPORTING, SIR. >
< MY COMPLIMENTS, TAI, ON SURVIVING THE BATTLE OF TRENWYTH AND MAKING IT BACK TO REPORT. HOW DID YOU MANAGE IT ? >
<NOT WITHOUT HELP, SIR. THERE WERE FOUR CIVILIANS AND AN ALLIANCE OFFICER ON THAT WORLD, ALSO IN HIDING FROM OUR ENEMIES.>
<THEY TREATED MY WOUNDS AND GAVE ME SHELTER, UNTIL THE WAY WAS CLEAR FOR US ALL TO GO. >
< DESPITE THE FACT THAT I, TOO, WAS AN ENEMY, AND THEY HAD ME PRISONER, THEY CHOSE TO FREE ME, SIR. >
< AND YOU ACCEPTED THIS MERCY-- FROM OUR ENEMIES-- JUST TO SAVE YOUR OWN LIFE ? >
<WEAKLING!>

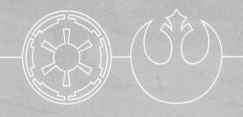

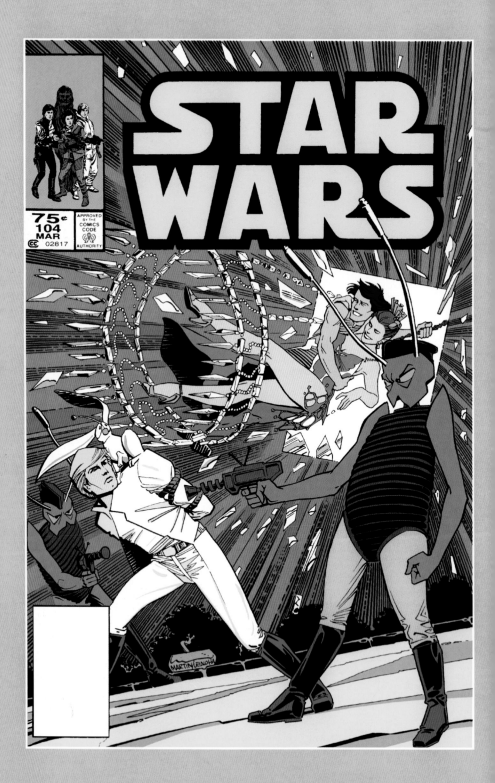

O DUFFY, *writer* CYNTHIA MARTIN, *penciler* NOT THE REAL CINDY, BUT AN INCREDIBLE SIMULATION, *inker* LYNIS OLIVER, *colorist* TOM ORZECHOWSKI, *letterer* ANN NOCENTI, *editor* JIM SHOOTER, *editor in chief*

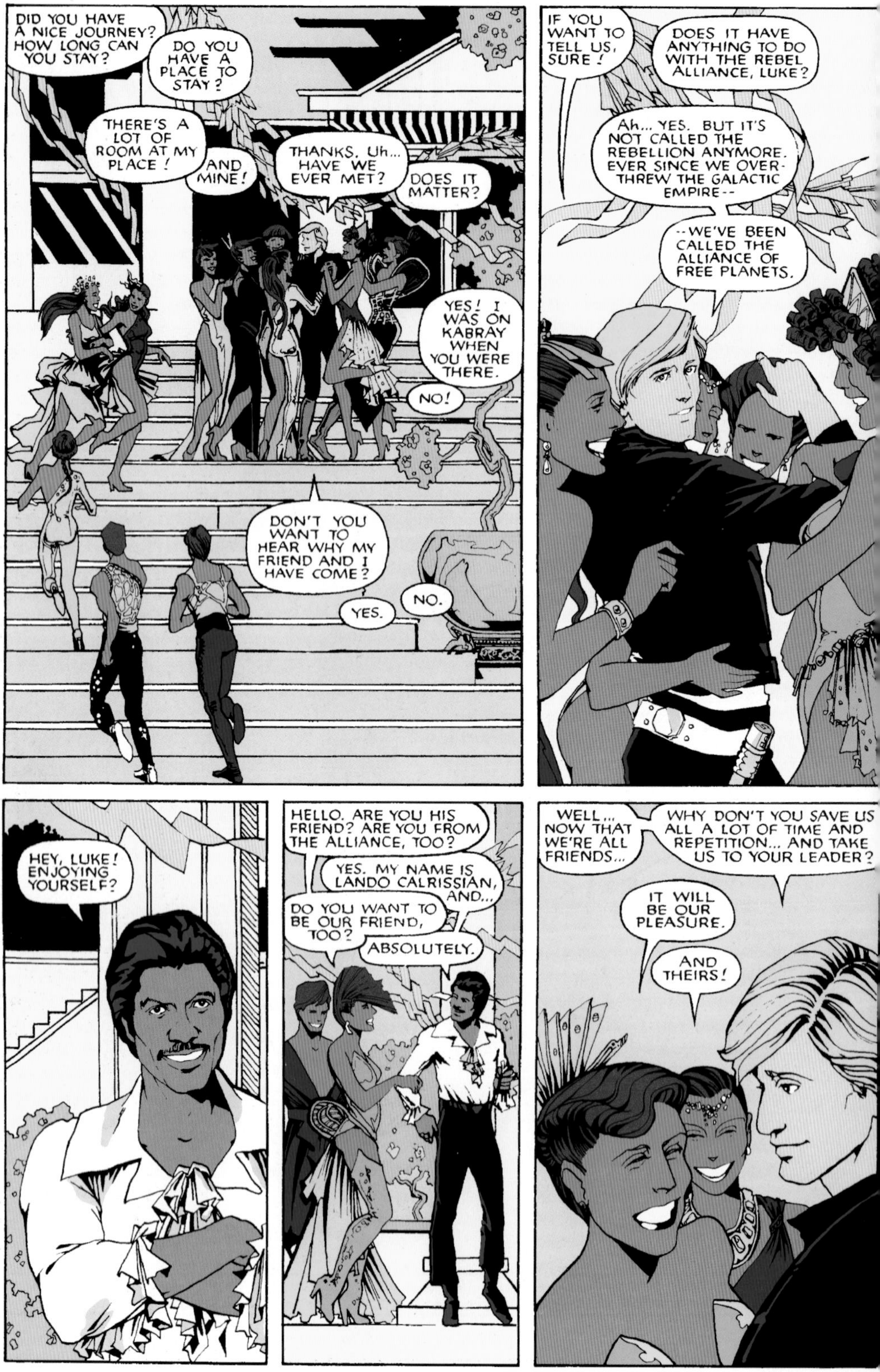
DID YOU HAVE A NICE JOURNEY? HOW LONG CAN YOU STAY?
DO YOU HAVE A PLACE TO STAY?
THERE'S A LOT OF ROOM AT MY PLACE!
AND MINE!
THANKS. Uh... HAVE WE EVER MET?
DOES IT MATTER?
YES! I WAS ON KABRAY WHEN YOU WERE THERE.
NO!
DON'T YOU WANT TO HEAR WHY MY FRIEND AND I HAVE COME?
YES.
NO.
IF YOU WANT TO TELL US, SURE!
DOES IT HAVE ANYTHING TO DO WITH THE REBEL ALLIANCE, LUKE?
Ah... YES. BUT IT'S NOT CALLED THE REBELLION ANYMORE. EVER SINCE WE OVER-THREW THE GALACTIC EMPIRE--
--WE'VE BEEN CALLED THE ALLIANCE OF FREE PLANETS.
HEY, LUKE! ENJOYING YOURSELF?
HELLO. ARE YOU HIS FRIEND? ARE YOU FROM THE ALLIANCE, TOO?
YES. MY NAME IS LANDO CALRISSIAN, AND...
DO YOU WANT TO BE OUR FRIEND, TOO?
ABSOLUTELY.
WELL... NOW THAT WE'RE ALL FRIENDS...
WHY DON'T YOU SAVE US ALL A LOT OF TIME AND REPETITION... AND TAKE US TO YOUR LEADER?
IT WILL BE OUR PLEASURE.
AND THEIRS!

LUKE, LANDO... MAKING YOURSELVES AT HOME, I SEE!

LEIA!

AND US, COMMANDER SKYWALKER-- JAHN, MARRUC, RAHUHL, AND BAHB.

I THOUGHT YOU BOYS WERE EAGER FOR A LITTLE REST HERE AT HOME BE- FORE WE BEGAN OUR MISSION... DID YOU AND LEIA JUST LAND?

LANDO AND I FIGURED YOU'D ARRIVED DAYS AHEAD OF US...

WE WERE SUPPOSED TO... BUT WE RAN INTO SOME RATHER INTERESTING DELAYS ON OUR WAY HERE...

I'LL TELL YOU ABOUT THEM ONCE WE HAVE EVERYONE ASSEMBLED.

GOOD. I WANT TO HEAR IT.

OH! ISN'T THAT HER HIGHNESS-- PRINCESS LEIA ORGANA?

OF COURSE IT IS! JUST LOOK AT HER!

WE'VE WANTED TO MEET YOU FOR THE LONGEST TIME! EVERY- ONE DOES!

YOU'RE EVEN PRETTIER THAN YOUR PICTURE.

HEY, BUZZ OFF! SHE ALREADY KNOWS ALL THE ZELTRONS SHE WANTS TO.

WE'RE ENOUGH ZELTRONS FOR ANYONE!

Oh, GOOD.

YOU JUST LET US KNOW, YOUR HIGHNESS. ANYONE HERE BOTHERS YOU, WE'LL... WE'LL... WE'LL FIX THEM! THAT'S WHAT!

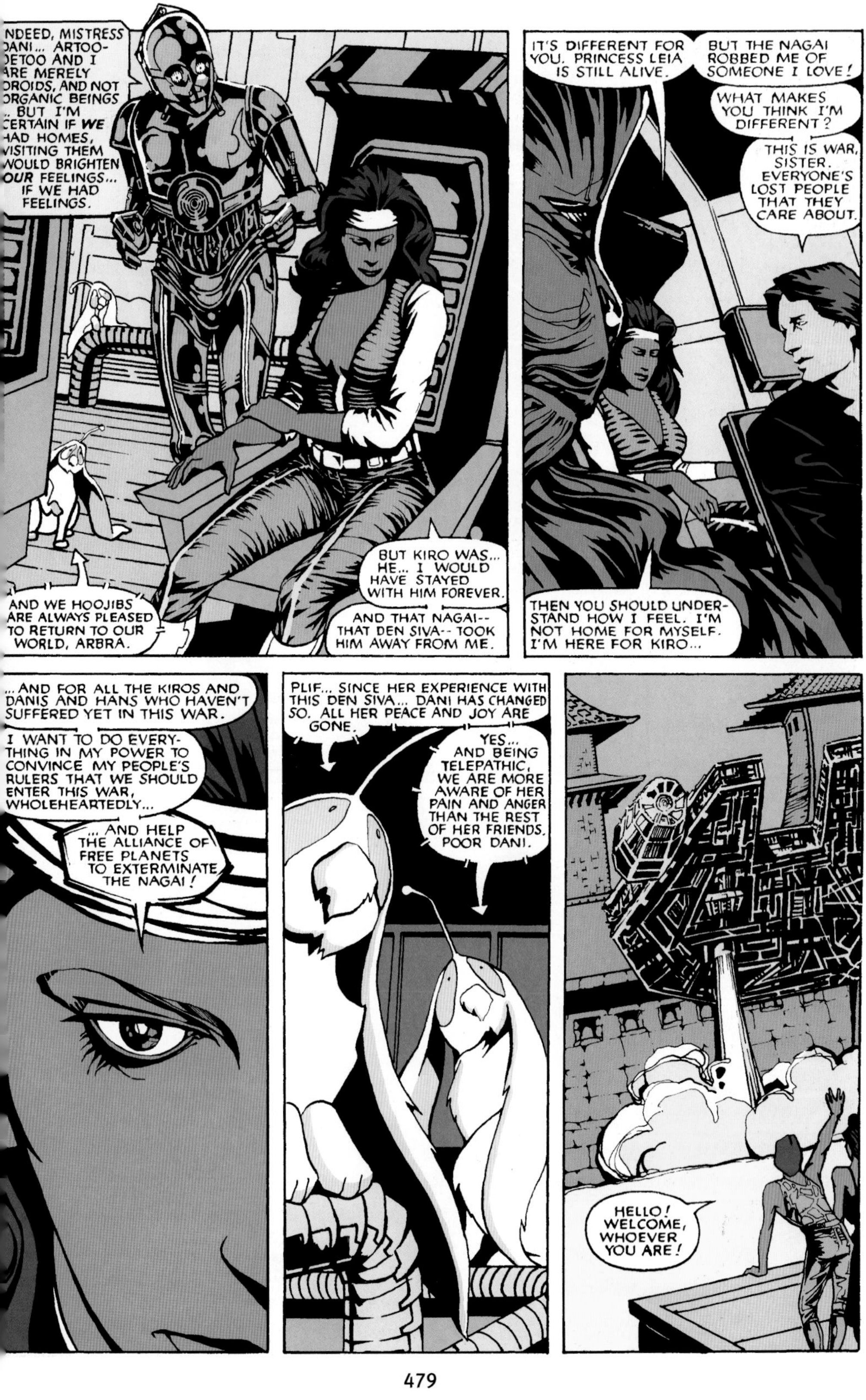
NDEED, MISTRESS DANI... ARTOO-DETOO AND I ARE MERELY DROIDS, AND NOT ORGANIC BEINGS .. BUT I'M CERTAIN IF WE HAD HOMES, VISITING THEM WOULD BRIGHTEN OUR FEELINGS... IF WE HAD FEELINGS.
AND WE HOOJIBS ARE ALWAYS PLEASED TO RETURN TO OUR WORLD, ARBRA.
BUT KIRO WAS... HE... I WOULD HAVE STAYED WITH HIM FOREVER.
AND THAT NAGAI-- THAT DEN SIVA-- TOOK HIM AWAY FROM ME.
IT'S DIFFERENT FOR YOU. PRINCESS LEIA IS STILL ALIVE.
BUT THE NAGAI ROBBED ME OF SOMEONE I LOVE!
WHAT MAKES YOU THINK I'M DIFFERENT?
THIS IS WAR, SISTER. EVERYONE'S LOST PEOPLE THAT THEY CARE ABOUT.
THEN YOU SHOULD UNDERSTAND HOW I FEEL. I'M NOT HOME FOR MYSELF. I'M HERE FOR KIRO...
...AND FOR ALL THE KIROS AND DANIS AND HANS WHO HAVEN'T SUFFERED YET IN THIS WAR.
I WANT TO DO EVERYTHING IN MY POWER TO CONVINCE MY PEOPLE'S RULERS THAT WE SHOULD ENTER THIS WAR, WHOLEHEARTEDLY...
... AND HELP THE ALLIANCE OF FREE PLANETS TO EXTERMINATE THE NAGAI!
PLIF... SINCE HER EXPERIENCE WITH THIS DEN SIVA... DANI HAS CHANGED SO. ALL HER PEACE AND JOY ARE GONE.
YES... AND BEING TELEPATHIC, WE ARE MORE AWARE OF HER PAIN AND ANGER THAN THE REST OF HER FRIENDS. POOR DANI.
HELLO! WELCOME, WHOEVER YOU ARE!

IT'S AS YOU PREDICTED, SIR DEN. THE MILLENNIUM FALCON HAS JUST LANDED ON ZELTROS.

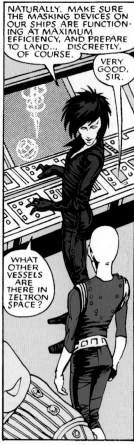

NATURALLY. MAKE SURE THE MASKING DEVICES ON OUR SHIPS ARE FUNCTION-ING AT MAXIMUM EFFICIENCY, AND PREPARE TO LAND... DISCREETLY, OF COURSE.

VERY GOOD, SIR.

WHAT OTHER VESSELS ARE THERE IN ZELTRON SPACE?

ANY OF THEM?

NONE THAT WE CAN DETECT, SIR. JUST A FEW SMALL, INSIGNIFICANT SHIPS.

WE TAKE THEM TO BE TRADING VESSELS, SIR. OR PLEASURE CRAFT. TOO SMALL FOR ANYTHING ELSE.

WELL, FIRST OFFICER HIROG, MAKE YOUR REPORT. HAS THAT BIG SHIP WE SPOTTED LEFT THE AREA YET?

WAS IT ANY-THING WE SHOULD ...er... WORRY ABOUT?

IT'S GONE, CAPTAIN HOOKYR... AND I DON'T THINK IT WAS ANY THREAT TO US, ANY MORE THAN THOSE OTHER SHIPS THAT WENT BY.

SO BIG AND CLUMSY... IT MUST HAVE BEEN A PLEASURE CRAFT, OR A TRADING VESSEL.

EXCELLENT. Mr. TAHKAY, SET A COURSE FOR ZELTROS. WE CONQUER IT TODAY...

...FOR CONQUEST IS THE GLORIOUS DESTINY OF OUR PEOPLE -- THE HIROMI!!!

OH, IT DOES MY HEART SUCH GOOD TO GREET YOU, COMMANDER SKYWALKER AND GENERAL CALRISSIAN. I CANNOT REMEMBER HAVING MORE WELCOME VISITORS AT ANY TIME DURING OUR REIGN.

CAN YOU, LEONIE?

NO, I CAN'T, ARNO... NOR NICER LOOKING ONES.

AND WITH SUCH SMILES, TOO.

AND SEE HOW HAPPY THEIR ARRIVAL HAS MADE OUR PEOPLE.

WHAT PLEASES OUR PEOPLE PLEASES ME. LET US HONOR OUR GUESTS WITH A PARTY.

EXCELLENT IDEA. PARTIES ALWAYS PLEASE ME.

PARTIES PLEASE EVERYONE!

YOUR MAJESTIES, WE'RE MORE THAN FLATTERED BY YOUR SUGGESTION...

WE'RE HONORED!

...BUT DON'T YOU WISH TO HEAR WHAT BUSINESS BROUGHT US, BEFORE YOU EXTEND SUCH MAGNIFICENT HOSPITALITY?

YES... BUT I THINK YOU DESERVE A PARTY ALREADY...

WE ZELTRONS FAVOR CANDOR, AND ADMIRE IT IN OTHERS.

BUT PLEASE... SATISFY YOUR SCRUPLES. TELL US OF THE LATEST NEWS FROM THE ALLIANCE...

YES. THEN WE CAN CELEBRATE YOUR ARRIVAL WITHOUT DISTRACTIONS!

CELEBRATING OUR ARRIVAL ALREADY?

I DIDN'T THINK YOU EVEN KNEW WE WERE HERE.

RWOORF

HAN!!!

LEIA...

LOOK AT HOW GLAD HER HIGHNESS AND THE GENERAL ARE TO SEE EACH OTHER!

HECK, EVERYONE'S GLAD TO SEE THE GENERAL ...I AM!

MAYBE... BUT DON'T YOU GO TRYING TO KISS HIM...

SPLENDID TO SEE YOU AGAIN, LUKE.

HI, PLIF. I'VE MISSED YOU, TOO.

RARF?

SURE, CHEWBACCA. YOU KNOW WE'RE ALWAYS HAPPY TO SEE YOU!

AND, SURROUNDED BY ZELTRON YOUNG LADIES AGAIN, I SEE.

I'M GETTING USED TO IT.

AH... NOW THAT WE'RE ALL HERE, PERHAPS WE COULD RESUME...

RIGHT. THE SOONER WE RESUME, THE SOONER WE CAN FINISH-- AND PARTY!

MAJESTIES... THE UNPLEASANT TRUTH IS THAT THE ALLIANCE IS AT WAR ONCE AGAIN. OUR OLD ENEMIES--

--THE REMNANTS OF THE EMPIRE-- HAVE ALLIED THEMSELVES WITH A FORCE OF RUTHLESS INVADERS KNOWN AS THE KNIVES... OR NAGAI.

ACTUALLY... NOT ALL OF THE NAGAI MAY BE AS BAD AS WE FIRST FEARED.

ON OUR WAY HERE, MY FOUR ATTACHES AND I HAD AN EXPERIENCE WHICH MAY EXPLAIN THEIR INVASION...

... AND EVEN GIVES ME HOPE THAT ONE DAY, WE MAY ACHIEVE PEACE WITH THEM.

THE ONLY PEACE ANY NAGAI DESERVES IS THE PEACE OF THE GRAVE! WE SHOULD KILL THEM ALL, QUICKLY...

DANI--!

AND THE ONLY REASON I SAY THAT IS THAT TORTURE IS NOT THE ZELTRON WAY!

482

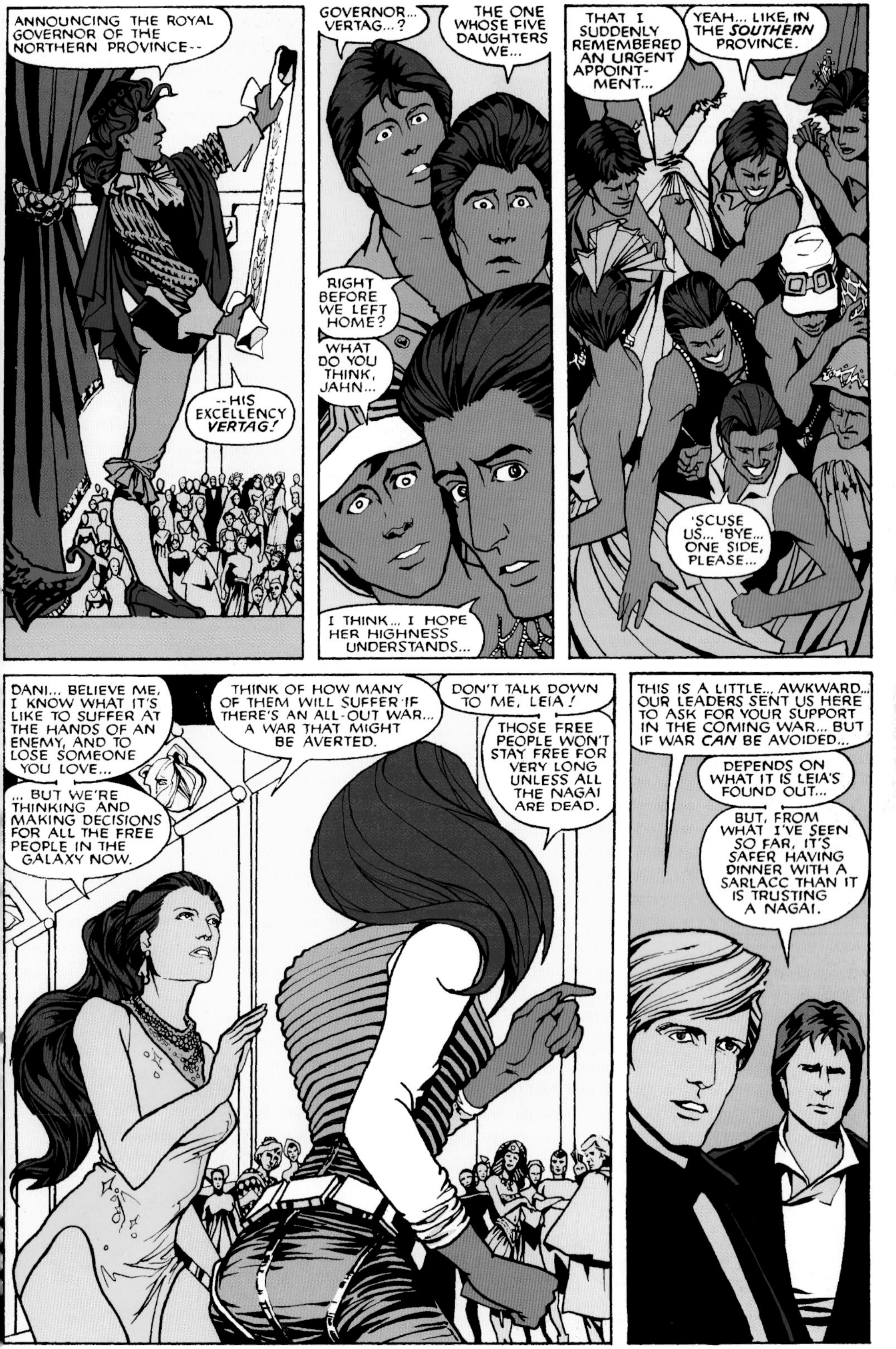
ANNOUNCING THE ROYAL GOVERNOR OF THE NORTHERN PROVINCE--
--HIS EXCELLENCY VERTAG!
GOVERNOR... VERTAG...?
THE ONE WHOSE FIVE DAUGHTERS WE...
RIGHT BEFORE WE LEFT HOME?
WHAT DO YOU THINK, JAHN...
I THINK... I HOPE HER HIGHNESS UNDERSTANDS...
THAT I SUDDENLY REMEMBERED AN URGENT APPOINT-MENT...
YEAH... LIKE, IN THE SOUTHERN PROVINCE.
'SCUSE US... 'BYE... ONE SIDE, PLEASE...
DANI... BELIEVE ME, I KNOW WHAT IT'S LIKE TO SUFFER AT THE HANDS OF AN ENEMY, AND TO LOSE SOMEONE YOU LOVE...
... BUT WE'RE THINKING AND MAKING DECISIONS FOR ALL THE FREE PEOPLE IN THE GALAXY NOW.
THINK OF HOW MANY OF THEM WILL SUFFER IF THERE'S AN ALL-OUT WAR... A WAR THAT MIGHT BE AVERTED.
DON'T TALK DOWN TO ME, LEIA!
THOSE FREE PEOPLE WON'T STAY FREE FOR VERY LONG UNLESS ALL THE NAGAI ARE DEAD.
THIS IS A LITTLE... AWKWARD... OUR LEADERS SENT US HERE TO ASK FOR YOUR SUPPORT IN THE COMING WAR... BUT IF WAR CAN BE AVOIDED...
DEPENDS ON WHAT IT IS LEIA'S FOUND OUT...
BUT, FROM WHAT I'VE SEEN SO FAR, IT'S SAFER HAVING DINNER WITH A SARLACC THAN IT IS TRUSTING A NAGAI.

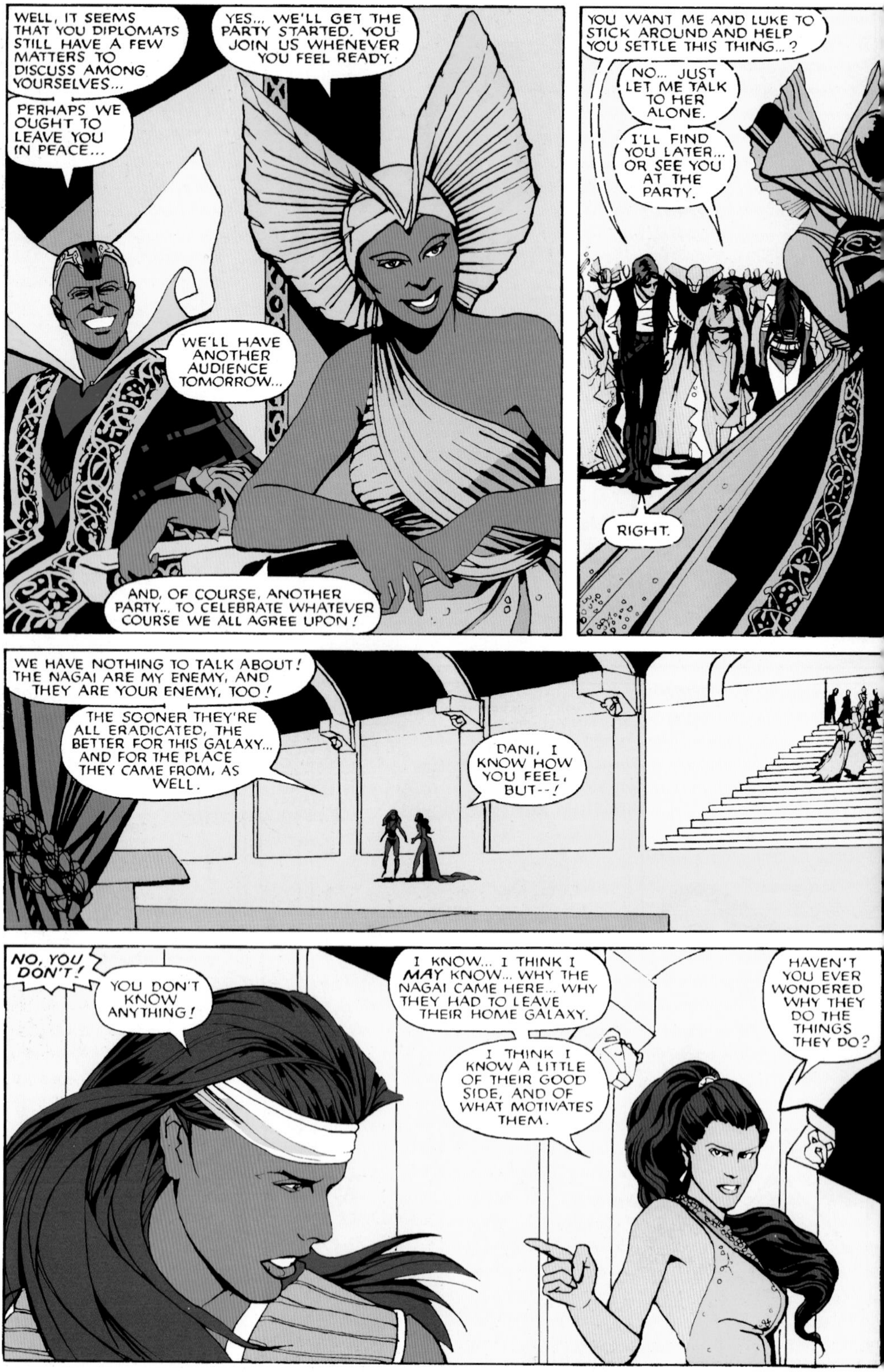
WELL, IT SEEMS THAT YOU DIPLOMATS STILL HAVE A FEW MATTERS TO DISCUSS AMONG YOURSELVES...
PERHAPS WE OUGHT TO LEAVE YOU IN PEACE...
YES... WE'LL GET THE PARTY STARTED. YOU JOIN US WHENEVER YOU FEEL READY.
WE'LL HAVE ANOTHER AUDIENCE TOMORROW...
AND, OF COURSE, ANOTHER PARTY... TO CELEBRATE WHATEVER COURSE WE ALL AGREE UPON!
YOU WANT ME AND LUKE TO STICK AROUND AND HELP YOU SETTLE THIS THING...?
NO... JUST LET ME TALK TO HER ALONE.
I'LL FIND YOU LATER... OR SEE YOU AT THE PARTY.
RIGHT.
WE HAVE NOTHING TO TALK ABOUT! THE NAGAI ARE MY ENEMY, AND THEY ARE YOUR ENEMY, TOO!
THE SOONER THEY'RE ALL ERADICATED, THE BETTER FOR THIS GALAXY... AND FOR THE PLACE THEY CAME FROM, AS WELL.
DANI, I KNOW HOW YOU FEEL, BUT--!
NO, YOU DON'T!
YOU DON'T KNOW ANYTHING!
I KNOW... I THINK I MAY KNOW... WHY THE NAGAI CAME HERE... WHY THEY HAD TO LEAVE THEIR HOME GALAXY.
I THINK I KNOW A LITTLE OF THEIR GOOD SIDE, AND OF WHAT MOTIVATES THEM.
HAVEN'T YOU EVER WONDERED WHY THEY DO THE THINGS THEY DO?

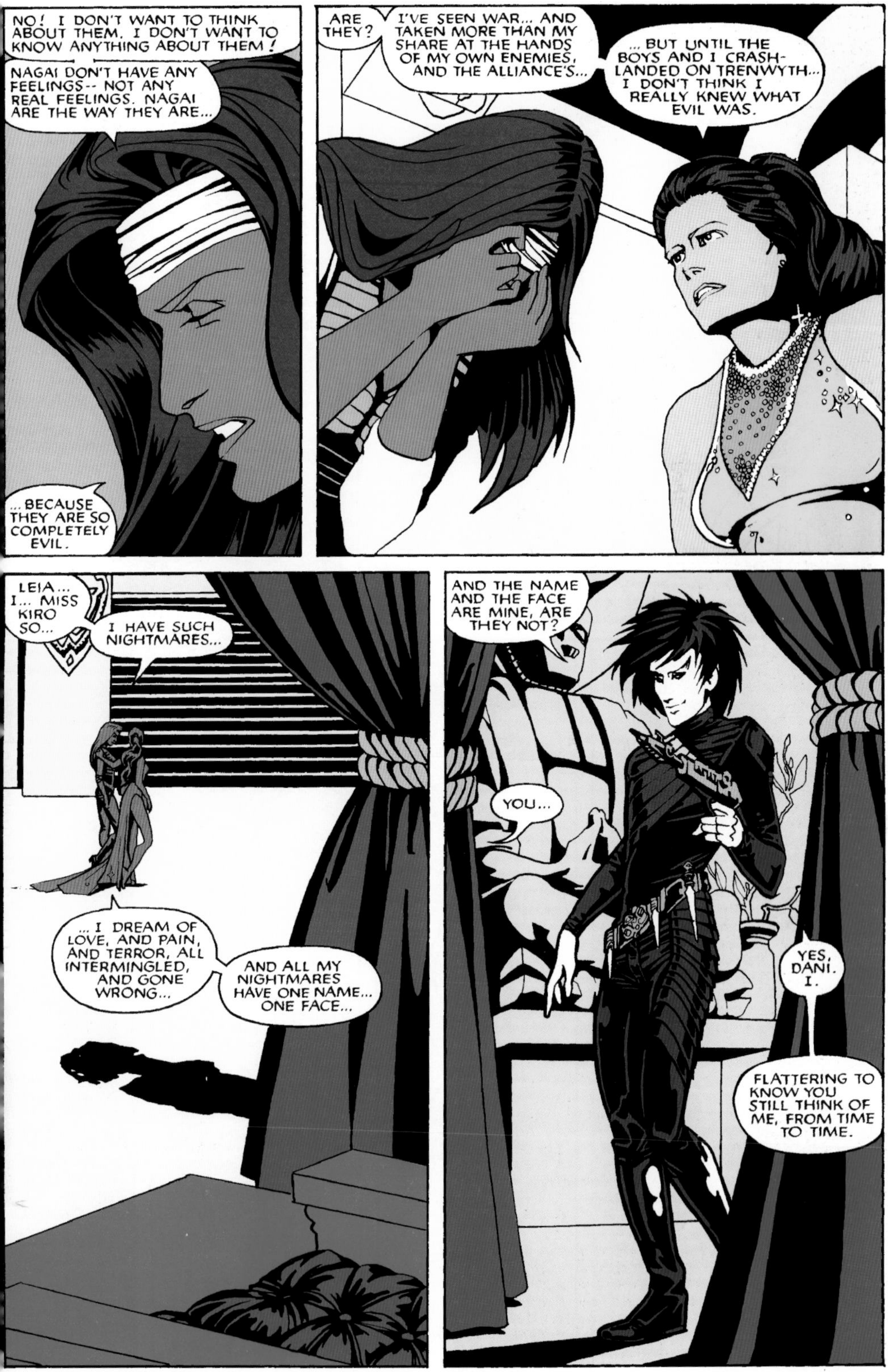
NO! I DON'T WANT TO THINK ABOUT THEM. I DON'T WANT TO KNOW ANYTHING ABOUT THEM!
NAGAI DON'T HAVE ANY FEELINGS-- NOT ANY REAL FEELINGS. NAGAI ARE THE WAY THEY ARE...
...BECAUSE THEY ARE SO COMPLETELY EVIL.
ARE THEY?
I'VE SEEN WAR... AND TAKEN MORE THAN MY SHARE AT THE HANDS OF MY OWN ENEMIES, AND THE ALLIANCE'S...
...BUT UNTIL THE BOYS AND I CRASH-LANDED ON TRENWYTH... I DON'T THINK I REALLY KNEW WHAT EVIL WAS.
LEIA... I... MISS KIRO SO...
I HAVE SUCH NIGHTMARES...
...I DREAM OF LOVE, AND PAIN, AND TERROR, ALL INTERMINGLED, AND GONE WRONG...
AND ALL MY NIGHTMARES HAVE ONE NAME... ONE FACE...
AND THE NAME AND THE FACE ARE MINE, ARE THEY NOT?
YOU...
YES, DANI. I.
FLATTERING TO KNOW YOU STILL THINK OF ME, FROM TIME TO TIME.

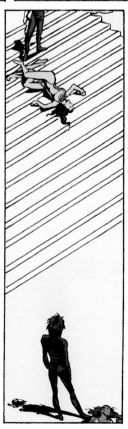

486

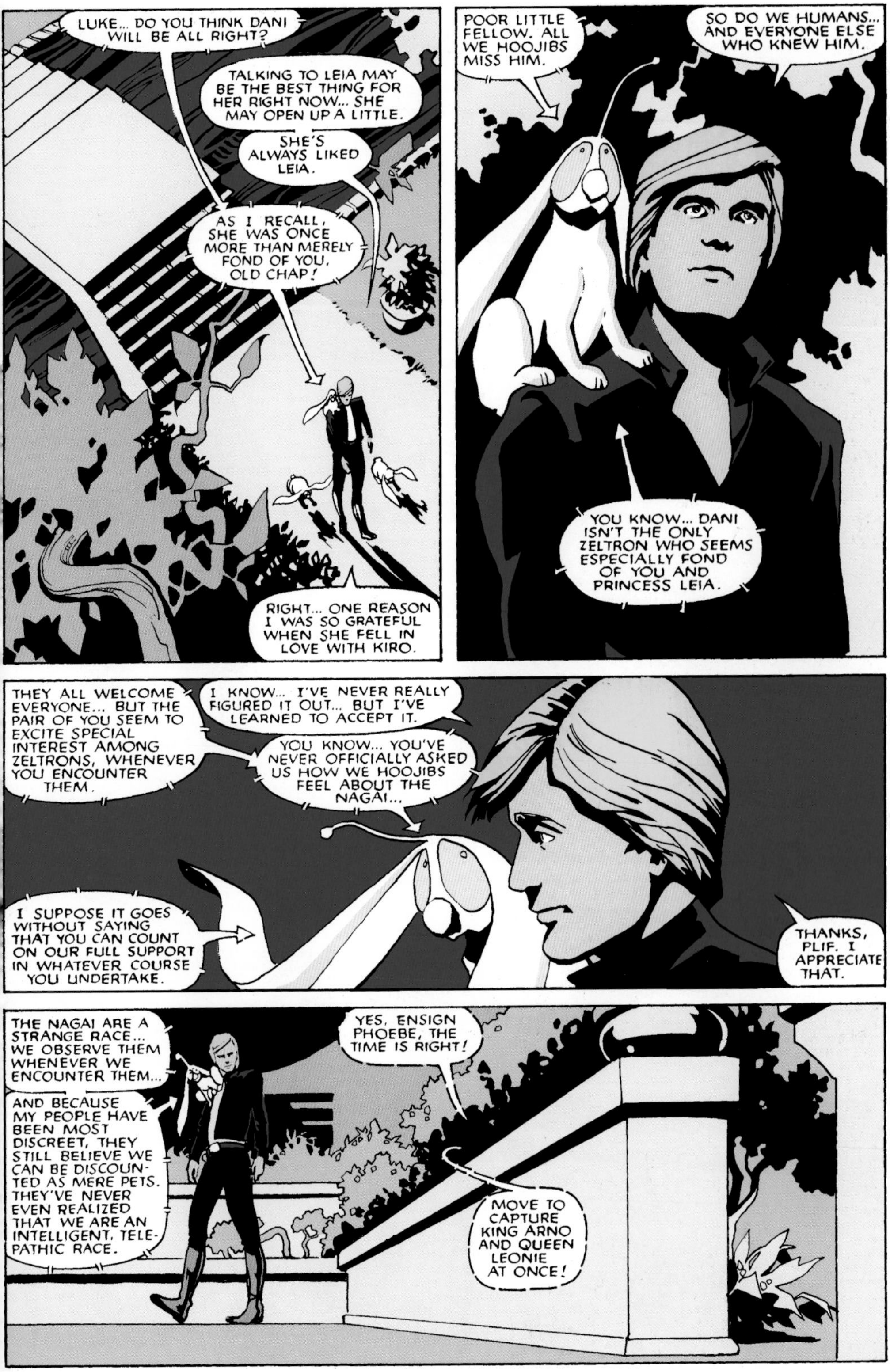
LUKE... DO YOU THINK DANI WILL BE ALL RIGHT?
TALKING TO LEIA MAY BE THE BEST THING FOR HER RIGHT NOW... SHE MAY OPEN UP A LITTLE.
SHE'S ALWAYS LIKED LEIA.
AS I RECALL, SHE WAS ONCE MORE THAN MERELY FOND OF YOU, OLD CHAP!
RIGHT... ONE REASON I WAS SO GRATEFUL WHEN SHE FELL IN LOVE WITH KIRO.
POOR LITTLE FELLOW. ALL WE HOOJIBS MISS HIM.
SO DO WE HUMANS... AND EVERYONE ELSE WHO KNEW HIM.
YOU KNOW... DANI ISN'T THE ONLY ZELTRON WHO SEEMS ESPECIALLY FOND OF YOU AND PRINCESS LEIA.
THEY ALL WELCOME EVERYONE... BUT THE PAIR OF YOU SEEM TO EXCITE SPECIAL INTEREST AMONG ZELTRONS, WHENEVER YOU ENCOUNTER THEM.
I KNOW... I'VE NEVER REALLY FIGURED IT OUT... BUT I'VE LEARNED TO ACCEPT IT.
YOU KNOW... YOU'VE NEVER OFFICIALLY ASKED US HOW WE HOOJIBS FEEL ABOUT THE NAGAI...
I SUPPOSE IT GOES WITHOUT SAYING THAT YOU CAN COUNT ON OUR FULL SUPPORT IN WHATEVER COURSE YOU UNDERTAKE.
THANKS, PLIF. I APPRECIATE THAT.
THE NAGAI ARE A STRANGE RACE... WE OBSERVE THEM WHENEVER WE ENCOUNTER THEM...
AND BECAUSE MY PEOPLE HAVE BEEN MOST DISCREET, THEY STILL BELIEVE WE CAN BE DISCOUNTED AS MERE PETS. THEY'VE NEVER EVEN REALIZED THAT WE ARE AN INTELLIGENT, TELEPATHIC RACE.
YES, ENSIGN PHOEBE, THE TIME IS RIGHT!
MOVE TO CAPTURE KING ARNO AND QUEEN LEONIE AT ONCE!

WELL! WHAT HAVE WE HERE?

EEP!!!

LUKE, ISN'T THAT...?

YES... IT'S ADMIRAL ACKBAR'S LONG-LOST AIDE, HIROG.

NICE TO SEE YOU, HIROG. HOW'S IT GOING?

AND WHAT'S THIS I HEAR ABOUT SOMEONE CAPTURING THE KING AND QUEEN?

YOU'LL NEVER KNOW, FOOL!

THANK GOODNESS!

BLIP

LUKE, SHALL WE...?

NOT YET, PLIF. I DON'T THINK WE'RE IN ANY DANGER... AND I WANT TO SEE WHAT GOES ON.

MIGHT BE KIND OF FUN.

THOUGHT YOU WERE PRETTY CLEVER, DID YOU?

WELL, CLEVER YOU MAY BE... BUT NOT CLEVER ENOUGH TO STAND IN THE WAY OF THE GLORIOUS DESTINY OF THE HIROMI!

NOW, TO FINISH TRANS-MITTING MY MESSAGE!

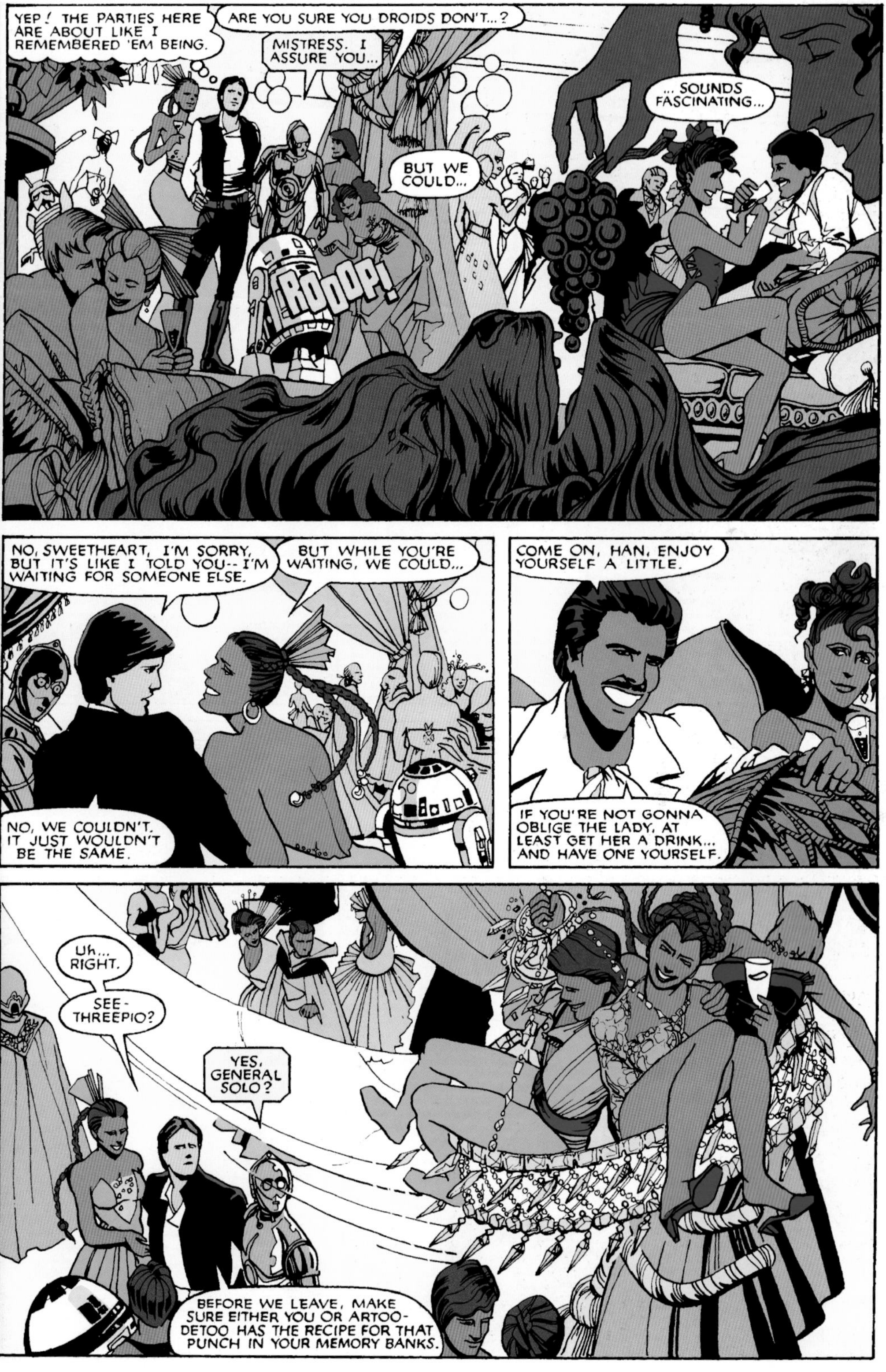
YEP! THE PARTIES HERE ARE ABOUT LIKE I REMEMBERED 'EM BEING.
ARE YOU SURE YOU DROIDS DON'T...?
MISTRESS. I ASSURE YOU...
BUT WE COULD...
ROOOP!
... SOUNDS FASCINATING...
NO, SWEETHEART, I'M SORRY, BUT IT'S LIKE I TOLD YOU-- I'M WAITING FOR SOMEONE ELSE.
BUT WHILE YOU'RE WAITING, WE COULD...
NO, WE COULDN'T. IT JUST WOULDN'T BE THE SAME.
COME ON, HAN, ENJOY YOURSELF A LITTLE.
IF YOU'RE NOT GONNA OBLIGE THE LADY, AT LEAST GET HER A DRINK... AND HAVE ONE YOURSELF.
Uh... RIGHT.
SEE-THREEPIO?
YES, GENERAL SOLO?
BEFORE WE LEAVE, MAKE SURE EITHER YOU OR ARTOO-DETOO HAS THE RECIPE FOR THAT PUNCH IN YOUR MEMORY BANKS.

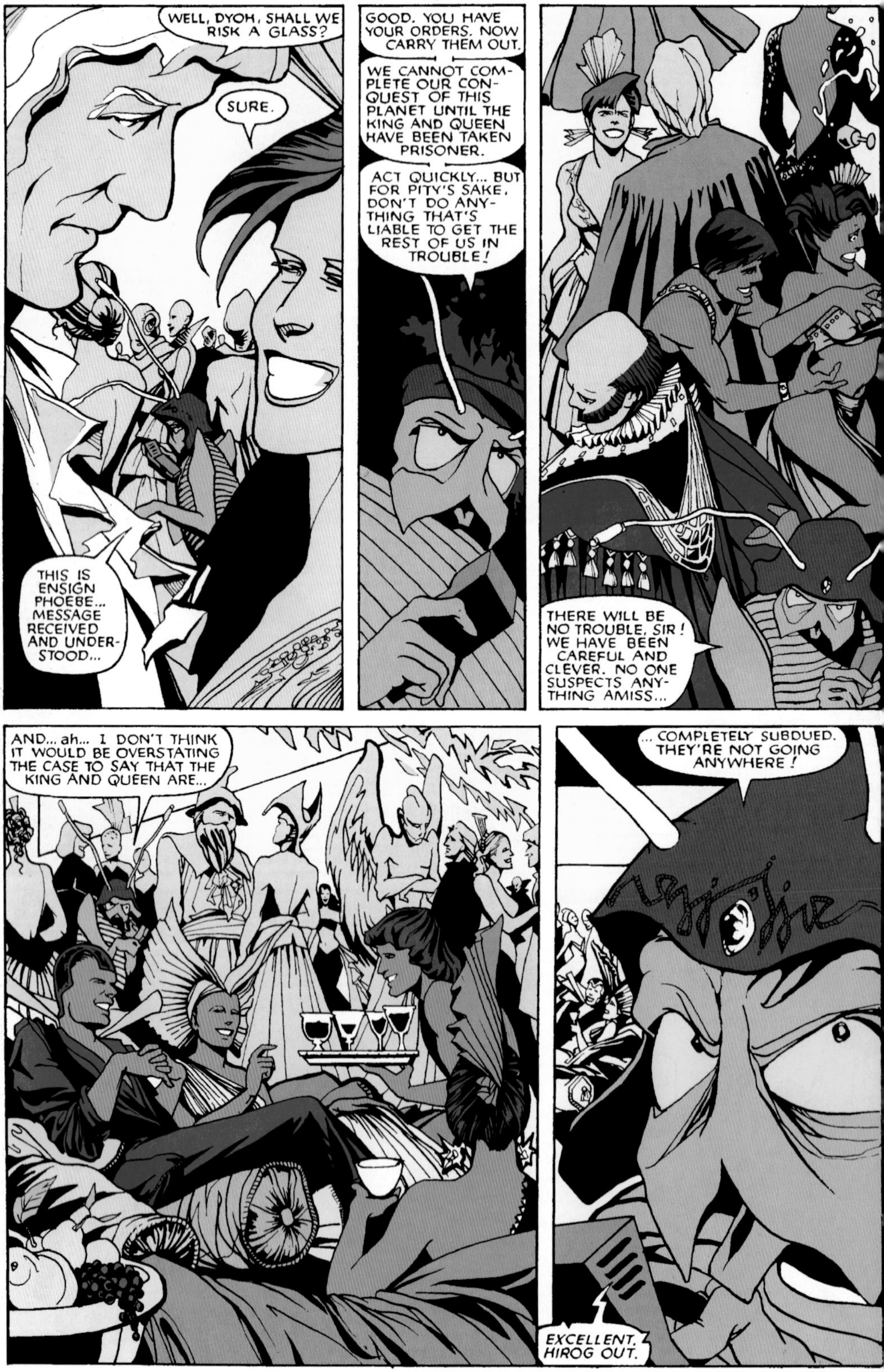
WELL, DYOH, SHALL WE RISK A GLASS?
SURE.
THIS IS ENSIGN PHOEBE... MESSAGE RECEIVED AND UNDERSTOOD...
GOOD. YOU HAVE YOUR ORDERS. NOW CARRY THEM OUT.
WE CANNOT COMPLETE OUR CONQUEST OF THIS PLANET UNTIL THE KING AND QUEEN HAVE BEEN TAKEN PRISONER.
ACT QUICKLY... BUT FOR PITY'S SAKE, DON'T DO ANYTHING THAT'S LIABLE TO GET THE REST OF US IN TROUBLE!
THERE WILL BE NO TROUBLE, SIR! WE HAVE BEEN CAREFUL AND CLEVER. NO ONE SUSPECTS ANYTHING AMISS...
AND... ah... I DON'T THINK IT WOULD BE OVERSTATING THE CASE TO SAY THAT THE KING AND QUEEN ARE...
...COMPLETELY SUBDUED. THEY'RE NOT GOING ANYWHERE!
EXCELLENT. HIROG OUT.

YES, MEN, IT HAS TAKEN US TWO MILLENNIA... YEARS OF PLANNING... OF WORKING... OF *HIDING*...

OF MAKING SURE NO ONE BEATS US UP... BUT AT LAST WE HAVE BEGUN!

SOON, THIS ENTIRE GALAXY WILL BE TRODDEN IN THE DUST BENEATH THE *SOLES* OF OUR *HIROMI BOOTS!*

LUKE, WAS IT WISE TO LET THEM TIE YOU?

PLIF, I'M A TRAINED JEDI KNIGHT. IF I WANT TO GET OUT OF THESE ROPES, THEY WON'T HOLD ME.

I'M ENJOYING THIS.

COMMANDER, SIT YOURSELF UPON THE VACANT THRONE... ASSUME YOUR RIGHT-FUL PLACE AS HOOKYR THE FIRST, NEW RULER OF ZELTROS.

NOTHING CAN STOP US NOW! THE GLORY OF THE HIROMI IS ASSURED! YAAYYY!

(AGAIN)

(AGAIN)

WHAT... WHAT COMES AFTER THE VICTORY CHEER?

I'M... I'M NOT SURE...

Ah... ONE MORE TIME... I THINK...

YOUR ILLUSTRIOUSNESS... HOW WOULD THE GLORY OF THE HIROMI PEOPLE BEST BE SERVED?

WELL... NOW THAT WE'VE COMPLETED THE CONQUEST... AND CHEERED, OF COURSE (THAT'S VERY IMPORTANT)... I THINK THE NEXT THING TO SERVE OUR DESTINY...

WOULD BE TO... SERVE LUNCH!

STILL THINK WE'RE IN DANGER, PLIF?

CERTAINLY NOT.

Oh, BOY!

I WONDER WHERE THEY KEEP THE FOOD AROUND HERE...

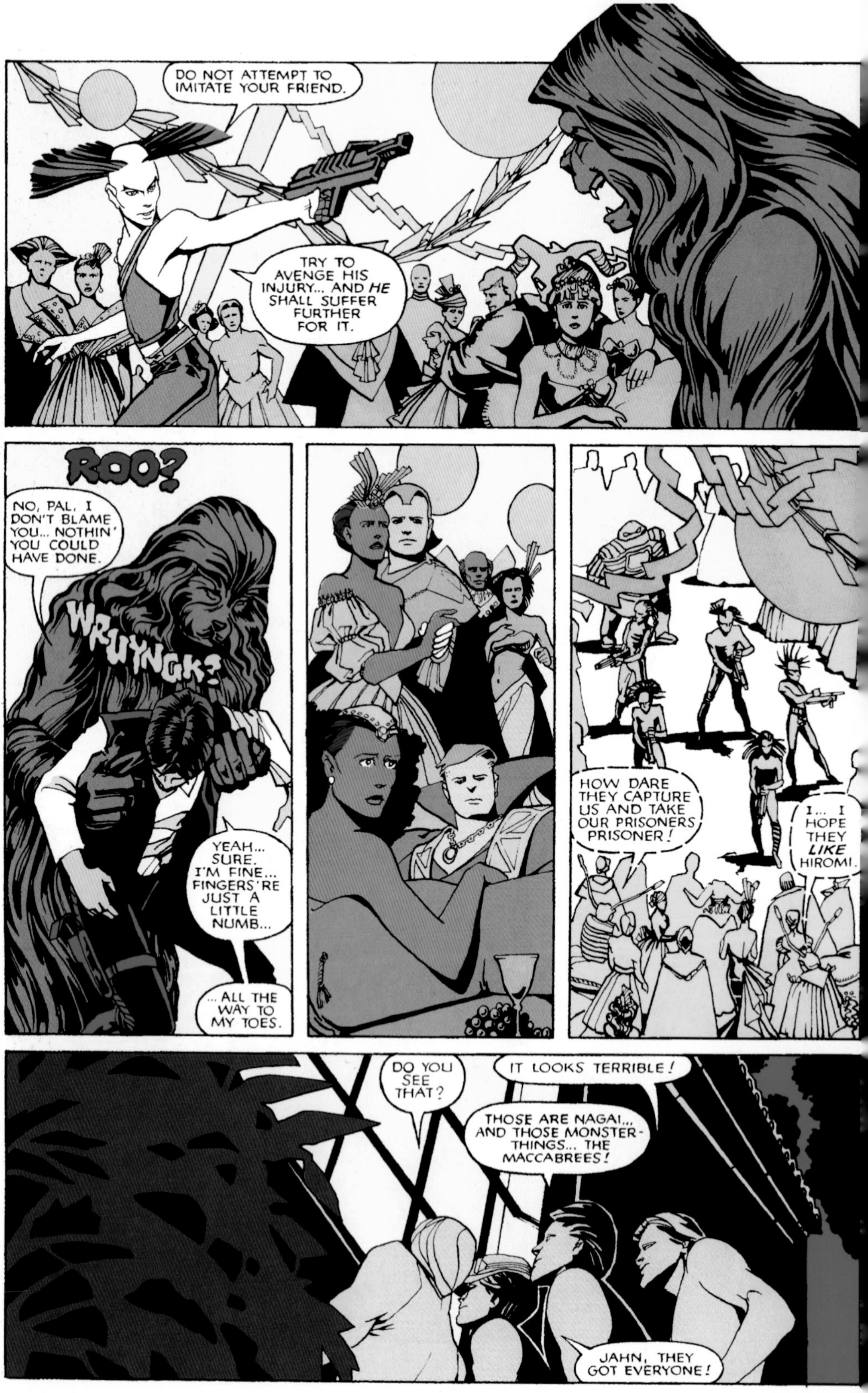
DO NOT ATTEMPT TO IMITATE YOUR FRIEND.
TRY TO AVENGE HIS INJURY... AND *HE* SHALL SUFFER FURTHER FOR IT.
ROO?
NO, PAL, I DON'T BLAME YOU... NOTHIN' YOU COULD HAVE DONE.
WRUYNGK?
YEAH... SURE. I'M FINE... FINGERS'RE JUST A LITTLE NUMB...
...ALL THE WAY TO MY TOES.
HOW DARE THEY CAPTURE US AND TAKE OUR PRISONERS PRISONER!
I... I HOPE THEY *LIKE* HIROMI.
DO YOU SEE THAT?
IT LOOKS TERRIBLE!
THOSE ARE NAGAI... AND THOSE MONSTER-THINGS... THE MACCABREES!
JAHN, THEY GOT EVERYONE!

NEXT: the party's over

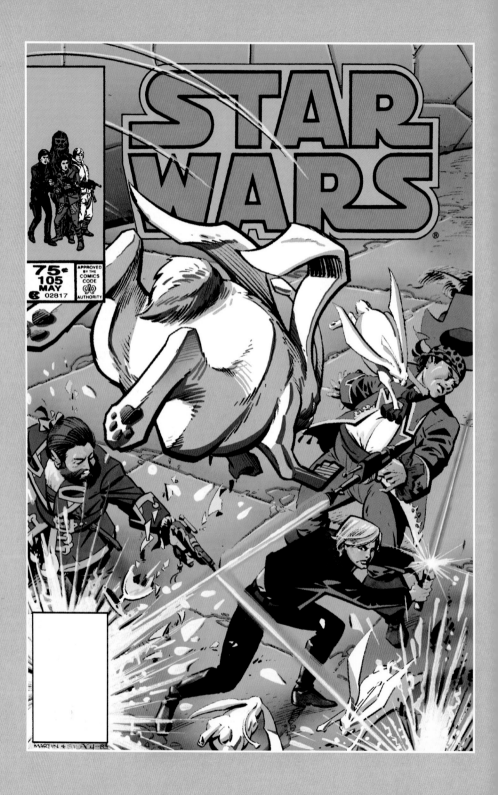

499

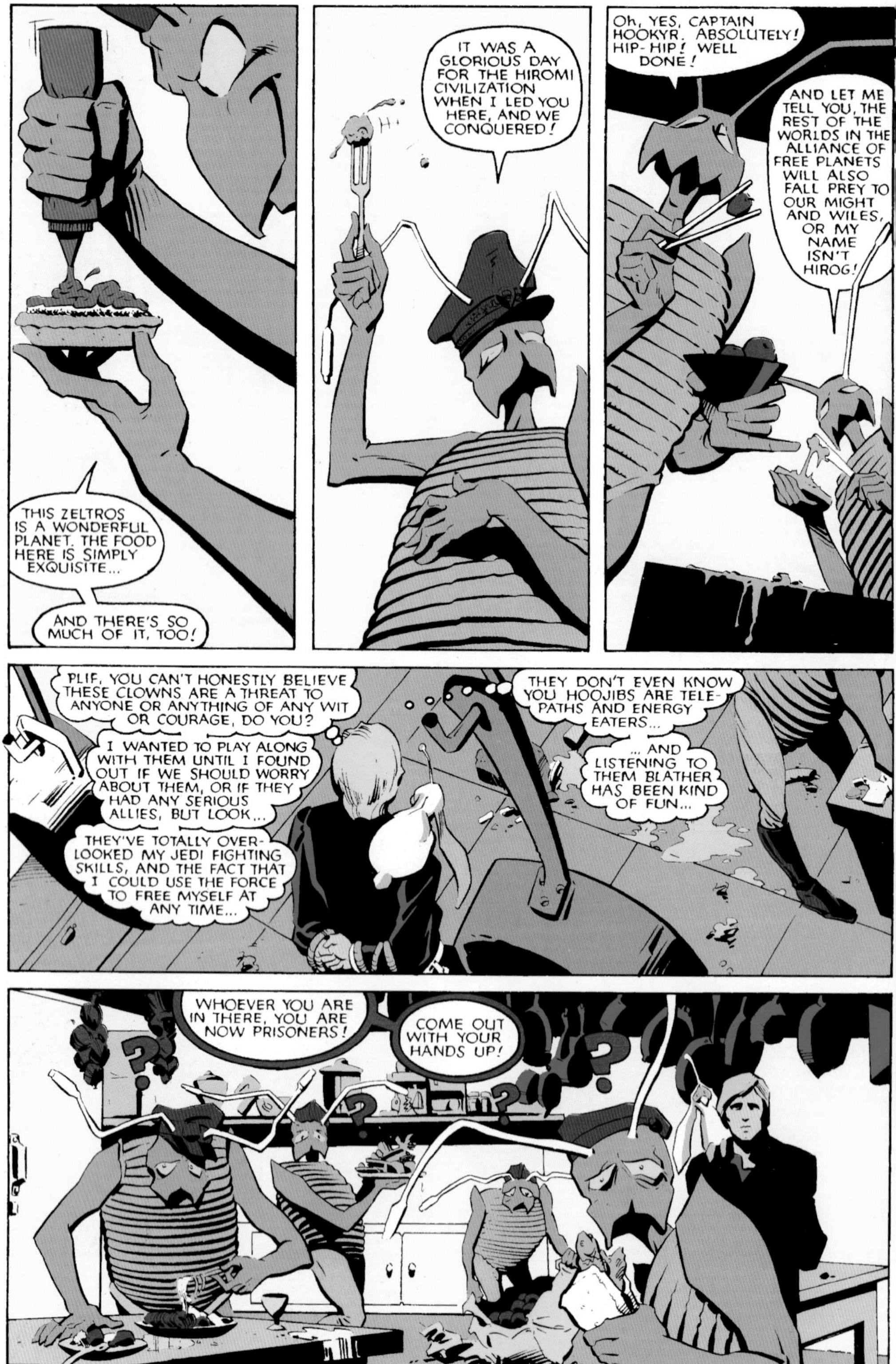

THIS ZELTROS IS A WONDERFUL PLANET. THE FOOD HERE IS SIMPLY EXQUISITE...
AND THERE'S SO MUCH OF IT, TOO!
IT WAS A GLORIOUS DAY FOR THE HIROMI CIVILIZATION WHEN I LED YOU HERE, AND WE CONQUERED!
Oh, YES, CAPTAIN HOOKYR. ABSOLUTELY! HIP-HIP! WELL DONE!
AND LET ME TELL YOU, THE REST OF THE WORLDS IN THE ALLIANCE OF FREE PLANETS WILL ALSO FALL PREY TO OUR MIGHT AND WILES, OR MY NAME ISN'T HIROG!
PLIF, YOU CAN'T HONESTLY BELIEVE THESE CLOWNS ARE A THREAT TO ANYONE OR ANYTHING OF ANY WIT OR COURAGE, DO YOU?
I WANTED TO PLAY ALONG WITH THEM UNTIL I FOUND OUT IF WE SHOULD WORRY ABOUT THEM, OR IF THEY HAD ANY SERIOUS ALLIES, BUT LOOK...
THEY'VE TOTALLY OVERLOOKED MY JEDI FIGHTING SKILLS, AND THE FACT THAT I COULD USE THE FORCE TO FREE MYSELF AT ANY TIME...
THEY DON'T EVEN KNOW YOU HOOJIBS ARE TELEPATHS AND ENERGY EATERS...
... AND LISTENING TO THEM BLATHER HAS BEEN KIND OF FUN...
WHOEVER YOU ARE IN THERE, YOU ARE NOW PRISONERS!
COME OUT WITH YOUR HANDS UP!

BASH!

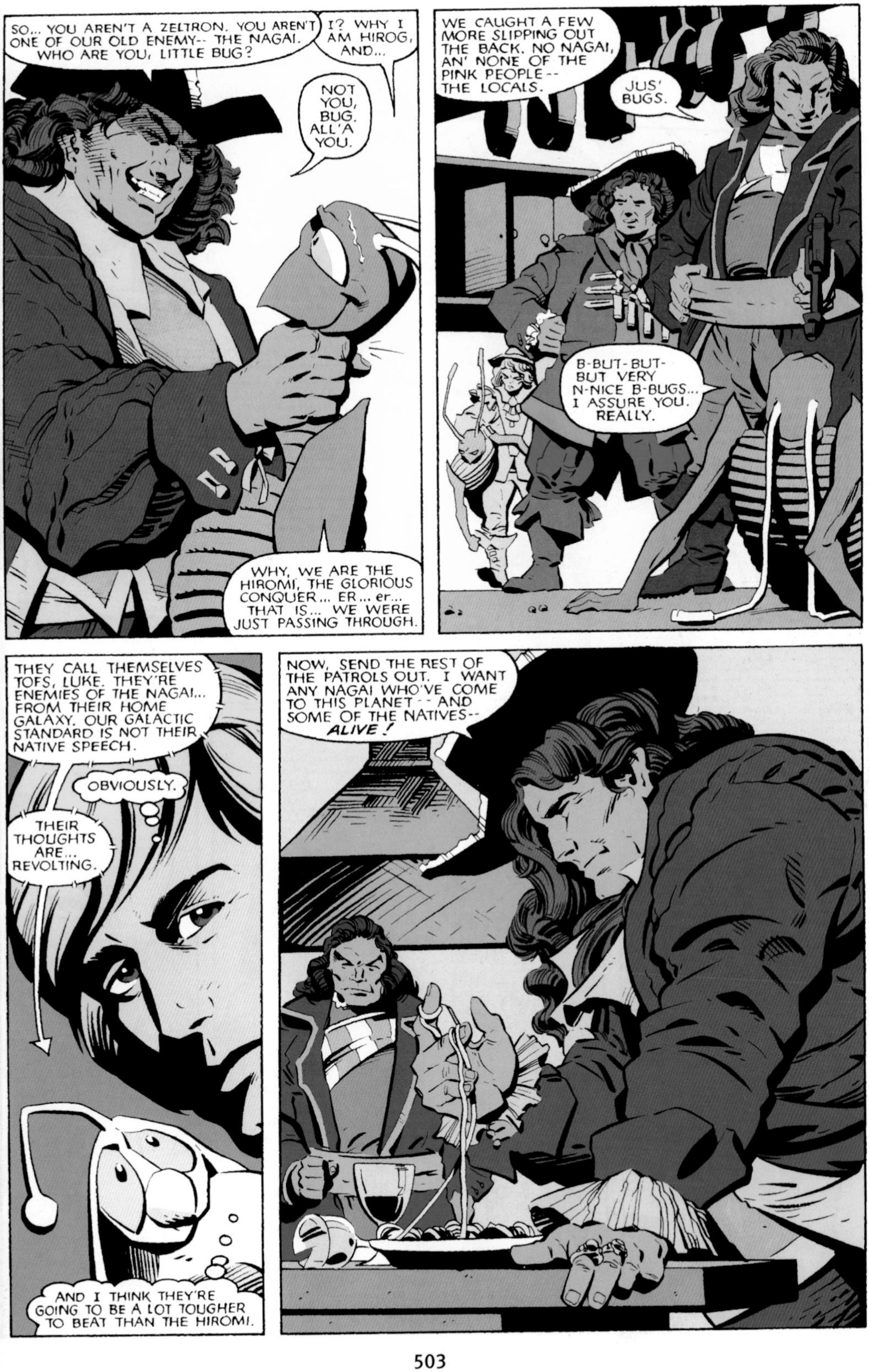
SO... YOU AREN'T A ZELTRON. YOU AREN'T ONE OF OUR OLD ENEMY-- THE NAGAI. WHO ARE YOU, LITTLE BUG?
I? WHY I AM HIROG, AND...
NOT YOU, BUG. ALL'A YOU.
WHY, WE ARE THE HIROMI, THE GLORIOUS CONQUER... ER... er... THAT IS... WE WERE JUST PASSING THROUGH.
WE CAUGHT A FEW MORE SLIPPING OUT THE BACK. NO NAGAI, AN' NONE OF THE PINK PEOPLE-- THE LOCALS.
JUS' BUGS.
B-BUT-BUT-BUT VERY N-NICE B-BUGS... I ASSURE YOU. REALLY.
THEY CALL THEMSELVES TOFS, LUKE. THEY'RE ENEMIES OF THE NAGAI... FROM THEIR HOME GALAXY. OUR GALACTIC STANDARD IS NOT THEIR NATIVE SPEECH.
OBVIOUSLY.
THEIR THOUGHTS ARE... REVOLTING.
AND I THINK THEY'RE GOING TO BE A LOT TOUGHER TO BEAT THAN THE HIROMI.
NOW, SEND THE REST OF THE PATROLS OUT. I WANT ANY NAGAI WHO'VE COME TO THIS PLANET-- AND SOME OF THE NATIVES-- *ALIVE!*

WH-WHO ARE THESE PEOPLE? WHY ARE THEY HERE?

THEY'RE CALLED THE NAGAI, SWEETHEART... AN' THE BIG CYBORGS ARE THEIR HEAVYWEIGHTS-- THE MACCABREE.

AN' YOU CAN BET THEY AREN'T HERE TO JOIN THE PARTY.

YOU SOUND PRETTY DISGUSTED, HAN.

HROWL!

YEAH, LANDO, LIKE CHEWIE SAID, THE SITUATION IS DISGUSTING.

WE COME HERE TO ZELTROS TO CONVINCE THEM TO JOIN THE ALLIANCE OF FREE PLANETS' DEFENSE AGAINST THE NAGAI...

YEAH... AND THE KING AND QUEEN GAVE US SUCH A BIG WELCOME... THAT A NAGAI INVASION RIGHT HERE CATCHES US FLAT-FOOTED.

HOW'S YOUR WOUNDED WRIST?

I'LL LIVE. IF I CAN GET MY HAND AROUND A BLASTER, I THINK I CAN FIRE IT.

BUT YOU WON'T GET YOUR HAND AROUND A BLASTER, ALIEN. WE NAGAI KNOW YOUR REPUTATION.

WE HAVE ALREADY DISPATCHED ANOTHER SQUADRON TO ROUND UP ANY OTHER OF YOUR ALLIES WHO MAY BE ON THIS PLANET...

IN FACT, IT'S TIME TO COMMUNICATE...

DEN SIVA? LIEUTENANT SIVA, ACKNOWLEDGE, PLEASE.

504

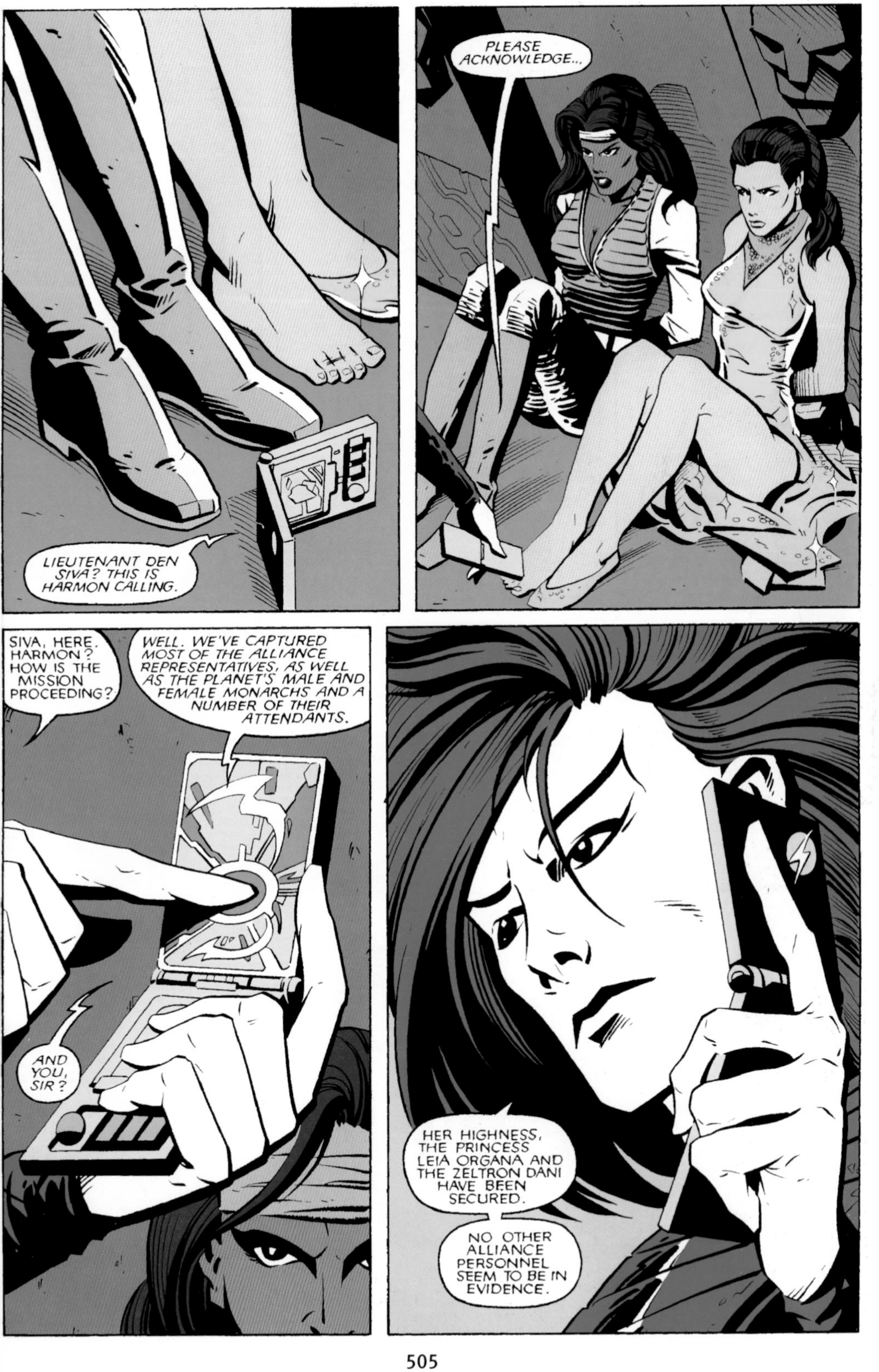
LIEUTENANT DEN SIVA? THIS IS HARMON CALLING.
PLEASE ACKNOWLEDGE...
SIVA, HERE. HARMON? HOW IS THE MISSION PROCEEDING?
WELL. WE'VE CAPTURED MOST OF THE ALLIANCE REPRESENTATIVES, AS WELL AS THE PLANET'S MALE AND FEMALE MONARCHS AND A NUMBER OF THEIR ATTENDANTS.
AND YOU, SIR?
HER HIGHNESS, THE PRINCESS LEIA ORGANA AND THE ZELTRON DANI HAVE BEEN SECURED.
NO OTHER ALLIANCE PERSONNEL SEEM TO BE IN EVIDENCE.

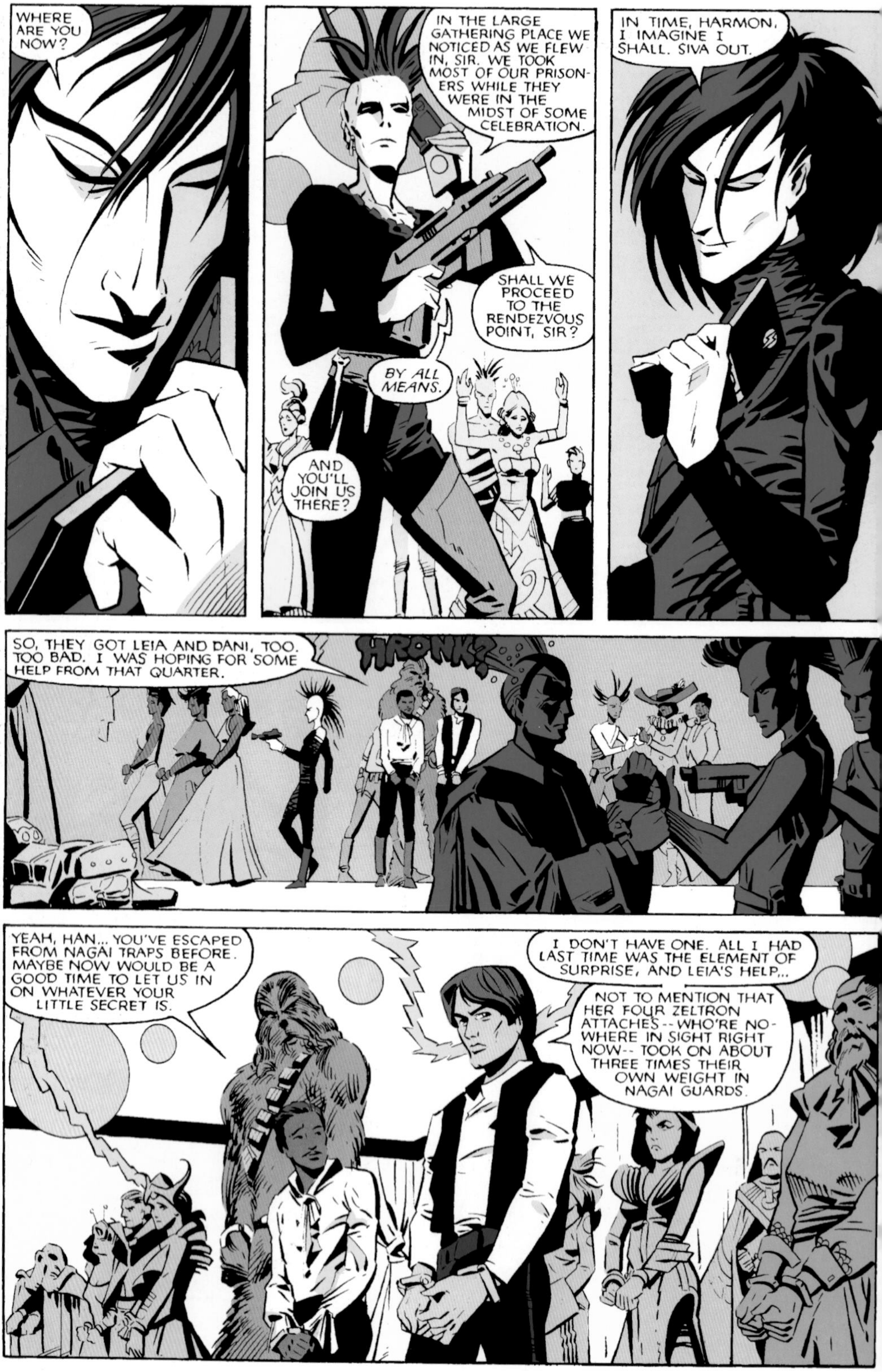
WHERE ARE YOU NOW?
IN THE LARGE GATHERING PLACE WE NOTICED AS WE FLEW IN, SIR. WE TOOK MOST OF OUR PRISONERS WHILE THEY WERE IN THE MIDST OF SOME CELEBRATION.
SHALL WE PROCEED TO THE RENDEZVOUS POINT, SIR?
BY ALL MEANS.
AND YOU'LL JOIN US THERE?
IN TIME, HARMON, I IMAGINE I SHALL. SIVA OUT.
SO, THEY GOT LEIA AND DANI, TOO. TOO BAD. I WAS HOPING FOR SOME HELP FROM THAT QUARTER.
HRONK?
YEAH, HAN... YOU'VE ESCAPED FROM NAGAI TRAPS BEFORE. MAYBE NOW WOULD BE A GOOD TIME TO LET US IN ON WHATEVER YOUR LITTLE SECRET IS.
I DON'T HAVE ONE. ALL I HAD LAST TIME WAS THE ELEMENT OF SURPRISE, AND LEIA'S HELP...
NOT TO MENTION THAT HER FOUR ZELTRON ATTACHES-- WHO'RE NOWHERE IN SIGHT RIGHT NOW-- TOOK ON ABOUT THREE TIMES THEIR OWN WEIGHT IN NAGAI GUARDS.

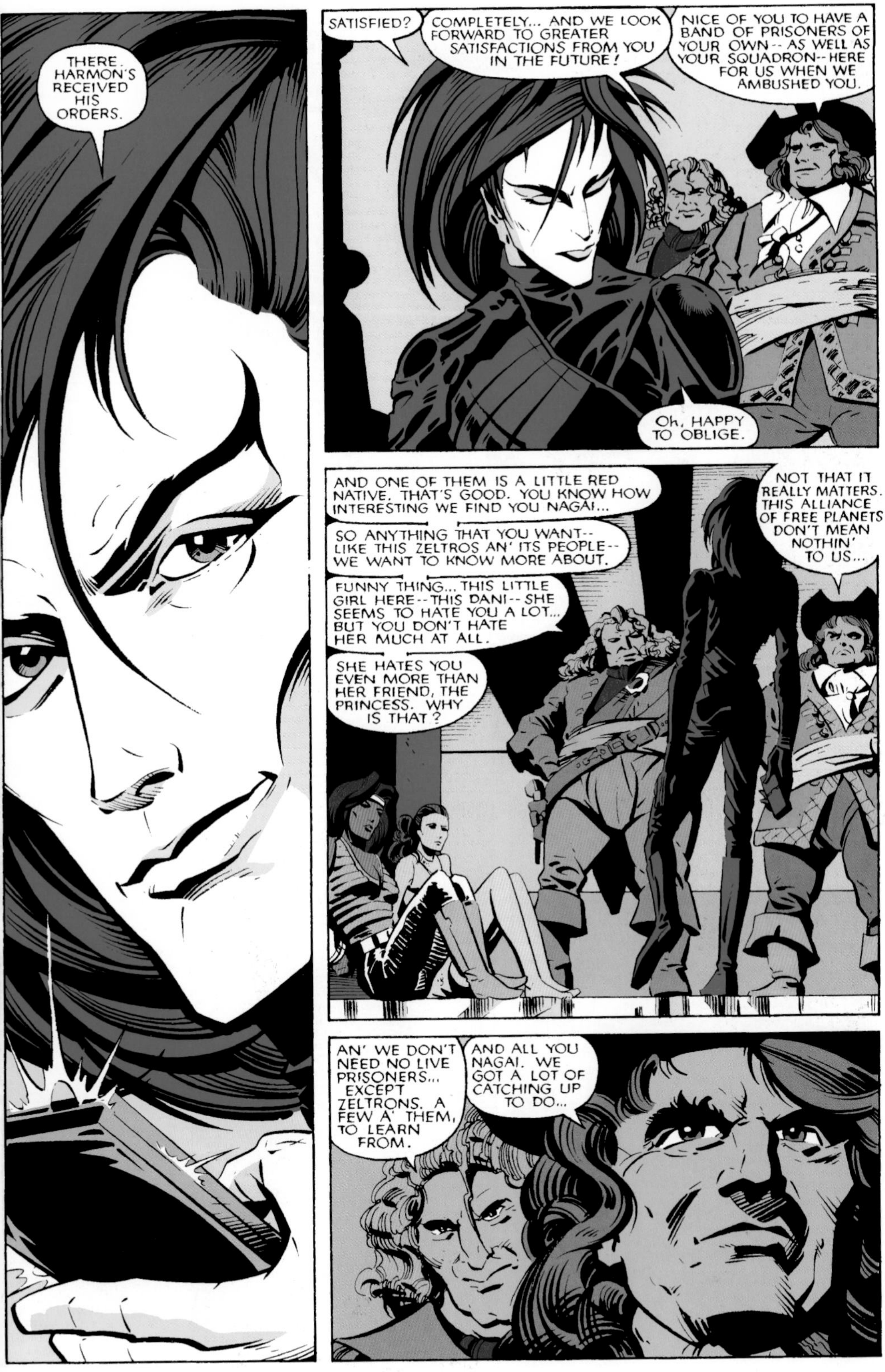
THERE. HARMON'S RECEIVED HIS ORDERS.
SATISFIED?
COMPLETELY... AND WE LOOK FORWARD TO GREATER SATISFACTIONS FROM YOU IN THE FUTURE!
NICE OF YOU TO HAVE A BAND OF PRISONERS OF YOUR OWN-- AS WELL AS YOUR SQUADRON--HERE FOR US WHEN WE AMBUSHED YOU.
Oh, HAPPY TO OBLIGE.
AND ONE OF THEM IS A LITTLE RED NATIVE. THAT'S GOOD. YOU KNOW HOW INTERESTING WE FIND YOU NAGAI...
SO ANYTHING THAT YOU WANT-- LIKE THIS ZELTROS AN' ITS PEOPLE-- WE WANT TO KNOW MORE ABOUT.
FUNNY THING... THIS LITTLE GIRL HERE--THIS DANI--SHE SEEMS TO HATE YOU A LOT... BUT YOU DON'T HATE HER MUCH AT ALL.
SHE HATES YOU EVEN MORE THAN HER FRIEND, THE PRINCESS. WHY IS THAT?
NOT THAT IT REALLY MATTERS. THIS ALLIANCE OF FREE PLANETS DON'T MEAN NOTHIN' TO US...
AN' WE DON'T NEED NO LIVE PRISONERS... EXCEPT ZELTRONS. A FEW A' THEM, TO LEARN FROM.
AND ALL YOU NAGAI. WE GOT A LOT OF CATCHING UP TO DO...

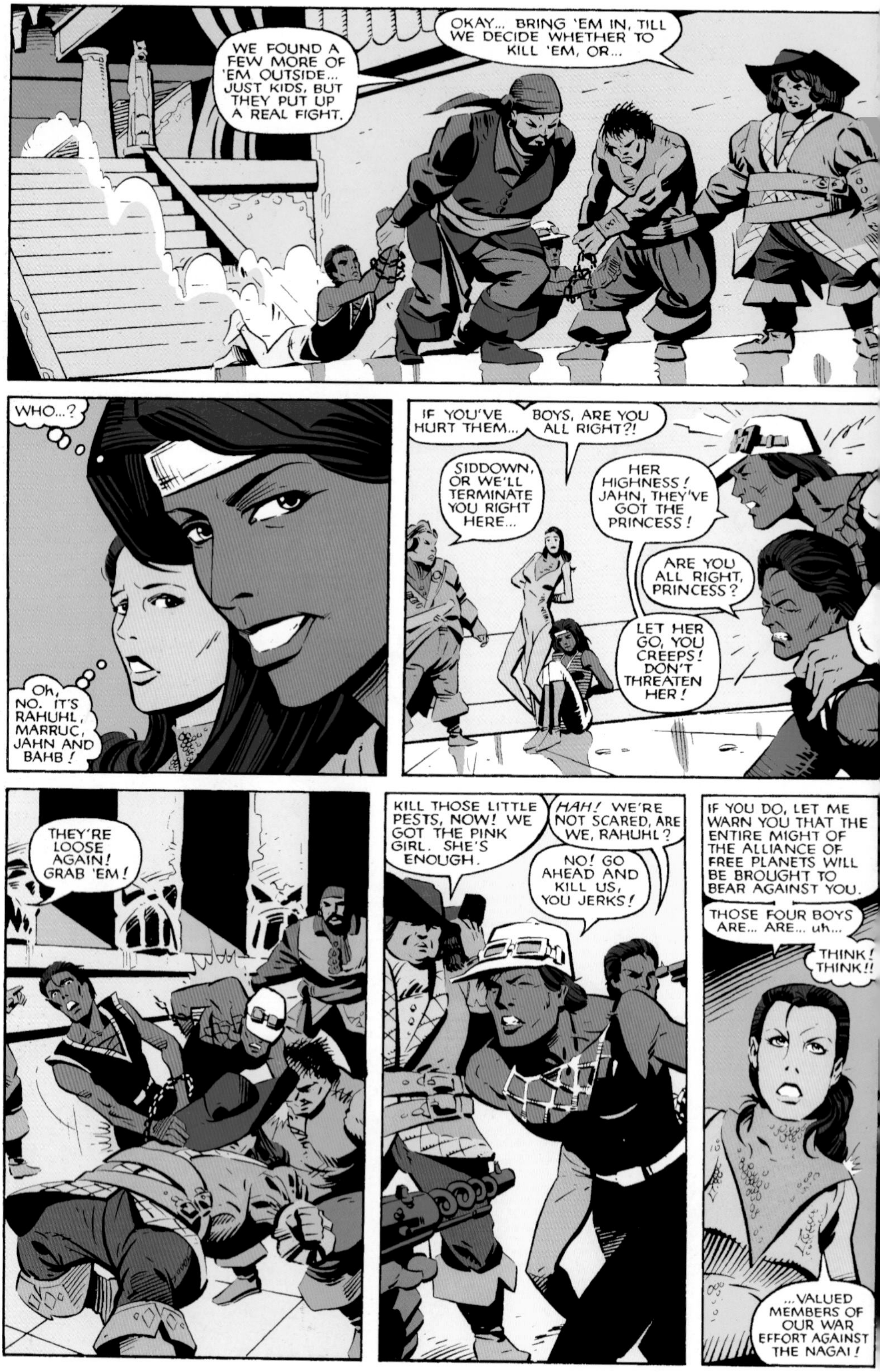
WE FOUND A FEW MORE OF 'EM OUTSIDE... JUST KIDS, BUT THEY PUT UP A REAL FIGHT.
OKAY... BRING 'EM IN, TILL WE DECIDE WHETHER TO KILL 'EM, OR...
WHO...?
Oh, NO. IT'S RAHUHL, MARRUC, JAHN AND BAHB!
IF YOU'VE HURT THEM...
BOYS, ARE YOU ALL RIGHT?!
SIDDOWN, OR WE'LL TERMINATE YOU RIGHT HERE...
HER HIGHNESS! JAHN, THEY'VE GOT THE PRINCESS!
ARE YOU ALL RIGHT, PRINCESS?
LET HER GO, YOU CREEPS! DON'T THREATEN HER!
THEY'RE LOOSE AGAIN! GRAB 'EM!
KILL THOSE LITTLE PESTS, NOW! WE GOT THE PINK GIRL. SHE'S ENOUGH.
HAH! WE'RE NOT SCARED, ARE WE, RAHUHL?
NO! GO AHEAD AND KILL US, YOU JERKS!
IF YOU DO, LET ME WARN YOU THAT THE ENTIRE MIGHT OF THE ALLIANCE OF FREE PLANETS WILL BE BROUGHT TO BEAR AGAINST YOU.
THOSE FOUR BOYS ARE... ARE... uh...
THINK! THINK!!
...VALUED MEMBERS OF OUR WAR EFFORT AGAINST THE NAGAI!

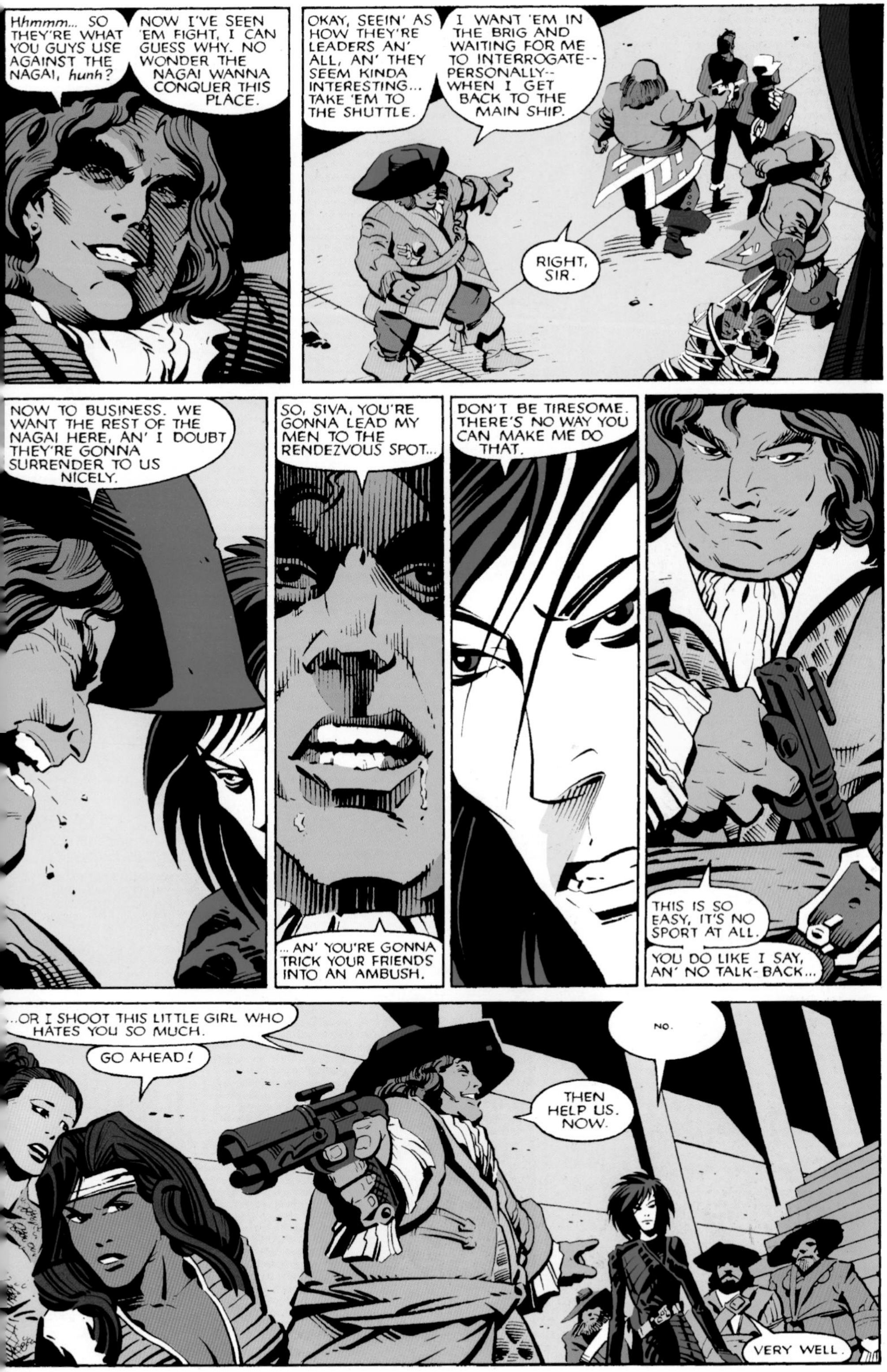
Hhmmm... SO THEY'RE WHAT YOU GUYS USE AGAINST THE NAGAI, hunh?
NOW I'VE SEEN 'EM FIGHT, I CAN GUESS WHY. NO WONDER THE NAGAI WANNA CONQUER THIS PLACE.
OKAY, SEEIN' AS HOW THEY'RE LEADERS AN' ALL, AN' THEY SEEM KINDA INTERESTING... TAKE 'EM TO THE SHUTTLE.
I WANT 'EM IN THE BRIG AND WAITING FOR ME TO INTERROGATE-- PERSONALLY-- WHEN I GET BACK TO THE MAIN SHIP.
RIGHT, SIR.
NOW TO BUSINESS. WE WANT THE REST OF THE NAGAI HERE, AN' I DOUBT THEY'RE GONNA SURRENDER TO US NICELY.
SO, SIVA, YOU'RE GONNA LEAD MY MEN TO THE RENDEZVOUS SPOT...
... AN' YOU'RE GONNA TRICK YOUR FRIENDS INTO AN AMBUSH.
DON'T BE TIRESOME. THERE'S NO WAY YOU CAN MAKE ME DO THAT.
THIS IS SO EASY, IT'S NO SPORT AT ALL.
YOU DO LIKE I SAY, AN' NO TALK-BACK...
...OR I SHOOT THIS LITTLE GIRL WHO HATES YOU SO MUCH.
GO AHEAD!
NO.
THEN HELP US. NOW.
VERY WELL.

SO, WHADDAYA GOT BLASTERS FOR?

YOU COME WITH US!

OF COURSE.

AN' SHUT THE DOOR BEHIND YOU. LOOK AT THE VERMIN YOU'RE LETTING IN.

HEY, YEAH! TARGET PRACTICE!

BORP

STOP THAT, YOU BULLIES! THEY'RE NOT VERMIN! THEY'RE--!

PRETENDING TO BE SIMPLE ANIMALS, DANI. DON'T SPOIL THAT. AS LONG AS HOOJIBS ARE TELEPATHIC AND AGILE...

...THEY CAN ALWAYS BE OUT OF HARM'S WAY BEFORE THESE TOFS SHOOT.

SEE? THE TOFS ARE GETTING FRUSTRATED... THEY'VE LOST INTEREST.

YES... LIKE MOST BULLIES, THEY HATE BEING SHOWN UP!

PLIF? WHAT'S THE SITUATION OVERALL?

THINGS HAVE BEEN BETTER, I'M AFRAID, BUT WE ARE MENDING MATTERS AS BEST WE CAN.

A PARTY OF NAGAI HAVE CAPTURED MOST OF THE ZELTRON DIGNITARIES, GENERALS SOLO AND CALRISSIAN, CHEWBACCA AND THE DROIDS...

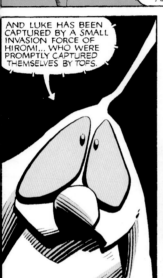

AND LUKE HAS BEEN CAPTURED BY A SMALL INVASION FORCE OF HIROMI... WHO WERE PROMPTLY CAPTURED THEMSELVES BY TOFS.

≥Whew!≤ DO WE HAVE A PLAN?

LUKE WILL TAKE CARE OF STARTING THE ACTION AT HIS END. HE'D LIKE YOU TO BE AWARE THAT, WHILE THE TOFS WILL USE A SABER OR A BLASTER, A CLUB IS THEIR WEAPON OF CHOICE.

MY PEOPLE AND I WILL EVEN THE ODDS IN OUR USUAL FASHION...

...AND CONTINUE TO ACT AS VERMIN...

...VERMIN WHO ARE VERY SKILLED AT STAYING OUT OF HARM'S WAY, I MIGHT ADD.

SO, JUST WHAT IS THIS THING, ANYWAY?

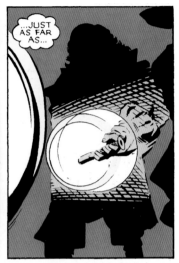

515

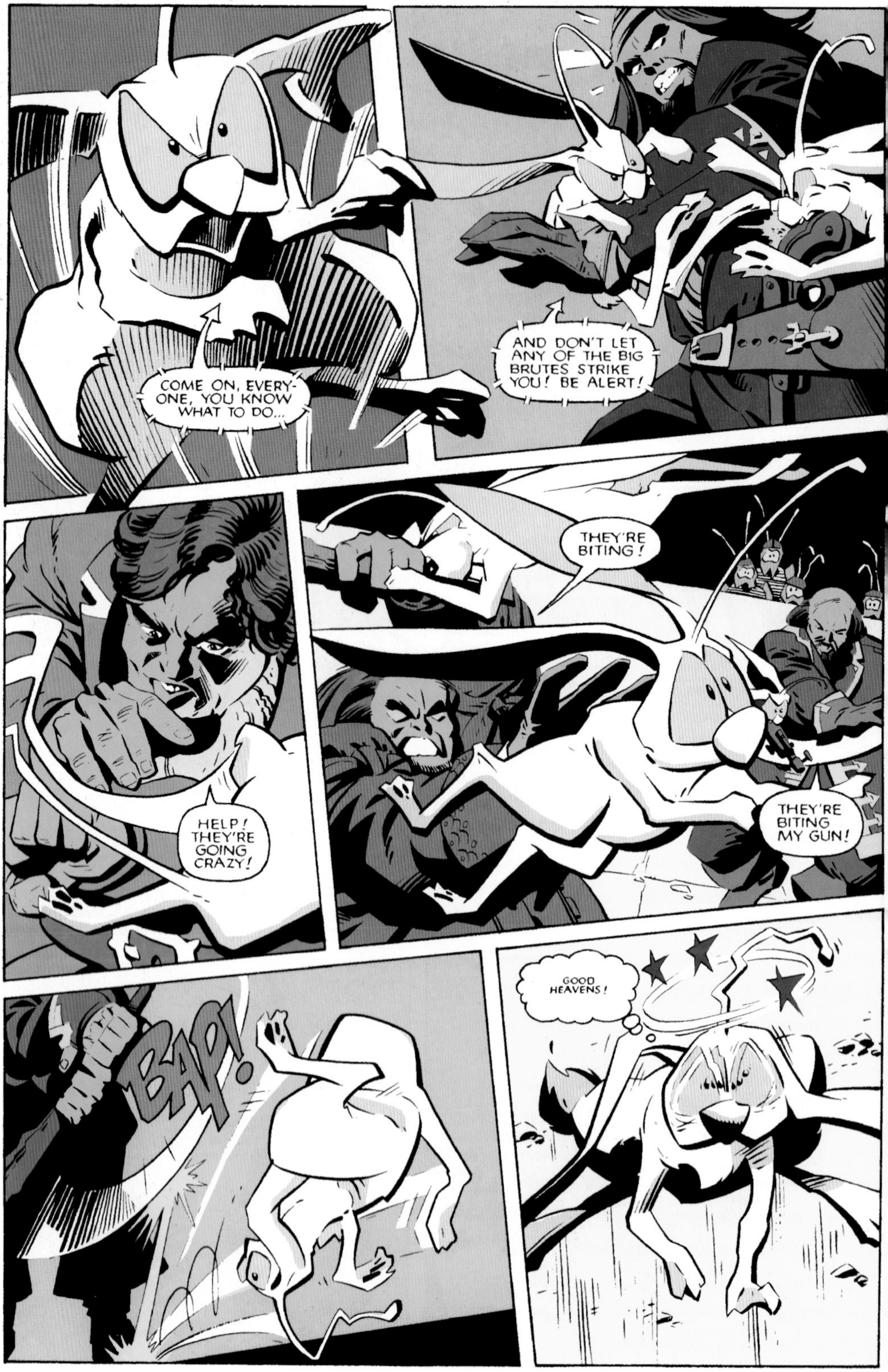
COME ON, EVERY-ONE, YOU KNOW WHAT TO DO...
AND DON'T LET ANY OF THE BIG BRUTES STRIKE YOU! BE ALERT!
THEY'RE BITING!
HELP! THEY'RE GOING CRAZY!
THEY'RE BITING MY GUN!
BAP!
GOOD HEAVENS!

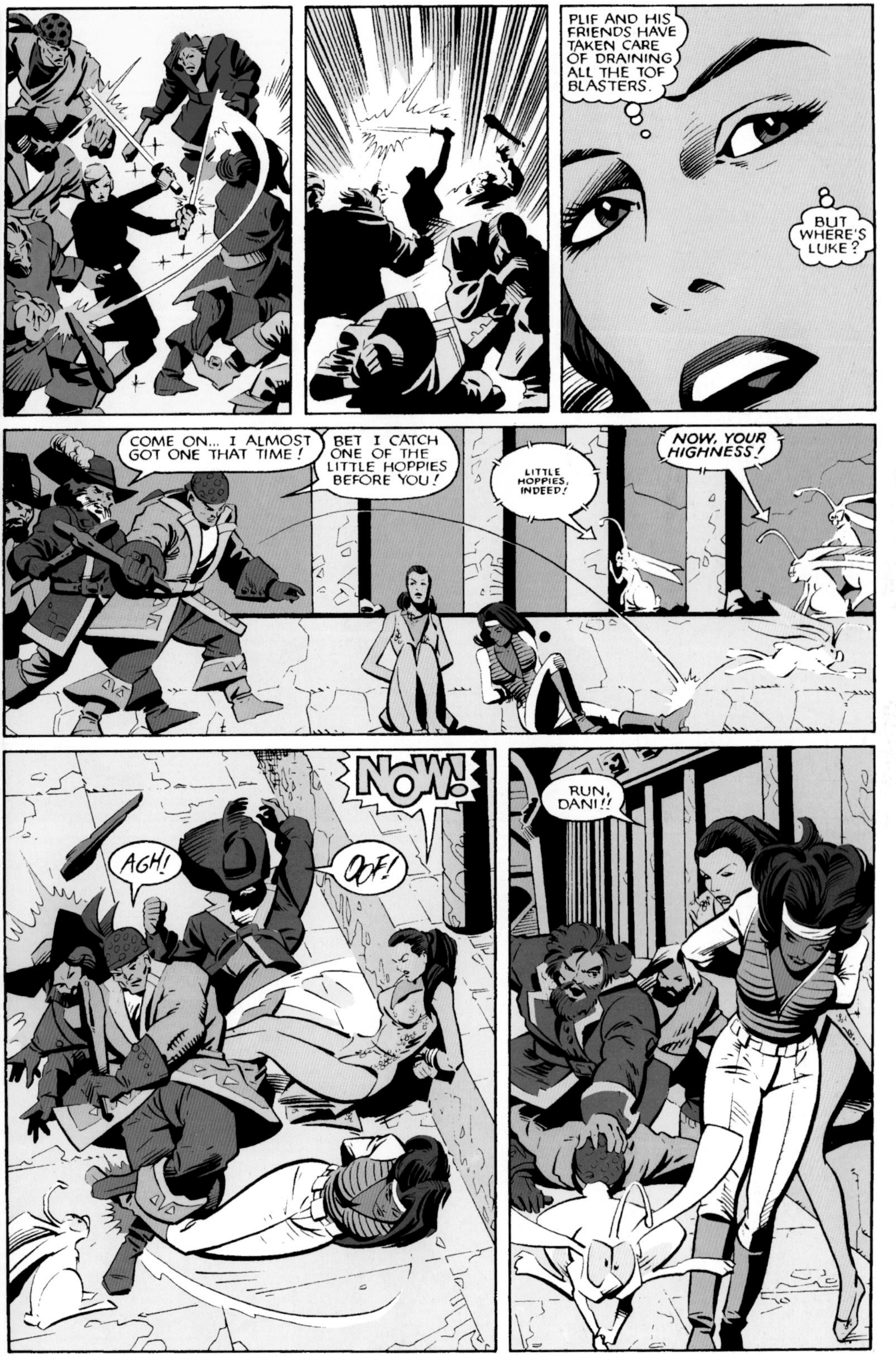
PLIF AND HIS FRIENDS HAVE TAKEN CARE OF DRAINING ALL THE TOF BLASTERS.
BUT WHERE'S LUKE?
COME ON... I ALMOST GOT ONE THAT TIME!
BET I CATCH ONE OF THE LITTLE HOPPIES BEFORE YOU!
LITTLE HOPPIES, INDEED!
NOW, YOUR HIGHNESS!
NOW!
AGH!
OOF!
RUN, DANI!!

BLAST 'EM!
GO AHEAD... FOR ALL THE GOOD IT DOES YOU!
HEY... WHAT'S HAPPENING?!
NOTHING!
I KNOW THAT! I MEANT, WHY NOT? WHY DON'T OUR GUNS WORK?
WHO CARES? THERE'S ONLY TWO OF THEM, AN' WE STILL GOT OUR CLUBS.
I WOULDN'T TRY THAT IF I WERE YOU.
SAYS WHO?
ME.
PLUS THE ANGRIEST ASSORTMENT OF "LITTLE HOPPIES" YOU'RE EVER LIKELY TO ENCOUNTER!
AND US!!!

NICE TIMING, LUKE.

WE AIM TO PLEASE.

GO ON, JUST TRY SOMETHING! GO AHEAD!

WE DARE YOU!

SOMEONE GET ANOTHER ROPE, AND WE'LL TIE THEM UP SOME MORE!

LUKE... THERE ARE NAGAI HERE... AND THEY'VE TAKEN VIRTUALLY EVERYONE ELSE PRISONER...

EXCEPT MY ZELTRONS... THE TOFS TOOK THEM TO THEIR SHIP...

AND DEN SIVA... THE TOFS ARE FORCING HIM TO BETRAY THE OTHER NAGAI RIGHT NOW. WE HAVE TO PREVENT THAT...

WHY? THE NAGAI DESERVE TO DIE! AND DEN MORE THAN ANY OF THEM...

BECAUSE YOU LOVED KIRO, AND DEN KILLED HIM? BUT DO YOU HONESTLY BELIEVE, AFTER ALL THIS, THAT THE TOFS ARE ANY BETTER?

AND WHAT ABOUT THE PRISONERS? DO ALL THOSE ZELTRONS, AND LANDO, AND CHEWBACCA DESERVE TO DIE?

AM I GOING TO LOSE HAN ... JUST BE- CAUSE YOU DON'T WANT TO HELP DEN ... EVEN IN A GOOD CAUSE?

Oh...

ALL RIGHT! LET'S GO.

THE REST OF US WILL TAKE CARE OF YOUR BOYS, LEIA. TRUST US.

I DO.

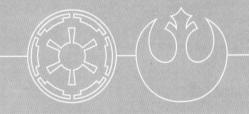

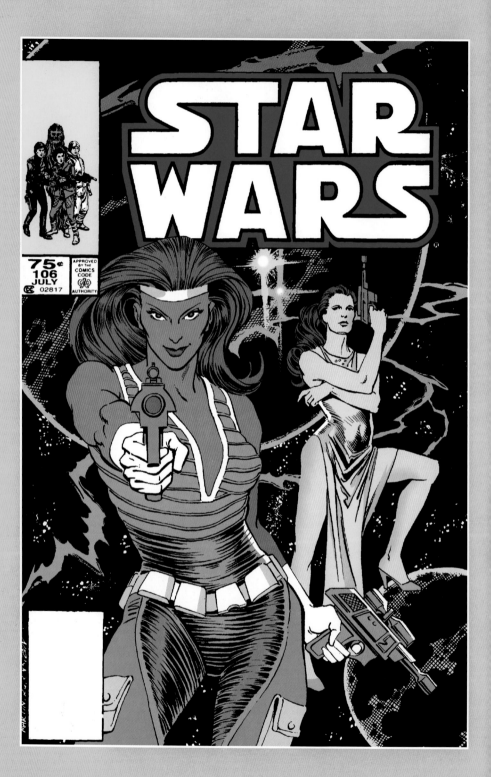

JO DUFFY
WRITER

CYNTHIA MARTIN
LAYOUTS

KEN STEACY
FINISHES

DAINA GRAZIUNUS, COLORIST
TOM ORZECHOWSKI, LETTERER

ANN NOCENTI
EDITOR

JIM SHOOTER
EDITOR IN CHIEF

TRULY, THIS IS A GLORIOUS DAY FOR OUR PEOPLE-- THE HIROMI!!

Oh, YES, CAPTAIN HOOKYR. NOTHING COULD BE MORE GLORIOUS THAN THIS!

THE PLANET OF ZELTROS HAS BEEN SAVED... OUR ALLIES-- LUKE SKYWALKER AND THE HOOJIBS-- ARE FREE... THE TOFS-- THOSE NEFARIOUS RAIDERS, HAVE BEEN ROUTED...

AND, MOST IMPORTANT OF ALL, NO ONE HURT ANY OF US!

NOW, LET'S HEAR IT FOR NOT GETTING HURT!

YAAAAY!

I'M GLAD NONE OF YOU GUYS WERE HURT, TOO.

HERE'S HOPING ALL OF YOU... AND PLIF'S FOLKS-- THE HOOJIBS-- ARE AS LUCKY...

...WHEN WE STAGE OUR ASSAULT ON THE MAIN TOF SHIP.

A-A-A-A-ASA-ASA-ASA...

ER... AH... DID YOU SAY ASSAULT?

SURE. A BUNCH OF MY FRIENDS-- AND OTHER MEMBERS OF THE ALLIANCE OF FREE PLANETS-- WERE TAKEN.

IT'S GOING TO TAKE MORE THAN MY MASTERY OF THE FORCE AND TRAINING AS A JEDI KNIGHT, AND MORE THAN THE HOOJIBS' TELEPATHY AND ENERGY-EATING ABILITIES TO FREE THEM.

IT'S GOING TO TAKE SKILL... DARING... CUNNING...

QUALITIES WHICH THE HIROMI LACK IN ABUNDANCE, LUKE.

I'LL HAVE MY LIGHT-SABERS... AND YOU CAN HAVE YOUR BLASTERS... OR ANY CLUBS AND BLADES THE TOFS WE CAPTURED WERE CARRYING.

WHAT ELSE COULD YOU ASK FOR?

Ah... REINFORCEMENTS?

A FAST SHIP TO TAKE US HOME?

LUNCH?

DON'T SHIRK, HIROG! THIS IS OUR CHANCE TO FULFILL OUR DESTINY AS HIROMI!

TRULY, WE HAVE ALWAYS BEEN LOYAL MEMBERS OF THE ALLIANCE OF FREE PLANETS...EXCEPT FOR TRYING TO CONQUER A FEW SMALL WORLDS FOR OUR- SELVES THAT NO ONE WANTED ANYWAY.

WE OWE IT TO OUR FRIENDS-- AND TO OUR RACE-- TO FREE THEM FROM THOSE... THOSE SPACE GANGSTERS!

YESSIR!

OH, WE'RE ALL GOING TO GET KILLED... I JUST KNOW IT.

LUKE, ARE YOU CERTAIN ABOUT THIS?

PLIF... WE HAVE A JOB TO DO, FOR THE SAKE OF THE OTHERS...

...SO WE'LL JUST HAVE TO MAKE THE BEST USE POSSIBLE OF THE TOOLS AT HAND.

IF THEY'RE REALLY INSPIRED, THE HIROMI MIGHT DO A GOOD JOB.

I'VE SEEN STRANGER THINGS THAN THAT HAPPEN.

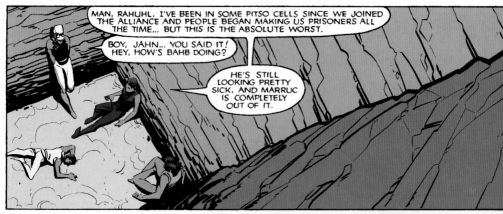

MAN, RAHUHL, I'VE BEEN IN SOME PITSO CELLS SINCE WE JOINED THE ALLIANCE AND PEOPLE BEGAN MAKING US PRISONERS ALL THE TIME... BUT THIS IS THE ABSOLUTE WORST.

BOY, JAHN... YOU SAID IT! HEY, HOW'S BAHB DOING?

HE'S STILL LOOKING PRETTY SICK, AND MARRUC IS COMPLETELY OUT OF IT.

I WISH THOSE TOFS HADN'T HIT THEM SO HARD WHEN THEY CAUGHT US.

YEAH. I WONDER HOW EVERYONE ELSE IS DOING...

IT'S TOUGH TO KEEP IT ALL STRAIGHT-- WE COME HOME TO ZELTROS, AN' THEN THE NAGAI INVADE, AN' CATCH HER HIGHNESS, AN' GENERAL SOLO, AND THE KING AND QUEEN AND EVERYONE...

AND THEN THESE TOFS-- WHOEVER THE HECK THEY ARE-- INVADE... AND CAPTURE US, AND ALL OUR FRIENDS, AND HALF OF THE NAGAI.

YEAH. Y'KNOW... WE'RE PRINCESS LEIA'S ATTACHÉS, SO IT'S OUR JOB TO PROTECT HER FROM BAD STUFF LIKE THAT.

AND WE CAN'T DO THAT, WHILE WE'RE STUCK IN HERE.

SO... YOU COME UP WITH A PLAN YET?

I THINK SO...

NOW LISTEN, YOU GUYS...

< WHAT HAVE YOU THERE? >

< FOOD FOR THE PRISONERS. *SUPREME* INSTRUCTED THAT THEY WERE TO BE KEPT HEALTHY AND WELL UNTIL HE ARRIVED TO DEAL WITH THEM PERSONALLY. >

< YES... THEY ARE INTERESTING PEOPLE, THESE ZELTRONS... AND I HEAR THEIR FEMALES ARE EVEN BETTER. >

< TRULY, IT IS WELL THAT WE CAME TO THIS GALAXY IN PURSUIT OF OUR OLD ENEMY-- THE NAGAI. >

< THAT FOOD YOU ARE TAKING IS FOR THE PRISONERS. >

< IF THEY ARE DISPLEASED... TELL THEM TO ADDRESS THEIR COMPLAINTS TO ME...! >

< INDEED. >

NOW--

OOWWW!

527

FOOLS!! DID YOU THINK I'D WALK IN HERE WITHOUT EXPECTING SOME STUNT?

JERKS!

IF YOU'RE UP TO THAT KIND OF TRICK, YOU'VE GOT ENOUGH ENERGY TO DO WITHOUT THIS MEAL... AND THE ONE AFTER.

AND CLEAN THIS MESS... OR YOU'LL GET NOTHING FROM US. EVER.

BUT... BUT, PLEASE... YOU GOTTA LET US OUTTA HERE.

AT LEAST LET MARRUC OUT... YOU REALLY HURT HIM BEFORE... AND WE WERE WORRIED... THAT'S WHY WE...

OUR INSTRUCTIONS SAID FOR YOU TO BE ALIVE AN' WELL FOR OUR BOSS WHEN HE GOT HERE...

DIDN'T SAY NOTHIN' ABOUT HAVIN' TO BE ALL FOUR OF YOU. THREE'LL PROBABLY DO.

GOT ANY MORE PLANS, JAHN?

WHILE, BACK ON ZELTROS...

528

LET'S BE QUIET, DANI. AFTER ALL THE TROUBLE LUKE AND THE HOOJIBS WENT TO TO RESCUE US, I'D HATE TO BE RECAPTURED...

... BY THE TOFS *OR* THE NAGAI!

NOT TO WORRY, LEIA... I'VE PROBABLY GOT MORE EXPERIENCE THAN YOU DO AT THIS TYPE OF WORK...

THERE THEY ARE... THE BAND OF TOFS ON THEIR WAY TO INTERCEPT AND CAPTURE THE BAND OF NAGAI WHO'D ALREADY TAKEN EVERONE ELSE PRISONER.

AND THERE HE IS WITH THEM -- THE NAGAI WHO RUINED MY LIFE --

-- DEN SIVA...

...DEN...

DANI, PLEASE... YOU MUSTN'T... YOU CAN'T.

DEN IS UNARMED... A HELPLESS PRISONER... AND HE GOT THAT WAY TRYING TO SAVE YOU FROM THE TOFS...

HE'S BETRAYING HIS OWN PEOPLE TO THEIR GREATEST ENEMIES FOR YOU... YOU WOULDN'T...

OF COURSE SHE WOULDN'T. IT WOULD MEAN GIVING US AWAY TO THE TOFS... AND DESTROYING ANY CHANCE EITHER WE OR DEN HAVE OF FREEING HAN AND LANDO AND CHEWBACCA...

AS WELL AS ALL THE ZELTRON LEADERS THE NAGAI HAVE CAPTURED.

YOU'RE RIGHT. I WOULDN'T. BUT I'D LIKE TO.

PLIF, ARE YOU OR ANY OF YOUR PEOPLE GETTING ANY INTELLIGIBLE THOUGHTS FROM THIS MAN?

NONE IN OUR LANGUAGE OR HIS OWN, LUKE... EXCEPT FOR INCREDIBLE, MALICIOUS HOSTILITY. HIS WILL IS VERY STRONG.

DON'T MAKE US GET UN-PLEASANT. TELL US HOW TO GET TO YOUR MAIN SHIP AND WHAT KIND OF A RECEPTION WE CAN EXPECT THERE.

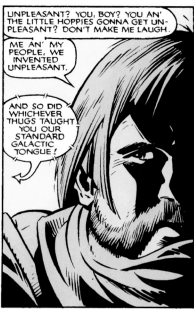

UNPLEASANT? YOU, BOY? YOU AN' THE LITTLE HOPPIES GONNA GET UN-PLEASANT? DON'T MAKE ME LAUGH.

ME AN' MY PEOPLE, WE INVENTED UNPLEASANT.

AND SO DID WHICHEVER THUGS TAUGHT YOU OUR STANDARD GALACTIC TONGUE!

NEVER MIND, LUKE!

WE WILL MAKE HIM TALK! WE PERFECTED UNPLEASANT!

THERE'S NOTHING-- EXCEPT EATING, CHEERING, AND NOT GETTING BEATEN UP-- THAT WE HIROMI LIKE BETTER THAN MAKING PEOPLE TALK.

NOW, TALK TO US! TALK! TALK! TALK

Y-Y-YOU B-B-B-BUGS ARE C-CRAZY!

YES, WE ARE! CRAZY ABOUT MAKING PEOPLE TALK! TOO BAD FOR YOU!

NOW, TALK!

THEREARE ONLYABOUTADOZEN ORSOOFUSLEFTON THESHIPIT'SATNINER STROKEZEROSEVE THREE

HE TALKED! *HE TALKED!* LET'S *HEAR* IT FOR THE RUTHLESS *HIROMI!*

BE *QUIET!* OR DO YOU WANT EVERY TOF IN THE AREA WHO'S NOT A PRISONER TO HEAR YOU AND COME INVESTIGATE?

ARE THERE ANY FREE TOFS WITHIN EARSHOT?

I DON'T PICK UP THOUGHTS FROM ANY.

WELL... I'M NOT SURE IT'S WISE-- OR PARTICULARLY NICE-- TO SCARE THEM LIKE THAT.

I SUSPECT THEY'LL GET OVER IT.

LOOK! WE'VE MADE IT SAFELY BACK TO OUR SHIP! SOFTLY, NOW...

YAAAAAAAAY!

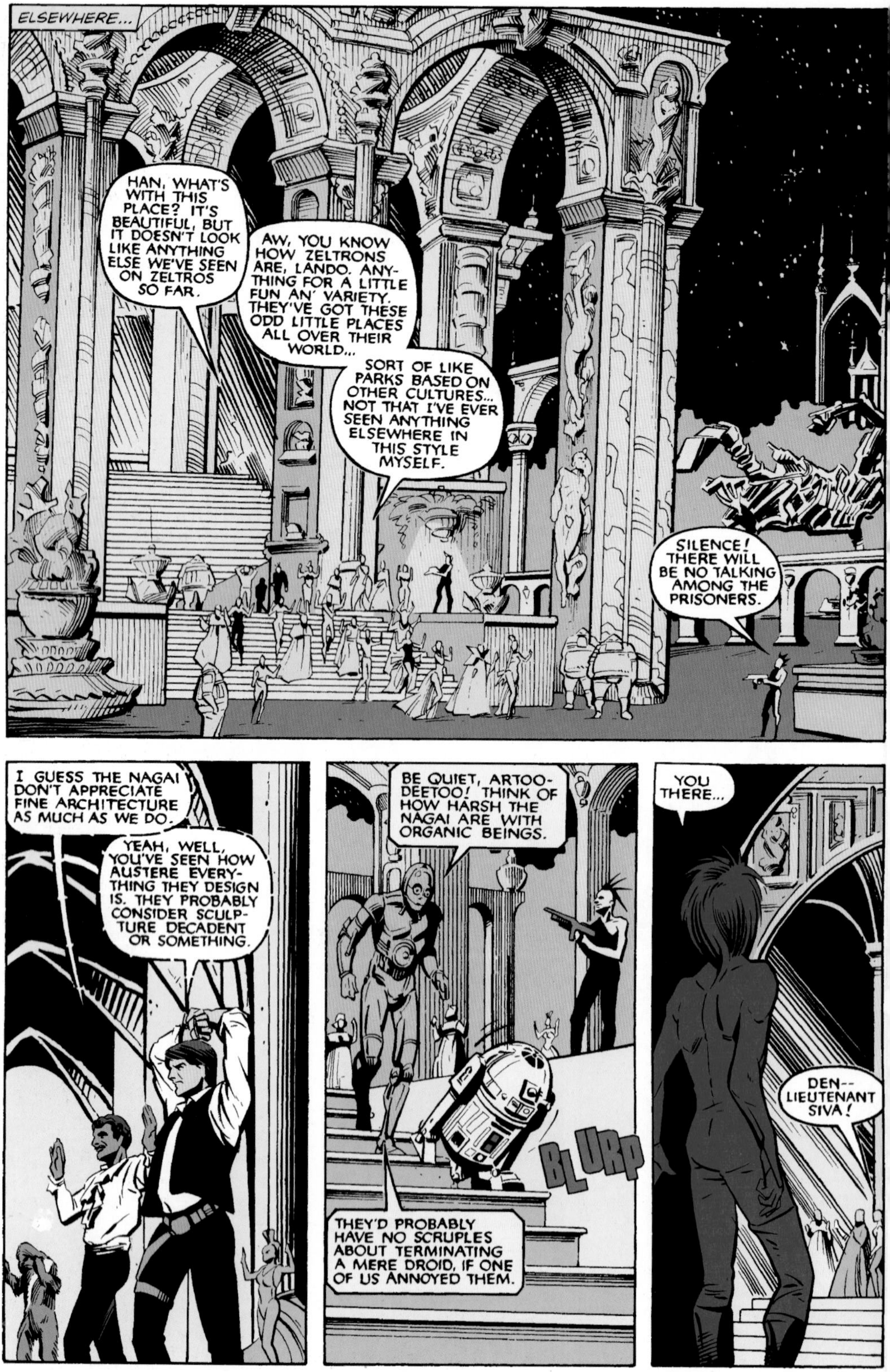
ELSEWHERE...
HAN, WHAT'S WITH THIS PLACE? IT'S BEAUTIFUL, BUT IT DOESN'T LOOK LIKE ANYTHING ELSE WE'VE SEEN ON ZELTROS SO FAR.
AW, YOU KNOW HOW ZELTRONS ARE, LANDO. ANY-THING FOR A LITTLE FUN AN' VARIETY. THEY'VE GOT THESE ODD LITTLE PLACES ALL OVER THEIR WORLD...
SORT OF LIKE PARKS BASED ON OTHER CULTURES... NOT THAT I'VE EVER SEEN ANYTHING ELSEWHERE IN THIS STYLE MYSELF.
SILENCE! THERE WILL BE NO TALKING AMONG THE PRISONERS.
I GUESS THE NAGAI DON'T APPRECIATE FINE ARCHITECTURE AS MUCH AS WE DO.
YEAH, WELL, YOU'VE SEEN HOW AUSTERE EVERY-THING THEY DESIGN IS. THEY PROBABLY CONSIDER SCULP-TURE DECADENT OR SOMETHING.
BE QUIET, ARTOO-DEETOO! THINK OF HOW HARSH THE NAGAI ARE WITH ORGANIC BEINGS.
BLURP
THEY'D PROBABLY HAVE NO SCRUPLES ABOUT TERMINATING A MERE DROID, IF ONE OF US ANNOYED THEM.
YOU THERE...
DEN-- LIEUTENANT SIVA!

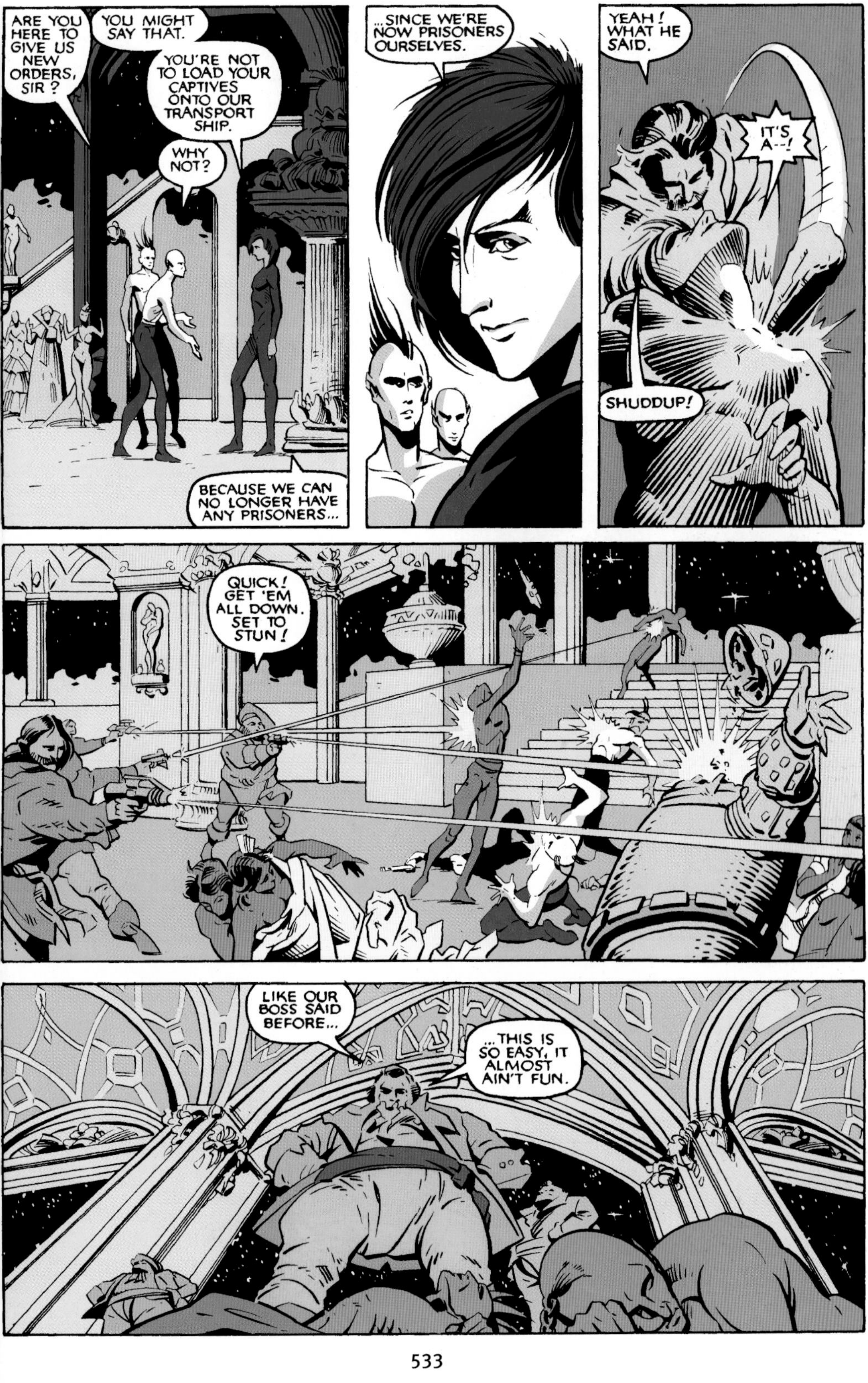
ARE YOU HERE TO GIVE US NEW ORDERS, SIR?
YOU MIGHT SAY THAT.
YOU'RE NOT TO LOAD YOUR CAPTIVES ONTO OUR TRANSPORT SHIP.
WHY NOT?
BECAUSE WE CAN NO LONGER HAVE ANY PRISONERS...
...SINCE WE'RE NOW PRISONERS OURSELVES.
YEAH! WHAT HE SAID.
IT'S A--!
SHUDDUP!
QUICK! GET 'EM ALL DOWN. SET TO STUN!
LIKE OUR BOSS SAID BEFORE...
...THIS IS SO EASY, IT ALMOST AIN'T FUN.

GRODONK!

NO, CHEWIE, I DON'T KNOW WHO'S FIRIN'...

...BUT THAT DON'T MEAN I'M NOT GONNA TAKE ADVANTAGE OF IT!

AROOO!

YOU HEARD THE MAN, FOLKS. THIS IS OUR CHANCE!

ULP!

POP!

OH, ARTOO! DON'T GET HURT!!!

ALL RIGHT!

YEAH!

LET'S SHOW THOSE GUYS!

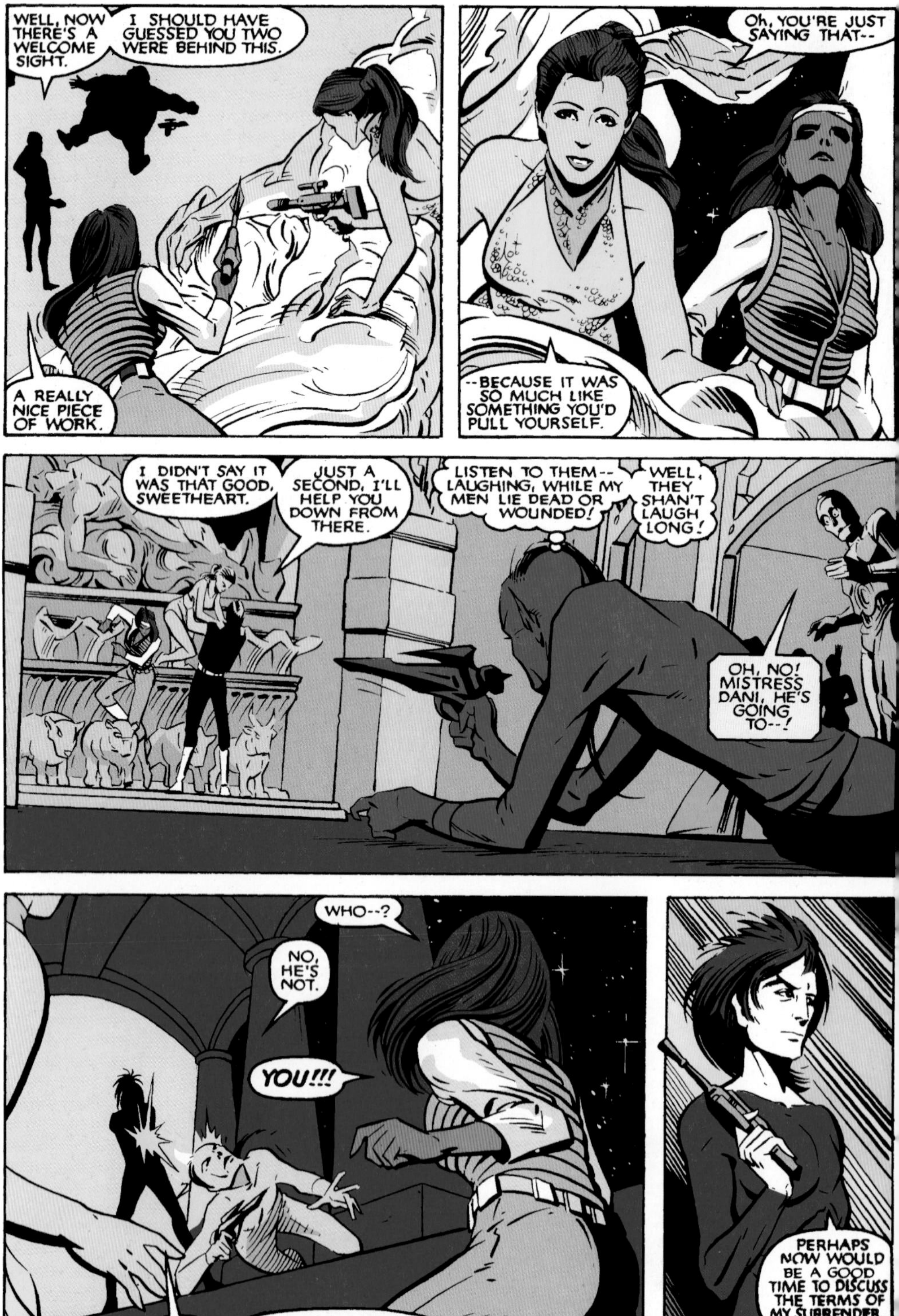
WELL, NOW THERE'S A WELCOME SIGHT.
I SHOULD HAVE GUESSED YOU TWO WERE BEHIND THIS.
A REALLY NICE PIECE OF WORK.
Oh, YOU'RE JUST SAYING THAT--
--BECAUSE IT WAS SO MUCH LIKE SOMETHING YOU'D PULL YOURSELF.
I DIDN'T SAY IT WAS THAT GOOD, SWEETHEART.
JUST A SECOND, I'LL HELP YOU DOWN FROM THERE.
LISTEN TO THEM-- LAUGHING, WHILE MY MEN LIE DEAD OR WOUNDED!
WELL, THEY SHAN'T LAUGH LONG!
OH, NO! MISTRESS DANI, HE'S GOING TO--!
WHO--?
NO, HE'S NOT.
YOU!!!
YES, DANI. I.
WELL, SINCE I SEEM TO HAVE TAKEN STEPS THAT WILL IRREVOCABLY CUT ME OFF FROM MY PEOPLE--
PERHAPS NOW WOULD BE A GOOD TIME TO DISCUSS THE TERMS OF MY SURRENDER...
...UNLESS... I COULD POSSIBLY INTEREST YOU IN A NEW ALLIANCE...?

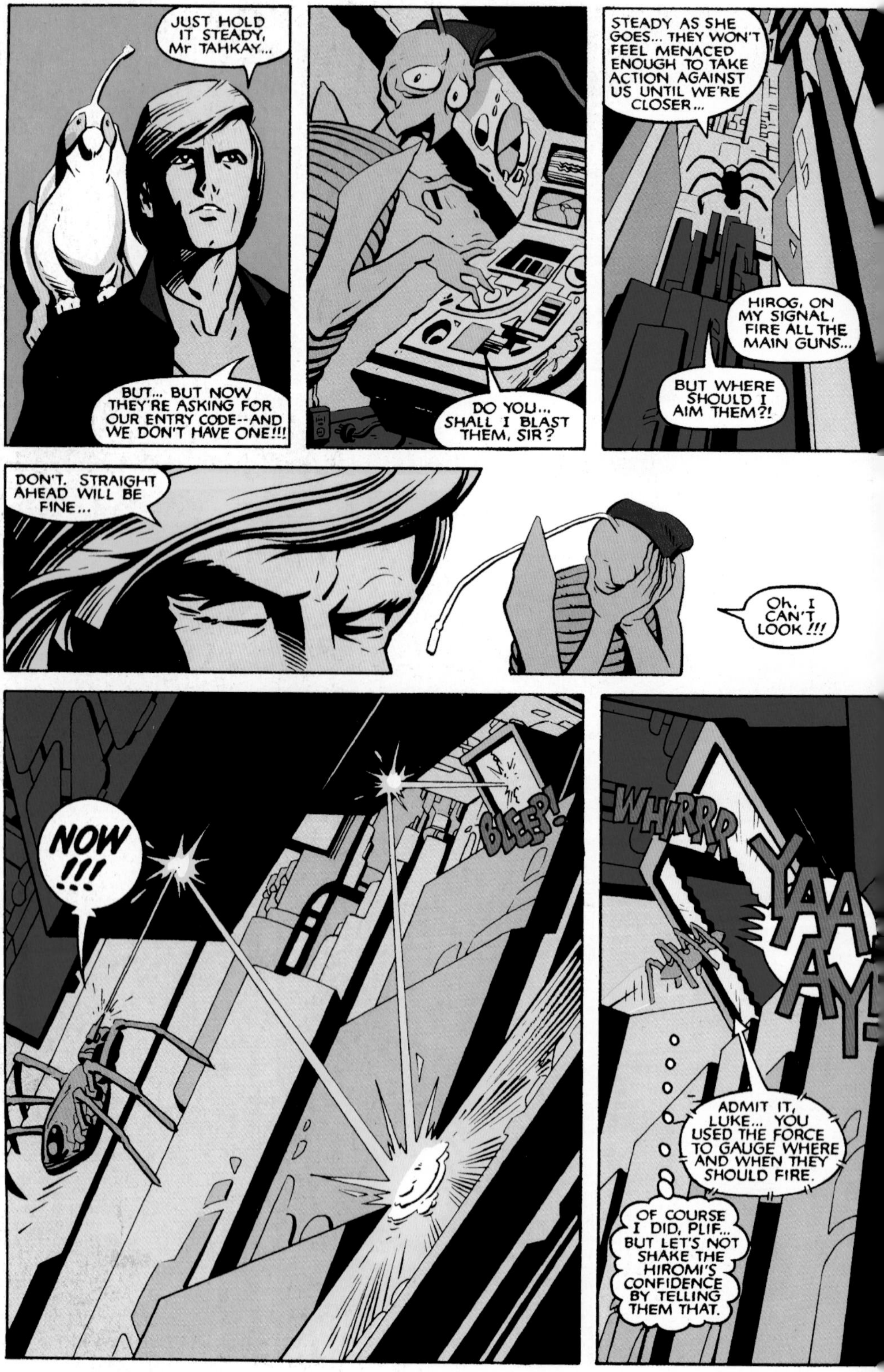
JUST HOLD IT STEADY, Mr TAHKAY...
BUT... BUT NOW THEY'RE ASKING FOR OUR ENTRY CODE--AND WE DON'T HAVE ONE!!!
DO YOU... SHALL I BLAST THEM, SIR?
STEADY AS SHE GOES... THEY WON'T FEEL MENACED ENOUGH TO TAKE ACTION AGAINST US UNTIL WE'RE CLOSER...
HIROG, ON MY SIGNAL, FIRE ALL THE MAIN GUNS...
BUT WHERE SHOULD I AIM THEM?!
DON'T. STRAIGHT AHEAD WILL BE FINE...
Oh, I CAN'T LOOK!!!
NOW!!!
BLEEP!
WHIRRR
YAAAAY!
ADMIT IT, LUKE... YOU USED THE FORCE TO GAUGE WHERE AND WHEN THEY SHOULD FIRE.
OF COURSE I DID, PLIF... BUT LET'S NOT SHAKE THE HIROMI'S CONFIDENCE BY TELLING THEM THAT.

A PRETTY ROUGH ONE. I FIGURE HALF OF US WILL DO WHAT WE CAN TO TAKE OUT THE SECURITY SYSTEMS-- LIVING AND MECHANICAL...

...WHILE THE REST FIND AND FREE THE KIDS...

OF COURSE... IT WOULD BE A LOT EASIER IF EVERYONE HELPED.

HOW ABOUT IT, GUYS? YOU FEEL LIKE COMING DOWN AND JOINING THE PARTY?

W-W-WELL... IF YOU'RE ABSOLUTE-LY SURE IT'S SAFE...?

SO WHICH JOB DO YOU GUYS WANT TO TAKE?

WHICH-EVER ONE YOU'RE DOING!

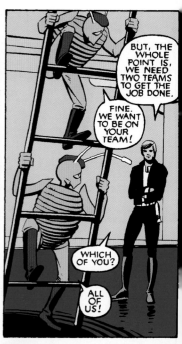

BUT, THE WHOLE POINT IS, WE NEED TWO TEAMS TO GET THE JOB DONE.

FINE. WE WANT TO BE ON YOUR TEAM!

WHICH OF YOU?

ALL OF US!

BUT WE HAVE TO SPLIT UP... HOW ABOUT IF YOU ALL STICK TOGETHER, AND I TAKE THE HOOJIBS WITH ME?

BUT... IF WE GO ALONE, WHO'LL PROTECT US?

WHY... YOU'LL PROTECT YOUR-SELVES!

WE WILL? WITH WHAT?

WHY... UH... WITH YOUR GLORIOUS HIROMI COURAGE! YOUR CUNNING! YOUR SKILLS!

THAT DAUNTLESS, MATCHLESS, LEGENDARY HIROMI SPIRIT...

COME ON, NOW! LET'S HEAR IT FOR THE GLORIOUS HIROMI...

YAAAY!

BESIDES, HE'S COUNTING ON US! NOW ONWARD, MEN. WE HAVE A JOB TO DO!

FEAR NOTHING!

ZRIK!

WH-WH-WH-WHAT HAPPENED TO THE LIGHTS...

I... SUSPECT THAT OUR ALLIES, THE GLORIOUS HOOJIBS, HAVE BEEN FEEDING OFF THE ENERGY IN THE SECURITY SYSTEMS. FORWARD...

Er... AND IF ANYONE WISHES TO HOLD HANDS UNTIL WE REACH A MORE BRIGHTLY LIT CORRIDOR...

... I, FOR ONE, SHALL ASK NO QUESTIONS AFTERWARDS!

EVERY SYSTEM EXCEPT LIFE SUPPORT IS SHUTTIN' DOWN, ONE CORRIDOR AFTER ANOTHER...

AN' THERE'S NOTHIN' WRONG WITH THE POWER SYSTEMS THAT I CAN SEE.

UNOBSERVANT LOUT!

AHA! AN AUSPICIOUS LOOKING DOOR IF EVER I'VE SEEN ONE! A CELL DOOR, I'VE NO DOUBT.

SHALL I BLAST IT, MEN?

OH, DO!

IT'S THEM! THE ZELTRONS WE'VE BEEN LOOKING FOR!

BUT, WHATEVER IS WRONG WITH MARRUC. HE LOOKS QUITE--

YOU!

EEP!!

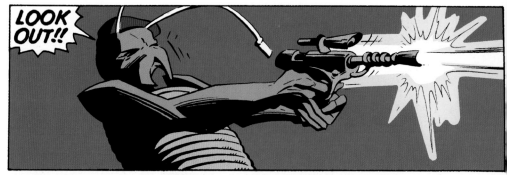

LOOK OUT!!

NICE SHOOTING, HIROG. LUCKY FOR ME YOU SPOTTED THAT TOF...

NOW WE BETTER CLEAR OUT OF HERE. TOUGH AS WE ALL ARE, I DON'T KNOW IF FIFTEEN OR SO OF US ARE ENOUGH TO TAKE ON THIS WHOLE GALLEON...

...SO I PLANTED SOME EXPLOSIVES IN A FEW OF THEIR MAIN SYSTEMS.

WE'D BETTER BE AWAY BEFORE THEY BLOW...

BE RIGHT WITH YOU, LUKE...

A TOF! WE ACTUALLY BEAT A TOF...

IN A FAIR FIGHT!

BY OUR-SELVES...

IMAGINE!!

SO, LET'S HEAR IT--

YAAAYAYY!

NEXT: OLD FRIENDS AND NEW UNITE FOR THE FINAL CHAPTER IN MARVEL'S CONTINUING ADVENTURES OF LUKE SKYWALKER--

ALL TOGETHER NOW!

PORTRAIT OF A JEDI MASTER!

YODA IN HIS SWAMPLAND HOME ON DAGOBAH, LOVINGLY PICTURED BY MARIE SEVERIN!

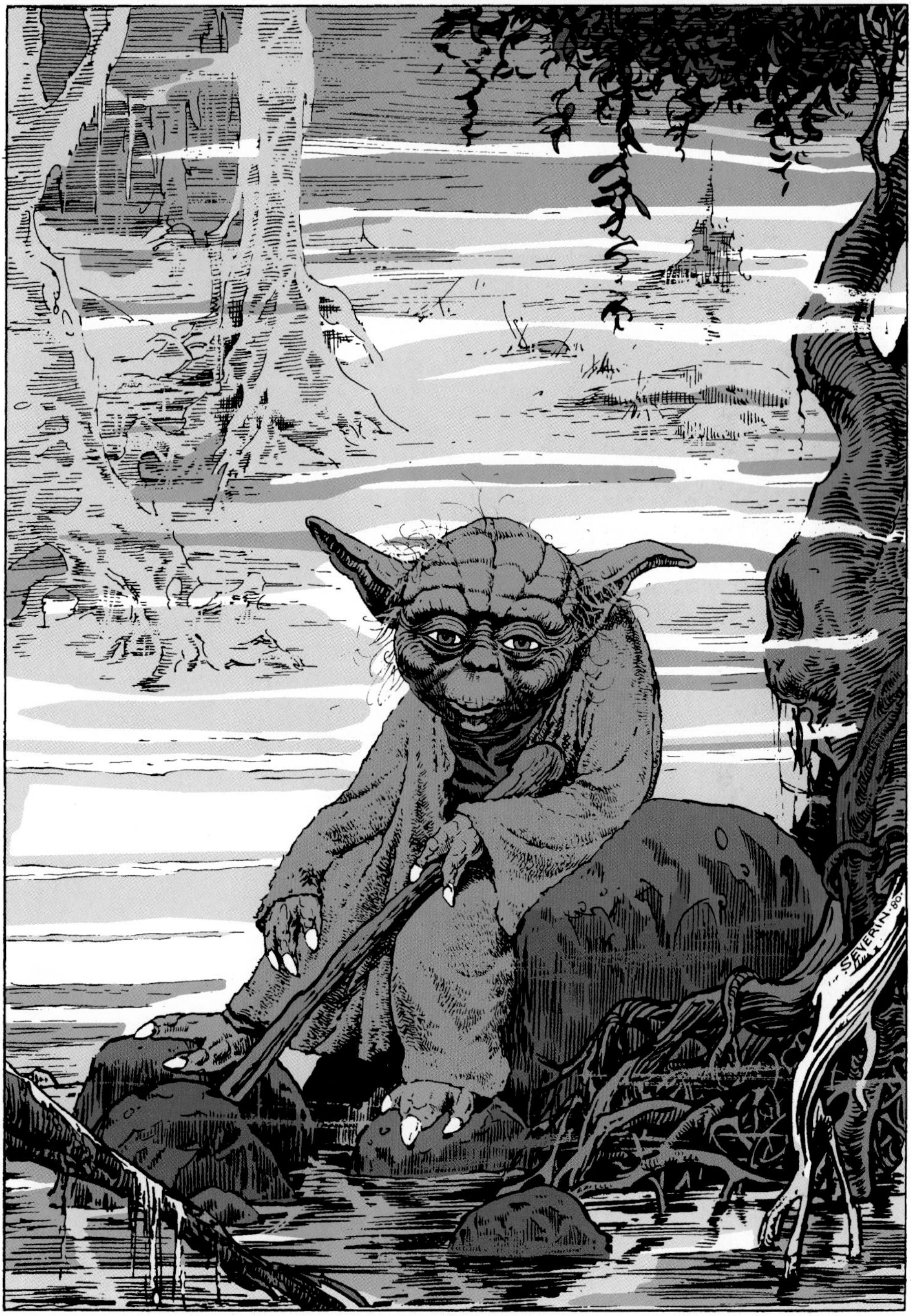

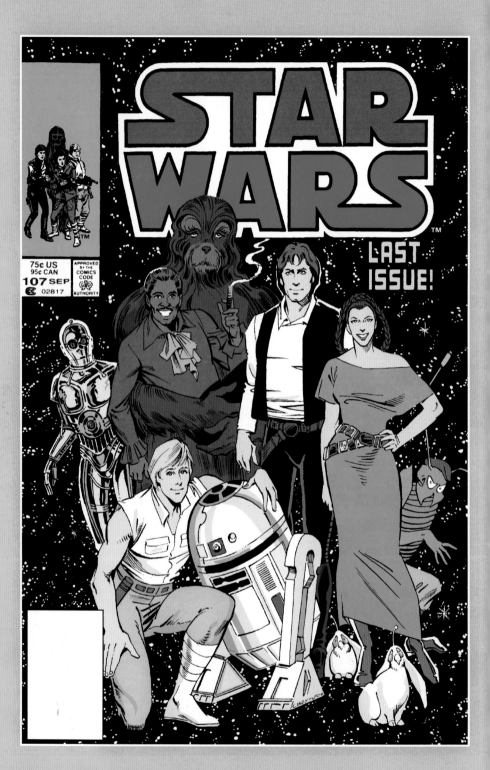

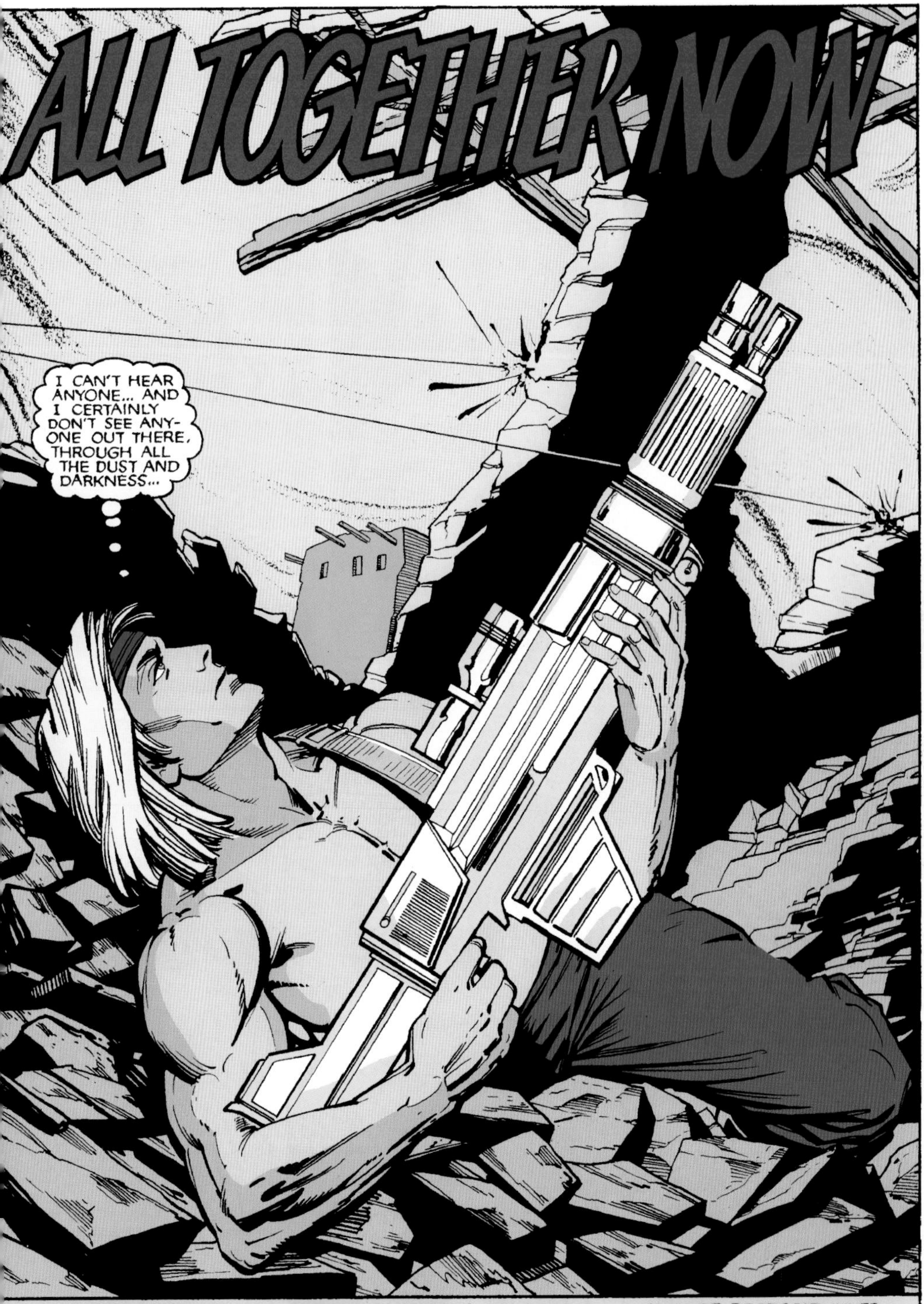
ALL TOGETHER NOW
I CAN'T HEAR ANYONE... AND I CERTAINLY DON'T SEE ANYONE OUT THERE, THROUGH ALL THE DUST AND DARKNESS...

JO DUFFY, WRITER CYNTHIA MARTIN, PENCILER WHILCE PORTACIO, INKER
TOM ORZECHOWSKI, LETTERER ELAINE LEE, COLORIST ANN NOCENTI, EDITOR JIM SHOOTER, EDITOR IN CHIEF

BLAM BLAM

AAIEEEGHK!

...BUT THAT DOESN'T MEAN THEY'RE NOT OUT THERE...

NOW... WHERE'S THE NEXT THREAT COMING FROM?

KNIFE!

BETTER GET YOUR HEAD DOWN, FRIEND. I'D HATE TO LOSE YOU.

A POINT WELL TAKEN, LUKE.

BUT SHARE YOUR SECRET WITH ME. HOW DO YOU ALWAYS KNOW WHEN THE TOFS ARE ABOUT TO START SNIPING AT US?

FOR THAT MATTER... HOW DID YOU KNOW I WAS BEHIND YOU? YOU CANNOT HAVE HEARD ME!

SHING

I DIDN'T... I FELT YOU... THE *FORCE* THAT SURROUNDS US ALL CAN TELL YOU MANY THINGS...

...ONCE YOU'VE LET YOURSELF BECOME SENSITIVE TO IT.

AH, YES... THE *FORCE*. YOU LEARNED WONDERFUL THINGS, WHEN YOU TRAINED IN THE WAYS OF THE JEDI KNIGHTS. HAVE YOU EVER CONSIDERED SHARING SOME OF YOUR KNOWLEDGE WITH MY PEOPLE-- THE NAGAI?

THERE'LL BE TIME ENOUGH TO CONSIDER CULTURAL EXCHANGE BETWEEN NAGAI AND THE ALLIANCE OF FREE PLANETS, AFTER WE WIN THE WAR WE HAVE ON OUR HANDS RIGHT HERE.

SPEAKING OF WHICH-- DO ANY OF YOU OVER THERE SEE OR HEAR ANYTHING WE SHOULD BE AWARE OF?

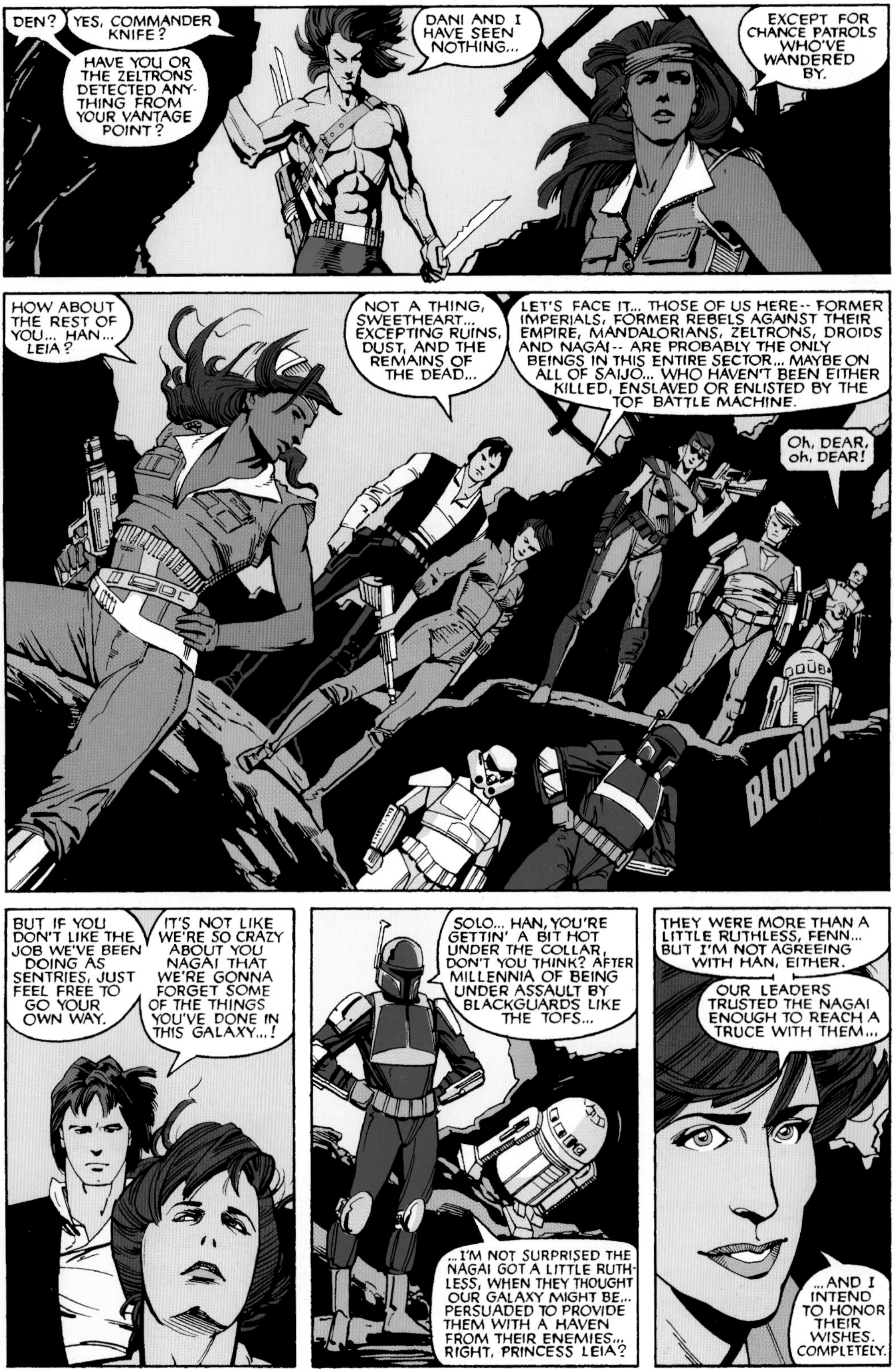
DEN?
YES, COMMANDER KNIFE?
HAVE YOU OR THE ZELTRONS DETECTED ANYTHING FROM YOUR VANTAGE POINT?
DANI AND I HAVE SEEN NOTHING...
EXCEPT FOR CHANCE PATROLS WHO'VE WANDERED BY.
HOW ABOUT THE REST OF YOU... HAN... LEIA?
NOT A THING, SWEETHEART... EXCEPTING RUINS, DUST, AND THE REMAINS OF THE DEAD...
LET'S FACE IT... THOSE OF US HERE-- FORMER IMPERIALS, FORMER REBELS AGAINST THEIR EMPIRE, MANDALORIANS, ZELTRONS, DROIDS AND NAGAI-- ARE PROBABLY THE ONLY BEINGS IN THIS ENTIRE SECTOR... MAYBE ON ALL OF SAIJO... WHO HAVEN'T BEEN EITHER KILLED, ENSLAVED OR ENLISTED BY THE TOF BATTLE MACHINE.
Oh, DEAR, oh, DEAR!
BLOOP!
BUT IF YOU DON'T LIKE THE JOB WE'VE BEEN DOING AS SENTRIES, JUST FEEL FREE TO GO YOUR OWN WAY.
IT'S NOT LIKE WE'RE SO CRAZY ABOUT YOU NAGAI THAT WE'RE GONNA FORGET SOME OF THE THINGS YOU'VE DONE IN THIS GALAXY...!
SOLO... HAN, YOU'RE GETTIN' A BIT HOT UNDER THE COLLAR, DON'T YOU THINK? AFTER MILLENNIA OF BEING UNDER ASSAULT BY BLACKGUARDS LIKE THE TOFS...
...I'M NOT SURPRISED THE NAGAI GOT A LITTLE RUTHLESS, WHEN THEY THOUGHT OUR GALAXY MIGHT BE... PERSUADED TO PROVIDE THEM WITH A HAVEN FROM THEIR ENEMIES... RIGHT, PRINCESS LEIA?
THEY WERE MORE THAN A LITTLE RUTHLESS, FENN... BUT I'M NOT AGREEING WITH HAN, EITHER.
OUR LEADERS TRUSTED THE NAGAI ENOUGH TO REACH A TRUCE WITH THEM...
...AND I INTEND TO HONOR THEIR WISHES. COMPLETELY.

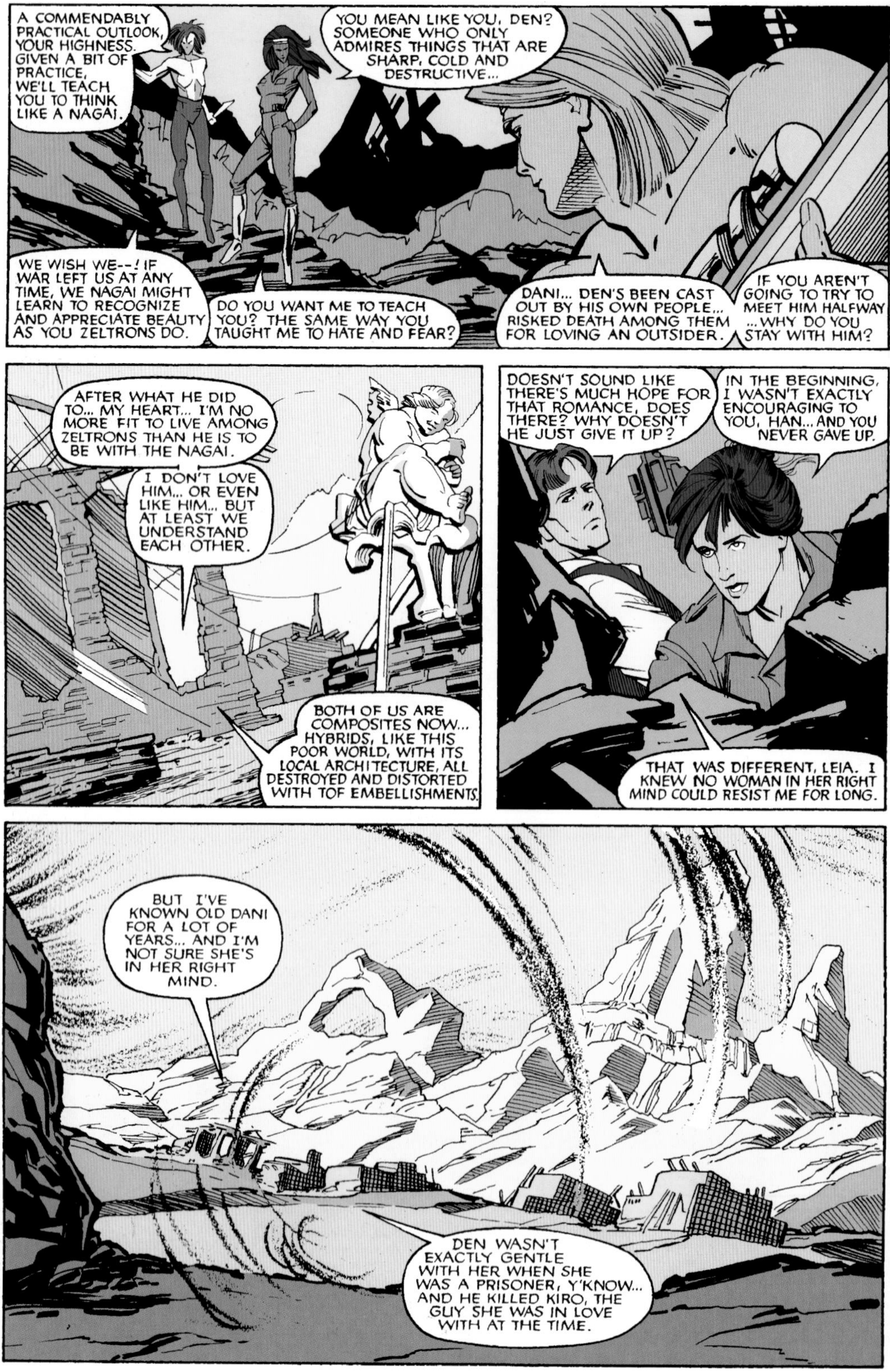
A COMMENDABLY PRACTICAL OUTLOOK, YOUR HIGHNESS. GIVEN A BIT OF PRACTICE, WE'LL TEACH YOU TO THINK LIKE A NAGAI.
YOU MEAN LIKE YOU, DEN? SOMEONE WHO ONLY ADMIRES THINGS THAT ARE SHARP, COLD AND DESTRUCTIVE...
WE WISH WE--! IF WAR LEFT US AT ANY TIME, WE NAGAI MIGHT LEARN TO RECOGNIZE AND APPRECIATE BEAUTY AS YOU ZELTRONS DO.
DO YOU WANT ME TO TEACH YOU? THE SAME WAY YOU TAUGHT ME TO HATE AND FEAR?
DANI... DEN'S BEEN CAST OUT BY HIS OWN PEOPLE... RISKED DEATH AMONG THEM FOR LOVING AN OUTSIDER.
IF YOU AREN'T GOING TO TRY TO MEET HIM HALFWAY ...WHY DO YOU STAY WITH HIM?
AFTER WHAT HE DID TO... MY HEART... I'M NO MORE FIT TO LIVE AMONG ZELTRONS THAN HE IS TO BE WITH THE NAGAI.
I DON'T LOVE HIM... OR EVEN LIKE HIM... BUT AT LEAST WE UNDERSTAND EACH OTHER.
BOTH OF US ARE COMPOSITES NOW... HYBRIDS, LIKE THIS POOR WORLD, WITH ITS LOCAL ARCHITECTURE, ALL DESTROYED AND DISTORTED WITH TOF EMBELLISHMENTS.
DOESN'T SOUND LIKE THERE'S MUCH HOPE FOR THAT ROMANCE, DOES THERE? WHY DOESN'T HE JUST GIVE IT UP?
IN THE BEGINNING, I WASN'T EXACTLY ENCOURAGING TO YOU, HAN... AND YOU NEVER GAVE UP.
THAT WAS DIFFERENT, LEIA. I KNEW NO WOMAN IN HER RIGHT MIND COULD RESIST ME FOR LONG.
BUT I'VE KNOWN OLD DANI FOR A LOT OF YEARS... AND I'M NOT SURE SHE'S IN HER RIGHT MIND.
DEN WASN'T EXACTLY GENTLE WITH HER WHEN SHE WAS A PRISONER, Y'KNOW... AND HE KILLED KIRO, THE GUY SHE WAS IN LOVE WITH AT THE TIME.

TEMPERS ARE FRAYING AND I'M NOT SURPRISED, CONSIDERING WHAT'S AT STAKE HERE, AND HOW SMALL OUR CHANCES OF SUCCEEDING--

--AT THIS MISSION ADMIRAL ACKBAR AND MON MOTHMA ASSIGNED US.

WE MUST PUT ASIDE OUR PERSONAL FEELINGS AND GRUDGES... IT IS OUR ONLY HOPE.

NOW, I KNOW MOST OF YOU ARE FAMILIAR WITH THE PLANET SAIJO, ONE OF THE WORLDS ON THE RIM OF THE GALAXY. ONE OF THE EARLIEST BATTLES BETWEEN OUR PEOPLE AND YOU NAGAI WAS FOUGHT THERE...

...JUST AS IT HAD PREVIOUSLY BEEN THE SITE OF SOME OF THE BLOODIEST AND BITTEREST DISPUTES BETWEEN US, WHEN SOME OF THOSE HERE STILL SUPPORTED THE GALACTIC EMPEROR, AND THE REST WERE IN REBELLION AGAINST HIM.

THE WORLD ITSELF IS SPARSELY POPULATED, AND ITS INHABITANTS HAVE RAISED ONLY THE MOST PRIMITIVE OF STRUCTURES...

...BUT IT HAS EVER THRIVED AS A SPACEPORT AND A TRADING POST AMONG THE OUTER WORLDS.

SINCE WE LEARNED OF THE NAGAI INCURSIONS THERE, LONG BEFORE WE ACCEPTED THEM INTO OUR ALLIANCE, WE HAVE HAD OUR FINEST INTELLIGENCE AGENTS IN THE OUTER WORLDS KEEPING TRACK OF ALL THE COMINGS AND GOINGS ON SAIJO...

AND WE NOW KNOW, WITH ABSOLUTE CERTAINTY, THAT NEITHER THE NATIVES NOR THE NAGAI ARE IN POWER THERE.

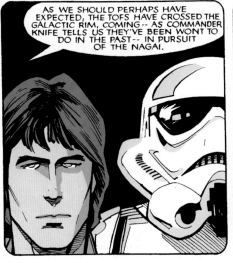

AS WE SHOULD PERHAPS HAVE EXPECTED, THE TOFS HAVE CROSSED THE GALACTIC RIM, COMING-- AS COMMANDER KNIFE TELLS US THEY'VE BEEN WONT TO DO IN THE PAST-- IN PURSUIT OF THE NAGAI.

AND THE SUPREME COMMANDER OF ALL THEIR FORCES ON THIS EXPEDITION HAS MADE SAIJO HIS PERSONAL BASE -- THE BASE OF OPERATIONS OF THE CROWN PRINCE OF TOF, HEIR TO THE THRONE OF THEIR ENTIRE CIVILIZATION.

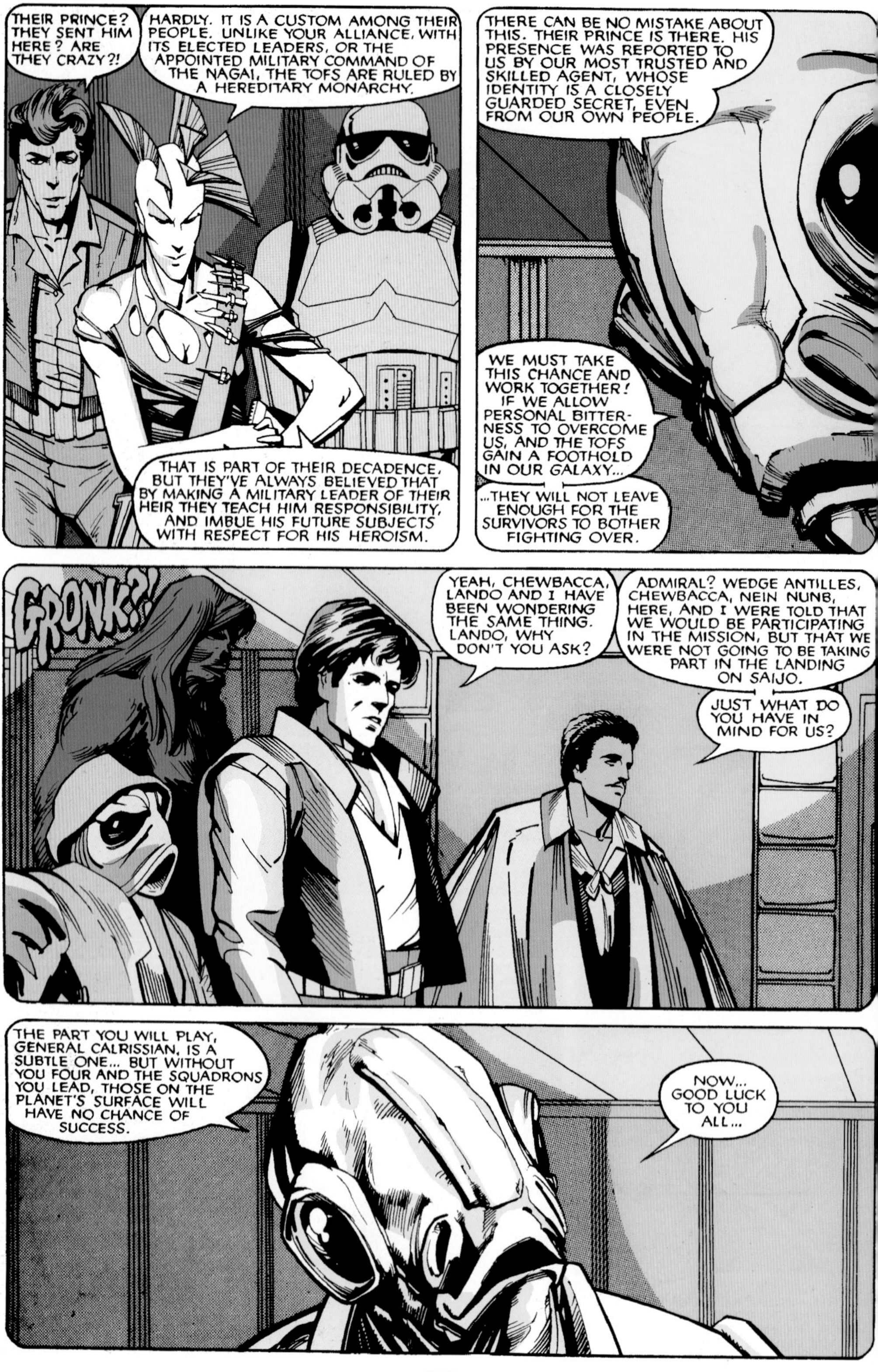
THEIR PRINCE? THEY SENT HIM HERE? ARE THEY CRAZY?!
HARDLY. IT IS A CUSTOM AMONG THEIR PEOPLE. UNLIKE YOUR ALLIANCE, WITH ITS ELECTED LEADERS, OR THE APPOINTED MILITARY COMMAND OF THE NAGAI, THE TOFS ARE RULED BY A HEREDITARY MONARCHY.
THAT IS PART OF THEIR DECADENCE, BUT THEY'VE ALWAYS BELIEVED THAT BY MAKING A MILITARY LEADER OF THEIR HEIR THEY TEACH HIM RESPONSIBILITY, AND IMBUE HIS FUTURE SUBJECTS WITH RESPECT FOR HIS HEROISM.
THERE CAN BE NO MISTAKE ABOUT THIS. THEIR PRINCE IS THERE. HIS PRESENCE WAS REPORTED TO US BY OUR MOST TRUSTED AND SKILLED AGENT, WHOSE IDENTITY IS A CLOSELY GUARDED SECRET, EVEN FROM OUR OWN PEOPLE.
WE MUST TAKE THIS CHANCE AND WORK TOGETHER! IF WE ALLOW PERSONAL BITTERNESS TO OVERCOME US, AND THE TOFS GAIN A FOOTHOLD IN OUR GALAXY...
...THEY WILL NOT LEAVE ENOUGH FOR THE SURVIVORS TO BOTHER FIGHTING OVER.
GRONK?!
YEAH, CHEWBACCA, LANDO AND I HAVE BEEN WONDERING THE SAME THING. LANDO, WHY DON'T YOU ASK?
ADMIRAL? WEDGE ANTILLES, CHEWBACCA, NEIN NUNB, HERE, AND I WERE TOLD THAT WE WOULD BE PARTICIPATING IN THE MISSION, BUT THAT WE WERE NOT GOING TO BE TAKING PART IN THE LANDING ON SAIJO.
JUST WHAT DO YOU HAVE IN MIND FOR US?
THE PART YOU WILL PLAY, GENERAL CALRISSIAN, IS A SUBTLE ONE... BUT WITHOUT YOU FOUR AND THE SQUADRONS YOU LEAD, THOSE ON THE PLANET'S SURFACE WILL HAVE NO CHANCE OF SUCCESS.
NOW... GOOD LUCK TO YOU ALL...

AND MAY THE FORCE BE WITH YOU." NOT A BAD SEND-OFF, WHEN YOU THINK OF IT.

WITH WHAT'S COMING UP, THE MORE THAT'S POSITIVE WE HAVE WITH US, THE BETTER.

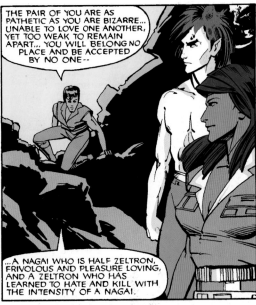

THE PAIR OF YOU ARE AS PATHETIC AS YOU ARE BIZARRE... UNABLE TO LOVE ONE ANOTHER, YET TOO WEAK TO REMAIN APART... YOU WILL BELONG NO PLACE AND BE ACCEPTED BY NO ONE--

...A NAGAI WHO IS HALF ZELTRON, FRIVOLOUS AND PLEASURE LOVING, AND A ZELTRON WHO HAS LEARNED TO HATE AND KILL WITH THE INTENSITY OF A NAGAI.

FUNNY, I THOUGHT YOU NAGAI LIKED HYBRIDS... OR WAS THAT JUST WHAT YOU TOLD BEY WHEN HE WANDERED INTO YOUR SECTOR OF SPACE, SO THAT YOU COULD GAIN HIS CONFIDENCE AND CONVINCE HIM TO BETRAY THE REST OF US?

BEY WAS HALF CORELLIAN, LIKE YOU, SOLO... BUT HE WAS ALSO HALF NAGAI... HALF MY BROTHER. FOR THAT I WELCOMED HIM.

AND HE WAS WEAK! FOR YOUR SAKE, HE ALSO BETRAYED US NAGAI.

IN FUTURE, WHEN I DEAL WITH THOSE WHO ARE NOT TRUE NAGAI, I SHALL REMEMBER THAT!

THIS IS THE MERRI-WEATHER... BULK CRUISER MERRIWEATHER, REQUESTING LANDING CLEARANCE, THAT WE MAY CONDUCT NORMAL TRADE. WE BRING SUPPLIES FROM TOF CENTRAL.

SAIJO? HAVE WE PERMISSION TO LAND?

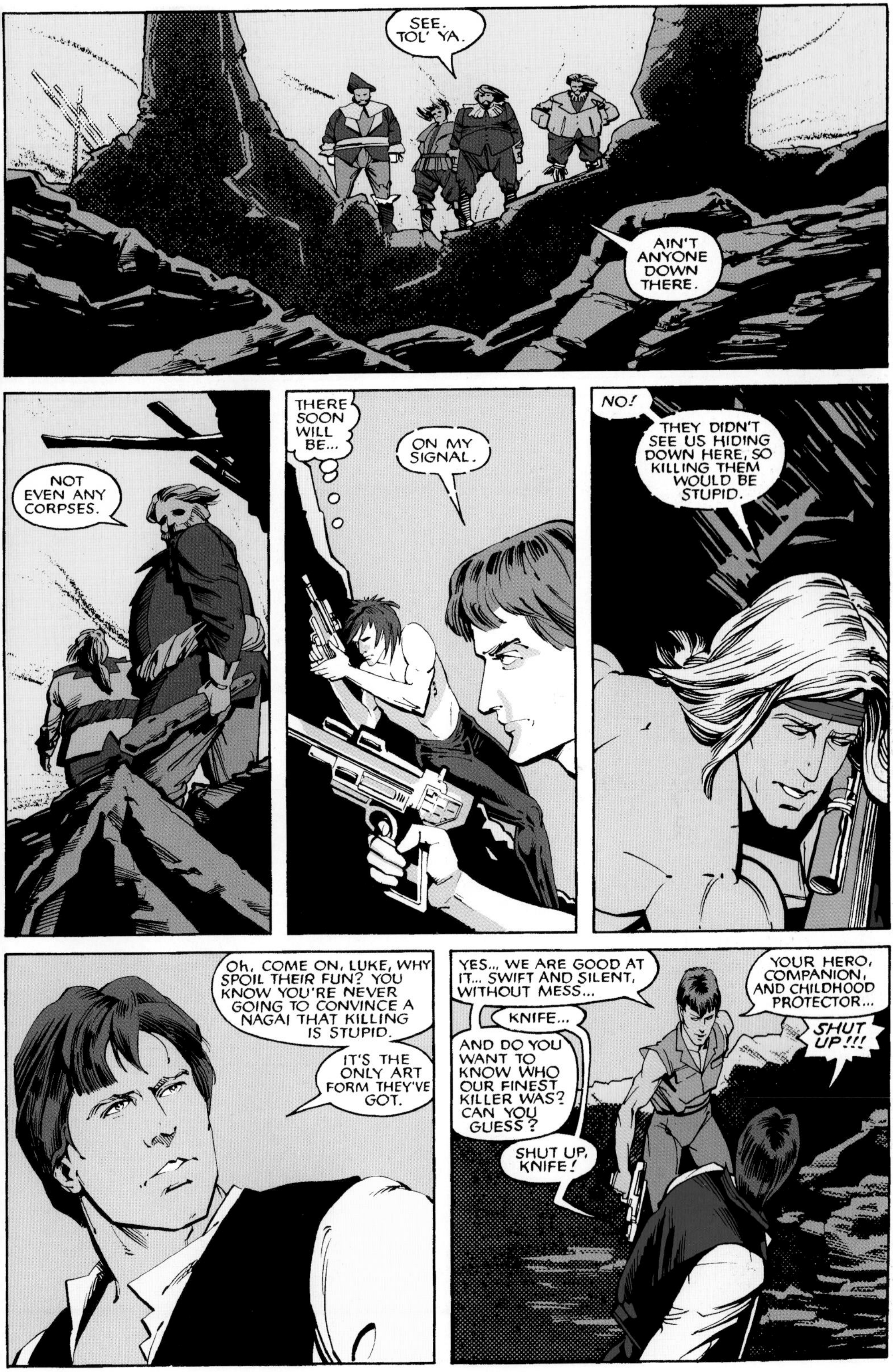
SEE. TOL' YA.
AIN'T ANYONE DOWN THERE.
NOT EVEN ANY CORPSES.
THERE SOON WILL BE...
ON MY SIGNAL.
NO!
THEY DIDN'T SEE US HIDING DOWN HERE, SO KILLING THEM WOULD BE STUPID.
Oh, COME ON, LUKE, WHY SPOIL THEIR FUN? YOU KNOW YOU'RE NEVER GOING TO CONVINCE A NAGAI THAT KILLING IS STUPID.
IT'S THE ONLY ART FORM THEY'VE GOT.
YES... WE ARE GOOD AT IT... SWIFT AND SILENT, WITHOUT MESS...
KNIFE...
AND DO YOU WANT TO KNOW WHO OUR FINEST KILLER WAS? CAN YOU GUESS?
SHUT UP, KNIFE!
YOUR HERO, COMPANION, AND CHILDHOOD PROTECTOR...
SHUT UP!!!

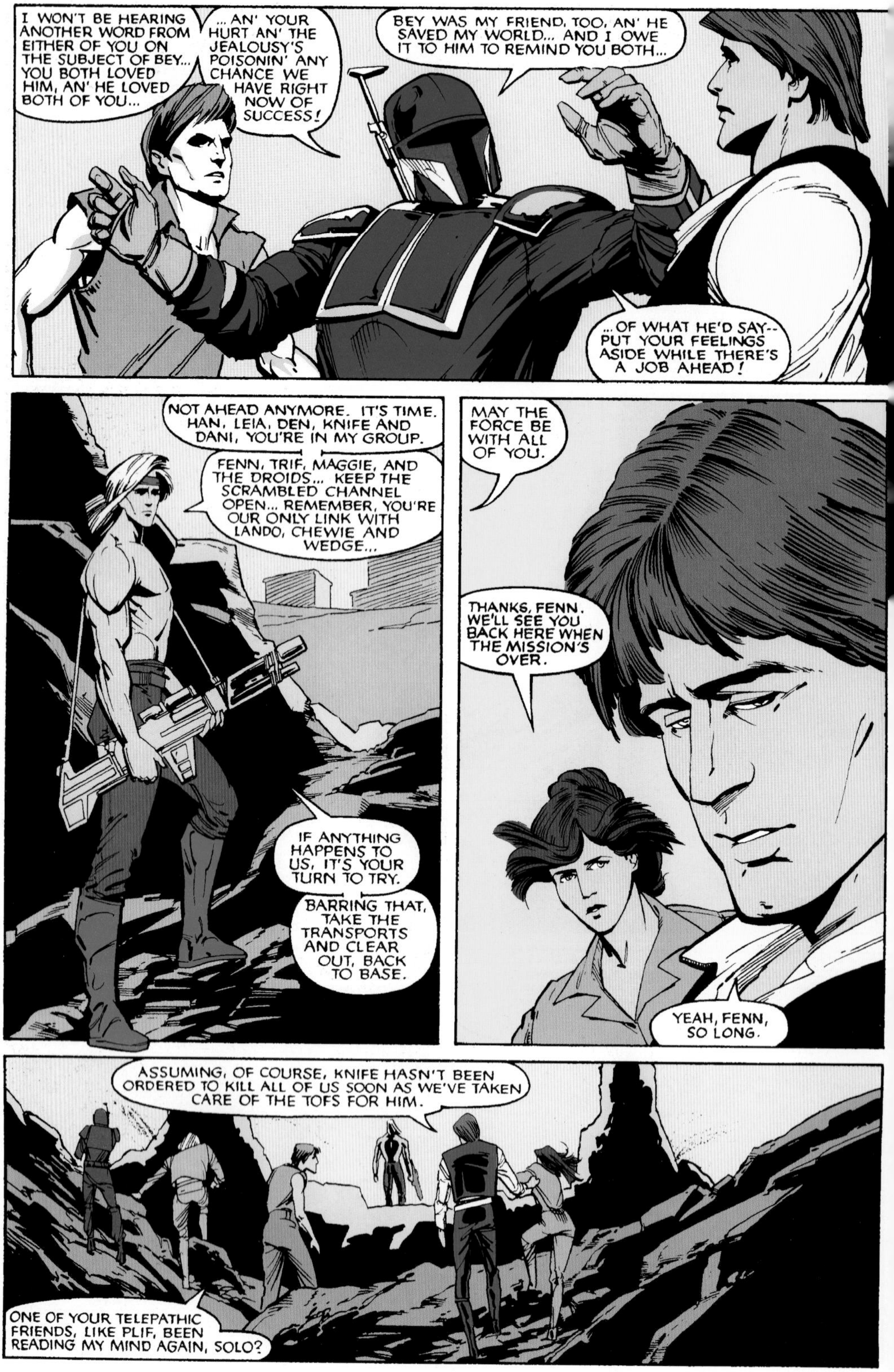
I WON'T BE HEARING ANOTHER WORD FROM EITHER OF YOU ON THE SUBJECT OF BEY... YOU BOTH LOVED HIM, AN' HE LOVED BOTH OF YOU...
...AN' YOUR HURT AN' THE JEALOUSY'S POISONIN' ANY CHANCE WE HAVE RIGHT NOW OF SUCCESS!
BEY WAS MY FRIEND, TOO, AN' HE SAVED MY WORLD... AND I OWE IT TO HIM TO REMIND YOU BOTH...
...OF WHAT HE'D SAY-- PUT YOUR FEELINGS ASIDE WHILE THERE'S A JOB AHEAD!
NOT AHEAD ANYMORE. IT'S TIME. HAN, LEIA, DEN, KNIFE AND DANI, YOU'RE IN MY GROUP.
FENN, TRIF, MAGGIE, AND THE DROIDS... KEEP THE SCRAMBLED CHANNEL OPEN... REMEMBER, YOU'RE OUR ONLY LINK WITH LANDO, CHEWIE AND WEDGE...
IF ANYTHING HAPPENS TO US, IT'S YOUR TURN TO TRY.
BARRING THAT, TAKE THE TRANSPORTS AND CLEAR OUT, BACK TO BASE.
MAY THE FORCE BE WITH ALL OF YOU.
THANKS, FENN. WE'LL SEE YOU BACK HERE WHEN THE MISSION'S OVER.
YEAH, FENN, SO LONG.
ASSUMING, OF COURSE, KNIFE HASN'T BEEN ORDERED TO KILL ALL OF US SOON AS WE'VE TAKEN CARE OF THE TOFS FOR HIM.
ONE OF YOUR TELEPATHIC FRIENDS, LIKE PLIF, BEEN READING MY MIND AGAIN, SOLO?

NO ONE'S BEEN READING ANYTHING, KNIFE. PLIF AN' THE HOOJIBS ARE THE ONLY TELEPATHS WE'VE GOT... AND NONE OF THEM ARE ALONG ON THIS MISSION...

AND DON'T YOU AND YOUR FRIENDS PLAN, IF YOU CAN, TO BETRAY US AT MISSION'S END?

BUT IT WASN'T HARD TO GUESS YOUR PLANS. I KNOW HOW YOU NAGAI THINK.

PERHAPS NOT, SOLO. BUT YOU'VE BEEN FAR MORE FORGIVING OF YOUR OTHER ENEMIES THAN YOU ARE TOWARD US NAGAI...

NO. WE'RE NOT LIKE YOU.

FENN'S STAFF PILOTS... TRIF AND MAGGIE-- WERE ONCE IMPERIALS, YET THEY REMAIN UNCHALLENGED. I BELIEVE YOUR RESENTMENT OF COMMANDER KNIFE AFFECTS YOUR VIEW OF OUR ENTIRE RACE!

I NEED NO ONE TO SPEAK FOR ME, DEN... I THINK SOLO KNOWS, IN HIS HEART, THAT I AM NOT THE MONSTER HE WOULD LIKE TO BELIEVE ME.

I AM A LEADER OF MY PEOPLE, AND A SERVANT OF THEIR PEOPLE. I LOVE MY WORLD.

FOR NAGI-- FOR THE NAGAI-- I WOULD DO AS BAD AS I HAVE DONE AGAIN, OR WORSE, WITHOUT REGRET OR HESITATION.

AS WOULD I, KNIFE... AND I THINK THEY WOULD, TOO, FOR EACH OTHER, OR FOR THE SAKE OF THE FREE WORLDS THEY SERVE.

I THINK... WE ARE NOT SO DIFFERENT, AFTER ALL.

AND I SAY WE ARE.

AND I CHEER THE DIFFER- ENCES.

ALL OF YOU... PLEASE DROP IT UNTIL WE COMPLETE THE JOB.

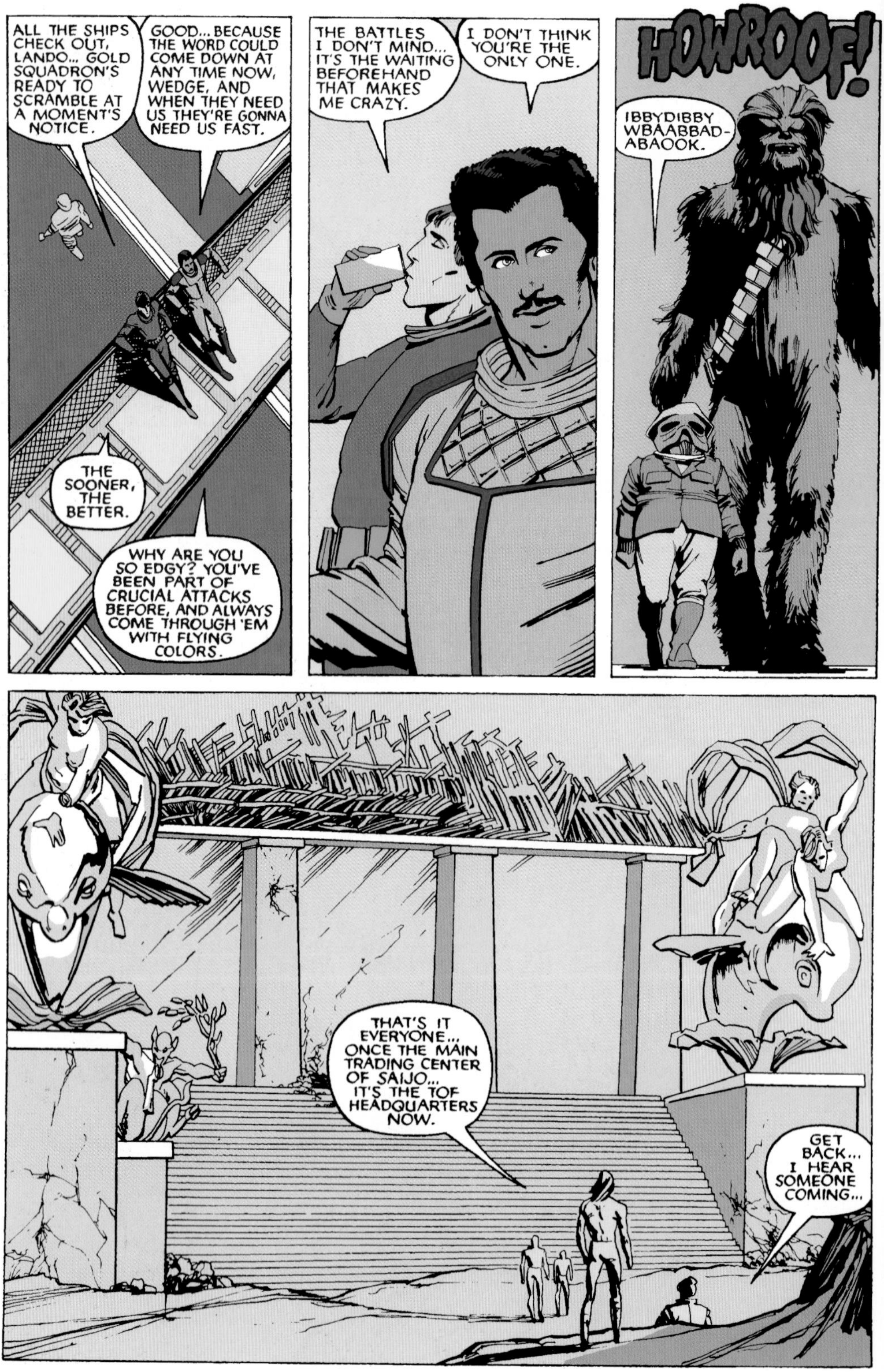
ALL THE SHIPS CHECK OUT, LANDO... GOLD SQUADRON'S READY TO SCRAMBLE AT A MOMENT'S NOTICE.
GOOD... BECAUSE THE WORD COULD COME DOWN AT ANY TIME NOW, WEDGE, AND WHEN THEY NEED US THEY'RE GONNA NEED US FAST.
THE SOONER, THE BETTER.
WHY ARE YOU SO EDGY? YOU'VE BEEN PART OF CRUCIAL ATTACKS BEFORE, AND ALWAYS COME THROUGH 'EM WITH FLYING COLORS.
THE BATTLES I DON'T MIND... IT'S THE WAITING BEFOREHAND THAT MAKES ME CRAZY.
I DON'T THINK YOU'RE THE ONLY ONE.
HOWROOF!
IBBYDIBBY WBAABBAD-ABAOOK.
THAT'S IT EVERYONE... ONCE THE MAIN TRADING CENTER OF SAIJO... IT'S THE TOF HEADQUARTERS NOW.
GET BACK... I HEAR SOMEONE COMING...

COME ON, MOVE IT ALONG... THE PRINCE WANTS TO INTERVIEW ALL NAGAI TAKEN ALIVE ... PERSONALLY.

FASTER, YOU!

I THINK AN OPPORTUNITY HAS JUST PRESENTED ITSELF.

SAY NO MORE.

COME ALONG, KNIFE.

LADY LUMIYA... TRULY, WE CANNOT ADEQUATELY EXPRESS OUR GRATIFICATION...

...AT YOUR HAVING FORSAKEN YOUR NAGAI COMRADES AND JOINED YOUR-SELF TO OUR CAUSE.

NO THANKS ARE NECESSARY, PRINCE SERENO.

I VOWED TO DARTH VADER, MY OLD MASTER, THAT I WOULD LAY DOWN MY LIFE FOR THE DESTRUCTION OF LUKE SKYWALKER AND THE ALLIANCE OF FREE PLANETS.

THE NAGAI WERE ONLY USEFUL TO ME SO LONG AS THEY SEEMED LIKELY TO FULFILL THAT END.

NOW THAT THEY'VE ALLIED THEMSELVES WITH SKYWALKER, WELL...

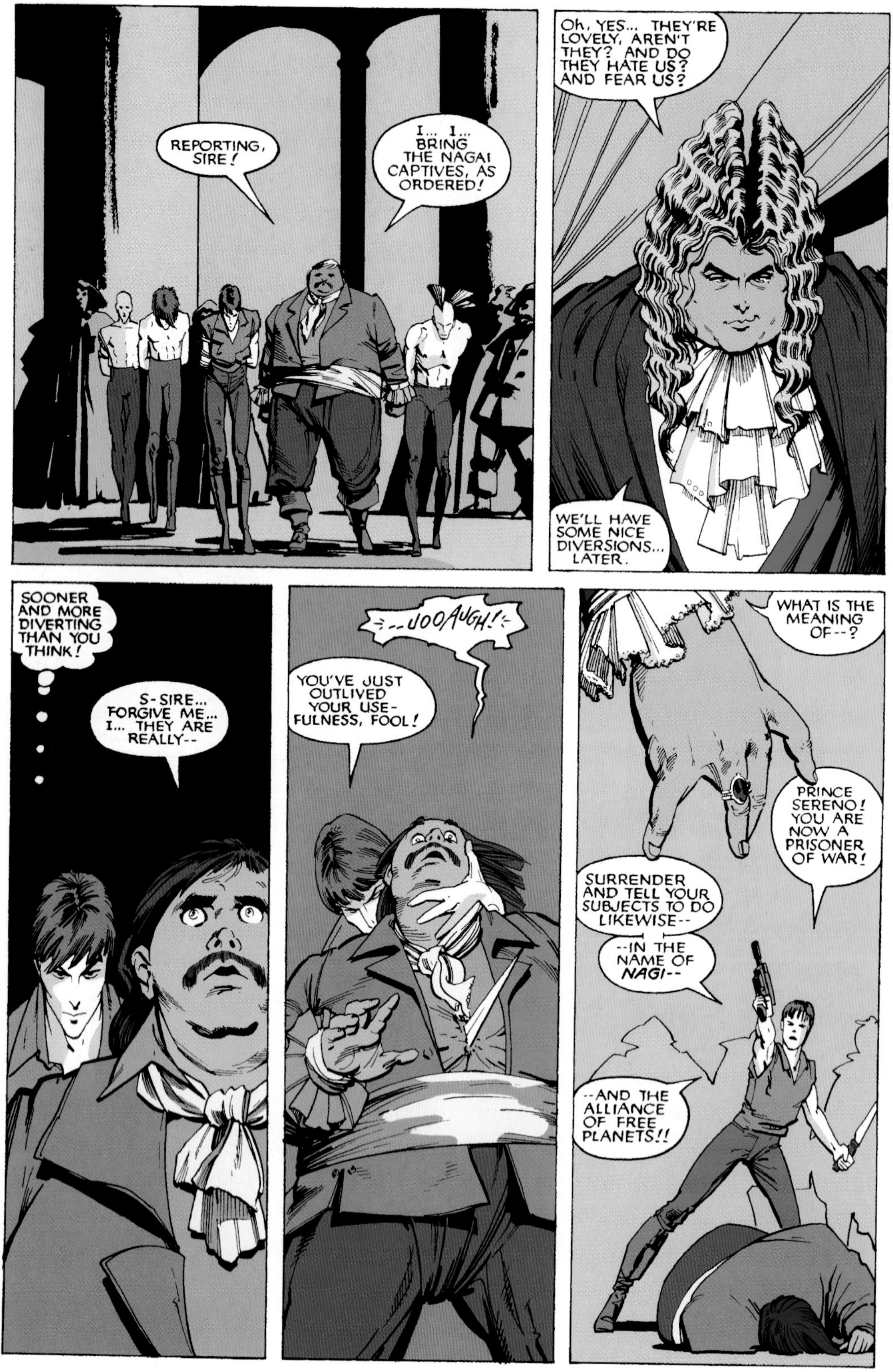

REPORTING, SIRE!
I... I... BRING THE NAGAI CAPTIVES, AS ORDERED!
Oh, YES... THEY'RE LOVELY, AREN'T THEY? AND DO THEY HATE US? AND FEAR US?
WE'LL HAVE SOME NICE DIVERSIONS... LATER.
SOONER AND MORE DIVERTING THAN YOU THINK!
S-SIRE... FORGIVE ME... I... THEY ARE REALLY--
--JOOAUGH!--
YOU'VE JUST OUTLIVED YOUR USE-FULNESS, FOOL!
WHAT IS THE MEANING OF--?
PRINCE SERENO! YOU ARE NOW A PRISONER OF WAR!
SURRENDER AND TELL YOUR SUBJECTS TO DO LIKEWISE--
--IN THE NAME OF NAGI--
--AND THE ALLIANCE OF FREE PLANETS!!

EVERYONE'S IN PLACE, LUKE... GET YOUR LIGHT-SABRE HANDY...

...AND LET'S GIVE KNIFE AND DEN MORE SUPPORT THAN THEY PROBABLY DESERVE!

RIGHT!

HAVE NO FEAR, SERENO! THE FOOL IS TAKEN CARE OF...

UHN

AND MY BLASTER WAS SET TO STUN, SO THAT YOU MAY QUESTION HIM AT YOUR LEISURE, LATER.

THAT'S LUMIYA'S VOICE! COME ON, DANI! THEY'RE GOING TO NEED US!

BLAST! I KNEW IT WAS GOING TOO SMOOTHLY.

REMEMBER, OUR OBJECTIVE IS THE PRINCE. WE'VE GOT TO TAKE HIM ALIVE!

RIGHT!

ATTENTION, MERRIWEATHER... BULK CRUISER MERRIWEATHER, DO YOU READ ME?

THERE IS A HOSTILE PRESENCE IN FORCE ON SAIJO. THEY ARE ATTACKING THE PRINCE. WE NEED AIR SUPPORT!

LOCATE AND DESTROY THEIR MAIN BASE.

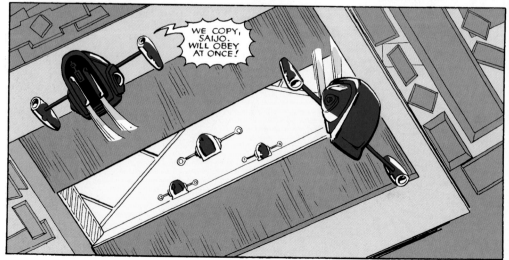

WE COPY, SAIJO. WILL OBEY AT ONCE!

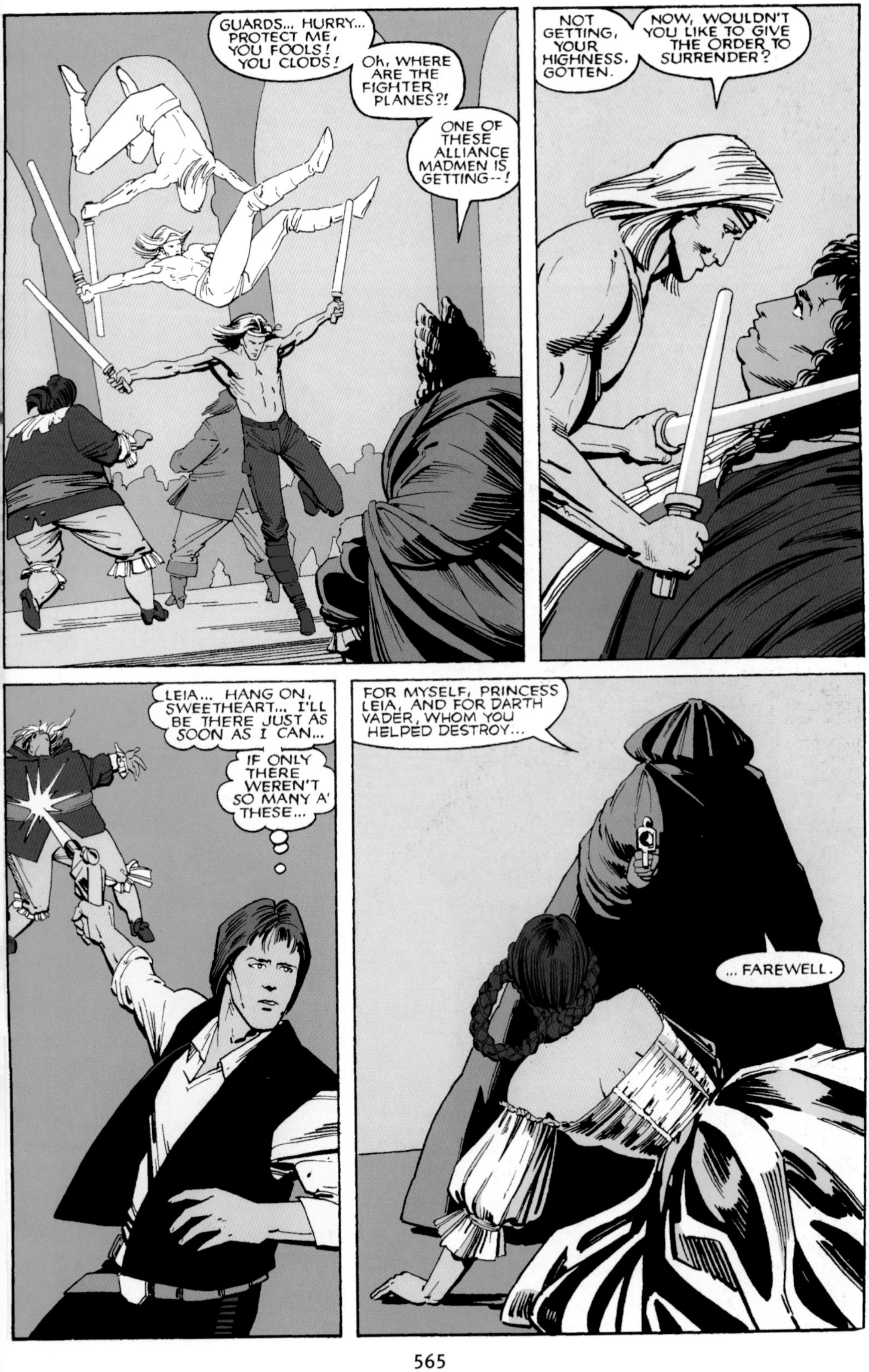
GUARDS... HURRY... PROTECT ME, YOU FOOLS! YOU CLODS!
Oh, WHERE ARE THE FIGHTER PLANES?!
ONE OF THESE ALLIANCE MADMEN IS GETTING--!
NOT GETTING, YOUR HIGHNESS. GOTTEN.
NOW, WOULDN'T YOU LIKE TO GIVE THE ORDER TO SURRENDER?
LEIA... HANG ON, SWEETHEART... I'LL BE THERE JUST AS SOON AS I CAN...
IF ONLY THERE WEREN'T SO MANY A' THESE...
FOR MYSELF, PRINCESS LEIA, AND FOR DARTH VADER, WHOM YOU HELPED DESTROY...
... FAREWELL.

AND AFTER YOU-- KNIFE...

NO... IF I MAKE A BREAK FOR IT, SHE'LL...

I CAN'T LEAVE HIM TO DIE...

YYOOO

LEIA! ARE YOU...?

I'M FINE, HAN...

BUT... LUMIYA WAS SHOT BY ONE OF THE TOFS!

SHE LEFT ME NO ALTERNATIVE.

WHAT WAS THAT, LANDO? I DIDN'T QUITE COPY. OUR LINK-UP THROUGH FENN'S BASE MUST BE A LITTLE FAULTY.

I SAID, START BREAKING OUT THE DRINKS AND THE PARTY HATS.

EVERYTHING'S UNDER CONTROL UP HERE.

WE DESTROYED ABOUT HALF OF THE SMALL SHIPS, AND THEN THE MERRIWEATHER SURRENDERED TO US.

AEROOR

GOOD WORK.

AND NOW, YOUR HIGHNESS, I THINK YOU'VE STALLED LONG ENOUGH. GIVE THE ORDER FOR THE REST OF YOUR PEOPLE TO SURRENDER.

OH... VERY WELL, THAT'S ENOUGH, EVERYONE...

BUT... YOU, THERE... YOU COULD HAVE SAVED ME.

WHY DID YOU BETRAY ME AND HELP THEM?

BECAUSE I'M ONE OF THEM.

HIM!

OUR TRUSTED AGENT AMONG THE TOFS ALL THIS TIME HAS BEEN...

BEY.

BEY...

I MAY NOT BE TRUE CORELLIAN... OR TRUE NAGAI...

BUT I COULDN'T STAND BACK AND LET THE TOFS DESTROY BOTH SIDES... AND YOU WITH THEM.

COME ON... I KNOW YOU STILL FEEL A LITTLE ROCKY AFTER THAT STUN BLAST... BUT WHEN A GUY COMES AS FAR AS OL' BEY HAS FOR YOU...

...THE LEAST YOU CAN DO IS MEET HIM HALFWAY.

MY IDENTITY WAS A CLOSELY CON-CEALED SECRET FROM MOST OF THE ALLIANCE, HAN... BECAUSE THE ADMIRAL WASN'T SURE HOW PEOPLE WOULD TAKE THE KNOWLEDGE THAT I WAS HELPING THEM.

Y DO SUR TO M

WELL, uh... NATURALLY. I MEAN, IT FIGURED. YOU'D...

...WANT TO BE HERE...

TO... PROTEC YOUR BROTH AN' ALL...

I CAME HERE TO PROTECT BOTH MY BROTHERS. YOU'RE PART OF MY FAMILY, TOO.

Oh, YEAH, SURE. BOTH OF US.

NATURALLY. I KNEW THAT'S WHAT YOU MEANT.

LET'S GET HIS HIGHNESS BACK TO THE ALLIANCE BAS AS QUICKLY AS POSSIBLE. I'VE SIGNALED FENN TO REMAIN IN CHARGE HERE.

IT'S WONDERFUL. DO YOU KNOW WHAT THIS MEANS?

SURE. FOR THE FIRST TIME IN A LONG, LONG TIME, ALL OF US, AS RACES AND AS INDIVIDUALS, HAVE A FAIR CHANCE AT MAKING PEACE.

AND I HOPE... NO, I KNOW... WE CAN DO IT!

FIN